Re-viewing Hitchcock

Re-viewing Hitchcock

New Critical Perspectives

**Edited by
Robert E. Kapsis**

THE BRITISH FILM INSTITUTE
Bloomsbury Publishing Plc, 50 Bedford Square, London, WC1B 3DP, UK
Bloomsbury Publishing Inc, 1359 Broadway, New York, NY 10018, USA
Bloomsbury Publishing Ireland, 29 Earlsfort Terrace, Dublin 2, D02 AY28, Ireland

BLOOMSBURY is a trademark of Bloomsbury Publishing Plc

First published in Great Britain 2026 by Bloomsbury
on behalf of the
British Film Institute
21 Stephen Street, London W1T 1LN
www.bfi.org.uk

The BFI is the lead organisation for film in the UK and the distributor of Lottery funds for film. Our mission is to ensure that film is central to our cultural life, in particular by supporting and nurturing the next generation of filmmakers and audiences. We serve a public role which covers the cultural, creative and economic aspects of film in the UK.

Copyright © Robert E. Kapsis, 2026

Robert E. Kapsis has asserted his right under the Copyright, Designs and
Patents Act, 1988, to be identified as author of this work.

For legal purposes the Acknowledgments on pp. xvi–xvii constitute an
extension of this copyright page.

Cover design: Louise Dugdale
Cover image: Original Dye Transfer Print from 'The *Vertigo* Project' by Jean Curran – *Kim in the Green Light*.
Alfred Hitchcock, *Vertigo*, and the images of Alfred Hitchcock are trademarks and likeness rights of Alfred Hitchcock, LLC. All Rights Reserved 2018.

All rights reserved. No part of this publication may be: i) reproduced or transmitted in any form, electronic or mechanical, including photocopying, recording or by means of any information storage or retrieval system without prior permission in writing from the publishers; or ii) used or reproduced in any way for the training, development or operation of artificial intelligence (AI) technologies, including generative AI technologies. The rights holders expressly reserve this publication from the text and data mining exception as per Article 4(3) of the Digital Single Market Directive (EU) 2019/790.

Bloomsbury Publishing Plc does not have any control over, or responsibility for, any third-party websites referred to or in this book. All internet addresses given in this book were correct at the time of going to press. The author and publisher regret any inconvenience caused if addresses have changed or sites have ceased to exist, but can accept no responsibility for any such changes.

A catalogue record for this book is available from the British Library.

A catalog record for this book is available from the Library of Congress.

ISBN: HB: 978-1-8390-2620-1
PB: 978-1-8390-2619-5
ePDF: 978-1-8390-2622-5
eBook: 978-1-8390-2621-8

Typeset by Integra Software Services Pvt. Ltd.
Printed and bound in India

For product safety related questions contact productsafety@bloomsbury.com.

To find out more about our authors and books visit www.bloomsbury.com
and sign up for our newsletters.

Contents

List of Contributors x
Acknowledgments xvi

    Introduction 1
    Robert E. Kapsis

Part One Enduring Triumphs 11

1   *The Lodger* (1926): The First True Hitchcock Movie 13
    Henry K. Miller

2   The Two *Blackmails* from 1929: A Reputation Crosses the Sound Barrier 21
    Bryony Dixon

3   "No Manners at All and Always Seeing Things": The Return of Hitchcock's Vanished Englishwomen in *The 39 Steps* (1935) and *The Lady Vanishes* (1938) 31
    J. E. Smyth

4   *Rebecca*'s Gendered Reception from 1940 to the Present 43
    Patricia White

5   *Shadow of a Doubt* (1943) and *Notorious* (1946): Two Hollywood—and Definitively American—Masterworks 54
    Thomas Schatz

6   Re-viewing *Rear Window* (1954) 68
    Janet Staiger

7 *North by Northwest* (1959): Nothing but Entertainment 78
Thomas Leitch

Part Two Changing Receptions 91

8 "A Director Who Can Impose His Own Personality on His Pictures": British Critics and *Sabotage* (1936) 93
James Chapman

9 *The Man Who Knew Too Much* (1956) as a Critical Lens on American Culture 106
Paula Marantz Cohen

10 "She Isn't Quite Herself Today": *Psycho* (1960) before and after Queer Theory 115
David Greven

11 #MeToo and Angry Nature: The Changing Tides of Approaches to *The Birds* (1963) 128
Lucy Bolton

12 *Vertigo* (1958) and *Marnie* (1964): Two Reception Histories on Steroids 140
Robert E. Kapsis

13 *Rope* (1948): A Late Bloomer 158
Neil Badmington

Part Three Films on an Upwards Trajectory 167

14 *Downhill* (1927): "The Most Discussed Film Director in England" 169
Henry K. Miller

15 *Under Capricorn* (1948): Hitchcock, Melodrama, and the Christian Imagination 175
Richard Allen

16 The Reception History of Hitchcock's *The Trouble with Harry* (1955) 182
Sidney Gottlieb

17 More Blessed to Give: Tracking the Reception of Alfred Hitchcock's *Mr. & Mrs. Smith* (1941) 198
Elizabeth L. Bullock

18 Criminal Indifference: The Strange Case of *The Wrong Man* (1956) 210
Jason P. Isralowitz and Robert E. Kapsis

Part Four Four Reception Anomalies 227

19 Hitchcock and His Critics: The Fall and Rise of *Strangers on a Train* (1951) 229
Robert E. Kapsis

20 *Frenzy* (1972): "Dark, Nasty, Full of Bile"… and a Masterpiece? 242
Tania Modleski

21 *Topaz* (1969): "One of the Most Uneven Films in the History of Cinema" 252
James Chapman

22 What the Two Versions of *The Man Who Knew Too Much* Reveal about Film Criticism in the USA and Britain 262
Robert E. Kapsis

Part Five Hitchcock's Television Series 269

23 The Final Frontier: Hitchcock's Television Work 271
Thomas Leitch

24 Toward a New Appreciation of *Alfred Hitchcock Presents*, *The Alfred Hitchcock Hour*, and Shamley Productions 279
Christina Lane

25 Life after Death: Preserving and Promoting Hitchcock's TV Persona 289
Robert E. Kapsis

26 Travels in Hitchcock's Multiverse 303
Joel Gunz

Part Six Global Hitchcock: Beyond the USA and the UK

27 Hitchcock and *L'Écran français*: At the Roots of the *Politique des auteurs*?
Tifenn Brisset

28 Hitchcock in Germany—A Germanic Hitchcock?: Transnational Genre, Art Cinema, and Auteurism in 1970s/1980s *Filmkritik* and in the Work of Harun Farocki and Christian Petzold
Jaimey Fisher

29 Alfred Hitchcock and Italian Film Criticism: "A Good Second-Rate Director"
Francesca Cantore and Andrea Minuz

30 Alfred Hitchcock's Cinema in the USSR and Post-Soviet Russia: Loud Absence
Sergei Kapterev

31 Tracing Hitchcock in South Korea: From *I Confess* to *Decision to Leave*
Hye Seung Chung

32 Hitchcock in Japan: Invisibility and Hypervisibility
Daisuke Miyao

33 Introducing Hitchcock to Communist China: Two Decades of Reception and Popularization
Sun Yi

34 Hitchcock in Spain
Dona M. Kercher

35 Hitchcock's Audiences in Mexico: From Movie Theaters to TV
Ana Rosas Mantecón

36 Hitchcock in Argentina: Some Preliminary Findings
Dona M. Kercher

Coda A A "Signature Pattern": The Importance of Music in Hitchcock's Films 414
Jack Sullivan

Coda B Deserter or Honored Exile? Views of Hitchcock from Wartime Britain 421
Charles Barr

Index 428

Contributors

Richard Allen is Chair Professor of Film and Media Art at the School of Creative Media, City University of Hong Kong. He is the author of *Hitchcock's Romantic Irony* (2007), which examines the relationship between sexuality and style in Hitchcock's work, together with fifteen scholarly articles on Hitchcock. He organized the Hitchcock Centennial Conference in 1999 and is the co-editor of three anthologies on Hitchcock. From 2001 to 2018 he edited, with Sid Gottlieb, *The Hitchcock Annual*. His newest book is *Storytelling in Hindi Cinema: Doubles, Deception, and Discovery* (2025).

Neil Badmington is Professor of English Literature in the School of English, Communication and Philosophy at Cardiff University. He is author of four books (two are on Hitchcock), editor of over twenty volumes (including *Alfred Hitchcock: Critical Evaluations of Leading Filmmakers*, in four volumes, 2014) and author of many essays. He has written regularly for the *Times Literary Supplement*. His most recent book, *Perpetual Movement: Alfred Hitchcock's* Rope, was published by State University of New York Press in July 2021 as part of the Horizons of Cinema series edited by Murray Pomerance. It was ten years earlier, in 2011, when *Hitchcock's Magic*, his first book on Hitchcock, was published and distributed in the USA by the University of Chicago Press.

Charles Barr is Professor Emeritus, School of Media, Language and Communication Studies at the University of East Anglia. He has written extensively on British Cinema and on Hitchcock, including an overlap between the two in the classic *English Hitchcock* (1999). His other work on Hitchcock includes *Vertigo*, BFI Classics (2012) and, more recently, in collaboration with Alain Kerzoncuf as coauthor, *Hitchcock Lost and Found: The Forgotten Films* (2016). For many years, he served on the editorial board of *The Hitchcock Annual*.

Lucy Bolton is Professor of Film Philosophy at Queen Mary University of London, where she specializes in film philosophy, film stardom, and feminist approaches to filmmaking and film theory. She is the author of *Film and Female Consciousness: Irigaray, Cinema and Thinking Women* (2011), and *Contemporary Cinema and the Philosophy of Iris Murdoch* (2019). She is the co-editor of *Lasting Screen Stars: Images that Fade and Personas that Endure* (2016, winner of BAFTSS Best Edited Collection 2017). She has published widely on film philosophy and film stardom and is the co-editor of the book series *Visionaries* (EUP) on women filmmakers. Her writings include book-length chapters on Hitchcock's *Marnie* and on Tippi Hedren's career stint with Hitchcock during the filming of *The Birds* and *Marnie*, as well as Hedren's star image and female genealogy.

Tifenn Brisset has a doctorate in philosophy and is a lecturer in film studies in the Language, Literature, Performing Arts, Information and Communication, Journalism Department (UFR LLASIC) at Grenoble Alpes University, France. Her doctoral thesis focused on the links between philosophy and the cinema of Alfred Hitchcock. Her essays on Hitchcock have appeared in several publications, including *The Hitchcock Annual* (forthcoming), *L'Avant-Scène Cinéma* (2022), *(d')Après Hitchcock* (2022), *La Furia Umana* (2021), *Influxus* (2016), *CinémAction* (2015), and *Film International* (2013).

Elizabeth L. Bullock is a cinema, art history, and humanities instructor at the City Colleges of Chicago and at Dominican University, River Forest. Bullock earned her Humanities MA from the University of Chicago's Cinema and Media Studies program. Her publications include "Naughts and Crosses: Marital and Cinematic Gamesmanship in Alfred Hitchcock's *Mr. & Mrs. Smith*" in *The Hitchcock Annual* (2021) and "Imaginary Women in Hitchcock's *Vertigo* and Akerman's *Jeanne Dielman*" in *Vertigo 65* (forthcoming).

Francesca Cantore is Assistant Professor of Film at Sapienza University of Rome. She has published *Il trasformista: Alberto Sordi, l'Italia, il cinema* (2023) and coauthored *Divorzio all'italiana: Regia di Pietro Germi* (2024). Her research has appeared in national and international academic journals (*Journal of Italian Cinema & Media Studies*, *L'Avventura*, *La Valle dell'Eden*, etc.) and in volumes by publishers such as Peter Lang, Il Mulino, Marsilio, and Il Saggiatore.

James Chapman is Professor of Film Studies at the University of Leicester and former editor of the *Historical Journal of Film, Radio, and Television*. He has published on the history of spy cinema and television, including *Licence to Thrill: A Cultural History of the James Bond Films* (3rd edn, 2024), *Hitchcock and the Spy Film* (2018) and *Saints and Avengers: British Adventure Series of the 1960s* (2002) as well as a standalone monograph on *Dr. No: The First James Bond Film* (2022). He has also published articles on Hitchcock for *The Hitchcock Annual* and the *Historical Journal of Film, Radio and Television*.

Hye Seung Chung is Professor of Film and Media Studies at Colorado State University. She is the author of *Hollywood Asian: Philip Ahn and the Politics of Cross-Ethnic Performance* (2006), *Kim Ki-duk* (2012), *Hollywood Diplomacy: Film Regulation, Foreign Relations, and East Asian Representations* (2020), and *Cinema under National Reconstruction: State Censorship and South Korea's Cold War Film Culture* (2024). She is also the coauthor (with David Scott Diffrient) of *Movie Migrations: Transnational Genre Flows and South Korean Cinema* (2015) and *Movie Minorities: Transnational Rights Advocacy and South Korean Cinema* (2021).

Paula Marantz Cohen is Distinguished Professor of English and Dean Emerita of the Pennoni Honors College at Drexel University, Philadelphia. Cohen is the author of six nonfiction books, including *Alfred Hitchcock: The Legacy of Victorianism* (2022). She is also the author of six novels. Her essays, stories, and reviews have appeared in the *Yale Review*, *American Scholar*, *Southwest Review*, *Times Literary Supplement*, *Raritan*, *Hudson Review*, and *Wall Street Journal*—as well as *The Hitchcock Annual*, *Alfred Hitchcock Centenary Essays*, *Companion to Alfred Hitchcock*, *Hitchcock's America*, and other publications. Her latest piece on Hitchcock—a review essay of Edward White's critically acclaimed book, *The Twelve Lives of Alfred Hitchcock: An Anatomy of the Master of Suspense* (2021) appeared in the *Times Literary Supplement*.

Bryony Dixon is a curator at the BFI National Archive, responsible for the silent film collection. She has researched and written on many aspects of early and silent film as well as programming for a variety of film festivals and events worldwide. She is the author of *The Story of Victorian Film* (BFI Screen Stories series 2023), *Silent Films* (BFI Screen Guides, 2011) and has written numerous articles and book chapters on silent cinema and archiving. She has been a regular contributor to Sight & Sound and the BFI's DVD BluRay publications. She has been lead curator on a number of the BFI's major film restorations, including Underground (1928), Shooting Stars (1927), The Great White Silence (1924), South (1919) and all nine surviving Hitchcock silent films.

Jaimey Fisher is Professor of German and Cinema and Digital Media at the University of California, Davis, and also the Director of the University of California (system-wide) Humanities Research Institute (UCHRI), based at UC Irvine. He is the author of *German Ways of War: Affective Geographies of War Films* (2022), *Treme* (2019), *Christian Petzold* (2013), and *Disciplining Germany: Youth, Reeducation, and Reconstruction* (2007). He has also edited/coedited volumes on film, including *New German Cinema and Its Global Contexts* (2025), *The Berlin School and Its Global Contexts* (2018), *Generic Histories of German Cinema* (2013), as well as on theory—*Spatial Turns: Space, Place, and Mobility in German Culture* (2010) and *Critical Theory: Current State and Future Prospects* (2001).

Sidney Gottlieb is Professor of Communication and Media Studies at Sacred Heart University, Fairfield, Connecticut. He edits *The Hitchcock Annual*. His work on Hitchcock includes two volumes of *Hitchcock on Hitchcock* (1995 and 2015), *Alfred Hitchcock: Interviews* (2003), and, most recently, in collaboration with Donal Martin as co-editor, *Haunted by Vertigo: Hitchcock's Masterpiece Then and Now* (2021).

David Greven is Professor of English at the University of South Carolina. He publishes in the fields of nineteenth-century American literature and film studies. His books include a volume on the Merchant–Ivory film *Maurice* (1987) for the revived Queer Film Classics series edited by Thomas Waugh and Matthew Hays (2023); *Ryan Murphy's Queer America*, coedited with Brenda Weber (2022); *Intimate Violence: Hitchcock, Sex, and Queer Theory* (2017), *Queering the Terminator* (2017), and *Ghost Faces: Hollywood and Post-Millennial Masculinity* (2016). His essays on film have appeared in journals such as *Screen*, *Quarterly Review of Film and Video*, *Journal of Cinema and Media Studies*, *Genders*, *Studies in Gender and Sexuality*, *Postmodern Culture*, *The Hitchcock Annual*, *Film International*, *Flow*, *Jump Cut*, *Refractory: A Journal of Entertainment Media*, *CineAction*, and *Cineaste* and in critical collections such as *The Cambridge Companion to Alfred Hitchcock*, *Close-Up: Great Cinematic Performances*, *Patricia Highsmith on Screen*, *Reading Sex and the City*, *Action Chicks*, and *Reading the Bromance: Homosocial Relationships in Film and Television*. He is currently writing a book on Hitchcock's 1950s films and the American gothic which is under contract with Oxford University Press.

Joel Gunz is a writer, filmmaker, host of the annual HitchCon International Alfred Hitchcock Conference and publisher of *The Hitchcockian Quarterly*. His essay "The Influence of Paul Klee on the Films of Alfred Hitchcock" was published in *Critical Insights: Alfred Hitchcock* (2017). His 2021 film essay analyzing Hitchcock's surrealist influences, *Spellbound by L'Amour Fou*, was selected by several film festivals and won Best Short Documentary at the Medusa Film Festival. He is also president of MacGuffin Media, presenting online film screenings followed by scholarly panels and discussions.

Jason P. Isralowitz is the author of *Nothing to Fear: Alfred Hitchcock and the Wrong Men* (2023). He is a partner at the law firm Hogan Lovells. A native of Queens, Isralowitz graduated from Boston University's College of Communication with a bachelor's in journalism and holds a JD from the University of Pennsylvania Law School. He has practiced law in Manhattan since 1993.

Robert E. Kapsis is Professor Emeritus of Sociology and Film Studies at Queens College and the Graduate Center of the City University of New York. He is author of *Hitchcock: The Making of a Reputation* (1992); the e-book version was released in 2022. Shortly after its publication, Kapsis developed "Multimedia Hitchcock," an innovative, interactive software project. Originally conceived as a pedagogical tool for his college courses on Hitchcock, the project grew into an interactive kiosk exhibited at MoMA, the Academy of Motion Picture Arts and Sciences, and other museums and nonprofit institutions celebrating the Hitchcock Centennial in 1999. Kapsis is also editor of *Nichols and May: Interviews*, *Woody Allen: Interviews, Revised and Updated* (2016), *Jonathan Demme: Interviews*, *Charles Burnett: Interviews*, and *Conversations with Steve Martin*; and coeditor (with Kathie Coblentz) of *Clint Eastwood: Interviews* and *Woody Allen: Interviews* (2006). He is currently working on a book on Hitchcock's posthumous reputation, to be published by Bloomsbury.

Sergei Kapterev is Senior Researcher at the Research Institute of Film Art in Moscow. He received his Ph.D. from the Tisch School of the Arts at New York University in 2005; his dissertation ("Post-Stalinist Cinema and the Russian Intelligentsia, 1953–1960: Strategies of Self-Representation, De-Stalinization, and the National Cultural Tradition") was published in 2008. Since 2001, he has been a regular contributor to *Kinovedcheskie zapiski*. Dr. Kapterev's English-language articles on Eisenstein and on the reception of American films in the Soviet Union during the early Cold War period have appeared in *Studies in Russian and Soviet Cinema* and *Kritika* respectively.

Dona M. Kercher is Professor Emerita of Spanish and Film, Assumption University, Worcester, Massachusetts. She is author of *Latin Hitchcock: How Almodóvar, Amenábar, De La Iglesia, Del Toro and Campanella Became Notorious* (2015).

Christina Lane is Professor of Film Studies in the Department of Cinematic Arts and Associate Dean of Graduate Studies in the School of Communication at the University of Miami. She is the Edgar Award-winning author of the book, *Phantom Lady: Hollywood Producer Joan Harrison, The Forgotten Woman behind Hitchcock* (2020). In addition to the books *Feminist Hollywood: From Born in Flames to Point Break* (2000) and *Magnolia* (2011), she has published numerous journal articles. She has contributed essays related to Hitchcock and his female collaborators to *Authorship and Film* (2003), *Hitchcock and Adaptation: On the Page and Screen* (2014), and *The Hitchcock Annual*.

Thomas Leitch recently retired from the University of Delaware, whose Film Studies program he had directed for thirty years. His extensive writings on Alfred Hitchcock include *Find the Director and Other Hitchcock Games* (1991), *The Encyclopedia of Alfred Hitchcock* (2002), *A Companion to Alfred Hitchcock* (2011), and many essays for *The Hitchcock Annual*. His most recent books are *The Scandal of Adaptation* (2023) and *Engagements with Adaptation* (2025).

Henry K. Miller is a Lecturer in Film Studies at Anglia Ruskin University, an Affiliated Lecturer at the University of Cambridge, and Honorary Senior Research Fellow at the Slade School of Fine Art, University College London. His most recent book is *The First True Hitchcock* (2022). He is also the co-editor, with Rachel Garfield, of *DWOSKINO: the gaze of Stephen Dwoskin*, shortlisted for the 2023 Kraszna-Krausz Book Awards, and editor of *The Essential Raymond Durgnat* (2014). He was researcher on Brighid Lowe's film *Together with Lorenza Mazzetti* (2023).

Andrea Minuz is Full Professor of Film and Media History at Sapienza University of Rome, Department of Art History and Performing Arts. He has published essays in multiauthored volumes and various articles in academic journals. His books as author include *La Shoah e la cultura visuale: Cinema, memoria, spazio pubblico* (2010); *L'invenzione del Luogo: Spazi dell'immaginario cinematografico* (2011); *Viaggio al termine dell'Italia: Fellini politico* (2012), *Political Fellini: Journey to the End of Italy*

(2018), and *Quando c'eravamo noi: La crisi della sinistra nel cinema italiano da Berlinguer a Checco Zalone* (2014). He is cocurator for the book series Italian Frame for Mimesis.

Daisuke Miyao is Professor and Hajime Mori Chair in Japanese Language and Literature at the University of California, San Diego. Miyao is the author of *Japonisme and the Birth of Cinema* (2020), *Cinema Is a Cat: A Cat Lover's Introduction to Film Studies* (2019), *The Aesthetics of Shadow: Lighting and Japanese Cinema* (2013), and *Sessue Hayakawa: Silent Cinema and Transnational Stardom* (2007). He is also the editor of *The Oxford Handbook of Japanese Cinema* (2014) and the co-editor of *The World of Benshi* (2024) with Michael Emerich, and *Transnational Cinematography Studies* (2017) with Lindsay Coleman and Roberto Schaefer.

Tania Modleski is the Florence R. Scott Professor Emerita of English at the University of Southern California. Her groundbreaking book, *The Women Who Knew Too Much: Hitchcock and Feminist Theory,* first appeared in 1988. A second edition came out in 2005, and a third edition appeared in 2015.

Ana Rosas Mantecón is a Professor and Researcher in the Anthropology Department of the Universidad Autónoma Metropolitana Iztapalapa in Mexico. She specializes in audience research and cultural policies related to cinema and other cultural institutions (museums and cultural heritage). She is author of *Ir al cine. Antropología de los públicos, la ciudad y las pantallas* (Going to the cinema. Anthropology of audiences, the city and the screens, 2017) and *Pensar los públicos* (Thinking about audiences, 2023). She has authored several articles, many historical in nature, that approach film exhibition from a social and cultural perspective.

Thomas Schatz is Professor Emeritus, Department of Radio-Television-Film at the University of Texas at Austin. He has written four books about Hollywood films and filmmaking. These include *Hollywood Genres*, one of the standard academic texts on the subject; *The Genius of the System*, a highly acclaimed book about the "studio system" during Hollywood's classical era; and *Boom and Bust: American Cinema in the 1940s*. His writing on film has appeared in the *New York Times*, *Premiere*, *The Nation*, and *Film Comment*. His work has also appeared in scholarly anthologies, such as *The Cambridge Companion to Alfred Hitchcock* (2015). His current projects include *Power Surge: Conglomerate Hollywood and the Studio System's Last Hurrah* and *Universal Pictures*.

J. E. Smyth is a writer, critic, Professor of History at the University of Warwick, and the author of several books, including *Fred Zinnemann and the Cinema of Resistance* (2014), *Nobody's Girl Friday* (2018), and *Mary C. McCall Jr.: The Rise and Fall of Hollywood's Most Powerful Screenwriter* (2024). Her research has been supported by the Getty Foundation, the British Academy, and the Academy of Motion Picture Arts and Sciences. She has written for the *Los Angeles Review of Books*, *Cineaste*, *Times Literary Supplement*, *Sight and Sound*, and *Written By*.

Janet Staiger is the William P. Hobby Centennial Professor Emeritus of Communication in the Department of Radio-Television-Film and Professor Emeritus of Women's and Gender Studies at the University of Texas at Austin. Staiger broke ground in film studies with her coauthorship of *The Classical Hollywood Cinema: Film Style and Mode of Production to 1960* (1985, with David Bordwell and Kristin Thompson). Staiger was also one of the earliest film and media scholars to explore reception studies, culminating in her 1992 book, *Interpreting Films: Studies in the Historical Reception of American Cinema*. She has subsequently published three more books and one coedited anthology in this area: *Perverse*

Spectators: The Practices of Film Reception (2000), *Blockbuster TV: Must-See Sitcoms in the Network Era* (2000), *Media Reception Studies* (2005), and *Political Emotions* (2010, coedited with Ann Cvetkovich and Ann Reynolds). In "Creating the Brand: The Hitchcock Touch" (*The Cambridge Companion to Alfred Hitchcock*, 2015), she applied a reception approach to Hitchcock's career, especially his efforts at self-promotion and branding.

Jack Sullivan is Professor of English at Rider University, New Jersey. He has published six books, including *Hitchcock's Music* (2006), the first in-depth study of the role music plays in Hitchcock's films. He has written for the *New York Times*, *Wall Street Journal*, *Opera*, *Washington Post*, *Boston Globe*, *New Republic*, *Chicago Tribune*, *Irish Times*, *Musical America*, *Chronicle of Higher Education*, *Literature/Interpretation/Theory*, *American Record Guide*, *Hitchcock Annual*, *Newsday*, *USA Today*, *Kurt Weill Newsletter*, *Harper's*, and in volumes for Wiley-Blackwell, Palgrave Macmillan, York University Press, Scribner's, Chelsea House Library of Literary Criticism, R. R. Bowker, and Prentice Hall. He has also contributed program notes for Carnegie Hall, the Metropolitan Opera, Spoleto USA, the New Jersey Symphony, and the Wexford Opera Festival. His media appearances include CBS, CNN, the BBC, and NPR, where he has been both a guest and a host. His 2013 script for the New York Philharmonic's "Hitchcock!", a presentation of Hitchcock's film music at Lincoln Center, was narrated by Alec Baldwin and Sam Waterston.

Patricia White is Director of the Aydelotte Foundation for the Liberal Arts and Centennial Professor of Film and Media Studies at Swarthmore College, Pennsylvania. Her books include *Rebecca* (BFI Film Classics, 2021); *Women's Cinema/World Cinema: Projecting Contemporary Feminisms* (2015), and *Uninvited: Classical Hollywood Cinema and Lesbian Representability* (1999), and, with Timothy Corrigan, *The Film Experience* (now in its sixth edition with Bedford St. Martin's, 2021). Her recent essays have appeared in *The Oxford Handbook of Queer Cinema* (2021), *Ulrike Ottinger: Film, Art, and the Ethnographic Imagination* (2024), *Studies in World Cinema*, and *Film Quarterly*. She is a member of the *Camera Obscura* editorial collective.

Sun Yi is Associate Professor in the College of Media and International Culture at Zhejiang University. Her recent publications have appeared in *Screen, Adaptation, New Review of Film and Television Studies*, and *Journal of Film and Video*.

Acknowledgments

I am grateful to those contributors to this book whose encouragement motivated me to forge ahead during challenging phases of this endeavor. The names of these contributors are listed here chronologically starting with the earliest and ending with the most recent influencers: Sid Gottlieb, Richard Allen, Thomas Schatz, Tom Leitch, Neil Badmington, Janet Staiger, Patricia White, Charles Barr, James Chapman, Henry Miller, Jennifer Smyth, David Greven, Christina Lane, Daisuke Miyao, Jaimey Fisher, Dona M. Kercher, and Ana Rosas Mantecón. Special appreciation goes to Toby Miller, who, as a reviewer of my original BFI proposal, urged me to adopt a more global approach in tracing the reception of Hitchcock and his legacy. Further, as an advisor, he helped put me in touch with several film scholars from territories outside of the USA and Great Britain, especially from Latin America and Asia.

I'm grateful to the editorial staff of Bloomsbury/BFI, especially my publisher Rebecca Barden, whose early commitment to *Re-viewing Hitchcock* helped keep it on track, continuity editor Emily Lovelock, who was instrumental in transforming a partly inchoate manuscript into a thematically more unified and finely tuned collection, and editorial assistant Rex Cleaver, who put in the long hours necessary for getting the manuscript cleared for production. Special thanks to Stephanie Carral, production editor at Bloomsbury, and Kelly Labrum, project manager at Integra, for their skillful and tireless guidance in steering this challenging and complex project in the right direction.

I would also like to thank the following for permission to reprint their material:

The Hitchcock Annual for permission to reprint abridged versions of: Charles Barr, "Deserter or Honored Exile? Views of Hitchcock from Wartime Britain," *Hitchcock Annual*, 2004–2005, pp. 1–24 (see Coda B); and Richard Allen, "*Under Capricorn*: Hitchcock, Melodrama, and the Christian Imagination," *Hitchcock Annual*, vol. 23, 2019, pp. 107–140 (see Chapter 15).

The University of Chicago Press for permission to print a revised and expanded version of: Robert E. Kapsis, *Hitchcock: The Making of a Reputation*, Chicago, Ill.: University of Chicago Press, 1992 (see Chapter 22).

Yale University Press for permission to reprint selections from Jack Sullivan, *Hitchcock's Music*, New Haven, Conn.: Yale University Press, 2008 (see Coda A).

Columbia University Press for permission to publish a revised and updated version of Dona Kercher, *Latin Hitchcock: How Almodovar, Amenabar, De la Iglesia, Del Toro and Campanella Became Notorious*, New York: Columbia University Press, 2015 (see Chapter 34).

Grateful acknowledgment is also made to the following sources for use of images: Figures 12.6, 25.2, 25.3, and 25.4 reproduced with permission of the Alfred Hitchcock Estate, courtesy of the Academy of Motion Picture Arts and Sciences. Additional acknowledgments to Toyota for Figures 25.5, and to Apple for Figure 25.8. Figures in Chapters 3 and 8 are reproduced with permission from the BFI Archives. The contributors made every effort to contact copyright holders of images reproduced in *Re-viewing*

Hitchcock. Regrettably, contact was not possible in every instance. We welcome correspondence from those entities that we have been unable to trace.

I would like to express my gratitude to Leland Faust, executor of the Hitchcock Estate, and to the Hitchcock family for their support and encouragement throughout this project. The estate's assistance in securing many of the permissions required for this book was invaluable.

Finally, I would like to thank my wife, Susan Marsden Kapsis, for her emotional support during the three-plus years I worked on the book, as well as for her incisive comments and editorial suggestions.

Introduction

Robert E. Kapsis

Re-viewing Hitchcock: New Critical Perspectives introduces a reception approach as a new way of conceiving Alfred Hitchcock's career. This historical reception focus assesses the effect of changes in critical discourse over several decades, mainly in the USA and Great Britain but also globally, in shaping the "meaning" of Hitchcock's works relative to the impact of other extratextual factors. The book analyzes the historical fate of well over half of Hitchcock's films (and also includes a section on his television work), thus providing significantly more coverage of his body of work than found in most extant anthologies. The volume's dominant strategy is to carve out Alfred Hitchcock's career—in terms of different film trajectories based on whether a film is perceived as a success throughout its historical run or whether it traverses an uneven path—from down to up, up to down, or some combination of both.

The book is comprised primarily of essays written especially for this volume by a diverse team of eminent Hitchcock scholars, academic film critics, and film historians; it also includes a small sampling of relevant previously published articles and commentaries, typically in an abridged form, as well as a few essays that have been adapted from previous published works. The inclusion of these pieces ensures comprehensive coverage that pays homage to important voices in Hitchcock's reception history.

Part I: Enduring Triumphs

Chapters 1–7 focus on the historical reception of several Hitchcock films that received high marks from audiences and critics alike when first released and have continued to do so up to the present. The films in this rarified category include *The Lodger* (1926), *Blackmail* (1929), *The 39 Steps* (1935), *The Lady Vanishes* (1938), *Rebecca* (1940), *Shadow of a Doubt* (1943), *Notorious* (1946), *Rear Window* (1954), and *North by Northwest* (1959). The combination of textual and extratextual factors impacting the popular and critical perceptions of each of these nine films is complex and, ultimately, unique to each film.

Hitchcock himself called *The Lodger* "the first true Hitchcock movie," in his famous interview with François Truffaut. In the first chapter of *Re-viewing Hitchcock*, Henry K. Miller reveals that this was a widely held view among his British critics well before Hitchcock said it, partly because of the rave reviews that the film received on its debut in 1926 and release in 1927. He then charts the film's changing reputation—from a standard to which Hitchcock ought to return to the skeleton key to the rest of his oeuvre.

Made in 1929, during the transition to the sound picture, Hitchcock's *Blackmail* morphed into two films: an all-silent version and a part-talkie film with music and some dialogue scenes. In her chapter on *Blackmail*, Bryony Dixon discusses the changing reputation of both versions—each of which, she reports, continues to gain ground in the ranking of his best works, especially the "silent talkie" version—still the better known of the two.

J. E. Smyth's chapter on how modern Englishwomen are represented in *The 39 Steps* (1935) and *The Lady Vanishes* (1938) is itself a brilliant testimony of what is enduring and "triumphant" about the reception of these two films. "For decades," writes J. E. Smyth, "research on Hitchcock's representation of women has tended to focus on his post-1940 films produced in Hollywood." Re-examining the director's two most popular and critically acclaimed English films of the 1930s, Smyth deftly "reconstructs the [historical] contexts for Pamela, Iris, and Miss Froy onscreen while emphasizing the resonant, offscreen feminist identities of theater legend and activist Dame May Whitty, star Margaret Lockwood, and *Times* film critic Dilys Powell." Critical of the bulk of auteurist and psychoanalytic approaches to *The 39 Steps* and *The Lady Vanishes*, which, she argues, "obscured the films' images of modern Englishwomen at home and abroad," Smyth's offering represents a fresh, empirically rich, and historically anchored alternative to Hitchcock Studies.

Patricia White makes the case that *Rebecca* (1940), Hitchcock's first US film, was guaranteed a warm reception. The film was produced and launched by Selznick International Pictures in the wake of *Gone with the Wind*'s unprecedented publicity campaign, and it built on the success of the bestselling Daphne du Maurier novel from which it was adapted. A box-office success, the film brought Hitchcock his first Oscar nomination for best director, and it won in two of its eleven nominated categories: best cinematography and best picture. As the only Hitchcock film to win the top award, *Rebecca* remained an ambivalent object for the director. It was Selznick, whose fingerprints were all over the film's casting, production values, and script, who took home the Oscar: not Hitchcock. This ambivalence has been at the heart of the film's place in Hitchcock criticism, where, according to White, it rivals *Vertigo* for the attention of feminist scholars.

Shadow of a Doubt (1943) and *Notorious* (1946) have figured prominently in Hitchcock's oeuvre and evolving reputation from the outset. Both were critical and commercial hits upon initial release; both were central to the early proponents of Hitchcock's auteur stature (especially François Truffaut in his groundbreaking 1966 study, *Hitchcock*); and the stock in both films, according to Thomas Schatz, has continued to rise over the years, as analyses have steadily broadened and grown more nuanced. As Schatz points out, the production history of both films impacted favorably in advancing Hitchcock's critical standing as he effectively served as a "hyphenate" producer-director on both films, and in fact he received producer as well as director credit on *Notorious*, as he would on every subsequent film in his career. Imbedded as an addendum in Schatz's chapter is a long extract from a Charles Barr essay from 2004–2005 that provides a retrospective reconsideration of how British critics viewed Hitchcock during the decade of the 1940s—especially the period encompassing World War II.

Rear Window (1954) was highly praised upon its release, and, over the past seventy years, critics have maintained their esteem for its achievements. In this chapter, Janet Staiger reviews a few of the more ubiquitous strategies for approaching *Rear Window* that have surfaced over the years. Arguably, most controversial has been ideological criticism—an approach that analyzes a film to argue something about its place within larger discursive behaviors in culture. Although the first reviews of *Rear Window* asserted numerous possible social messages that the film was conveying, the most notable, according to Steiger, were the feminist arguments in the mid 1970s about how spectators may be engaging with films. As Steiger wisely cautions us here, designating a film as feminist (or racist, etc.) should not be based on content or aesthetics alone but rather on its actual effect on a particular set of spectators.

The reception history of *North by Northwest* is an interesting case. Widely regarded as one of Hitchcock's finest achievements, the film, unlike the others in this select group, has inspired relatively little critical commentary. The reason for this, writes Thomas Leitch, is that

> [*North by Northwest*] does not tick any of the boxes that have inspired much recent work on Hitchcock. It is not British, not an adaptation of an earlier novel or play or story, not a product of Hitchcock's long-term collaboration with a particular studio like Selznick International, Warner Bros., Paramount, or Universal, and not an especially fraught representation of heterosexual romance.

"Bracketed by *Vertigo* and *Psycho,* two masterpieces that have inspired reams of commentary," he continues, "it has maintained a sterling reputation as 'the Hitchcock picture to end all Hitchcock pictures.'"

Part II: Changing Receptions

Sabotage (1936), *The Man Who Knew Too Much* (1956), *Rope* (1949), *Vertigo* (1958), *Psycho* (1960), *The Birds* (1963), and *Marnie* (1964) were not highly praised by a critical mass of influential mainstream journalistic critics when they were released but over time have figured prominently and dramatically in both journalistic and scholarly reassessments of Hitchcock's work. Collectively, the essays in this section make the case that many of these shifts are a reflection of the movement in critical discourse from auteur theory's dominance in the 1960s and 1970s to feminist film theory's ascendancy and prominence during the 1970s and 1980s (as discussed, for example, in the sections on *Vertigo*, *Marnie*, and the remake of *The Man Who Knew Too Much*) and beyond that with the rise, more recently, of queer studies and other anti-auteurist tendencies in film scholarship (see especially the chapters on *Psycho*, *Rope*, and *The Birds*). Among the most striking reception patterns reported in this section is the one meticulously described in the opening essay on *Sabotage*, where James Chapman establishes through his exhaustive archival research that the film's debut in 1936 deeply divided the critics, especially in Britain, and claims further that the film has continued to divide subsequent generations of Hitchcock scholars both in Britain and the USA. At the same time, he reports that the contemporary reviews in England were united in their assessment that *Sabotage* "was very much Hitchcock's film: that it bore his unique stylistic imprint and distinctive directorial flourishes"—compelling evidence, in fact, that "the discursive language of contemporary reviews in Britain during the 1930s was very similar to what later became the auteur theory, even if the term itself yet held no currency. British critics recognized Hitchcock as an auteur long before *Cahiers du Cinéma* or Andrew Sarris."

Part III: Films on an Upwards Trajectory

Chapters 14–18 consider several of Hitchcock's lesser-known films, including *Downhill* (1927), *Under Capricorn* (1949), *The Trouble with Harry* (1955), *Mr. & Mrs. Smith* (1941), and *The Wrong Man* (1956) which have been reevaluated upwards by critics and academics in recent years—films that I strongly suspect will continue to be taken more seriously in the years to come. The writers assigned to these films

(Henry K. Miller, Richard Allen, Sidney Gottlieb, Elizabeth L. Bullock, and Jason P. Isralowitz and Robert E. Kapsis, respectively) are all quite explicit about their expectation and the reasons they anticipate that their film has the power to be more highly regarded in the future. In various degrees, they are all of the opinion that the film they were assigned is "a signature work in [Hitchcock's] canon"—to borrow a phrase from Allen. "We often think of Hitchcock," writes Allen,

> as a modernist director, working within the idiom of popular cinema, a self-conscious master of style and form who complicates the vocabulary of melodrama that he inherits from nineteenth-century and twentieth-century popular cinema. This is certainly the case. Yet, at the same time, as *Under Capricorn* attests, we can equally understand Hitchcock's achievement as a perpetuation and renewal of the tradition of nineteenth-century melodrama under the influence of its complex late-nineteenth-century and early-twentieth-century forms.

Sidney Gottlieb articulates a similar strategy in the final paragraph of his defense of *The Trouble with Harry*:

> [As] important as it is to expand our interpretations of [the film], I think the key critical task and challenge is to integrate it more fully into our comprehensive appreciation and understanding of Hitchcock. It may not be in all ways the equal of, say, *Shadow of a Doubt*, *Rear Window*, *Psycho*, or *Vertigo*, but it stands up well alongside them as a useful, perhaps even necessary complement. If we want to get a full and true sense of his powerful and probing engagement with, to name a few of his main subjects ... the burden of the past, the inevitability of trauma, the volatility of desire ... we must look closely at not only the "classics" mentioned above but also his somewhat different take on all those subjects in *The Trouble with Harry*. If we are to take Hitchcock seriously, we need to take *The Trouble with Harry* seriously.

Similarly, Miller and Bullock each convincingly makes the case that reassessing an earlier work of Hitchcock's such as *Downhill* (Miller) or a more recent but also largely forgotten one such as *Mr. & Mrs. Smith* (Bullock) could stimulate a reviewing or reframing of Hitchcock's entire body of work in refreshingly new ways. Finally, Isralowitz and Kapsis recount the story of how *The Wrong Man*, which remains one of Hitchcock's least heralded masterworks, had a rough go of it early in its reception history but that over the years the film has increasingly been championed by world-renowned filmmakers (e.g., Martin Scorsese, Steven Spielberg, and Guillermo del Toro) and by prominent film critics and scholars as well.

Part IV: Four Reception Anomalies

The four films discussed here don't conveniently fall within the trajectories previously described. The reception history of *Strangers on a Train* in Great Britain and the USA (Chapter 19) is an anomaly in the sense that the archival research findings deviated sharply from the rags-to-riches path implied in the literature. Chapter 20 examines *Frenzy* (1972), Hitchcock's next to last film, which also provides an interesting variation of the reception stories described in the previous two sections. When first released, many reviewers, especially in the USA, characterized *Frenzy* as one of Hitchcock's greatest films. However, as Tania Modleski reminds us here, the film has not fared well over time, demonstrating the power of feminist thought, especially during the 1970s and 1980s, in shaping Hitchcock's reputation (compare Kapsis 1992), though in this essay she treats the film with more respect and awe than in her 1988 critique. Chapter 21 focuses on the strange case of *Topaz* (1969), a vastly underappreciated Hitchcock film that has been resistant to critical rehabilitation altogether, while Chapter 22, the last essay in this section, examines another Hitchcock film that has lost favor—the original 1934 version of *The Man Who Knew Too Much*—and explores what its demotion reveals about the state of film criticism in the USA and Britain.

Part V: Hitchcock's Television Series

The focus of Chapters 23–26 is on recent reassessments of Hitchcock's television series from the 1950s and 1960s. One of the cases Thomas Leitch references in his opening essay is Jan Olsson's excellent book *Hitchcock à la Carte* (2015), which begins with the author raising the following query:

> Where to place Alfred Hitchcock's television work in relation to his cinema within this rich cocktail of artistry and self-serving promotion still poses a critical dilemma. In this sweep of media, with a magazine in his name (*Alfred Hitchcock's Mystery Magazine*, 1956–) and a phalanx of book anthologies, all elements feed off each other. The [relative] lack of scholarly attention to small-screen Alfred … seems to indicate that the television venture stands thematically decoupled from Hitchcock's cinema and at best resides among the footnotes to his film work. I argue that rather than just an intertwined strand in the larger fabric of the Hitchcock oeuvre, it represents a resounding echo chamber for reception and reputation.
>
> (Olsson 2015: 9)

One of the highlights of the TV section is a new and revelatory essay by Christina Lane on the inner workings of Hitchcock's TV production team, which emphasizes the extent to which Hitchcock's contribution to the series was overshadowed by Joan Harrison, who, between 1956 and 1959, reigned as a key producer of the show and suggests that a reviewing may be warranted of the many teleplays under her creative watch that were not directed by Hitchcock.

Another highlight of the TV section is an essay by Robert E. Kapsis, drawing from his archival research of Hitchcock family records of distribution deals relating to Hitchcock's television series from the 1950s and 1960s, including several plans at different times to develop a new series or related ventures based on the original. Among the intriguing subplots revealed in Kapsis's account is the extent to which the Hitchcock family and its team of advisers have been proactive in monitoring and nurturing the favorable reception of Hitchcock's TV work along with other projects related to his TV persona and brand, and doing so not only in the USA but also worldwide.

Another eye-catching finding reported by Kapsis, especially given the volume's overarching focus on the historical reception of Hitchcock's body of work, is that the success of his television show and the greater fame it had brought him caused Hitchcock to worry about how this might adversely impact on the reception of his feature films. As Hitchcock's daughter explains it, her father felt that he would now have to factor in the possibility that his new celebrity status could become a distraction for his increasing fan base. Take, for example, his cameo appearances. Hitchcock thought that it might make sense for him to start programming his "little walk-ons" earlier in his films—well before jump-starting the film's major plot line, because of his concern that audiences might be distracted by the thought of when in the film he would be making his cameo appearance, and yet, at the same time, Hitchcock wouldn't want to deny his fans from being able to say, "There he is. There he is." In other words, Hitchcock reasoned that by planting his cameo appearances earlier in his films, his fans would be less likely to be distracted.

The closing essay by Joel Gunz points to new ways of conceptualizing the relationship between Hitchcock's TV show and his feature films, with implications for how these works might be received in the years to come.

Part VI: Global Hitchcock: Beyond the USA and the UK

"The power of the cinema, in its purest form, is so vast because it can go over the whole world," said Alfred Hitchcock in 1964. "On a given night a film can play in Tokyo, West Berlin, London, New York, and the same audience is responding emotionally to the same things." This, the final and longest section (Chapters 27–36), explores the critical reception of Hitchcock's films in four Western and Eastern European Countries (France, Germany, Italy, and Soviet and post-Soviet Russia), three Asian countries (South Korea, Japan, and Mainland China), and three Spanish-speaking countries (Spain, Mexico, and Argentina). While it was impossible to include chapters on every country and region that has been touched by Hitchcock's work, it is my hope that this limited sampling of countries and regions will prove an inspiration and a starting point for future scholars interested in examining Hitchcock's legacy in other nations and territories.

The results reported in this section affirm that Hitchcock's films have reached audiences worldwide, and always have, but challenge the notion that they have found the same audience, responding the same way, wherever they are shown. The following overview of this section was prepared by Robert E. Kapsis, with assistance from Toby Miller, who reviewed the original book proposal and spearheaded the expansion of the book to include this international component.

There are distinct issues that arise when approaching film globally and evaluating Hitchcock in this broader milieu. For example, this volume addresses the question, inter alia, of the stability and instability of Hitchcock as a sign, as an author and a set of texts. It shows how seemingly similar films and television programs can have different meanings and valences, depending on the identities, historicities, and locations of their audiences, be they journalistic, scholarly, popular, or governmental. This is especially the case with famous cultural producers, such as Hitchcock, and all the more so when the original texts are dubbed, subtitled, promoted, distributed, and interpreted beyond their points of origin. Hitchcock is too well known to be understood, so well traveled and multivocal is his sign.

And the US cinema that he inhabited for most of his working life was multicultural. Hitchcock used to reprimand anti-Hollywood Britons with, "There are no Americans. America is full of foreigners" (quoted in Truffaut with Scott 1967: 54). It was a place laden with difference. In the 1930s, the industry's peak body termed this "drawing into the American art industry the talent of other nations in order to make it more truly universal" (quoted in Higson and Maltby 1999: 5). That notion of universality has been a touchstone since, to the point where people around the world fancy themselves to be experts on US culture and life because of their encounters with imported film.

We must take great care in imagining there is a singular, stable Hitchcock just because he helped to innovate, standardize, and yet individuate the form and style of the classical era. And we can discern echoes of his work and even signature in a Swedish action director like Mats Helge Olsson (Gustafsson and Kääpä 2021: 162) as well as art-cinema auteurs in Pedro Almodóvar (Kercher 2015), Claude Chabrol (Bazin 2019: 108), and Neil Jordan (Pramaggiore 2007: 53, 146, 201–202 n. 11), just as Hitchcock himself parroted and refined others. His enormously varied reception and influence are nowhere clearer than in the chapters to come.

Chapters 27, 28, 29, and 30 focus on the historical reception of Hitchcock's films in France, Germany, Italy, and Soviet and post-Soviet Russia. An empirically based reassessment of Hitchcock's early canonization by the French is the focus of Tifenn Brisset's essay that opens this section. Next, Jaimey Fisher's essay on Hitchcock in West Germany focuses on Hitchcock's changing status as its industry shifted into the New Wave-ish "New German Cinema." Fisher explores how Hitchcock's reception eventually became so positive that, by the early 1980s, West Germany's key film journal, *Filmkritik*, dedicated numerous special sections to his films, including commentary on *Topaz*, *Frenzy*, and *Torn Curtain* by critic-filmmakers like Harun Farocki and Hartmut Bitomsky among others. Farocki would make a rare feature film—*Betrayed*, his only one—that paid conspicuous homage to *Vertigo*. And Farocki's student-collaborator Christian Petzold, now among Germany's most celebrated directors, has repeatedly cited a *Filmkritik* essay on *Vertigo* by Farocki as a primary influence on his own cinema. Such citations underscore how important the reception of a figure like Hitchcock can be not only for critics and audiences but for other filmmakers as well.

One of the interesting discoveries reported by Francesca Cantore and Andrea Minuz in their chapter on the critical reception of Hitchcock in Italy is that while Hitchcock, often praised by the film critics, was rarely viewed as he had been in France and Germany as a brilliant auteur or filmic genius. Rather, in Italy he was seen mainly as "a good second-class director" whose films were entertaining and technically sound but "had little to do with art and the predominant idea of cinema of postwar Italian culture."

A highpoint of Sergei Kapterev's chapter on the ramifications of Hitchcock's long delayed reception in Russia is his account of Hitchcock's influence on Soviet films at a time when Hitchcock's cinema was officially banned but, nevertheless, could be seen by a rather small group of Soviet people living both outside and inside the USSR. Combining archival research with recollections of Hitchcock's fans and detractors, Kapterev, a resident of Moscow, is ideally positioned to provide readers of this volume with a credible and absorbing picture of the history of the filmmaker's absence and presence within the Soviet and Russian cultural systems.

The next three chapters, 31, 32, and 33, focus on the historical reception of Hitchcock's films in South Korea, Japan, and Mainland China—an assignment to which all three of our contributors (Hye Seung Chung, Daisuke Miyao, and Sun Yi, respectively) reported finding methodologically challenging. Typical was Hye Seung Chung's lament over doing archival film research in South Korea: "Most evidence will be journalistic, anecdotal, and fragmented […] historical film research in South Korea can be very challenging: there are no archival clippings collections as in the Margaret Herrick Library [of the Academy of Motion Pictures Arts and Sciences] or NYPL's Billy Rose Collection."

To overcome this deficiency in the availability of historical reception data, Hye Seung Chung locates "Hitchcockian" elements in South Korean cinema through a cross-cultural comparative analysis of *Vertigo* and Park Chan-wook's *Decision to Leave* (2022). Although Park has denied Hitchcock's influence in the production of his Cannes award-winning film, both South Korean and Western critics have detected many parallels between these two mysteries which both center on the voyeurism and scopophilia of a lovestruck detective. Combining intertextual analysis with a global reception approach, Chung frames

Decision to Leave as an unofficial remake of *Vertigo*, which updates Hitchcock's midcentury masterpiece by introducing themes touching on migration, multiculturalism, and global inequity.

Turning next to Daisuke Miyao's essay on Hitchcock in Japan, we learn that none of Hitchcock's Hollywood films were released there until after World War II had ended in 1945. Following the attack on Pearl Harbor in 1941, the Japanese government had banned American films from being screened in Japan. Then, from August 1945–1952, Japan was occupied by the Allied Army. The top priority of the Occupation government was to publicize the American way of life—democracy and capitalism—and using Hollywood films to do so. Hitchcock's crime films were not ideal products for that purpose, and, hence, their releases were delayed or did not happen at all. The first Hitchcock film released after the war was *Shadow of a Doubt* (1943) in December 1946. *Suspicion* (1941) followed it in February 1947. *Rebecca* (1940) had to wait until 1949, *Foreign Correspondent* (1940) in 1946, and *Lifeboat* (1943) never.

Sun Yi's essay on the early reception of Hitchcock in Mainland China begins in 1979 with the reception of *Rebecca*, the first Hitchcock film imported into China, and ends in 1999 with the commemorative articles celebrating the 100th anniversary of Hitchcock's birth. One of the highlights of her essay is looking at the initial reception of Hitchcock's work in the late 1970s and early 1980s, especially of *Rebecca* and then *Spellbound*, which were the first Hitchcock films imported to China following the end of the Cultural Revolution and the birth of the less repressive cultural-political climate taking root there. An intriguing issue raised by Sun Yi is accounting for why scholarly attention was now paid to Hitchcock and how this "discovery" of him functioned within the context of China's reopening up to Western culture. Another high point of Sun Yi's essay is demonstrating how the reception of Hitchcock's films helped transform the critical language of Chinese film criticism.

The final three essays (Chapters 34, 35, and 36) examine the historical reception of Hitchcock's films in Spain, Mexico, and Argentina. Until the release of Kercher's book *Latin Hitchcock* about Hitchcock's reception in the Spanish-speaking world, his impact had been largely ignored. For this volume, Kercher has produced an abridged version of sections from her original study. In addition, she updates the evolving critical relationship between the master and Spanish filmmakers by focusing on how Carlota Pereda adapts his aesthetics and genre tropes. Next, Ana Rosas Mantecón contributes a chapter on Hitchcock in Mexico, which, among other things, builds on Kercher's earlier research regarding the initial reception of Hitchcock's films in Mexico City. In the final chapter, Kercher similarly builds on her earlier work on Argentina by highlighting the taxidermy motif in recent films by Fabián Bielinsky and Benjamín Naishtat.

Collectively, several of the global chapters suggest new lines of inquiry: Consider *Vertigo* and the fact that its reception history is detailed in several of the global section essays—most notably, in the chapters on Germany, Spain, Argentina, and South Korea. One consequence of having such rich comparative data is that it becomes possible to gauge the extent to which the speed of *Vertigo*'s assent as a critical favorite in the USA was more unique or more typical of its reception history in other countries.

A few final comments regarding the uniqueness of this volume: Music is a signature element in Hitchcock's work and yet has often been ignored or slighted in the writings of Hitchcock scholars. In this volume, music gets its due, and this is where the expertise of one of our contributors, part-time musicologist Jack Sullivan comes into play both as a contributor and advisor (see Sullivan 2006). Sullivan's addendum to the volume tracks the importance of music to Hitchcock's reception across several films, including *Blackmail*, *Rebecca*, and *Vertigo*.

One consequence of carving up the Hitchcock legacy in the manner we have in this volume is that the historical fate of such a recasting or reordering of his films touches on many of the perspectives and approaches characteristic of the anthologies already out there, thereby making this volume potentially attractive as a pedagogical tool for Hitchcock courses at the undergraduate level, introductory courses in film studies, and for Hitchcock scholars and film students at the graduate level. In addition, the present volume, focusing as it does on the historical fate of well over half of Hitchcock's films (including a section on his work in TV), provides a particularly comprehensive overview of the director's reception history. It is our hope that the volume's versatility will inspire a new generation of students and scholars to consider the importance of how Hitchcock has been—and continues to be—received, critiqued, and understood.

References

Bazin, André (2019) *The Film Critic as Philosopher*: *André Bazin on Euro-Japanese Cinema*, *1949–1958*, vol. II, trans. and ed. R. J. Cardullo, Mumbai: Curato.
Bennett, Tony (2007) *Critical Trajectories*: *Culture*, *Society*, *Intellectuals*, Malden, Mass.: Blackwell.
Chartier, Roger (1989) "Texts, Printings, Readings," in Lynne Hunt (ed.), *The New Cultural History*, Berkeley, Calif.: University of California Press, pp. 154–175.
Chartier, Roger (2005) "Crossing Borders in Early Modern Europe: Sociology of Texts and Literature," trans. Maurice Elton, *Book History*, 8: 37–50.
Gustafsson, Tommy, and Pietari Kääpä (2021) *The Politics of Nordsploitation*: *History*, *Industry*, *Audiences*, New York: Bloomsbury Academic.
Higson, Andrew, and Richard Maltby (1999) "'Film Europe' and 'Film America': An Introduction," in Andrew Higson and Richard Maltby (eds), *"Film Europe" and "Film America"*: *Cinema*, *Commerce and Cultural Exchange*, Exeter: University of Exeter Press, pp. 1–31.
Kapsis, Robert (1992) *Hitchcock: The Making of a Reputation*, Chicago, Ill.: University of Chicago Press.
Kercher, Dona (2015) *Latin Hitchcock*, New York: Wallflower Press.
Modleski, T. (1988) *The Women Who Knew Too Much: Hitchcock and Feminist Theory*, London and New York: Routledge.
Olssen, Jan (2015) *Hitchcock à la Carte*, Chapel Hill, NC: Duke University Press.
Pramaggiore, Maria (2007) *Irish and African American Cinema: Identifying Others and Performing Identities*, *1980–2000*, Albany, NY: State University of New York Press.
Sullivan, Jack (2006) *Hitchcock's Music*, New Haven, Conn.: Yale University Press.
Truffaut, François, with Helen G. Scott (1967) *Hitchcock*, New York: Touchstone.

PART ONE

Enduring Triumphs

Chapter 1
The Lodger (1926)
The First True Hitchcock Movie

Henry K. Miller

In an oft-cited article published in the year of Hitchcock's death, Ivor Montagu recounts an incident at a party thrown by his mentor Adrian Brunel, some time in late 1926 or early 1927, when the three men were working for Gainsborough Pictures. The question arose: "For whom, primarily, do we make films?" (Montagu 1980: 190). The other guests were film people, probably including Leila Stewart, publicity chief of Gainsborough's distributor, W. & F. Some of them said the public. Others said the boss. Hitchcock's answer was the press. Becoming known to the public as a director "would be the only way you became free to do what you wanted," and that meant courting the critics. Montagu himself had been working as a newspaper critic for the *Observer* when he first had dealings with Hitchcock, early in 1926, at the time of the first screenings of Hitchcock's directorial debut, *The Pleasure Garden*, and of the production of the first film of Hitchcock's that Montagu worked on, *The Lodger*.

Hitchcock's own account of *The Lodger*, best known in the version he gave to Truffaut, gives the critics a pivotal role. According to Hitchcock (Truffaut 1967: 35), W. & F. disliked the first cut of the film—on the tape he mentions "the head of their publicity department, a woman," presumably Stewart—and shelved it.[1] But after a couple of alterations were made, primarily at Montagu's suggestion, though Hitchcock was characteristically unforthcoming about naming him, *The Lodger* was at last given a trade show and was "acclaimed as the greatest British film made up to that date" (Truffaut 1967: 35). The critics' hosannas silenced the distributor's doubts, and Hitchcock's future was assured. *The Lodger* was remembered, in effect, as "the first true 'Hitchcock movie'" well before Hitchcock described it thus to Truffaut, and it remains the best known of his silent films. Unsurprisingly, its critical reputation has been closely bound up with Hitchcock's authorial identity. When he was still establishing himself in London, *The Lodger* was a lodestar that critics urged him to steer by, and after he had achieved fame and fortune in Hollywood, its entrails were retrospectively examined for portents of the major works that had followed.

The crucial trade show to which Hitchcock referred took place in September 1926, but the critics were part of *The Lodger*'s story well before then. At that relatively early stage in the history of British film criticism, most "critics" were general film correspondents, writing for the newspapers. Discrete reviews did appear in some papers, on occasion, as well as in the trade press, consisting of four weekly papers in 1926–1927, but much of what the general film correspondents wrote, including critical remarks amounting to reviews, appeared in general film columns, among opinion, gossip, and reportage—some of it about Hitchcock. The production of *The Lodger* was covered by the same writers who would go on to review it, starting with the first night of shooting, in February 1926, which was reported in more than one newspaper.

One critic who was there that night, A. Jympson Harman of the *Evening News*, one of the principal London papers, not only visited the studio on at least one further occasion but was also shown footage from *The Lodger*'s famous staircase scene, the shooting of which had been attended by other critics and probably by Harman as well, even before the rest of the film had been shot. Meanwhile, Harman's opposite number, Walter Mycroft of the *Evening Standard*, both reported on the film and enabled Hitchcock to film on location in his newspaper's offices—though copies of both the *News* and the *Standard* appear in the finished film, with the difference having some bearing on the plot. Within a few months of the film's release, Mycroft and Hitchcock were working alongside one another at British International Pictures—on whose poaching of Hitchcock from Gainsborough Mycroft had had the exclusive.

Hitchcock's recollection of the critics calling *The Lodger* "the greatest British film made up to that date" is only an exaggeration in the sense that formulations of this kind are the stock-in-trade of film critics, apt to be repeated without a backward glance. Mycroft, writing in the *Sunday Herald*, called it the "boldest and most original thing ever done on the British screen" (*Illustrated Sunday Herald*, September 19, 1926, p. 16). Harman began his *Evening News* column: "An Englishman of 26 has made a film masterpiece" (*Evening News*, September 20, 1926, p. 9). Another critic who had reported on the film's production, Iris Barry, writing in the *Daily Mail*, called it a "triumph" that "can more than hold its own against any foreign production" (*Daily Mail*, September 15, 1926, p. 7).[2] (The background against which *The Lodger* appeared was a political campaign, in which the *Mail*, reaching a mass, middle-class readership, took a leading part, to turn back the tide of American films washing over Britain and promote the domestic product.) Barry, who was a personal friend of Hitchcock and Alma Reville, inserted similar remarks—"a positive shock, so unlike anything else"—along with a still from the film into her book *Let's Go to the Pictures*, published just two months later, in November 1926 (Barry 1926: 235–236). In the *Daily Express*, the *Mail*'s principal rival, G. A. Atkinson called *The Lodger* "beyond question, the best screen-thriller produced to date" (*Daily Express*, September 15, 1926, p. 3). Earlier in the year, Atkinson had been given a private preview of *The Pleasure Garden* before it had been trade-shown, and now he quoted himself: "'When [Hitchcock] is in a position to produce a drama entirely to his own liking, it is safe to prophesy that he will create a sensation.' That prophecy was amply fulfilled yesterday" (*Daily Express*, September 15, 1926, quoting *Sunday Express*, February 14, 1926, p. 10).

The film was not due to open to the public until January 1927. The September trade show was primarily for the benefit of prospective exhibitors and the trade journalists who served them. Within the film business, there was some resistance to allowing newspaper critics into such screenings, and not all newspapers covered them since their readers would not be able to see the films for months to come. Within a few years, separate press screenings, nearer to the time of release, became the norm, but in the meantime there was no consistent approach to rereviewing films. Some of those who had reviewed the trade show might devote a few words in their column as a reminder, while others—notably Mycroft in this case—might not mark the actual release at all.

As was customary for major films, *The Lodger* opened at a single prominent West End venue, the Marble Arch Pavilion, on Monday, January 17, four weeks before its general release, and this was the "hook" for most critics. There does not seem to have been a press show, but there were some significant notices in advance of the 17th, presumably based on the trade show four months earlier. G. A.

Atkinson wrote in a preview of the coming week's releases on Friday, January 14, that *The Lodger* "has been generally acclaimed as the best British film yet produced," almost word-for-word the formulation Hitchcock remembered (*Daily Express*, January 14, 1927, p. 6). Two days later, in a similar preview section in the *Sunday Express*, he wrote: "Masterpiece of ingenious treatment" (*Sunday Express*, January 16, 1927, p. 4). Also on Sunday, January 16, the *Observer*'s critic Maurice Willson Disher praised *The Lodger*, interestingly, as an example of the quality of "the Gainsborough directors" rather than that of Hitchcock, whom he did not name (*Observer*, January 16, 1927, p. 13).[3] (*The Sunday Times*, the *Observer*'s main rival, did not then consistently review films.)

On the day of release, the *Daily Mail* ran a small notice, in amidst miscellaneous news items, titled "Good British Film." Signed "The Film Critic" and almost certainly written by Iris Barry, it does not name Hitchcock and ends with the claim that *The Lodger* "contains the largest closeups ever seen on the screen" (*Daily Mail*, January 17, 1927, p. 7). Atkinson, meanwhile, in a column of short reviews, wrote that Hitchcock was "indisputably a screen-genius" (*Daily Express*, January 17, 1927, p. 7). Harman had reviewed the September trade show at some length, by contemporary standards, but did so again in January nonetheless: "The aim of the director, Mr. Alfred Hitchcock, was to produce in the spectator something of the air of bewilderment and fear which the characters of the story experienced," he wrote (*Evening News*, January 17, 1927, p. 9). "'The Lodger' is an essay in that impressionistic treatment which will in its time entitle filmmaking truly to be called an art."

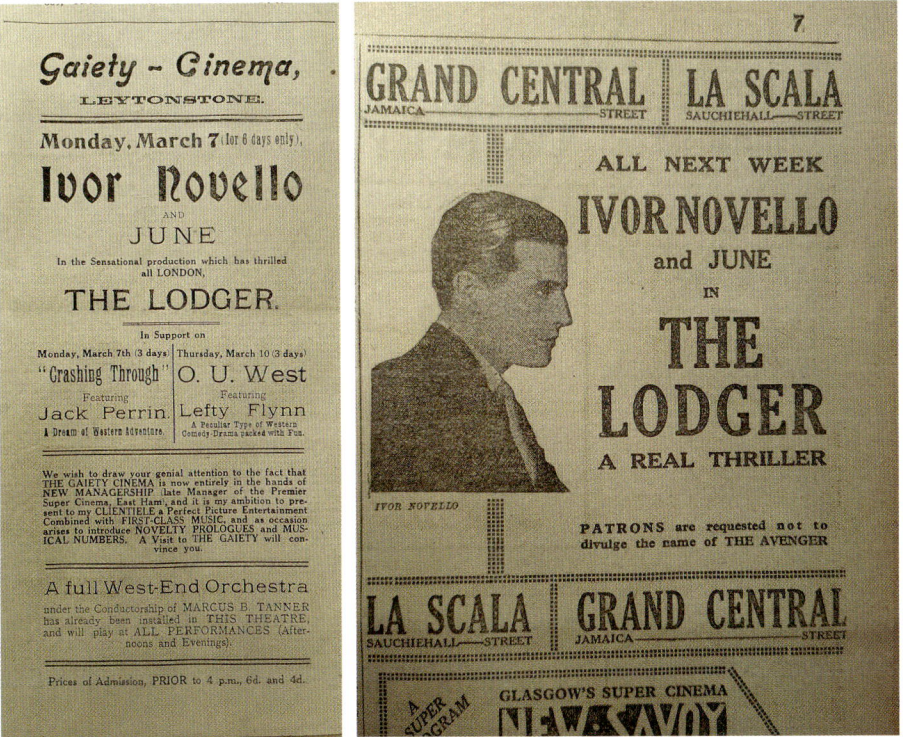

Figure 1.1 Advertisements for *The Lodger*, one anticipating the *Psycho* campaign against spoilers.

Leytonstone Express and Independent, March 5, 1927, p. 1; Glasgow *Evening Times*, March 12, 1927, p. 7.

Although *The Lodger*'s general release date was given as February 14, in fact it opened before then in two English regional centres, Birmingham and Manchester, as well as in Dublin, and was reviewed by critics in all three cities. The *Birmingham Post*'s anonymous reviewer took issue with the kissing, writing that although Ivor Novello and June "are what are called 'good-lookers,'" nevertheless "the picture would not be harmed by the excision of many of the 'close ups' of the pair, more especially when they are engaged with 'osculatory exercises'" (*Birmingham Post*, January 31, 1927, p. 5).

Meanwhile the *Irish Independent*'s reviewer, also anonymous, remarked on "the queues which lined up outside the Metropole" to see it (February 1, 1927, p. 9). The *Manchester Evening Chronicle* reviewed the film during this early engagement—at the Gaiety Theatre, one of the city's leading venues—but the *Manchester Guardian* did not, presumably because the *Guardian*'s film critic, C. A. Lejeune, was based in London, but it is still striking that Lejeune did not review *The Lodger*.[4]

Lejeune was a friend of Hitchcock and would remain one for decades to come, and although her weekly column was often free of reviewing, she did write standalone reviews on occasion. In late 1926 and early 1927, she wrote up *Ben-Hur*, *Faust*, *Metropolis*, and, at the start of February, Maurice Elvey's *Hindle Wakes*, produced by Victor Saville. Lejeune's first brief mention of *The Lodger*, in early March, was in a column devoted to the art of cutting in which *Hindle Wakes* was her main example (*Manchester Guardian*, March 5, 1927, p. 11). It was not until June, by which time *The Lodger* was well into its general release and Hitchcock's next film, *Downhill*, had been trade-shown, that she offered the view, in an instalment of her weekly column subtitled "Britain's Baby," one of the first significant profiles of Hitchcock to be published anywhere, that *The Lodger* was "the best film made in England up to the end of last year," another judgement almost identical to the one Hitchcock remembered (*Manchester Guardian*, June 11, 1927, p. 9).

In some ways the most notable early commentary on *The Lodger*, though it was dispatched from London, appeared in a paper serving a city where the film had not yet been shown, the *New York Sun*. This was the work of John Grierson, recently a regular critic for the paper, now back in Britain, where he would soon form around him the documentary film unit that took and made his name. Grierson's first comment on *The Lodger*, in the issue dated March 12, 1927, was "bogey-bogey murder and mystery stuff, laid on with a shovel as in the days of ancient hokum, but its tedium is relieved by some excellent camera work" (*New York Sun*, March 12, 1927, p. 8). *The Lodger* had been represented to Grierson as one of a group of "English films produced in the last year which are believed to be better than the average American picture," and he was keen to pour cold water on all of them, being convinced, or at any rate wishing to give the impression that he was convinced, that "England does not take its cinema very cinematically." A week later, however, returning to the subject of English directors, he gave Hitchcock more credit, calling him "the most outstanding of them, graduated by stages from commercial art. He is a young man of twenty-six, with a fine sense of camera, but somewhat untutored emotionally. He is very good with types and experiences of which he has personal knowledge. His worst fault is a tendency to stage trickery" (*New York Sun*, March 19, 1927, p. 8).

Grierson's remarks are notable largely because he repeated them at greater length some four years later, after he had made his own mark as a filmmaker and was engaged in proselytizing a very different conception of cinema from the one offered by the commercial features industry in which Hitchcock was employed; and because these later remarks—unlike most such remarks—eventually became a known quantity, to be discussed or dismissed, through their republication in his book *Grierson on Documentary*, whose first edition appeared in 1946. "In trying new material," wrote Grierson of *Rich and Strange*, "Hitchcock has found himself outside both his experience and his imagination," and this departure from the world he knew "has caught him short," leading him to rely on "the smart touch," the "clever little pieces" that, according to Grierson, the highbrows loved (Hardy 1946: 49–51). It is also worth noting, however, that Grierson's remarks do not depart as radically as it may seem from the consensus on Hitchcock—if one can speak of such a thing—that had been formed by early 1927.

It is true that *The Lodger* was hailed as the best British film that had yet been produced, and that Hitchcock was hailed as a master and a screen-genius on the strength of it. But it is also true that the same critics doing the hailing had a low estimation of his material. "The story, it must be confessed, is not wholly effective," wrote Mycroft after the trade show (*Evening Standard*, September 15, 1926, p. 3). "The narrative, apart from the producer's brilliantly clever treatment of it, is unsatisfactory," wrote Atkinson on the day of its release (*Daily Express*, January 17, 1927, p. 7). Lejeune, in "Britain's Baby," published after Grierson's columns appeared, but extremely unlikely to have been influenced by them, called the material of *The Lodger* "slight and sensational" (not a term of praise here) and hoped that one day "he may surprise us all, and himself among the number, by making a picture that is as good in its conception as in its execution" (*Manchester Guardian*, June 11, 1927, p. 9).

Grierson ultimately demanded that Hitchcock should make a film in the industrial North or Midlands "with the personals in their proper places and the life of a community instead of a benighted lady at stake" (Hardy 1966: 74), as if there were a way of ranking the matter of Hitchcock's films—desire, obsession, guilt, madness—against other, purportedly more serious things. Grierson was at least prepared to say directly what he thought was important, but he was incapable of seeing what the matter of Hitchcock's films really was, possibly because it was embodied in the form of the thriller or melodrama (then more or less interchangeable terms). More sympathetic contemporaries like Lejeune may not have been able—within the scope of brief notices, written on tight deadlines, for newspaper readers—to identify the meaning beneath the surface, but they saw what was meaningful.

Both Lejeune and Barry, the latter presumably writing actually on the day of the film's first screening, September 14, 1926, since her article appeared the following morning, tried in their first responses to evoke the film's opening sequence. "Mr. Alfred Hitchcock, the talented young director," wrote Barry, "opens it with a terrified, screaming woman's head, and swiftly follows with brilliant impressions of newspaper offices, the B.B.C., and paperboys all bruiting abroad the news of a murder" (*Daily Mail*, September 15, 1926, p. 7). Lejeune, for her part, aligned *The Lodger* with the "modern film" that "describes nothing—it hints, suggests, sketches, flashes from expression to expression," and wrote that when its director "wants to create a sense of dark mystery for his theme he opens with a series of cuts and flashes of mouths screaming, faces horrified and distorted, newspaper telegrams, rushing news-vans, words on a sky sign, words across the ether, all sorts of startled images" (*Manchester Guardian*, March 5, 1927, p. 11). Both writers knew that these were more than "smart touches," and that something vital was at stake.

*

In common with the vast majority of silent films, *The Lodger* practically disappeared from view in the 1930s and 1940s, but its reputation was kept alive, and in such a way that it became treated as the forerunner, along with *Blackmail*, of the series of British thrillers that made Hitchcock's international reputation in the mid-1930s. The pairing of *The Lodger* and *Blackmail* began almost as soon as the latter was released, notably in Paul Rotha's immensely influential book *The Film Till Now*, published in 1930, in which *The Lodger* is represented as Hitchcock's "most sincere work" and *Blackmail* as his return to a "progressive mood" after the "series of unpretentious pictures" (Rotha 1930: 232) from *Downhill* to *The Manxman*, for which Rotha had little regard. Some twenty years later, in Lindsay Anderson's study of Hitchcock in *Sequence*, *The Lodger* is "the basis of Hitchcock's style" (Anderson 2004: 412), with *Blackmail* the next film to build on it, and *The Man Who Knew Too Much*, the first of the major thrillers, the next after that, with lengthy gaps between in each case. For Anderson and his colleagues on *Sequence* and *Sight and Sound*, and for the two leading newspaper critics of the time, Dilys Powell of the *Sunday Times* and Richard Winnington of the *News Chronicle*, *The Lodger*, *Blackmail*, and the 1930s thrillers constituted the heights from which Hitchcock had fallen—with the exception of *Shadow of a Doubt*—in Hollywood. Few if any American critics could have seen *The Lodger*, but the British perspective was reproduced in the second edition of *The Film Till Now*, with its fat supplement by Richard Griffith of the Museum of Modern Art, published in 1949.

The Lodger was not centrally involved in the revaluation of Hitchcock from the mid-1950s onwards, a process whose inception it is the convention to attribute to the critics of *Cahiers du cinéma*, though it took on a quite different character in the English-speaking world. On the occasion of Hitchcock's first retrospective at the Museum of Modern Art in 1963, some fourteen years after Griffith had lamented his having fallen prey to "production supervision and star values" (Rotha and Griffith 1949: 557), Peter Bogdanovich, in a publication accompanying the season, followed precedent by lumping in *The Lodger* with *Blackmail* and the 1930s thrillers before asserting that Hitchcock's American films were "in every way more personal and mature, more controlled and original, more artful and serious" (Bogdanovich 1963: 3–4) than the films he had made in England, which Bogdanovich nonetheless rated "the best films ever made in that country." Bogdanovich is unlikely to have meant that *Secret Agent* was a better film than *The Red Shoes*, or that *The Man Who Knew Too Much* (1956) was more original than *The Man Who Knew Too Much* (1934); he was engaging in brute-force hucksterism. But hucksterism has its uses, and the swelling of Hitchcock's reputation brought attention, eventually, to his whole body of work, *The Lodger* included. It became, for the most part, the stuff of programme notes, capsule reviews, passages in career-survey books and biographies, and shorter ones in newspaper articles and magazine features.

Writing of this kind tends to blend biographical-historical and critical discourses, often with a strong bias towards the former, and that has proved to be the case with *The Lodger*, burdened as it is by the "first true Hitchcock" label its maker affixed to it. Ivor Montagu's claim that his edits saved *The Lodger* and with it Hitchcock's nascent career, part of Hitchcock lore since the 1940s, has informed not only accounts of the film's making but practically everything that has been written about it, partly because Montagu's story seems to provide a key to the mystery of how Hitchcock became Hitchcock. In Tom Ryall's *Alfred Hitchcock and the British Cinema*, and in many other sources, *The Lodger* is seen as the happy outcome of Hitchcock's education in European art cinema, made possible by his social betters in the Film Society, of which Montagu was the chairman, including the influence of Soviet montage theory and practice. *The Lodger* itself—the film not the myth—is somewhat peripheral to these discussions, and in reality there was no such influence, while the still pervasive idea that it was "the first true Hitchcock" obscures the fact that the most "Soviet" sequence in *The Lodger*, the opening that so struck its first critics, is quite unlike anything else in the Hitchcock oeuvre. Nevertheless, *The Lodger* has been subjected to serious critical scrutiny, notably by Maurice Yacowar in his pioneer work *Hitchcock's British Films* (1977), by William Rothman in *The Murderous Gaze* (1982), by Leslie Brill in *The Hitchcock Romance* (1988), by Richard Allen in "*The Lodger* and Hitchcock's Aesthetic" (2001–2002), by Michael Williams in *Ivor Novello: Screen Idol* (2003), by Jessica Brent in "Beyond the Gaze" (2004), by Murray Pomerance in "Light, Looks, and *The Lodger*" (2009), and by David Trotter in "Hitchcock's Modernism" (2010).

With the American films long ago ensconced in the canon, *The Lodger* is no longer bracketed with *Blackmail* and the 1930s thrillers but treated as the precursor of a wider range of films. In his landmark book *English Hitchcock*, published on Hitchcock's centenary, Charles Barr remarks that Hitchcock's earliest literary influences were the "fascinatingly complementary figures" of John Buchan, "the novelist of action and adventure," progenitor of the 1930s thrillers, and Marie Belloc Lowndes, "the novelist of interior drama," author of *The Lodger* (Barr 1999: 15). For Barr, the gendered "Buchan/Belloc Lowndes dialectic" structures Hitchcock's whole career so that in his reading, at least by implication, *The Lodger* is aligned more with the likes of *Rebecca* than it is with thrillers like *The 39 Steps*. My own work, in *The First True Hitchcock*, extends this argument, identifying in *The Lodger*—for the first time, so far as I am aware—an uncanny anticipation of *Vertigo*.

As the romance between the titular Lodger and Daisy, the daughter of the house, blooms, he buys her a dress he has seen her modelling in the course of her job as a living mannequin in a West End salon. Later in the film, having been accused of being the serial killer, he tells her his secret—that he is not the killer but the brother of one of his victims, whose death he is trying to avenge—by means of a flashback to his sister's murder. In the flashback, his sister is wearing the same dress he has just bought Daisy (see Fig. 1.2). The Lodger, just like Scotty in the later film, wants his new love to resemble an old one—only in this case it is his sister. It is difficult to imagine this being made explicit, and of course there is the possibility that it was an accident of some kind—perhaps, for example, in the script at the time of shooting it was not his sister but his girlfriend or fiancée. But there is also to be weighed the claim in Patrick McGilligan's biography that Hitchcock's sister Nellie "took a job as a mannequin for a job in

Figure 1.2 The titular Lodger (Ivor Novello) with his sister (Eve Gray), moments before her murder.

The Lodger, dir. Alfred Hitchcock, prod. Gainsborough Pictures, 1926

Oxford Street" (McGilligan 2003: 16).[5] Possibly all this seemed less strange at the time, but it is at least evidence that a century after its release the last word on *The Lodger* has not been heard.

Notes

1. In the published version, the publicity chief's sex is omitted.
2. For an account of Barry's time on the *Daily Mail*, see my article "In Northcliffe Jail: Iris Barry, Film Journalist" (Miller 2024).
3. My thanks to Pamela Hutchinson for identifying "M.W.D."
4. For an overview of Hitchcock and Lejeune's friendship, see my article "Sympathetic Guidance: Hitchcock and C. A. Lejeune" (Miller 2015).
5. McGilligan's book is without references, so it is difficult to know where this information came from — hence its absence from my own book.

References

Allen, Richard (2001–2002) "*The Lodger* and the Origins of Hitchcock's Aesthetic," *Hitchcock Annual*, vol. 10, pp. 38–78.
Anderson, Lindsay (2004) "Alfred Hitchcock," in *Never Apologise: The Collected Writings*, London: Plexus, pp. 410–421.
Barr, Charles (1999) *English Hitchcock*, Moffat: Cameron & Hollis.
Barry, Iris (1926) *Let's Go to the Pictures*, London: Chatto & Windus.
Bogdanovich, Peter (1963) *The Cinema of Alfred Hitchcock*, New York: The Museum of Modern Art Film Library.
Brent, Jessica (2004) "Beyond the Gaze: Visual Fascination and the Feminine Image in Silent Hitchcock," *Camera Obscura*, 19 (1) (55): 77–111.
Brill, Leslie (1988) *The Hitchcock Romance*: *Love and Irony in Hitchcock's Films*, Princeton, NJ: Princeton University Press.
Hardy, Forsyth (ed.) (1946) *Grierson on Documentary*, London: Collins.
Hardy, Forsyth (ed.) (1966) *Grierson on Documentary*, rev. edn, London: Faber & Faber.
McGilligan, Patrick (2003) *Alfred Hitchcock: A Life in Darkness and Light*, Chichester: Wiley.
Miller, Henry K. (2015) "Sympathetic Guidance: Hitchcock and C. A. Lejeune," *Hitchcock Annual*, vol. 20, pp. 33–64.
Miller, Henry K. (2022) *The First True Hitchcock*: *The Making of a Filmmaker*, Oakland, Calif: University of California Press.
Miller, Henry K. (2024) "In Northcliffe Jail: Iris Barry, Film Journalist," *Journal of Early Popular Visual Culture*, 21 (4): 57–67.
Montagu, Ivor (1980) "Working with Hitchcock," *Sight and Sound*, 49 (3): 189–193.
Pomerance, Murray (2009) "Light, Looks, and *The Lodger*," *Quarterly Review of Film and Video*, 26 (5): 425–433.
Rotha, Paul (1930) *The Film Till Now*, London: Jonathan Cape.
Rotha, Paul, and Richard Griffith (1949) *The Film Till Now*: *A Survey of World Cinema*, London: Vision Press.
Rothman, William (1982) *Hitchcock: The Murderous Gaze*, Cambridge, Mass.: Harvard University Press.
Ryall, Tom (1986) *Alfred Hitchcock and the British Cinema*, London: Croom Helm.
Trotter, David (2010) "Hitchcock's Modernism," *Modernist Cultures*, 5 (1): 123–139.
Truffaut, François, and Helen G. Scott (1967) *Hitchcock*, New York: Simon & Schuster.
Williams, Michael (2003) *Ivor Novello*: *Screen Idol*, London: British Film Institute.
Yacowar, Maurice (1977) *Hitchcock's British Films*, Hamden, Conn.: Archon Books.

Chapter 2
The Two *Blackmails* from 1929
A Reputation Crosses the Sound Barrier

Bryony Dixon

Alfred Hitchcock's *Blackmail* (1929) was, and is, all about "reputation." At the time when it was conceived and made, Hitchcock intended it to carry his reputation as a film director across the Rubicon of silent to sound film and into the future. The reputation of the film itself, that is the sound version, was hailed by contemporaries as transformative in the transition to sound. It had a particular appeal to the British audience to whom it gave hope in the face of poor imported sound films and badly made part-talkies, and the figure of Hitchcock was seen as central to the film's success. Added to this was the fact that not only had he produced this exceptional sound film, but he had also made a sublime silent version that was greeted with enthusiasm by audiences and critics alike. Its reputation now cements it as a classic in the canon of silent films.

Then there is *Blackmail's* subsequent reputation. As Mark Glancy wrote in his chapter, "Hitchcock and Film Nationalism," which contains an excellent condensed historiography of writings on the film both at the time and more recently: "from the time of its release until the present day, *Blackmail* has inspired extensive critical and scholarly attention … Like other classic films then, *Blackmail* has endured because it suited the interests of successive waves of critics and audiences" (2007: 186).

Because of who made it and when it was made, *Blackmail* will, of course, continue to be useful. It is lovely to write about and to pick apart. It has a delightful symmetry, which would be even more elegant if Hitchcock had been allowed his original ending. It serves as a perfect case study to explain the transition to sound film as well as Hitchcock's interests, ambitions, filmmaking style and methods. And, as Glancy has documented, the process of examining *Blackmail* as an example of clever construction started from the time it was made. Tom Ryall (1986) likewise points to this early usage in a 1936 Film Society event in London, which used clips from Hitchcock films to demonstrate sound technique, and in the same year a screening of *Blackmail* for the purposes of comparison with Lewis Milestone's dialogue-heavy *The Front Page* (1931) at the Everyman Cinema, in Hampstead, one of the first repertory cinemas where films were studied for their artistry.

Contemporaries in the small world of film criticism in the late 1920s Britain were just as avid as later historians to point out the film's clever features. As Kenneth Macpherson, editor of *Close Up* put it, "We are not burning to make a written orderliness of the implications, but we are interested to do so, because it is a film of essentially an examinable nature and of a nature that once examined, is far and away the most significant determinant to unification of sound-sight, deliberately and sustainedly that we have yet had" (1929: 257).

Edgar Anstey, writing twenty years later, notices the same quality (1949: 240–241):

The coming of the sound film might have been expected to offer a special threat to Hitchcock's imagery. Most other directors were in the deepest despair. The beautiful, economical eloquence of the silent image now, they cried, was lost. The camera henceforth was to be tied to the ponderous, unselective sound recording equipment; imagination would be rooted to the studio floor. The contribution which Hitchcock made to the release of less optimistic directors from this gloomy misconception has come to be symbolized in a simple trick that he employed in *Blackmail* and which is less remarkable in itself than in the possibilities which it revealed (and the affection in which it is held by writers on the cinema).

Blackmail's reputation and the fame of its director meant that the film's physical and cultural survival was assured. It was one of the British Film Institute's earliest acquisitions into the National Film Archive in the 1940s, directly from John Maxwell at Associate British Pictures, and it was screened regularly at the National Film Theatre from 1952 onwards. Significantly, it made it into the legendary "360 Classics" list, a repertory programme of the world's best films selected by the BFI archive's Keeper of Fiction Film. Claude Chabrol and Éric Rohmer wrote about it enthusiastically in 1957, in their book *Hitchcock: The First Forty-Four Films*, and it has been regularly screened, taught and written about by generations of cinephiles ever since.

The growth in reputation of the silent version of *Blackmail* is more recent, although, again, contemporary observers saw it, and some, such as Paul Rotha, thought it superior. Good prints of the silent version were not generally available for a while, except to the collectors and very serious enthusiasts, but in 1982 the BFI printed it up on 35 mm and circulated it to those cinemas that could show silent film, and it was well received as an elegant example of late silent film art. The availability of the film led to the intense scrutiny of the two versions by Charles Barr in an article in *Sight and Sound* (spring 1983) and in further detail in his book *English Hitchcock* in 1999, which seems to have sparked an interest in this game of textual analysis. His thoroughness has left us with little to say on the matter, although I will come on to explain some of the findings of the restoration of the film in 2012, which confirm his conjectures.

In recent decades, the trend for big orchestral treatments of the canon of classics of silent cinema has further enhanced the reputation of the silent version. The BFI toured both versions during the Hitchcock centenary in 1999. In 2008, I introduced the film in front of several thousand people, crammed into the Piazza Maggiore at Bologna's Il Cinema Ritrovato Festival, to see the film with Neil Brand's wonderful Herrmann-esque score for full orchestra. Then, in 2012, it got the five-star restoration treatment as part of the "Hitchcock 9," a project by the BFI National Archive that I worked on, as lead curator with the technical team headed up by Kieron Webb and Ben Thompson, to restore all his surviving silent films. This formed the BFI's contribution to the cultural programme surrounding the London Olympics, putting Alfred Hitchcock on a level with other British cultural icons such as Shakespeare and Dickens—enhancing his reputation with a general public not well versed in their own film history. From here, the film travelled the world, with its largest crowd—a staggering 25,000 seated on the Odessa Steps in 2014 (see Fig. 2.1).

Figure 2.1 25,000 spectators watch *Blackmail* at the 2014 Odessa International Film Festival.
Courtesy of BFI National Archive.

I mentioned earlier some discoveries that were made during the project to restore the silent films that have a bearing on the reputation of Hitchcock as a director and the silent/sound versions of *Blackmail*. As we compared the different prints and negatives and attempted to reconstruct some of the most cut-about films, the sophistication of the filmmaking, from his first film as director, became evident; this was not juvenilia. *The Pleasure Garden* (1926), for example, which now has almost a reel's length of extra footage compared to previously available versions, restored to their place in the film, scenes and shots that revealed Hitchcock's subtle use of symbolism and clarity of structure: a half-eaten apple glimpsed after a wedding-night scene (see Fig. 2.2) or a close-up of a cup of tea with a floating tea leaf in it. (For those who knew the old wives' tale, this presages trouble in the form of the arrival of a stranger.) Hitchcock would continue to use these motifs of which the knife as a constant reminder of the murder in *Blackmail* is a similar example.

From his first film then, we can see the trademark touches that marked Hitchcock out as one of the cleverest filmmakers of his generation. This is not to say that all his films were great successes, and he was working within a complex commercial environment with modest budgets; furthermore, despite a reasonable amount of autonomy, he was a studio employee with the usual constraints. Nevertheless, we can see Hitchcock building his reputation as the various projects arose. His strategy, as Ivor Montagu had it in his oft-quoted reminiscence of Hitchcock declaring that he made films not for audiences or studio bosses but "for the press," by means of peppering his films with clever flourishes that they would write about, seems to have worked. *Blackmail*'s clever expressionistic uses of sound were planned by Hitchcock in a wholly deliberate way for the press to pick up on—and here we are, still talking about them today.

Figure 2.2 The symbolism of a bitten apple in *The Pleasure Garden* (1926). Courtesy of BFI National Archive.

Immersed in Hitchcock's silents during the restoration project, my colleagues and I began to build up a vocabulary of techniques that Hitchcock used in his films. One that strikes me as relevant here is an example from *The Ring* (1927) showing that the prescient Hitchcock saw early on that sound film was coming and that any director who was going to survive the transition needed to be both on top of the technology and also capable of supplying that extra dimension to the narrative construction of the film. This would convince audiences that sound film was not just, in his damning phrase, "photographs of people talking." So, take, for example, the famous "shock cut" Hitchcock uses in the sound version of *Blackmail*, where Alice White wandering the streets of London in her fugue state after stabbing the artist sees the flopped arm of a drunk, mirroring in her mind the arm of the dead artist. On the cut, the scream we expect from her is seen to be coming from the landlady as she finds the artist's body. According to Barry Salt, this is the first example in film history of the shock cut: as he defines it, "a cut to a different scene, accompanied by a sharp discontinuity in the accompanying sound" (1990: 284). We can compare this to a scene in *The Ring* where Hitchcock uses a similar cut but using a visual representation of a sound. Early in the film, two pairs of characters are having private conversations on either side of a Gypsy caravan, from which Clare Greet, as a fortune teller, is mischievously eavesdropping on both. Instead of clumsily cutting between each pair, Hitchcock shows her listening to the illicit flirting of one couple (Mabel and Bob Corby). At this point, a shot of a kettle boiling over elicits her sudden reaction to the "sound." Crossing the room to deal with the kettle, she is then facing the right direction to look through the opposite window to listen in to the conversation of the other pair (Jack and the fight promoter). The image of the whistling kettle in this case acts as a kind of inaudible sound bridge in the same way as the audible scream in *Blackmail*. It's a device Hitchcock uses again; for example, the famous screaming landlady/train whistle in *The 39 Steps* (1935). He uses several visual "sound" cues in the silent *Blackmail*, such as the shot of the shop's doorbell in the breakfast scene, the "sound" of which makes Alice jump and drop the knife, and an aural interruption indicated by a shot of a ringing bell in the inspector's office.

This demonstrates that Hitchcock had a repertoire of filmmaking tricks up his sleeve, ready to use in his hybrid film. And he could also develop new ones. The device of the distorted soundtrack, as in the over-loud canary singing in its cage, the shop bell and the gossip talking in the breakfast scene, from which Alice (and we) can eventually only hear the word "knife," must have been a new technique developed on the hoof by Hitchcock and his new sound crew. As Hitchcock, the arch manipulator, had foreseen, interviewers focused on the impressive flourishes that he wanted them to notice. The whole issue of how the sound film was made seems to have caught the public interest even as it was being made. As the RCA sound equipment arrived at Elstree and the plans for the film changed, there was some effort to document the process for the press. Michael Powell took some production stills, and there were visits to the set by journalists (see Fig. 2.3).

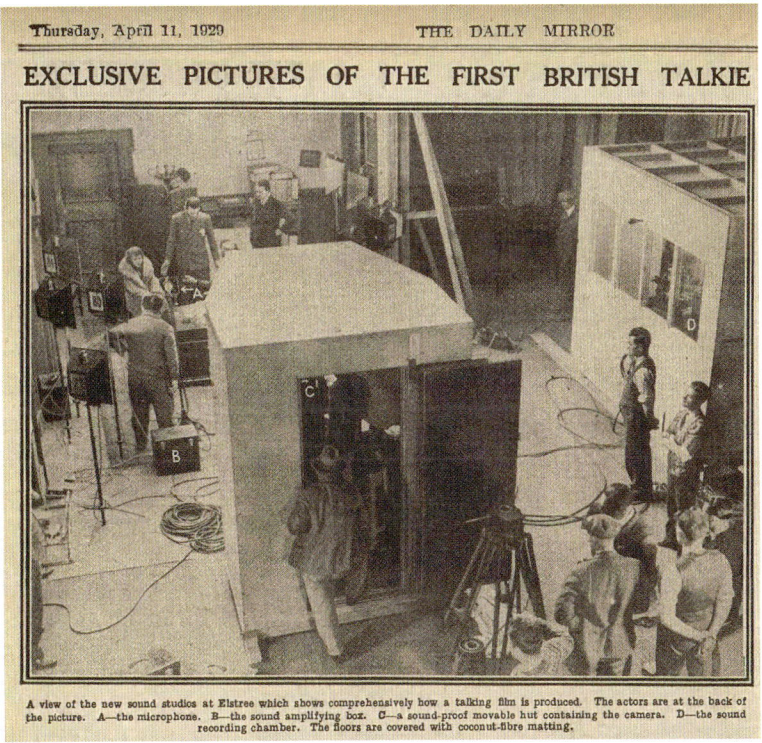

Figure 2.3 Exclusive visit to the set of *Blackmail* showing the sound stage with Hitchcock on the left facing the actors.

Daily Mirror, 11 April 1929, BFI Reuben Library.

Principal photography commenced in February when much of the silent-version footage was filmed, but it seems likely that the RCA Phototone equipment, which Maxwell had secured for the new sound stage in Elstree studios, must have been on the way or being tested. It was already installed and working by press announcements on April 1 and 6. Hitchcock seems to have delighted in the story, much repeated in later life, that his bosses didn't know till the premiere that he was making a full talkie; perhaps they should have read the papers as *Daily Mirror* journalists seemed to have known in April. On an "exclusive" set visit to the studio, to see the new wonder technology in action, they described *Blackmail* as "the first British full length talking film," which doesn't sound like they were talking about a part-talkie. Other prestigious set visits were arranged to the studio during the shoot—most notably in May by the Duke and Duchess of York (the future George VI and Queen Mary).

In trying to determine how clever Hitchcock was being with shooting scenes and sequences that could be used for both silent and sound versions during the making of *Blackmail*, it is useful to be aware of the chronology. Not much time passed between the start of the silent-version shooting and the decision by the studio to do a sound version with music and effects and with whatever percentage of dialogue. Music must have been commissioned some time before the sound reshoots in April and then recorded. We also know that a theme was incorporated into this score (in the scene where Alice, walking through the city, passes the West End theatre) from the song "Miss Up to Date," which Cyril Ritchard was performing in March in the stage revue *Love Lies*. This was later marketed as a tie-in with the film. All of which suggests that decision-making on the sound components of the film were happening rapidly between the silent footage being filmed and the sound retakes, where in another clever move Hitchcock cleverly integrated the lyrics of the song into the meaning of the seduction scene.

In terms of the editing and integration of the two versions, the restoration project revealed that the opening sequence, with the Flying Squad vehicle racing through the streets of London, was slightly poorer in quality than the rest of the print, which all came directly from the original negative, suggesting that the scene was duplicated footage. This would support the idea that the silent version was made *after* the sound version. It was unlikely they expensively reshot the police-van sequence so the original negative of this scene was likely used in the sound version and then duplicated for the silent edit. This confirms that the making of the two versions overlapped.

The restoration project of Hitchcock's silent films as a whole revealed that Hitchcock, in line with studio practice in Britain, always made two negatives. This was the practice everywhere but was done in different ways. In larger, better financed studios, such as those in Hollywood, they used two or more cameras to record two negatives simultaneously. In British studios, it was more usual to use one camera crew to film each shot twice, sequentially. The purpose of assembling two negatives made up from the different shots is to have two versions to print from, partly as backup in case of processing errors or accidents and partly to have a version (they are usually called A and B negatives) from which to make additional prints for export. This was in the days before intermediate duplicating film stocks were available so that all prints had to be made directly from the assembled negatives to avoid any loss of quality (although occasionally they did have to make duplicates as we have seen). We could see this very clearly in the case of *The Ring* (1927), where we have the domestic version at the BFI National Archive and which we compared with a French version from another collection (Dixon and Webb 2012). Comparison of the two, reveals that the shots vary very slightly, so we can deduce that the individual shots were filmed, then immediately reset and reshot with the same camera.

Why does this matter? Again this is about whether or not, and how far ahead of the decision to do a part talkie, Hitchcock planned to leapfrog his rivals by making a full talking picture. Was it premeditated?

Charles Barr's detailed analysis of the two versions of *Blackmail* in his chapter from *English Hitchcock*, reveal that silent footage and sound reshoots are mixed up in both versions. There are shots from the sound reshoots in the silent version (you can tell from cast changes). Barr speculated that two negatives were made for the film, having observed that most of the individual shots of the sound and silent versions are different, even for those sections which previous writers had assumed were shot silent and then simply had soundtrack (music and effects) added. The comparisons made during the restoration process confirm this.

Barr details several instances of difference in the opening reel, which was designed to be free of dialogue—the shot of the New Scotland Yard sign is one example that can be seen clearly. It is impressive how actors and crew could recreate shots so they were near identical. My personal favorite pair of shots takes place in the early sequence where Frank and the other detective have just arrived at the upstairs room of a poor tenement, where their suspect is in bed. The villain is ostensibly reading a newspaper while keeping a close eye on the detectives in the reflection of a mirrored lamp. We see him holding the paper smoking a cigarette, whose ash is about to fall. It falls. One might assume that you couldn't recreate the accidental falling of ash from a cigarette. But if you compare the frames before the ash falls and the frame after, in the sound and silent versions, you can see the actor's hands are in a slightly different position vis-à-vis the photos on the newspaper, leading us to conclude that they did indeed retake the shot and stage the falling of the cigarette ash (see Fig. 2.4). It seems unlikely that anyone would go to this trouble if it were not necessary to have near identical shots.

From this we can say that the sound and silent versions were made from the two sets of shots that went to make up the edited negatives. Hitchcock clearly planned many long sequences where he didn't have to use recorded dialogue—the whole first reel, much of the scene after the murder, Alice's long walk through London at night, and the final chase. In fact, the dialogue sequences make up surprisingly little of the film. But, crucially, this didn't seem to matter. Where part-talkies, made that year, were proudly announcing the percentages of sound to silent running time, *Blackmail* was hailed as the first full talkie. It went down a storm. It was designed to be a success, and it was, receiving plaudits even in the usually hostile American press. *Variety* called it

> a piece of craftsmanship which makes the stuff which has come over so far look like nobody's business. Not just a talker but a motion picture that talks. Alfred J. Hitchcock has solved the problem of making a picture which does not lose any film technique and gains effect from dialog. It will have the same effect on American technique that German films had half a dozen years ago.
>
> (*Variety*, July 10, 1929, p. 24)

Hitchcock had pulled off a considerable coup, masking the inadequacies of the technology at his disposal in early 1929. With a modest amount of dialogue, a lead actress that had to have her words spoken by someone else, no noise-reduction equipment, boom mics or postproduction dubbing, it is remarkable that his hybrid film was not the mess that other films of the time were. And yet, for all that Hitchcock dazzled the press with his clever touches, he had also produced a decent film that "talked" and had authenticity.

Hitchcock's choice of subject, "the study in fear," as Kenneth Macpherson called it, was a masterstroke. It built on his former success, *The Lodger* (1926) and played to the cinemagoing audience, who he understood well. He was one of them, after all. That solid lower-middle-class London background—shopkeepers and cab-drivers or semi-professionals in the burgeoning service industries of the capital—had

Figure 2.4 The sound version of *Blackmail* at a point where cigarette ash falls and the same frame in the silent version.

the most to lose from the blunt instrument that was the Law. It was all too easy to slip just one notch down the social ladder into the abyss of poverty from which it was almost impossible to climb out. This is what makes the artist, Crewe, so attractive to Alice: he seems to float above society's conventions, and it's what makes Tracy the blackmailer so desperate; he is on that slippery slope, in the opening reel, towards the state of the career criminal for whom the Law has no forgiveness or latitude. Hitchcock knew that his audience, made up largely of this class, would understand the fear of blind justice.

It is relevant because this is the rationale for the long opening sequence in which the Flying Squad rush to a poor part of the city to arrest a suspect, which is one of the most important parts of the film. Originally it was matched, as per Charles Bennett's source play, by the neat but tragic ending, where the girl is sucked under and processed by the system, as the underclass criminal is, in this opening sequence. It's widely misunderstood by later writers, perhaps because it's very long as an opening montage, which are usually only a couple of minutes in the classical filmmaking mode. Tom Ryall likens it to a documentary treatment. To my mind, this is all drama. It opens like a 1930s crime picture with the spinning wheels of a police van racing through the city streets. And any thoughts of documentary seriousness are surely undermined by the sampler on the wall above the wanted man's bed (difficult to spot even for the ardent film restorer) which reads "The Lord helps those who help themselves," a phrase famously *not* from the Bible and a classic piece of Hitchcockian humor.

Harry Watt, as it happens a famous documentarist and director of *Nightmail* (1936), in his perceptive article, "Reseeing *Blackmail*" from *World Film News* in April 1937, saw no such documentary tendency but put his finger on Hitchcock's essential driver:

> Of course, the quality of the sound was frightful. Burps and hoops punctuated the conversations. Anny Ondra mouthed her shop-girl's words in front of the camera, while Joan Barry minced Mayfair into the microphone off the set. But in spite of all this the fact remains that in *Blackmail* Hitch didn't think of sound as a new trick to put words into his characters' mouths—he thought of it as a new dramatic medium, something with which to build up suspense, drama, and interest. In the silent sections he used music. Music for reels at a time. And it worked. The action was quicker and just as intense. There was no feeling of artificiality through lack of speech. And where there was speech it was used almost wholly for dramatic effect, not to prove to the audience that the actors had uvulas and larynxes.

So contemporaries clearly felt that apart from some clunkiness in the sound recording, which we can forgive, given the technology available to him (and still a great deal better than other films of those years), the film as a whole integrated dialogue and sound to the benefit of the film as a whole. Apart from his expressionistic use of sound, which was the film's greatest achievement, the score and effects also went some way to smoothing out any clunkiness. Jack Sullivan's work on the use of music in Hitchcock's films suggests, in the regrettable absence of information about the process, that "the patterns are so astonishingly consistent with Hitchcockian music in later films—music frequently cued by Hitchcock's extensive, immaculately preserved music notes—that it is reasonable to suppose he controlled it a great deal" (Sullivan 2006: 3; see also Coda A).

This seems plausible—he must have had extensive requirements for the music—but we may never know. As director of a silent film, Hitchcock wouldn't have had much control about scoring for previous projects, this being largely a matter for the exhibitor and only occasionally for producers. However, in the case of *Blackmail*, we can only surmise that, like the visuals for the film, the music was developed in its different iterations as the plans changed for the film. Roger Manvell and John Huntley made these observations in 1957:

> Britain was fortunate that her first true production in sound proved to be a film of some distinction— Alfred Hitchcock's *Blackmail* ... the musical accompaniment had already been considered on the basis of a "live" orchestral accompaniment in the cinemas and *Blackmail* offers a recorded example of a silent film score, with only occasional, if interesting, concessions to sound film technique ... the musical score is composed of material supplied by Campbell and Connelly, compiled and arranged by Hubert Bath and Harry Stafford. It is played by The British International Symphony Orchestra conducted by John Reynders.
>
> (Manvell and Huntley 1975: 27)

The credit information is borne out by the main titles of the film, but otherwise information on the score is scarce. Elizabeth Weis (1982: 52) conjectures that the score is unlikely to have been developed first for the silent version on the basis that Campbell and Connelly were basically song publishers, but it could be they were tentatively commissioning library music for use in film, as other publishers like HMV were, in the febrile atmosphere of 1929 when cinema orchestras were being laid off all over the country. It's worth noting that the main players, Reynders, Bath, and Stafford, were all working flat out on other film projects for British International Pictures at the same time, including *Kitty* and *Under the Greenwood Tree,* both near contenders with *Blackmail* for the first British sound film.

John Reynders conducted the score for the recording of the sound version with the newly formed British International Pictures Symphony Orchestra, and it was also issued in disc form for those cinemas still stuck with that format. Nothing of the *Blackmail* score was published, and we know nothing of any of the composers except for one, Charles Williams, and that only anecdotally. He was a conductor of cinema orchestras and a prolific composer of light music for film, best known now for the iconic "The Devil's Gallop." It is possible that Williams was one of several writing for Campbell and Connelly. Whether traces of these musicians' style are discernible in the score I leave to the musicologists.

So, Hitchcock had planned not to survive but to thrive in the new world of sound film. He had chosen his subject wisely for mass appeal and to build on his previous success, *The Lodger.* As well as being well prepared with his repertoire of filmmaking techniques, he had also pivoted in the face of changing technology and studio demands and skillfully integrated his material to produce two exceptional films in two distinct modes. *Blackmail* rescued Hitchcock's reputation after the tepid response to his previous two films, *Champagne* (1928) and *The Manxman* (1929) and confirmed his status as a top director. Of course, even after stepping so neatly over the sound barrier, his future was not all plain sailing. As a studio man, he still had to do projects he may not have chosen, but his reputation was now his to lose—he never really did—and it is in part the effort he put into *Blackmail* that clinched it.

References

Anstey, E. (1949) "Development of Film Technique in Britain," in Roger Manvell (ed.), *Experiment in the Film*, London: Grey Wall Press, pp. 240–241.
Barr, C. (1983) "Blackmail Silent & Sound," *Sight and Sound*, 52 (2): 122.
Barr, C. (1999) *English Hitchcock*, Moffat: Cameron & Hollis.
Chabrol, C., and É. Rohmer (1957) *Hitchcock: The First Forty-Four Films*, Oxford: Roundhouse, pp. 21–24.
Dixon, B., and K. Webb (2012) "Restoring Hitchcock," *Journal of Film Preservation*, 87: 89–95.
Glancy, M. (2007) "*Blackmail* (1929): Hitchcock and Film Nationalism," in J. Chapman, M. Glancy, and S. Harper (eds), *The New Film History: Sources, Methods, Approaches*, Basingstoke: Palgrave Macmillan, pp. 185–200.
Huntley, J., and M. Roger (1975) *The Technique of Film Music*, 2nd edn, London: Focal Press.
Macpherson, K. (1979) "As Is: By the Editor," *Close Up*, 5 (6): 447.
Manvell, R. (ed.) (1949) *Experiment in the Film*, London: Grey Walls Press.
Rotha, P. (1930) *The Film Till Now*: *A Survey of World Cinema*, New York: Jonathan Cape & Harrison Smith.
Ryall, T. (1986) *Alfred Hitchcock and the British Cinema*, 2nd edn, London: Croom Helm.
Salt, B. (1990) *Film Style and Technology*, London: Starword.
Sullivan, J. (2006) *Hitchcock's Music*, New Haven, Conn.: Yale University Press.
Watt, H. (1937) "Reseeing *Blackmail*," *World Film News*, April, p. 15.
Weis, E. (1982) *The Silent Scream: Alfred Hitchcock's Sound Track*, Rutherford, NJ: Fairleigh Dickinson University Press.

Chapter 3

"No Manners at All and Always Seeing Things"

The Return of Hitchcock's Vanished Englishwomen in *The 39 Steps* (1935) and *The Lady Vanishes* (1938)

J. E. Smyth

The cumulative bibliography on women in Alfred Hitchcock's films would crush even the Master of Suspense, but most of the scholarship and popular fantasizing has focused on the director's post-1940 Hollywood films, including *Rebecca* (1940), *Spellbound* (1945), *Notorious* (1946), *Rear Window* (1954), *Vertigo* (1958), *North by Northwest* (1959), *Psycho* (1960), *The Birds* (1963), and *Marnie* (1964). Hitchcock's blondes are a recognizable collection, pinned by the male gaze, occasionally finding surface empowerment through Edith Head's costumes, but ultimately condemned to matrimony or murder. Though Ingrid Bergman had a memorable role as a psychoanalyst in *Spellbound*, in Hitchcock's American thrillers, women's paid jobs are almost always tied to selling sex. Even spies Eve (Eva Marie Saint) in *North by Northwest* and Alicia (Bergman again) in *Notorious* have to bed down with their marks and be "rescued" by other men. Secretaries (Janet Leigh in *Psycho* and Tippi Hedren in *Marnie*) and barmaids (Anna Massey in *Frenzy*, 1972) fare even worse. Despite patrician Lisa Fremont's (Grace Kelly) provenance as a fictionalized model for businesswoman Anita Colby (Lemire 2000: 70–73), *Rear Window*'s heroine is still perversely focused on marrying the greying remains of L. B. Jefferies (James Stewart).

It's tempting to shrug off Hitchcock's representational tendencies during this period of his career as a reflection of the postwar USA's cultural return to misogyny and more restrictive gender roles, but the director's work was not always so hypersexualized and anti-feminist. To locate what Charles Barr has termed Hitchcock's "strong and often sympathetic parts for women" (1999: 14–15), spectators need to tighten their belts, abandon his big-budget Hollywood features, and return to the 1930s and English austerity.[1]

The 39 Steps and *The Lady Vanishes* have endured as the most transatlantically successful films from Hitchcock's English era. Domestically, *The 39 Steps* was acclaimed "the most popular film of the year" (*Nottingham Evening Post*, December 4, 1935), and even in Scotland, critics dubbed Hitchcock the "King of British thriller-directors" (*Dundee Evening Telegraph*, January 4, 1936). American critics saw *The 39 Steps* as "the British *It Happened One Night*" (*Screenland*, September 1935, p. 53) and as a breakthrough foreign film. A few years later, *The Lady Vanishes* opened to universal acclaim, and the éminence grise of American culture, Gilbert Seldes, complained that Hollywood had lost its touch, bested by Hitchcock's "eccentric people," "enlightened comedy," and "camera shifts connected by sound effects" (Seldes 1939). He needn't have worried. By 1939, Hitchcock belonged to American producer David O. Selznick. Stunned and resentful that the director had abandoned England for a lucrative Hollywood contract (and within weeks of the onset of World War II), London *Times* critic Dilys Powell rewrote praise of *The Lady Vanishes*. Under her watch, the film became the high point of national film production because its ensemble artistry defined the collective, idiosyncratic national spirit on the brink of war—not because it was a Hitchcock film (*Sunday Times*, April 9, 1939, p. 4; March 16, 1941, p. 3; January 16, 1949, p. 2).

Despite Powell's reputation as a prominent feminist,[2] neither she nor any of her colleagues noticed that *The Lady Vanishes* and *The 39 Steps* are the only pre-Hollywood Hitchcock films to feature women unencumbered by the patriarchy; they are free of onscreen husbands (*The Man Who Knew Too Much*, 1934), policemen fathers (*Young and Innocent*, 1937), and other creepy male relatives (*Jamaica Inn*, 1939). Increasingly from the 1960s and the rise of professional film studies scholarship and Hitchcock studies, the heroines of *The 39 Steps* and *The Lady Vanishes* have been marginalized in favor of onscreen women more compliant with dominant theoretical discourses testifying to the objectification, fetishization, and victimization of women. This essay offers some historical alternatives to more traditional film studies and Hitchcock scholarship.

Adapting [to] Independent Englishwomen

Although women were never integral to the plots of John Buchan's espionage novels featuring Richard Hannay, twenty years and multiple editions after the 1915 publication of *The Thirty-Nine Steps*, screenwriters Charles Bennett and Ian Hay helped Hitchcock transform the all-male cast of the classic imperialist spy novel into a hectic three-night, three-woman thriller. As Hannay (Robert Donat) dodges a lethal ring of foreign agents and local policemen, he is supported by a sophisticated Mata Hari type (German star Lucie Mannheim) and submissive Scottish farmer's wife (English stage actress Peggy Ashcroft) but meets his match in the blonde, middle-class Pamela (Madeleine Carroll) aboard a train.

The 39 Steps has been explored by a range of film historians over the years, including Barr, Charles Silet, Mark Glancy, Toby Miller, and Noel King, but none of these men has been particularly interested in why Pamela is on that train north or speculated on her possible profession (given that a third of all Englishwomen worked outside the home in 1935, not an unreasonable question). For male scholars Pamela is just "the blonde from the train" (Silet 2009: 114)—initially dismissed by Glancy because she is not displayed like a sexual object. According to Glancy, her 1930s outfit resembles a "a nun's habit," and her glasses (necessary for anyone trying to read the *Times* in poor light on a rumbling train) are "spinsterish" (Glancy 2003: 55).[3] Pamela's professional attire—known as sportswear to contemporary designers, clients, and the media—was of a type favored by middle-class and working-class women on both sides of the Atlantic to help them get from work to evening without having to change (Arnold 2009). The style was not only worn on screen by Carroll but was also favored off screen by women in the British film industry, including screenwriter and film editor Alma Reville (Fig. 3.1). Hannay may gate-crash the Scottish by-election meeting, but Pamela, escorting the real speaker, has a reason to be there. All contextual evidence from her attire to her familiarity with the members and speaker suggest that she is an English political party member working for an English-born candidate for the Scottish seat. It was a well-established form of Westminster colonialism (or "British" politics) and derives from Buchan's novel, when Hannay seeks help from Sir Harry, a dim but well-meaning English laird living on his Scottish estate who is standing for the local seat. Bennett and Hitchcock cut Sir Harry from the film adaptation but fashioned Pamela out of the remains of the political scenes.[4]

Women in Great Britain had been working as mostly Liberal and Conservative mayors, councillors, and civil servants long before they became Members of Parliament in 1918 (Thackery 2010).[5] In 1935 alone, sixty-seven women stood as candidates, and nine were elected or reelected, including Florence Horsbrugh, the Conservative MP for Dundee (*Dundee Evening Telegraph and Post*, October 29, 1935, p. 1). Post-suffrage-era British women over twenty-one not only stood for local and regional political office but also served in powerful women's networks for social change (Rasmussen 1983; Graves 1994; Hannam 2010). Pamela's appearance alongside a range of older female party members at the front of

Figure 3.1 Left to right: Madeleine Carroll and Alma Reville, wearing versions of the working woman's sportswear, and Hitchcock. Production still from *The 39 Steps*, directed by Alfred Hitchcock.

© Gaumont-British Picture Corporation 1935. All rights reserved.

the house and the roughly 50:50 mix of men and women of all ages in the audience were not remarkable for the era. Sadly, however, it was unusual for British cinema of the 1930s to portray women in national politics. Anna Neagle's performances in *Victoria the Great* (1937) and *Sixty Glorious Years* (1938) were about the limit.

A member of the political establishment, Pamela is unimpressed with Hannay, a dashing, trench-coat-clad bachelor with a penchant for jumping off moving trains. Even when handcuffed to him on a double bed, she spends most of her screen time disarming him with total, glacial put-downs. Her glasses, posh Home Counties accent (especially grating in a Scottish landscape), and sportswear ensemble with prominent shirtwaist and wide lapels (another reference to early-twentieth-century working women's attire) contribute to her air of authority that contrasts with Hannay, the dishevelled, romantic outsider. Though they grow to tolerate one another in the closing sequence at a London music hall, there's no kiss; their hands merely join discreetly in the final shot. Hannay's wrist is the only one still manacled; cool and collected Pamela is free.

Before turning to acting, Madeleine Carroll had earned her BA from Birmingham University at age twenty and had even taught in a girls' school for a time (*Lancashire Daily Post*, December 27, 1935, p. 6). Publicists undoubtedly felt they had to manage Carroll's "cultured Birmingham girl" image. One article attested to the "realistic" physical and verbal abuse Carroll had to endure on her escape with Donat's Hannay ("*39 Steps* Stars Pained by Realism," pressbook, 1935). Another claimed, "She hated to be mastered … But she learned to like it from the MAN who put the MAN in roMANce." However, behind the headlines, Carroll was more robust than her asthmatic male co-star, who "caught 'flu' from running about in the Shepherd's Bush studios' waterlogged recreation of the Scottish Highlands ("All Wet," *Picturegoer*, March 23, 1935, p. 32). Although acclaimed for her verbal and physical comedy in *The 39 Steps*, Carroll migrated to Hollywood later in the decade, where she wasted whatever talent she displayed for Hitchcock playing a succession of well-bred and lifeless heiresses and princesses (*Lloyds of London*, 1936; *It's All Yours*, 1937; *The Prisoner of Zenda*, 1937).

In *The Lady Vanishes*, Margaret Lockwood's Iris would be even more empowered, assuming Donat/Hannay's narrative role as the undoubted, outspoken protagonist of Launder's and Gilliat's European espionage script, originally written in 1936 as *Lost Lady*. Like Hannay, she is also introduced as a "foreigner" abroad—an independent traveler of means. Though Buchan described Hannay's occupation as a mining engineer in the British Empire's African colonies, when he comes to England, he is contemplating a permanent move to the life of a gentleman living off the interest from his investments. In the script, Hannay's imperialist origins are airbrushed for a more lily-white Canadian ancestry; his occupation is not discussed (Barr 1999: 149). He is, by default, an unattached gentleman of leisure living in a walk-up flat in Portland Place—the ultimate wish fulfillment of a 1930s male spectator fighting off the impact of the economic depression.

Margaret Lockwood's Iris appears even more independently wealthy than Hannay or Pamela (her sportswear ensembles and handbags are monogrammed with her initials), and, as she confesses to her two girlfriends (played by Googie Withers and Sally Stewart), she only gets engaged to an anonymous "check chaser" because she is bored and has "done everything." In fact, Iris (based more faithfully on the heroine in Ethel Lina White's *The Wheel Spins* [1936] than Bennett's and Ian Hay's invention of Pamela in Buchan's male-dominated novel) represents that rarest and most exhilarating of screen heroines: an elegant, entitled, single woman, living easily and without apology in post-suffrage England (and on holiday in Central Europe), whose financial assets, class, education, and sex mean that she can control just about any civilized situation she encounters. Yet, apart from Patrice Petro, Hitchcock scholars have rarely given Iris the attention she deserves.

In Launder's and Gilliat's script, Iris becomes a metaphor for Great Britain's geographic and political identity in the 1930s, moving from splendid isolation at the hotel resort to the humiliations of appeasement in her efforts to secure allies to find Miss Froy to creating a coalition of fellow English passengers against the gaslighting foreigners. Iris initially takes her independence for granted, but it is tied to a tightrope, acceptance–rejection context as a wealthy, single woman in 1930s English society. As Virginia Woolf noted in *Three Guineas* (1938), educated, middle-class Englishwomen had made some progress toward equality, post-suffrage, and were even part of the social and political Establishment dramatized on screen (Pamela), even if it was largely due to their links to or support of powerful men (Iris's unseen father, Pamela's MP employer). However, their numbers were not yet substantial enough to successfully contest dominant inequalities. Although working-class women had potential in organizing across gender lines to defy employers, Woolf identified the truly powerful woman of the post-suffrage era as the independently wealthy, educated working woman: "She need no longer use her charm to procure money from her father or brother… she can express her own opinions … she can declare her genuine likes and dislikes. In short, she need not acquiesce; she can criticize" (Woolf 2011: 132). It could be a character description of Iris. But, as Woolf and others have pointed out, this new woman was threatened by the rise of European fascism (De Grand 1976; Mouton 2010).

The Lady Vanishes also suggests that it isn't only women who are vulnerable to England's crumbling status in contemporary Europe. In the hilarious opening sequence, the hotel manager first communicates details of an avalanche and train delay in Italian, French, and German before relaying it in English (thereby relegating the English tourists to the lowest level on the European cultural totem pole). Consequently, holidaying cricket aficionados Caldicott (Naunton Wayne) and Charters (Basil Radford) are the last to join the queue for a room and are compelled to share the maid's room. Iris, Miss Froy (May Whitty), and Iris's two female traveling companions have mastered the language of money to get the best access to food and board. Though Iris has almost no contact with Miss Froy prior to boarding the train, the older woman's knowledge of foreign languages (and awareness of the perils of Central Europe in the 1930s) mean that they become the third English couple on the train (after Charters and Caldicott and the adulterous "Todhunters"). After Iris's accident (taking the brunt of a blow to the head intended for Miss Froy), her personal borders are threatened. Miss Froy takes care of Iris, and, when Froy is abducted, Iris returns the diplomatic favor, protecting the rights of another Englishwoman in a country that does not respect the dominance of the English or of women abroad. The fact that all of this was written in 1936 and shot in January 1938, a few months before the Anschluss (March 12–13, 1938), the Sudetenland crisis (September 1938), the Munich Agreement (September 30, 1938), and the announcement of the Pact of Steel (May 22, 1939) gives *The Lady Vanishes* an aura of political prescience far beyond any other film of its era.[6]

Eminent Victorians

Although wealthy, confident women were plentiful in Hollywood films of the 1930s (*It Happened One Night*, 1934; *Theodora Goes Wild*, 1936; *Stage Door*, 1937; *Topper*, 1937; *The Mad Miss Manton*, 1937), Lockwood's Iris is more atypical of classic English screen women (her fellow countrymen, the misogynist and chauvinist Caldicott and Charters, label her masterful aura as "American"). She may be younger than Miss Froy, but Iris shows little desire to please or to be looked at by men; she simply wants obedience. When men won't obey her and help her find Miss Froy—whether it is Paul Lukas's patronizing Freudian doctor, or the tweedy music scholar, Gilbert (Michael Redgrave), or even the train porters—

Lockwood's steely-eyed contempt and uncompromising mouth are bracing to watch. In White's novel, Iris is less impervious to the disapproving looks of other passengers or to doubts about her "story" of the missing Miss Froy. But on screen, Lockwood's Iris defies the rules for romantic ingénues and doesn't step back or apologize for who she is and what she wants. Paced by Hitchcock, Lockwood moves the narrative along as fast as any train and won't wait for anyone to catch up with her.

When Iris does sit down briefly with Redgrave's Gilbert—a combination of two dithering academic men in White's novel—he confesses his fascination for her … because of her resemblance to his father (no Oedipus or Dr. Freud in this romance). Like the old gentleman, Gilbert tells Iris, "You haven't any manners at all, and you're always seeing things." In a film "saturated with signifiers of Englishness" (Barr 1999: 198), White, Launder, Gilliat, and Lockwood created a heroine who remained refreshingly at odds with contemporary views on what constituted appropriate femininity or good manners—English, American, or European. Furthermore, in being likened to Gilbert's father, Iris is a woman out of step with the times, even Victorian in her eccentric individualism—and she doesn't give a damn for Gilbert's approval either. She is not even listening to Gilbert's compliment but is busy looking elsewhere, spurning the accepted codes of feminine objectification to look on her own terms. In ignoring Gilbert's romantic appeal to look at him, Iris uncovers more proof of Miss Froy's existence written on the train window. Like Gilbert's father, Iris will "never desert a lady in trouble," though the older generation's paternal sexual "chivalry" has been replaced with solidarity between women.

As Lockwood's Iris transcends what is considered to be feminine in 1938, so does Whitty's Miss Froy, who turns out to be not just a sweet-faced English governess in need of rescue but a spy working undercover in a Central European country—a combination of northern Italy and Germany—since 1932. When she is rescued, thanks to the efforts of Iris, Gilbert, and a Cockney nun in heels (Catherine Lacey), Miss Froy won't stay still like an obedient feminine object; she dashes off over the snowy hills in the middle of a gun battle. Patriarchal and oedipal rules don't apply to her; remember, as she tells Iris, her name is not "Freud," but "OY! Not EUD: Froy … To rhyme with joy" (Launder and Gilliat 1936–1938: 50; see Fig. 3.2).

In 1938, Hitchcock was the country's most widely publicized film director, but Whitty was arguably the more famous of the two—an unquestioned legend in entertainment history. One local Cambridge newspaper didn't even use the film's title or Hitchcock to promote the film but simply alerted readers that "Dame May Whitty Vanishes at the Rex Cinema" (*Cambridge Daily News*, February 1, 1939, p. 4). The first stage and screen actress to receive a damehood, Whitty played on both sides of the Atlantic with Ellen Terry, Irene Vanbrugh, and Richard Mansfield and was part of Lena Ashwell's female-dominated company, which employed female stagehands, scenery shifters, lighting technicians, and stage managers ("Iris Intervenes," 1915). She was also a staunch advocate for women's suffrage, chairing the Actresses' Franchise League, campaigning in London's East End (*Votes for Women*, January 9, 1914, p. 227; February 12, 1915, p. 162), and, alongside Sylvia Pankhurst, publishing letters during World War I warning the prime minister that women would return to active campaigning if their demands for equality weren't met (Whitty et al. 1916). After suffrage was achieved in Great Britain, she was a founding member of British Equity, the actors' union, campaigning for a standard contract, the elimination of abuses by producers and directors, and the growth of benevolence funds for up-and-coming and unemployed actors (*The Era*, May 21, 1930, p. 6; *The Stage*, 1938). The union's first meeting was held in her Covent Garden parlour, and, throughout the 1930s, she chaired all the meetings. Married to English actor-manager Ben Webster, she rarely used her married name. By the time she played Miss Froy, her daughter Margaret was a headlining Broadway director, responsible for Maurice Evans's successful

Figure 3.2 Froy, not Freud: *The Lady Vanishes*' feminists, Dame May Whitty (Miss Froy) and Margaret Lockwood (Iris Henderson), take tea.
The Lady Vanishes, directed by Alfred Hitchcock. © Gainsborough Pictures 1938. All rights reserved.

productions of *Richard II* and *Hamlet*. Throughout the 1930s and 1940s, Margaret Webster was at the center of a group of influential women producers and directors that included Cheryl Crawford and Theresa Helburn.

Whitty's off-screen career was certainly better known to the public than Miss Froy's work in espionage, but her history as a working Englishwoman off screen is entwined in her role as Miss Froy, providing a kind of extratextual inspiration and example for Lockwood's generation of women in an era when fascism was rolling back post-Great War gains in gender equality (Fig. 3.3). French, Swiss, and most Italian women still could not vote, and the Nazis had eroded the gains in education, work, and political representation women had made in Germany's Weimar Republic. The many facets of Whitty's career and public image attested to a long history of women's political and social advocacy, with ties to feminism, labor, and charitable work for the arts. Whitty wasn't just a star. She was a leader during a period in late-nineteenth and early-twentieth-century history when women dominated English and American theatrical

Figure 3.3 Michael Redgrave's Gilbert points to May Whitty's exhausted Miss Froy, but it is Margaret Lockwood's Iris who must keep her nerve for the next generation of women.

The Lady Vanishes, directed by Alfred Hitchcock. © Gainsborough Pictures 1938. All rights reserved.

companies. She was not just a working mother but was also a woman who raised a daughter to become a director in an increasingly male-dominated theatrical profession.

Women's Off-screen Allies?

Lockwood's and Whitty's roles would never have been possible without writers Frank Launder and Sidney Gilliat, who maintained and developed Iris's independence in the novel and transformed Miss Froy from an unassuming governess into a British spy (Smyth 2023). After the screenwriters fell out with Hitchcock over film publicity suggesting that Hitchcock had written *The Lady Vanishes*, the duo moved into directing and producing their own films. Their scripts include an array of independent working women and characters, from Patricia Roc's war worker (*Millions Like Us*, 1943) to Margaret Rutherford's unflappable school mistress (*The Happiest Days of Your Life*, 1950), but their follow-up script for Lockwood, *Night Train to Munich* (1940), gave her a more passive role with little of Iris's intellectual and physical speed (Powell, *Sunday Times*, July 28, 1940, p. 3). Rather than providing the film's momentum, she played the damsel in distress—the decorative object that needed moving to safety. While Lockwood's point-of-view shots motivated cutting in *The Lady Vanishes* and Redgrave and Lockwood appeared in two-shots as they worked to find Miss Froy, Rex Harrison's Gus/Herzog is a more dynamic and solo action man in *Night Train to Munich*. In *The Lady Vanishes*, Gilbert may playfully take on the role of Holmes to her Watson, but he is still Iris's faithful watch/lapdog. Only at the end, when allegedly at Hitchcock's insistence, the screenwriters abandoned White's plotlines for a shootout and runaway-train sequence, does Gilbert assume the action-man role and leave Iris behind with the rest of the passengers. Even then, it is a collaborative effort as Lacey's working-class nun, with Iris's help, takes over Charters's role in changing over the points and getting them to safety.

Although in contrast to Hollywood, film studios in Greater London were less inclined to hire women behind the camera in the 1930s in major creative or administrative roles (Carman 2015; Smyth 2018; Bell 2021), Hitchcock credited wife Alma Reville and secretary Joan Harrison as his principal collaborators while publicizing *The Lady Vanishes* (Maloney 1938). More than a few "English Hitchcocks" were based on the work of female writers, such as Marie Belloc Lowdnes (*The Lodger*, 1913; filmed 1926), Josephine Tey (*A Shilling for Candles*, 1936; filmed as *Young and Innocent*, 1937), and White. Hitchcock and Reville continued to work with women screenwriters in Hollywood, including Harrison, who turned scriptwriter at the end of the 1930s, and Jay Presson Allen (*Marnie*, 1964), but *The Lady Vanishes*' story of female solidarity and the refusal to be silenced stands out, particularly in the wake of a renewed interest in independent women in 1930s cinema and post-#MeToo.

Despite actress Tippi Hedren's claims of the director's abuse in the 1960s, Hitchcock's respect for Margaret Lockwood over Michael Redgrave was obvious in 1938. Redgrave, primarily a theater actor, felt he "had made a mistake" when he went to the sound stages at Islington and found working with Hitchcock tense and difficult (Redgrave 1983: 121–124). A member of John Gielgud's Old Vic company, Redgrave preferred the theater director's chaotic, collaborative, and more time-consuming style to Hitchcock's brisk, stick-to-the script approach on set, and, since Gielgud had hated working for Hitchcock in *Secret Agent* (1936) and three years later would later dismiss the medium in his memoirs (Gielgud 1939: 284–286), Hitchcock may not have been particularly well disposed toward Redgrave. Redgrave even claimed that Hitchcock made his infamous "actors are cattle" quip on set.

In contrast, Hitchcock treated Lockwood like the film professional she was. Though she was also a theater-trained RADA graduate, Lockwood had her start in films and by 1938 was a star after her breakthrough role in *Bank Holiday*, as a working-class nurse. The year producer Ted Black gave her top billing over Redgrave, her salary at Gainsborough was an impressive £6,000, the equivalent of £525,000 in today's currency (Lockwood 1955: 67).[7] Although Lockwood is almost never quoted in any Hitchcock Studies, 1930s and 1940s journalists adored her because she "had not got a star complex" (*Picturegoer*, July 29, 1939). Like May Whitty, she had "mid-Victorian charm," which set her apart from the usual run of modern glamor girls (*Picturegoer*, May 14, 1938, p. 15), and was unapologetic in admitting her favorite pastime away from work: eating ("She Loves a Good Feed!" *The News*, February 18, 1938, p. 11). In her 1955 autobiography, *Lucky Star*, she remembered *The Lady Vanishes* as "one of the films I have enjoyed most in my career," and the film's publicity supported her performance of a mid-Victorian maverick who wasn't afraid of standing up against men. One *Sunday Post* photograph shows her glowering at Lukas's Dr. Hartz, prompting the journalist's caption: "Gesh, dames are getting mighty tough nowadays. If it wasn't for Michael Redgrave, lovely Margaret Lockwood would flatten Paul Lukas" (January 22, 1939, p. 24).

Like Carroll, success in a Hitchcock film brought Lockwood to Hollywood, but, unlike Carroll, Lockwood considered Hollywood to be "the most dead-alive place on earth, like a seaside resort out of season" and found ingénue roles in North American historical epics equally dull (Tims 1989: 94). She refused to dye her hair blonde for Darryl Zanuck and told outraged American reporters that "British films are best" (*The Era*, January 19, 1939, p. 1). The British press was staunchly against losing her to Hollywood ("Don't Send Margaret Lockwood to Hollywood Again!" *Lancashire Daily Post*, January 22, 1941, p. 4), and, along with *The Lady Vanishes*' alumni, actors Naunton Wayne, Basil Radford, and Redgrave, and writers Launder and Gilliat, the actress sustained the national film industry though war and postwar challenges, offering film content and style that were distinctly different—and refreshingly offbeat—compared with Hollywood. Later Lindsay Anderson (1949) and Stanley Kauffmann (1959), following Dilys Powell, would continue to highlight *The Lady Vanishes* as the peak of national film production and the best film Hitchcock made, even after he moved to more lucrative opportunities in America (*New Republic*, August 10, 1959). But with the rise of professional film studies, with its heavy reliance on psychoanalysis and theories of the male gaze, and histories of Hollywood and "British" film production that ignored the presence of women behind the camera and in the wider culture, the power of *The Lady Vanishes* waned. Philip French was one of the few critics to promote the film and its rare scenes of class and feminism in 2012, but it was *Vertigo* and its very different portrait of women that topped *Sight and Sound*'s critics' poll.

It may strike some as ironic that Hitchcock seems to have tolerated confident, intelligent women on screen who did their own looking back in the 1930s, while media critics and academic Hitchcock fans have seemed less comfortable with Iris and made no effort to connect her and Pamela's perspectives to women's wider social, political, and cultural emancipation in the 1930s and its attempted erasure under European fascism. It is worth emphasizing that Dr. Hartz's psychoanalytic explanations for Iris's "hallucinations" of an imaginary Miss Froy, designed to curb her authority as a wealthy Englishwoman and belief in her point of view, are rooted in the misogyny of the male establishment, Freudian psychoanalysis, and the university system (which also supported Film Studies as an academic discourse from the 1960s) and are ultimately designed to camouflage the abduction and attempted murder of another woman and rewrite the past. Iris set aside these explanations as foreign nonsense—like any sound English Victorian nonconformist. And, as Miss Froy reminds us, her surname is not Freud. A few of us listened to her.

Notes

1   Barr's approach in *English Hitchcock* (1999) recovers the specifically "English" working-class and middle-class cultures on screen and the English-born filmmakers off screen that dominate Hitchcock's early work for the British film industry. Following suit, in this essay, I use "English," signifying a specific 1930s context, while being well aware of the wider political baggage attending institutional histories and readings of "British national cinema."

2   The Oxford-educated critic was the model for academic Phoebe Tucker in Dorothy L. Sayers's *Gaudy Night* (1935).

3   Silet incorrectly states that Pamela is reading a book (2009: 111), but it is a newspaper with neatly creased white pages. Male film scholars writing in the second half of the twentieth century assumed women on trains read novels—perhaps passing the time waiting for a dashing young man to drop by their carriage. But Pamela,

a political professional, quite obviously is reading her trade paper—*The Times*—for events in Westminster and not for the film reviews.

4 However tempting it may be to credit the invention of Pamela to another working woman, Hitchcock's collaborator, scenarist, and wife Alma Reville, no documentation exists to support her direct involvement.

5 Ironically, Constance Markiewicz, the first woman to be elected to Parliament, never took her seat in Westminster. As a member of Sinn Féin, she would not swear allegiance to the King (Haverty 2016).

6 Sidney Gilliat discusses the political background of *Lost Lady/The Lady Vanishes*, which involved some shooting in Yugoslavia before the government tossed the film crew out, in his oral history for Bectu, the Broadcasting, Entertainment, Communications and Theatre Union (May 15, 1990), available here: https://historyproject.org.uk/interview/sidney-gilliat. See also Smyth 2023.

7 Lockwood only lost top billing to Redgrave in 1986, when Rank reissued the film and released a new pressbook (*The Lady Vanishes*, 1986: BFI). This transition points to the wider masculinization of film authorship and publicity in the second half of the twentieth century.

References

The 39 Steps (1935) Pressbook, Berkhamsted: British Film Institute Special Collections.

"Actresses Franchise League" (1914) *Votes for Women*, January 9, p. 227.

"All Wet" (1935) *Picturegoer*, March 23, p. 32.

Anderson, L. (1949) "Alfred Hitchcock," *Sequence*, 9 (autumn): 113–123.

Arnold, R. (2009) *The American Look*, London: I. B. Taurus.

Barr, C. (1999) *English Hitchcock*, London: BFI.

Bell, M. (2021) *Movie Workers*, Urbana, Ill.: University of Illinois Press.

"British Equity" (1930) *The Era*, May 21, p. 6.

Buchan, J. (1915) *The Thirty-Nine Steps*, London: Chatto & Windus.

Cambridge Daily News (1939) February 1, p. 4.

Carman, E. (2015) *Independent Stardom*, Austin, Tex.: University of Texas Press.

Carroll, S. (1935) "*The 39 Steps*," *Sunday Times*, June 9.

De Grand, A. (1976) "Women Under Italian Fascism," *The Historical Journal*, 19 (4): 947–968.

"Don't Send Margaret Lockwood to Hollywood" (1941) *The Lancashire Daily Post*, January 22, p. 4.

"Dundee Candidate's Street Campaign" (1935) *Dundee Evening Telegraph and Post*, October 29, p. 1.

French, P. (2012) "My Favourite Hitchcock: *The Lady Vanishes*," *The Guardian*, July 24.

George, R. (1939) "Hollywood Now Comes to Us: Margaret Lockwood on New Situation," *The Era*, January 19, p. 1.

Gielgud, J. (1939) *Early Stages*, London: Macmillan.

Gilliat, S. (1990) Oral History, May 15, Broadcasting, Entertainment, Communications and Theatre Union (Bectu) Archives, https://historyproject.org.uk/interview/sidney-gilliat.

Glancy, M. (2003) *The 39 Steps*, London: I. B. Taurus.

Graves, P. M. (1994) *Labour Women: Women in British Working Class Politics, 1918–1939*, Cambridge: Cambridge University Press.

Hannam, J. (2010) "Women as Paid Organizers and Propagandists for the British Labour Party between the Wars," *International Labour and Working-Class History*, 77 (spring): 69–88.

Haverty, A. M. (2016) *Constance Markievicz: Irish Revolutionary*, Dublin: The Lilliput Press.

"Hollywood Takes a Back Seat" (1939) *The Sunday Post*, January 22, p. 24.

"Iris Intervenes at the Kingsway" (1915) *The Queen: The Lady's Newspaper*, October 23, p. 761.

Kauffmann, S. (1959) "*North by Northwest*," *The New Republic*, August 10.

"Kingsway Hall Meeting" (1915) *Votes for Women*, February 12, p. 162.

The Lady Vanishes (1938) UK pressbook, Berkhamsted: British Film Institute Special Collections.

The Lady Vanishes (1986) UK pressbook, Berkhamsted: British Film Institute Special Collections.

Launder, F., and S. Gilliat (1936–1938) *The Lady Vanishes*, shooting script, Berkhamsted: British Film Institute Special Collections.
Lemire, E. (2000) "Voyeurism and the Postwar Crisis of Masculinity in Rear Window," in J. Belton (ed.), *Alfred Hitchcock's Rear Window*, Cambridge: Cambridge University Press, pp. 57–90.
Lockwood, M. (1938) "Margaret Lockwood Writes on Glamour," *Picturegoer*, May 14, p. 15.
Lockwood, M. (1955) *Lucky Star*, London: Oldham's.
Maloney, R. (1938) "What Happens After That," *New Yorker*, September 2, p. 25.
McCarthy, H. (2012) "Whose Democracy? Histories of British Political Cultures between the Wars," *The Historical Journal*, 55 (1): 221–238.
Miller, T., and N. King (2012) "Accidental Heroes and Gifted Amateurs: Hitchcock and Ideology," in L. Poague and T. Leitch (eds), *A Companion to Alfred Hitchcock*, Malden, Mass.: Wiley-Blackwell, pp. 425–451.
Mouton, M. (2010) "From Adventure and Advancement to Derailment and Demotion: Effects of Nazi Gender Policy on Women's Careers and Lives," *Journal of Social History*, 43 (4): 945–971.
Nottingham Evening Post (1935) December 4.
Petro, P. (2009) "Rematerializing the Vanishing Lady: Feminism, Hitchcock, and Interpretation," in L. Poague and M. Deutelbaum (eds), *A Hitchcock Reader*, Malden, Mass.: Wiley-Blackwell, pp. 126–136.
Powell, D. (1939) "Undiscovered England: A National Character for Our Films," *Sunday Times*, April 9, p. 4.
Powell, D. (1940) "War Film Triumph," *Sunday Times*, July 28, p. 3.
Powell, D. (1941) "Short Story Films," *Sunday Times*, March 16, p. 3.
Powell, D. (1949) "Films of the Week," *Sunday Times*, January 16, p. 2.
Rasmussen, J. S. (1983) "The Political Integration of British Women," *Social Science History*, 7 (1): 61–95.
Redgrave, M. (1983) *In My Mind's I*, New York: Viking.
"Robert Donat and Madeleine Carroll in Spy Thriller" (1935) *Lancashire Daily Post*, December 27, p. 6.
Screenland (1935) September, p. 53.
Seldes, G. (1939) "Three English—Three Thousand American: Personal Reactions to Recent Films," in *The Movies and the People Who Make Them*, New Haven, Conn.: Theatre Patrons, pp. 309–310.
"She Loves a Good Feed!" (1938) *The News*, February 18, p. 11.
Silet, Charles (2009) "Through a Woman's Eyes: Sexuality and Memory in *The 39 Steps*," in L. Poague and M. Deutelbaum (eds), *A Hitchcock Reader*, Malden, Mass.: Wiley-Blackwell, pp. 109–121.
Smyth, J. E. (2018) *Nobody's Girl Friday: The Women Who Ran Hollywood*, New York: Oxford University Press.
Smyth, J. E. (2023) "Lost Lady/*The Lady Vanishes*: A Historian's Whodunnit," *Cineaste*, 48 (3): 34–39.
"A Spy Mystery Set in Scotland" (1936) *Dundee Evening Telegraph*, January 4.
Thackery, D. (2010) "Women and Conservative Activism in Early Twentieth-Century Britain," *Journal of British Studies*, 49 (4): 826–848.
Tims, H. (1989) *Once a Wicked Lady*, London: W. H. Allen & Co.
Truffaut, F. (1968) *Hitchcock/Truffaut*, London: Weidenfeld & Nicholson.
White, E. L. (1997) *The Lady Vanishes/The Wheel Spins*, London: Bloomsbury.
Whitty, M., S. Pankhurst et al. (1916) "Suffragists' Letter to the Prime Minister," *Church League for Women's Suffrage*, January, p. 6.
Woolf, V. (2011) *Three Guineas*, London: Penguin.

Chapter 4
Rebecca's Gendered Reception from 1940 to the Present

Patricia White

Of course, it was old-fashioned in 1938 when it was written—I remember critics saying it was a queer throwback to the 19th-century Gothic novel. But I shall never know quite why it seized upon everyone's imagination, not just teenagers and shop girls, like people try to say now, but every age, and both sexes.

DAPHNE DU MAURIER (DU MAURIER AND MALET 1993)

Yes, it has stood up quite well over the years. I don't know why.

ALFRED HITCHCOCK (TRUFFAUT 1985: 129)

Rebecca's steady reputation as a classic, and its influence over generations of (notably female and queer) viewers and scholars through remakes and reissues is an important determinant of Hitchcock's international cultural legacy, one that challenges the idea of male genius and makes room for collaboration and contradiction (including "saving" Hitchcock from being "canceled"). This essay positions the film's popular standing since its release in relation to factors including genre, adaptation, studio labor, marketing, and audience reception, before examining the decisive contributions of criticism by anglophone feminist scholars on the film's place in film studies.

If Rebecca, the absent presence in Daphne du Maurier's novel of that title and its 1940 film adaptation, is a fundamentally unstable signifier, the film *Rebecca* itself has remained solidly, stolidly "classic." Hyped as a quality production by Selznick International and United Artists at the time of its release, it was well received by reviewers; Frank Nugent called it "altogether brilliant" in his *New York Times* review (March 29, 1940). In 1940, Hitchcock was a well-known director, and keen curiosity about his first US film no doubt contributed to critical and popular interest in *Rebecca*. But neither his expert direction, nor his self-promotion was the primary motor of the film's initial success. Audiences, primed by du Maurier's bestseller and by the publicity and box-office success of Selznick's *Gone with the Wind* (1939), still in theaters, made *Rebecca* "the most popular picture of 1940" (*Boxoffice Barometer*, 1940). Classic status was clinched when the film won the Oscar for best picture, a feat no other Hitchcock film would accomplish. Moreover, *Rebecca*'s appeal was both timely and lasting. As an adaptation of a popular novel, it hit a nerve with anxious women on the eve of World War II. Its rerelease in 1944 amid a wartime cycle of gothic women's pictures was just the first of many repeat appearances before audiences in theaters and on television over the decades that attest to its enduring significance. *Rebecca* is an indisputably canonical film but not (only) because Hitchcock made it.

This chapter takes a closer look at "*Rebecca*'s women" to understand its legacy. The plural and the possessive in the phrase "*Rebecca*'s women" connote the multiplicity and partisanship of feminist approaches to the film. The plural refers to the women who contributed creatively; to the fascinating women at the center of its tale; and to the fans, critics, and scholars who have kept it so prominent in the overlapping canons of "classical Hollywood cinema" in general, and "Hitchcock's films" in particular.

Production, text, reception: these categories structure my short book on the film for the BFI Classics series. In Chapter 1, "Rebecca's Story," I take up the question of authorship—the story of the film's production has been told as a struggle between Hitchcock and Selznick for creative control—ultimately over fidelity to du Maurier's original text. While the novelist declined involvement in the production, women like Joan Harrison were decisive. In Chapter 2, "Rebecca's Style," I offer a reading of the film that focuses on its successful cinematic staging of the preoccupation of the female gothic with ambivalent relationships between and among women. And in Chapter 3 "Rebecca's Grip," I talk about the film's persistence in history and popular memory as well as in feminist scholarship. Whether or not we take *Rebecca* as itself a feminist text, it has a rich feminist legacy. It bears repeating: few films of the undisputed cultural standing of *Rebecca*—it counts as a classic whether measured by merit or popularity—can claim women's centrality to all three components. Each of these dimensions bears on Hitchcock's critical standing into the post-#MeToo era.

Production

Rebecca's status as a middlebrow classic has arguably cost it a seat in the Hitchcock pantheon. Hitchcock himself contributed to this state of affairs in the famous exchange between the director and François Truffaut on the film in the interview facilitated by interpreter Helen Scott that appeared as Truffaut's book *Hitchcock*.

> FT: Are you satisfied with *Rebecca*?
> AH: Well, it's not a Hitchcock picture; it's a novelette, really. The story is old-fashioned; there was a whole school of feminine literature at the period, and though I'm not against it, the fact is that the story is lacking in humor.

Truffaut, to his credit, disagrees with the director's assessment, venturing that Hitchcock's later films drew on *Rebecca*'s mastery of atmosphere. Certainly, first-time access to Hollywood resources expanded Hitchcock's toolkit. Auteurist critics following Truffaut have found plenty of Hitchcock touches in the film, notably the moving subjective camera. But the production of the film at Selznick International, over which Hitchcock had less control than he would over many of the films considered his masterpieces, has thwarted a full-on embrace of *Rebecca* by the Hitchcock critical establishment.

Hitchcock's disavowal of the film is widely credited to his chafing under the control David O. Selznick exercised over the director's first contracted picture with the studio. Selznick imprinted all aspects of the film, from script to casting to special effects. He famously excoriated the script treatment submitted by Hitchcock and Harrison (and an uncredited Alma Reville, Hitchcock's spouse) for its lack of fidelity to the source text: "We bought *Rebecca* and we'll make *Rebecca*." Certainly the men's working relationship, with its starkly contrasting methods and priorities, offers a plum historical case of artistic collaboration in the studio system, as the work of Leonard Leff and Thomas Schatz has richly demonstrated.

The studio's marketing too positioned *Rebecca* squarely as a Selznick production, and reviewers privileged producer over director. At that time, Selznick's selling power was directly tied to his ability reliably to adapt and exploit women's bestsellers. Like *Gone with the Wind*, *Rebecca* made an aggressive appeal to a women's moviegoing market that would only become more crucial as the decade wore on. Kyle Edwards' research in the Selznick archives documents the centrality of adaptation to the studio's production strategy and its prominence in its marketing campaigns. Both *Gone with the Wind* and *Rebecca* were well-appointed adaptations of female-authored bestsellers whose emotional volatility spoke to the contradictions of white middle-class anglophone femininity at midcentury. Loyalty to the book, and credit to Selznick for the adaptation's fidelity, ensured the film's reputation as a classic more than its display of a directorial signature.

In her definitive feminist critical study *The Women Who Knew Too Much: Hitchcock and Feminist Theory* (1988), Tania Modleski opens her brilliant reading of *Rebecca* by quoting Hitchcock's exchange with Truffaut. With the dismissive term "novelette" and his evocation of "feminine literature," Hitchcock makes clear his discomfort with the source material; the skirmish over possession of the film is also with Daphne du Maurier, whom Hitchcock does not even mention by name. Critic Robin Wood's initial assessment of the film in his influential *Hitchcock's Films*, Modleski points out, also invokes the "novelette" to characterize the feminized subject matter. Critics echo Hitchcock's sensitivity to what I call "undue feminine influence" over the project—du Maurier's text and the female audience's skewing of the film market, both of which echo *Rebecca*'s haunting of the living in the film's narrative. If *Rebecca* is among the "best-loved" (*Chicago Tribune*) Hitchcock films, but not among its most critically respected, it is because of its association with du Maurier's novel and with the broader women's culture with which it has become nearly synonymous.

Rebecca, the novel and film, found initial enthusiastic reception in the context of late 1930s and early World War II transatlantic popular culture and attendant transformations of the gendered public sphere. The 1930s economic disaster and the rise of fascism in Europe interrupted some of the most overt gains of the feminist movement. But the US workforce included 11 million women during the decade despite efforts to prioritize male workers (Hapke 1995: xiii). Women were primary targets of consumer culture, including books and movies, and women seized professional opportunities in the culture industries. Hitchcock's "whole school of feminine literature" perhaps stood in for a publishing industry that supported a significant number of women writers, editors, and publicists. In the film industry, studio hierarchies clearly favored men, and people of color were structurally excluded during its "golden age." But Hollywood did present viable career options for white women beyond acting. It is this professional context of women's participation in filmmaking that auteurist criticism of *Rebecca* has ignored.

The twenty-first century has seen a robust turn to historical research in feminist scholarship. J. E. Smyth opens her study *Nobody's Girl Friday*: *The Women Who Ran Hollywood* (2018), by pointing to the healthy representation of women in studio employment records reported annually in the trade journal *Film Daily* during the 1930s and 1940s. Women worked as screenwriters, editors, designers, script coordinators, publicists, journalists, and agents. Dorothy Arzner has been widely touted as the only women studio director during this period, but she came up through ranks that included many other women, and she continued to work with some of them. Women took on many roles in the film industry, at many levels, including department heads.

A tantalizing glimpse of the culture is offered in the 1938 comic novel *I Lost My Girlish Laughter*, recently reissued with an introduction by Smyth. Published under the pseudonym Jane Allen, the autobiographical work was written by Silvia Schulman, once personal secretary to David O. Selznick at MGM, in collaboration with playwright Jane Shore. In the novel, Selznick is mercilessly caricatured in the figure of sexist, narcissistic studio head Sidney Bland. While the book's narrator shows how a smart and capable woman taken on as a secretary might find her way to the center of Hollywood power and decision-making, she was subjected to routine sexual harassment and not recognized or compensated appropriately. Interviews with Marcella Rabwin, Selznick's executive assistant during the production of *Gone with the Wind* and *Rebecca*, seem to corroborate much of Schulman's account.

A standout in this recent feminist film historiography, Christina Lane's biography *Phantom Lady: Hollywood Producer Joan Harrison, the Forgotten Woman Behind Hitchcock* (2020), details not only how much this ambitious young woman contributed to *Rebecca* and other Hitchcock projects (including producing his TV show) but also sheds light on the context in which the film's ambivalent sexual politics took form. Her account of how *Rebecca* came to be Hitchcock's first US film also brings the roles of several other women to light (see Fig. 4.1).

Harrison, a smart and stylish Englishwoman, quickly moved up from working as Hitchcock's assistant to writing and producing. She was working with Hitchcock on his last UK film, *Jamaica Inn* (1938)—also adapted from a du Maurier novel—when she read the galleys of what would become the author's

Figure 4.1 Hitchcock reading from du Maurier's *Rebecca* as he discusses the film with Joan Harrison.

Peter Stackpole/The LIFE Picture Collection/Shutterstock.

megahit, *Rebecca*. Meanwhile, Kay Brown, Selznick's New York agent, who had been instrumental in the acquisition of *Gone with the Wind*, equally excited, brought the book to the producer's attention. At the time, Selznick was courting Hitchcock, who was ready to take on the scale of Hollywood filmmaking and to flee the shadow of war over Europe. As part of the negotiations, Hitchcock visited the USA with his family and Joan, and, on this trip, Harrison became friendly with Brown.

Despite having to overcome du Maurier's dissatisfaction with the film version of *Jamaica Inn*, the two women went to work, with Selznick International London agent Jenna Ressair, to secure the rights to the property they favored for the collaboration, *Rebecca*. When Hitchcock finally signed with Selznick, the promising producer–director partnership was underwritten with du Maurier's transatlantic popularity with women. Harrison's position was specified in Hitchcock's studio contract, and she was involved with the film throughout pre- and postproduction. She worked on the script through all stages of *Rebecca*, making revisions during production, and earning invaluable on-set skills that she would use in her later work as a producer. After Hitchcock moved on to *Foreign Correspondent*, she stayed on to do rewrites and implement Selznick's extensive reshoots and pickups. Her ability to function in this producer capacity worked well at the independent studio; even as Selznick tried to put a finger in every pie, he was unable to supervise everything. Harrison was nominated, together with playwright Robert E. Sherwood, for an Oscar for *Rebecca*'s screenplay. In fact, in her first year in Hollywood, she was also nominated for the screenplay for Hitchcock's *Foreign Correspondent*.

While Reville wasn't signed to Selznick International, she too collaborated with Hitchcock and Harrison on the treatment, and Joan Fontaine remembers her being on set every day, referring to them as a triumvirate. There was also behind-the-scenes input from Irene Mayer Selznick. All of these women were fans of the novel. Harrison and Reville presented a united front during the casting process, which Selznick hoped to exploit for publicity, as he'd done with *Gone with the Wind*, finding Fontaine "coy and simpering" in her screen test. As the process wore on, Brown sought the opinion of the "ladies" in Selznick's New York office on batches of screen tests collected in England by Ressair. But, as Lane points out, there's quite a difference between a casting call for Scarlett O'Hara and one for the gauche and mousy heroine of *Rebecca*—a figure strikingly at odds with the kind of woman working behind the scenes on the film.

The casting and script negotiations around *Rebecca* staged a small-scale drama around the meaning of New Womanhood in the 1930s. Selznick quashed any attempts to make the heroine more modern or the proceedings more "humorous," demanding fidelity to what du Maurier characterized as a "rather grim" novel. Fortunately, the key element of *Rebecca*'s subversive gender and sexual politics was never contested in these negotiations: the titular character would remain absent from the screen—Selznick eagerly approved Hitchcock's approach to this challenge. Rebecca would be present in almost every other element of the film: music, mise-en-scène, camera movement, editing, special effects, the behavior of the central trio of heroine, husband, and housekeeper.

The Film Text

How did *Rebecca*'s women in the film's diegetic universe make the film a touchstone of twentieth-century women's popular culture? How did the narrative itself raise questions of gendered authority and value? Hitchcock was one of many top talents who made his mark directing women's pictures in studio-era Hollywood.

"Hitchcock infused [*Rebecca*] and several other [film]s, with an oblique intimation of female frigidity producing strange fantasies of persecution, rape and death–masochistic reveries and nightmares, which cast the husband into the role of the sadistic murderer" (Elsaesser 1985: 180).

Thomas Elsaesser's lurid description of the cycle of films he calls "the Freudian feminist melodrama of the forties" undermines his use of the term "feminist" (Elsaesser 1985: 179). Moreover, as an auteurist critic, he overlooks the influence of the female gothic as a literary genre on the 1940s films. Du Maurier revived the gothic genre for the twentieth century, with ambivalent effects and great commercial impact. A throwback historically, "*Rebecca*'s women" may have been conceptualized in reaction to feminism, but this does not preclude it from being an important framework for the genre's revival, transposition, and interpretation. It bears emphasizing that *Rebecca*'s gender politics are not particularly progressive—it offers for identification a doormat with daddy issues, kills off its stereotypically sinister lesbian-coded character, glorifies the British aristocracy, and ignores race and empire. However, feminist *Rebecca* criticism, in excavating all these matters and more, has been uniquely productive. Work by Judith Mayne, Mary Ann Doane, Alex Doty, Modleski, Rhona Berenstein, and many others stages a confrontation with the reigning auteurist paradigm by engaging approaches including psychoanalysis, queer theory, and adaptation, genre, and production culture studies.

The gothic is about the isolation of a woman: in the institution of marriage, in the class divisions of the marriage economy. Narratologically, the gothic is concerned with relationships between and among women. The centrality of the heroine's predecessor, first wife or ancestor, stages a female oedipal drama of separation and succession. A genre originated by women writers and kept in print by women audiences, the gothic was primed for cinematic adaptation. As Doane notes, the audiovisual medium suited the gothic's emphasis on appearances and the centrality of the woman's look. Rather than displaying what Laura Mulvey famously called "to-be-looked-at-ness" (Mulvey 1975: 11), the heroine of Rebecca must look convincingly. Joan Fontaine in the role of "I," did so, earning a best actress nomination. (She earned the award itself for reprising aspects of her performance the next year in *Suspicion*, 1941, directed by Hitchcock and written by Harrison and Reville with Samson Raphaelson.)

In his insistence that Hitchcock and Harrison stay close to du Maurier's text in their adaptation, Selznick crucially recognized that "I" was an important site for audience identification.

> Every little thing that the girl does in the book, her reactions of running away from the guests, and the tiny things that indicate her nervousness and her self-consciousness and her gaucherie are all so brilliant in the book that every woman who has read it has adored the girl and understood her psychology, has cringed with embarrassment for her, yet has understood exactly what was going through her mind.
>
> (Selznick 1972: 260–261)

It's not hard to extend that identification to Selznick himself, as does his biographer David Thompson, and even to Hitchcock, who deploys his signature traveling point-of-view shots to put the viewer in her sensible shoes. An identification with a passive heroine is an important divergence from the usual male oedipal pattern, as Teresa de Lauretis elaborates in her synthesis of feminist psychoanalytic approaches in "Desire in Narrative" (1984). And identifying with "I" is far from comfortable. In addition to exhibiting a cringing timidity, she represents a conservative version of socialized femininity (white, middle-class, infantilized) with which some of us are taught from early on to identify and many more are taught to idealize. What is feminist about this?

The discomfort itself is telling, as is the fact that Rebecca and "I" are doubles: One is on screen nearly all the time but doesn't have a name; the other's initials are scattered over the entire mansion while she is never glimpsed in the flesh. Rebecca is the good girl's dark other, and there are both colonial and sexual connotations to that darkness. Unlike *Jane Eyre*, in which Rochester's former wife is from Jamaica and thus explicitly connected with the history of British colonialism, *Rebecca* carries only a trace of racialization in the arguably Jewish connotations of the title character's name—meaning "to ensnare." *Rebecca*'s sexual difference from "I" is much more apparent in the text than a potential ethnic difference. *Rebecca* is sensual, confident, and competent, while I is prim and naïve. That perhaps "I" wants to have, not to be, Rebecca is argued by Rhona Berenstein in "'I'm Not the Sort of Person Men Marry': Monsters, Queers, and Hitchcock's *Rebecca*" (Berenstein 1995). Lesbian readings of the film, like Berenstein's, and my own in "Female Spectator, Lesbian Specter" (White 1991), take *Rebecca*'s preoccupation with difference between women as a catalyst for or a symptom of desire, most overtly displayed by Mrs. Danvers' attentions to the dead Rebecca's effects. "*Rebecca*'s women" carries a possessive, erotic sense, referring to those seduced by Rebecca the character through *Rebecca* the novel or film.

Queer readings of the film are historically grounded in the era's sexual politics and in du Maurier's biography. Lesbianism—or sapphic modernism—was a literary theme in the 1920s. *The Well of Loneliness* had been tried and found obscene in Britain in 1928 (and found not so in the USA in 1929); Lillian Hellman's *The Children's Hour* ran on Broadway from 1934 to 1936. In film, *Maedchen in Uniform* (dir. Leontine Sagan, 1931) was released in the USA as an art film, around the same time Garbo and Dietrich kissed women in their movies. Margaret Forster's fascinating and widely read biography of du Maurier reports that the author first encountered her own desire for women at boarding school in France. The school's headmistress, known as "Ferdie," later became a member of the du Maurier household. But, unlike du Maurier's sisters Angela and Jeanne, who lived with female life partners, Daphne largely dismissed her own "Venetian"—family slang for lesbian—tendencies. Nevertheless, she was sometimes an ardent suitor of women. Forster reports that she pursued an affair with Gertrude Lawrence, and she was in love with her publisher's wife. Du Maurier described Ellen Doubleday as a "Rebecca," which she meant as a compliment, a reference to the idealized Rebecca in whom we are all led to believe until Maxim defames her. But, Forster argues, du Maurier generally kept the "boy in a box," as the author put it, tapping this androgynous creative power in her writing.

In the novel *Rebecca*, the revelation that the dead woman's idealized image is built on a fiction allows the heterosexual couple to live ever after—I won't say happily, as the book relegates them to a gloomy life of exile. Or convincingly, as the narrator has to forgive the husband for, and collude with him on covering up, the murder of her predecessor. (Significantly, and unlike the Code-bound film, the novel also allows Danvers to live on.) But we could also see that collapse of illusion as a revelation that the intensity of I's feeling for Rebecca is due not to jealousy but to desire. The heroine's overt belief in Rebecca's unspeakably evil nature could thus be read as a projection of internalized homophobia. But if I can't always convince my students that I is a lesbian, I can usually persuade them that Mrs. Danvers is.

Of *Rebecca*'s women, it perhaps this character who has been most rehabilitated since the film's original release. It's not that Mrs. Danvers' formidable status, and Judith Anderson's performance, have not long been appreciated. Her salary (which far exceeded Fontaine's), her Oscar nomination, and her reviews show she was integral to the film's success. It's Danvers' madness, which homophobic discourse attributed to the sterility of lesbianism, that can now be celebrated as desire's excess. Take, for example, the camp tribute to the character in *Brave Smiles*, a play by the Five Lesbian Brothers. Even at the time of the film's production, the censors recognized Danvers' special relationship with Rebecca. Joe Breen objects to "quite inescapable inferences of sex perversion" in the script; contemporary reviewers noted Danvers' "dark hypnotic charm" and "sinister menace." Berenstein's historical research shows queer audiences were also attuned to this dimension of the text's appeal (Berenstein 1998).

Eroticism between women is very much on display in *Rebecca*'s famous West Wing where Danvers comes very near to actually … What? Seducing "I" or driving her mad? In the first of two scenes set in Rebecca's rooms, Danvers coaxes I to touch the dead woman's clothes and imagine her rituals and routines; in the second, she urges the young woman, fleeing from her disgrace at the ball, to jump to her death. With the heroine dressed in a facsimile of a gown Rebecca once wore and Danvers in her customary floor-length black gown, the scene is temporally ambiguous, as if multiple generations of women are performing an ambiguous pas de deux in perpetuity in this space. In its long history as a lesbian classic, *Rebecca* immerses viewers in this gothic mise-en-scène. The spell cast by *Rebecca* is heard in Waxman's score, as Jack Sullivan demonstrates in Coda A.

Whether or not we concur with Smyth that women "ran the show" in 1930s and 1940s Hollywood, it is significant that Hitchcock launched his Hollywood career at the period's midpoint, in 1940. *Rebecca* kicked off a decade of Hollywood women's pictures—Freudian feminist melodramas—that captured and shaped changing gender roles and relationships between and among women in the USA and beyond. The central trio of *Rebecca*'s women—Rebecca, Danvers, and I—complemented, in flashy supporting roles, by the inimitable Florence Bates and the great Gladys Cooper (a longtime du Maurier family friend)—offered multiple points of entry for female audiences.

Reception

We realized that this film was being shown again because the people of the community had paid it the rare honor of wanting it back. Rebecca possesses a quality so unique, so ingratiating that we hazard a guess that it will be brought back again and again and always at the command of the people.

REBECCA UA PRESSBOOK, 1944

As I've argued, female audiences were well primed for Selznick's "picturization" of 1938's bestselling novel. Du Maurier's *Rebecca* captured a fiercely loyal reading public almost immediately in both UK and US releases, selling out several print runs in advance. The property was soon adapted as a play in England by du Maurier herself, and in the USA by Orson Welles as a radio drama. With the film rights presold and publicity buildup around casting, readers eagerly anticipated the adaptation.

Helen Taylor's emphasis on the memory of *Gone with the Wind*'s fans across generations of women in her wonderful study, *Scarlett's Women*, provides a model for *Rebecca*'s cultural importance. Taylor delves into the appeal of the fantasy of the antebellum American South for British readers and viewers. Although I have not done ethnographic research like Taylor's, I do believe that the fantasy of English aristocracy is similarly key to *Rebecca*'s popularity with American audiences. Selznick adapted Mitchell's and du Maurier's novels back to back, and linked them in his studio's promotion and release strategy. Connected as bestselling "women's fiction," the properties promulgated contradictory fantasies of gender, race, class, and nation. And, for US audiences, *Rebecca* rallied support for England before the USA entered World War II.

The enthusiastic reception of *Rebecca* in both markets closes a circle regarding "the whole school of feminine literature" and its culture-industry cadres. Brown, Harrison, Mayer Selznick, and Joan Fontaine were all fans of du Maurier's book who brought that passion and insight to the actual making of the film. Fans too felt possessive, like the woman who wrote to Selznick bemoaning Fontaine's casting (calling her a "silly nincompoop"). For many, *Rebecca* was not a "Hitchcock" picture: it was and is a du Maurier adaptation.

Of course, these female consumers became even more important to the industry during wartime, as Hollywood studios looked for successful formulae to appeal to the homefront audience. *Rebecca* was rereleased as soon as 1944 by United Artists, and various elements of its success were incorporated into other films. Joan Fontaine was cast in *Suspicion*, *Jane Eyre*, and *Frenchman's Creek* (another du Maurier adaptation). Selznick and Hitchcock would make *Notorious* and *Spellbound* together.

Interest in the women's pictures of the 1940s on the part of feminist film scholars secured *Rebecca* a central place in cinema studies. The film begs a psychoanalytic approach—if a more nuanced one than Elsaesser's quoted above. Modleski drew on her work on the history of women's genres and pleasures in her tour-de-force reading, "Never to Be 36 Years Old: *Rebecca* as Female Oedipal Drama," a kernel for her influential book on Hitchcock, *The Women Who Knew Too Much* (Modleski 1988). De Lauretis built on Modleski's reading as well as Mulvey's originary essay, "Visual Pleasure and Narrative Cinema" (1975), comparing the role of the ancestral female portraits of *Rebecca* and *Vertigo* in relaying desire through narrative (see Fig. 4.2). Mary Ann Doane's essay on *Rebecca* and the Max Ophuls film *Caught*, "The Inscription of Femininity as Absence" (1981) emphasized the lack of fit between classical cinema's specular and narrative mechanisms and representations of female subjectivity and desire, noting the period's "obsession with … psychical mechanisms associated with the female—chiefly masochism, hysteria, and paranoia" (Doane 1981: 196). In my own reading of *Rebecca*, I challenged Doane's claim that that "in positing … a female spectator … it is no longer necessary to invest the look with desire" by positing a specifically lesbian spectator (White 1981: 197). In addition to theorizations drawing on psychoanalysis, feminist film scholars pursued historical approaches, putting Hollywood woman's pictures in cultural and economic context. Doane's own work on the female consumer gaze offers a valuable approach to *Rebecca*'s historical reception.

The marketing campaign for *Rebecca* addressed fans as if they were Rebeccas rather than Is—or, more accurately, as Is looking to become Rebeccas—with "the *Rebecca* Luxury Wardrobe" and high-end furnishings. Kay Brown, from a social registry background, supervised the fashion tie-in, though it seems to have missed its window when the film's release was delayed until April. Note that self-adornment and home decorating are presented as forms of deception and masquerade in the film; female consumers are enlisted on the side of subterfuge and excess. Rebecca was, we are told by Mrs. Danvers, in one of her campiest lines, "most particular about her sauces." Interestingly, it was instead I's pullover sweater and matching cardigan that *Rebecca* made fashionable. The twinset became the costume of the young woman independent earner, known in some parts as the "Rebecca."

Ultimately, it is the doubleness of the gothic—its conservatism and its radicality—that makes *Rebecca*'s women interesting, and legion. From the female workers who both colluded with and steered the culture industry, to the heroine's crisis of curiosity, to the material and aspirational bonds among audience members forged by marketing, there is no "woman" in the singular that *Rebecca* invokes or explains. Moreover, while *Rebecca*'s women may overlap with "Hitchcock's women," they exceed any framing of their labor, their origin, or their loyalty in terms of the Master. *Rebecca* is perhaps the only Hitchcock film that doesn't need his name attached to retain its importance in film history. It isn't just a matter of giving

Figure 4.2 Mrs. de Winter (Joan Fontaine) and Mrs. Danvers (Judith Anderson) under the watchful eye of Caroline de Winter.
Rebecca, directed by Alfred Hitchcock. © Selznick International Pictures 1940. All rights reserved.

Selznick, or du Maurier, or Harrison and Reville, the credit they deserve, it's about recognizing authorship as performance and collaboration, appreciating genre as intertextual and contextual, and acknowledging the good taste and possessiveness with which female audiences have always driven the history of the movies.

Rebecca remains culturally important not just as a triumph of the Hollywood studio system but also as a test object for ideas about and experiences with the intimate intertwining of women and popular culture in the twentieth century. *Rebecca* is, in key ways, by, for, and about women. The appeal of a novel by a popular woman writer was immediately grasped by professional women, who facilitated its adaptation by a director and a Hollywood showman, who, each in his own way, was attuned to questions of female representation. Repeated remakes, reissues, and copies generated memories transferred across generations, within families and locales not necessarily resembling the ones centered by the text. And the specificities of its story and its telling speak to psychic aspects of individuation and their social organization that invite feminist, queer, class-conscious, and anti-imperialist readings. *Rebecca*'s classic status points to an array of sometimes contradictory factors that suggest that the film's meaning is as multiple and unstable as Rebecca's after all.

References

Allen, Jane (2019) *I Lost my Girlish Laughter*, New York: Vintage.
Berenstein, Rhona J. (1995) "'I'm Not the Sort of Person Men Marry': Monsters, Queers, and Hitchcock's *Rebecca*," in Corey K. Creekmur and Alexander Doty (eds), *Out in Culture*: *Gay*, *Lesbian and Queer Essays on Popular Culture*, Durham, NC: Duke University Press, pp. 239–261.
Berenstein, Rhona J. (1998) "Adaptation, Censorship, and Audiences of Questionable Type: Lesbian Sightings in *Rebecca* (1940) and *The Uninvited* (1944)," *Cinema Journal*, 37 (3): 16–37.
de Lauretis, Teresa (1984) *Alice Doesn't: Feminism, Semiotics, Cinema*, Bloomington, Ind.: Indiana University Press.
Doane, Mary Ann (1981) "Caught and *Rebecca*: The Inscription of Femininity as Absence," in Constance Penley (ed.), *Feminism and Film Theory*, London and New York: Routledge and BFI Publishing, pp. 216–228.
Du Maurier, Daphne (1938) *Rebecca*, New York: Doubleday.
Du Maurier, Daphne, and Oriel Malet (1993) *Letters from Menabilly: Portrait of a Friendship*, London: Weidenfeld & Nicolson.
Elsaesser, Thomas (1985) "Tales of Sound and Fury: Observations on the Family Melodrama," in Bill Nichols (ed.), *Moves and Methods*: *An Anthology*, vol. II, Berkeley, Calif.: University of California Press, pp. 165–189.
Forster, Margaret (1993) *Daphne du Maurier*, London: Chatto & Windus.
Hapke, Laura (1995) *Daughters of the Great Depression*: *Women*, *Work*, *and Fiction in the American 1930s*, Athens, Ga.: University of Georgia Press.
Lane, Christina (2020) *Phantom Lady: Hollywood Producer Joan Harrison—The Forgotten Woman behind Hitchcock*, Chicago, Ill.: Chicago Review Press.
Leff, Leonard J. (1999) *Hitchcock and Selznick*: *The Rich and Strange Collaboration of Alfred Hitchcock and David O. Selznick in Hollywood*, Berkeley, Calif.: University of California Press.
Mayne, Judith (1988) *Private Novels, Public Films*, Athens, Ga.: University of Georgia Press.
Modleski, Tania (1988) *The Women Who Knew Too Much*: *Hitchcock and Feminist Theory*, New York: Methuen.
Mulvey, Laura (1974) "Visual Pleasure and Narrative Cinema," *Screen*, 16 (3): 6–18.
Rabwin, Marcella (1999) *Yes, Mr. Selznick: Recollections of Hollywood's Golden Era*, New York: Dorrance.
Selznick, David O. (1972) *Memo from David O. Selznick*: *The Creation of Gone with the Wind*, edited by Rudy Behlmer, New York: Viking Press.
Smyth, J. E. (2018) *Nobody's Girl Friday*: *The Women who Ran Hollywood*, New York: Oxford University Press.
Thomson, David (1972) *Showman: The Life of David O. Selznick*, New York: Knopf.
Truffaut, François, with Helen G. Scott (1985) *Hitchcock*, rev. edn, New York: Simon & Schuster.
White, Patricia (1991) "Female Spectator, Lesbian Specter: The Haunting," in Diana Fuss (ed.), *Inside/Out: Lesbian Theories*, *Gay Theories*, New York: Routledge, pp. 142–172.
White, Patricia (2021) *Rebecca*, London: Bloomsbury.
Wood, Robin (1969) *Hitchcock's Films*, 2nd edn, New York: Castle.

Chapter 5

Shadow of a Doubt (1943) and *Notorious* (1946)

Two Hollywood—and Definitively American—Masterworks

Thomas Schatz

Ever since their initial release, both *Shadow of a Doubt* (1943) and *Notorious* (1946) have been critical darlings. Both were among the best reviewed films in the year against stiff competition at the very peak of Hollywood's classical studio era, and both have fared exceptionally well with succeeding generations of critics. In fact, as of this writing, *Shadow of a Doubt* is one of the rare films with a 100 percent rating on the review aggregator Rotten Tomatoes (based on fifty-three reviews, most of them written for reissues and festival screenings long after initial release), while *Notorious* clocks in at 96 percent (on forty-eight reviews) (Rotten Tomatoes 2024a, 2024b). Indeed, it's fair to say that *Shadow of a Doubt* and *Notorious* are among the few Hitchcock films that were well received initially and have seen their stature rise over time. That said, both films had their naysayers when they first appeared—as did Hitchcock, who was lambasted by a contingent of British critics and professionals for migrating to Hollywood and signing with prestige producer David O. Selznick. Moreover, the terms of both films' reception have shifted considerably over time, especially with the onslaught of auteurism in the 1960s and the rise of academic film studies and scholarly publishing in the 1970s and beyond. Thus, while both *Shadow of a Doubt* and *Notorious* now are firmly ensconced in the Hitchcock canon, each has seen its share of critical churn—along with Hitchcock's own stature—in the intervening decades.

The Critical Reception of *Shadow of a Doubt* in Britain and America

Made while Hitchcock was still finding his footing in America and in Hollywood, *Shadow of a Doubt* was his sixth picture since migrating from England in 1939 and signing a long-term contract with

Selznick (Schatz 1997: 87). He began that stint with two very British pictures and two resounding critical and commercial hits: *Rebecca* (1940), winner of the best-picture Oscar, and *Foreign Correspondent* (1941). Two of his next three—*Mr. & Mrs. Smith* (1941), an offbeat foray into romantic comedy, and *Saboteur* (1942), a war-themed cross-country chase film—were set in America, and both did poorly by Hitchcock's standards with critics and audiences alike. Between those two subpar pictures, Hitchcock directed *Suspicion* (1942), another film set in Britain and an obvious follow-up to *Rebecca*, which won an Academy Award for Joan Fontaine, who starred in both films. *Suspicion* also scored with critics and moviegoers.

So Hitchcock's early track record in Hollywood was somewhat uneven, and by 1942 he had yet to make a distinctly American film. As if to rectify that, Hitchcock summoned the playwright Thornton Wilder, fresh from his Pulitzer Prize–winning Broadway hit *Our Town*, and the two went to work on *Shadow of a Doubt*. Setting up camp in Santa Rosa, California, they collaborated closely on the screenplay while Hitchcock prepared the production—a truly singular picture at the time, shot entirely on location and in the community in which the story is set (see Fig. 5.1).[1]

A disquieting companion piece to *Our Town*, Wilder's paean to small-town America, *Shadow of a Doubt* probed the dark side of a seemingly ideal American family and its idyllic community. The story

Figure 5.1 Production still from *Shadow of a Doubt*, directed by Alfred Hitchcock.
© Universal Pictures 1943. All rights reserved. Courtesy of the Alfred Hitchcock Trust.

centered on two discontents, a visiting uncle from somewhere back East, and his namesake niece, who reconnects with her Uncle Charlie but comes to realize that he is a serial killer of wealthy widows. The production boasted a tremendous cast, headlined by Teresa Wright in just her fourth film, after garnering two nominations and an Oscar win in her first three, and Joseph Cotten, a sudden star after his breakthrough performances in *Citizen Kane* (1941) and *The Magnificent Ambersons* (1942).[2]

Shadow of a Doubt was released in January 1943 in the USA and two months later in the UK, and it was a solid commercial and critical hit on both sides of the war-torn Atlantic. *Film Daily* ranked it the sixteenth best-reviewed film of the year on the basis of the top-ten lists of seventy-six "representative critics and commentators" (*1944 Film Daily Year Book*, p. 105). It was vying with stiff competition as the war boom went into high gear along with Hollywood's (and the entire nation's) conversion to war production; in fact, every one of *Film Daily*'s top-ten films that year was a war-related title.

Interestingly enough, British critics tended to be more sensitive to *Shadow of a Doubt*'s ironic treatment of the small-town milieu and archetypal family, and to Hitchcock's probing of the disturbances lurking beneath the complacent surface. Dilys Powell, one of England's top critics, wrote in the *Sunday Times* that for Hitchcock, like the novelist G. K. Chesterton, "the most exciting detective stories and thrillers" were those that "record some minor infamy" within a familiar locale. Unlike *Saboteur* and *Foreign Correspondent*, in which the sprawling story "dissipated interest" as the narrative scope widened, *Shadow of a Doubt* finds Hitchcock "returning to the enclosed crime" in a tale that sets "the welcoming home" and "the solidity and ordinariness of the background" against "the strangeness of murder" and "the cunning and underlying savagery of the criminal" (*Sunday Times*, March 28, 1943). An unsigned rave review in the *New Statesman* took much the same tack, opening with this bald statement: "'Shadow of a Doubt' is the best film Hitchcock has made. No need this time for darksome mills, car chases, ticking clocks, scrambles over the Statue of Liberty" (*New Statesman*, March 28, 1943). Instead, we are given something much more quotidian. "Crime and ordinary life rarely consort together on the screen" the way they do in this film, said this critic, as an average family welcomes a beloved and distinguished visitor who is actually a "psychopath," and whose "natural sympathy" with his niece leads to her discovery of his murderous ways. "If the film has a fault," concluded the reviewer, "it is that Hitchcock is too tender-hearted and shuffles a bit at the end. But it comes off, shuffle and all."

Another top British critic, *The Observer*'s C. A. Lejeune, noted that "Hitchcock's new film is a choice one of its kind," with its depiction of the average family enhanced by the film's "naturalism," not only the location shooting but also the sound design, particularly the frequent use of "overlapping dialogue" and of "unrelated conversations carried on between several people at one time" (*The Observer*, March 28, 1943). That led Lejeune to speculate that "Hitchcock has been taking an intensive course of Orson Welles"—whose *The Magnificent Ambersons* was released just weeks earlier in the UK—"unless one assumes" the reverse, that Welles has been studying Hitchcock. The comparisons to *The Magnificent Ambersons* came up in several *Shadow of a Doubt* reviews, including Dilys Powell's, who clearly saw Welles influencing Hitchcock. She, too, mentioned the distinctive sound design and "the interrupted broken conversation, the dialogue drowned in chatter." And she closed her review with further speculation. "I do not think I was mistaken in seeing the Welles influence elsewhere in this admirably made film," wrote Powell, "in the use of closeups, the pictorial handling of the solitary figure, and the suggestion of the voice overheard" (see Fig. 5.2).

The initial critical response to *Shadow of a Doubt* in the USA was equally enthusiastic. The New York reviews were so uniformly upbeat that Universal Pictures, which produced and distributed the Selznick-packaged picture, took out full-page ads in *Variety*, *Motion Picture Herald*, *Film Daily*, and other trade

Figure 5.2 The Welles-style framing of Teresa Wright's Charlie.

papers highlighting the Gotham reviews. These ads were aimed primarily at exhibitors since Universal did not own its own theater chain and was eager to book *Shadow of a Doubt* in the fiercely competitive and overheated first-run theatrical marketplace. It's worth noting here that the trade papers also reviewed virtually all major studio releases, providing a first line of critical response just prior to the film's release. These, too, were geared mainly to potential exhibitors. *Film Daily*, for example, ran an unsigned review on January 8, 1943, that opened with this all-caps headline: "ACE MELLER WITH SOCKO B. O. POWER VIA ACTING, ACTION AND HITCHCOCK'S FLARE FOR SUSPENSE" (*Film Daily*, January 8, 1943). The review then listed several reasons for this "appraisement," beginning with this: "Hitchcock's handling of a power-packed meller [melodrama] in an American venue (most of the action takes place in California community of modest size) will add realism and consequence to the story in the eyes and estimation of the nation's entertainment-seekers." One week later, Universal planted four full-page ads in *Film Daily* featuring the New York critics' response to *Shadow of a Doubt*, which appeared up front in the paper on every other page (*Film Daily*, January 15, 1943, pp. 3, 5, 7, 9).

Receiving the most prominent play in this ad campaign was the *New York Times* review by Bosley Crowther, who at the time was that widely acknowledged dean of American film critics (and would continue to be until the 1960s). The ad reproduced the first two paragraphs of Crowther's review, which were indeed glowing, culminating in the assertion that Hitchcock's capacity to induce "mental anguish" both in his characters and in moviegoers "is of championship proportions" in *Shadow of a Doubt*, rendering it "a sheer delight" (*New York Times*, January 13, 1943). The quoted portion of the review stopped there, conveniently enough, before Crowther abruptly pivoted to "the principal fault—or rather the sole disappointment" in the film, which was Hitchcock's failure to fully deliver on the "tremendous promise" of the setup and the steadily intensifying conflict between the two principals. Once young Charlie learns that her beloved, cosmically connected Uncle Charlie "is really a murderer of rich, fat widows wanted back East," wrote Crowther, "the story takes a decidedly anticlimactic dip and becomes just a competent exercise in keeping the tightrope taut."

That was a minority opinion among American critics, however, who consistently praised Wright's performance and her character's gritty determination to protect her family and to rid the community of Uncle Charlie. Moreover, many favorably compared *Shadow of a Doubt*'s payoff to the infamously tacked-on "happy ending" to *Suspicion*. The *Time* magazine review, for instance, stated, "This Hitchcock masterpiece has the same general theme as *Suspicion*—the slow, terrible growth of fear of a loved one. But *Shadow*, from beginning to end, is a surpassingly better picture. Its horror is compounded by its setting: an exquisitely commonplace family in a familiar small California town" (*Time*, January 18, 1943). The unsigned staff review described the film's steady, unnerving buildup as "a crescendo of terror" and circled back to *Suspicion* in closing: "Unlike *Suspicion*, *Shadow* hits few false notes, maintains suspense to the end."

The Initial Critical Response to *Notorious*

Between *Shadow of a Doubt* and *Notorious*, Hitchcock directed two films, both of which contributed to his growing stature. The first was *Lifeboat*, a war film packaged by Selznick and financed and distributed by 20th Century Fox. Released in January 1944, it was a solid hit, earning Hitchcock an Oscar nomination for best director (one of four nominations for an award he never won). Then came *Spellbound*, a Selznick International production released by United Artists in October 1945 and an enormous hit—on a par with *Notorious*, in fact. The film was a well-crafted star vehicle for Ingrid Bergman, who was under contract to Selznick and coming off *Casablanca* (1942), *For Whom the Bell Tolls* (1943), and an Oscar-winning performance in *Gaslight* (1944). A deft melding of noir intrigue and high-gloss romance, *Spellbound* co-starred Gregory Peck as a troubled veteran who wins the heart of Bergman's psychoanalyst as she cures his amnesia and clears him of a murder charge. It was the third-biggest hit in 1945 and appeared on over 400 ten-best critics' lists, and it was nominated for six Oscars including best picture and best director (*1946 Film Daily Year Book*, p. 111; *1947 Film Daily Year Book*, p. 119).

Thus, Hitchcock's stature was stronger than ever when *Notorious* was released in August 1946, giving him back-to-back runaway hits. Packaged by Selznick and sold to RKO, which financed and released the picture, *Notorious* actually outpaced *Spellbound* at the box office although it finished only eighth in a year loaded with hits at the very peak of Hollywood's war boom. *Notorious* was a critical hit as well but not quite on *Spellbound*'s level, appearing on 177 top-ten lists (*1947 Film Daily Year Book*, p. 119). And it was nominated for two Academy Awards—for the original screenplay by Ben Hecht (who also scripted *Spellbound*) and for Claude Rains' supporting role—but it scored no Oscar wins.

The contemporaneous reviews of *Notorious*, in both the trades and the popular press, were uniformly positive; indeed, most were outright raves. But they varied widely in their treatment—or even their acknowledgment—of the film's narrative, thematic and moral complexities. Some of the stronger and more insightful reviews appeared in the trade papers, which were obliged to provide a plot synopsis to give exhibitors a sense of the film's commercial assets and audience appeal, its "adult" dimensions, and its "exploitation" value. W. R. Weaver's front-page review in *Motion Picture Daily*, for instance, opened by asserting the marquee value of co-stars Cary Grant, Bergman and Rains, who along with Hitchcock and Hecht "guarantee that the attraction will open to terrific attendance" and also noted the film's "provocative" and "exploitable" elements (*Motion Picture Daily*, July 24, 1946). Chief among these was the star-crossed love affair between Grant's American agent and Bergman's bereft daughter of a German-American traitor, whom Grant recruits to penetrate a ring of Nazis (led by Rains) operating in

Rio. After laying out the setup, Weaver spent much of the review pondering the film's moral dilemmas, particularly the behavior of Grant's superiors who "begin to look pretty seedy" when they encourage Bergman, who falls in love with Grant before getting her assignment, to accept Rains' unexpected proposal of marriage. This ratchets up the suspense in "typically Hitchcock" fashion, said Weaver, with the film's "final, suspenseful sequence" favorably resolving matters. "Nevertheless, the spectacle of American agents employing an unfortunate, if somewhat dissolute, young woman to marry a German agent to obtain information … is not one to send proud Americans out of the theatre singing 'My Country Tis of Thee.'"

Whether this moral ambiguity is a selling point and an opportunity for "sensational exploitation" was left open by Weaver, and he didn't mention *Notorious*'s tense but remarkably subdued climax in which the reunited lovers walk out of Rains' mansion, leaving him (and his mother) to face the wrath of their fellow Nazis. Other trade-press critics did deal more directly with that remarkable payoff, although few knew quite what to do with it. Among the more effective assessments was Red Kann's *Motion Picture Herald* review, headlined "Suspense Supreme," which closed with this:

> The romantic formula, of course, dictates that Grant will get the girl, but by what devices and through what dangers are not readily apparent as the action proceeds. The FBI is never mentioned. A gun is neither shown nor fired. Uranium ore is referred to, but the atom bomb, never. The love passages are long, delicate and decidedly pulsating. These are some of the nuances and representative of … the suavity and smoothness in evidence here. Hitchcock's direction, in short, is superb; his attraction, a winner.
>
> (*Motion Picture Herald*, July 27, 1946)

The staff review in *Film Daily*, on the other hand, closed with the odd (and mistaken) assertion that "Rains' death at the hands of his co-plotters spells a happy ending for the lovers" (*Film Daily*, July 25, 1946). A more accurate but still problematic account of the finale appeared in *Harrison's Reports*, which noted that "Grant rescues Ingrid from the spies without as much as a scuffle," which is deemed "a typical Hitchcock ending, done masterfully" (*Harrison's Reports*, July 27, 1946). The subdued climax was indeed masterful, but it was in fact quite atypical of Hitchcock's finales, which invariably involved a good deal more than a scuffle (see Fig. 5.3).

Mainstream press critics in both the USA and the UK were equally upbeat, although they tended to treat *Notorious* in more general terms than the trade press and were even more circumspect about the film's moral and thematic complexities. One notable exception in the USA was Bosley Crowther in his cogent *Times* review. He opened by stating that Hitchcock, Hecht, and Bergman, "the ones most responsible for *Spellbound*," have teamed on "another taut, superior film" (*New York Times*, August 16, 1946). What distinguished *Notorious* was "the remarkable blend of love story with expert 'thriller,'" which was crucially enhanced by "the uncommon character of the girl." In a "forthright and daring" maneuver, wrote Crowther, Hecht and Hitchcock present Bergman's character as "a lady of notably loose morals." That laxity is attributed to her being "the logically cynical daughter of a convicted American traitor," although on a deeper level it was the "integrity of her nature" that led Bergman's heroine to take on the espionage job and see it through to the bitter and possibly fatal end. That integrity, said Crowther, was "the prop that holds the show." Crowther was impressed, too, with the romantic and sexual tangle in *Notorious*, which was handled by Hecht and Hitchcock "with sophistication and irony" and comes across as "a frank, grownup amour"—i.e. an intimate sexual relationship. "And Miss Bergman and Mr. Grant

Figure 5.3 Devlin (Cary Grant) coming to Alicia's (Ingrid Bergman) rescue.
Notorious, directed by Alfred Hitchcock. © RKO Radio Pictures and Vanguard Films 1946. All rights reserved.

have played it with surprising and disturbing clarity." Here he cited the couple's legendary three-minute kiss—shot in tight closeup with appropriate pauses to accommodate the Production Code (see Fig. 5.4)—although he did not mention the film's equally renowned set pieces: the couple's desperate wine-cellar search intercut with the cocktail party (and diminishing wine supply) upstairs, and the couple's final escape abetted by Rains as his fellow Nazis look on. Clearly, Crowther was more interested in conveying the film's grown-up amour than in discussing Hitchcock's expert thriller.

British critics, for the most part, focused on Bergman's performance and star power as well as Hitchcock's direction. "The story is not notably original," wrote Joan Lester in England's Sunday *Reynold's News*, for example. "Yet in Director Hitchcock's hands, and with the beauty of Bergman, this old material takes on new life" (Lester 1947). And in a *Daily Herald* piece headlined "Impossible Ingrid," P. L. Mannock noted the many improbabilities that lead to Bergman's American agent bedding down with Rains' Nazi (*Daily Herald*, February 14, 1947). But "credibility takes a back seat" in the film thanks to Hitchcock's "brilliant, prankish touch" and to Bergman's "star magnetism." Campbell Dixon dug just a bit deeper in his *Daily Telegraph* review, noting the "vulgar" terms in which Bergman's character was presented and developed (*Daily Telegraph*, February 17, 1947). But then came the Bergman default: "If the film recovers from its tawdry start, and indeed it gets better and better as it goes on, that is largely because Miss Bergman possesses, as perhaps no other actress does, beauty, talent and a fresh spontaneous charm."

Figure 5.4 Grant and Bergman's three-minute kiss.

It's important to note here that *Notorious*, unlike *Shadow of a Doubt*, did have a few high-profile detractors in Britain who saw the film as a consummate example of Hitchcock squandering his talents while enjoying the superior resources and remuneration that Hollywood provided. This contingent of critics and industry insiders comprised "a minority, but an articulate and influential one," as Charles Barr points out in his excellent essay, "Deserter or Exile? Views of Hitchcock from Wartime Britain" (Barr 2004: 1; see also Coda B). Barr briefly recounts the group's trashing of *Notorious*, quoting several critics including Richard Winnington, whose review in the *News Chronicle* well indicated their take. "*Notorious* can be said to glitter with a deadly sickness," wrote Winnington. "Alfred Hitchcock has gone out, at all costs, for polish, at the price of originality and suspense and story" (*News Chronicle*, February 15, 1947). Barr counters the negative reviews with Paul Dehn's rave in the *Sunday Chronicle*, which deemed *Notorious* a "magnificent" picture, arguing that every word and gesture "has its proper place and point in this melodrama's vehement unraveling," and that every shot and sequence "is cut brilliantly to correct measure" (*Sunday Chronicle*, February 16, 1947). Those countervailing views, according to Barr, clearly signaled "the complexities of the discourse about Hitchcock in 1940s Britain" (2004: 18).

A Critical Turn: Hitchcock and Auteurism

In surveying the contingent of Hitchcock-bashers in 1940s Britain, Barr mentions in passing a 1949 article by Lindsay Anderson, a rising young film critic (he was then in his mid-twenties) who would become a leading filmmaker in the Free Cinema documentary movement in the 1950s and the British New Wave in the 1960s. Published in the fall 1949 issue of the film journal *Sequence* and entitled, simply, "Alfred

Hitchcock," the piece was strident, pithy, and influential—both as a last gasp, so to speak, of the vocal group of critics and industry types lamenting Hitchcock's flight to Hollywood and the work he produced there, and also as an odd antecedent to the auteur polemic that would soon be roiling in France, with Hitchcock at the center of the storm (see Anderson 1972). Indeed, Anderson was a precursor of sorts to Truffaut, Godard, and the other Parisian critics-turned-filmmakers who were the chief architects of both auteurism and, later, the French New Wave. Anderson's piece also dealt directly with *Shadow of a Doubt* and *Notorious* and thus warrants consideration here in some detail.

Anderson began by noting that "Hitchcock's long career has been intimately bound up with the history of cinema," and he presented a brief overview of that career through the 1920s and 1930s. "Hitchcock's best films are in many ways very British," argued Anderson, "in their humor, their lack of sentimentality, their avoidance of the grandiose and the elaborately fake" (1972: 48). These qualities were "threatened" when Hitchcock went to work for Selznick, which committed him "to all that is worst in Hollywood—to size for its own sake, … to the star system for its own sake, to glossy photography, high-toned settings, lushly hypnotic musical scores." All of which were readily evident in *Rebecca* and Hitchcock's subsequent Hollywood films with the notable exception of *Shadow of a Doubt*, "a film which might be construed as an attempt—his last—to justify himself as a director." For Anderson, Hitchcock, in *Shadow of a Doubt*, displayed "an everyday realism that is reminiscent of his earlier days," but also "a subtlety of characterization distinctly superior to them." In a view that recalls Crowther's, he also contended that *Shadow of a Doubt* "is at its best in the first half," particularly in establishing its small-town setting and in developing Cotten's and Wright's characters. But the film failed "to sustain excitement and surprise" in the "later reels," wrote Anderson, and lapsed into "a simple thriller." Nonetheless, in his view it remained Hitchcock's "best American film" (Anderson 1972: 48–57).

Anderson saw *Notorious*, on the other hand, as symptomatic of Hitchcock's growing "preoccupation with technique, to the detriment of the material." In fact, he contended that technique in all of Hitchcock's work from *Spellbound* onward "ceases to be a means and becomes an end in itself." What these Hollywood films lack "is the wholeness of their predecessors." Films like *The 39 Steps* and *The Lady Vanishes* "succeed as works of art (however minor) because they attain a perfect, satisfying balance between content and style; the enlargement which Hitchcock's style has undergone in Hollywood had been accompanied by no equivalent intensifying or deepening of sensibility or subject matter." He went on to note that "*Notorious* presents an unpleasant but by no means uninteresting situation, which is thrown away largely because characterization is sacrificed to a succession of vulgar, superficial effects" (Anderson 1972: 57–59).

Anderson's article caused quite a stir and, according to Barr, "undeniably helped to fix a view of Hitchcock's decline that was dominant for at least a decade in English-language criticism" (Barr 2004: 2). That statement is certainly debatable. Any long-standing view of Hitchcock's "decline" after migrating to Hollywood was held by a minority of British critics and professionals, while his stature with mainstream critics in both the UK and the USA clearly was steadily growing. That said, Hitchcock was actually at a low ebb professionally in 1949, having suffered three consecutive disappointments following *Notorious*: his last Selznick picture, *The Paradine Case* (1947) and his first two pictures as an independent producer-director, *Rope* (1948) and *Under Capricorn* (1949). And he would suffer another setback with *Stage Fright* in 1950. But Hitchcock's career then began a stunning resurgence that began with *Strangers on a Train* (1951) and accelerated throughout the decade, particularly after he signed a multipicture deal with Paramount in 1953 that yielded *Rear Window* (1954), *To Catch a Thief* (1955), *The Man Who Knew Too Much* (1956), *Vertigo* (1958) and *Psycho* (1960).

Barr's reference to "English-language criticism" is notable here as well—an obvious nod to the young French critics writing for *Cahiers du Cinéma* in the 1950s, who fashioned *la politique des auteurs* with Hitchcock as the film author par excellence. Claude Chabrol and Éric Rohmer were perhaps Hitchcock's strongest advocates at *Cahiers*, but it was François Truffaut who convinced him to submit to a series of interviews in the early 1960s that were the basis for the now-legendary book, *Hitchcock* (aka *Hitchcock/Truffaut*), published in English in 1967 (Truffaut 1967). By then, the *Village Voice* critic Andrew Sarris's "Notes on the Auteur Theory in 1962" had appeared in the American journal *Film Culture*, with Hitchcock firmly situated in the "Pantheon" of great directors (Sarris 1962–1963), and Robin Wood's *Hitchcock's Films*, the first book-length auteur study in English, had been published in the USA (Wood 1965).

Shadow of a Doubt and *Notorious* figured into both of those groundbreaking studies, albeit along radically different lines. For Wood, the two films represent sins of omission. *Hitchcock's Films* effectively inverted Anderson's general argument that Hitchcock's best work came early in his British period. Instead, Wood espoused a view held by many early auteurists that Hitchcock's style and directorial personality developed over time, particularly after his move to Hollywood. Hence, Wood's decision to focus on eight films from Hitchcock's "mature" period: *Strangers on a Train* and *Rear Window* along with his six most recent films—*Vertigo*, *North by Northwest* (1959), *Psycho*, *The Birds* (1963), *Marnie* (1964), and *Torn Curtain* (1966)—which, in his view, comprised "an astonishing, unbroken chain of masterpieces and the highest reach of his art to date" (Wood 1965: 17, 26).

Truffaut, on the other hand, found evidence of Hitchcock's distinctive style and his characteristic thematic concerns throughout his entire oeuvre. Moreover, *Shadow of a Doubt* and *Notorious* were each singled out within *Truffaut/Hitchcock* as a favorite of one of the two filmmakers. Truffaut pointed out that Hitchcock frequently identified *Shadow of a Doubt* as "the one you prefer" amongst all his films (Truffaut 1967: 109). "I wouldn't say *Shadow of a Doubt* is my favorite picture," replied Hitchcock, although he allowed that he may have "given that impression" (Truffaut 1967: 109). The two agreed that Thornton Wilder proved to be an ideal collaborator and that in Uncle Charlie they created the consummate Hitchcock antagonist—the only film besides *Psycho* "in which your central figure is a villain," pointed out Truffaut, and a sympathetic one at that (1967: 111).

Truffaut opened the conversation about *Notorious* by identifying it as "truly my favorite Hitchcock picture" and "the very quintessence of Hitchcock" (1967: 120). The two discussed the film's noirish stylization as well as the director's collaboration with Ben Hecht to create what Truffaut terms "a model of scenario construction" (1967: 122; Fig. 5.5). They also considered the moral and dramatic complexity of the triangulated romance. "The story of *Notorious* is the old conflict between love and duty," said Hitchcock. "Cary Grant's job—and it's a rather ironic situation—is to push Ingrid Bergman into Claude Rains's bed. One can hardly blame him for seeming bitter throughout the story, whereas Claude Rains is a rather appealing figure, both because his confidence is being betrayed and because his love for Ingrid Bergman is probably deeper than Cary Grant's" (Truffaut 1967: 124). Truffaut also deemed Rains's character "undeniably your best villain," although he went on to rank Cotten's antagonist in *Shadow of a Doubt* and Walker's in *Strangers on a Train* in that category as well (1967: 125).

Shadow of a Doubt, *Notorious*, and Hitchcock Scholarship

The onslaught of auteurism—and Hitchcock's central position in that critical discourse—along with the subsequent development of film studies in academia turned Hitchcock criticism into a veritable cottage industry for trade and scholarly publishers alike. That output is far too varied and voluminous

Figure 5.5 The "noirish" stylings of *Notorious*.

to even begin to summarize here, although a few strains are worth mentioning in so far as *Shadow of a Doubt* and *Notorious* are concerned. One of these strains emerged rather abruptly with the publication of Laura Mulvey's "Visual Pleasure and Narrative Cinema" in the fall 1975 issue of the British film journal *Screen*. Mulvey's aim was to appropriate psychoanalytic theory "as a political weapon, demonstrating the way the unconscious of patriarchal society has structured film form" (1975: 6). She posited that classical Hollywood narration situates woman as the object of desire and the motivation but not the agent of action and invariably presents "woman as image" and "man as the bearer of the look." This was the basis of course for her notion of the "male gaze"—the interdependent tripartite "look" of the movie camera, the spectator, and the (predominantly male) protagonist.

Mulvey devoted only two of the article's thirteen pages to Hitchcock—and specifically to *Rear Window* and *Vertigo*, in which the male gaze fundamentally shapes the narrative proceedings. Her piercing, cogent analysis took hold, to say the least, sparking arguments that have raged ever since—most intensely in the 1980s, when Hitchcock studies and feminist film criticism went into another register. This robust discourse reached a culmination of sorts with Tania Modleski's *The Women Who Knew Too Much: Hitchcock and Feminist Theory*, published in 1989. Modleski opened by describing Mulvey's 1975 essay as "the founding document of psychoanalytic feminist film theory," and she built an analytic schema that both counters and complements it (Modleski 1989: 1). Modleski analyzed the presence and occasional prevalence of the female gaze (and female agency) in a wide range of Hitchcock films throughout his career, paying special attention (in case-study chapters devoted to *Rebecca* and *Notorious*) to his remarkable run of "woman's pictures"—and female star vehicles—during his tenure with Selznick. She was especially interested in the curious play of genre in *Notorious*, aptly observing that "one of the main interests of the film lies in the way it combines elements of film noir, an essentially male genre, in which man is the active investigator of woman, and the female Gothic, in which woman is assigned an investigative role" (Modleski 1989: 60). She found this same genre blending at work in both *Spellbound* and *Shadow of a Doubt*, which, like *Notorious*, were released just as noirs like *Laura* (1944), *Double Indemnity* (1944), and *The Big Sleep* (1946) solidified the male-centric dimension of the period style.

Feminist readings of Hitchcock's woman's pictures broadened the auteurist approach to his work and also signaled an increasingly sophisticated treatment of style and genre. Robin Wood contributed to this effort in "Ideology, Genre, Auteur," an essay first published in *Film Comment* in 1977. The essay deftly compared *Shadow of a Doubt* to Frank Capra's *It's a Wonderful Life* (1946), both of which turn on a "central tension" involving "the disturbing influx of film noir into the world of smalltown domestic comedy" (Wood 1977: 47). Moreover, both films "have as a central ideological project the reaffirmation of the family and smalltown values"—something Capra convincingly pulls off, argued Wood, while it rings "completely hollow" in *Shadow of a Doubt* with its dark romance and underlying sexual tensions (see Fig. 5.6) and its famously ambiguous tag scene (Wood 1977: 47, 51). Hitchcock seemed well aware of that

Figure 5.6 Young Charlie notices the ring is engraved with someone else's initials.

irony, telling Truffaut that the final exchange outside the church between young Charlie and the detective indicates that she "will be in love with her Uncle Charlie for the rest of her life"—after killing him in self-defense in the previous scene (Truffaut 1967: 112). Wood wasn't so sure of Hitchcock's intent and his awareness of the film's deeper resonance, however, and he closed his essay with this zinger: "Its roots in the Hollywood genres, and in the very ideological structure it so disturbingly subverts, make *Shadow of a Doubt* so much more suggestive and significant a work than Hitchcock the bourgeois entertainer could ever have guessed" (Wood 1977: 51).

Wood incorporated "Ideology, Genre, Auteur" into *Hitchcock's Films Revisited*, a 1989 book that included *Hitchcock's Films* in its entirety (the book was then out of print), along with nine new chapters, most of which examined earlier Hitchcock films that were "neglected" in the previous study—and all of which temper the strident auteurism of his previous Hitchcock study with more contemporary theoretical approaches. His close reading of *Notorious*, for instance, appears in a chapter entitled "Star and Auteur: Hitchcock's Films with Ingrid Bergman," building on the work of Richard Dyer, Andrew Britton and others in the burgeoning subfield of "star studies" (Wood 1989).

Despite Wood's second thoughts about Hitchcock's authorial intent and creative authority over *Shadow of a Doubt*, it's clear that he considered it a masterwork of 1940s Hollywood cinema. But the implicit message in "Ideology, Genre, Auteur" is that *Shadow of a Doubt* is less firmly fixed in the Hitchcock canon than *Notorious*—a view that continually crops up in later reviews and analyses. Dave Kehr, in a brief 1985 review in *Chicago Reader*, opened by calling *Shadow of a Doubt* "Alfred Hitchcock's first indisputable masterpiece" (*Chicago Reader*, April 5, 1985). But he also credited Wilder for creating "*Our Town* turned inside out." Alan Stanbrook, writing in the *Daily Telegraph* on the occasion of a BBC airing in 1998, called *Shadow of a Doubt* "a gem … that is too little known but ranks among the best work [Hitchcock] did in America" (*Daily Telegraph*, July 18, 1998). And he went on to say that Hitchcock "always had a soft spot for the film and it is indeed one of his best," but is lesser known because it lacks the enduring star power and memorable set pieces of his anointed classics, including *Notorious*. *Shadow*'s greatest strength, in Stanbrook's view, is that the film "is all of one piece"—a well-crafted, internally coherent thriller that is carried from beginning to end by Hitchcock's inimitable style and two incomparable performances. Roger Ebert made the same argument, writing in 2011 that *Shadow* "is framed so distinctly in the Hitchcock style that it plays firmly and never breaks out of the story." Only in retrospect did the film's implausible and occasionally absurd narrative elements rear their heads "and the weaknesses grow evident" (Ebert 2011). Thus, his summary judgment: "As plots go, this one is not a masterpiece, but it works because it generates suspense" (Ebert 2011). Ebert assigned *Shadow of a Doubt* four stars—his highest ranking, which he also bestowed on *Notorious*. But one suspects that he never quite sorted out his feelings about a film that Hitchcock continually referred to as his favorite and perhaps his best. Nor did Robin Wood, who in a 2004 piece, "Hitchcock and Fascism," wrote that "*Shadow of a Doubt* remains the most perennially disturbing of all [Hitchcock's] films" (Wood 2004: 40).

Notes

1. *Shadow of a Doubt* was based on an original story by Gordon McDonell, and Sally Benson contributed to the shooting of the script after Wilder left for military service.
2. Wright's nominations were for *The Little Foxes* (1941) and *The Pride of the Yankees* (1942); her Oscar win was for best supporting actress in *Mrs. Miniver* (1942).

References

Anderson, Lindsay (1972) "Alfred Hitchcock," in Alfred LaValley (ed.), *Focus on Hitchcock*, New York: Prentice Hall, pp. 48–59. First published in 1949.

Barr, C. (2004–2005) "Deserter or Honored Exile: Views of Hitchcock from Wartime Britain," *Hitchcock Annual*, vol. 13, pp. 1–24.

Ebert, R. (2011) "Uncle Charlie Brings Excitement to a Small Town," November 9, https://www.rogerebert.com/reviews/great-movie-shadow-of-a-doubt-1943#google_vignette

The Film Daily (1944) "Ten Best Pictures of 1943," in *The 1944 Film Daily Year Book of Motion Pictures*, ed. J. Alicoate, p. 105.

The Film Daily (1946) "Ten Best Pictures of 1945," in *The 1946 Film Daily Year Book of Motion Pictures*, ed. J. Alicoate, p. 111.

The Film Daily (1947) "Ten Best Pictures of 1946," in *The 1947 Film Daily Year Book of Motion Pictures*, ed. J. Alicoate, p. 119.

Harcourt-Smith, S. (1947) "'The Best Years of Our Lives' and 'Notorious,'" *Tribune*, undated (BFI clips file).

Lester, J. (1947) "*Notorious*," *Reynold's News*, February 16.

Modleski, T. (1989) *The Women Who Knew Too Much: Hitchcock and Feminist Theory*, London and New York: Routledge.

Mulvey, L. (1975) "Visual Pleasure and Narrative Cinema," *Screen*, 16 (3): 6–18.

Rotten Tomatoes (2024a) "*Notorious*," https://www.rottentomatoes.com/m/1015287-Notorious

Rotten Tomatoes (2024b) "*Shadow of a Doubt*," https://www.rottentomatoes.com/m/1018688-shadow_of_a_doubt

Sarris, A. (1962–1963) "Notes on the Auteur Theory in 1962," *Film Culture*, 27: 1–8.

Schatz, T. (1997) *Boom and Bust: Hollywood in the 1940s*, New York: Scribner's.

Truffaut, F. (1967) *Hitchcock*, New York: Touchstone/Simon & Schuster.

Wood, R. (1965) *Hitchcock's Films*, New York: A. S. Barnes.

Wood, R. (1977) "Ideology, Genre, Auteur," *Film Comment*, 13 (1): 46–51.

Wood, R. (1989) *Hitchcock's Films Revisited*, New York: Columbia University Press.

Wood, R. (2004–2005) "Hitchcock and Fascism," *Hitchcock Annual*, vol. 13, pp. 25–63.

Chapter 6
Re-viewing *Rear Window* (1954)

Janet Staiger

As with several other of Alfred Hitchcock's films, *Rear Window* (1954) was highly praised upon its release, and, over the past seventy years, critics have maintained their esteem for its achievements. While it has not remained untouched in several ways, its ubiquity as a memorable and very smart film has sustained its position as one of the major pieces of cinematic creativity. In this chapter, I will review three strategies of approaching *Rear Window* that have occurred: analysis and evaluation of its narrative and narrational tactics, ideological criticism, and critical appreciation via referentiality, quotation, parody, and satire.

Analysis and Evaluation of Narrative and Narrational Tactics

The initial public response to *Rear Window* was praise, with some critique of the film's narrative and narrational tactics. Numerous initial reviewers describe the film as a strong genre picture: "unusually good piece of murder mystery entertainment" (*Variety*, July 14, 1954, pp. 165–166); "the second most entertaining picture (after *The 39 Steps*) ever made by Alfred Hitchcock" (*Time*, August 2, 1954, p. 72); "a tense and exciting exercise in his new melodrama" (Crowther 1954: 18); "a humdinger of a thriller" (Zunser 1954: 15); a "masterpiece" (*Newsweek*, August 9, 1954, p. 80); and an "exciting new whodunit" (*Life*, August 16, 1954, p. 89).

Genre was not the only angle into the film. While noting the value to storytelling, critics recognize the technical feats on display. Robert Kass describes the film as "odd": "Odd because it departs almost entirely from the suspenseful thriller which is associated with Hitchcock's name, and odd, too, because it is all but lacking in any sort of formal plot ... [it is] bewildering but delightful, a 'bop' movie ... a most engaging summer comedy" (1954: 383). Steve Sondheim concludes it is Hitchcock's "best picture in many years" (2000: 168) because "Hitchcock's brilliance is his wit, and his flawless technique for using that wit to support and counterpoint suspense" (2000: 169).

Initial reviewers did have some reservations, primarily about narrational tactics. While appreciating Hitchcock's genre achievements, Bosley Crowther in the *New York Times* opines, "Mr. Hitchcock's film is not 'significant.' What it has to say about people and human nature is superficial and glib. But it does expose many facets of the loneliness of city life and it tacitly demonstrates the impulse of morbid curiosity" (*New York Times*, August 6, 1954, p. 18). John McCarten in the *New Yorker* writes that the narrative's premise does not have credibility, and he thinks the experiment of remaining in the same room is "foolishness" (1954: 51). In *Commonweal*, Philip T. Hartung remarks that "as a chiller '*Rear Window*' is somewhat disappointing" although it is about "characterization." Overall, the film is "often talky and artificial" (Hartung 1954: 463). While appreciating Hitchcock's "enthusiasm for sheer technique," Arthur Knight decides that that "seems to impose such synthetic restrictions, such absurdly artificial limitations upon the action of his films that the plot is all but swamped by the pyrotechniques" (1954: 31). Ernest Borneman concludes it is a "gimmick film" (1954: 18) although he does appreciate its reminder to him of pleasures of the silent cinema. Derwint May, writing in *Sight and Sound*, declares *Rear Window* to have "gracelessness" and "unevenness" with the thriller interrupted by a "half-hearted plot of love and character" (1954: 89–90). Another British reviewer, P.H., summarizes the film as "little more than an ingenious, heartless, intermittently entertaining exercise in technique" (1954: 129).

Within the complaints is apparent a sort of rejection of semiexperimental techniques in narration that are favored over a transparent and straightforward presentation of a plot in a typical generic formula. As Robert Kapsis argues, from the 1930s to the late 1960s, most important US academic and journalistic critics prize "realism" and films "which dealt with serious social issues" (1992: 12). Hence, what later critics and filmmakers enjoy—the film's games with storytelling—appear to some writers in 1954 as roadblocks to a straightforward engagement with a good, exciting story. Yet, by 1955, other analysts quickly and overtly reject those preferences. Claude Chabrol in an essay, "Les Choses sérieuses," rejects undervaluing *Rear Window*, concluding after an extended analysis of formal qualities of the film, "*Rear Window* affords me the satisfaction of greeting the piteous blindness of the sceptics with a gentle and compassionate hilarity" (1955: 139). In a review for its revival in 1962 for the British *Sunday Times*, Dilys Powell exclaims, "I can't see it too often" (*Sunday Times*, April 1, 1962), and Penelope Gilliatt declares, "it is brilliantly cinematic" (*Observer*, April 1, 1962).

Indeed, rapidly in the next few years after the film's release, the critics "appealed to four major intertextual discourses: psychoanalysis, authorship, generic conventions of Hollywood filmmaking, and current social issues" to analyze and evaluate *Rear Window* (Staiger 1992: 89). Later (the 1960s to mid 1980s), they would add modernist and reflexive strategies to the repertoire of narrative and narrational strategies they find in the film (Staiger 1992: 81–85).

Because this is an extensively analyzed film, this chapter can only skim over some of the excellent discussions of *Rear Window*. As Robin Wood so famously asks in 1965, "Why should we take Hitchcock seriously?" (Wood 1965: 7), numerous writers find all sorts of reasons to analyze and evaluate his films. In their famous conversation, François Truffaut and Hitchcock discuss *Rear Window* with Truffaut hypothesizing that Hitchcock liked the source story by Cornell Woolrich "because it represented a technical challenge: a whole film from the viewpoint of one man, and embodied in a single, large set." Hitchcock replies, "Absolutely. It was a possibility of doing a purely cinematic film" (1967: 159). Hitchcock repeats this characterization in an interview about the film with *Take One* in 1968: "I chose this picture because of all the films I have made, this to me is the most cinematic" (1968: 40). In both conversations, Hitchcock proceeds to provide clear explanations for what counts as cinematic to him. However, other analysts note that the film has qualities related to other media. For instance, John Belton provides an extended discussion of *Rear Window* as a "limit-text" for a "theatrical" film because of its treatment of space (1988: 1121–1138). And Richard Combs argues that the film has a structure of fairy tales (à la Propp) as its basis (2014: 1–35).

Still, the primary focus of analysis is usually on technique. For instance, Belton argues that Hitchcock's point-of-view shots place spectators in the character's position (1980: 11), providing expressionistic (nonrealistic aspects to the mise-en-scène) and constructivist (editing) aesthetics, both of which are formalistic because "they explore the means of artistic representation" (1980: 9). David Bordwell disagrees with the general proposition about how to understand what a spectator is experiencing. He writes "A film ... does not 'position' anybody. A film cues the spectator to execute a definable variety of operations" (1985: 29). Coming from his cognitive approach, Bordwell acknowledges that "*Rear Window* ... has long been used as a small-scale model of the spectator's activity" (1985: 40) but redefines what that might mean. This issue in particular will matter for ideological criticism of the film.

What is presented on the screen, however, elides all that is off screen as James MacDowell points out: "I will be arguing that Hitchcock's cinema should encourage us to see ellipses and other forms of elision as having the potential to be key expressive features in a filmmaker's arsenal" (2010: 78). Besides temporal games (what happens while Jeff is asleep, for instance), Hitchcock uses the ellipses and other occlusions to "establish point of view, convey narrative focus, and reinforce underlying themes" (MacDowell 2010: 99).

Still much occurs onscreen to affect the film. Michel Chion (1992) emphasizes sound, pointing out that although the fourth side of the courtyard is seldom seen, sound is constantly implying that space's existence. In his book-length study, *Hitchcock's Music*, Jack Sullivan declares, "*Rear Window* is Hitchcock's most daring experiment in popular music. Its pop-song surrealism is the forerunner of *American Graffiti, Mona Lisa, After Hours*, and many other films, but the way tunes and street sounds drift through the soundtrack, in and out of windows and the protagonist's dreams, is unique" (2006: 169).

Points of view, editing, cinematography, and sound are not the only techniques of narrative/narrational interest. Costumes, especially those outfits of the female protagonist, provoke commentary. Listing five functions of dresses in the film, Sarah Street points out their "narrative development, the delineation of gender relations, the articulation of the class theme, star images and the development of the 'masquerading blonde,' and finally the role of costume in the film's authorship" (2000: 91). Obviously, acting also matters as James Naremore's 1988 discussion of it provides an extensive description.

Scholars often move from details about the narrative and narrational qualities to make arguments about themes in the film, using theses about psychology/psychoanalysis, authorship, genre, current social issues, and modernism as support to describing and analyzing the film. Although numerous lines of commentary exist, one strong psychological/psychoanalytical one involves issues around *Rear Window*'s portrayal of masculinity, particularly provoked by the primary protagonist, L. B. "Jeff" Jefferies, being confined mostly to a wheelchair. Thus, his near immobilization allows further analogical discussion. John Fawell argues that Hitchcock has empathy for "the feel of human loneliness and alienation" and his voyeurism "is more nourishing than demeaning for the viewer" (2001: 5). Consequently, the film's critical attack is less on the female than the male: "*Rear Window* represents an unambiguous, sometimes even vicious, broadside on the male psyche and male sexual insecurity" (Fawell 2001: 6). In a 2008 essay, I place *Rear Window* into the male melodrama genre, pointing out that Jefferies displays the classic "fallen man" lapse from proper masculinity with his broken leg as both literal and symbolic. However, David Baker (2008) believes that Lisa represents to Jeff the "monstrous feminine" with the film offering a double genre plotline of the detective story as masculine and active and the romance as feminine and passive.

Another combination of these analytical and thematic discussions of the characters occurs around whether (or how) Jefferies might be understood as a peeping tom. Even one of the characters in the film observes that Jefferies is something of a voyeur, encouraging this sort of analysis. Raymond Durgnat concludes that "the accusations of Jeff and Lisa remain, which is one reason why the film becomes, spiritually, one of Hitchcock's more interesting films" (1974: 237). However, in a conversation with Peter Bogdanovich in 1963, Hitchcock objects to describing Jefferies' behavior as weird, arguing he thinks it is normal behavior. With an intense shot-by-shot analysis, Stefan Sharff (1997) agrees with Hitchcock. Robert Benton (1984) goes further with a psychoanalytic approach, arguing the entire film should be considered a dream.

These thematic strands raise questions of authorship and social content. Andrew Sarris makes the clever argument that Hitchcock is too entertaining: Hitchcock's "reputation has suffered from the fact that he has given audiences more pleasure than is permissible for serious cinema" (1968: 58) while placing Hitchcock in Sarris's "pantheon" (top) author group, summarizing him as "the supreme technician of the American cinema" (1968: 57). Still the personal and social matters raised in the film produce observations about understanding *Rear Window* within broader social life. Although other valuable analyses occur (in, for instance, works by Maurice Yacowar [2010], Louis Phillips [1985], and Thomas Harris [1987]), Armond White's argument is that *Rear Window* is "a social study, relevant to issues of individual survival in the modern world," a world "with the difficult or dehumanizing structures of social life" (2000: 119).

Another coalition of textual analysis draws upon perceptions of modernism. An early articulation of this occurs in Jean Douchet's 1960 essay, claiming "*Rear Window*: It is there that Hitchcock elaborates his very concept of cinema (that is to say of cinema in cinema), reveals his secrets, unveils his intention" (Douchet 1986: 2). Yet, Slavoj Žižek, distinguishing between modernism and postmodernism, forwards the argument that Hitchcock works in the latter style because modernism "'gentrifies' the disquieting uncanniness of its object" (Žižek 1992: 2) while postmodernism "estrange[s] its very initial homeliness: 'You think what you see is a simple melodrama … [but] you've totally missed the point'!" (1992: 2).

Throughout the tenure of *Rear Window*'s existence as a film, theses about how to describe it are as plentiful as textual approaches. In 1983, Philip Strick states that the only question of the day is whether it is the best of Hitchcock's films (1983: 38). While that is still debatable, less so is Edward White's 2021 claim: "*Rear Window* is Hitchcock's definitive film."

Ideological Criticism

A major strand of considering *Rear Window* has been to use it as an exemplar for larger discursive behaviors in culture. In other words, it stands in for something else. Although the first reviews of *Rear Window* asserted numerous possible social messages that the film was possibly conveying, most notably here are the feminist arguments beginning in the early 1970s about how films may be typifying culture. Neither Marjorie Rosen in 1973 nor Joan Mellon, also in 1973, address *Rear Window*; however, Molly Haskell in her *From Reverence to Rape* in the same year criticizes Grace Kelly's character as having a "chic vacuous personality" (1987: 269).

It is obviously Laura Mulvey's initial commentary in 1975 about "visual pleasure" that initiates a more complex psychoanalytical thesis about how to consider how "women" may function in cinema. "Realism"—the goal for Rosen, Mellon, and Haskell—is less the point than how, in Mulvey's analysis, a male spectator can employ a woman for masculine psychoanalytical opportunities. Specifically, Mulvey references *Rear Window* and *Vertigo* (1958) as providing looks which are "oscillating between voyeurism and fetishistic fascination" (1975: 15). Taking off from Douchet's analysis of the film, Mulvey suggests that Jefferies' (and by association male spectators') voyeurism is enhanced especially when Lisa moves from being a spectator watching the events as directed by Jefferies to an actor when invading Thorwald's apartment. This initial and important analysis serves as one primary foundation for many further arguments about how the film (and any film) operates within larger cultural dynamics.

Jokingly, or not, Wood begins his 1983 discussion of these same two films referring to his 1965 question about taking Hitchcock seriously as now becoming "'Can Hitchcock be saved for feminism?'" (Wood 1983: 30). Tania Modleski, in response, points out that Wood's question shifts the criterion by which to judge Hitchcock's films from "moral complexity" to "political correctness" (1988: 3). She claims that Wood "proceeds to minimize the misogyny in them and to analyze both *Rear Window* and *Vertigo* as exposés of the twisted logic of patriarchy, relatively untroubled by ambivalence or contradiction ... For Wood, political 'progressiveness' has come to replace moral complexity" (Modleski 1988: 3).

Modleski exemplifies a third phase of feminist criticism in which the variability of spectators (sex, gender, race, sexuality, class, and so forth) must be considered when evaluating any possible ideological consequences. For *Rear Window*, Modleski concludes that some Hitchcock films "do allow for the (limited) expression of a specifically female desire and that such films ... trace a female oedipal trajectory, and in the process reveal some of the difficulties for women in becoming socialized in patriarchy" (1988: 2). She remarks that "women are not where they appear to be, locked into male 'views' of them, imprisoned in their master's dollhouse" (Modleski 1988: 85).

Concurrent with Modleski's work (and to whom she refers) are the contributions of Teresa de Lauretis and other scholars. Modleski explains de Lauretis's thesis: "identification on the part of women at the cinema is much more complicated than feminist theory has understood: far from being simply masochistic, the female spectator is always caught up in a double desire, identifying at one and the same time not only with the passive (female) object, but with the active (usually male) subject" so that Hitchcock is not "utterly misogynistic" or sympathetic but displays "a thoroughgoing ambivalence about femininity" (Modleski 1988: 2–3). Taking up a self-avowed spectator position of a 1980s feminist reader, Jeanne Allen states, "I will argue that the position of the female spectator, myself included, for *Rear Window* affords the pleasure of critically engaging the analysis of the traps and lures of heterosexual romance as presented by the constructed persona (not the historical person) 'Hitchcock,'" permitting for a feminist reader "an empathic compromise" (1988: 33).

Subsequent responses over the next decade produce multiple dynamics to be considered. Carol Mason considers class conflicts within the "sexual politics of looking ... [so that Lisa] also symbolizes the threat of white women's economic mobility" (1991: 111). Robert Corber points out that multiple historical features affect spectatorship as subjectivity is "an ongoing, continuous construction that is renewed daily through the individual's always provisional encounter with the institutions, discourses, and practices that structure her/his relation to the world" (1993: 4). Thus, his reading of *Rear Window* in the middle of the "anti-Stalinist project of Cold War liberals" (Corber 1993: 12) stresses that "the film's emphasis in the climatic scene in Jeff's resemblance to Thorwald indirectly ratifies the liberal critique of postwar American culture" that the separation of public and private are being obliterated (1993: 105). In something of a bravura performance, Lee Edelman creates a complicated argument of Lisa as female versus the anus, with the film's "repudiated pulsions of the anus" (1999: 79).

Rejections and nuances of the various theses about spectators and *Rear Window* continue, indicating the ongoing place the film holds in academic discourse as an exemplar. Particularly useful essays are from Elise Lemire (2000), Florence Jacobowitz (2011), and David Greven (2015).

Referentiality, Quotation, Parody, Satire

After the strategies of praise and ideological criticism, the third strategy of engagement with *Rear Window* has been noting its referentiality and the instances of quotation, parody, and satire, usually in the same medium (film and television) as *Rear Window*. A recent example and riff on the film is *The Woman in the House across the Street from the Girl in the Window* (2022) whose title certainly gives away the plot. A scholar might venture to guess that this strategy took a while to appear and mature. However, Hitchcock knew a good plotline and used it himself in his television episode, "Mr. Blanchard's Secret," in *Alfred Hitchcock Presents*, December 23, 1956. While the female protagonist who writes mysteries is convinced her neighbor Mr. Blanchard has murdered his wife, it turns out his secret is something much less sinister and much more comedic; he has fixed her antique lighter which she thought he had stolen. Hitchcock and his writers were obviously laughing at his own successful storyline and characters, employing referentiality and parody for the knowledgeable viewer. Indeed, Patrick McGilligan describes the television episode as "a mild satire of *Rear Window*" (2003: 543).

In this strategy, it is important to distinguish between critical observations about any reflexivity of *Rear Window* and the subsequent responses of parody and other referential evaluations to *Rear Window*. As Robert Stam and Roberta Pearson point out, "Jean Douchet, writing in Cahiers du Cinema [sic] in 1960, was among the first to point out the reflexive dimension of *Rear Window*" (1983: 136). They agree and expand Douchet's point by explaining how this is occurring: "A paradigmatic instance of reflexivity, the film performs the metalinguistic dismantling of the structures of scopophilia and identification operative in dominant cinema generally and in Hitchcock's own films particularly, even while exploiting those very structures" (1983: 136).

Other scholars expand on Douchet's thesis about the film's reflexivity. Belton notes that while Hitchcock's point-of-view shots place spectators in characters' positions, the film is "also Hitchcock's most self-reflective work" (1980: 11). He also claims that Hitchcock made the actor Raymond Burr, who plays Thorwald, move like the producer David O. Selznick, who Hitchcock believed meddled in his films. Belton stresses, "The Selznick reference only confirms the notion that *Rear Window* is 'about the cinema'" (1980: 11). Other scholars also expand on how and whether the film can be described as reflexive. For instance, Fawell provides a litany of such discussions and mentions that "Jeff [is] to be seen as a stand-in for the filmgoer" (2001: 123) because of his voyeurism, preference for fantasy, and paralyzed position; indeed, "Jeff's window [serves as] a metaphor for a movie screen" (Fawell 2001: 125) with the other windows functioning "as silent films" in "recognizable film genres" (2001: 128). Lawrence Howe argues that while *Rear Window* is about scopophilia, it is also about fears of being seen: "scopophobia" (2008: 17). Jeff's position changes as should the spectators in relation to "one's own position with regard to watching" (Howe 2008: 19).

Benton cautions, however, against arguing that the effect of such self-referential maneuvers about film as film is particularly modernist: "But Hitchcock's techniques, especially in this film, do not distance the viewer, nor do they serve to deconstruct the filmic technique. On the contrary, especially in *Rear Window*, they seem, paradoxically, to serve to increase the manipulative power of the film" (Benton 2000: 492). In an extended argument, Patricia Ferrara agrees that what Hitchcock is doing in *Rear Window* is not exploring "theories of film viewership" (1985: 21) but how "people relate to one another through seeing" (1985: 23).

To resolve this question about the implications of the possible reflexivity of *Rear Window* (whether to view the plot parallels with watching cinema as a critique and critical challenge to the spectatorship experience), R. Barton Palmer in 1986 introduces the notion of "meta" into the conversation. He argues that Hitchcock's "later American films, in short, are neither 'classic' nor 'modernist,' but rather 'metafictional'" (Palmer 1986: 4–5). Quoting Patricia Waugh, Palmer explains that "'metafictional novels tend to be constructed on the principal [sic] of a fundamental and sustained opposition: the construction of a fictional illusion (as in traditional realism) and the laying bare of that illusion'" (1986: 5). Palmer argues this occurs for *Rear Window*. David Roche concurs in his own extended discussion of the film within his subcategory of "allegories of spectatorship." These are films with complex commentaries not only about spectatorship but also "of creations as well, of the cinematic apparatus" (Roche 2022: 106). *Rear Window* suggests "spectatorship is [not just scopophilia but] also a cognitive, intellectual and collective activity … *Rear Window* also dramatizes the diversity within a given audience and its interpretations, notably based on variables including gender and occupation" (Roche 2022: 111–112).

Figure 6.1 One of the many homages to *Rear Window*, and its original scene. In this episode of *The Simpsons*, Bart begins to grow suspicious that neighbor Ned Flanders has murdered his wife.

Rear Window, directed by Alfred Hitchcock © Patron Inc. and Paramount Pictures 1954. All rights reserved. "Bart of Darkness" directed by Jim Reardon. Written by Dan McGrath. *The Simpsons*, Season 6, Episode 1. © 20th Century Fox Television 1994. All rights reserved.

While the discussion of *Rear Window*'s own acts of referentiality has become more nuanced since the film's appearance, equally developed have been external examples directed toward the film through the pleasures of allusion, quotation, parody, even satire. All sorts of cultural actors have engaged in this. This sort of behavior rapidly followed the film's release as evidenced by Hitchcock's own play in "Mr. Blanchard's Secret" (1956). However, fellow filmmakers have often turned to Hitchcock for inspiration. White (2000) provides an extended analysis of Brian De Palma's references to *Rear Window* in De Palma's *Sisters* (1972) and within *Blow-Up* (1966), *The Conversation* (1974), and *Blow Out* (1981). The film has been remade several times, explicitly in *Disturbia* (2007) and the made-for-television movie *Rear Window* (1998) starring Christopher Reeve who, in 1995, had been paralyzed in a horse-riding accident, and, more obliquely, such as in the very recent *The Woman in the House across the Street from the Girl in the Window* and *Kimi* (2022). All of these are rather serious references to and uses of the original.

More playful, however, are all sorts of instances of light-hearted allusions. As of November 17, 2023, a fan wiki for *Rear Window* lists sixteen instances. It includes examples from *The Flintstones* (1961), *Get Smart* (1969), *The Simpsons* (1994), *Castle* (2013), and *Family Guy* (2017) (see Fig. 6.1).

The range of these dates indicates both the immediate and long-lasting impact of the film and the presumption by the writers and directors of popular culture that audiences will recognize the source.

In some ways, the history of the reception of *Rear Window* is boring. The film was immediately praised and remained highly evaluated. However, its legacy is more than as just an outstanding film. It has provoked much commentary over its seventy years, helping scholars sort out issues of concern to analyzing and evaluating cinema.

References

Allen, J. (1988) "Looking through 'Rear Window': Hitchcock's Traps and Lures of Heterosexual Romance," in Deidre Pribram (ed.), *Female Spectators: Looking at Film and Television*, London: Verso, pp. 31–44.

Baker, D. (2008) "Seeing Is Believing: Detective and Romance in *Rear Window*," *Screen Education*, 51 (spring): 125–130.

Belton, J. (1980) "Dexterity in a Void: The Formalist Esthetics of Alfred Hitchcock," *Cineaste*, 10 (3): 9–18.

Belton, J. (1988) "The Space of *Rear Window*," *Modern Language Notes*, 103 (5): 1121–1138.

Belton, J. (ed.) (2000) *Alfred Hitchcock's Rear Window*, Cambridge: Cambridge University Press.

Benton, R. J. (1984) "Film as Dream: Alfred Hitchcock's *Rear Window*," *Psychoanalytic Review*, 71 (3): 483–500.

Bordwell, D. (1985) *Narration in the Fiction Film*, Madison, Wisc.: University of Wisconsin Press.

Borneman, E. (1954) "*Rear Window*," *Films and Filming*, 1 (2): 18.

Chabrol, C. (1955) "Les Choses sérieuses [Serious Things]," *Cahiers du cinéma*, April, p. 46. Reprinted in Jim Hillier (ed.), *Cahiers du Cinéma: The 1950s, Neo-Realism, Hollywood, New Wave*, trans. Liz Heron, Cambridge, Mass.: Harvard University Press, 1985, pp. 136–139.

Chion, M. (1992) "The Fourth Side," in S. Žižek (ed.), *Everything You Always Wanted to Know about Lacan (But Were Afraid to Ask Hitchcock)*, London: Verso, pp. 155–160.

Combs, R. (2014) "*Rear Window*: Fairy-Tales in a Butcher's Yard," *Hitchcock Annual*, vol. 19, pp. 1–35.

Corber, R. (1993) *In the Name of National Security: Hitchcock, Homophobia, and the Political Construction of Gender in Postwar America*, Durham, NC: Duke University Press.

Deutelbaum, M., and L. Pogue (eds) (1986) *A Hitchcock Reader*, Ames, Iowa: Iowa University Press.

Douchet, J. (1986) "Hitch and His Public," *Cahiers du cinéma*, 113 (November), trans. Verena Conley. Reprinted in M. Deutelbaum and L. Pogue (eds), *A Hitchcock Reader*, Ames, Iowa: Iowa University Press, pp. 7–15.

Durgnat, R. (1974) *The Strange Case of Alfred Hitchcock or the Plain Man's Hitchcock*, Cambridge, Mass.: MIT Press.

Edelman, L. (1999) "*Rear Window*'s Glasshole," in Ellis Hanson (ed.), *Out Takes*: *Essays on Queer Theory and Film*, Durham, NC: Duke University Press, pp. 72–96.
Fawell, J. (2001) *Hitchcock's* Rear Window: *The Well-Made Film*, Carbondale, Ill.: Southern Illinois University Press.
Ferrara, P. (1985) "Through Hitchcock's *Rear Window* Again," *The New Orleans Review*, 12 (3): 21–30.
Freedman, J. (ed.) (2015) *The Cambridge Companion to Alfred Hitchcock*, New York: Cambridge University Press.
Greven, D. (2015) "Hitchcock and Queer Sexuality," in J. Freedman (ed.), *The Cambridge Companion to Alfred Hitchcock*, New York: Cambridge University Press, pp. 122–142.
Harris, T. (1987) "*Rear Window* and *Blow-Up*, Hitchcock's Straight Forwardness vs. Antonioni's Ambiguity," *Literature/Film Quarterly*, 15 (1): 60–63.
Hartung, P. T. (1954) "Look Now," *Commonweal*, 60 (August 13), p. 463.
Haskell, M. (1987) *From Reverence to Rape: The Treatment of Women in the Movies*, 2nd edn, Chicago, Ill.: University of Chicago Press.
Hitchcock, A. (1972) "*Rear Window*," *Take One*, 2, no. 2 (Nov-Dec 1968), 18–20, rpt. in *Focus on Hitchcock*, Ed. Albert J. LaValley (Englewood Cliffs, NJ: Prentice-Hall, 1972), 40–6.
Hitchcock, A., and P. Bogdanovich (1963) *The Cinema of Alfred Hitchcock*, New York: Museum of Modern Art Library.
Howe, L. (2008) "Through the Looking Glass: Reflexivity, Reciprocality, and Defenestration in Hitchcock's *Rear Window*," *College Literature*, 35 (1): 16–37.
Jacobowitz, F. (2011) "Hitchcock and Feminist Theory from Rebecca to Marnie," in T. Leitch and L. Poague (eds), *A Companion to Alfred Hitchcock*, Maiden, Mass.: Wiley-Blackwell, pp. 452–471.
Kapsis, R. E. (1992) *Hitchcock*: *The Making of a Reputation*, Chicago, Ill.: University of Chicago Press.
Kass, R. (1954) "Film and TV," *Catholic World*, 179 (August), p. 383.
Knight, A. (1954) "Documenting the West," *Saturday Review*, 37 (August 21), pp. 30–31.
Leitch, T., and L. Poague (eds) (2011) *A Companion to Alfred Hitchcock*, Malden, Mass.: Wiley-Blackwell.
Lemire, E. (2000) "Voyeurism and the Postwar Crisis of Masculinity in *Rear Window*," in J. Belton (ed.), *Alfred Hitchcock's* Rear Window, Cambridge: Cambridge University Press, pp. 57–90.
MacDowell, J. (2010) " What We Don't See, and What We Think It Means: Ellipsis and Occlusion in *Rear Window*," *Hitchcock Annual*, vol. 16, pp. 77–101.
Mason, C. (1991) "*Rear Window*'s Lisa Freemont: Masochistic Female Spectator of Post-War Socioeconomic Threat?" Social and Political Change in Literature and Film: Florida State University Conference on Literature and Film, 16, pp. 109–121.
May, D. (1954) "*Rear Window* and Dial M for Murder," *Sight and Sound*, 24 (2): 89–90.
McCarten, J. (1954) "Hitchcock Confined Again," *The New Yorker*, 30 (25): 50–51.
McGilligan, P. (2003) *Alfred Hitchcock: A Life in Darkness and Light*, New York: Regan Books.
Mellen, J. (1973) *Women and Their Sexuality in the New Film*, New York: Dell Publishing.
Modleski, T. (1988) *The Women Who Knew Too Much: Hitchcock and Feminist Theory*, London and New York: Routledge.
Mulvey, L. (1975) "Visual Pleasure and Narrative Cinema," *Screen*, 16 (3): 6–18.
Naremore, J. (1988) *Acting in the Cinema*, Berkeley, Calif.: University of California Press.
P.H. (1954) "*Rear Window*, USA, 1954," *Monthly Film Bulletin*, 21 (248): 129.
Palmer, R. B. (1986) "The Metafictional Hitchcock: The Experience of Viewing and the Viewing of Experience in *Rear Window* and *Psycho*," *Cinema Journal*, 25 (2): 4–19.
Phillips, L. (1985) "Through a Glass Darkly; A Consideration of Alfred Hitchcock's 'Rear Window'," *The Armchair Detective*, 18 (2): 190–193.
"*Rear Window*," (1954) https://movies.fandom.com/wiki/Rear_Window_(1954)/In_Popular_Culture
Roche, D. (2022) *Meta in Film and Television Series*, Edinburgh: Edinburgh University Press.
Rosen, M. (1973) *Popcorn Venus*, New York: Avon Books.
Sarris, A. (1968) "Hitchcock," in *The American Cinema: Directors and Directions 1929–1968*, New York: E. P. Dutton & Co., pp. 56–61.
Sharff, S. (1997) *The Art of Looking in Hitchcock's* Rear Window, New York: Limelight Editions.
Sondheim, S. (2000) "*Rear Window*," in J. Belton (ed.), *Alfred Hitchcock's* Rear Window, Cambridge: Cambridge University Press, pp. 168–170.

Staiger, J. (1992) *Interpreting Films: Studies in the Historical Reception of American Cinema*, Princeton, NJ: Princeton University Press.

Staiger, J. (2008) "Film Noir as Male Melodrama: The Politics of Film Genre Labeling," in Lincoln Geraghty and Mark Jancovich (eds), *The Shifting Definitions of Genre: Essays in Labeling Films, Television Shows and Media*, Jefferson, NC: McFarland & Company, pp. 71–91.

Stam, R., and R. Pearson (1983) "Hitchcock's *Rear Window*: Reflexivity and the Critique of Voyeurism," *enclitic*, 7 (1): 136–145.

Street, S. (2000) "'The Dresses Had Told Me': Fashion and Femininity in *Rear Window*," in J. Belton (ed.), *Alfred Hitchcock's* Rear Window, Cambridge: Cambridge University Press, pp. 91–109.

Strick, P. (1983) "*Rear Window*," *Films and Filming*, 350 (November), pp. 38–39.

Sullivan, J. (2006) *Hitchcock's Music*, New Haven, Conn.: Yale University Press.

Truffaut, F. (1967) *Hitchcock*, New York: Simon & Schuster.

White, A. (2000) "Eternal Vigilance in *Rear Window*," in J. Belton (ed.), *Alfred Hitchcock's Rear Window*, Cambridge: Cambridge University Press, pp. 118–140.

White, E. (2021) "Crime, Mystery, and All Things Thrilling," *Crime Reads*, April 13.

Wood, R. (1965) *Hitchcock's Films*, New York, Paperback Library.

Wood, R. (1983) "Fear of Spying," *American Film*, 9 (2): 28–35.

Yacowar, M. (2010) *Hitchcock's British Films*, 2nd edn, Detroit, Mich.: Wayne State University Press.

Žižek, S. (1992) "Introduction: Alfred Hitchcock, or, The Form and Its Historical Mediation," in S. Žižek (ed.), *Everything You Always Wanted to Know about Lacan (But Were Afraid to Ask Hitchcock)*, London: Verso, pp. 1–12.

Zunser, J. (1954) "Hitchcock's Scariest in Years Comes to Town," *Cue*, August 7, p. 15.

Chapter 7
North by Northwest (1959)
Nothing but Entertainment

Thomas Leitch

Taking advantage of the public persona that had become even better known through his introductions to each episode of *Alfred Hitchcock Presents*, the director introduced *North by Northwest* with a three-minute trailer labeled "A GUIDED TOUR WITH ALFRED HITCHCOCK" in which, posing as a tour guide, he addressed the audience directly about the tonic importance of vacations. Despite the downsides of "sand and sunburn" or "mountain climbing and a charley horse," he intoned, "we should all have some kind of holiday" and suggested "a quiet little tour—say about two thousand miles. I have just made a motion picture, *North by Northwest*, to show you some of these delights." In a summary keyed to the principal geographic locations of the film, New York, Chicago, and Rapid City, South Dakota, he drolly contrasts and often commingles menace and delight. As Eva Marie Saint, playing industrial designer Eve Kendall, offers to join Cary Grant's character, Roger O. Thornhill, in the upper sleeping-car berth where she has hidden him from the police—who wrongly suspect him of murdering diplomat Lester Townsend inside the United Nations—Hitchcock remarks, "A train may be an old-fashioned way to travel, but an upper berth is a lovely place to go when it's your time to go." As a Freightliner rig hurtles toward Grant, who is standing in its way trying to flag it down in order to escape the crop-dusting plane that has targeted him for death, Hitchcock announces, "The people are all so friendly in the great outdoors." And he touts "the serene nobility of Mount Rushmore" as Eve, spotting the assassin leaping toward her and Thornhill as they try to descend the face of the monument, screams in terror. In short, Hitchcock concludes, the film promises "nothing but entertainment—a vacation from all your problems, as it was for me" (see Fig. 7.1). Whether or not they have ever seen this trailer, later commentators have almost without exception taken their cue from this final judgment, agreeing that *North by Northwest* is nothing but entertainment. The differences among them arise from the very different ways they parse that phrase.

The film wasted no time in establishing its credentials as highly effective entertainment. In its opening week at Radio City Music Hall, it earned $209,000, setting Music Hall records for both the best opening week and the best nonholiday week and making it the top grossing film in the USA (*Variety*, September 2, 1959, p. 5). Its combined gross of $404,056 for its first two weeks was enough to set

Figure 7.1 In the trailer for *North by Northwest*, Hitchcock, acting as a travel agent, pronounces the film "nothing but entertainment."

North by Northwest, directed by Alfred Hitchcock. © Metro-Goldwyn-Mayer 1959. All rights reserved.

another record for the Music Hall, where it remained for a total of seven weeks, retaining its status as the nation's top-grossing film ("Box Office," 1959).

The film was greeted by the best reviews of Hitchcock's career. Although *Variety* acknowledged that "[s]econd thoughts on the film will produce the feeling that there are loose ends and stray threads that are never quite bound up or followed through," its anonymous reviewer described the film as quintessential Hitchcock, "the Alfred Hitchcock mixture as before—suspense, humor, and comedy," and added, "Seldom has the concoction been served up so delectably" (*Variety*, June 29, 1959). Jack Moffitt, of the *Hollywood Reporter*, announced that "[a] packed audience at the preview loved every moment of this Alfred Hitchcock thriller" (*Hollywood Reporter*, June 30, 1959). Describing the film as a team effort, Moffitt singled out Robert Burks' cinematography, George Tomasini's editing (especially of the soon-to-become-famous crop-dusting scene), Bernard Herrmann's evocative musical score, and the special effects by A. Arnold Gillespie and Lee LeBlanc for special praise. His highest plaudits were reserved for Cary Grant's playfully befuddled impersonation of Thornhill, a Madison Avenue advertising man hopelessly out of his depth; Eva Marie Saint's surprisingly smoldering performance as Thornhill's seducer, a character miles removed from the waiflike roles that had established Saint onscreen; Ernest Lehman's witty and inventive original screenplay, which swiftly plunged Thornhill into life-threatening adventures without ever shattering his self-possessed sense of entitlement; and Hitchcock's direction of the project, the longest and most self-consciously epic of his American films, which Moffitt called "pure entertainment" (*Hollywood Reporter*, June 30, 1959). The *New York Times* called *North by Northwest* "the year's most scenic, intriguing, and merriest chase" (August 7, 1959, p. 28). The *New Yorker* more specifically labeled it "the brilliant realization of a feat [Hitchcock] has unintentionally been moving toward for more than a decade—a perfect parody of his own work," and added, "Hitchcock demonstrates himself to be a master parodist, for the picture […] first flawlessly reproduces all his celebrated mannerisms, and then methodically puffs them all out of shape with a swaggering look-at-me exaggeration" (Balliett 1959).

Critics of the film's first release in the UK echoed this note. John Waterman welcomed Hitchcock's recovery from the decline that *Vertigo* had seemed to indicate: "All is still for the best in the best of all nightmare worlds" (*Evening Standard*, October 15, 1959, p. 19). The anonymous reviewer for the *Guardian*, noting that the film, though certainly not Hitchcock's best, may have been his most characteristic, explained, "Hitchcock has always seemed to care less for his film stories than for the opportunities provided by them for a show of his special tricks of virtuosity. But his interest in detail and this cavalier treatment of the narrative as a whole have never gone quite so far as in 'North by North-West'" (*Guardian*, October 17, 1959, p. 3). Isabel Quigly, observing that "[t]he Hitchcock guarantee is one of the most foolproof things in an often foolish industry. You know, whether the film is first-rate or not, that you are going to have fun there: because Hitchcock himself is invincibly good fun and pretty well everything he touches becomes so too," characterized *North by Northwest* as "reassuringly surprising as you might expect" (*Spectator*, October 23, 1959, p. 17). C. A. Lejeune developed this last point further: "In the old days we went to a Hitchcock film in order to be startled. Now we go in order to relax. We know exactly what to expect." Just as important, "[w]e know, too, what not to expect. A story with a social message. […] Hitchcock himself is honest as the day, but he is old-fashioned enough to believe that the first purpose of the screen is to endue its customers with pleasure" (*Observer*, October 18, 1959, p. 25). Recalling that "[i]n the past one has occasionally felt that the director was losing, in the hugeness and wealth of the United States, his own sharp self," Dilys Powell announced: "Not this time. […] In 'North by North-West' he has filled the screen with the extravagance of America, but he has used the extravagance without ever subordinating to it his own wicked ingenuity. In the middle of all that size he has made the absurdities of the adventure seem almost possible" (Powell 1989: 156). Penelope Houston, writing for *Sight and Sound*, noted the film's structural echoes of *The 39 Steps* and *Saboteur*, whose breathtaking finale it transferred from the Statue of Liberty to Mount Rushmore, and joined Waterman in comparing it favorably to *Vertigo*, whose relative commercial failure the year before had shocked and saddened the director:

> Critics who like to see Alfred Hitchcock's films as so many cryptograms to be puzzled over for hidden symbols are going to have a hard time with *North by Northwest*. This is the purest piece of entertainment filmmaking we have had from him for some years; it is also, which does not inevitably follow, the most purely entertaining.
>
> (Houston 1959)

Although François Truffaut would tell Hitchcock only a few years later that "*North by Northwest* is the picture that epitomizes the whole of your work in America" (Truffaut 1985: 380), the director confessed at the time of its release that "*Vertigo* is much more important to me than *North by Northwest*" (Domarchi and Douchet 1959: vii). If none of these early reactions finds the film especially searching or profound, that perspective is eminently in keeping with the larger public's view of Hitchcock in 1959 as the gravely jocose Master of Suspense whose elevation to the heights of the cinematic pantheon by François Truffaut, Andrew Sarris, and Robin Wood, who identified *Rear Window*, *Vertigo*, and *Psycho* as Hitchcock's signature accomplishments, lay still a few years ahead.

These glowing contemporaneous reviews lay a surprisingly detailed groundwork for the film's unique status in Hitchcock's oeuvre. From the day it was released, its reputation has never flagged. Sixty-five years later, it is still regarded as one of Hitchcock's finest achievements. An online column for SlashFilm ranked it third among Hitchcock's greatest films. The *Independent*, *Far Out*, and *Parade* all ranked it fourth. *Esquire* ranked it fifth (Nicholson 2020). Rotten Tomatoes ranked it sixth, with a Tomatometer approval score of 97 percent. IndieWire, while ranking it only twelfth, acknowledged that even if it is not "the ultimate Hitchcock movie […] it may be the most entertaining" (Blauvelt and Chapman 2024).

Ever since its first release, critics have consistently regarded *North by Northwest* as rewardingly well-crafted entertainment. Its highly artificial man-on-the-run plot has dated remarkably little in the years since. The exceptionally entertaining qualities its first reviewers found in the film stem from a return to the formula most closely associated with Hitchcock's Gaumont British thrillers of the 1930s: a delighted determination to shift its tone without warning from comical to threatening and back again, often in the middle of a scene. After displaying unparalleled mastery in the dexterity of these tonal shifts, which left audiences uncertain from moment to moment whether they should react with laughter or fear, in the 1934 *The Man Who Knew Too Much* and *The 39 Steps*, Hitchcock had largely abandoned them in his more homogeneous American melodramas from *Rebecca* to *Vertigo*. But Ernest Lehman's endlessly resourceful screenplay puts them front and center once more, not only in the film's signature set pieces, the crop-duster's attack on Thornhill in an isolated Indiana cornfield and the climactic chase atop the Mount Rushmore memorial, but in any number of comical moments that pop up unexpectedly during the most menacing situations and moments of surprising violence that threaten Thornhill, who seems determined to ignore the peril into which so many apparently anodyne scenes have suddenly plunged him. Plied with bourbon and placed behind the wheel of a car headed for the edge of a cliff, Thornhill recovers just enough to escape his killers in a wildly inebriated car chase and to act as if everything is nicely under control. Encountering the killers among the passengers in a crowded elevator during his return with his skeptical mother (Jessie Royce Landis) to the Plaza Hotel in search of George Kaplan, the nonexistent secret agent for whom he has been mistaken, Thornhill wordlessly calls his mother's attention to them, only to suffer comically acute embarrassment when her direct question to them—"Excuse me, but you gentlemen aren't really trying to kill my son, are you?"—provokes everyone in the elevator except Thornhill to gradually rising laughter (see Fig. 7.2).

Thornhill's brief meeting with Lester Townsend at the United Nations ends with shocking suddenness when one of the killers throws a knife at Townsend's back and a press photographer captures a shot of Thornhill standing over the corpse clutching the weapon. Thornhill's every encounter with Eve aboard the 20th Century Limited is a decorous tango of mutual flirtation and double entendres. Trying to escape the police when the train arrives in Chicago, Thornhill dons a redcap porter's uniform, and the police, discovering the ruse, descend on every redcap in the station, grabbing them, brusquely examining each of their faces, and then moving on to the next candidate as Thornhill, safely out of his disguise, attempts to shave in a men's room using the ludicrously small razor Eve has supplied him with as a fellow shaver regards him with thinly disguised contempt. The hijinks Thornhill improvises at the auction in order to escape from police custody lead one exasperated attendee to respond to his suspicion that a painting offered for sale might be fake by telling him, "You're no fake. You're a genuine idiot".

Thornhill's reunion with Eve at Mount Rushmore's Memorial View Building ends with her shooting him, though he returns to life in the following scene. His escape from the hospital room—where he has been confined to prevent him from further interfering in the federal government's long-range campaign against suavely menacing spy Phillip Vandamm (James Mason)—takes him through an exterior window far above the street to an adjoining window which leads him to another hospital room. There, a young female occupant, sitting up in bed, cries, "Stop!" and then, putting on her glasses and presumably recognizing him as Cary Grant, repeats more tenderly, "Stop," before he tut-tuts at her and takes his

Figure 7.2 Perhaps the most embarrassing moment in *North by Northwest* comes early on, when Roger Thornhill (Cary Grant) cannot hide from the elevator full of bystanders when his mother (Jessie Royce Landis) asks the two assassins (Adam Williams and Robert Ellenstein) he has surreptitiously pointed out to her whether they're really trying to kill him.

Figure 7.3 Its impudent finale on Mount Rushmore goes far to establish *North by Northwest* as "the Hitchcock picture to end all Hitchcock pictures."

leave. And the film interrupts the cliff-hanging finale atop Mount Rushmore (see Fig. 7.3) in the middle of Thornhill's attempt to pull Eve to safety by dissolving to a postlude in which Thornhill and Eve, presumably now married, are reenacting the scene aboard the train returning them to New York, capped by a final miniature shot of the train entering a tunnel, whose suggestion of sexual consummation inspired Hitchcock to label it "one of the most impudent shots I ever made" (Truffaut 1985: 107–108).

For all these reasons, the film is widely regarded as pure entertainment that is nothing but entertainment, providing a diverting two-hours-plus of pleasure without any of the distracting depths that adulterate *Rear Window*, *Vertigo*, or *Psycho*. Every ounce of its appeal is available to casual viewers who rejoice so wholeheartedly in its improbable plot, geographical sweep, brilliant set pieces, iconic performances, sparkling dialogue, and impossibly broad range of tones that they feel no need to return to it ever again—or, if they do return to it, will watch it hoping for exactly the same experience they had the first time around. As Luc Moullet wrote in reviewing the film's 1959 release in France in *Cahiers du Cinéma*, "the film is beautiful because we see that it is fake, that it hides nothing, that it gives nothing" (Moullet 1993: 195). Despite Robert E. Kapsis's observation that "future generations of critics would find deeper meanings, subtleties, and ironies in the film" (Kapsis 1992: 55), so many of these deeper meanings are rooted in contemporaneous reviewers' reactions to the film that *North by Northwest* has largely continued to be regarded as the exemplary reviewer's film, one that offers so much entertainment to a first-time viewer that the only second thoughts it inspires concern the unlikeliness of its artifices.

For this reason, the film has provoked relatively little critical commentary that goes beyond its initial reviewers' enthusiastic catalogues of its virtues as nothing but entertainment. It has been particularly neglected by Hitchcock scholars. David Sterritt's 1993 *The Films of Alfred Hitchcock* makes no reference to it. Tania Modleski's *The Women Who Knew Too Much: Hitchcock and Feminist Theory*, Christopher Orr's *Hitchcock and the Twentieth Century*, Stephane Duckett's *Hitchcock in Context*, and Bruce Isaacs' *The Art of Pure Cinema: Hitchcock and His Imitators* pass over it in virtual silence, even though it is one of Hitchcock's most characteristic and widely imitated films. There is no essay devoted to it in Richard Allen and Sam Ishii-Gonzalès's collection *Alfred Hitchcock: Centenary Essays*, in Sidney Gottlieb and Christopher Brookhouse's *Framing Hitchcock: Selected Essays from the Hitchcock Annual*, or in David Boyd and R. Barton Palmer's *Hitchcock at the Source: The Auteur as Adapter*. Its reputation, as *Far Out* summarizes it, is that of a canonical Hitchcock film, "a commercial powerhouse" that is "one of the finest thrillers you will ever see" (*Far Out*, n.d.) while being at the same time not a particularly interesting film for critics or scholars to explore because its pleasures are so obvious, perhaps even superficial. It does not tick any of the boxes that have inspired much recent work on Hitchcock. It is not British, not an adaptation of an earlier novel or play or story, not a product of Hitchcock's long-term collaboration with a particular studio like Selznick International, Warner Bros., Paramount, or Universal, and not an especially fraught representation of heterosexual romance. Bracketed by *Vertigo* and *Psycho*, two masterpieces that have inspired reams of commentary, it has maintained a sterling reputation as "the Hitchcock picture to end all Hitchcock pictures" (Lehman 1999: vii), as Ernest Lehman described his aspiration in writing its screenplay, even though it is not mysterious in the specific sense of presenting problems, inconsistencies, or obscurities commentators have felt obliged to plumb.

Broadly speaking, commentators on the film have chosen as their point of departure either Hitchcock's description of it as nothing but entertainment or Moullet's edict that the film is fake, and either disputed the verdict at hand or accepted it and explored its implications. The status of *North by Northwest* as an unexcelled crowd-pleaser despite, rather than because of, its stylish implausibility is established as early as 1965 by Robin Wood, who calls it "a very, very good light comedy" notable for its "immense superiority" not only to *Goldfinger*, a representative James Bond film that Wood sees as essentially disposable entertainment, but also to Hitchcock's earlier man-on-the-run films because of its success in melding the omnipotent image of the superspy epitomized by Bond with the glossy image of the advertising executive sucked into an espionage plot he keeps insisting has nothing to do with him (Wood 1989: 141, 133). In short, Wood is bent on rescuing the film from its status as mere entertainment.

Introducing his 1975 study guide to the film, John P. Frayne is less interested in challenging Wood's reading of Hitchcock than its tone when he says that Hitchcock's "genuine popularity is beyond question, though critical reaction is divided. Some writers, like Robin Wood, treat him with a solemnity appropriate for Shakespeare. Other critics consider Hitchcock a fine craftsman who has wasted his talents on superficial subject matter" (Frayne 1975: 77). James Chapman challenges Wood's verdict more substantively in 2014 by arguing that "the relationship between Hitchcock and the James Bond movies is more complex than has generally been allowed" (Chapman 2014: 176). Hitchcock, Chapman notes, was considered to direct the first Bond feature, the ultimately unproduced James Bond of the Secret Service, by producer Ivar Bryce, who told Ian Fleming that *North by Northwest* was "the most terrific Bond-style thriller—almost plagiarizing—and superb. […] It is exactly the picture we are trying to make" (Chapman 2014: 157). In the only essay in the twenty-six volumes of the *Hitchcock Annual* in which *North by Northwest* plays a leading role, Chapman examines both Bond's echoes of Hitchcock and Hitchcock's echoes of Bond before concluding the essay, tellingly titled "Hitchcock and Bond," with an extended comparison of the two franchises as commercial projects.

Writing four years later in *Hitchcock and the Spy Film*, Chapman suggests more generally that "the reference points for *North by Northwest* are not so much specific texts as the spy genre as a whole" (Chapman 2018: 226). Calling Hitchcock's film "a transitional film in the history of spy cinema," Chapman follows Martin Rubin in locating it "on the cusp of what [Rubin] terms the genre's 'classical period' […] and its 'modern period,' beginning around 1960" (Chapman 2018: 236; see Rubin 2001: 119). For Chapman, *North by Northwest*, "the least political of Hitchcock's spy films," is "a key film—perhaps the key film—in the history of spy cinema," largely because it "exemplifies the process of 'genre upscaling' that occurred in American cinema during the 1950s" (Chapman 2018: 228, 235, 234; for a further account of "genre upscaling," see Thompson and Bordwell 1994: 394). In addition, it occupies a pivotal place in its director's career as well, for "it represents a point of convergence between the two thriller modes" represented by "sensational melodramas" like *The Lady Vanishes* and *Foreign Correspondent* and the "realist mode" of *Secret Agent* and *Notorious*, which placed "greater emphasis on psychological realism and character motivation" even as its unblinkered view of the Cold War foreshadows "the ideological and moral ambiguity of the existential thriller" (Chapman 2018: 227).

If Chapman treats *North by Northwest* as an exemplary entry in the Hitchcock universe that is prophetic in "exploring the political and social anxieties of mid-twentieth century America" (Chapman 2018: 235), Lesley Brill wastes no time in his influential study *The Hitchcock Romance* in centering *North by Northwest*, placing it at the heart of Hitchcock's canon because of its linkage of two different kinds of romance, the tropes of Hollywood romantic comedy and "the relatively fabulous kind of narrative we associate with folklore and fairy tale and their literary and cinematic offspring" (Brill 1988: 5). For Brill, the artifice of *North by Northwest* is inseparable from the broader stylization of romance, a genre he finds essential to understanding Hitchcock's films precisely because it allows a safe way to approach and share matters of the heart.

Other commentators have taken the film's artifice as their starting point. Leonard J. Leff's production history of the film methodically traces the stages by which *The Wreck of the Mary Deare*, the project for which MGM had originally brought together Hitchcock and Lehman, was abandoned when they realized that neither of them was as interested in the project as in creating the ultimate Hitchcock film, originally titled *In a Northwesterly Direction*; the problems that arose in the course of plotting and casting the film and negotiating with MGM over the budget, the control Hitchcock wrestled to achieve over its production, and its residual rights; the challenges of creating pivotal scenes set but not shot inside the United Nations complex and on Mount Rushmore; and the film's financial success as "the year's sixth top-grossing film" (Leff 1986: 59). George M. Wilson has called it "a kind of wry apologia for the sort of illusionistic art—more particularly, for the sort of illusionistic cinema—that Hitchcock, paradigmatically, has always practiced" (1979: 1161). James Naremore, focusing more narrowly on Cary Grant's star performance as Thornhill, celebrates Grant's combination of "the light-comic sophistication of an Alfred Lunt and the music hall clowning of a Charlie Chaplin with the glamour of a fashion model and the athleticism of a Hollywood action hero" (Naremore 1993: 5; see also Naremore 1988: 213–235).

Pursuing this last argument further, Marian Keane links Cary Grant's performance as Thornhill to the performances to which the film's outlandish premise—a middle-aged, twice-divorced executive, mistaken for a secret agent who himself is a nonexistent fiction created to draw suspicion away from the real secret agent working against the sinister Phillip Vandamm, must embrace the role into which he has been thrust in order to survive, clear his name, and earn a happy ending—drives Thornhill, on the one hand, and the performances of author figures like Vandamm (who is constantly criticizing Thornhill's performance as a wronged innocent), the Professor (Leo G. Carroll) who represents the United States Intelligence Agency, and Hitchcock himself. Disputing Raymond Durgnat's remark, "I find the film hard to justify as a bildungsroman, simply because Thornhill seems on his way back to Madison Avenue" as it closes (Durgnat 1974: 313), Keane observes that Thornhill's dilemma is that

> he does not know about the world he inhabits, how it works or what lies in store for him; he also does not know, on a deeper level, what he is to do. His manner of surviving his thrownness in the world he discovers himself to inhabit relies upon his intelligence and physical agility and most importantly on his comic wit.
>
> (Keane 1993: 216)

Her approach, based in part on her reading of Stanley Cavell's *Pursuits of Happiness: The Hollywood Comedy of Remarriage*, is developed further by Cavell's own essay on *North by Northwest*, which takes the film's title as a cue to emphasize its determined rewriting of *Hamlet* that foregrounds "Grant/Thornhill [and Hamlet] as surrogate for Hitchcock" (Cavell 1981: 770).

The line Keane and Cavell take is informed by, and in turn enriches, a series of discussions of *North by Northwest* as an anatomy of modern American national identity. This premise, which had already informed Raymond Durgnat's extended discussion of the film, is developed by Richard Millington, who notes that

> the maneuvers Thornhill teaches himself […] not only describe a tactics of self-discovery but define a stance toward the experience of living within American culture, a strategy for the reclamation of "American character." The capacity for analysis that Thornhill achieves and enacts, his ability to see the covert shapes and structures that ideology gives to experience, is precisely what his situation demands—and insofar as his situation represents our own, it is the ability that we, too, must discover if we are to recover our own American characters from the conditions the film makes manifest.
>
> (Millington 1999: 150)

Pursuing this line further, Frank M. Meola treats *North by Northwest* as "a particularly rich consideration of American artifice and identity-confusion" from the viewpoint of an outsider from England who "intuits the American awareness—clear in writers from Brockden Brown to Emerson, Poe, and Hawthorne—of threats to the soul" in all his works, "dwell[ing] on the precariousness of social forms and the dangers of the forces beyond yet within them" in *Vertigo* and *Psycho*, the darker films that bracket *North by Northwest*, and "look[ing] toward self-invention as a solution only if it puts us further in touch with what we might term life-affirming energies" (Meola 2000–2001: 35, 36, 35). And Jennifer L. Jenkins pointedly links the ideals of romance Brill had found central to Hitchcock's work to a specifically American self-mythologizing impulse: "The philosophy of marriage in *North by Northwest* is a singularly democratic one: a volitional union of equals, hard-won by strife and commitment to an idea greater than themselves. A more perfect union, as it were" (Jenkins 2017: 254).

An alternative strand of commentary pioneered by structuralist and poststructuralist theorists uses the film's artifice to ground more general theories of representation, or anti-representation. Peter Wollen approaches the film's structure on the same terms that Vladimir Propp had developed early in the twentieth century to analyze Russian folktakes and fairy tales, though he suggests supplementing Propp's emphasis on absences or lacks as narrative motivations with a system of exchanges, in order to demonstrate both the kinship between *North by Northwest* and the romance that Brill would explore in more humanistic terms and to valorize the structural study of narrative as a perfectly reasonable way to approach more complex stories (Wollen 1976).

Writing a year earlier, Raymond Bellour proposes a far more radical approach to the film's artifice. Illustrating his position by an extended shot-by-shot analysis of the crop-dusting sequence (see Fig. 7.4),

Figure 7.4 The film's celebrated crop-dusting sequence serves as the basis for Raymond Bellour's extended analysis of its representational system.

Bellour fleshes out his premise that Hollywood cinema, like psychoanalysis, depends on "a system of representations in which the woman occupies a central place only to the extent that it [is] a place assigned to her by the logic of masculine desire" (Bellour 2000: 93) with the more specific argument that the film's several levels of alternation reveal an oedipal logic: "the systematic accumulation of symmetries and dissymetries [that is, alternation] through the filmic chain decomposed by the work of a generalized segmentation constantly mimics and reproduces (because the one produces the other) the schema of family relations that founds the narrative space" (2000: 205). Employing spatial models of analysis echoing Bellour's, Fredric Jameson identifies "the contradiction that informs the film" as "the conceptual incoherence or inconsistency between the ideological opposition of public and private (and that between the equally stereotypical terms of open and closed)" (Jameson 1992: 71). Tom Cohen's pun-heavy remarks about the film in *Hitchcock's Cryptonomies* are driven by the phrase "think thin," the self-directed memo Thornhill asks his secretary to put on his desk in the film's opening sequence, which requires "a zero figure—[the nonexistent agent George] Kaplan, Roger 'O.'—to counter its own emptiness, stalled figurative traffic and endemic superficiality as cinematic trait" (Cohen 2004: 20). Cohen notes the ways Lester Townsend's "liquefied library," in which books are replaced by cabinets holding liquor bottles, "incorporates the film's own bookish departure from *Hamlet* into a translation of the biblio-archive into cinematic mnemonics" and concludes that the nonexistent compass direction inscribed in the film's title "involves an irreversible loss of aura and anthropomorphism, echoed in the directive to 'think thin'" (Cohen 2004: 21). The most radical reading, or anti-reading, of all is Christopher D. Morris's demonstration that every sign in the film, beginning with its title, amounts to an "implication that language is self-cancelation" (2002: 203). Borrowing from Jacques Derrida's essay on undelivered letters, Morris challenges "[t]he dominant master narrative in criticism of *North by Northwest* [which] holds that its ending finds Thornhill matured and its ambiguities resolved in favor of love" (2002: 208), observing that many scenes in the film feature audiences who miss or misinterpret important evidence, suggesting that the film's own audience is equally blind and concluding that "[t]rue 'grounds' of identity in *North by Northwest* are nonexistent" (2002: 209). Indeed, "*North by Northwest*'s questioning of the master narratives of self, country, and love works to undermine the grounds of understanding of film criticism," including whatever interpretations Morris or Hitchcock himself might offer: "Whatever is conveyed to the viewer is outside the director's control. The director is as helpless as the viewer in enforcing an interpretation on the interior content of the film, in defining its direction" (Morris 2002: 209, 213).

Another recent analysis pushes the analysis of the film in a direction that is both new and surprisingly familiar. David Greven pairs *North by Northwest* with the more obviously queer *Psycho* to argue that "the queerness of *North by Northwest* lies in Hitchcock's denaturing of what heterosexual desire and romance mean, and his interest in depicting Thornhill as a man transformed into a complex human being through the development of his love for Eve" (2017: 34) who is "not just a queer figure but a stand-in for the homosexual male" (2017: 45)—Leonard, the villainous sidekick played by Martin Landau, who, when he "seized upon the homosexuality and urged Hitchcock to permit its subtle depiction," was told, "I don't make message movies, Martin" (see Leff 1986: 52). As a result of the film's narrative structure and Landau's more veiled indications of Leonard's sexuality, *North by Northwest* emerges as "a no-man's film, one that decenters the heterosexual male hero and leaves narrative up for identificatory grabs. […] His [Thornhill's] plight provides and establishes a normative premise within which queer negotiations can occur, a cover story for covert queer struggles" (Greven 2017: 42). Like Brill, whose analysis of the Hitchcock romance he both queers and valorizes, Greven closes the circle of commentary on *North by Northwest* by noting the film's exemplary status: "Grant, who embodies 'male femininity' as

[Andrew] Britton put it, blurs the lines of identification, the screen protagonist who elicits queer desire while pursuing, and being pursued by, the woman" (Greven 2017: 51).

Unlike the reviewers who praised *North by Northwest* on its first release for its power to entertain, Hitchcock scholars who have taken up the film since then have largely approached it as an example of some more general thematic or representational tendency they found more interesting, more worth talking about, than the film itself: Wood's defense of Hitchcock's supremacy to the genre thrills of James Bond, Brill's mapping of the Hitchcock romance, Naremore's examination of cinematic performance, Keane and Cavell's exploration of comedies of remarriage, Millington's anatomy of America, Bellour's analysis of symbolic blockage, Greven's determination to queer Hitchcock. The most notable exception to this rule is Murray Pomerance's analysis of the film in *An Eye for Hitchcock*, which makes a point of not "forcing the work into the perspective of any single theoretical mode" (2004: 5). For Pomerance, Thornhill's adventures constitute a history of "confused identity […] plaited with the history of situational ambiguity and the history of the development of the technology of disguise" (2004: 14). He singles out the auction sequence as presenting "a testament to Roger's gaining full control of his identity in a role directed by others" whose expectations he alertly notes and seeks to fulfill (Pomerance 2004: 56).

The enduring status of *North by Northwest* as nothing but entertainment raises important questions the label might seem to conceal. The Alfred Hitchcock who told Martin Landau that he didn't make message movies thought of himself, and consistently presented himself, as an entertainer. More scholarly critics, taking their cues from Éric Rohmer, Claude Chabrol, François Truffaut, and Robin Wood, systematically resolved to rescue him from the status of a mere entertainer by emphasizing his thematic or semiotic seriousness. Part of the price for this rescue was a relative neglect of *North by Northwest* and Hitchcock's other most successfully entertaining films in favor of more obviously challenging films. But, in fact, Hitchcock at his best both challenges and entertains, as the epithet Master of Suspense already indicates. Even when he is not at his best, in films from *Champagne* (1928) to *Topaz* (1969), both impulses are clearly present. Instead of treating Hitchcock as an entertainer who invites his audience of guests to relax and enjoy themselves, analysts moved to wonder whether relaxation is really consistent with the kinds of pleasures his films provide might better treat him as a filmmaker whose formidable accomplishments depend not on transcending entertainment but on providing superior entertainment—someone who entertains both guests and ideas, considering and playing with them inveterately, hypothetically, and with his own distinctive brand of hospitality, as he does so memorably in *North by Northwest*.

Acknowledgments

I wish to express my gratitude to Ian O'Sullivan, of the BFI Reuben Library, for his invaluable help in tracking down British reviews of *North by Northwest*'s initial release.

References

Balliett, W. (1959) "Hitchcock on Hitchcock," *New Yorker*, August 8.
Bellour, R. (2000) "Symbolic Blockage," in C. Penley (ed.), *The Analysis of Film*, Bloomington: Indiana University Press, pp. 235–350.
Blauvelt, Christian, and Wilson Chapman (2024) "The 25 Best Alfred Hitchcock Movies, Ranked," IndieWire, July 23.
Brill, L. (1988) *The Hitchcock Romance*: Love and Irony in Hitchcock's Films, Princeton, NJ: Princeton University Press.

Cavell, S. (1981) "*North by Northwest*," *Critical Inquiry*, 7 (4): 761–776.
Chapman, J. (2014) "Hitchcock and Bond," *Hitchcock Annual*, vol. 19, pp. 153–190.
Chapman, J. (2018) *Hitchcock and the Spy Film*, London: I. B. Tauris.
Cohen, T. (2004) *Hitchcock's Cryptonomies*, vol. II: *War Machines*, Minneapolis, Minn.: University of Minnesota Press.
Domarchi, J., and J. Douchet (1959) "An Interview with Alfred Hitchcock," trans. Lahcen Hassan and Darlene Sadlier, *Cahiers du Cinéma*, 102 (December): vii.
Durgnat, R. (1974) *The Strange Case of Alfred Hitchcock*, Cambridge, Mass.: MIT Press.
Frayne, J. P. (1975) "*North by Northwest*," *Journal of Aesthetic Education*, 9 (2): 77–95.
Greven, D. (2017) *Intimate Violence*: *Hitchcock, Sex, and Queer Theory*, New York: Oxford University Press.
Houston, P. (1959) "*North by Northwest*," *Sight and Sound*, July.
Jameson, Fredric (1992) "Spatial Systems in *North by Northwest*," in S. Žižek (ed.), *Everything You Always Wanted to Know about Lacan (But Were Afraid to Ask Hitchcock)*, London: Verso, pp. 47–72.
Jenkins, J. L. (2017) "The Philosophy of Marriage in *North by Northwest*," in R. B. Palmer, H. B. Pettey, and S. M. Sanders (eds), *Hitchcock's Moral Gaze*, Albany, NY: State University of New York Press, pp. 253–269.
Kapsis, R. E. (1992) *Hitchcock*: *The Making of a Reputation*, Chicago, Ill.: University of Chicago Press.
Keane, Marian (1993) "The Designs of Authorship: An Essay on *North by Northwest*," in J. Naremore (ed.), North by Northwest: *Alfred Hitchcock, Director*, New Brunswick: Rutgers University Press, pp. 210–220.
Leff, L. (1986) "Hitchcock at Metro," in M. Deutelbaun and L. Poague (eds), *A Hitchcock Reader*, Ames, Iowa: Iowa State University Press, pp. 41–61.
Lehman, E. (1999) " Introduction," *North by Northwest*, London: Faber & Faber, pp. vii–xi.
Meola, F. M. (2000–2001) "Hitchcock's Emersonian Edges," *Hitchcock Annual*, pp. 23–46.
Millington, R. (1999) "Hitchcock and American Character: The Comedy of Self-Construction in *North by Northwest*," in J. Freedman and R. Millington (eds), *Hitchcock's America*, New York: Oxford University Press, pp. 135–154.
Morris, C. D. (2002) *The Hanging Figure*: *On Suspense and the Films of Alfred Hitchcock*, Westport, Conn.: Praeger.
Moullet, L. (1993) "*North by Northwest*," in J. Naremore (ed.), North by Northwest: *Alfred Hitchcock, Director*, New Brunswick: Rutgers University Press, pp. 195–197.
Murrian, Samuel (2025) "The 15 Best Alfred Hitchcock Movies of All Time, Ranked," *Parade*, February 15.
Naremore, J. (1988) "Cary Grant in *North by Northwest*," in *Acting for the Cinema*, Berkeley, Calif.: University of California Press, pp. 213–235.
Naremore, J. (1993) "Introduction: Spies and Lovers," in North by Northwest: *Alfred Hitchcock, Director*, New Brunswick: Rutgers University Press, pp. 3–19.
Nicholson, Tom (2020) "The 18 Best Alfred Hitchcock Movies," *Esquire*, www.esquire.com/uk/culture/film/a33979236/alfred-hitchcock-movies
Pomerance, M. (2004) "A Great Fall: Action North by Sincerity Northwest," in *An Eye for Hitchcock*, New Brunswick: Rutgers University Press, pp. 14–57.
Powell, D. (1989) "Hitch among Cliff-Hangers," in D. Powell, *The Golden Screen*: *Fifty Years at the Films*, ed. George Perry (London: Pavilion, 1989), pp. 156–157.
Ross, Graham (2022) "Alfred Hitchcock's 20 Greatest Films, from *Rebecca* to the *Birds*," *Independent*, August 26.
Rubin, M. (2001) *Thrillers*, Cambridge: Cambridge University Press.
Thomas, Lee, and Jack Whatley (2020) "Ranking All 52 Surviving Feature Films Directed by Alfred Hitchcock," *Far Out*, August 13.
Thompson, K., and D. Bordwell (1994) *Film History*: *An Introduction*, New York: McGraw-Hill.
Truffaut, F., with Helen Scott (1985) *Hitchcock*, rev. edn, New York: Simon & Schuster.
Underhill, Fiona (2021) "Alfred Hitchcock's 20 Best Films Ranked," *SlashFilm*, August 26.
Wilson, G. M. (1979) " The Maddest MacGuffin: Some Notes on *North by Northwest*," *Modern Language Notes*, 94 (5): 1159–1172.
Wollen, P. (1982) "*North by Northwest*: A Morphological Analysis," in *Readings and Writings*: *Semiotic Counter-Strategies*, London: Verso, pp. 18–33.
Wood, R. (1989) *Hitchcock's Films Revisited*, New York: Columbia University Press.

PART TWO

Changing Receptions

Chapter 8

"A Director Who Can Impose His Own Personality on His Pictures"

British Critics and *Sabotage* (1936)

James Chapman

Sabotage was the fourth of what Raymond Durgnat called Hitchcock's "classic thriller sextet" in the mid 1930s—preceded by *The Man Who Knew Too Much* (1934), *The 39 Steps* (1935) and *Secret Agent* (1936), followed by *Young and Innocent* (1937) and *The Lady Vanishes* (1938)—and was by some distance the most divisive of them in its critical reception (Durgnat 1974: 20). *Sabotage* was an adaptation of Joseph Conrad's 1907 novel *The Secret Agent*, the different title necessitated because Hitchcock's previous film, based on W. Somerset Maugham's *Ashenden*, had been titled *Secret Agent*. In an interview for *Film Weekly*, Hitchcock averred that the sequence of spy pictures had not been planned: "It was purely a coincidence that three of my films in succession—*The Man Who Knew Too Much*, *The 39 Steps* and *Secret Agent*—should all have a background of spying. I am not setting out to be an expert on screen spies" (*Film Weekly*, May 23, 1936, p. 28).

Sabotage has always seemed something of an odd film out not only within the sextet but also among the thirty-one Hitchcock films based on literary sources. The emergence of critical interest in Hitchcock within adaptation studies—exemplified by R. Barton Palmer and David Boyd's collection *Hitchcock at the Source* (2011) and Mark Osteen's *Hitchcock and Adaptation* (2014)—has offered new ways of understanding the narrative and thematic structures of Hitchcock's films that does not involve a reductive form of auteur theory. It would probably be fair to say that two broad generalizations can be made about Hitchcock's films based on novels: that most were based on "popular" writers—including Marie Belloc Lowndes (*The Lodger*), Clemence Dane and Helen Simpson (*Enter Sir John*—the source text for *Murder!*), John Buchan (*The Thirty-Nine Steps*), Josephine Tey (*A Shilling for Candles*—the source for *Young and Innocent*), Ethel Lina White (*The Wheel Spins*—the source for *The Lady Vanishes*) and Daphne du Maurier (*Jamaica Inn*, *Rebecca*)—and that they usually had an arm's-length relationship to the source text. Hitchcock professed that he was not interested in filming more "literary" novels. He told François Truffaut that he would never film a work such as *Crime and Punishment* because "in Dostoyevsky's novel there are many, many words and all of them have a function … [To] really convey that in cinematic terms, substituting the language of the camera for the written word, one would have to make a six- to ten-hour film" (Truffaut 1986: 85–86). However, as Paula Marantz Cohen contends, *Sabotage* was "the one movie of his career that is based on an irrefutably great work" (Marantz Cohen 1995: 30).

Joseph Conrad was one of the first English modernists: his novels—including *Heart of Darkness*, *Lord Jim*, *Nostromo*, *The Secret Agent* and *Under Western Eyes*—were characterized by their moral pessimism, their narratives of despair, and their introspective, rootless protagonists. F. R. Leavis felt that *The Secret Agent* was "one of Conrad's two supreme masterpieces" (the other was *Nostromo*) and "one of the two unquestionable classics of the first order that he added to the English novel" (Leavis 1948: 220). A recurring feature of the critical scholarship on Hitchcock has been the reasons put forward as to why he chose to film *The Secret Agent*—a novel that in tone and style is so different from the other works that he turned to for source material. Donald Spoto, for example, suggests that "Hitchcock must have chosen Conrad's novel because he shared several of its concerns: the banality of evil, the transference of guilt, the disaffection and unsteadiness in human relationships, the duplicity inherent in the enterprise of espionage and the enterprise of tracking down spies" (Spoto 1983: 156). Éric Rohmer and Claude Chabrol offer another possible explanation that arises from Hitchcock's own professional ambitions as a filmmaker. They argue that *Sabotage* was "a film whose sole purpose was personal prestige" and that he made it in order to demonstrate "that he was a director of international status" (Rohmer and Chabrol 1988: 47).

There is some credence to this argument. In the 1930s, Hitchcock's reputation was shaped by John Grierson's oft-quoted labeling of him as "the world's best director of unimportant pictures" (Hardy 1981: 108). *Sabotage* presented an opportunity to make a more serious film that would nevertheless be done "with such dazzling virtuosity that it would evoke the best of Hollywood without sacrificing a certain British chic" (Rohmer and Chabrol 1988: 48). By the mid 1930s, Hitchcock's career ambitions were orienting toward Hollywood: it is surely significant in this regard that his first visit to the USA was to promote *Sabotage* in 1937 (McGilligan 2003: 201). Hitchcock's three previous films had attracted good notices in America, especially from the New York critics, and the Gaumont-British Picture Corporation evidently had high hopes for *Sabotage*, which, with its American star (Sylvia Sidney; see Fig. 8.1), was part of the studio's ambitious strategy to grow its presence in the US market (Sedgwick 1996).

Sabotage opened in London in December 1936, where it premiered at the Tivoli, once a showcase cinema on the Strand, but by the mid 1930s being eclipsed as a premiere venue by newer cinemas clustered around Leicester Square, before going into the London suburbs, after which it was showing across the country throughout the first six months of 1937. While there is no evidence of distributor's receipts, John Sedgwick's statistical analysis of popular film preferences using the "POPSTAT" method—which calculates the relative popularity of individual films based on the length of their run in selected cinemas and taking into account the seating capacity of those cinemas—suggests that *Sabotage* was the fifty-second most popular film released in Britain in 1936 and the twelfth most popular British film: it was therefore less successful than *Secret Agent* (seventeenth overall and third most popular British film of 1936) but within the range that would probably be considered a middling success (Sedgwick 2000: 262–276). The exhibitors' trade paper *Kinematograph Weekly* thought it a "very good general entertainment" and an "outstanding booking for all classes" (December 10, 1936, p. 25). However, the fan magazine *Picturegoer*, whose readership comprised regular cinemagoers, found the film "a trifle ponderous and slow … The picture presents interesting characters and provides quite good entertainment, although looked at dispassionately it is all rather vague and involved in plot" (*Picturegoer*, December 19, 1936, p. 105).

British Critics and *Sabotage* (1936)

Figure 8.1 The Verlocs at home: a tense domestic scene for Sylvia Sidney and Oscar Homolka. *Sabotage*, directed by Alfred Hitchcock. © Gaumont British Picture Corporation 1936. All rights reserved. Still provided courtesy of the BFI Archive.

This chapter focuses on contemporary British critical responses to *Sabotage*, drawing upon a range of primary sources across both the quality and popular and the national and regional press. I have chosen to focus on the British context for two reasons. First, and as I have argued elsewhere (Chapman 2025), the 1920s and 1930s saw the emergence of what might be described as a proto-auteurist discourse within mainstream British film criticism. A common feature of newspaper film reviews, especially those written by critics who did not come from a literary or theatre background, was the idea that the best films revealed a unifying creative agency that should be attributed to the director. In his book *The Film Till Now* (1930), for example, Paul Rotha anticipated Andrew Sarris's "Notes on the Auteur Theory" by three decades:

> If a film is to be a unity, clear cut and single-minded, the director alone must preconceive it and communicate its content to the audience through groups of interpreters of his vision, under his supreme command. The construction of a film from the first conception to the final product must be under the absolute control of the director.
>
> (Rotha 1967: 110–111)

A handful of directors during the interwar period—Ernst Lubitsch, René Clair, Fritz Lang, King Vidor and Frank Borzage were the most often cited, while Orson Welles and Preston Sturges were later additions to the canon—were characterized by the recurring thematic and formal properties of their films. Hitchcock was the one British director included in this elite group. Sydney Carroll's review of *The 39 Steps* for the *Sunday Times* exemplifies how Hitchcock was being constructed as an auteur long before the auteur theory had emerged as a critical tool:

> Every film of real quality bears the unforgettable stamp of its creator. Individuality is a rare and precious thing. In moving pictures it is exceptionally hard to discover. When it is there, however, it usually assumes a force and a distinction unmistakably attributable to its director alone. In *The Thirty-Nine Steps* [sic], now showing at the New Gallery, the identity and mind of Alfred Hitchcock are continuously discernible, in fact supreme.
>
> (*Sunday Times*, June 9, 1935, p. 4)

The second reason for focusing on Britain is that it offers the opportunity to range beyond those who might be called the "usual suspects"—James Agate, Iris Barry, C. A. Lejeune, Dilys Powell, Richard Winnington—and to include a broader and more diverse range of contemporary critics, especially those representing the popular and regional press.[1]

The contemporary critical reception of *Sabotage* needs to be understood in this context insofar as it was seen first and foremost as a Hitchcock film, characterized by his distinctive directorial touches, rather than as, say, a Gaumont-British film or as a vehicle for Sylvia Sidney. For example, George Campbell, writing for the topical weekly magazine *The Bystander*:

> Alfred Hitchcock has his faults, but amongst his many admirable qualities is this: He has style. Ninety-nine pictures out of a hundred might have been made by anybody. But not Hitchcock's. His work is as unmistakable as Alexander Korda's, or Lubitsch's or René Clair's. His range, in atmosphere and character, is not very wide, but in his own field he is supreme. His setting is London, his characters are the Cockneys he has studied with such a shrewd and penetrating eye, his theme is the capacity for deeds of darkness and of horror that lie beneath the commonplace of London life.
>
> (*The Bystander*, December 16, p. 446)

The film critic of *The Civil and Military Gazette*—a daily paper catering for the British community in India—was also an unlikely proto-auteurist:

> It is notorious that nobody cares about film directors. Yet you are defied to see *Sabotage*, one of the most exciting thrillers in years, without being aware of Alfred Hitchcock who directed it. "Hitch" has a style, which is something only a handful of directors have. It is an intelligent, highly individual style. A picture by him carries its maker's mark as definitely as a Noel Coward play or a Rolls-Royce car.
>
> (*The Civil and Military Gazette*, April 23, 1937, p. 11)

And "R.G." (the *Manchester Guardian*), while rather less favorably disposed toward the film, noted Hitchcock's ability to mould the source material:

> This is a talkie adaptation of Conrad's *The Secret Agent*, but instead of Conrad's air of mystery we have Hitchcock's atmosphere, and instead of Conrad's prose Hitchcock's camera technique. This

atmosphere and this technique we have had before … Whether the story is taken from Maugham or Conrad makes little difference: a melodrama will be made of it, and will be a melodrama in Alfred Hitchcock's manner. It is excellent that there should be in the British film industry a director who can impose his own personality on his pictures; but when these pictures are all the same type, there is a sameness about them.

(*Manchester Guardian*, December 3, 1936, p. 6)

The review concluded with an echo of John Grierson: "Why should Hitchcock's vigorous talent be expended only on 'thrillers'? Why does he continue to say with such brilliance so little?"

While *Sabotage* was universally seen as Hitchcock's film, however, there were divergent views on where it ranked among his work. Some reviewers heralded it as his best to date. F. S. Jennings, writing for theatrical weekly *The Era*, averred that "Alfred Hitchcock … is entitled to consider this melodrama as his best talkie" (*The Era*, December 9, 1936, p. 15). *The Scotsman* felt that "Alfred Hitchcock's new film strengthens his position as Britain's foremost director. It has the close observation and ingenious situations characteristic of his work; but here those qualities are not demonstrated for their own sake but take their place naturally in the continuity and construction of the story" (April 13, 1937, p. 15). Sydney Carroll thought it ranked among the very best British films:

The picture *Sabotage* is another of those British films any producing company can be proud of. The direction is by Alfred Hitchcock. Once again, "Hitch" has proved his particular genius. He extracts the utmost out of each subject he handles. Joseph Conrad's story *The Secret Agent* is suited to the screen medium. It is sinister and dramatic. Charles Bennett has made a good play. The dialogue, by Ian Hay and Helen Simpson, is economic and telling. The cast has been well chosen. We are given a superb series of London backgrounds—traffic-laden streets peopled with the exact types we meet with any day of the week. No stagey cockneys strut upon the street. In gesture, manner and dialect, they are really lifelike figures, while here and there is evidence of the cosmopolitan.

(*Sunday Times*, December 6, 1936, p. 66)

P. L. Mannock (*Daily Herald*) was a little more qualified but rated the film highly: "On the whole, Alfred Hitchcock's *Sabotage*, at the Tivoli, is better than his last, *Secret Agent*. Again we are given a good innings of this brilliant director's capricious sense of melodrama" (*Daily Herald*, December 4, 1936, p. 17). And Frank Evans (*Newcastle Evening Chronicle*) thought that it fell just short of greatness:

After the slight disappointment occasioned by *The Secret Agent* [sic], this film answers the highest hopes that Alfred Hitchcock will make a really great film. I mean "great" in every sense of the word. For *Sabotage* is great in some respects; technically it is one of the cleverest films ever made, superbly directed, acted and cut.

(*Newcastle Evening Chronicle*, March 9, 1937, p. 11)

An unlikely admirer of *Sabotage* was Graham Greene, who was jobbing as a film critic for the *Spectator* between 1935 and 1940. (The *Spectator* was—and is—a weekly publication leaning to the political right; however, it has a history of employing left-wing art and film critics, including not only Greene but also his successor, Basil Wright, a self-declared Marxist.) Greene was no fan of Hitchcock, whom he regarded as "tricky, not imaginative": "Hitchcock's films—especially *The Man Who Knew Too Much*—are simply made up of tricks, in their plots as well as their direction" (Parkinson 1993: 399). However, Greene was surprisingly positive about *Sabotage*:

> I have sometimes doubted Mr Hitchcock's talent. As a director he has always known exactly the right place to put his camera (and there is only one right place in any scene), he has been pleasantly inventive with his sound, but as a producer and as a writer of his own scripts he has been appallingly careless: he has cared more for an ingenious melodramatic situation than for the construction and continuity of his story. In *Sabotage* for the first time he has really "come off."
>
> *Sabotage* is not, of course, Conrad's *Secret Agent*. That dark, drab passionate tale of Edwardian London could never find a place in the popular cinema, and only M. Jacques Feyder, I think, the director of *Thérèse Raquin*, could transfer its peculiar qualities—of madness and despair and four-wheelers and backstreets—to the screen. But Mr Hitchcock's "variations on a theme" are on a different level from his deplorable adaptation of Mr Maugham's *Ashenden*. This melodrama is convincingly realistic, perhaps because Mr Hitchcock has left the screenplay in other hands.
>
> (*The Spectator*, December 11, 1936, p. 54)

While Greene evidently did not appreciate that Hitchcock had been as fully involved in scripting *Sabotage* as his other films, he felt that the film "retains some of the ruthlessness of the original" and that for once Hitchcock's directorial flourishes did not detract from the story: "This ingenious and pathetic twist"—in reference to the killing of Verloc—"is stamped as Mr Hitchcock's own, but unlike so many of his ideas in the past it is an integral part of the story." Otherwise Greene felt that "Hitchcock has been helped by admirable dialogue, written by Mr Ian Hay and Miss Helen Simpson, and a fine cast … with only two weak members" (those were John Loder and child actor Desmond Tester as Stevie, for whose "prep school accent I feel an invincible distaste") (*The Spectator*, December 11, 1936, p. 56).

Some of the most effusive reviews of *Sabotage* came from the local press. These sources demonstrate that critical admiration for Hitchcock was not limited to the metropolitan critics. For example, the *Reading Standard* thought it one of Hitchcock's best:

> Ever since the first days of British sound films, Alfred Hitchcock has been regarded as one of the finest of our directors, and the early promise he showed with *Blackmail*, the first English thriller, has been sustained. His latest film, *Sabotage*, seems destined to rank among the classics of the screen.
>
> (April 2, 1937, p. 66)

The *Worthing Gazette* headed its review "A Brilliant British Film" and suggested that "it is the direction of Alfred Hitchcock that lifts this film clean out of the ordinary. Hitchcock has a flair for finding film drama in the smallest incidents of everyday life, and he has employed it to great effect in *Sabotage*" (March 10, 1937, p. 3). The *Mearns Leader and Kincardineshire Mail* told its readers, "You must see *Sabotage*, Alfred Hitchcock's latest masterpiece, which is at the Picture House this week. 'Hitch' is on the theme he likes best—melodrama with the suspense kept at high pitch throughout" (February 25, 1937, p. 15). The *Leominster Picture News* suggested that it did not disappoint: "You will remember with pleasure previous Alfred Hitchcock thrillers *The Man Who Knew Too Much*, *39 Steps* [sic] and *Secret Agent*. Well, *Sabotage* is right up to the usual Hitchcock standard of excellence" (May 1, 1937, p. 10). The *Royal Leamington Spa Courier and Warwickshire Standard* agreed: "Alfred Hitchcock, the brilliant 'crime' director, has produced a sufficiently good film in *Sabotage* to claim for it the qualification 'the British film that calls for no apology'" (February 12, 1937, p. 8).

While most local film review columns were relatively brief, some offered fuller notices. These sometimes demonstrated a quite sophisticated understanding of the medium. One such was the *Chester Chronicle*, which picked *Sabotage* as its "Film of the Week" on March 20, 1937:

> Was it a deliberate sense of irony or a well-meaning desire to enlighten the darkness of the "fans" that caused Alfred Hitchcock to preface *Sabotage* (at the Gaumont Palace) with a dictionary definition of the title word? Anyway, he was taking no chances. He might simply have called the film "The Wrecker," but "*Sabotage*" is less commonplace, in spite of the damaging effect of so many Soviet State trials! With the cooperation of Oscar Homolka, and a distant acknowledgement of his indebtedness to Joseph Conrad, who wrote the story and called it *Secret Agent* [sic], the Gaumont-British director has made another melodrama with a difference.

The unnamed reviewer was one of the few to highlight the self-reflexive quality of *Sabotage*, or what would now be described as its meta-cinematic apparatus:

> The screen-craft and observation are brilliant. You see a cinema within a cinema—an intriguing development of the old play-within-a-play idea. On the screen at which you are looking you see Sylvia Sydney and John Loder; on the screen within Robertson Hare and Tom Walls. The idea has been used before, as a novelty; here it is part of the dramatic action.
>
> (March 20, 1937, p. 12)

However, *Sabotage* was not universally admired. Some reviewers found it too morbid and bleak despite its undoubted technical excellence. One such was C. A. Lejeune (the *Observer*), usually a champion of Hitchcock's, but who thought *Sabotage* was his "least likeable" film. While she recognized that it was a "quite masterly piece of film technique," the overall tone was too bleak:

> The keynote of *Sabotage* is complete destruction. Not only is the main plot concerned with a conspiracy to blow up Piccadilly Circus and terrorise London, but everything that is human and innocent and ordinary in the picture seems consecrated to the needs of ruthlessness. The young schoolboy brother of the heroine, the only really sympathetic character in the piece, is smashed to pieces with a time bomb in a London omnibus. With him go a puppy, an amiable old lady, a friendly conductor, and all the most cheerful group of sentimental commonplaces that Hitchcock can gather together in one locale. Following this event, the heroine sticks her husband in the stomach with a carving-knife, and a kindly old anarchist blows up the corpse and himself to glory with another hand grenade, leaving the murderess free to marry the Scotland Yard detective. And all this destruction is neatly contrived with two pots of explosive kept in the back bedroom of a bird-shop and labelled, with cherubic Hitchcock menace, "Tomato Ketchup" and "Strawberry Jam."
>
> (*The Observer*, December 6, 1936, p. 16)

Lejeune accepted that the bus sequence "is superbly timed" and "calculated to wring every whither in the audience." "But," she added, "I believe—and I stick to it—that there is a code in this sort of freehanded slaughter, and Hitchcock has gone outside the code in *Sabotage*." Hitchcock, who paid more attention to critics than his public comments about them would suggest, seems to have taken Lejeune's criticism to heart. He later told Truffaut—in response to Truffaut's comment that the killing of a child in a film "comes close to an abuse of cinematic power"—that "I made a serious mistake in having the little boy carry the bomb … The boy was involved in a situation that got him too much sympathy from the audience, so that when the bomb exploded and he was killed, the public was resentful" (Truffaut 1986: 144).

Lejeune's distaste for *Sabotage* was extreme, but it demonstrates that admiration for the film was not unconditional. Nor was hers a lone voice. No reviews regarded *Sabotage* as a bad film, but several found it flawed in certain respects. Criticisms focused on its narrative construction, a consistent complaint being that the bomb-on-the-bus sequence in the middle of the film rendered the rest of it anticlimactic. The *Northern Whig and Belfast Post* pronounced: "An opportunity of making an outstanding British film has been missed by Alfred Hitchcock in his latest picture, *Sabotage* … Unfortunately, except for a flashing moment or two, the suspense falls flat, and a film that starts off at a high level ends with a feeling of disappointment" (December 9, 1937, p. 10). The *Belfast News Letter* considered the bus journey "one of the most suspenseful sequences yet screened," but the rest of the film was something of a letdown: "Unfortunately the brilliancy of the passage makes the rest of the film an anticlimax and the deep personal concern in the fate of the actors is impaired" (March 2, 1937, p. 11). James Agate (*The Tatler*) was evidently underwhelmed:

> I went the other day to see *Sabotage* at the Tivoli, and must regretfully say that I was disappointed. To begin with, why change the title? *Sabotage* sounds like industrialism, and is therefore dull. Somehow or other I couldn't manage to believe in the blowing-up of the bus. It looked rather as if somebody had blown up a matchbox and then magnified it. And, of course, even if one believed it, nobody is going to stand for the blowing-up of the little boy … I have great admiration for Alfred Hitchcock as a director. But it seems to me that the best he can now do is to try his hand for a change at something different from suspense. Criticism should be constructive. Therefore let the brilliant producer, since he appears to like Joseph Conrad, leave behind buses and bombs and give us a film of *Nostromo*, *Almayer's Folly*, or even that lovely book, *Victory*, if Shepherd's Bush can provide the desert island.
> (*The Tatler*, December 23, 1937, p. 532)

The bus sequence was the most commented upon moment of *Sabotage*—both at the time and since—although no other reviewer was quite as blunt as "E.H.E." (*Sunderland Echo*): "The suspense is overwhelming. One lives with that bomb for every second of the time. It is almost a relief when it goes off and hurtles Desmond and a bus load of people into eternity" (*Sunderland Echo and Shipping Gazette*, March 9, 1937, p. 5).

A consequence of the reception of *Sabotage* as "a Hitchcock film" was the marginalization of Joseph Conrad in many of the reviews. Graham Greene was an exception in this regard. Some reviews did not even mention Conrad; others merely noted in passing that the film was based on *The Secret Agent*. The relatively few reviews that offered a comparison between the film and its source text tended to agree that Hitchcock had downplayed the psychological character study of the novel in preference for an exploration of the mechanics of suspense. *The Times*, for example, maintained that

> Mr Hitchcock concentrates so much on the building up of an atmosphere of suspense, with typical and rather too frequent expressions of Cockney humour, that he does not realize how much he is

thinning the atmosphere by becoming absorbed in the timing and theatrical mechanics of the bomb. He neglects the character of Verloc which Conrad made so subtle and contradictory.

(December 7, 1936, p. 12)

The British Film Institute's *Monthly Film Bulletin* noted the same point: "Whereas in the book interest centres on the psychology of Verloc, the film is mainly a drama of suspense. The individual genius of Hitchcock is very clearly shown in the distinctive and original direction" (December 1936, p. 213). The *Worthing Herald* was one of the few sources to attach any cultural currency to the Conrad connection: "This film is strong meat, it grips and enthrals. The name of Conrad is sufficient indicator of the excellence of the story: there isn't a dull moment in the whole 70 minute run of the picture" (March 6, 1937, p. 7).

There is one aspect of the contemporary reception discourse of *Sabotage* that anticipated later theoretical preoccupations of Hitchcock scholarship: its realism. It seems unusual today to describe Hitchcock as a realist director when so much Hitchcock scholarship—exemplified by Laura Mulvey (1975) and William Rothman (1983)—has highlighted the oneiric quality of his films. However, the discursive terms in which contemporary British critics understood realism were not the same as later philosophical interventions in film theory. Realism was understood not in a psychological sense but rather in terms of an authenticity in background and detail. Even Grierson realized that "Hitchock is the only English director who can put the English poor on the screen with any verisimilitude" (Hardy 1981: 110). A recurring theme of contemporary reviews of *Sabotage* was the authenticity of the London settings. The review from the *Chester Chronicle* already quoted felt that the locations "give verisimilitude to the film, which is shot" exclusively in the workaday world of London" (March 20, 1937, p. 12). The *Worthing Gazette* declared that "it is the direction of Alfred Hitchcock that lifts this film clean out of the ordinary. Hitchcock has a flair for finding film drama in the smallest incidents of everyday life, and he has employed it to great effect in *Sabotage*" (March 10, 1937, p. 3). P. L. Mannock compared the "real" London of *Sabotage* favorably with the fictional "Everytown" of Korda's production of *Things to Come* (1936):

Unlike H. G. Wells, with his "Everytown," he [Hitchcock] knows the vivid force of putting real places on the screen. The Zoo Acquarium, the Lord Mayor's Show [Fig. 8.2], Chelsea Power Station and a recognisable London figure strongly in this tense melodrama of Scotland Yard shadowing the perpetrators of a series of explosions.

(*Daily Herald*, December 4, 1936, p. 17)

The only example I have found of this discourse being questioned is by the film correspondent of the *Yorkshire Post*, who responded to an interview with Hitchcock while he was making *Sabotage* in which the director was quoted as saying "I maintain that reality is the most important factor in the making of a successful film": "I am a confirmed admirer of Mr Hitchcock's gifts, but I should not have thought that in his 'thrillers' he was aiming at 'reality.' The excitement they offer seems to me artificial, dreamlike, and it often suffers, I have felt, from the incoherence of a dream" (July 14, 1936, p. 8).

Sabotage has continued to divide opinion in subsequent critical assessments. For many Hitchcock scholars, it tends to be regarded as an interesting failure that does not fit into the overall pattern of his Gaumont-British films. William Rothman, for example, contends that "*Sabotage* is not a major achievement. It does not successfully integrate its moments of horror with the theatricality demanded by the Hitchcock thriller format, which for the first time seems to constrict rather than liberate Hitchcock" (1982: 175). Charles Barr finds the disparate elements of the film problematic: "*Sabotage* is at once

Figure 8.2 Putting on the Lord Mayor's Show: the authentic London admired by critics in *Sabotage* was largely a cinematic sleight of hand.

a political thriller, a Conrad adaptation, and a psychodrama, and the three layers don't fully mesh; in a sense, it is delivering three stories in one, in a rich and uneven narrative that lasts barely 75 minutes" (1999: 175). In contrast, Raymond Durgnat considers *Sabotage* "the profoundest film of Hitchcock's thriller period, and perhaps of his career" (1974: 137). And Neil Sinyard concurs that "the solidity of the settings and supporting characterizations, the ruthless outrageousness of its plotting, and the tragic and ironic love story that is its core, give the film a profundity and compassion beyond anything Hitchcock made in this country" (Sinyard 1983: 35).

If there is a discernible trend within more recent scholarship, it has been the identification of *Sabotage* as an early instance of Hitchcock's meta-cinematic apparatus. Hitchcock criticism has long since claimed the films of his American maturity such as *Rear Window* (1954) and *Vertigo* (1958) as being "about cinema": others, including Marant Cohen (1995) and Barr (1999), have drawn attention to the oneiric, dreamlike quality of some of the British films. *Sabotage*, a film in which much of the narrative is set in the space of a slighty rundown suburban London cinema, is ripe for such a reading, most obviously in the killing of Verloc (Oskar Homolka), in which Mrs Verloc (Sylvia Sidney) appears to be acting in a near trancelike state (see Fig. 8.3). For scholars such as Cohen and Mark Osteen (2014), there is something else at play. Hitchcock's self-conscious highlighting of the "filmic" qualities of the "literary" text signals his authorial identity in a film that, perhaps because of the novel's status as a "classic," is closer tied to the source text than most of his others. And that this context informs the changes that Hitchcock—and his writers Charles Bennett, Ian Hay, and Alma Reville—made to the source text. While the strictures of

Figure 8.3 Hitchcock at the movies: The director on the set of the Bijou Cinema in *Sabotage*.

censorship would have prevented the film's Verloc from being the owner of a pornographic bookshop, the decision to turn him into a cinema-owner, rather than any other slightly disrespectable lower-middle-class profession, seems particularly noteworthy.[2]

In *Hitchcock's British Films*, Maurice Yacowar contends that "*Sabotage* was immediately hailed as a brilliant work and has lost very little ground since" (1977: 206). In fact, as this chapter has shown, its contemporary reception in Britain was rather more mixed, some reviewers claiming it as an outstanding British film while others were more equivocal. Where the contemporary reviews were united, however, was in their assessment that *Sabotage* was very much Hitchcock's film: that it bore his unique stylistic imprint and distinctive directorial flourishes. This prompts us to reconsider the relationship between Hitchcock's British films and the auteur theory. It had previously seemed to me that auteur-focused readings of Hitchcock's British films (such as Yacowar's) were problematic insofar as they took a critical construction of Hitchcock formed in the 1950s and 1960s, and based largely on his later American films, and applied it retrospectively to the British films, highlighting those aspects that fit the auteur Hitchcock and marginalizing those that did not. However, the discursive language of contemporary reviews was very similar to what later became the auteur theory, even if the term itself yet held no currency. British critics had recognized Hitchcock as an auteur long before *Cahiers du Cinéma* or Andrew Sarris.

Notes

1 Some local newspapers simply adapted the sample reviews of films suggested in exhibitors' press books. This accounts for the very similar wording of the reviews in numerous local papers, including the *East Kent Times* ("The film portrays in dramatic fashion the efforts of terrorists to paralyze the working of London, and the ways in which the menace is finally stamped out by the forces of law and order"; May 1, 1937, p. 3), the *Peterborough Standard* ("It portrays in dramatic fashion the efforts of terrorists to paralyse the workings of a great city, and the way in which the menace is finally stamped out by the forces of law and order"; March 5, 1937, p. 8), and the Boston *Mercury and Guardian* ("Alfred Hitchcock brings the authentic London scene to the screen in *Sabotage*, which portrays in dramatic fashion the efforts of terrorists to paralyse the workings of a great city and the way in which the menace is finally stamped out by the forces of law and order"; May 28, 1937, p. 9).

2 Earlier studies of *Sabotage* as a novel-into-film adaptation, such as Anderegg (1975), were more concerned with the hoary old chestnut of fidelity to the source text.

References

Anderegg, M. A. (1975) "Conrad and Hitchcock: *The Secret Agent* inspires *Sabotage*," *Literature/Film Quarterly*, 3 (3): 215–225.
Barr, C. (1999) *English Hitchcock*, Moffat: Cameron & Hollis.
Chapman, J. (2025) "'The Director of the Film Is the Man who Chiefly Matters': How British Critics Invented the Auteur Theory," in R. Shail and S. Hall (eds), *Film Critics and British Film Culture: New Shots in the Dark*, Edinburgh: Edinburgh University Press (forthcoming). pp. 23–37.
Durgnat, R. (1974) *The Strange Case of Alfred Hitchcock; or The Plain Man's Hitchcock*, London: Faber & Faber.
Hardy, F. (ed.) (1981) *Grierson at the Movies*, London: Faber & Faber.
Leavis, F. R. (1948) *The Great Tradition*, London: Chatto & Windus.
Marantz Cohen, P. (1995) *Alfred Hitchcock: The Legacy of Victorianism*, Lexington, Ky.: University Press of Kentucky.

McGilligan, P. (2003) *Alfred Hitchcock*: *A Light in Darkness and Light*, Chichester: John Wiley & Sons.
Mulvey, L. (1975) "Visual Pleasure and Narrative Cinema," *Screen*, 16 (3): 6–18.
Osteen, M. (2000) "'It Doesn't Pay to Antagonize the Public': *Sabotage* and Hitchcock's Audience," *Literature/Film Quarterly*, 28 (4): 259–268.
Osteen, M. (ed.) (2014) *Hitchcock and Adaptation*: *On the Page and Screen*, Lanham, Md.: Rowman & Littlefield.
Palmer, R. B., and D. Boyd (eds) (2011) *Hitchcock at the Source*: *The Auteur as Adaptor*, Albany, NY: State University of New York Press.
Parkinson, D. (ed.) (1993) *The Graham Greene Film Reader*: *Mornings in the Dark*, Manchester: Carcanet Press.
Rohmer, É., and C. Chabrol (1988) *Hitchcock*: *The First Forty-Four Films*, trans. Stanley Hochman, New York: Ungar.
Rotha, P. (1967) *The Film Till Now*: *A Survey of World Cinema*, rev. edn with new material by R. Griffith, London: Spring Books.
Rothman, W. (1982) *Hitchcock*: *The Murderous Gaze*, Cambridge, Mass.: Harvard University Press.
Sedgwick, J. (1996) "Michael Balcon's Close Encounter with the American Market, 1934–36," *Historical Journal of Film, Radio and Television*, 16 (3): 333–348.
Sedgwick, J. (2000) *Popular Filmgoing in 1930s Britain*: *A Choice of Pleasures*, Exeter: University of Exeter Press.
Sinyard, N. (1983) *The Films of Alfred Hitchcock*, London: Admiral Books.
Spoto, D. (1983) *Alfred Hitchcock*: *The Dark Side of Genius*, London: William Collins.
Truffaut, F., with H. G. Scott (1986) *Hitchcock*, London: Paladin.
Yacowar, M. (1977) *Hitchcock's British Films*, Hamden, Conn.: Archon Books.

Chapter 9

The Man Who Knew Too Much (1956) as a Critical Lens on American Culture

Paula Marantz Cohen

Alfred Hitchcock's career spans the life of classical narrative film. But the relevance of his movies extends beyond this. They continue to be enjoyed by film enthusiasts and studied by aspiring filmmakers. They also continue to be the subject of interpretive analysis by critics. To me, the hallmark of Hitchcock's greatness is this enduringly interpretive fertility. A great work of art is never used up; it continues to yield insight that may have never been dreamt of by its creator and that continues long after that creator's death and in the wake of even the most radical societal change. This is true for Hitchcock, specifically for those films that were made at the height of his career and popularity when the resources available to him were greatest and when he had acquired enough access to American culture to understand it while still being new enough to the country to view it with fresh eyes.

The single film that Hitchcock remade, *The Man Who Knew Too Much*, offers an especially productive lens in this respect. It marks itself as a specifically American film while also being the remake of a film made in Britain earlier in Hitchcock's career. In the twenty-two years between the 1934 film and the 1956 remake, the vocabulary of film criticism came to encompass a host of new variables and, more importantly, Hitchcock's interest and investment in his adopted country deepened. By remaking this film as a specifically American film set abroad (in Marrakesh and in London), he was able to tap into ideas regarding American exceptionalism, globalization, tensions in patriarchal culture and gender norms that would evolve long after this film debuted and, indeed, long after his death. While all of Hitchcock's films have the capacity for sustained insight into our culture, this film seems uniquely able to support this kind of insight. We can talk about Hitchcock now with as much vigor as we did fifty years ago; through this film in particular, we can trace what is seen to be important in American culture.

The 1934 version of *The Man Who Knew Too Much* was made at a crucial point in Hitchcock's British career. He had successfully made the transition to sound, found his footing in the suspense genre, and established his characteristic pacing and humor (Krohn 2000). The film was widely praised by both British and American newspapers. The 1956 remake was initially less well received. This was a period when the Hollywood film was generally seen as lacking in artistry and ideas. The popular newspapers of the day liked it with reservations, giving the advantage to the earlier, British version (Kapsis 1992: 43–45).

In the 1934 film, the female character occupied the central role. She was an expert shot, engaged in an international skeet-shooting competition, and was shown to be part of an elite British social set, high-spirited and irreverent with regard to established behavior. By extension, she was also an unconventional wife and mother. The film was short (75 minutes), fast-paced, and packed with humorous bits. The 1956 film, by contrast, seemed, initially at least, more conventional, even, one could say, less Hitchcockian. It was two hours in length and was criticized at the time for lacking the pace and suspense as well as the quirky humor of the British original. This tells us something about how we judge contemporaneous works of art, failing to see the ways in which they may push against established conventions or evolve beyond, even transcend, earlier work. In the case of the 1956 film, the variables that made it seem conventional at its release were the very variables that, from a somewhat later vantage point (or from a perspective outside of American society) would take on more resonance and mark it as an exceptionally interesting and original work.

I should add that a group of critics at the time of the 1956 release focused its criticism of the film on its status as a commercial Hollywood product. This strand of loosely Marxist critique pervaded so-called highbrow circles and was propounded by the *New Yorker* and *The Nation*. For these publications, the use of Technicolor and VistaVision, along with the presence of major film stars in the principal roles, was seen as a form of vulgar popularizing. In an apparent concession to its entertainment value, the *New York Times*'s review by Bosley Crowther praised the film: "Even in mammoth VistaVision, the old Hitchcock thriller-stuff has punch" (*New York Times*, May 17, 1956, p. 37).

By the mid 1960s, the view that the 1956 film lacked craftmanship began to undergo revision and be seen as a layered, character-based exploration, i.e., "more than a thriller," as François Truffaut would observe in his interview with the filmmaker. Hitchcock supported this view when he stated that the earlier film was the work of "a talented amateur and the second was made by a professional" (1985: 89). (Read in the context of his conversation with Truffaut, it may seem that Hitchcock was pandering to or momentarily swayed by the perspective of his interviewer.)

The elevation of Hitchcock as an auteur by *Cahiers du Cinéma* critics like Truffaut helped this film become influential in other circles. Yet even with the ascendency of his American-made films under auteur theory, the 1956 *Man Who Knew Too Much* was not placed in the "first rank" of Hitchcock films during this period of reassessment. Robin Wood's 1965 *Hitchcock's Films*, for example, doesn't deal directly with it (an omission rectified in his revised 1989 *Hitchcock's Films Revisited*).

In the 1970s and 1980s, a new kind of revisionism sets in for Hitchcock's films with the advent of feminist theory. Laura Mulvey uses Hitchcock's Hollywood films as exemplars of the destructive and coercive "male gaze" of classic narrative cinema. The 1956 *Man Who Knew Too Much*, with its use of the male star, James Stewart, and of the ultra-wholesome Doris Day, contributes to this critique. Both William Rothman and Ina Rae Hark make a point of highlighting the more patriarchal aspects of the American remake in comparison to the 1934 version with its much more central and powerful female protagonist.

Yet, as Kapsis notes, the rerelease of the film in theaters in the mid 1980s ushered in a more positive view, helped by the general rise of attention to Hitchcock as an auteur (1992: 150–154). Moreover, the feminist perspective denigrating Hitchcock was complicated by Tania Modleski, Robin Wood, and others (including myself) in the late 1980s, 1990s, and beyond, who saw Hitchcock's Hollywood films as engaging in a critique of patriarchy alongside a support of it. *The Man Who Knew Too Much* could now be understood as an anatomy of marriage and gender roles as they exist in a patriarchal and conformist society. In a rare exception, Joel W. Finler, writing in 1992, continues to see the 1934 film as superior and the 1956 version as "one of Hitchcock's weakest films," citing earlier critics like Ray Durgnat and John Russell Taylor, who agreed with him. I tend to see Finler's reaction as conditioned by his belief that Hitchcock, during this period, was too intent on reaching a large, international audience (Finler 1992: 110–111).

I would suggest that a more nuanced view of the film becomes more pronounced in the wake of Doris Day's roles following the release of this film, as she became increasingly associated with highly conventionalized, sexually insinuating romantic comedies. (Day's persona, as a perky, virtuous Everywoman, elicited the famous remark by Oscar Levant: "I knew Doris Day before she was a virgin.") Day's role in *The Man Who Knew Too Much* serves as a kind of transition between her earlier career as a singer with big bands and her role as the romantic interest or wife in later romantic comedies. Her films with Rock Hudson are especially emblematic of coercive ideas about patriarchy and heterosexuality (given that Hudson was gay and the studios assiduously promoted him as heterosexual).

In short, in *The Man Who Knew Too Much*, Day seems positioned between her past and future roles: she plays a former celebrity singer who has now settled down to being the wife of a Midwestern physician while still harboring qualities of self-assertion associated with her former life on the New York and London stage. She also draws on her still prominent reputation, and her singing becomes the means by which she saves her child. This positioning retrospectively encourages us to see the strains associated with being an assertive professional woman and being a submissive wife. In reality, Day, like Hudson, was deeply insecure, nothing like the wholesome figures she played on screen (Kaufman 2008)—a façade not explored by Hitchcock in this film but certainly made central to the representation of the female lead in *Vertigo*. Murray Pomerance also sees the film as a playful "Oedipal marriage," given its use of the mother–son bond and compares it with the pathological version of this in the 1951 *Strangers on a Train* (2013: 233). One could also say that it points us forward to the mother–son pathology of *Psycho*.

The above perspective has been extended and further complicated by responses to the 1956 film in the 2000s. These bring to bear more extreme critiques of both mothering and heterosexuality, finding in it motifs that go against the grain of traditionally normative ideas about gender and family. David Greven and Richard Corber have both explored these ideas. Greven sees Hitchcock as showing a marked identification with his female heterosexual characters while also being fascinated by queer male characters (in the case of this film, the character played by Reggie Nalder as the dapper, enigmatically menacing gunman retained to shoot the diplomat in the Royal Albert Hall). Corber sees the film as reflecting Cold War paranoia and homophobia.

At the same time, other issues have come into play as this film has gotten more attention from critics. In 2019, for example, Matthew Bolton looked closely at its structure, using the idea of adaptation as the template. Where the pre-Truffaut assessments of craft were at the expense of the later version, Bolton sees Hitchcock as very much in control of his material (2019: 170). Behind Bolton's treatment are issues in adaptation theory (Smith 1980) in which the relationship between original and adaptation is explored without the sense that one is more authentic or privileged than the other, a perspective of particular value in thinking about the 1956 film.

The film's American inflection, despite (and indeed because of) having no scenes set in America, has also been highlighted. The expansive social critique of postmodern and, particularly, postcolonial criticism informs this analysis. A number of critics have remarked on the McKennas' relationship to the North African setting that opens the film. There is the remark made by young Hank on the way to their hotel in Marrakesh comparing their surroundings to Las Vegas, his statement that his father had "liberated" Africa during the war, and his careless knocking off of the veil of a local woman on a bus (see Fig. 9.1).

Though all this comes from the mouth and actions of a child, it nonetheless rings of smug assumptions that have been passed down to him and that circulate among privileged circles in the West. Also significant is the scene in the Moroccan restaurant where Stewart's character expresses frustration at being unable to sit or eat in Western fashion and, later, in the marketplace, when he is accosted by the French undercover agent whose blackface makeup Stewart's fingers smear as the man, having been stabbed, falls to the ground and whispers his secret message (Fig. 9.2).

These incidents create a context with which to deconstruct white privilege and hegemony even as these things are superficially upheld. Some suggestion of this reading is present in Murray Pomerance's British Film Institute (BFI) treatment of the film, which begins with a reference to Edward Said's *Orientalism*, a text that critiques the tendency of Westerners to artificially exoticize the East. Tatjana Jukić takes this further in drawing a correlation between the way Africa is subordinated to Western influence, values, and power, and the way Day's character, Jo McKenna, is subordinated to her husband.

Another interesting angle on the film has been introduced by Pomerance with regard to class elements in both the 1934 and 1956 versions of the film. He makes note of the decor and clothing in both and pays special attention to speech, observing that the accent, idiom, and style of repartee in the 1934 film reflect Hitchcock's acute awareness of British class distinctions. In the 1956 version, this awareness is repeated during the scenes with the British characters. Upper-class friends of Jo's waiting at the Savoy

Figure 9.1 The McKenna family's eventful arrival to Marrakesh at the beginning of *The Man Who Knew Too Much*. *The Man Who Knew Too Much*, directed by Alfred Hitchcock. © Paramount Pictures 1956. All rights reserved.

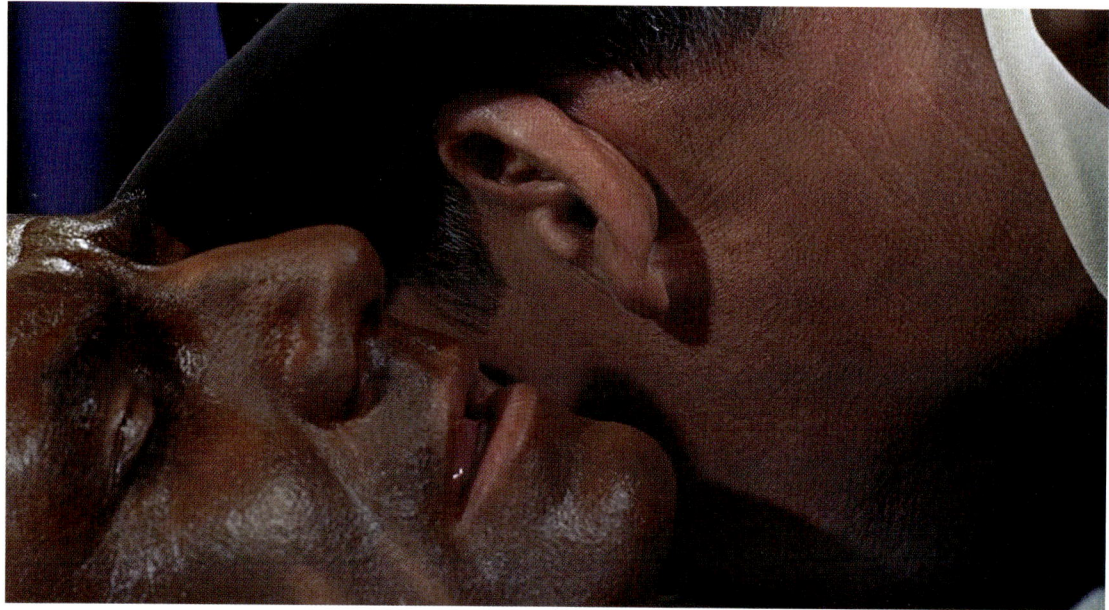

Figure 9.2 The dying Bernard (Daniel Gélin) reveals the assassination plot to a stunned Ben (James Stewart).

contrast in dress, manner, and verbal style the lower-middle-class Draytons whom the McKennas have met in Marrakesh and who kidnap Hank. Yet these distinctions are mostly buried or blurred in this version of the movie. One could argue that American indifference toward class is replaced by a more rigid notion of gender and of American exceptionalism. In a particularly acute Hitchcockian touch that emphasizes the confused power dynamic in marriage, he chooses to give the female character the male nickname "Jo."

The musical and general sound aspects of the film have also come under analysis. The background musical score was composed by Hitchcock's favored musical director Bernard Herrmann, but two pieces written by others stand out as exceptionally memorable. One is "Que Será, Será," sung twice by Day—first in a duet of Jo with her son; later, as Jo tries to communicate with him when he is imprisoned in an upstairs room of the embassy, and he whistles an accompaniment. The song, by Jay Livingston and Ray Evans, won the Academy Award for best song in 1956 and continues to be a familiar standard. The second piece is "Storm Clouds Cantata" by Arthur Benjamin, with Herrmann doing the conducting that also figured in the 1934 version of the film and that was reused to cue the attempted assassination attempt (Fig. 9.3).

Murray Pomerance, in his BFI monograph, is especially eloquent on the subject of sound in this film. He discusses, for example, the use of the cantata over the opening credits:

> the cymbalist's culminating crash [is] artfully mixed by the sound engineers with the humming motor of the Casablanca–Marrakech bus, so that the vehicle is transformed into an echo of the orchestral gesture, an instrumentation. The action thus become orchestral, we are cued for special attention to matters acoustic, not just the pained whine of the bus but the little boy's chatter, the squealing brakes as the driver swerves and the veil is yanked off, the staccato bark of the angry Arab's voice, the calming suavity of Bernard's response: instrumentations all.
>
> (Pomerance 2016: 77)

Figure 9.3 An advertisement for the Royal Albert Hall concert, conducted by Bernard Herrmann.

Pomerance goes on to note how perfectly the sequence in the Royal Albert Hall is orchestrated, with the pistol shot as a kind of instrument in the performance of the work (see Fig. 9.4).

One could say that the orchestration of the event here—a metonym of sorts for the kind of work involved in making a film—is disrupted by Jo McKenna's scream, differentiating the artificially plotted aspect from the human reality where lives can actually be lost or saved through a moment of visceral expression. Elisabeth Weis, in discussing this scene, also notes that both versions of the film are attuned to the interplay of sound and silence and use music effectively. However, she argues that the 1956 version is more sophisticated in preparing the audience for the use of the cantata as the moment for the attempted assassination, reflecting greater awareness and control on Hitchcock's part of how the variables involved could be used to heighten suspense (Weis 1986: 107–108). Jack Sullivan, also discussing how Hitchcock used music in the 1956 version, quotes the filmmaker's statement that he was careful to "not disturb the musical unity of the cantata" in the Royal Albert Hall sequence, playing it at the same volume both in the lobby and inside the theater, while the music sung toward the end of the film by Day is modulated so as to give us a sense of how it would be heard loudly up close in the main area of the embassy and then faintly by the boy, captive in a room upstairs (Sullivan 2011: 223–224; see also Coda A).

This singing by Day, which hearkens back to her character's earlier career, gives her agency and makes possible the successful conclusion. Her first rendering of the song "Que Será, Será," when she dances with Hank, and her second performance in the embassy (Fig. 9.5), to which he responds with whistling, can both be said to establish their bond. This connection between them can be said to override the suppression represented by her husband, who drugs her and originally takes precedence over her in his search for the "wrong" Ambrose Chapel.

Figure 9.4 The assassin plans to mask his gunshot with the crash of Herrmann's cymbals.

Figure 9.5 Jo (Doris Day) sings "Que Será, Será" at the top of her voice, hoping her kidnapped son will hear.

Although *The Man Who Knew Too Much* has not traditionally been included in a discussion of Hitchcock's most revered films such as *Rear Window*, *Vertigo*, and *Psycho*, this too has begun to change. As previously noted, Robin Wood acknowledged his omission and rectified it in his revised *Hitchcock's Films Revisited*. Its recent inclusion in the BFI series is further evidence of its rise in stature. In this monograph, Pomerance sees the film as a complex exploration of American identity and culture. He notes that it prepares the way for *Vertigo*, which explores how artifice and stereotype function to prop up but also to erode the credibility of the dominant culture. *Vertigo* will cast the same actor, Stewart, in the lead as the mentally unbalanced detective protagonist. That representation helps us see the gaps in the persona of the superrational Dr. McKenna, a man who must drug his wife in order to control his own rising sense of panic. Here is a case where a later film can be said to gloss an earlier one. Robin Wood had suggested something along the same lines when he noted that the literal fear of Scottie in *Vertigo* is a repressed fear in *The Man Who Knew Too Much* (1989: 364–365).

It is now possible to read Hitchcock's American films as a kind of extended commentary on his own family, which had settled in America, and a perspective on the growth to adulthood of his daughter Patricia. I have argued in my book, *Alfred Hitchcock: The Legacy of Victorianism*, for the significance of the filmmaker changing the kidnapped child from a girl in the early version to a boy in the later one as a way to distance himself from the anxiety associated with his daughter's maturing and separation. The fact that Patricia Hitchcock decided to become an actress, against the preference of her father, may have felt like a kind of kidnapping by the very industry that had shaped his career and made his fortune (P. M. Cohen 1995: 122).

Finally, I would note that there are elements in the 1956 film that point to trends in the future of representation. The use of Doris Day's persona, for example, strikes me as a self-conscious move that would become more pronounced in avant-garde circles with filmmakers from Robert Altman to Andy Warhol who capitalized upon celebrity and the glamour and artifice of the movie star in their work. The song, "Que Será, Será," sung by Day in the movie, would, as noted, go on to top the music charts, reflecting a symbiosis of media, arguably begun with "Somewhere Over the Rainbow" in *The Wizard of Oz* in 1942 (O'Leary 2021). This points toward the kind of intensive tie-in marketing that would be fully exploited as movies became more expensive to make and linked to more saturated forms of promotion. The film also presents a model of American family life already familiar to audiences from recent television sitcoms like *Father Knows Best*, which debuted in 1954 (followed by *Leave It to Beaver* in 1957 and *The Donna Reed Show* in 1958). The film uses some of the same wholesome imagery associated with the nuclear family in these shows while subtly pointing out the fissures and darker implications of that family model (something Hitchcock had already explored in his earlier American film, *Shadow of a Doubt* in 1943). Another essay on this film might place it alongside the sitcoms of the era and consider how Hitchcock's own entry into television in 1955 with *Alfred Hitchcock Presents* often reflects some of the tensions, present in the 1956 film, in a more condensed form and using his own persona to supply ironic commentary.

It is a tribute to Hitchcock's greatness as a filmmaker that *The Man Who Knew Too Much* has been able to support such evolving and multifaceted critical analysis. It speaks to us about things we care deeply about: family, nation, the vulnerability of children, the nature of gender roles, the tensions and sacrifices that accompany a career, the role of espionage and terrorism in pursuit of ideals, the issue of trust, and the general unpredictability of life. But it is also, as *New York Times* reviewer Crowther had noted in 1956, an enormously entertaining film. The ability to link penetrating social criticism with mass entertainment is a feat that only the greatest artists are able to accomplish.

References

Bolton, M. (2019) "The Director Who Knew Himself: Remaking the Romance in *The Man Who Knew Too Much*," *Hitchcock Annual*, vol. 23, pp. 165–200.

Cohen, P. M. (1995) *Alfred Hitchcock: The Legacy of Victorianism*, Lexington, Ky.: University of Kentucky Press, 1995.

Cohen, T. (1995) "Beyond 'The Gaze': Žižek, Hitchcock, and the American Sublime," *American Literary History*, 7 (2): 350–378.

Corber, R. (1993) *In the Name of National Security*: *Hitchcock*, *Homophobia*, *and the Political Construction of Gender in Postwar America*, Durham, NC: Duke University Press.

Finler, J. W. (1992) *Hitchcock in Hollywood*, New York: Continuum.

Greven, D. (2013) "Cruising, Hysteria, Knowledge: *The Man Who Knew Too Much* (1956)," *Psycho-Sexual*, Austin, Tex.: University of Texas Press.

Griffin, M. (2018) *All That Heaven Allows*: *A Biography of Rock Hudson*, New York: HarperCollins.

Hark, I. R. (1999) "Revealing Patriarchy: Why Hitchcock Remade *The Man Who Knew Too Much*," in W. Raubicheck and W. Srebnick (eds), *Hitchcock's Rereleased Films*: *From Rope to Vertigo*, Detroit, Mich.: Wayne State University Press, pp. 209–220.

Jukić, T. (2013) "*The Man Who Knew Too Much*: Žižek and the Balkans," *European Journal of English Studies*, 17 (2): 160–175.

Kapsis, R. E. (1992) *Hitchcock*: *The Making of a Reputation*, Chicago, Ill.: University of Chicago Press.

Kaufman, D. (2008) *Doris Day*: *The Untold Story of the Girl Next Door*, London: Virgin Books.

Krohn, W. (2000) *Hitchcock at Work*, New York: Phaidon Press.

Mulvey, L. (1975) "Visual Pleasure and Narrative Cinema," *Screen*, 16 (2): 6–18.

O'Leary, B. (2021) "A Brief History of Movie Tie-In Singles," Medium, August 26. https://medium.com/fanfare/a-brief-history-of-movie-tie-in-singles-75f8b2e87725

Pomerance, M. (2013) *Alfred Hitchcock's America*, Cambridge: Polity Press.

Pomerance, M. (2016) *The Man Who Knew Too Much*, London: British Film Institute and Bloomsbury Publishing.

Rothman, W. (1984) *Hitchcock*: *The Murderous Gaze*, Cambridge, Mass.: Harvard University Press.

Said, E. (1978) *Orientalism*, New York: Pantheon Books.

Smith, B. H. (1980) "Narrative Versions, Narrative Theories," *Critical Inquiry*, 7 (1): 213–236.

Sullivan, J. (2011) "Hitchcock and Music," in T. Leitch and L. Poague (eds), *A Companion to Alfred Hitchcock*, Oxford: Blackwell Publishing, pp. 219–236.

Truffaut, F., with H. G. Scott (1985) *Hitchcock/Truffaut*, rev. edn, New York: Simon & Schuster.

Weis, E. (1986) "Consolidation of a Classical Style: *The Man Who Knew Too Much*," in M. Deutelbaum and L. Poague (eds), *A Hitchcock Reader*, Ames, Iowa: Iowa State University Press, pp. 102–108.

Wood, R. (1969) *Hitchcock's Films*, New York: Castle Books.

Wood, R. (1989) *Hitchcock's Films Revisited*, New York: Columbia University Press.

Chapter 10
"She Isn't Quite Herself Today"
Psycho (1960) before and after Queer Theory

David Greven

"We all go a little mad sometimes—haven't you?" Norman Bates (Anthony Perkins) says to the doomed Marion Crane (Janet Leigh) in Alfred Hitchcock's 1960 film *Psycho*, both making a declaration and pleading for solidarity. The solidarity between these characters emerges from the madness they share, hers a fugue state, his a state of mind; the distinctions between them, however, would appear to be more significant, distinctions that specifically lie in the representation of their gendered and sexual identities. *Psycho* famously kills off its main character Marion halfway through the picture, when she has stopped off at the Bates Motel, run by the shy young man Norman, set up as her protector and rescuer (see Fig. 10.1). Marion stole $40,000 from her boss's client in hopes of being able to free her lover Sam (John Gavin) from the debt that he claims prevents him from marrying her; she is murdered in the shower right after she has decided to go back to Phoenix, Arizona and return the money. Ostensibly, Marion is killed by Norman's pathologically jealous and possessive mother, known as "Mrs. Bates" or "Mother." When Lila Crane (Vera Miles), Marion's sister, faces off against Norman Bates, revealed as the true "Mrs. Bates," at the climax, the film stages a confrontation that will be endlessly replayed in the genre of the slasher-horror film, *Psycho*'s most obvious cinematic legacy.

While its seemingly central story about a lonely, marriage-minded, and increasingly desperate woman's odyssey across dark nighttime highways demands continuous analysis, the film's chief influence lies in its particular configuration of recurring tropes of the slasher-horror genre: the sexually confused, gender-bending, ultimately inscrutable young man capable of murderous violence, usually directed against women; the disturbing and herself murderous mother who shields her son as she unsheathes her own killing tools; and the female investigator. The slasher-film genre, pioneered by John Carpenter's *Halloween* (1978), makes *Psycho* its template, as masked killers such as Michael Myers go on creative killing sprees, largely targeting sexually active teens.

The film critic David Thomson holds *Psycho* responsible for the cinematic bloodbath that occurred in its wake—not only for the bloody mayhem of the slasher film but also for the ways in which American culture has become inured to graphic violence, indiscriminately rendered. I have a certain sympathy for Thomson's argument here. Murder has indeed become a disquietingly obsessive trope in entertainment's

Figure 10.1 Anthony Perkins' Norman Bates in *Psycho*.
Psycho, directed by Alfred Hitchcock. © Shamley Productions 1960

diverse fields—with film, television, news channels, and endless cable shows devoted to the subject. A routine episode of any TV crime series contains information and imagery about human savagery so graphic as to seem pornographic.

In order to lay the blame for this at Hitchcock's door, however, Thomson reverts to a view of the artist that one might have imagined Robin Wood disabused us of in the 1960s. He emphasizes Hitchcock's stated view of *Psycho* as "a fun picture," indeed a funhouse. While *Psycho* has been read by some as a black comedy, especially given its lines such as Norman Bates's "Mother isn't quite herself today," few audience-goers would describe the film as "fun." Not only the infamous shower murder and its brutality but also the film's somber tone make an impact on the viewer, one deepened by the film's bleak finale where the death drive wins, Mother's skull face, superimposed on that of the once sympathetic Norman, its signature. Thomson does make an important point about the film in one of the last chapters: the "loneliness is more interesting in *Psycho*, and more pioneering, than the violence, the sex, or the terrific assertion of 'pure' cinema" (2009: 128).

Psycho's reception history indexes the emergence of queer theory as a methodology. The film was received initially as a "perverse" text, a work in poor taste that uneasily combined black humor and unprecedented graphic content, in this case related primarily to violence but also to sexuality. The film's fusion of unsettling, transgressive themes caused a ripple effect in criticism, leading critics to struggle over its specific fusion of female-centered narrative, quasi-explicit treatment of homosexuality, gender-bending themes and fears, and a tone that hovered over or oscillated between comedy and bleak pessimism. The film was then read as a homophobic text in the era of Vito Russo's *The Celluloid Closet* and the first AIDS decade, with readings that focused on the images of Norman Bates as "swishy" and mincing, adding to the view of the film as phobic towards the effeminate male and therefore same-sex desire (a welter of concerns that clearly need to be unpacked). The third phase of reception heralded the film as queer and even gay-affirming. More recently, the film has come to be viewed as an anti-trans text.

This chapter has two goals. First, I will explore *Psycho* as a self-reflexive work that critically analyzes its own gendered themes. It conducts this self-analysis by establishing that its seemingly distinct narrative halves—heterosexual female and queer male, respectively—are deeply imbricated. Second, I will consider the film's critical reception as a metonymic genealogy of queer and trans theory.

Bird by Bird: Phallic Mothers, Vulture Mothers

Psycho is a grim vision of American life, by turns tormenting, terrifying, and heartbreaking. But it is also an exciting film, an excitement that emerges, I argue, from its paired subversive interests in, on the one hand, a woman who acts on her desires, even if in so doing she meets with disastrous consequences, and, on the other, a man whose sexual identity is highly marked by tropes of gender ambiguity, a male figure who is represented as queer in all of the multivalent senses of this term. A madwoman and a queer male each get a chance to have film narrative all to themselves; if the conservatism of the film lies in the fates that await each of the characters, its radicalism emerges from the opportunities the film grants itself to explore both female sexuality and queer sexuality, especially in relation to each other, sexualities that are both abnegated within patriarchy.

The violence with which *Psycho*'s narrative splits into two distinct parts, the woman's narrative transforming into the male's, is powerfully allegorized by the onscreen violence of the film's famous shower murder sequence, a montage sequence that literally cuts film into bits. While concerns with gender and sexuality link the film's intersecting narratives, these concerns also appear to undergo a profound transformation in the second half. Norman's queer one would seem to be violently opposed to Marion's heterosexual female one. As a woman's narrative transforms into a queer male's narrative, the woman must be annihilated. It would appear that the two halves of this film are irreconcilable, that the woman's narrative must cede to the male's. I am revising the paradigms of Raymond Bellour, who argues that *Psycho* fulfils the demands of oedipal narrative by enforcing a transition from the female-dominated narrative to a male-dominated one. Marion Crane's "neurosis" cedes to Norman Bates's "psychosis" (2000: 238–261).

Yet, while the differences between these two halves of the film must be noted, there is, ultimately, a way in which the film serves one continuous, organic narrative with no real disruption in theme, only one in audience identification with the protagonist. This shift in the locus of audience identification is so vividly, violently enacted by the murder of Marion that it effectively obscures the consistency with which the film pursues what is ultimately revealed as its major theme: the triumph of the phallic feminine. This is certainly a strange theme for a film that features as its central sequence the murder of a woman; but then again, during this sequence and for much of the film, the audience believes, or is assumed to believe, that an elderly woman marshals the massive physical force to annihilate a young woman, as well as an adult male detective (Arbogast). Marion's agency in the first half of the film is depicted as active even as her wild, contradictory actions suggest the feminine malady of hysteria. The character of Lila Crane (Vera Miles), Marion's sister, is, if anything, even more forthright and driven than Marion, a woman who acts, moves forward, demands and acquires agency.

Norman's queer male narrative is itself colonized by the forces of the feminine—specifically, of the phallic feminine—in a way that extends the suggestions of phallic femininity in Marion: The character of Mother, as Norman imagines her, is a prime example of the phallic mother, vulturelike in her associations with menace and death, Medusan in her power to kill. What we have in *Psycho*, ultimately, are two distinctly gendered narratives that are nevertheless also, despite the genuine differences between them, one narrative of phallic femininity, or perhaps more properly the varieties of phallic femininity.[1]

What specifically concerns me in *Psycho*, then, is the way in which the film constructs the queer male as the opponent of both femininity and of the heterosexual order but, more importantly, represents femininity as a supremely powerful force that subsumes male identity. If misogynistic and homophobic elements inhere in this work, there is also something of a radical statement being made in terms of the film's interests in the feminine and the queer, even as they are shown to be in opposition to one another. To understand what *Psycho* is saying about women and homosexual men, you have to get it from the Mother—that is, the Mother half of Norman's mind.

If we are always already studying male fantasies of women here, in Hitchcock's hands male fantasy itself becomes the subject of analysis; *Psycho* is a self-analysis that foregrounds the central preoccupations of his cinema. Because of Hitchcock's greatness as a filmmaker and because of the peculiar obsessions of his oeuvre, his films offer an extraordinary opportunity to study misogyny and homophobia in works that foreground an awareness of their social and psychic costs even as they display misogynistic and homophobic tendencies.

That *Psycho* is a self-analysis is a point worth emphasizing. Many critics have described Hitchcock as a self-reflexive filmmaker. To cite a recent example, Sebastian Smoliński discusses *The Lodger: A Story of the London Fog* (1927), with justification often called the first true Hitchcock film, in terms of the "metapicture" and "the self-reflexive quality of the image" (2024: 30–31). The self-consciousness of *Psycho* is not unique to this work, given that we can say that *Rear Window* and *Vertigo*, among other Hitchcock films, are deeply self-conscious, pursuing a critique of their central themes of voyeurism, obsession, and fantasies of femininity. But *Psycho*'s self-consciousness is tied to an explosive series of cultural and aesthetic shifts. Its gory aspects, however subtly conveyed, and the frank sexuality of its opening scene alone mark the film as a break with the Production Code and signal the imminent demise of the studio system. Marion Crane's single-minded and isolated journey bespeaks a new agency for cinematic women, even if the road movie on which she embarks leads to Hell. Norman Bates's descent into an unreachable void of psychosis echoes Marion's journey towards death. The film at numerous points conveys its understanding of the paired and parallel trajectories of these dual protagonists, and in conveying this self-awareness, *Psycho* makes it possible to theorize its knowingness about shifts in gender and sexuality as a form of queer critique. A brief examination of the film yields insights into this dimension of its sensibility.

When the Woman Acts

Marion's desire for the man she loves and hopes to marry, Sam Loomis, is what propels her descent into madness; her narrative is specifically concerned with the ways in which her acting out on her desires not only leads to her death but also draws out complex and disturbing aspects of her character. The film is a strikingly ambivalent statement about female sexuality, especially when considered in terms of Hitchcock's fascination with the female star throughout his films, a fascination given a thorough deconstruction in *Psycho*, which so brazenly dispatches the female star early on.

When the camera swoops, from its omniscient, panning views of the city of Phoenix, Arizona, in the opening shots, into a hotel room, it discovers a couple, Marion and Sam, who have just had sex on their lunch hour (Marion's lunch is uneaten). Marion's narrative will be about restoring the unseen scene of heterosexual fulfillment, a presumptive Paradise from which she, and the viewers, by the time of the postcoital scene with which the film narrative proper begins, have already been expulsed. In her narrative, Marion not only represents femininity but also stands in for the heterosexual couple, her boyfriend Sam being crucially introduced in the opening scene and not seen again until after Marion's onscreen death, though he is heard in voice-over meant to simulate Marion's interior mental dialogue. Yet, as a woman who acts out on her desires, making a bid for social agency, she deviates from normative codes of gendered identity. Her propulsive quest for Sam, legitimate sex (i.e., sanctified by marriage), and for marriage wrests narrative away from the patriarchal order, which then makes every determined effort to regain control, as evinced by her famous encounters with her boss, who does a double take when he sees her fleeing with the Texas oilman Cassidy's $40,000; the highway cop with the blindingly opaque sunglasses; the used-car salesman (who unites in her mind with the cop, who physically reappears at the used-car lot, as both inquisitors discuss whether Marion is a "wrong one" in her fantasy); and, it must be added, with Norman, insofar as he represents the punitive force of the law and morality in his obscenely retributive murder of her. What Marion Crane shares with Norman is a flight from gendered normativity; if we all go a little mad sometimes, flights of madness in the film allow Marion access to masculine agency and Norman to feminine identity, mainly in the form of his fantasies of the maternal but also in certain key aspects of his deportment.

The character of Lila Crane, who goes on a search for her sister Marion after her disappearance and suspected robbery, was long an overlooked character. Played by a minor star, Vera Miles, and part of the "shadow couple," in the phrase of Raymond Bellour, of Lila and Sam, the main couple being Marion and Sam, Lila was considered at best the secondary lead. Alexander Doty, however, championed Lila as a "brash, heroic dyke" (2000: 180). In response to Doty's revaluation of Lila, Tania Modleski, author of the great feminist study of Hitchcock, *The Women Who Knew Too Much*, writes,

> I find no evidence in the film that Lila is attracted to women; indeed, she does not interact with any woman in the film … Lila is punished as a woman—for usurping male investigative powers when she discovers the body of Mrs. Bates … And ultimately, dyke or no dyke, Lila needs to be rescued by Marion's lover, Sam.
>
> (Modleski 2015: 165–166)

Carol Clover introduces Lila Crane as prototype for the Final Girl only to qualify her value as such:

> The Final Girl sequence is prefigured, if only rudimentarily, in *Psycho*'s final scenes, in which Lila (Marion's sister) is caught reconnoitering in the Bates mansion and nearly killed. Sam (Marion's boyfriend) detains Norman at the motel while Lila snoops about (taking note of Norman's toys). When she perceives Norman's approach, she flees to the basement. Here she encounters the treated corpse of Mrs. Bates and begins screaming in horror [Fig. 10.2]. Norman busts in and is about to strike when Sam enters and grabs him from behind [Fig. 10.3]. Like her generic sisters, then, Lila is the spunky inquirer into the Terrible Place: the one who first grasps, however dimly, the past and present danger, the one who looks death in the face, and the one who survives the murderer's last stab.
>
> (Clover 2014: 39)

After having persuasively laid out the foundations of the Final Girl in Lila, Clover proceeds to delineate all the ways in which Lila is not a Final Girl. Lila "enters the film midway and is sketchily drawn"; there is no depiction of her act of "self-defense." In contrast, the Final Girl of the slasher is the main character in

Figure 10.2 Lila Crane (Vera Miles) learns the truth.

Figure 10.3 John Gavin's Sam Loomis apprehends Norman in the film's climax.

the film as well as the "Girl Scout, the bookworm, the mechanic. Unlike her girlfriends (and Marion Crane) she is not sexually active." The Final Girl's vigilant watchfulness, her registering of dangers that her friends overlook, verges on "paranoia … Above all she is intelligent and resourceful in a pinch" (Clover 2014: 39).

That Lila currently stands as both the film's secondary lead and decisive figure for both feminist (Clover) and queer (Doty) critique signals something crucial about the volatile energies of *Psycho*, its power to reflect its own moment and a contemporary one. The moment where Lila catches her own reflection in a series of refracted mirror images allegorizes not only her duality—as supporting character and theoretical linchpin—but the film's status as period and postmodern text.

Hitchcock's use of one element of film grammar further emphasizes *Psycho*'s self-consciousness. Extreme close-ups—of Marion while she is driving and being lacerated by punitive voices in her head, of the highway cop who purports to help but only blindingly obliterates with his mirror-shade stare, of Mother's laughing skull face, of Norman's eerie smile at the end as Mother visually aurally, thematically swallows him whole—threaten to break through the screen and devour the viewer. Marion's eerie smile as, in close-up, she listens to the chorus of critical voices in her head while night-driving and Norman's eerie smile when he speaks in Mother's voice at the close are self-reflexive gestures aimed at both trapping and violating the viewer, our sense of safe distance from the screen.

Braudy and Durgnat: Early Queer Theory

Psycho's reception history far exceeds the space I have in this chapter. The film was initially met with apprehension that either amplifies or belies its massive box-office success. "You'd better have a strong stomach," the reviewer for *Time* magazine warned. As Royal S. Brown summarizes, the initial reviews "did not concentrate on the brilliance of the montage" in the shower murder sequence, "nor did they show much awareness of the film's complex interweaving of text and subtext" (1994: 25). Taking the film seriously at the time was something one could admit to only under duress. When Robin Wood submitted his first piece on *Psycho*, anticipating his great book *Hitchcock's Films*, the editor of an English film journal told him that he had apparently failed to get the fact that the film was a joke. (*Cahiers du cinéma* would eventually publish Wood's essay.)

Psycho's volatile themes and images, its knowing self-analysis, drew out early attempts to theorize its gendered and sexual politics, making the film and its critical reception arguably the first queer theory texts. While neither Leo Braudy, best known for his 1976 study *The World in a Frame: What We See in Films*, nor Raymond Durgnat, who wrote *The Strange Case of Alfred Hitchcock* (1974) and a late work devoted to his most famous film, *A Long Hard Look at* Psycho, were specifically invested in wrestling with matters of gender and sexuality in their writings of the 1960s, their essays on *Psycho* from this period revealingly demonstrate that to discuss the film seriously was to theorize gender and sexuality.

Braudy writes critically of the famous series of interviews that the French filmmaker François Truffaut conducted with Hitchcock, resulting in the well-known book. Braudy contends that Truffaut's questions skim the Hitchcockian surface. What particularly interests me is Braudy's treatment of Hitchcock on the romantic and always already heterosexual couple. Identifying Hitchcock's "comedies" and "tragedies" as "almost like genres," he notes that the romantic couple plays a key role in Hitchcock's efforts to bring "his audience from the detachment of irresponsible spectators to the involvement of implicated participants" (Braudy 1968: 24). In the comedies, the couple serves as "surrogates in a series of adventures that turn out happily" (Braudy 1968: 24). In the tragedies, however, matters take a different turn. His tragedies "have no such romantic couple for ease of audience identification and sympathy" (Braudy 1968: 24). Remarking on Truffaut's observation that *Psycho* offers no one with whom the audience can identify, Braudy describes Marion Crane and Sam Loomis as maintaining "a melancholic relation in which sex and money are the prime topics of conversation" (Braudy 1968: 24). There is much more to unpack in this essay, but let me offer one nugget of insight: "Through Hitchcock's manipulation of point of view and moral sympathy, we have entered the shell of his personality and discovered the rooted violence and perverse sexuality that may be in our own natures. Our desire to save Norman is a desire to save ourselves" (Braudy 1968: 27).

From Homophobic to Queer-Affirming to Transphobic

In my book on Hitchcock and queer theory, *Intimate Violence*, I chart the movement from readings of *Psycho* that declare it a homophobic work to readings such as Alexander Doty's, that salvage the film from charges of homophobia to celebrate it as queer and resistant. Because I chart Hitchcock's queer critical history in this book, I will limit my discussion of it to some especially salient moments.

Echoing the early writing of Manny Farber, who condemned Hitchcock for presenting homosexuals negatively (in what was therefore also a notable example of early antihomophobic film criticism, however one feels about Farber's critique), John Hepworth critiques "Hitchcock's Homophobia" in his essay by that name. Hepworth emphasizes the depiction of Norman Bates as effeminate and concludes that the film invites the viewer to read the character in homophobic terms.[2]

Surprisingly enough, the major queer theorists who emerged in the late 1980s and 1990s did not discuss *Psycho* at length. The question of Hitchcock's homophobia animated a crucial, shaping text for queer theory, but it was *Rope* (1949), not *Psycho*, that concerned D. A. Miller in his essay "Anal *Rope*." In 1991, Miller, in an argument too complex to be summarized here, argues that Hitchcock's refusal to make a film with any cuts expresses the director's fused fears of castration and sodomy, figured as the core, defining practice of gay male sexuality (Miller 1991: 134). In his essay "*Rear Window*'s Glasshole," Lee Edelman challenges Laura Mulvey's theory of the male gaze, elaborated in her famous essay "Visual Pleasure and Narrative Cinema," first published in 1975 in *Screen*, by arguing that it is the phobically hidden figure of the anus rather than the castrating effect of the woman's body that bedevils the heterosexual protagonist. Patricia White and Tania Modleski have critiqued these theorists' exclusive emphasis on issues of queer male sexuality, ignoring the roles of women in the films and larger feminist issues.[3]

In his essay "How Queer Is My *Psycho*?" Alexander Doty champions Lila Crane as the lesbian heroine. In making a positive case for a queer, rather than "gay" or "homophobic," *Psycho*, Doty broke new ground in Hitchcock studies, allowing critics to explore the subversive nature of Hitchcock's gendered depictions and their implications for sexuality. Patricia White's writings on *Rebecca* and Lucretia Knapp on *Marnie* offer similarly open-ended explorations of the Hitchcock film's queer possibilities.

In more recent writing on *Psycho*, the issue of the representation of transgendered characters has been viewed as particularly vexed, so much so, in fact, that two critics stage a dialogue in print on this subject, one that sheds valuable light.

In "The New Border War? An Intergenerational Exchange on Bad Trans Horror Objects," an article published in 2022, Dan Vena and Islay Burgess compare notes on trans representation and historical divides within trans commentary. The impetus for their dialogue is Chris Vargas's three-part poster series "Trans Video Store" featured at the Museum of Transgender History & Art (MOTHA) (see Fig. 10.4).[4] The series displays a hand-drawn catalog of videocassette-styled covers of historic trans films. Mimicking staff picks at a local video store, these selections, which include controversial entries such as *Psycho* and *Silence of the Lambs* (dir. Jonathan Demme, 1991), were chosen by Vargas through conversation with other trans individuals and represent the artist's mission to bring "a cohesive visual history of transgender culture into existence."

Vena elaborates,

Figure 10.4 Trans Video Store, Museum of Transgender History & Art (MOTHA).

Artwork: Chris Vargas.

I was motivated to record this dialogue between Burgess and myself because of the initial discomfort I felt toward the Transgender Media Portal's research assistants censoring important horror films from Vargas's depiction of trans cinema history. I was angry, and more than that, I was afraid at the ease at which they, as members of a younger generation, disregarded texts that were meaningful to other (older) trans individuals.

(Vena and Burgess 2022: 189)

Burgess responds

For me, "bad" trans objects are authored by cis creators who, knowingly or not, reinforce harmful stereotypes that make it difficult for trans viewers to identify with these media works. However, I disagree with your framing of my generation's approach to these objects as simply a dismissal. Instead, I think of it as an act of mourning.

(Vena and Burgess 2022: 190)

Psycho vexes the issues both commentators raise. In the infamous psychiatrist's explanation scene after Norman Bates is revealed as the impersonator of Mrs. Bates (see Fig. 10.5), the district attorney, one of the none-too-inspiring officials sternly listening to the psychiatrist Dr Simon's (Simon Oakland) musings, responds to the question Sam Loomis raises as he sits beside Lila Crane, whom he rescued from "Mrs. Bates"/Norman. "Why was he … dressed like that?" Sam asks. The DA responds immediately, before the psychiatrist can, "He's a transvestite," which prompts Dr. Simon's "Ahh, not exactly." The psychiatrist elaborates,

Not exactly. A man who dresses in woman's clothing in order to achieve a sexual change … or satisfaction … is a transvestite. But in Norman's case, he was simply doing everything possible to keep alive the illusion of his mother being alive. And whenever reality came too close, when danger or desire threatened that illusion, he'd dress up, even to a cheap wig he brought. He'd walk about the house, sit in her chair, speak in her voice … He tried to be his mother. [A sad smile.] And now … he is. [A pause.] That's what I meant when I said I got the story from the mother.

Joseph Stefano's screenplay adaptation of Robert Bloch's novel has been justly praised—except for this infamous psychiatrist scene. Robin Wood and Raymond Durgnat have both defended it, however.

As a response to the charges of transphobia, and not in any manner to diminish their importance, I do believe that we need first to address the film's own effort to address the root causes of Norman's illness, including his dressing up in women's clothes when presented as an aspect of his illness. It does us well to remember that the postwar era was heavily marked and shaken up by the published research of Alfred C. Kinsey. Talk of transvestism was in the air, making the DA's response to Sam Loomis understandable if not persuasive. As Joanne Meyerowitz summarizes, Kinsey "saw crossdressing and crossgender identification as male phenomena and used them to speculate about sex differences in the capacity for psychological conditioning. In his usual style, he did not condemn transvestites or transsexuals," although he did "disapprove of the genital surgery requested by male-to-female transsexuals" (Meyerowitz 2001: 72).[5]

Figure 10.5 Dr. Fred Richman (Simon Oakland) discusses Norman's motivation.

Clearly, Kinsey provides no get-out-of-transphobia-jail-free card. I do however believe that *Psycho*'s various phobic aspects need, each one, to be explored and re-situated within the film's historical contexts. To state the obvious, contemporary trans theory was not available to the filmmakers of *Psycho*, even as they made a film within an era that was awash in a new awareness of transgender life, identity, and desire. Christine Jorgensen, who served in the US Army during World War II, became a celebrity in the 1950s when she publicized the sex reassignment surgery she underwent in Europe, becoming the first person known to have done so in the USA. (Irving Rapper made a commercial narrative film about Jorgensen released in the 1970s.)

Psycho, along with works such as *Glen or Glenda* (dir. Ed Wood, 1953) and *Homicidal* (dir. William Castle, 1961), can be considered as the vanguard of the public discussion of transgender issues rather than any kind of definitive statement about them. If we frame *Psycho* as the start of a conversation about trans identity rather than a summary judgment of an identity of which the film could not plausibly be considered aware, we approach it more productively. Overall, and most importantly, *Psycho* remains useful as a work that draws out the theorist of gender and sexuality, in its myriad forms, in us all.

Notes

1 The very conception of phallic femininity is itself, of course, most significantly a male fantasy. In its Freudian elaboration, the phallic feminine is embodied in the disturbing and uncanny figure of the phallic mother. If Freud's concepts are entirely controvertible in terms of actual people and experiential life, they are nevertheless

useful for the study of representation, especially representation that is itself as brazenly Freudian as Hitchcock's films generally are, *Psycho* especially.

2 Hepworth's essay, "Hitchcock's Homophobia," is collected in *Out in Culture: Gay, Lesbian, and Queer Essays on Popular Culture*, edited by Corey K. Creekmur and Alexander Doty (see Hepworth 1995). *Out in Culture* includes both Robin Wood's response to Hepworth and Hepworth's rebuttal to Wood's own.

3 White discusses both Miller's "Anal *Rope*" and Edelman's "*Rear Window*'s Glasshole."

4 I profusely thank Chris Vargas for generously sharing these three high-resolution images of their artwork.

5 Here is the cited passage in Meyerowitz's article in full: "Sex researcher Alfred Kinsey's vision of sexual taxonomy continued to evolve after he published his first landmark volume on human sexuality, and his research into sexual subcultures went beyond his initial studies of homosexuality and prostitution. In the late 1940s and early 1950s, he developed a new interest in crossdressing and cross-gender identification … He began to interview transvestites and transsexuals, and [placed] his emerging vision of gendered behavior and gender identity within the scientific theories of his day. Kinsey rejected the prevailing views, preferring instead a behaviorist model of gender. He saw crossdressing and crossgender identification as male phenomena and used them to speculate about sex differences in the capacity for psychological conditioning. In his usual style, he did not condemn transvestites or transsexuals, but he disapproved of the genital surgery requested by male-to-female transsexuals. It was here that Kinsey hit the limits of his well-known sexual liberalism in which he approved of all sexual variations that did not involve coercion."

References

Braudy, L. (1968) "Hitchcock, Truffaut, and the Irresponsible Audience," *Film Quarterly*, 21 (4): 21–27.
Braudy, L. (1976) *The World in a Frame: What We See in Films*, New York: Doubleday.
Brown, R. S. (1994) *Overtones and Undertones: Reading Film Music*, Berkeley, Calif.: University of California Press.
Clover, C. (2014) *Men, Women, and Chain Saws: Gender in the Modern Horror Film*, Princeton, NJ: Princeton University Press and British Film Institute.
Doty, A. (2000) "How Queer Is My *Psycho*?" in *Flaming Classics: Queering the Film Canon*, London and New York: Routledge, pp. 155–188.
Durgnat, R. (2002) *A Long Hard Look at* Psycho, Berkeley, Calif.: BFI Publishing, distributed by The University of California Press.
Edelman, L. (1999) "*Rear Window*'s Glasshole," in E. Hanson (ed.), *Out Takes: Essays on Queer Theory and Film*, Durham, NC: Duke University Press, pp. 72–97.
Edelman, L. (2004) *No Future: Queer Theory and the Death Drive*, Durham, NC: Duke University Press.
Greven, D. (2017) *Intimate Violence: Hitchcock, Sex, and Queer Theory*, London and New York: Oxford University Press.
Hepworth, J. (1995) "Hitchcock's Homophobia," in C. K. Creekmur and A. Doty (eds), *Out in Culture: Gay, Lesbian, and Queer Essays on Popular Culture*, Durham, NC: Duke University Press, pp. 186–197.
Meyerowitz, J. (2001) "Sex Research at the Borders of Gender: Transvestites, Transsexuals, and Alfred C. Kinsey," *Bulletin of the History of Medicine*, 75 (1): 72–90.
Miller, D. A. (1991) "Anal *Rope*," in D. Fuss (ed.), *Inside/Out: Lesbian Theories, Gay Theories*, London and New York: Routledge, pp. 119–141.
Modleski, T. (2015) *The Women Who Knew Too Much: Hitchcock and Feminist Theory*, 3rd edn, London and New York: Routledge.
Modleski, T., and D. Greven (2015) "An Interview with David Greven," in T. Modleski, *The Women Who Knew Too Much: Hitchcock and Feminist Theory*, 3rd edn, London and New York: Routledge, pp. 153–168.
Smoliński, S. (2024) "*The Lodger* (1927): Contaminating British Silent Cinema," in L. Robinson and M. Robson (eds), *One Shot Hitchcock: A Contemporary Approach to the Screen*, New York: Oxford University Press, pp. 19–37.

Thomson, D. (2009) *The Moment of* Psycho: *How Alfred Hitchcock Taught America to Love Murder*, New York: Basic Books.

Vena, D., and I. Burgess (2022) "The New Border War? An Intergenerational Exchange on Bad Trans Horror Objects," *Journal of Cinema and Media Studies*, 61 (2): 189–193.

White, P. (2004) "Hitchcock and Hom(m)osexuality," in R. Allen and S. Ishii-Gonzalès (eds), *Hitchcock: Past and Future*, London and New York: Routledge, pp. 215–217.

Chapter 11
#MeToo and Angry Nature
The Changing Tides of Approaches to *The Birds* (1963)

Lucy Bolton

The idiosyncratic personality of Alfred Hitchcock is a dominant cultural phenomenon, lending his name to many elements of filmmaking form and style, from sophisticated blondes to dolly zooms, and certainly to macabre humor. *The Birds* was marketed very much around Hitchcock's reputation and celebrity. The trailer, featuring Hitchcock waxing lyrical about how lucky birds are to be treated so well by humans in that they are given beautiful cages and that their feathers adorn ornate hats, was not only bleakly subversive but also prepared the audience for the revolt of the birds to come in the movie. Hitchcock sits down to eat a roast chicken, and only then does the conflict between his words and his actions seem to put him off his food. The final shot of the trailer is a panic-stricken Tippi Hedren bursting into the room and screaming "They're coming!" The publicity campaign focused on Hitchcock in several ways, not only the delicious prospect of his perverse sense of humor (the trailer quotes him as saying "*The Birds* could be the most terrifying motion picture I have ever made!") but also on his selection of Tippi Hedren as his leading lady, widely—and favorably—reported as a replacement for his beloved Grace Kelly. Magazines that covered the Cannes premiere of the film not only complimented Hedren's performance but also referred to the arduous physical experience of working with the thousands of birds and the injuries that Hedren sustained ("La remplaçante," 1963: 4–5; Lombart 1963).[1] This reveals that knowledge of the intensity of the production was in public circulation at the time, and so the level of outrage that the onset tales provoked in the twenty-first century reflects a shift of priorities and interests in public reception.

The nonchalance, if not humor, with which Hedren's injuries were considered in 1963 is certainly no longer the prevailing response. Hedren's account in her 2016 memoir of the abuse and assault that she suffered at the hands of Hitchcock throughout the making of *The Birds* and *Marnie*, and how he followed through on his promise to ruin her career by refusing to release her from her contract with him, presaged the viral expansion of the #MeToo movement in 2017. At the same time, developments in film theories and critical approaches have shifted attention away from maternal oedipal dramas and psychoanalytic paradigms, and toward the punishment of humans by abused nature. The film's significant contemporary reputation is grounded therefore in two popular discourses: female empowerment and survival, and the environmental horror of humans vs. nature. These current perspectives mean that *The Birds* is a film of great cultural relevance and popularity and also that there is a willingness to accept it on its own terms, eschewing the need to work out what it all means.

The reputation and indeed notoriety of *The Birds* has come to be dominated by Hitchcock's sexual harassment and abuse of Hedren. In 2018, at the age of eighty-eight, Hedren fronted an advertising campaign for Gucci in a series of advertisements for jewelry (Fisher, 2018). In January 2024, Tippi Hedren is ninety-four, and social media is jam-packed with images, GIFs, stills and fan art that demonstrate the popular esteem in which she is held. Her image as Melanie Daniels has become iconic: it forms the basis of innumerable fancy-dress outfits, skits, social-media content, and artwork. There is a Barbie version of Melanie, complete with ravens enmeshed in the doll's hair; and the green suit, designed by Edith Head, formed a major installation as part of the Hollywood Costume exhibition at the Victoria & Albert Museum in London in 2012 (Lodwick 2012: 208). Hedren is also matriarch of a unique Hollywood female genealogy, with her daughter Melanie Griffith (aged six during the making of *The Birds*) and granddaughter Dakota Johnson not only shoring up Hedren's seniority and status but also perpetuating the legendary conflicts and trauma through their own interviews (Bolton 2016: 99–112; Fernandez 2021). The relationship between Hitchcock and Hedren has formed the basis of several dramatic works, including the television drama *The Girl* (dir. Julian Jarrold, 2012) and the play *Double Feature* (John Logan, 2024), as well as countless magazine cover stories and newspaper articles (Adams 2012; Borelli-Persson 2016). It is fair to say that since the release of Hedren's memoir, the lurid tales of Hitchcock's obsession with Hedren, his coercive controlling behavior, and the sexual assault that she describes, have all but obliterated the other reputational elements of the film in popular culture. This is not to say that Hedren's memoir was the first mention of these matters. Donald Spoto conducted an exposé of Hitchcock's treatments of many of his leading ladies in *Spellbound by Beauty*, originally published in 1999, which formed the basis of *The Girl*. Also, the challenges of the shoot involving live birds, and the injuries sustained by Hedren in the prolonged shooting of the attack scenes, were described in publicity for the movie at the time, and in scholarly and critical works.[2] Remarkable also is the evident concentration of Hedren's professional achievements on the two films she made with Hitchcock, which chimes with her claims that he threatened to—and succeeded in—ruining her career. Hedren tells how she learned that François Truffaut, among several other filmmakers, had approached Hitchcock asking to work with Hedren but was told she was not available: he would not release her from her contractual obligations (Hedren 2016: 74). Despite many television appearances, and indeed film roles, it is undeniable that she was never seen in a role that was as complex and challenging as those of Melanie Daniels or Marnie. A glimpse of what we could have seen from Hedren is afforded to us by her supporting role in Charlie Chaplin's *A Countess from Hong Kong* (1967), where she shares the screen with Marlon Brando and acquits herself with dignity and confidence.

Ian Buchanan writes, "Tippi Hedren's acting has been much criticised, but her brittle posture is perfectly done. Fragile and precious, but always too stiff, she is like a porcelain figure seesawing on a knife's edge" (2002: 115). This statement buys into the frailty of Hedren as Daniels as many others have done and fails to acknowledge the strength and self-reliance that she exhibits, along with the elegance and poise. The irresistible attraction of Melanie Daniels is in great measure down to her audacity and her physicality: not only does she rise to the challenge of Mitch's "gag" in the pet shop (where he knew all along that Melanie was a society girl, not a shop assistant) by choosing to play an elaborate gag on him in return (delivering the lovebirds as a surprise), but she demonstrates her resourcefulness and physical confidence at every

Figure 11.1 Melanie Daniels manages the boat, the oar, and the motor with ease.

turn. She sets off in her car to drive the coast road to Bodega Bay, locates the homestead and personnel of the Brenner family, and manages the outboard motor on the boat with ease. There is great spectatorial pleasure to be had in the bafflement of the men who aid her in the fulfilment of her prank: They do not seem to expect a woman who looks like Melanie to be able to manage the boat, the motor, or the physical demands of carrying out the task (see Fig. 11.1). She is independent and liberated—physically and financially, and probably sexually.

The eroticism of her pursuit of Mitch, focused on the romantically suggestive lovebirds, along with the revelations about her society shenanigans, clearly establishes Melanie as a woman of the world, an equal to Mitch in romantic, intellectual, and sexual terms, and Hedren embodies the amused demeanor and physical determination to make this a convincing characterization. That is not to say that the performance is one-note. As I have discussed elsewhere, there are elements in Hedren's walk, slightly wobbling on her high heels, that convey a vulnerability of which she might not be aware (Bolton 2020). However, she also displays temper in response to Mitch's taunting about her jumping into fountains naked and resilience in the face of Lydia's hostility and Cathy's entreating to come to her party. All this confirms that weakness or frailty are not a part of Melanie's way of being in the world, evident in fact from our first sighting of her turning and smiling in appreciative amusement at the wolf whistle she receives when heading for Davidson's pet shop (see Fig. 11.2).

A slight wobble in Melanie's self-confidence is displayed when she responds to Mitch's query about "a mother's love" with the angry pronouncement "My mother? Don't waste your time!" She turns away from Mitch, and the camera, and reveals in a tearful voice that she doesn't know where her mother is. This is one of the chinks in the mystery of the film that has invited psychoanalytical responses over the years, along with the presence of Mitch's overbearing mother, Lydia, and the absent father whose

Figure 11.2 Melanie appreciates the boy's wolf whistle.

portrait dominates the Brenner family living room. Psychoanalytic film theory has been used by many critics and scholars—drawing on Lacan, Freud and Oedipus—including Bellour, Spoto, Truffaut, and Žižek, to explain the reason why the birds attack. For Žižek, the birds embody a deranged maternal superego, derived from Lydia's hysterical response to the perceived threat that Melanie represents to taking her son away. For Fredric Jameson, who sees the film as a "taming of the shrew" story, the birds "can always, in one way or another, be read as spilling out of Tippi Hedren's psyche" (1992: 48). Early feminist analyses of the film, such as the work by Jacqueline Rose, Susan Lurie, and Margaret Horowitz, were also psychoanalytic and focused, broadly, on the problem of Lydia, and the threat posed to the family, and to patriarchy, by Melanie.

John P. McCombe describes this psychoanalytic work on *The Birds* as the "'Lacanization' of Hitchcock studies" (McCombe 2005: 65). McCombe himself considers the film in the framework of Romanticism, focusing on what he perceives as the film's romantic interest in "a natural world that overpowers rational calculation and causality" (2005: 64). In her highly influential BFI Classic volume on the film, published in 1998, Camille Paglia similarly invokes the British Romantic tradition, arguing that *The Birds* is "in the main line of British Romanticism, descending from the raw-nature tableaux and sinister femmes fatales of Coleridge" (Paglia 1998: 7). Paglia also describes how she felt the overwhelming power of the film when she saw it as a teenager, and that she now views it as "a perverse ode to woman's sexual glamour, which Hitchcock shows in all its seductive phases, from brittle artifice to melting vulnerability" (1998: 7). Paglia's monograph successfully shifts the scholarly emphasis onto the complexity and significance of Melanie Daniels as a woman, rather than simply a pawn in the Brenner family oedipal drama. Paglia describes how, as the pet shop scene comes to an end and Melanie plans her revenge on Mitch Brenner, she is "lost in conspiratorial thought, her eyes mischievously darting and her face glowing with autoerotic glee" (1998: 27; see Fig. 11.3).

Paglia also pays attention to Mrs Bundy, and the "great restaurant episode," which Paglia describes as "a play within a play," given the number of characters, the arguments they represent, and the detailed, collective dialogue whereby several characters put forward different arguments for the bird attacks (1998: 69).

In more recent feminist work on the film, attention has turned toward the significance of the women in the film more broadly. For example, Hildy Miller considers the historical period in which *The Birds* is set and proposes that the film reflects the reality for women during the Kennedy era. Miller describes how "a flock of women characters—principally, Melanie, Annie, Lydia, and Cathy—manifests that female existence" (2020: 136). Miller's compelling argument is that these women in the film are straining at the boundaries of their roles in the patriarchy of this era and that we cannot know whether the film's patriarchal attitudes stem from Hitchcock or the culture reflected in the film, or both (2020: 137). Miller is furthering and consolidating what Paglia began, which is to confirm that Melanie is "a force to be reckoned with on both land and water" (2020: 139). Considering her as possessing many features of the gothic heroine, Miller describes how Melanie is repeatedly confined physically despite being brighter and quicker than all the other characters. Considering Annie, Miller sees her as refining traditional gender roles and as someone whose lifestyle choices make her seem a "sort of proto-hippie" rather than a pitiable victim of unrequited love. Miller's overall argument about the women in *The Birds* is a positive and hopeful one that sees the film's ending as offering Melanie the prospect of a mother's love, from Lydia, which she has previously lacked, and that Melanie and Cathy are likely to participate in the coming social changes of the 1960s. This approach to the film, which historicizes the characters socially and culturally, also focuses on the relationships of women in the film to each other, and to milestones in feminism, such

Figure 11.3 Melanie contemplates her revenge on Mitch with glee.

as the publication of Betty Friedan's *The Feminine Mystique* in February 1963 (*The Birds* was released in March). This feminist scholarship shifts attention away from approaches that limit the understanding of women's experience, such as auteurism or Lacanian psychoanalysis, and refocuses the critique in order to explicate the ways in which women's lives shape, and are shaped by, the film as a cultural object.

Other theoretical perspectives have also been brought to bear upon the film, and queer readings by scholars Lee Edelman (2004) and David Greven (2017) have opened out ways of looking in Hitchcock, and in *The Birds* in particular. Whether it is Annie Hayworth's look of longing after Melanie, or positioning the birds as sinthomosexual in the promotional tagline "*The Birds* is coming," queer orientations toward the film enable the complexity of sexual and social dynamics to be drawn out (Greven 2017: 218). Greven describes the misogyny inherent in the final attack of the birds on Melanie, likening it to a rape scene, and also identifies Melanie's "hyperfemininity" and "active phallic desire" (2017: 219). Through focusing on the multifaceted nature of Melanie Daniels, and Hedren's performance, Greven is able to identify her as "one of Hitchcock's richest female characters, someone who develops into authentic personhood over the course of the narrative" (2017: 219). This is true, but perhaps only up until the final sequence, when Melanie is reduced to catatonia by the bird attack. In one devastating shot, as Melanie is laid on the settee, bloodied and almost lifeless, she crosses her hands across her chest. In this posture, she resembles more a statue on a sarcophagus than a high-society playgirl. She literally assumes the posture of the dead (see Fig. 11.4).

In one of the most original and compelling conflations between feminist and queer approaches, Jack Halberstam considers that the "harpies" in the film are attacking in order "to break down the structures of heterosexual desire and replace them with a female homosexuality" (2000: 135–136). There is certainly a network of judgments and connections formed between women in the film. Mrs Bundy and Melanie

Figure 11.4 Melanie resembles a corpse in a coffin following the bird attack.

have a strong discussion about the bird attacks in which Melanie presents the evidence and Mrs Bundy dismisses her, as well as her arguments. Annie makes it clear to Melanie that she still has feelings for Mitch, without explicitly telling her what she wants her to do—or not do. Lydia and Annie are friends, and Lydia comes to feel warmly toward Melanie following the care Melanie shows for Cathy and the need Melanie has for care from Lydia. These dynamics, far more than the swiftly confirmed attraction between Mitch and Melanie, are the driving, developing, emotional structures of the film. There are resolutions, of different sorts, to the hostility expressed toward Melanie initially by Lydia, then by Mrs Bundy, and by the mother in the Tides Restaurant who screams at Melanie that she must be to blame, resulting in a strong slap to bring her to her senses delivered by Melanie herself (see Fig. 11.5).

As scholarly approaches have evolved in the twenty-first century, it seems that several areas have opened up for *The Birds* to invade. Ian Buchanan uses the schizoanalytic thinking of Deleuze and Guattari to move away from Žižek's nihilism about the film's ending to reframe it as far from a desire for annihilation and more Melanie's "crushing realisation that she cannot live up to the demands of the new character she has fashioned for herself" (2002: 117). For Buchanan, it is more a question of Melanie realizing the price she will have to pay for becoming-woman, than that the film is "just another (boring?) oedipal melodrama" (2002: 106). The appeal of rejecting the imposition of an oedipal framework on the film is compelling, and yet the idea that Melanie's ascent of the stairs to her assault and mutilation is in some way a suicidal escape from her heteronormative future seems again to deprive her character of agency and hope.

Another philosophical approach to the film has come from ecocriticism and ecohorror. Film critic Kim Newman, in his compendium *Nightmare Movies*, considers *The Birds* to be "the seminal revolt-of-

Figure 11.5 The women in the Tides Restaurant turn on Melanie.

nature film" (2011: 88). Indeed, back in 1998, Camile Paglia cites Federico Fellini's name for the film as being an "apocalyptic poem" and claims that Hitchcock is directly addressing the theme of "destructive, rapacious nature" (Paglia 1998: 7). Ecocriticism as a field of scholarship, originating in relation to literature and environmental issues, has developed as a field of film studies since the 1990s and is now a thriving subdiscipline. In an inventive and persuasive article, Bruno Lessard develops his idea of what he calls "the Hitchcockian Bird-Event," proposing that Hitchcock merges human and animal subjectivities "and their multifaceted expressions in a particular cinematic time characterised by the void and relationality" (2010: 151). Expressed in its most basic—but compelling—concepts, Lessard's argument is that the film binds humans and birds together on the same plane of cinematic subjectivity, creating a "problematic relation." The film then unfolds this relation in a series of events—the bird attacks—which unfold in cinematic time, and these events emerge out of empty-time. By way of example, Lessard analyzes the jungle gym scene, demonstrating how Melanie sits and smokes, waiting, conveying impatience. The spectator realizes, through the cuts away from Melanie and to the jungle gym, that the birds are massing. Our gaze becomes aligned with Melanie's when she follows the flight of one bird who lands on the jungle gym, revealing the number of birds who have settled there. We then see Melanie's shocked face as she rises to assess the number of birds (see Fig. 11.6). This, Lessard argues, shows how Hitchcock not only directs our attention to the impending "bird event" but also to the moments before and after the event. In this way, "his characters thus become links or traces between attacks, and the temporal flow of the film is thus decelerated to allow the presence of empty-time frames" (Lessard 2010: 161). Lessard is getting at Hitchcock's use of motion and stillness in the film. In the empty-time, characters are waiting to be assigned a position in the expressive pattern: "it is not the meaning of the bird attacks that matters

Figure 11.6a Melanie sits and smokes, waiting with impatience.

Figure 11.6b Melanie realizes the birds have massed.

but the functioning of the attacks between empty-times and how these empty-times are constructed" (Lessard 2010: 162). The birds are not imposed from outside, but they are bodies in the film, along with human bodies, who are shown to enter into new relations. Lessard highlights the exquisitely constructed scene where the faces of Mitch, Melanie, and Lydia are incrementally revealed from a low-angled camera as they occupy empty-time listening to the birds flying away after their invasive attack on the Brenner house. Lessard observes, "When the three characters are in the frame, desperately waiting for the birds to go, one perceives that Hitchcock's emerging tableau vivant truly expresses the novel concept of the event that he ingeniously constructs in his film" (2010: 163).

Not driven by a desire to understand why the birds attack, a film-philosophical approach such as Lessard's attempts to account for the novelty and ingenuity of the experience that *The Birds* affords. Lessard calls for us to pay attention to the "movement and emergence of bodies," human and avian, "as they relate to a process of effectuation that could not exist without the void acting as that which enables appearance in the first place" (2010: 164). This approach offers insight into the moments of silence and apparent inaction, or foreboding, and also to the conventionally perplexing ending, where the occupants of Bodega Bay have changed. There are different types of bodies in the community now, and Lessard's conclusion is that "the characters come to terms with the attacks and accept that their embodied presence in the world will be tied forever to insecurity and imbalance" (2010: 165). The world has changed, but persists, despite the claims by the drunken Charles McGraw that, with the bird attacks, the end of the world has arrived (see Fig. 11.7).

In the twenty-first century, particularly since 2016, *The Birds* has been claimed by audiences and feminist critics as a Tippi Hedren star text and monument to Hitchcock's sadistic treatment of his fledgling star. Hedren's star status has been explosively bolstered by fourth-wave feminist approaches

Figure 11.7 The world has changed and so has its habitation.

to her survivorship of the abuse she endured, her empowerment, her matriarchy, and the proliferation of her iconic style on internet platforms. She is credited with being responsible for the development and growth of the Vietnamese nail-salon industry, having arranged for the women refugees from South Vietnam to be taught the art of manicures in the 1970s (Phan 2016: 87).[3] She established the Shambala Preserve for exotic, endangered, big cats in 1972 and has become widely known for her love of animals, including a period of time when lions shared her house and for the making of the film *Roar* (Hedren 2016: 199–232). Hitchcock's treatment of Hedren on and off set is now seen as epitomizing his sadistic and cruel personality, enabling the film itself to emerge from behind auteurist discourses to speak to the post-#MeToo critical and fan communities, LGBTQ scholars and audiences, as well as to be seen as a seminal and influential horror film. As this chapter has shown, the film's multivalence ensures its contemporary broad and eclectic appeal with audiences, as well as being the subject of continuing interest among Hitchcock scholars.

As a scholarly text, the film has been subject to a variety of disciplinary approaches, theoretical and critical. Much of the discourse around the film for the first forty years was driven by the desire to understand why the birds attack. Currently, the film is seen more as a seminal "revolt of nature" picture, and critical approaches are less concerned to explain the film than to demonstrate and analyze the unique and powerful vision of the world of the film. The plethora of reproductions and adaptations of images available online are a fine example of John Orr's observation about "the enduring power of [Hitchcock's] moving images" (2005: 1). *The Birds* is surely one of the most enduring of Hitchcock's films, and there is irony that the popularity of the film with social media is founded so heavily on Hedren, when her career oblivion was allegedly Hitchcock's aim. As Mitch dabs at Melanie's head wound from the seagull, she challenges what he is putting on her hair, and he replies, "just some peroxide." This line always elicits laughter in contemporary audiences, suggesting that the focus is more on Melanie's character and her perfectly constructed appearance than it is on the bird that pecked her. Today, audiences are far happier to accept the mystery, and embrace the weirdness of the film. Laura Mulvey considers that "both Tippi Hedren's characters, in *Marnie* and *The Birds* (1963), are designed, as it were, to attract the male gaze, both erotic and investigative, that I analyzed in 'Visual Pleasure and Narrative Cinema'" (Mulvey 2021: 221). As the decades have passed since, that gaze has also become appreciative and affectionate, and predicated on respect.

Notes

1. In "La Remplaçante de Marilyn… et celle de Grace Kelly" (*Noir et Blanc*, January 4, 1963, pp. 4–5), the unnamed author writes that Grace Kelly was lucky to have been saved from the attacking birds that Hedren was subject to.
2. Camille Paglia goes into detail about the challenges of the shoot in her BFI Classic (1998: 13–15 and 89–93).
3. See also the website of the Vietnamese Heritage Museum, https://vietnamesemuseum.org/details/ms-tippi-hedren, where Hedren is described as "the Godmother of the Vietnamese Nail Industry."

References

Adams, T. (2012) "Escaping from Obsession," *The Observer Magazine*, December 16.
Bolton, L. (2016) "Melanie Griffith: Wild Girl and Working Woman," in L. Bolton and J. Lobalzo Wright (eds), *Lasting Screen Stars*: Images that Fade and Personas that Endure, Basingstoke: Palgrave Macmillan, pp. 99–112.
Bolton, L. (2020) "'The Brunette with the Legs': The Significance of Footwear in *Marnie*," in E. Ezra and C. Wheatley (eds), *Shoe Reels*: The History and Philosophy of Footwear in Film, Edinburgh: Edinburgh University Press, pp. 166–179.
Borelli-Persson, L. (2016) "Tippi Hedren Talks Alfred Hitchcock, Edith Head, and Her Granddaughter, Dakota Johnson," *Vogue*, November 17.
Buchanan, I. (2002) "Schizoanalysis and Hitchcock: Deleuze and *The Birds*," *Strategies*, 15 (1): 105–118.
Edelman, L. (2004) *No Future*: Queer Theory and the Death Drive, Durham, NC: Duke University Press.
Fernandez, A. (2021) "Dakota Johnson Says Alfred Hitchcock 'Ruined' Grandmother Tippi Hedren's Career," *People*, November 12.
Fisher, L. A. (2018) "Tippi Hedren Lands a Gucci Campaign at 88 Years Old," *Harper's Bazaar*, May 17.
Friedan, B. (1963) *The Feminine Mystique*, New York: Norton.
Greven, D. (2017) *Intimate Violence*: Hitchcock, Sex, and Queer Theory, New York: Oxford University Press.
Halberstam, J. (2000) *Skin Shows*: Gothic Horror and the Technology of Monsters, Durham, NC: Duke University Press.
Hedren, T. (2016) *Tippi*: A Memoir, New York: HarperCollins.
Jameson, F. (1992) "Spatial Systems in *North by Northwest*," in S. Žižek (ed.), *Everything You Always Wanted to Know about Lacan (But Were Afraid to Ask Hitchcock)*, London and New York: Verso, pp. 47–72.
Lessard, B. (2010) "'It's the End of the World!' The Paradox of Event and Body in Hitchcock's *The Birds*," *Film-Philosophy*, 14 (1): 144–173.
Lodwick, K. (2012) "The Treasure Hunt," in D. Nadoolman Landis (ed.), *Hollywood Costume*, London: V&A Publishing, pp. 202–211.
Lombart, J. (1963) "Le Festival de Cannes a donne le coup de grâce a la nouvelle vague," *Bonnes Soirées*, no. 2156, June 9, pp. 12–15.
McCombe, J. P. (2005) "'Oh, I see…': *The Birds* and the Culmination of Hitchcock's Hyper-Romantic Vision," *Cinema Journal*, 44 (3): 64–80.

Miller, H. (2020) "Refiguring *The Birds* as Modern Female Gothic in the Kennedy Era," *Rocky Mountain Review*, 74 (2): 133–155.

Mulvey, L. (2021) "The Metaphor of the Beautiful Automaton Reanimated: Artifice, Illusion, and Late Style in Vertigo," in S. Gottlieb and D. Martin (eds), *Haunted by Vertigo*: *Hitchcock's Masterpiece Then and Now*, East Barnet: John Libbey, pp. 219–233.

Newman, K. (2011) *Nightmare Movies*: *Horror on Screen since the 1960s*, London: Bloomsbury.

Orr, J. (2005) *Hitchcock and 20th Century Cinema*, London and New York: Wallflower Press.

Paglia, C. (1998) *The Birds*, London: BFI.

Phan, D. T. (2016) "Unpretty Nails: Addressing Workers Rights Violation within the Vietnamese Nail Salon Industry," *Asian Pacific American Law Journal*, 21: 81–143.

Schaefer, J. C. (2015) "Must We Burn Hitchcock? (Re) Viewing Trauma and Effecting Solidarity with *The Birds* (1963)," *Quarterly Review of Film and Video*, 32 (4): 329–343.

Spoto, D. (1992) *The Art of Alfred Hitchcock*: *Fifty Years of His Motion Pictures*, centennial edn, New York: Doubleday (Anchor Books).

Spoto, D. (2008) *Spellbound by Beauty*: *Alfred Hitchcock and His Leading Ladies*, London: Hutchinson.

Chapter 12
Vertigo (1958) and *Marnie* (1964)
Two Reception Histories on Steroids

Robert E. Kapsis

The film art world standing of both *Vertigo* and *Marnie* has improved dramatically over the decades as the impact of changing critical trends (e.g., the rise of auteur theory, attentiveness to gender and social class inequality, etc.) shaped how the two films were interpreted and remembered by critics and filmmakers.

Reactions to *Vertigo* during Its Initial Run in 1958

Audiences viewing *Vertigo* during its initial release in 1958 as well as first-time viewers attending the 1984 revival had not anticipated such a downbeat film. The film's early publicity suggested it would be akin to the popular romantic thrillers associated with the Paramount Hitchcock. There were no hints at all of *Vertigo*'s uniqueness. Consider, for example, the well-chosen elements in a twenty-word radio spot for the film: "See Alfred Hitchcock's greatest, *Vertigo*, Paramount's Technicolor, VistaVision, thriller, starring James Stewart, Kim Novak … and don't tell the ending." Except for the teaser about not revealing the ending, the ad in no way distinguishes *Vertigo* from *Rear Window* (1954), *To Catch a Thief* (1955), and *The Man Who Knew Too Much* (1956), Hitchcock's other recent Paramount successes.

    Financially, *Vertigo* was disappointing. After its first year of release, it earned significantly less than *Rear Window*, *To Catch a Thief*, and *The Man Who Knew Too Much* during comparable periods.[1] Hitchcock's decision to reveal the solution to the mystery two-thirds of the way through the film annoyed some critics (see, e.g., Knight, *Saturday Review*, June 7, 1958; cf. Lejeune, *London Observer*, August 10, 1958) and probably many filmgoers as well. The film's unexpected tragic ending was yet another element that disappointed viewers expecting a more conventional Hollywood finish. At no time during *Vertigo*'s publicity campaign did Hitchcock really prepare audiences for these significant deviations from the standard Hitchcock thriller, nor did the film reviews alert moviegoers to dramatic departure from what they had come to expect from Hitchcock. Indeed, many reviewers for daily newspapers characterized *Vertigo* as vintage Hitchcock (*New York Times*, 29 May, 1958; *New York Daily News*,

May 29, 1958; and *Los Angeles Examiner*, May 29, 1958). None divulged the film's surprise ending or commented on any other unusual twists and turns of its plot. The real surprise for filmgoers came, I suggest, when they discovered how different the film was from the usual Hitchcock work. The problem with *Vertigo*, then, was not that the initial reviews kept audiences away. Rather it was that the early filmgoers who saw it were disappointed because of its deviations from the more conventional Hitchcock thriller and, thus, complained about the film to family, friends, and acquaintances. One of the only hints of *Vertigo*'s uniqueness was the early print ad—designed by Saul Bass and featuring the spiral motif which subsequently was dropped and replaced by a more conventional ad because of Paramount's suspicion that the artsy ad had contributed to the film's weak box-office returns early in the campaign (see Figs 12.1 and 12.2).

Still widely held is the belief (see, e.g., Burr 2023) that, as a whole, the first generation of reviewers, both in America and England, had responded negatively to *Vertigo* and that is what caused audiences to stay away. Contrary to that view, we find, at least among the daily newspaper reviewers in the USA, that the critical response to *Vertigo* was generally very positive. *New York Times* chief critic Bosley Crowther's reaction was typical. Like other New York reviewers, Crowther chose not to jeopardize audience enjoyment by divulging any of Hitchcock's surprises, except to mention that *Vertigo* was based on a story by the same authors of "that excellent French mystery, *Diabolique*. That film, if you remember, told of a terribly devious plot to simulate a murder that didn't happen" (May 29, 1958). In a follow-up

Figure 12.1 Saul Bass's iconic poster.

Vertigo, directed by Alfred Hitchcock. © Alfred J. Hitchcock Productions 1958. All rights reserved. Poster Courtesy Universal and the Alfred Hitchcock Estate. The Academy of Motion Pictures Arts and Sciences.

Figure 12.2 Additional artwork for *Vertigo*.

piece, Crowther (*New York Times*, June 1, 1958) suggests that Hitchcock had recently become worried that Henri-Georges Clouzot, the director of the critically acclaimed *Wages of Fear* (1952) and *Diabolique* (1955), might overtake him as the international "Master of movie suspense." (Press releases for recent Clouzot films had characterized him as "the French Hitchcock.") According to Crowther, with *Vertigo*, Hitchcock had successfully met the challenge by making a romantic thriller that compared favorably with some of Hitchcock's greatest triumphs, including *Notorious* (1946) — a film Crowther had included on his "top ten" list for 1946. "Making characters grow important and sympathetic in the midst of peril," says Crowther, "is one [situation] that is obviously mastered by Mr. Hitchcock and M. Clouzot. Let us hope that each will go right on trying to do it better than the other has done in successive films" (Crowther, *New York Times*, June 1, 1958). A majority of daily newspaper reviewers would probably have agreed that with *Vertigo* Hitchcock had successfully met the Clouzot challenge (for important exceptions, see Scheuer, *Los Angeles Times*, May 29, 1958, and the bulk of British reviews, as reported by Barr (2012: 24; 2021: 77–78).

Critics for the more prestigious and intellectual weekly magazines and monthly journals, however, were of a different opinion. Judging from their earlier glowing reviews of *The Wages of Fear* and *Diabolique*, these critics clearly preferred the French Clouzot to the Hollywood Hitchcock.[2] To these critics, who were partly responsible for the film's early bad reputation, *Vertigo* was even more defective than Hitchcock's other recent productions. As longtime Hitchcock nemesis John McCarten, writing in the *New Yorker*, put it, "Alfred Hitchcock; who produced and directed the thing, has never before indulged in such farfetched nonsense" (*New Yorker*, June 7, 1958; see also Knight, *Saturday Review*, June 7, 1958; Hatch, in the *Nation*, June 14, 1958). Reviews of *Vertigo* in more middlebrow magazines, such as *Time* (June 16, 1958) and *Newsweek* (1958), were also highly critical of the film. Like McCarten, *Newsweek*'s critic complained that Hitchcock had "overdone his deviousness, overreached the limits of credibility" (June 2, 1958).

While mainstream and highbrow reviewers may have disagreed in their overall assessment of *Vertigo*, they shared the view that Hitchcock's work belonged in the realm of popular entertainment, not art. By contrast, a few trade-paper reviews—precursors of the later auteurist analyses of the film—pointed to *Vertigo* as "an artistic and entertainment triumph" (*Film Daily*, May 14, 1958) and proof of Hitchcock's "absolute genius" (*Hollywood Reporter*, May 12, 1958). Hitchcock exhibited "absolute genius," according to the *Hollywood Reporter* review, because he was able to inspire each of his collaborators "to rise above their usual competence." Moreover, the review expressed the belief that Hitchcock had demonstrated that the thriller genre could be a vehicle for "the greatest form of emotional drama." Interestingly, the review concluded that "*Vertigo* was one of the most fascinating love stories ever filmed"—an opinion that would become widespread among American critics during the 1970s, when the auteur theory dominated film criticism. *Vertigo* also inspired a number of teenage viewers who in time would themselves become distinguished film directors. Brian De Palma recalls seeing the film during its first run and being bowled over by it: *Vertigo* made "an incredible impression on me way before I was interested in making movies. [There] was something about the way the story was told and the cinematic language used in it that connected to me, even though, at that point [1958], I was studying to be an engineer" (De Palma, NPR, 2016). Martin Scorsese has also chronicled the huge impact *Vertigo* had on him when he was a teenager:

> I went to a big screen at the Capitol Theatre with my friends who were 15 years old … and even though the film was not received well at the time, we responded to the film very strongly. Didn't know why. I couldn't really tell why, couldn't tell what was happening, but we really went with the picture and remembered it, and it took years for us to see it again.
>
> (Scorsese, BFI 2012)

As for *Vertigo*'s reputation among the more academic and scholarly film publications of the period, the two existing American journals engaged in serious criticism, *Film Quarterly* and *Film Culture*, did not even bother to review it. Like the critics for the more prestigious and intellectual magazines, their contributors found the films of French thriller-director Henri-Georges Clouzot (*The Wages of Fear* and *Diabolique*) much more to their liking (see *Film Culture*, May–June 1955).

Reactions to *Marnie* during its Initial Run in 1964

Unlike the broad range of viewer response (or nonresponse) to *Vertigo* during its initial run, the reaction to *Marnie*'s debut six years later, especially among journalistic critics, was uniformly negative and, in several cases, quite hostile in tone—with reviewers from the USA (Kapsis 1992: 122–124) and England (Moral 2013: 144–148), with few exceptions, faulting the film for its loose plot, its simpleminded Freudian assumptions, and its numerous technical deficiencies such as the cardboard look of the exterior shot of the inner-city block where Marnie lived as a child (Fig. 12.3). Annoyance over what was perceived as Hitchcock's growing pretentiousness was likely the major reason why during its initial run journalistic critics responded so negatively to the film. A frequent charge among critics both in America and England was that Hitchcock was taking himself far too seriously, with the result that he had dispensed with his best collaborators. As a *New York Times* critic put it, "A strong suspicion arises that Mr. Hitchcock is

Figure 12.3 The much criticized exterior shot of the inner-city block where Marnie lived as a child.
Marnie, directed by Alfred Hitchcock. © Alfred J. Hitchcock Productions 1964. All rights reserved.

taking himself too seriously—perhaps the result of listening to too many esoteric admirers … When a director decides he's so gifted that all he needs is himself, he'd better watch out!" (E. Archer, *New York Times*, July 23, 1964). Two weeks earlier, a reviewer for *London's Evening News* had echoed a similar sentiment (July 9, 1964). And, as I have detailed elsewhere (see Kapsis 1988, 1992), Hitchcock's efforts at around the time of *The Birds* (1963) and *Marnie* (1964) to transform his reputation from that of popular entertainer to serious artist not only affected the making of *Marnie* but also contributed significantly to the film's negative critical reception (see also Moral 2013). Most critics wanted a film consistent with what they had come to expect from the acknowledged master of suspense. From that vantage point, *Marnie* was not a "true" Hitchcock film. Following the unrelenting gloom of *Psycho* (1960) and *The Birds* (1963), many critics had hoped Hitchcock would return to making films more in the spirit of such works as *North by Northwest*, *Rear Window*, and *To Catch a Thief*.

Hitchcock and Academic Film Criticism during the 1970s and 1980s

Shifting trends in academic film criticism, most notably during the 1970s when the auteur approach came to dominate film studies, helped catapult Hitchcock's reputation to that of great "film artist." Films such as *Vertigo* (1958) and *Marnie* (1964), which earlier had been denounced or ignored by the vast majority of intellectual reviewers during their initial release, were rediscovered as forgotten masterpieces by academic and other more serious critics under the influence of the auteur perspective.

The auteur phase of Hitchcock criticism began most visibly in 1965 with the publication of Robin Wood's *Hitchcock's Films* and lasted until roughly the late 1970s. Auteurist reassessments of *Vertigo* and *Marnie* during this period were overwhelmingly favorable and emphasized Hitchcock's total mastery of the film medium (see, e.g., Belton 1969; Cameron and Jeffrey 1965; Huss and Silverstein 1968; Spoto 1976; Yacowar 1977).

Unlike the heavily publicized appearance of Truffaut's *Hitchcock* in 1967, the publication two years earlier of Wood's study, the first book-length treatment of Hitchcock's films in English, went largely unnoticed by American and British journalistic critics. By contrast, academic film critics, especially in the USA, were quick to recognize Wood's work as a pioneering effort in the exegesis of Hitchcock's art. For example, in his introduction to *Focus on Hitchcock*, the first collection of critical readings on Hitchcock, published in 1972, Albert J. LaValley acknowledged the importance of Wood's study, describing it as "a key document in the Hitchcock controversy" and "essential reading for Hitchcock enthusiasts."

One of Wood's major points is that, like other works of art, Hitchcock's films disturb, leaving a "nasty taste in the mouth"—a correlate to Hitchcock's sense of a precarious moral order, most profoundly expressed in his later films, especially *Vertigo* and *Marnie*. With this work, Wood established himself as the first critic in print to declare *Vertigo* as "Hitchcock's masterpiece to date, and one of the four or five most profound and beautiful films that the cinema has yet given us," while regarding *Marnie* (again going against the grain) as perhaps Hitchcock's most mature work, explaining away so-called technical deficiencies such as the phony look of Marnie's childhood neighborhood as artistically inspired flourishes (see Fig. 12.3). In fact, years later he would quip, "If you don't like *Marnie* (the film), you don't really like Hitchcock; and if you don't love Marnie (the woman), you don't really love cinema."

Since the 1970s, a number of academic film scholars heavily influenced by psychoanalytic and feminist theory (e.g., Mulvey 1975; Modleski 1988) have also been drawn to *Vertigo* and *Marnie*—especially to *Marnie*. (Until recently, the vast majority of film scholars attracted to *Marnie* had been women.) In contrast to the auteur critics who glorified directorial authority (and the vast majority of whom were male), the feminist critics "implicitly challenge and decenter directorial authority by considering Hitchcock's work as the expression of cultural attitudes and practices existing to some extent outside the artist's control" (Modleski 1988: 3). No work has had a greater influence in steering feminist film criticism in this direction than Laura Mulvey's essay "Visual Pleasure and Narrative Cinema," which first appeared in the British journal *Screen* in 1975. Mulvey takes as her starting point "the way film reflects, reveals and even plays on the straight, socially established interpretation of sexual difference that controls images, erotic ways of looking and spectacle" (1975: 412). According to Mulvey and other early feminist film critics, many of Hitchcock's films, including *Vertigo* and *Marnie*, were works that functioned as if made exclusively for the pleasure of the male spectator, reflecting not Hitchcock's own distinct vision but rather the ethos of patriarchal society (see also Bellour 1977; Bergstrom 1979; Flitterman 1978).

On the other hand, starting in the late 1980s, there was a growing trend among feminist critics to concentrate on films that allowed women's experiences to be "voiced" and "visualized." Consider, for instance, Tania Modleski's book on Hitchcock: *The Women Who Knew Too Much*, where she argues that "insofar as Hitchcock's films repeatedly reveal the way women are oppressed in patriarchy, they allow the female spectator to feel an anger that is very different from the masochistic response imputed to her by some feminist critics" (Modleski 1988: 5). In her chapter on *Vertigo*, Modleski discusses the implication of Hitchcock giving away the secret of the film well before the end and thereby making the viewer privy to "the female point of view"—to Judy's thoughts and feelings: "However much we may be invited to condemn her as duplicitous in her 'double desire,' we must also see the way she is used and cast aside or tortured and finally killed off, as man desperately tries to sustain a sense of himself that necessitates the end of woman" (Modleski 1988: 100; see Fig. 12.4).

Feminist critics have increasingly approached *Marnie* from a similar vantage point (see, e.g., Bailin 1982; Piso 1986; Silverman 1983; see also Knapp 2009). Rebecca Bailin, for example, maintains that the female "voice" or "discourse" in *Marnie* was about violence in women's experience. Marnie is ill because of "something that happens to women at the hands of men" (Bailin 1982: 27). Not only is Marnie's stealing connected to her trauma, but it is also shown as a response to sexism. Indeed, as Bailin points out, in the film's opening scene there is the suggestion that Strutt has sexually harassed her (1982: 28). A more sociological approach is Michele Piso's 1986 essay which attempts to integrate such feminist concerns within a Marxist framework. According to Piso, the film's central tension and particular pathos is not really psychological or oedipal at all, as many earlier feminists had postulated (see, e.g., Bailin 1982; Silverman 1983), but "the class antagonism between Mark and Marnie, with her mother standing not only for a purely private and hideous past but also as the twisted embodiment of social repression and sexual exploitation" (Piso 1986: 289). According to Piso, Mark's desire to possess Marnie relates to his class position as owner of a midsized publishing firm; that is, Mark is a man of considerable property. Moreover, his unquestioned view of himself as a capitalist, argues Piso, is what led him to rape Marnie. But was it a rape? By the 1980s, this had become a contentious issue among Hitchcock scholars—a controversy that has persisted to this day (see, e.g., Bailin 1982; Greven 2017; Kapsis 1988, 1992; Modleski 2005, 2016a; Pomerantz 2017; Wood 1965). Figure 12.5 is a chronologically arranged series of five frame captures drawn from frequently cited shots from the film's controversial rape sequence.

Figure 12.4 Madeleine Elster (Kim Novak) before her transformation in *Vertigo*.

Vertigo (1958) and *Marnie* (1964) 147

Figure 12.5 Images from the controversial rape sequence in *Marnie*.

The Fate of *Vertigo* and *Marnie* after Hitchcock's Death in 1980

Sociologists Kurt Lang and Gladys Lang (1988) have suggested several reasons to account for the durability of a reputation including "the availability of others who, after the artist's death, have a stake in preserving or giving a boost to that reputation [and] the artist's own efforts, in his lifetime, to protect or project his reputation" (Lang and Lang 1988: 86). The revival and reception of "classic" Hitchcock films three years after the director's death provides a good illustration of this process. Of the fifty-four films that Hitchcock directed over a fifty-year period, he had commercial control over five of them: *Rope*,

Rear Window, *The Trouble with Harry*, *The Man Who Knew Too Much*, and *Vertigo*. (Ownership rights reverted to Hitchcock eight years after the films were first released.) These films, dating from the ten-year period between 1948 and 1958, had been taken out of circulation by Hitchcock during the early 1970s. According to Richard Schickel (1985), who had interviewed Hitchcock around that time, Hitchcock had decided to hold these films "off of television and away from revival houses as a legacy for his wife, Alma, and his daughter, Patricia." Keeping them off the market, Hitchcock believed, would increase their economic value. Another possibility, as Schickel (1985) has speculated, is that Hitchcock's decision to keep these films out of circulation until after his death was related to his wish to maintain some control over his posthumous reputation. Once dead, Hitchcock could no longer control what might be published about him. Libel laws, for instance, could no longer protect him from slander. However, what he could do, before he died, was to prevent these films from being shown until after his death. It would then be up to the guardians of his estate to determine a propitious time for releasing them. And, as it turned out, the reissue of these films, starting in 1983, couldn't have been better timed for managing Hitchcock's posthumous reputation.

Three months before the reissue of *Rear Window*, the first of the five "lost" films to be released, Donald Spoto came out with his controversial biography, *The Dark Side of Genius: The Life of Alfred Hitchcock*. A longtime champion of the view of Hitchcock as a serious artist (see his earlier book, *The Art of Alfred Hitchcock: Fifty Years of His Motion Pictures*, 1976), Spoto in his later book characterized Hitchcock as a tormented artist with a dark and malicious streak. Behind Hitchcock's façade of high joviality and good-naturedness, Spoto claimed, lurked a tormented and mean-spirited individual with the sexual maturity of an adolescent. This sexual immaturity and Hitchcock's cruelty, says Spoto, came to a head during the filming of *Marnie*, when he declared his affection for the film's star, Tippi Hedren, who rebuffed him. After that incident, according to Spoto, Hitchcock did all he could to ruin her career. In *Hitchcock: The Making of a Reputation*, I had speculated that the reissue of these five classic Hitchcock films just three weeks after Spoto's book came out was no coincidence and that, in fact, the revival of these films did help to "deflect the Hitchcock debate away from Spoto's 'revelations' about Hitchcock's questionable conduct to the films themselves" (Kapsis 1992). Coincidence or not, the reissue of these five films did help deflect the Hitchcock debate away from Spoto's charges against Hitchcock to the greatness and power of each of the reissued films—*Vertigo* and *Rear Window* in particular.

Before reporting on the critical response to *Vertigo* during the mid 1980s, we should call attention to the film's unique standing within the film art world at around the time of its reissue in late 1983. Less than two years earlier, in 1982, and for the first time, *Vertigo* had cracked the influential *Sight and Sound* critic's poll, ranking eighth in the top ten of the so-named "greatest films of all time." And this had happened despite the film being commercially unavailable for viewing since the early 1970s. Furthermore, Hitchcock had been especially scrupulous throughout the 1970s in his efforts to keep all copies of *Vertigo* out of circulation. Reportedly, when James Stewart wanted to show a clip of *Vertigo* during a retrospective of his work at the Berlin Film Festival in 1982, he was refused. Yet, in a little cinema in a Berlin neighborhood, 16mm versions of both *Vertigo* and *Rear Window* were being freely screened. It was only with extreme difficulty that the American Film Institute was able to secure an extract from *Vertigo* when it presented Hitchcock with its Life Achievement Award (*The Times*, November 15, 1983).

And, according to Martin Scorsese, *Vertigo* had become the film that "all the filmmakers in the seventies were trying to find copies of"—the lost picture everyone "was looking for" (interviewed in *Hitchcock/Truffaut*, documentary, dir. Kent Smith). Todd McCarthy, formerly the *Hollywood Reporter*'s chief film critic, recalls "going to see it at a clandestine screening in Los Angeles with one of its greatest champions, François Truffaut" (*Hollywood Reporter*, August 2, 2012). Interest in *Vertigo* was also fueled by the release in 1976 of two Hitchcock-inspired films—Brian De Palma's *Obsession* and Martin Scorsese's *Taxi Driver*—both with scores by Bernard Herrmann reminiscent of music he composed for *Vertigo* as well as for other Hitchcock films. Promotional materials circulating around the time of *Obsession*'s release emphasized the film's roots in the Hitchcock tradition. Overall, this promotional strategy backfired, with a majority of critics concluding that the film fell considerably below the high standards set by Hitchcock; in fact, a number of these critics used their reviews of *Obsession* as an excuse for rhapsodizing about *Vertigo* and thereby contributing to the *Vertigo* mania that preceded the film's rerelease in the early 1980s (see Kapsis 1992: 196–199).

Turning next to the critical response to *Vertigo* following its 1983–1984 reissue, we find among American journalistic critics a wide spectrum of upbeat auteur-inspired reviews (see, e.g., Gleiberman, *Boston Phoenix*, December 27, 1983; Kehr 1984; Wilmington, *LA Weekly*, November 25–December 1, 1983). Typical was Dave Kehr's who wrote:

> It is still the question that divides film aesthetics, separating critics who believe in the expressive power of popular filmmaking from those who see art only in the highbrow asceticism of a Bergman or an Antonioni, separating those who believe that film has its own artistic properties and potentials from those who measure achievement only by older, more established values. When Judy returns from the beauty parlor, her hair now dyed to match Madeleine's, she walks straight toward Scotty—straight toward the camera and us—and it is the first time in the film that a figure has emerged from the depths of the image to come to us, the first time we are met on the surface of the screen rather than drawn into it.
>
> (Kehr 1984)

In addition, several of the reviews also reflected sensitivity to feminist concerns (see, e.g., Wilmington, *LA Weekly*, November 25–December 1, 1983). Shortly before the film's rerelease, Wood (1983) had published in the popular film magazine *American Film* his revisionist essay on *Vertigo* and *Rear Window* where he offered an affirmative answer to the question, "Can Hitchcock be saved for feminism?" In light of Wood's "feminist" reading of *Vertigo* and Spoto's recently published "revelations" about Hitchcock's hostility toward women, it is understandable that a feminist reading of *Vertigo* would make sense to a number of viewers. However, even for reviewers most receptive to the film's uncompromising indictment of romantic love, the feminist viewpoint functioned as but one of several ways of illuminating the film. Without the recent contributions from Wood and Spoto, film reviewers would probably have neglected raising feminist-related issues just as they had done three months earlier with *Rear Window*.

Among British reviewers during this same period, we find that little had changed since 1958—the year *Vertigo* first came out. The English view of Hitchcock as essentially a popular entertainer—a "lightweight"—and, therefore, not to be taken seriously—had lingered on, leading British reviewers in 1983–1984 to include different works on their list of preferred Hitchcock films. While *Rear Window* and *Rope* were the two most heavily favored among the reissued films, *Vertigo* ran, at best, a distant third, with many critics viewing it as highly overrated. In contrast to their American counterparts, British reviewers who liked *Vertigo* tended to concentrate on matters relating to plot construction and the building of suspense rather than on thematic concerns or mise-en-scène. That is, the British were more interested in reassessing *Vertigo*'s effectiveness as a thriller than in exploring its probings into psychopathology and its indictment of romantic love. Not surprisingly, a number of British reviewers also wrote more favorably about *The Trouble with Harry*—a film Hitchcock had often described as characteristically English—compared to *Vertigo* (see Kapsis 1992: 149–157).

Starting in the early to mid 1990s, evidence starts to build of a profound shift in attitude about *Vertigo* occurring among British critics following the film's dizzying successes in *Sight and Sound* magazine's influential "Greatest Films of All Times" poll—climbing to fourth in 1992, second in 2002, and then, most dramatically of all, in 2012, replacing *Citizen Kane* in the coveted number 1 spot before slipping back to the number 2 slot in the 2022 poll. Focusing on the results from the 2012 poll, Nick James, editor of *Sight and Sound*, was quoted remarking that

> these results reflected a dramatic transformation in the "culture of film criticism"—and that "the new cinephilia" seems to be not so much about films that strive to be great art, such as *Citizen Kane*, and that use cinema's entire arsenal of effects to make a grand statement, but more about works that have personal meaning to the critic.

James continued:

> *Vertigo* is the ultimate critics film because it is a dreamlike film about people who are not sure who they are but who are busy reconstructing themselves and each other to fit a kind of cinema ideal of the ideal soulmate. In that sense it's a makeover film full of spellbinding moments of awful poignancy that show how foolish, tender and cruel we can be when we're in love.

And *Vertigo* works that way, says James, "especially if you watch it more than once. It is a film that grows and grows on you" (*Independent*, August 3, 2012). But perhaps even more significantly, according to the *Guardian*'s arts correspondent Mark Brown, *Vertigo*'s rise to the top "reflects the remarkable change in fortune Hitchcock has had with critics, some of whom [including critics and other spokespersons for BFI's own *Sight and Sound* magazine] once looked down on him as little more than a Hollywood thriller director." These days, continues Brown, "the BFI, which is currently showing a retrospective of the director's films, believes Hitchcock should be studied in schools alongside Shakespeare and Dickens" (*Guardian*, August 1, 2012).

The following extract from a 2021 essay focusing on *Vertigo*'s afterlife in art provides, overall, a good overview of this latest phase of *Vertigo* mania:

> *Vertigo* is everywhere. You can purchase a mug, laptop case, phone case, tote bag, clock, duvet cover, notebook, pillows [even playing cards, see Fig. 12.6]. The paratextual universe that encompasses this detritus of fandom is but one engine that keeps *Vertigo* circulating in our cultural landscape. Critical and scholarly writing is another. New insights and discoveries continue to abound as well as new questions borne from the many contextual and disciplinary frames through which *Vertigo* is filtered.[3] This seems to happen with particular fervor on the heels of anniversaries, with the film's rerelease in different formats (e.g., VHS, Laserdisc, DVD, Blu-ray), with special limited runs in theaters, and especially with its usurpation of *Citizen Kane* (1941) at the top spot on *Sight and Sound*'s much revered "Greatest Films of All Time" list in 2012.
>
> (Gottlieb and Martin 2021: 117)

Figure 12.6 *Vertigo* themed playing cards.
Courtesy Universal and the Alfred Hitchcock Estate.

What this overview of *Vertigo* mania failed to mention, however, is the instrumental role that renowned film directors have continued to play in advancing and maintaining *Vertigo*'s unique standing in global film culture. Every decade since 1992, *Sight and Sound* has asked "the world's leading directors" to list the ten films they believe to be "the greatest of all time." The scope of the poll has expanded significantly over time:

> Though it has always been global and inclusive in scope, the poll has expanded significantly each decade. In 1992, 101 directors voted; fast-forward to 2012, when 358 filmmakers took part. [In 2022], for the fourth edition of the poll, we received ballots from 480 directors. This electorate spans experimental, arthouse, mainstream and genre filmmakers from around the world. In every case, the voter is a director of note.
>
> (www.bfi.org.uk.directors'100)

In the 2022 poll, *Vertigo* achieved the sixth spot behind *Jeanne Dielman 23 quai du Commerce, 1080 Bruxelles* (1975) (fifth); *Tokyo Story* (1953) (fourth); *The Godfather* (1972) (third); *Citizen Kane* (1941) (second); and *2001: A Space Odyssey* (1968) (first). American director James Gray was one of those surveyed who had included *Vertigo* on his list of the ten greatest films of all time and who on numerous occasions during the past decade had also singled out the scene in *Vertigo* where Judy emerges from the bathroom as Madeleine as the most powerful scene in all of cinema (Fig. 12.7):

> The nature of desire is unceasingly complex and multilayered, and [*Vertigo*] is about all the trappings of desire. That [Scottie] could only love [Judy] when the idea of her glamour and her social class was

Figure 12.7 Kim Novak's transformation in *Vertigo*.

what he hoped it would be. When she's Judy, that's not enough for him. She has to be Madeleine. She has to be dressed up. She has to drive that green Rolls. She has to present [herself] in a certain way. The idea there, which is so amazing, is that all desire can be reduced to the idea of a fetish. It's fantastic. It's brilliant. I mean, that movie is, like, crazy great. [Why?] Because desire is the motivator for our behavior.

(Gray 2022)

[Social class is] not discussed in American life very much—there's a notion that social or economic class divides don't exist when of course they do. But that wasn't always true in film—think of John Ford, it's always all over his films. The idea of *Vertigo* is partly genius because of social class—the idea is he has to make Kim Novak up to the fancier version of Kim Novak in order to rekindle his obsession. So class becomes part of [the] story.

(IndieWire, December 12, 2013)

My impression is that many other film directors who have long been in awe of *Vertigo* would not dispute Gray's somewhat over-the-top take on this classic sequence.

Harder to gauge than *Vertigo*'s is *Marnie*'s cultural and critical standing since the 1980s. Special occasions or anniversaries for reviewing *Marnie* have been relatively few and far between. Ditto the number of important film directors who have openly embraced the film. The great Italian director Bernardo Bertolucci's love of *Marnie* is a striking exception. More typical, I suspect, is James Gray's relatively low opinion of *Marnie* and of much of Hitchcock's other output after *Psycho*, especially *The Birds*. Here is what Gray told a *Film Comment* interviewer (in October 2013), shortly after his 2013 film *The Immigrant* was shown at the 51st New York Film Festival:

> Gray: I hate *The Birds*. It's terrible … I can't sit through it! The incredible set piece with the crows landing … on the jungle gym—it has things great in it. But to sit through it is painful.
> Film Comment: A lot of critics and film theorists love it … They like *Marnie* too.
> Gray: I know. I can't go with *Marnie*. People I love and respect love *Marnie*, so I feel like I'm an idiot. It feels really awkward to me. It feels stiff …
> Film Comment: It's sloppy.
> Gray: After *Psycho*, his films kind of lose their sheen and beauty.

And yet *Marnie* continues to generate a great deal of intense interest and commitment, especially among academics. Compare, for example, Murray Pomerance's chapter on *Marnie* (2004: 130–169) with his book-length treatment for the BFI thirteen years later (Pomerance 2017). Thomas Leitch and Leland Poague, coeditors of *A Companion to Alfred Hitchcock* (2011), expressed surprise

> by the number of contributors who wrote at length about *Marnie*. In view of the fascinating differences that emerge from the considerations of *Marnie* in the essays by Tania Modleski, Brigitte Peucker, William Rothman, and Florence Jacobowitz, however, we were happy to be surprised, and we trust our readers will share our pleasure.
>
> (Leitch and Poague 2011: 5)

Moreover, several updated volumes devoted to Hitchcock have added new material on *Marnie* (see, e.g., Deutelbaum and Poague 2009; Modleski 2005, 2016a; Moral 2013; Rothman 2012).

Among the most illuminating of the newer pieces are several that approach *Marnie* from a queer perspective (see, e.g., Modleski 2005 and Greven 2017; and, earlier, Knapp 1993). For example, Greven views *Marnie* as:

> one of the richest explorations of what [he calls] queer resilience: a continuous level of self-reliance and fortitude within structures of stifling social conformity that emphasizes visible manifestations of gender and sexual normativity [and argues that], while lesbian overtones are certainly present, the film is more interested in presenting its solitary heroine's sexuality as onanistic. The forms of intimate violence that Hitchcock's films frequently depict find a newly politicized urgency in *Marnie*.
>
> (Greven 2017: 23–24)

Some of this growing interest in *Marnie* is no doubt also related to the negative backlash that Spoto's attacks and those by others (e.g., Tippi Hedren in her 2016 memoir) on Hitchcock's character had precipitated or triggered (see, e.g., Brody 2016; Moral 2013). Still, there is testimony that these new and recurring revelations about the darker side of Hitchcock, while damaging to the more sanitized view of him that some critics had once held, did not necessarily diminish their view of him as a great filmmaker. In fact, for *New Yorker* critic Richard Brody, the new revelations had the opposite effect. "*Marnie* is the film," he writes,

> in which Hitchcock's method reaches the breaking point—in which Hitchcock, the master of control, loses control. When I first saw the movie, decades ago, I was still unaware of the horrifying backstory to

its creation—Hitchcock's sexual harassment of its star, Tippi Hedren ... The greatness of Hitchcock's artistry, the musical sublimity of his images and the emotional power of his stories, isn't separable from his carnality—rather, his greatness depends upon the worst and most bestial aspects of his character. Without them, he'd be the artisan of cinematic cuckoo clocks, and what's all too often celebrated in the name of Hitchcock mania is precisely an abstracted craft that's isolated from its source of power, from its dynamic principle, from its raison d'être.

(Brody 2016)

Similarly, the renowned Hitchcock scholar Richard Allen seems also to have attempted to distance himself from some of the excesses of Hitchcock mania and of *Vertigo* mania in particular:

My favorite Hitchcock film is *Marnie*, though it is by no means his best. The reason I like *Marnie* so much is that it manages to be both highly self-conscious in style and achingly heartfelt ... The film is perhaps a love story in which the sick Marnie is rendered fit for love by the good intentions and unflagging persistence of Mark, but equally one can read the film as the forcible subordination of a vital, independent woman who has no desire for men or the patriarchal institution of marriage.

(Allen 2015; see also Allen 2007, chapter 6)

Summary and Conclusion

This chapter has documented how the film art world standing of both *Vertigo* (1958) and *Marnie* (1964) improved dramatically over the decades as the impact of changing critical trends (e.g., the rise of auteur theory, attentiveness to gender and social class inequality, etc.) shaped how these two Hitchcock films were interpreted and remembered by journalistic film reviewers, academic film critics/scholars, and filmmakers. Today, both films are highly regarded among academic film scholars. But, as this chapter reveals, *Marnie*'s reputation among journalistic film critics and film directors has been more nuanced, reserved, and, at times, even contentious. As reported earlier, director James Gray expressed some reserve about *Marnie* when he declared: "After *Psycho*, [Hitchcock's] films kind of lose their sheen and beauty." Musicological research is another area where *Vertigo* and *Marnie* might be fruitfully examined in relation to each other, most notably in studies assessing the impact of Bernard Herrmann's musical scoring on the reception history of the two films. Compared with their immediate embrace of his *Tristan and Isolde*-inspired music for *Vertigo*, Herrmann scholars have been slow to recognize "the dramatic power and intricate musical design" of his score for *Marnie*, which Herrmann himself considered among the greatest of his works (Schneller 2011: 55). Compare Jack Sullivan's (2006: 222–234) detailed commentary on the scoring for *Vertigo* with his paltry or scant coverage of *Marnie*'s (pp. 274–6): See Coda A, especially the section on *Vertigo*, which is adapted from Sullivan's chapter on *Vertigo* 222–234. Increasingly, however, Herrmann experts are acknowledging that his music for *Marnie* is also top-tier and warrants closer study, especially when it comes to gaining a better understanding of how music composition can be designed to mimic the form of a film itself and in the process make the film more dramatically powerful (Schneller 2011: 97). Elevating the reputation of the musical scoring for *Marnie* might in time also impact favorably on how future generations of journalistic film critics will come to view *Marnie* as a film.

Acknowledgment

Portions of this chapter covering reception history predating 1990 are adapted from Kapsis (1992).

Notes

1 Wikipedia's summary of the box-office data on the film is accurate: "While *Vertigo* did break even upon its original release, earning $3.2 million in North American distributor rentals against its $2,479,000 cost, it earned significantly less than other Hitchcock productions" (October 20, 2024, 6:21 a.m.).

2 See, for example, John McCarten's reviews of *The Wages of Fear* (*New Yorker*, February 26, 1955) and *Diabolique* (*New Yorker*, November 26, 1955). Another favorite of the highbrows was British director Carol Reed, whose concern with character development and "sound psychological motivation" they preferred over Hitchcock's tendency to sacrifice plausibility in favor of maximizing audience effects. Such was the case made in a review of *Strangers on a Train* (1951) appearing in the *Saturday Review* (July 14, 1951).

3 Of the recent scholarly writings on *Vertigo*, one of the best is David Greven's essay, "The Dark Side of Blondeness: *Vertigo* and Race" (2018), where he makes one of the strongest cases yet for scrutinizing Hitchcock's entire body of work from a racial perspective. If, as I have suggested, the Carlotta story in *Vertigo* is an allegory of a suppressed narrative of blackness and passing, the fact that Judy wears the necklace and therefore aligns herself with this nineteenth-century female ancestor functions as a moment of racial confession, however involuntary and/or unconsciously motivated. The *unheimlich* aspects of *Vertigo* extend beyond male fears of women; they touch upon the larger, deeper, more insidious fears of a racial otherness that can never be acknowledged but that lurks sorrowfully and threateningly within Hitchcock's work (Greven 2018: 77).

References

Allen, R. (2007) *Hitchcock's Romantic Irony*, New York: Columbia University Press.
Allen, R. (2015) "Interview," SimplyCharly.com, February 10.
Bailin, R. (1982) "Feminist Readership, Violence, and *Marnie*," *Film Reader*, 5: 24–35.
Barr, C. (2012) *Vertigo*, BFI Classics. Basingstoke: Palgrave Macmillan.
Barr, C. (2021) "Hitchcock and *Vertigo*: French and Other Connections," in S. Gottlieb and D. Martin (eds), *Haunted by* Vertigo: *Hitchcock's Masterpiece Then and Now*, East Barnet: John Libbey, pp. 78–94.
Bellour, R. (1977) "Hitchcock, the Enunciator," *Camera Obscura*, 2: 69–94.
Belton, J. (1969) "Mechanics of Perception," *Cambridge Phoenix*, 16 (October).
Bergstrom, J. (1979) "Enunciation and Sexual Difference (Part 1)," *Camera Obscura*, 3–4: 32–69.
Brody, R. (2016) "*Marnie* Is the Cure for Hitchcock Mania," *New Yorker*, August 17.
Burr, T. (2023) "*Vertigo* Is Still the Best Movie Ever. Or the Worst Movie Ever. Discuss," *Washington Post*, May 9.
Cameron, I., and R. Jeffery (1965) "The Universal Hitchcock," *Movie*, 12: 21–24.
De Palma, B. (2016) "Interview," National Public Radio, July.
Deutelbaum, M., and L. Poague (eds) (2009) *A Hitchcock Reader*, 2nd edn, Hoboken, NJ: Wiley-Blackwell.
Flitterman, S. (1978) "Woman, Desire, and the Look: Feminism and the Enunciative Apparatus in Cinema," *Cine-Tracts* 2 (fall): 63–68.
Gottlieb, S., and D. Martin (eds) (2021) *Haunted by* Vertigo: *Hitchcock's Masterpiece Then and Now*, East Barnet: John Libbey.
Gray, J. (2022) "5 Films that Are Worth Rediscovering," A. Frame. https://newsletter-dev.oscars.org/what-to-watch/post/james-gray-5-films-that-are-worth-rediscovering

Greven, D. (2017) *Intimate Violence*: *Hitchcock, Sex, and Queer Theory*, New York: Oxford University Press.
Greven, D. (2018) "The Dark Side of Blondeness: *Vertigo* and Race," *Screen*, 59 (spring): 59–79.
Hedren, T. (2016) *Tippi*: *A Memoir*, New York: William Morrow.
Hitchcock O'Connell, P., and L. Bouzereau (2003) *Alma Hitchcock*: *The Woman Behind the Man*, New York: Berkeley Books.
Huss, R., and N. Silverstein (1968) *The Film Experience*, New York: Harper & Row.
Kapsis, R. (1988) "The Historical Reception of Hitchcock's *Marnie*," *Journal of Film and Video*, 40 (3): 46–63.
Kapsis, R. (1992) *Hitchcock*: *The Making of a Reputation*, Chicago, Ill.: University of Chicago Press.
Kehr, D. (1984) "Hitch's Riddle," *Film Comment*, 20 (3): 9–18.
Knapp, L. (2009) "The Queer Voice in *Marnie*," in M. Deutelbaum and L. Poague (eds), *A Hitchcock Reader*, 2nd edn, Hoboken, NJ: Wiley-Blackwell, pp. 295–311.
Lane, C. (2020) *Phantom Lady*: *Hollywood Producer Joan Harrison—The Forgotten Woman Behind Hitchcock*, Chicago, Ill.: Chicago Review Press.
Lang, G. E., and K. Lang (1988) "Recognition and Renown: The Survival of Artistic Reputation," *American Journal of Sociology*, 94 (1): 79–109.
LaValley, A. J. (ed.) (1972) *Focus on Hitchcock*, Englewood Cliffs, NJ: Prentice Hall.
Leitch, T., and L. Poague (eds) (2011) *A Companion to Alfred Hitchcock*, Hoboken, NJ: Wiley-Blackwell.
Modleski, T. (1988) *The Women Who Knew Too Much*: *Hitchcock and Feminist Theory*, New York: Methuen.
Modleski, T. (2005) *The Women Who Knew Too Much*: *Hitchcock and Feminist Theory*, 2nd edn, London and New York: Routledge.
Modleski, T. (2016a) *The Women Who Knew Too Much*: *Hitchcock and Feminist Theory*, 3rd edn, London and New York: Routledge.
Modleski, T. (2016b) "Remastering the Master: Hitchcock after Feminism," *New Literary History*, 47 (spring): 135–158.
Moral, T. L. (2013) *Hitchcock and the Making of* Marnie, rev. edn, Lanham, Md.: Scarecrow Press.
Mulvey, L. (1975) "Visual Pleasure and Narrative Cinema," *Screen*, 16 (autumn): 6–18.
Piso, M. (1986) "Mark's *Marnie*," in M. Deutelbaum and L. Poague (eds), *A Hitchcock Reader*, Ames, Iowa: Iowa State University Press, pp. 288–303.
Pomerance, M. (2004) *An Eye for Hitchcock*, New Brunswick: Rutgers University Press, pp. 130–169.
Pomerance, M. (2017) *Marnie*, BFI Classics, Basingstoke: Palgrave Macmillan.
Rothman, W. (2012) *Hitchcock*: *The Murderous Gaze*, 2nd edn, Stony Brook, NY: State University of New York Press.
Sarris, A. (1983) "The Critical Anatomy of Alfred Hitchcock," *Village Voice*, October 18.
Schickel, R. (1985) "The Final Mystery," *On Cable*, June: 55–104.
Schneller, T. (2011) "Unconscious Anchors: Bernard Herrmann's Music for *Marnie*," *Popular Music History*, January 1, p. 97.
Scorsese, M. (2012) On *Vertigo*, BFI, YouTube, August 12.
Silverman, K. (1983) *The Subject of Semiotics*, New York: Oxford University Press.
Spoto, D. (1976) *The Art of Alfred Hitchcock*: *Fifty Years of His Motion Pictures*, New York: Hopkinson & Blake.
Spoto, D. (1983) *The Dark Side of Genius*: *The Life of Alfred Hitchcock*, New York: Balantine.
Sullivan, J. (2006) *Hitchcock's Music*, New Haven, Conn.: Yale University Press.
Wexman, V. W. (1986) "The Critic as Consumer: Film Study in the University, *Vertigo*, and the Film Canon," *Film Quarterly*, 39 (3): 32–41.
White, P. (2021) *Rebecca*, BFI Classics, London: Bloomsbury Academic.
Wood, R. (1977) *Hitchcock's Films*, 3rd edn, South Brunswick and New York: A. S. Barnes.
Wood, R. (1983) "Fear of Spying," *American Film*, 7 (1): 28–35.
Wood, R. (1989) *Hitchcock's Films Revisited*, New York: Columbia University Press.
Yacowar, M. (1977) *Hitchcock's British Films*, Hamden: Shoestring Press.

Chapter 13
Rope (1948)
A Late Bloomer

Neil Badmington

The reception of *Rope* is a tale of form, technique and—eventually—queer sex. *Rope* was Alfred Hitchcock's first color production and his first film after his contract with David O. Selznick had reached its end. Selznick had brought Hitchcock to California from England in the late 1930s, but their working partnership—which ran from *Rebecca* (1940) to *The Paradine Case* (1947)—favored Selznick creatively and financially, and so Hitchcock opted to strike out independently once he had fulfilled his contractual requirements. This desire for greater freedom led to his founding a production company called Transatlantic Pictures with Sidney Bernstein, a prominent figure in the British film industry.

Transatlantic's first release was an adaptation of Patrick Hamilton's play, *Rope* (also known as *Rope's End* in the USA). The play tells the tale of two young men who murder one of their friends, hide his corpse in a chest in their London flat, and throw a party while the body is still in the trunk. The drama unfolds in real time over the course of a single evening and builds toward the discovery of the crime by an eccentric poet named Rupert Cadell. Hamilton's plot has notable echoes of the case of Nathan Leopold and Richard Loeb, two students at the University of Chicago who murdered fourteen-year-old Robert Franks in 1924. Influenced by Nietzsche and seeing themselves as superior to others, Leopold and Loeb believed that they had perpetrated "the perfect crime," but they were soon caught and charged. Patrick Hamilton insisted that he had not been influenced by the case (Hamilton 1929: ix), but his claim is, as one of the author's biographers puts it, "simply not credible" (French 1993: 101).

Hitchcock's film kept the basic premise of Hamilton's play but shifted the setting to New York, added characters, altered names, and adjusted various other nuances. Hollywood's strict Production Code meant that there could be no open reference to the possibility that the two central male characters—Brandon and Phillip—were involved in a sexual relationship with each other (Badmington 2021: chapter 1; Billheimer 2019: chapter 17). In preserving the way in which Hamilton's drama took place in real time over the course of a single evening, Hitchcock made an unusual, experimental formal choice: *Rope* is made up of just eleven long shots that range from roughly two and a half minutes to nearly ten minutes in duration, during which the camera roams fluidly around the apartment in which almost all of the action takes place. What is more, half of *Rope*'s ten cuts are "masked," in that they attempt to hide the fact that a break in filming has occurred. Contrary to the claims of many, however, the film was neither shot in one take nor made to appear that way: five of *Rope*'s cuts are regular and completely obvious.

The release of the film in August 1948 was supported by a $450,000 marketing campaign, in which the formal and technical innovation of *Rope* was stressed repeatedly. For instance, a publicity booklet produced by Warner Bros. stressed how the film "demanded careful and constant rehearsal and split second timing on the part of the technical crew which worked on the picture. […] The camera moves around more than ever, but only to keep the audience on top of the action" (Warner Bros. 1948). An accompanying statement from Natalie Kalmus, the head of the Color Control Department at Technicolor, celebrated Hitchcock's command of color, and the director himself remarked on the challenges of shooting long takes in a confined space: "Whole sides of the apartment slide away, and the camera follows the actors as they move through the apartment. In order to achieve successful production of this unique technique, a simplified method of securing dolly shots without crane, boom, or tracks was devised" (Warner Bros. 1948).

Meanwhile, in a publicity interview that appeared in *Popular Photography* in 1948, Hitchcock explained how the film's experimental form required careful preparation:

Rope was a miracle of cueing. […] Even before the set was built I worked out each movement on a blackboard in my home. Then in the studio, the stage (actually a stage within a stage, made noiseless by constructing a special floor one and one-half inch above the regular one, soundproofed with layers of Celotex and carpet) was marked with numbered circles. These indicated where each specific camera stop had to be made, and when.

(Hitchcock 1997: 280)

Hitchcock reserved his highest self-praise, however, for a technical element that lay outside the windows of Brandon and Phillip's apartment:

[T]he most magical of all the devices was the cyclorama—an exact miniature reproduction of nearly 35 miles of New York skyline lighted by 8,000 incandescent bulbs and 200 neon signs requiring 150 transformers.

On film the miniature looks exactly Manhattan at night as it would appear from the window of an apartment at 54th Street and First Avenue […]. And since all the major action of *Rope* takes place in the living room of this apartment, with the spectators constantly viewing the background, it was impossible to use process shots or a backdrop. Both would have been too flat. We had to remember the core of the arc of view. So we had to employ the scale cyclorama and devise a "light organ" that not only would light the miniature and its panorama of buildings, but also could give us changing sky and cloud effects varying from sunset to dark—all seen from the apartment—to denote the passing of time.

In the 12,000 square feet of the cyclorama, the largest backing ever used on a sound stage, the spectator sees the Empire State, the Chrysler, and the Woolworth buildings; St. Patrick's, Radio City, and hundreds of other landmarks […]. Each miniature building was wired separately for globes ranging from 25 to 150 watts in the tiny windows. […] Twenty-six thousand feet of wire carried 126,000 watts of power for the building and window illumination—all controlled by the twist of an electrician's wrist, via a bank of 47 switches, as he sat at the light organ high up and far behind the camera.

(Hitchcock 1997: 277–278)

The marketing campaign set the tone for much of the early reception of the film, and the emphasis upon technique and form was reproduced regularly in press coverage of *Rope* around the time of its release. Reviewing the film in the *New York Times* the day after the premiere, for instance, Bosley Crowther began by noting how Hitchcock's "fondness […] for cinematic tours de force" had led the director to try "the trick of shooting a full-length picture in one set and in one continuous scene" (*New York Times*, August 27, 1948, p. 12). "The novelty of the picture," he continued, "is not in the drama itself, it being a plainly deliberate and rather thin exercise in suspense, but merely in the method which Mr. Hitchcock has used to stretch the intended tension for the length of the little stunt" (p. 12).

A little over two months later, a review in the *Gloucester Citizen* newspaper in the United Kingdom devoted most of its three columns to technical matters. "When you see 'Rope,'" the uncredited piece began,

> you will be seeing a film that has made history. To the ordinary cinemagoer the film will look very much like any other technical films [sic]. Just what has made it a milestone in film production will not be noticeable to the audiences. It appears to have the normal sort of camera work; its long, medium and closeup shots do not give any idea of the offstage activity which went to achieve them.
>
> (*Gloucester Citizen*, November 27, 1948)

Contemporary coverage of *Rope* in publications such as *American Cinematographer* (Yates 1948) and the *New York Herald Tribune* (August 27, 1948, p. 10) focused on form and technique in a similar fashion.

When Éric Rohmer and Claude Chabrol wrote the very first book on Hitchcock's work in 1957, they framed *Rope* in the same way. The film, for them, was one of Hitchcock's formal "experiments" (Rohmer and Chabrol 1979: 25) that "serve[d] as a kind of technical rough draft" (1979: 90) for *Under Capricorn* (1949), which continued *Rope*'s commitment to long takes, though in a more subtle and less experimental manner. While Rohmer and Chabrol acknowledged in passing the issue of sexuality in *Rope* (1979: 92), what interested them most was Hitchcock's technique, which "seems to be the most important element in this film" (1979: 91), and the director's "thorough amalgamation of two stylistic genres, the realistic and the thriller" (1979: 94).

Six years later, in an article written for *Movie*, V. F. Perkins proposed that Hitchcock "challenged himself to solve a self-imposed problem" in "each of his major films" (Perkins 1963: 11). "The problem in *Rope*," he continued, "is, of course, the ten minute take, and the challenge is to produce, without the use of editing, a movie which is undeniably 'film'" (1963: 11). For Perkins, the length of the shots is Hitchcock's "main method of making us feel the confinement of his characters" (1963: 12), and this formal innovation is where the "true originality of *Rope* lies" (1963: 11). If "*Rope* makes us feel the power of evil" (1963: 13), it does so thanks to Hitchcock's technical mastery and chosen form.

In terms of the focus on form and technique, little changed in the reception of *Rope* when Robin Wood published the first book-length study in English of the director's work, *Hitchcock's Films*, in 1965. Although Wood, like Rohmer and Chabrol, alluded briefly to the film's "supposed homosexual tensions" (Wood 2002: 16), he was much more interested at this stage in the link between the film's form and the way in which "the camera becomes the spectator's eye" (2002: 78). When Wood revised his book extensively as *Hitchcock's Films Revisited* in 1988, however, he acknowledged that he and V. F. Perkins had "resolutely ignore[d]" in their analyses of *Rope* "what now seems its main source of fascination, the homosexual subtext" (2002: 233). By way of correction, *Hitchcock's Films Revisited* added a chapter titled "The Murderous Gays: Hitchcock's Homophobia," in which Wood began by highlighting what he simply could not see in 1965: "It has been often noted that the figure of the psychopath that recurs throughout Hitchcock's work is sometimes coded (with more or less explicitness) as gay (or in one case lesbian)" (2002: 366).

"Coded" is a key word here, for, as Wood goes on to note, Hollywood's censorship rules made identifying same-sex desire upon the screen impossible:

> But which, in fact, *are* Hitchcock's gay characters? It seems to me a matter far harder to determine that has often precipitously been claimed. […] [P]rior to the '60s, it was impossible openly to acknowledge even the existence of homosexuality in a Hollywood movie; consequently, homosexuality had to be coded, and discreetly, and coding, even when indiscreet, is notoriously likely to produce ambiguities and contradictions.
>
> (2002: 345–346)

Those "ambiguities and uncertainties" can be drawn out of *Rope*, Wood proposes, by asking a series of questions that Hitchcock's film does not allow us to answer definitively:

> *Do* Brandon and Phillip kiss (offscreen)? *Could* they? They are gay and they live together, but are they technically lovers? Today, everyone seems ready to answer in the affirmative, and to regard as very naïve people who didn't "get" this in 1948. The affirmative answer is quite possibly the correct one: I am not saying that it is wrong, only that we can't be so certain and may be thinking unhistorically. The problem doubtless derives from the fact that a Hollywood movie made in the late '40s could not possibly answer a question which it couldn't even raise. Even the matter of the apartment's sleeping accommodation is kept carefully ambiguous: at one point we are told that the telephone is "in the bedroom," which seems to imply that there is only one (and Janet/Joan Chandler's response, "How cozy," can certainly be taken as the film's most loaded comment on the issue); later, however, we hear of a *second* bedroom (neither is ever shown). It's not simply that *Rope* cannot tell us that the two men sleep together; it also cannot tell us clearly that they *don't*, since that would imply that they might.
>
> (2002: 350–351)

Rereading *Rope* forty years on from its release and over twenty years after the publication of the first edition of his book, Wood concluded by pointing the finger at the homophobic world in which Brandon and Phillip lived: "Ultimately, it was society that was responsible for David Kentley's death, and if the film does not and cannot say this, it can, however inadvertently, supply the evidence that enables *us* to say it" (2002: 353–354).

Wood's reassessment in 1988 brought *Rope*'s (homo)sexuality into view and, in doing so, began to alter the reception of the film. Two years later, drawing extensively upon new developments in the field of queer theory, D. A. Miller published an essay that truly shifted the terms of the debate. "Anal *Rope*" opened with an observation that "serious-minded criticism" of the film to date had exhibited a "technicist bias" that rendered existing scholarship "almost definitively shaped by a ritual of recounting and assessing the director's desire to do the film, as he put it, 'in a single shot,' or at any rate as nearly without benefit of montage as the state of the art allowed in 1948, when a camera only held ten minutes' worth of film" (Miller 1990: 114). This "technicist bias," however, usually carried with it a strange technicist error:

For one thing, contrary to all reasonable expectations, it has hardly managed to generate a single accurate account of the technique in question. Again and again, for instance, we are told that each shot in *Rope* runs to ten minutes, whereas the shots range variously from roughly three to nine minutes; or that Hitchcock blackened out the action every time he changed cameras, though only five of *Rope*'s ten cuts are managed this way. It is as though *Rope* criticism aimed less at a description than at a correction of Hitchcock's experiment, for whose irregularities and inconsistencies there is substituted a programmatic perfection that better supports the dream of a continuous film (not yet to mention whatever wishes might find fulfillment in that dream) than Hitchcock's actual shooting practice.

(Miller 1990: 114)

Alongside these inaccuracies, Miller identified a tendency for critics to ignore or downplay the sexuality of the film's two central characters:

Concerning the narrative homosexuality, on the other hand, [*Rope* criticism] affects a bored indifference that seldom goes beyond a brief banalizing acknowledgment […], as though to suggest that the idea and image of men kissing, sucking, fucking one another were altogether devoid of the fascination that, on the contrary, the problems of the mobile camera may be taken for granted to hold in abundance.

(1990: 117)

Miller corrected decades of criticism. Drawing upon Roland Barthes's development of Hjelmslev's distinction between connotation and denotation, he examined how "*Rope* exploits the particular aptitude of connotation for allowing homosexual meaning to be elided even as it is also being elaborated" (1990: 118). Like Robin Wood, Miller singled out Brandon's remark about how the telephone is "in the bedroom," but what Miller added was a more thorough thinking-through of what happens when this moment of connotation is contradicted later in the film by Mrs Atwater's reference to "the *first* bedroom" (which implies that there is another). Meanwhile, the film depicts Brandon as having no girlfriend (which means that "he may be homosexual," Miller observes) but also establishes that "he had a girlfriend once—he may not be" (1990: 119). In short, there is an "abiding deniability" (1990: 118) in *Rope* that is enabled and sustained by connotation and contradiction, an "undecidability that keeps suspicion just that, a thing never substantiated, never cleared" (1990: 119; see Fig. 13.1). Any "desire for proof […] remains a hopeless task" (1990: 123) because the film never delivers a definitive answer. Connotation, Miller concludes, is "the dominant signifying practice of homophobia," in that it constructs "an essentially insubstantial homosexuality" (1990: 119).

Although Miller is critical of the "technicist bias" in earlier analyses of *Rope*, his essay returns to the technical functioning of half of the ten cuts (the five "blackouts," as he calls them). "What *is* gay male sex, according to the film?" he asks. "Of all the body parts, positions, and practices that the term may be thought to encompass, around which in particular does *Rope* fantasmatically entwine itself?" (1990: 127):

The first four blackouts bespeak almost an eagerness to be revealing in this regard. When the camera closes in on the backside of a man's suit only to reward thus intensified expectation with blank darkness, one is invited to imagine that the camera's itinerary has been blocked or, what comes to the same thing, would otherwise have continued—and how otherwise but, with a kind of Xray vision, from

Figure 13.1 Brandon and Phillip—extremely close to each other but always in a state of "abiding deniability."
Rope, directed by Alfred Hitchcock. © Transatlantic Pictures 1948. All rights reserved.

behind the gorgeously tailored suit (*superbement coupé*, as a French critic put it) through the cleft of the buttocks all the way to the perforation of the anus itself, whose cavital darkness would in any case make no difference between an interrupted itinerary and one that had reached its proper destination? Under cover of these blackouts, two things get "hidden." One is the popularly privileged site of gay male sex, the orifice whose sexual use general opinion considers (whatever happens to be the state of sexual practices among gay men and however it may vary according to time and place) the least dispensable element in defining the true homosexual. The other is the cut, for whose pure technicity a claim can hardly be sustained at so overwhelmingly hallucinatory a moment, even if the script didn't link the word with a body wound of irreducible symbolic importance. ("It's nothing; it's just a little cut," says Phillip of his bleeding hand; everybody knows better.) Moreover, these two things, by seeming to come in place of one another, configure one and the same thing: the anus is a cut, and vice versa. The most immediate reason for wanting to hide the cut, then, is that it is imagined to be a penetrable hole in the celluloid film body; and though there are countless obvious and ordinary reasons for wanting to hide the anus, it is hidden here as what remains and reminds of a cut.

(Miller 1990: 127)

When *Rope* ends five of its eleven shots, however, with a regular cut that is visible and unobscured, "the cut is not only shown but shown as being the patron or props of what […] would be called normal male desire (to Rupert twice; to Janet and Mrs. Wilson once apiece)" (1990: 129). In its two approaches to editing, as in its connotation and contradiction, *Rope* binds itself to the wider work of homophobia.

Miller's essay has been a rich and regular reference point for critics with an interest in the film's treatment of sexuality, even if those critics have sometimes taken issue with Miller's conclusions. In *Intimate Violence: Hitchcock, Sex, and Queer Theory*, for instance, David Greven proposes that "While they may contain homophobic elements, Hitchcock's films more acutely critique homophobia as one of the strategies used to inculcate and reinforce the heterosexual economy of gender and sexuality" (2017: 113). For Greven, although the actions of Brandon and Phillip in *Rope* are "hideously destructive" (2017: 119), it is not enough to infer a simple homophobic causality, according to which the two men kill purely because they are gay. The society against which the two young men rebel "also imprisons and delimits them" (2017: 119), and the body of law that forbids murder is the same body of law that forbids their desire for each other. Brandon and Phillip's sense of superiority, Greven continues, "is, at least on some level, an expression of mourning and rage that is most likely related to their sexuality. Further, what they principally chafe against may be not only the overt homophobia but also the stifling silences around the issue in their culture" (2017: 119). The murder is, in short, "a counterassault on heterosexual society" (2017: 120). Inviting his readers to "venture beyond the limits of Miller's argument," Greven concludes that *Rope* "is less a negative image of homosexuality than it is a film that explores homosexuals' negative images about their own identities" (2017: 134).

Although I have focused in this chapter on the dominant themes of form, technique, and sexuality in the reception of *Rope*, I do not mean to imply that all discussions of the film fall neatly into these categories. Other scholars have offered analyses that address, among other things, *Rope*'s treatment of architecture (Jacobs 2007), time (Damasio 2006), Cold War politics (Matthews 2010), and food (McKittrick 2016; Olsson 2015), and the film's use of humor (Smith 2000) and music (Clifton 2013; Paulin 2017; Schroeder 2012). Meanwhile, in *Hidden Hitchcock*, D. A. Miller returned to Brandon and Phillip's apartment more than two decades after the publication of "Anal *Rope*" in order to examine the strange tension between perfection and error that becomes apparent when a "Too-Close Viewer" uses modern technology such as a DVD player to reveal a "perverse counternarrative" based on small continuity errors that would probably have been invisible to audiences in 1948 (Miller 2016: 4–5). If *Rope* is one of Hitchcock's most constrained works, the reception of the film has been anything but.

References

Badmington, N. (2021) *Perpetual Movement*: *Alfred Hitchcock's* Rope, Albany, NY: State University of New York Press.
Billheimer, J. (2019) *Hitchcock and the Censors*, Lexington, Ky.: University Press of Kentucky.
Clifton, K. (2013) "Unravelling Music in Hitchcock's *Rope*," *Horror Studies*, 4 (1): 63–74.
Damasio, A. R. (2006) "How Hitchcock's *Rope* Stretches Time," *Scientific American*, 16 (1): 38–39.
French, S. (1993) *Patrick Hamilton*: *A Life*, London: Faber & Faber.
Greven, D. (2017) *Intimate Violence*: *Hitchcock, Sex, and Queer Theory*, New York: Oxford University Press.
Hamilton, P. (1929) *Rope*: *A Play*, London: Constable & Co.
Hitchcock, A. (1997) "My Most Exciting Picture," in Sidney Gottlieb (ed), *Hitchcock on Hitchcock*: *Selected Writings and Interviews*, London: Faber & Faber, pp. 275–284.
Jacobs, S. (2007) *The Wrong House*: *The Architecture of Alfred Hitchcock*, Rotterdam: 010 Publishers.
Matthews, K. L. (2010) "Reading, Guidance, and Cold War Consensus in Alfred Hitchcock's *Rope*," *Journal of Popular Culture*, 43 (4): 738–760.

McKittrick, C. (2016) *Hitchcock's Appetites*: *The Corpulent Plots of Desire and Dread*, London and New York: Bloomsbury.
Miller, D. A. (1990) "Anal *Rope*," *Representations*, 32 (fall): 114–133.
Miller, D. A. (2016) *Hidden Hitchcock*, Chicago, Ill.: University of Chicago Press.
Olsson, J. (2015) *Hitchcock à la Carte*, Durham, NC: Duke University Press.
Paulin, S. D. (2017) "Unheard Sexualities: Queer Theory and the Soundtrack," in R. Samer and W. Whittington (eds), *Spectatorship*: *Shifting Theories of Gender*, *Sexuality*, *and Media*, Austin, Tex.: University of Texas Press, pp. 77–95.
Perkins, V. F. (1963) "*Rope*," *Movie*, 7: 11–13.
Rohmer, É., and C. Chabrol (1979) *Hitchcock*: *The First Forty-Four Films*, trans. S. Hochman, New York: Ungar.
Schroeder, D. (2012) *Hitchcock's Ear*: *Music and the Director's Art*, London and New York: Continuum.
Smith, S. (2000) *Hitchcock*: *Suspense*, *Humour and Tone*, London: BFI.
Warner Bros. Pictures (1948) *A Photographic Production Notebook on Alfred Hitchcock's Rope*, Los Angeles, Calif.: Warner Bros. Folder 630, Alfred Hitchcock Collection, Margaret Herrick Library, Academy of Motion Picture Arts and Sciences, Beverly Hills, California.
Wood, R. (2002) *Hitchcock's Films Revisited*, rev. edn, New York: Columbia University Press.
Yates, V. (1948) "'*Rope*' Sets a Precedent," *American Cinematographer*, 29 (7): 230–231 and 246.

PART THREE

Films on an Upwards Trajectory

Chapter 14
Downhill (1927)
"The Most Discussed Film Director in England"

Henry K. Miller

Whereas *The Lodger* won instant critical acclaim that was sustained even during the years when it was practically invisible, and was always seen as quintessentially Hitchcockian, his next film, starring and based on a play cowritten by *The Lodger*'s leading man Ivor Novello, came and went on its original release and was effectively forgotten until Hitchcock's fame generated such an interest in his life and work that nothing he did would be allowed to remain undisinterred. If it is possible to imagine *The Lodger* having a critical reputation independent of Hitchcock—if, for example, he had had a career more like that of Victor Saville—then that is not the case with *Downhill*. It is a film that belongs to the complete retrospective season and the comprehensive film-by-film study, and according to Charles Barr, author of one such study, *English Hitchcock*, it "is not a film with a strong claim to being rescued from obscurity" (Barr 1999: 46). Nevertheless, it has inspired some significant insights into Hitchcock's art.

Aside from the question of the film's quality, the context for its original reception was a veritable glut of Hitchcock productions, within which *Downhill* was something of a legacy release. Like *The Lodger*, it was made for Gainsborough Pictures, but under very different circumstances. In May 1926, between the making and the first showing of *The Lodger*, Hitchcock had been poached by a new concern, then called British National but eventually called British International Pictures (BIP), which was even then constructing a new studio at Elstree, where the outer London suburbs met the Hertfordshire countryside. BIP, however, had a protracted gestation, and so in December 1926 Hitchcock agreed to return to Gainsborough to make *Downhill* and *Easy Virtue*. *Downhill* was finished quickly. It went into production on January 17, 1927, the day *The Lodger*, Hitchcock's third film, opened in London, and a week before *The Pleasure Garden*, his first film, went on general release; and it had its trade show on May 24, the day after the low-key release of his second film, *The Mountain Eagle*.

By the time *Downhill* opened to the public, in October 1927, Hitchcock had made and trade-shown not only *Easy Virtue*, destined to be similarly passed over, but also his first film for BIP, *The Ring*, and *The Ring*, which opened to the public in November, less than two months after *Downhill*, eclipsed both of the stopgap films—not least because from the point of view of Hitchcock's contemporaries in Wardour Street (the film trade) and Fleet Street (the press) it represented the future not the past, not only for Hitchcock but also for the big-spending new enterprise that had produced it.

Like *The Lodger* before it, *Downhill* had its trade show at the Hippodrome, a big Leicester Square entertainment hall near Gainsborough's offices, and was written up in the next day's papers. "Mr. Alfred Hitchcock, considered the most brilliant British director, has made a clever picture out of poor and, indeed, unsuitable and undramatic material," wrote Iris Barry in the *Daily Mail* (May 25, 1927, p. 8):

> The film abounds in clever things. One is a device which forcibly and economically shows how the girl makes up a garbled and convincing version of the truth when she spitefully accuses the hero of being her seducer.
> Mr. Hitchcock deliberately and against all film conventions shows up the squalid side of the luxurious dance club.
>
> (*Daily Mail*, May 25, 1927, p. 8)

The review ended there, conceivably victim of the *Mail*'s subeditors, whose practice was to cut for space, but evidently Barry did not have much time for the film. Meanwhile Walter Mycroft, in the *Evening Standard*, made the same argument—"The direction is much too important for the material" (May 25, 1927, p. 2)—but vacillated over a final judgement. After a brief synopsis up to the moment the film's protagonist is shown descending an escalator into the London Underground, Mycroft writes:

> The process is made thoroughly exciting owing to the ingenuity of Mr. Hitchcock. After his fade out from the escalator our youth as to the top part is revealed in evening dress. "Hullo," you say to yourself, "he's still a young man about town." Then the camera "pans," if that is the word, and reveals the lower half as well showing a tell tale napkin. "Oh, only a waiter," you decide. "Rather good that." But Mr. Hitchcock hasn't finished with you yet. The camera twists to show a Riviera scene and then twists some more whereby you discover that Mr. Novello isn't a waiter either. It is a theatre scene and he is a super.
>
> (*Evening Standard*, May 25, 1927, p. 2)

The slight infelicities of style register how quickly Mycroft's review had to be produced for publication, but from a single viewing it identifies and fairly accurately recounts the most memorable scene in the film (see Fig. 14.1). Nonetheless, though he was less articulate about what he thought was wrong with the film, he did not hold it in much higher regard than Barry, his colleague in the Film Society and a mutual friend of the Hitchcocks. (In his autobiography, Mycroft segues from a description of Barry as "very much the modern young woman of that day"—not a compliment—to one of Alma Reville as a woman of a similar stripe, the first he heard utter the word "bastard" (Mycroft 2006: 121).) Though *Downhill* may have pointed uphill for the British film industry, evidently it had not scaled the heights itself. In the *Sunday Express*, G. A. Atkinson, after a descant on Ivor Novello's star appeal—"purely erotic and emotional, and almost wholly, if not entirely, confined to women"—arrived at the judgement that Hitchcock had "produced from a mass of nonsense a masterpiece of cinematic treatment" (*Sunday Express*, May 29, 1927, p. 43).

Trade critics, though they were constrained by their close ties to the distributors to be more favorable than the newspaper critics, largely shared their view, with *Kinematograph Weekly*'s reviewer writing that Hitchcock "has got the utmost out of what is, at the best, a weak and rather intolerably sordid story" (May 26, 1927, p. 48). *Bioscope* said much the same (May 26, 1927, p. 43).

Figure 14.1 The theatre scene in *Downhill*, as described by Walter Mycroft.

A few weeks after the trade show, C. A. Lejeune decided to "take the excuse of his new film 'Downhill' to talk about Mr. Hitchcock" in her column in the *Manchester Guardian*, as she had not so far done, despite their friendship, under the title "Britain's Baby" (June 11, 1927, p. 9). "He has not, nor has any desire to have, the popular touch," she claimed, tying herself up in knots over the question whether he was "a conscious expressionist, or an expressionist in spite of himself." A little like her colleagues, she wrote that "the danger of a man possessing an individual and startling style is that he is apt not to be particular about the occasions on which he uses it," and that *Downhill* "carries out every promise of its predecessor without being at all a good film." The material of *The Lodger* she thought "slight and sensational," that of *Downhill* "downright bad […] I have never seen such an interesting production of rubbish nor a clever film which deserved quite so little praise."

Downhill was booked to have its first run at the Plaza cinema in Lower Regent Street, normally the shop window for Paramount, and so a sign of Gainsborough Pictures' aspirations for the film—it is possible that Gainsborough or its distributor W. & F. paid for the slot. It opened on Sunday, October 9, 1927, sharing the bill with *Chang*, Merian C. Cooper and Ernest B. Schoedsack's proto-documentary, a Paramount release that had been on at the venue for more than a month. Throughout *Downhill*'s fortnight at the Plaza, greatly adding to the buzz around the film as it approached its general release, Ivor Novello made personal appearances during the two evening programmes (see Fig. 14.2), interrupting the show to perform a scene from the film on stage: according to A. Jympson Harman, in the *Evening News*, "the change from screen to stage is accomplished without any break in continuity" (October 10, 1927, p. 9).

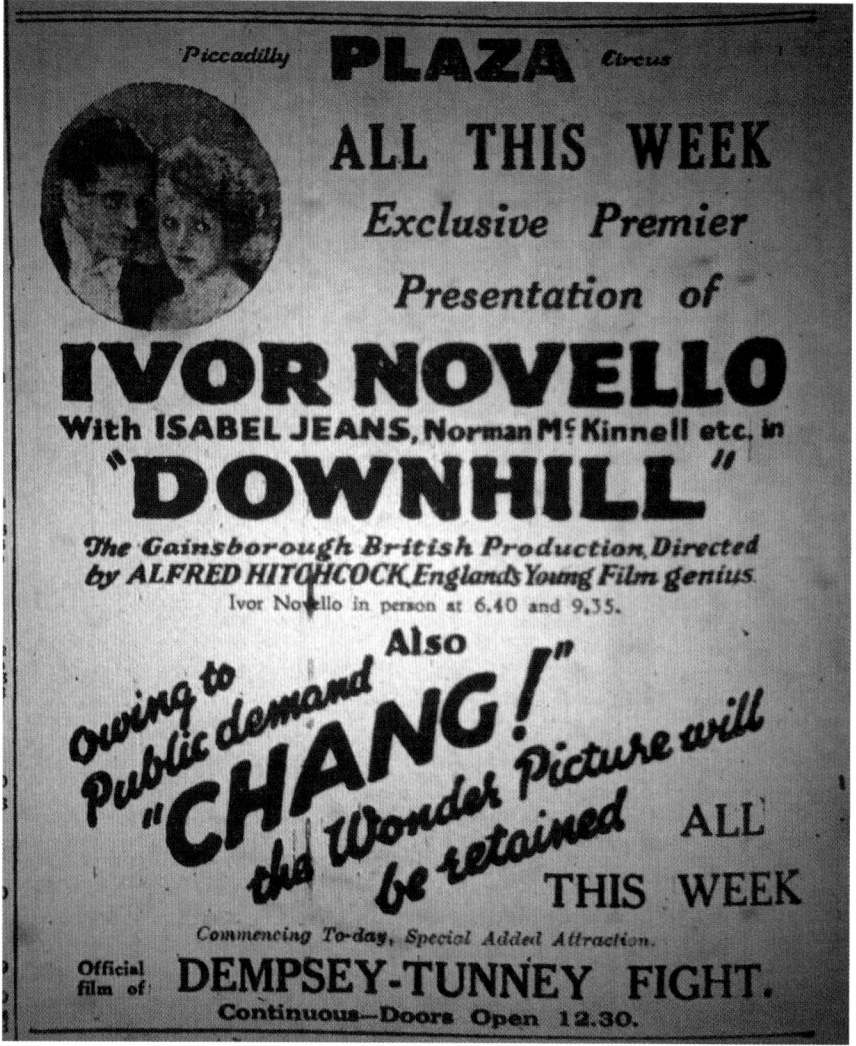

Figure 14.2 Advertisement for *Downhill* in the *Evening News*, October 10, 1927, p. 2.

As had been the case with *The Lodger*, some critics rereviewed *Downhill* on its release while others did not. Iris Barry used the occasion to comment on Hitchcock's prominence, calling him "the most discussed film director in England," deftly downplaying the new film and setting the scene for *The Ring* (*Daily Mail*, October 10, 1927, p. 17). Whereas *Downhill* and *Easy Virtue* "each possessed remarkable qualities," she wrote—note the use of the past tense for a film released the day before the article appeared, and another not yet released—with *The Ring* Hitchcock had "demonstrated once and for all that films worthy of exhibition throughout the world can be made in this country."

In much the same spirit, G. A. Atkinson, in the *Daily Express*, introduced *Downhill* as "a new production from Alfred Hitchcock, whose latest film, 'The Ring,' is one of the screen sensations of the year"—

evidently *Downhill* was not (*Daily Express*, October 10, 1927, p. 13). However, while other critics made only vague references to weak material, Atkinson, amplifying remarks he had made in his earlier review in the *Sunday Express*, made a frontal assault on the film's politics, which he saw as undermining the "public-school tradition," meaning the upper-middle-class code of conduct that, as he remarked, had "lost its fine edge owing to the levelling influence of the war." Nevertheless, Atkinson repeated that he was "willing to agree that from this mass of nonsense Mr Hitchcock has evolved a masterpiece of cinematic treatment." As had happened with *The Lodger*, Mycroft did not rereview *Downhill*, but the following month he too made a great fuss over *The Ring*—a film he later claimed to have helped Hitchcock write (Mycroft 2006: 36–37), putting his charitable response to *Downhill* in context.

Thirty years later, Rohmer and Chabrol wrote that the original critics' response to *Downhill* "now strikes us as severe and unjust" and that it was "possible to prefer it to *The Lodger*" (Rohmer and Chabrol 1979: 10). Very little seems to have been said about the film in the intervening three decades. Just like their predecessors, however, Rohmer and Chabrol saw *Downhill* as a mediocre story enlivened by Hitchcock's gifts as a "camera virtuoso" (1979: 11) and did not strain every rhetorical sinew to explain their apparent preference for it over *The Lodger*. The British and American critics who seized on the French writers' championing of Hitchcock tended not to adopt their specific verdicts beyond the general preference for the American films, and so it proved with *Downhill*. The most substantial scholarly works on the film, published by James Vest in the *Hitchcock Annual* in the mid-2000s, do not make great claims for its critical revaluation.

The most striking justification for *Downhill* is suggested by Raymond Durgnat's work, in particular his book *The Strange Case of Alfred Hitchcock*, published in 1974, and the magazine series from which it was expanded, published in *Films and Filming* in 1970. Over the years, one particular title-card from *Downhill* had been singled out for mockery, notably by its producer Michael Balcon—"Can I—won't I be able to play for the Old Boys?"—and insofar as the film had a reputation, it was summed up by this scene's comic plaintiveness. Durgnat defended the card itself but saw evidence in *Downhill* of Hitchcock being "in awe of the public school spirit" (1974: 74), thereby unwittingly reversing G. A. Atkinson's verdict. But Durgnat also saw in this apparent servility something more revealing of Hitchcock—very much not the product of a public-school education—and his audience.

In the book's introduction, Durgnat attempts to characterize Hitchcock's background as being shaped not only by the Catholicism in which he was schooled but perhaps even more so by the "Anglo-Saxon lower-class Protestantism" (1974: 45) that prevailed in early-twentieth-century London; both cultures, he commented, shared an emphasis on fear. For Durgnat, this fear was at once extramundane and corporeal—fear of God, fear of being caned by his Jesuit schoolmasters. In a paragraph that he did not incorporate into the book, perhaps because the section of the magazine series in which it appeared had already been reprinted in Arthur J. LaValley's *Focus on Hitchcock*, Durgnat went further in trying to adumbrate the peculiar mental climate that he felt he and Hitchcock more or less shared as sons of nearly neighbouring London suburbs (Durgnat 1970: 60): "Hitchcock's English world overlaps with that of Greene, or Orwell, with his vision of the semi-detached houses as so many 'cells of fear.'"[1]

It was a phrase that Durgnat used more than once, and he used it again in relation to Hitchcock in a *Sight and Sound* supplement published to mark Hitchcock's centenary. Orwell, he wrote,

> saw those long lines of terraced houses, all soot-blackened, as "cells of fear"—fear of non-respectability; fear of falling, morally or socially; fear of the quiet, neighbourly "English murder." All these fears make

Hitchcock motifs, though they're often transposed into movie daydream terms (posh rich slick heroes, smart exciting milieus). Or they're metaphored by nightmarelike thrillers, such as falls from edges and lofty faces (a God in the British Museum, the Statue of Liberty, four dead presidents).

(Durgnat 1999: 2)

The thought is completed by what Durgnat wrote twenty-five years earlier in the book version of *The Strange Case of Alfred Hitchcock*, where he again invoked Orwell in the section on *Downhill*; had he retained the "cells of fear" line from the 1970 version where it belonged, earlier in the book, it would constitute a reference back. *Downhill*, he wrote, "paraphrases that fear of social downfall which existed even more intensely during the economic miseries of the interwar years" particularly among the lower middle class whence Hitchcock came, and which made up such a high proportion of the cinema audience, and even more particularly among "those whom George Orwell, borrowing the phrase from a music hall song, described as the shabby genteel" (Durgnat 1974: 75). The hero of *Downhill* has a fear of social falling that everyone can relate to, even if he is falling from a higher rung; and that, for Durgnat, was Hitchcock's master fear, or one of them, so that in the Durgnatian imagination, *Downhill*, for all its shortcomings, expresses more directly what Hitchcock's other films only metaphored.

Note

1   It is unclear where or indeed whether Orwell actually used this phrase.

References

Barr, C. (1999) *English Hitchcock*, Moffat: Cameron & Hollis.
Durgnat, R. (1970) "The Strange Case of Alfred Hitchcock: Part Three," *Films and Filming*, 16 (7): 59–60.
Durgnat, R. (1974) *The Strange Case of Alfred Hitchcock, or The Plain Man's Hitchcock*, London: Faber & Faber.
Durgnat, R. (1999) "The Business of Fear," Hitchcock supplement, *Sight and Sound*, 9 (8): 2–11.
LaValley, A. J. (ed.) (1972) *Focus on Hitchcock*, Englewood Cliffs, NJ: Prentice Hall.
Mycroft, W. C. (2006) *The Time of My Life: The Memoirs of a British Producer*, Lanham, MD: Scarecrow Press.
Rohmer, É., and C. Chabrol (1979) *Hitchcock: The First Forty-Four Films*, trans. S. Hochman, New York: Frederick Ungar.
Vest, J. M. (2004) "Metamorphoses of *Downhill*: From Stage Play to Cinematic Treatment and Film," *Hitchcock Annual*, vol. 13, pp. 64–91.
Vest, J. M. (2005–2006) "The Making of *Downhill* and Its Impact on Hitchcock's Reputation," *Hitchcock Annual*, vol. 14, pp. 50–94.

Chapter 15
Under Capricorn (1948)
Hitchcock, Melodrama, and the Christian Imagination

Richard Allen

Hitchcock regarded his films as melodramas, as life with the dull bits cut out (Hitchcock 2015: 76–77), of which *Under Capricorn* (1949), in its reworking of gothic melodrama and its invocation of the "fallen woman," is an exemplary instance. However, many critics, with some notable exceptions like Charles Barr (1999: 74–77) and Robin Wood (1986: 327–335), have been reluctant to take Hitchcock seriously as a maker of melodramas. This is no doubt in part because of the negative connotations of excessive sentimentality attached to the term, which Hitchcock himself baulked at, but it is also because of the emphasis that critics, including myself (Allen 2007), have attached to Hitchcock's mastery of form and style, in which Hitchcock complicates the morality of melodrama. But, as I will argue in this chapter, we can also understand the complexity of form in Hitchcock as the complexity of melodrama itself. At least two transformations of melodrama are salient to understanding Hitchcock's films in general and *Under Capricorn* in particular.

First, late-nineteenth- and early-twentieth-century melodrama underwent a shift in moral characterization. While heroism and villainy were perhaps never in straightforward moral counter position to one another, in the late nineteenth century, a form of melodrama emerged in which the hero himself was sharply divided between good and bad traits and defined by moral ambivalence (Mayer 2004: 159). Divided-hero melodramas like Robert Louis Stevenson's *Jekyll and Hyde* (1886), Oscar Wilde's *The Picture of Dorian Gray* (1890), and Marie Belloc Lowndes's *The Lodger* (1913), had a profound influence on Hitchcock's formation as a storyteller. In *Under Capricorn*, the legacy of the divided hero is seen in the brooding Sam Flusky (Joseph Cotten), whose character in part draws on the persona of Uncle Charlie in *Shadow of a Doubt* (1943). His darkest impulses, class resentment, and suspicion of Hattie—Lady Henrietta (Ingrid Bergman)—are cultivated by the demonic Milly (Margaret Leighton), while his fundamental goodness is reflected in his tolerance and loyalty toward her during her descent into alcoholism. Charles Adare (Michael Wilding), who seeks to rescue her, is divided between his impulse to compete with Flusky and force himself upon Hattie, and his nobler, more altruistic instinct. Even Milly, who is in many ways the archetypal villain of melodrama, is a figure of some sympathy, for she is right to suspect Adare's motives. So melodrama, as *Under Capricorn* attests, may be complicated in its morality yet retain the lineaments of the form.

Second, as Linda Williams has argued in relationship to *Uncle Tom's Cabin* (1852), the Christian narrative of acquiescence to suffering, subsequent to the final great rescue in the afterlife, is complicated in secular melodrama by the fact that characters assume agency to overcome their condition in the here and now (Williams 2001: 48–65). Melodrama frequently has recourse to the rescue narrative to reconcile the dramaturgy of suffering with agency. Often it is the female innocent who suffers and the male hero who rescues, though from the beginning of the nineteenth century, melodrama had its share of plucky heroines (Rahill 1967: 49–52). *Uncle Tom's Cabin* is significant in this context, for it is the male character, Uncle Tom, who assumes a Christlike suffering and the female character, Eliza, the heroine, who escapes. Hitchcock's films in general not only question the male rescue formula in their divided heroes, they also bestow agency upon their heroines, even as they are made to suffer—sometimes, it seems, inordinately so. In *Under Capricorn*, Lady Henrietta is at once a martyr to suffering and an agent in her own redemption.

While the French critics writing in *Cahiers du cinéma* and elsewhere discerned the centrality of religious themes in Hitchcock and identified *Under Capricorn* as a signal instance of these themes, the topic of Hitchcock and religion has been sidelined in the literature. It is, I think, not simply that critics are embarrassed by the claims made by the French for Hitchcock's high moral tone but that they rightly take issue with the very idea of Hitchcock as a religious director that the French writers seem to espouse. Robin Wood, who embraces *Under Capricorn* as a melodrama of social injustice, dismisses as "claptrap" any association of the character of Milly with diabolism and original sin (Wood 1986: 334). The challenge is to recognize the religious inspiration in Hitchcock's work while acknowledging the transformations wrought upon it by the secular tradition of melodrama. Though he doesn't speak in terms of melodrama, the critic who comes closest to achieving this is Leslie Brill. Brill argues that it is the love between a man and a woman in Hitchcock's work that is the secular form of divine grace in a fallen world and that this love is typically redeemed by the faith of the woman in the man, though its realization is always threatened by demonic figures tinged with perversion (Brill 1988). This is the right sort of explanation if we are seeking to understand the Christian imagination in Hitchcock.

I will argue here that *Under Capricorn* is an articulate example of how the Christianity of pathos (Mâle 1986: 450) informs the very vocabulary of melodrama, even as the religious belief supported by affective piety recedes in its often secular world. We might say that in *Under Capricorn* Hitchcock declares his hand as a maker of melodramas and does so in terms that make explicit the indebtedness of melodrama to the rhetorical form of Christian affective piety, of sin, suffering, and redeeming love, even as the import of this story is transformed by being transposed into a secular story of suffering and redemption through love. A skeptic may respond that such indebtedness is rather easy to display in a costume picture set in the nineteenth century and that *Under Capricorn* is an exceptional film in Hitchcock's oeuvre. But while a full accounting would have to take into consideration Hitchcock's entire corpus, it is instructive nonetheless that Hitchcock should turn to making a film like *Under Capricorn* having launched his own company with Sidney Bernstein under the banner of Transatlantic Pictures, which gave him a kind of creative freedom that he had not tasted since he moved to America in 1939. The first film he made with his own production company, *Rope* (1948), has been considered a singularly important film, a clue to Hitchcock's overall preoccupations, both in its formal experimentation and in its frank exploration of human perversity, to which its experimental form is linked. Equally, but for different reasons, I would suggest that his second and last Transatlantic Picture, *Under Capricorn*, is also a signature work in his canon.

At the center of *Under Capricorn* lies the figure of the penitent Magdalen in the person of Lady Henrietta Flusky, as Ed Gallafent has pointed out (2005: 68–84). Mary Magdalen was, according to Christian mythology, a beautiful, aristocratic woman whose wealth allowed the indulgence of all the vanities attributed to women, but most specifically concupiscence, which led inexorably in the minds of the church fathers to prostitution (Jansen 2000). The penitent Magdalen, the reformed prostitute, became the patron saint of sinners and, according to tradition, spent many decades in prayer and flagellation in her mountain wilderness grotto for her sins. The fact that her sin was of a sexual nature connects her transgression to man's original sin and his essentially fallen nature, which Christ's sacrifice sought to assuage. This contrasts her character as a reformed sinner with Eve, the temptress, who caused the fall of mankind. Mary Magdalen is a critical figure for the evolution of the secular tradition of melodrama for, unlike the figure of Christ himself or the Virgin Mary, she provides a template for flawed innocence. Yet her contrition is so complete that she attains in tradition the saintly purity of the Virgin Mary herself (see Figs. 15.1 and 15.2).

The story of the Magdalen inspires the "fallen women" melodrama, so prevalent in nineteenth-century fiction and twentieth-century film, in which the woman of essential virtue is tarnished with ill repute and falls into a destitution which is at once physical and spiritual. A woman may fall in melodrama because of assault or abandonment, but the reason Henrietta suffers ill repute in *Under Capricorn* is because she has the temerity to follow her heart's desire in the face of social sanction. However, in contrast to standard fallen-woman stories, where the woman is denied marriage or cast out from marriage, Hattie's traumatic fall from society takes place as a consequence of marriage. At the origins of her fall is a sexual and social transgression—running away with the stable boy—which is then compounded by a homicide. Hattie elopes with Flusky, her stable-boy lover and then, confronted by her brutal unforgiving brother Dermot, who clearly deems her actions a violation of family honor, she shoots him in self-defense. This divides the newlyweds at the point of their union since Flusky, rather than Hattie, takes responsibility for the killing. Flusky, the "wrong man," is convicted and sent into penal servitude in Australia, where his lady follows him, desperate and destitute. In this sense, Flusky shares in Hattie's fall. Though he does not have very far to drop in social status, he carries the stigma of his social transgression and incarceration. The very title *Under Capricorn* suggests their fall spatially in the place "down under" and also their fall beneath the sign of sexual desire.

The portrayal of class injustice is a commonplace of melodrama; indeed, many critics have argued that it is central to an idiom that emerged at the turn of the nineteenth century to make sense of the dramatic shift from an aristocratic society based on tradition and custom to one governed by the marketplace and individual self-determination (McWilliam 2018: 171). *Under Capricorn* dramatizes the social injustice of an oppressive class system that classifies people as worthy or not on account of where they were born, and polices relationships based on differences in birth and social status. Hattie is the victim of an honor code mentality that dictates that a woman of her birth cannot marry beneath her on pain of death, where patriarchal class hierarchies are maintained by policing and controlling female sexuality through the threat of violence. It is this whole system that the love between the protagonists and Hattie's act of fratricide transgresses. Yet the killing and the sacrifices that issue from it also serve to activate the oppressive force of the class system, causing the weight of social ostracism and stigma to bear down on the couple, preventing them from finding comfort in each other and causing them to doubt the validity of their taboo-breaking love, even in the land of fresh starts and new opportunities that they now inhabit.

Figure 15.1 Henrietta (Ingrid Bergman), wearing the floral garland of Mary Magdalen, signifying purity of heart.

Figure 15.2 The bare feet of Henrietta, signifying penitence.

While Christianity seems to downplay the attainment of terrestrial justice in favor of justice in the afterlife, an ostensible concern with social justice is at the heart of Christ's teaching, as in the words that Matthew imputes to Jesus: "And I say unto you, it is easier for a camel to go through the eye of a needle than for a rich man to enter into the kingdom of God" (Matthew 19:24). In *Under Capricorn*, Flusky quotes a parable of Christ about the corrupting influence of wealth as he describes to Adare the deterioration of his relationship to Hattie. "There was nothing to talk about that we were willing to talk about. What is it that they say in the Bible? A great gulf fixed." This is a reference to the parable told by Jesus (Luke 16:19–31) of a rich man "dressed in purple and fine linen, who lived each day in joyous splendor," and a beggar, Lazarus, who was "covered with sores" and who longed "to be fed by the crumbs that fell from the rich man's table." The rich man dies and goes straight to Hell. When he sees Lazarus with Abraham in Heaven, he asks Lazarus to bring him water for he is burning in the fires, but Abraham informs him that this is impossible because, even if one might wish to cross the great gulf between Heaven and Hell, it is a gulf that cannot be traversed.

Flusky's allusion to this parable serves to evoke the way in which the couple have become both physically and spiritually isolated. Their isolation is articulated in *Under Capricorn* by Hitchcock's carefully orchestrated representation of the spatial divisions between upstairs and downstairs, especially through long-take camera movements that at once divide and unite them. Henrietta describes her bedroom to Adare in idealized terms—"this beautiful place, this beautiful room"—though it is very much a false heaven. Flusky, on the other hand, spends his time patrolling the downstairs with furrowed brow. As the long tracking shot that introduces Adare and the spectator to the house reveals, the downstairs is defined by the proximity of the very large living and dining room area to the hellish kitchen that is filled with cackling female ex-convicts kept in check by Millie's whip. Unlike Adare, who immediately seeks to bridge the divide upon his arrival as he sets about rescuing Hattie from an imaginary foe in her bedroom, Flusky remains downstairs throughout, until the point at which he finally ascends the staircase to comfort Hattie prior to rescuing her from Milly.

However, Flusky's biblical allusion equally draws attention to what he perhaps initially unconsciously believes, and then finally affirms when pessimism, skepticism, and Millie's influence take hold of him: the underlying reason for his separation from Henrietta is the great gulf between them in social status. Furthermore, the parable suggests that even though Flusky and Hattie had seemingly crossed the great divide through their marriage, their attempt to do so seems doomed to fail, and their failure in this matter seems predestined. Here we get close to the topic of original sin, which so exercised Hitchcock's French champions of the 1950s, but not quite in the form that those critics conceived it. If there is an original sin in *Under Capricorn*, it lies not in what happened in the Garden of Eden but, as Brill (1988: 262) perceptively suggests, in the rigid system of social status that overshadows the actions of the protagonists in the film and draws Flusky back into its orbit even in spite of himself.

Hitchcock's French critics speak extensively about original sin in Hitchcock's work, which they link to the idea of a "transfer of guilt." Chabrol and Rohmer write that guilt in Hitchcock "is perhaps less of a moral than of a metaphysical order. It is ... part of our very nature, the heritage of original sin" (1988: 128) or "the interchangeable guilt of all mankind" (1988: 149). We might call this the "metaphysical unconscious." However, examples of the "transfer of guilt" they cite are more prosaic and psychological. They involve individuals being assigned responsibility for something that they did not do, or, as in *Under Capricorn*, assuming responsibility for something someone else did. This "exchange" creates a connection between the two individuals involved, a circle of complicity or what Chabrol and Rohmer call a "community of sin" (1988: 114). Jacques Rivette provides an elegant analysis of this aspect of *Under*

Capricorn: "The transfer of the responsibility for sin had in the past divided the couple, one assuming the punishment, the other the guilt; this inadequately accepted sacrifice forces them to give themselves up to the intoxication of other mutual sacrifices, incessantly renewed" (1988: 99; see also Rivette 2018: 40). In the mind of the French critics, the link between the metaphysical and the psychological senses of the term seems partly forged by the psychoanalytic idea of an unconscious "transference" of guilt, where an attitude or emotion like guilt that belongs to one person is "unconsciously" adopted by another. However, this concept remains psychological; it does not properly take account of the objective, impersonal force of original sin. There is a better way to connect the two.

While Hattie is like the Magdalen in her penitence, at the same time she is fundamentally unlike her, for she does not ultimately accept the naming and shaming that accompanies her transgression and is a common feature of the "fallen woman" melodrama. On the contrary, her actions expose the edifice of social power and control that produces shame and guilt, even as that edifice persists. If we are to understand the invisible hand that produces shame and guilt, it is not something metaphysical at all but the all-too-human social constructs of status, class, and caste. The inevitability of these structures and the way they govern the lives of the protagonists in a melodrama like *Under Capricorn* is the shadow cast upon secular dramaturgy by original sin, which is sometimes so overwhelming that it feels like the hand of fate. The inherited moral hierarchies of class and caste societies that rank individuals according to their place in a social system are also where the "transfer of guilt" comes home to roost in the secular domain. For what is the honor code of patriarchal class and caste society other than a system based upon the "transfer of guilt," where the woman is a totemic vessel of purity and incipient bearer of shame for who she is and of guilt for what she does? Not only is the woman's fall from grace and loss of honor a shame borne by all that can only be assuaged by killing, she is "always already" shameful. That is, a woman born into an honor society of class or caste must from the beginning be hidden away or protected and cannot assume any kind of public agency. Hattie's quest for love, her unwillingness to bow to social pressure, her brave act of self-defense, her subsequent loyalty to Flusky, and her stoic resistance to suffering in *Under Capricorn* are a protest against all this.

We often think of Hitchcock as a modernist director, working within the idiom of popular cinema, a self-conscious master of style and form who complicates the vocabulary of melodrama that he inherits from nineteenth-century and twentieth-century popular cinema. This is certainly the case. Yet at the same time, as *Under Capricorn* attests, we can equally understand Hitchcock's achievement as a perpetuation and renewal of the tradition of nineteenth-century melodrama under the influence of its complex late-nineteenth-century and early-twentieth-century forms, where the moral Manicheism of classical melodrama was unsettled by a complex and ambivalent understanding of human motivation within a post-Romantic and post-Freudian world. More specifically, in *Under Capricorn*, a story about origins, Hitchcock and his collaborators revisit the nineteenth-century melodrama in a way that self-consciously reveals secular melodrama's own conditions of existence in the Western, Christian imaginary of a fallen, divided, and violent world that can only redeemed by grace in the form of love.

Acknowledgments

Excerpted with minor revisions from Richard Allen (2019) "*Under Capricorn*: Hitchcock, Melodrama, and the Christian Imagination," *Hitchcock Annual*, vol. 23, pp. 107–140. The research for this paper was supported by a grant from the Research Grants Council of the Hong Kong Special Administrative

Region, China (Project No. CityU 11600018). Many thanks to Sid Gottlieb and Christine Gledhill for their comments on an earlier draft and to Adrian Martin for supplying French source texts. A special appreciation to Robert Kapsis for his help in editing and overseeing the preparation of this shortened version.

References

Allen, R. (2007) *Hitchcock's Romantic Irony*, New York: Columbia University Press.
Barr, C. (1999) *English Hitchcock*, Moffat: Cameron & Hollis.
Brill, L. (1988) *The Hitchcock Romance*: *Love and Irony in Hitchcock's Films*, Princeton, NJ: Princeton University Press.
Gallafent, E. (2005) "The Dandy and the Magdalen: Interpreting the Long Take in Hitchcock's *Under Capricorn* (1949)," in John Gibbs and Douglas Pye (eds), *Style and Meaning*: *Studies in the Detailed Analysis of Film*, Manchester: Manchester University Press, pp. 68–84.
Hitchcock, A. (2015) "Why I Make Melodramas," in S. Gottlieb (ed.), *Hitchcock on Hitchcock*, vol. II, Berkeley, Calif.: University of California Press, pp. 76–77.
Jansen, K. L. (2000) *The Making of the Magdalen*: *Preaching and Popular Devotion in the Later Middle Ages*, Princeton, NJ: Princeton University Press.
Mâle, E. (1986) *Religious Art in France*: *The Late Middle Ages—A Study of Medieval Iconography and Its Sources*, trans. M. Mathews, Princeton, NJ: Princeton University Press.
Mayer, D. (2004) "Encountering Melodrama," in K. Powell (ed.), *The Cambridge Companion to Victorian and Edwardian Theatre*, Cambridge: Cambridge University Press, pp. 145–163.
McWilliam, R. (2018) "Melodrama and Class," in C. Williams (ed.), *The Cambridge Companion to English Melodrama*, Cambridge: Cambridge University Press, pp. 163–175.
Rahill, F. (1967) *The World of Melodrama*, University Park, Pa.: Pennsylvania State University Press.
Rivette, J. (2018) *Textes Critiques*, Post éditions.
Rohmer, É., and C. Chabrol (1988) *Hitchcock*: *The First Forty-Four Films*, New York: Continuum.
Williams, L. (2001) *Playing the Race Card*: *Melodramas of Black and White from Uncle Tom to O. J. Simpson*, Princeton, NJ: Princeton University Press.
Wood, R. (1986) *Hitchcock's Films Revisited*, New York: Columbia University Press.

Chapter 16

The Reception History of Hitchcock's *The Trouble with Harry* (1955)

Sidney Gottlieb

My aim in this essay is to survey and summarize critical commentary on Alfred Hitchcock's *The Trouble with Harry* in reviews that appeared on its first release in 1955 and on its rerelease in 1984 and also in essays in film journals and academic studies from the mid-1950s to the present day. Commentary on a Hitchcock film often both contributes to and reveals much about the overall conception at a particular time of Hitchcock as a filmmaker, with varying degrees of accuracy and idiosyncrasy. A common concern—sometimes a starting point, sometimes a concluding judgment, and sometimes a standard of evaluation and analysis—is whether or not the film is typical or atypical of Hitchcock, or whether it is superior or inferior Hitchcock. But at the same time as I try to plug my individual case study into that broader picture of Hitchcock, I also focus on the simultaneous story told by a close look at the body of commentary on *The Trouble with Harry*: the collaborative unfolding of the numerous layers of meaning and cinematic embodiment in this particular film. The picture of Hitchcock's reputation that emerges is a collage, and the history of *The Trouble with Harry* does not reduce easily to the kind of linear pattern that we often gravitate to and sometimes impose.

Early Promotion and Reviews in the USA

Initial reviewers of the film would probably have, like theater audiences, been prepared by watching the trailer, titled "Autumn in Vermont," the first half of which is a picturesque travelogue of the autumal scenery that is featured through the film and promoted as one of its main selling points. Reviewers, not just theater managers, may well have consulted the material in the detailed Paramount Showmanship Manual (1955) circulated with the film, containing numerous full-blown specimen reviews of the film that could be used, excerpted, or otherwise drawn from, and a variety of ads emphasizing that this film was "The Unexpected from Hitchcock!"—"Unexpected Romance … Unexpected Comedy … Unexpected Suspense."

Some ads aimed to have it all ways, announcing that the film contains "All You'd Expect from a Great Hitchcock Picture … Plus the Unexpected," and that it was "daringly different" but still a "Hitchcock shocker!"

Hitchcock not only directed his films but did what he could to direct the reception of them, and he repeatedly primed the audiences by describing *The Trouble with Harry* as "a comedy with a corpse" that will "make the audience laugh and scare them just a little" (quoted in Alpert 1955: 102) and repeatedly saying that it's "the pixy in me" that led to choosing this story to film (*Christian Science Monitor*, October 3, 1955, p. 10). In a prerelease article that came out under Hitchcock's name, even the title set out several lines that would be frequently followed in reviews, including a focus on the beautiful setting and an almost obligatory punning on the film's title: "Trouble with Vermont, It's Nice Place to Live or Die" (Hitchcock 1955). For many reviewers, the setting was the major attraction, and even in negative reviews the pictorial beauty was almost always mentioned and praised. The setting was the subject of one particularly fine critical analysis of the film, unexpectedly focusing on the unique qualities of sound in Vermont. Six months before the film's release, E. B. Radcliffe commented extensively on the "freshness and newness in common everyday sounds" throughout the film and how effectively they established the mood (*Cincinnati Inquirer*, April 3, 1955, section 3:8). He concludes by quoting Hitchcock on his use of the "fullness" of the "nighttime silence of the countryside": "I've never heard a silence that was so absolute … And at the same time so full of indefinable 'sounds.' It made a perfect, sinister, suggestive background for the gruesome whimsicalities of our picture."

When the film was released on October 3, 1955, the initial reviews were critical but by no means all negative. The *Hollywood Reporter*, noting how "whimsical" and "pixillated" the film is, states that it may be a film more for the "classes" rather than the "masses" (October 7, 1955). The review praises the scenery and the photography but notes numerous weaknesses, including that "few of the laughs are played against any straight character," that "All the scenes are funny, but they risk monotony by being funny in the same way," and that, finally, "because of his age, the thought of a physical relationship between [Edmund Gwenn and Mildred Natwick] is not particularly attractive." The review in *Variety* begins by saying that it is "not a catch-on-quick picture" and may have to settle for slow success, and concludes with high and discerning praise for the scenery, photography, wonderfully paired lovers, exceptionally good writing, and a particular appreciation for the "saucy talk" (*Variety*, October 12, 1955, p. 6).

Reviews in major newspapers often considered as opinion leaders were also mixed. For Bosley Crowther, the film is "a curiously whimsical thing," hampered by a "not particularly witty or clever script," indifferent direction, a "leisurely, almost sluggish pace," and "humor [that is] frequently strained" (*New York Times*, October 18, 1955, p. 46). He concludes with some appreciation of the film's "mild and mellow merriment" but makes clear in this and a follow-up review that what the film does best is not particularly valuable, calling "Alfred Hitchcock's candid opera bouffe (not boff)" (*New York Times*, October 23, 1955, p. X1). On the contrary, William Zinsser's two positive reviews of the film shrewdly anticipate that "Some moviegoers may find this picture too whimsical" but conclude that "most people should enjoy the comedy as much as Hitchcock obviously enjoyed making it" (*New York Herald Tribune*, October 18, 1955, p. 16; October 30, 1955, p. D1). He encourages audiences to make an adjustment and appreciate that he "spoofs the traditional murder movie"—and this includes the traditional Hitchcock film—directing with "rare sophistication," never crossing "the line between humor and offensiveness" despite a script "bursting with risque double meanings."

An overview essay by Richard Griffith briefly considers *The Trouble with Harry* as an example of how "Critics Disagree Over Values of New Pictures" (*Los Angeles Times*, November 23, 1955, p. 16). A reference to Zinsser's exuberant defense of the film's "overly whimsical characters" follows a quotation from an unnamed source that unhesitatingly describes the characters in the film as "desperately unreal, without depth" and our complete lack of "care [for] what happens to the corpse, or anyone who sees it," damning evidence confirming that "This is Alfred Hitchcock reaching bottom as a movie maker."

These latter comments echo the opinions expressed in the two most negative and dismissive reviews that I have found: Moira Walsh, writing in the Catholic-sponsored magazine *America*, not known for its support of anything daring or unconventional, notes that Hitchcock's attempt at humor in the film "rather spectacularly fails" (November 12, 1955), and John McCarten's review, in the *New Yorker*, usually associated with its appreciation of adventurous and challenging art in general, is tersely damning of more than this one film: "Alfred Hitchcock, whose work has been going downhill since he arrived in Hollywood, skids to preposterous depths in *The Trouble with Harry*. This is an overblown joke about a corpse" (October 29, 1955).

One of the most detailed early reviews in America is nearly as negative as McCarten's, but is by no means dismissive. Andrew Sarris presents Hitchcock as a director going "downhill," and sees *The Trouble with Harry* as yet another Hitchcock film "reaching for the smart touch" and as a result making films of fragmented moments rather than ones portraying "a procession of people and events … going somewhere" (1955: 31). While "ambitious," the film "sag[s] badly in the playing," and the overall conception "drag[s] along from scene to scene without much inner motivation" and substitutes what turns out to be only "pretty shots of the autumn foliage" for what should be a deeper "sense of milieu." But Sarris's essay is by no means simple director assassination: it is serious criticism to be reckoned with, and the concerns he raises in fact would be addressed and answered in years to come by serious critics more appreciative of Hitchcock's ambitions and accomplishments.

In an in-house report on the film several months after its release, summarizing and evaluating reviews to date, the studio of course did some cherry-picking, but there were plenty of cherries to be picked. In a full-page notice in *Paramount World* (February 1956, p. 10), their predictable PR hyperbole—"The nation's newspaper critics have … gone overboard in praise of this 'unexpected comedy-thriller'"— is at least supported by solid evidence, more than a dozen quotations from newspapers across the USA that do read as "rave reviews." And while Hitchcock was disappointed that the film was not more commercially successful and critically appreciated, which he attributed in part to the nature of the film's comedy and also what he thought was Paramount's lack of publicity effort (DeRosa 2001: 149), the studio spoke glowingly of "the film doing solid boxoffice business all over the country" (*Paramount World*, February 1956, p. 10) and highlighted stories of the great business this "thriller-killer-diller" film was doing.

The Trouble with Harry in England

The next wave of critical commentary came when the film was released in England, on March 26, 1956 (trade shown on March 20). Given Hitchcock's own insistence that the film exemplified a British kind of humor, one might predict an overwhelmingly warm response in England. This was not exactly the case, and, in fact, the reviews indicated a particular sensitivity to the issue of "taste"—and specifically "tastelessness." But on the whole, the level of serious attention and insight in the British reviews goes substantially beyond that of most of the American reviews, and even when the reviewer's appreciation is qualified and reserved, the specific qualifications and reservations are often based on careful analysis of Hitchcock's artistry and aims and the dynamics of audience expectation and response.

Before the film was released in England, it was summarized in detail and commented on appreciatively by Penelope Houston. Readers of her preview were primed to see a film "ghoulishly and irreverently parodying the conventions of the murder mystery," a "comedie noire" that brilliantly maintains its precarious balance between humor and bad taste (Houston 1956: 59). It is notable, she says, for "a team playing together with admirable precision" and filled with "quintessential Hitchcock" touches (Houston 1956: 59).

There was much high praise and thoughtful and appreciative analysis in subsequent reviews. Leslie Wood noted in particular Hitchcock's "superbly light touch," which prevented a "macabre story" from becoming "unpleasant or distasteful" and the "sure directorial touch" and "fine acting" combining in a film that shows "Hitchcock at his vintage best to delight filmmakers everywhere" (*Daily Film Renter*, March 22, 1956, p. 3). Alan Brien introduced his very positive review by "summing up" the film with a witty phrase that Hitchcock himself undoubtedly would have admired: "Esprit de corpse" (*Evening Standard*, May 3, 1956). Milton Shulman similarly recognizes that the film successfully overcomes what is unquestionably a fundamental and constant challenge confronted by the filmmaker and the audience: It is "directed with such amiable and casual relish that at times one forgets the basic tastelessness of the joke" (*Sunday Express*, May 6, 1956).

Predictably, others were not amused. Jympson Harman speculates that "This charming and witty flirtation with bad taste is Hitchcock's latest attempt to relieve his boredom with a reputation for being the best creator of screen thrills" but notes that "The Trouble With Hitch is that as soon as he dares to be different he gets into hot water with his admirers." He grants that the actors and director of *The Trouble with Harry* "handle the comedy with delightful composure and polite mirth," but the film ultimately "lacks variety," and the "funereal situation" of the film "palls on one occasionally" (*Evening News*, May 3, 1956). Harold Conway similarly finds much to admire in the film, "the most impudent shocker of his career," one that "turns death into a ghoulish farce," but only to a point. It's no surprise that Conway thinks of *Arsenic and Old Lace*, but Hitchcock's film doesn't measure up to that "corpse-larking" because Capra's characters were "charmingly mad" while Hitchcock's are "perfectly sane" and "too calculating for charm" (*Daily Sketch*, May 4, 1956). As a result, Conway says that he "chuckled shamelessly for an hour—until the joke began petering out." D. Granger's patience wears even thinner, and, in a completely negative review in the *Financial Times*, he complains of the "monotony" of what he describes as a "desperately whimsical murder story" focusing on a community "suffering from some kind of mass derangement" (May 7, 1956). The reviewer for the *Manchester Guardian* is far less severe and far more thoughtful but notes that the most worrisome aspect of the film is not that it is tasteless or overly whimsical but that it becomes "a bit of a bore" and "would all be much better if it were much less slow," a flaw that the reviewer attributes to Hitchcock's new predilection for "long, continuous 'takes'" (May 5, 1956, p. 5).

The two most influential reviewers at the time were anything but strong supporters of the film. While aiming not to be completely dismissive, C. A. Lejeune notes that "It is a coldblooded trifle at the best of times, and not everyone will appreciate its grisly sense of fun" (*Observer*, May 6, 1956). Dilys Powell was even more negative, concluding that *The Trouble with Harry* is ultimately a "boring little misfire," but she takes the time to set up an elaborate argument to support this judgment, which she admits is a highly personal one (*Sunday Times*, May 6, 1956). Perhaps with images like that shown in Figure 16.1 in mind, her premise is that "Jokes about death are chancy stuff in the cinema," and in explaining why she sat through Hitchcock's "cemetery joke … with a gravity bordering on the offensive," she very usefully puts this film in the context of others that similarly but more successfully present such "chancy stuff," including the Ealing comedies *Kind Hearts and Coronets* and *The Ladykillers* and especially Chaplin's *Monsieur Verdoux*, "heartlessly funny but with a serious dying fall, intent but with a shade of fantasy."

Ultimately, the positive reviews carry the day, in number and in persuasiveness. Fred Majdalany's review in the *Daily Mail* begins by admitting that dealing with death, especially as "the basis of a comedy," presents "a taste problem as perilous as a tightrope," but this is overcome by Hitchcock's "masterly

Figure 16.1 Miss Graveley and Captain Wiles nonchalantly banter over the body of Harry.
The Trouble with Harry, directed by Alfred Hitchcock. © Alfred J. Hitchcock Productions 1955. All rights reserved.

delicacy," ever present in a film that teaches us more about "the humour of the incongruous" than the "enormous unhumourous volumes on the nature of humour" (May 4, 1956). And in a follow-up review, as if directly rebutting Powell, Majdalany emphasizes that a major strength of the film is "the element of fantasy … presented with a straight casual face as actuality … [and] delicately managed" (*Daily Mail*, May 4, 1956).

The reviewer for the *TV Chronicle* joins the debate over the questionable taste of the film by chiding not Hitchcock but some commentators and audiences: "I find it difficult to forgive the daintiness of those who profess themselves to be shocked by Hitchcock's brilliant new comedie noire" (May 4, 1956). The reviewer engages in some sophisticated analysis to demonstrate how what could have been tasteless and "cataclysmically shocking" in the film is transformed into something "not only unshocking but exquisitely funny … due to Hitchcock's having somehow interposed the invisible equivalent of a theatrical gauze curtain between event and spectator." This is accomplished by dialogue "pitched … at a slight angle to reality," the "tact," "delicacy," and "reverence" of the characters, and by music—a rare mention in the early reviews of the great contribution of Herrmann's score—that "matches the dialogue's mood." A comparison of the film to J. M. Barrie's *Mary Rose*, blending the "fey and the forthright" (a particularly suggestive comment for those who know of Hitchcock's lifelong interest in this play), and a concluding emphasis on how Hitchcock's approach here is a "lyrical variation on his habitual one" nicely capture what several other reviews suggest are key elements of the film that must not be overlooked and add to our sense of what is Hitchcockian: that it is a wonderfully engaging "contemporary fairy tale" (Quigly, *Spectator*, May 11, 1956) and is "not without touches of poetry" (*Shell Magazine*, June 1956). British reviewers, as Hitchcock no doubt expected, emphasized the importance of appreciating the particular humor of the film but also shed much light on what is valuable in it beyond its humor.

The Trouble with Harry in France

Modest commercial success and mixed, though by and large positive, critical reception in America and England was followed in France by impressive and lingering audience popularity and appreciative commentary and serious analysis that played a substantial role in not only the critical history of *The Trouble with Harry* but also the development of auteur theory in general and in the emergence of Hitchcock in particular as a serious artist to be reckoned with. This is a complex story that has been told impeccably well by James Vest in the section on "French Responses to *The Trouble with Harry*" in his study of Hitchcock and France, so I need not repeat it here, but I will briefly summarize some of what he covers and gloss his comments in a few places.

The Trouble with Harry was previewed in an interview in *Cahiers du Cinéma* conducted by François Truffaut and Claude Chabrol that appeared more than a year before the film opened in Paris on March 14, 1956. The heart of the interview lies in the extensive statements by Hitchcock about his commitment to form, technical artistry, and audience engagement, but also his acknowledgment that these earnest young critics and about-to-be filmmakers were not wrong in noting certain recurrent themes in his films, such as confession and "an added dimension, somewhat or entirely, metaphysical" (Truffaut and Chabrol 2015: 198). But all this is prefaced by Hitchcock pitching his forthcoming film and presenting it in a now familiar way as a "comedy about a corpse" in the British manner and paying particular attention to its "color scheme" (Truffaut and Chabrol 2015: 191). Although he doesn't make the connection, it may not be simply coincidental that shortly after discussing a film prominently featuring an artist and his paintings Hitchcock likens himself to a painter for whom "the way of treating things … counts most" (Truffaut and Chabrol 2015: 192).

When the film was released, it was time for others to have their say about it, in a barrage of reviews. Truffaut wrote several, admiring the film but also noting that while it was filled with deep meaning, it was a puzzle that might take much effort to figure out, aided by Hitchcock's future films which always helped clarify what came before them (Vest 2003: 135). These were followed by four provocative reviews in the April 1956 issue of *Cahiers du Cinéma*. Éric Rohmer praises the film as a significant advance in Hitchcock's evolution as a "severe" and dark moralist, contemplating and commenting on the human predicament of living in a world of "aggressive malice" and guilt, not to mention death (1956: 36–38). Rohmer also notes the evolution of Hitchcock's style, now characterized by "elegance," "sobriety," and "poetry" (1956: 36–38). Jean Domarchi went so far as to say that *The Trouble with Harry* could be taken as "one of the keys to Hitchcock's world," presenting a spectacle where conscience has been erased and a group of people act comically irresponsible, as if the death of someone is "devoid of meaning" and a corpse is not a lesson in morality and mortality but "a simple cumbersome object that should be removed as quickly as possible" (Domarchi 1956: 40). Philippe Demonsablon allows that Hitchcock's works can be approached from a non-Catholic perspective but insists that *The Trouble with Harry* is a Catholic fable, perhaps illustrating that "To those who deprive themselves of looking at the world from God's point of view, the misery of the world without God appears" (1956: 40). And, finally, Jacques Rivette likens the film to a Kafkaesque parable, revolving around the unanswerable questions of whether humans are good or bad and whether "we should believe in the omnipotence of evil" or "refuse it" (1956: 41). In this film, "there always remains a secret behind a secret," unfathomable but foreboding and "suspicious" (Rivette 1956: 41).

Vest summarizes numerous other French reviews that praise a wide range of its qualities, including its humor, stunning use of color, dreamlike mood, and poetic presentation of serious moral and metaphysical themes (2003: 137–140). But what he found particularly significant is that while there were some dissenting notes, *The Trouble with Harry* was well received even among critics "generally resistant to the Hitchcock touch" (Vest 2003: 139), as well as by audiences at large. In this, Vest is following comments by Rohmer and Chabrol in the chapter on this film in *Hitchcock: The First Forty-Four Films*, the first book-length study of Hitchcock. This chapter expands on the review by Rohmer in *Cahiers*, in part by including some of the ideas proposed in the other *Cahiers* reviews, but also by emphasizing how *The Trouble with Harry* was a major turning point for Hitchcock's career and reputation: "The fact is that this film, disliked in the United States, is the one which in France did most for its director's reputation. After this film, people were willing to recognize him as an auteur rather than a mere technician" (Rohmer and Chabrol 1979: 134). When we think of the films of Hitchcock that the *Cahiers* critics gravitated toward, *Under Capricorn*, *Strangers on a Train*, *I Confess*, and *The Wrong Man* undoubtedly come first to mind. It is a real revelation to find that Rohmer and Chabrol include *The Trouble with Harry* in this group.

Ironically, the one French work always rightly associated with the elevation of Hitchcock's status as a filmmaker did not rely substantively on *The Trouble with Harry* to make this case. Based on interviews conducted in 1962, the material on this film in Truffaut's *Hitchcock* is far from enthusiastic, and while the momentum generated by the book certainly contributed to later serious attention to all of Hitchcock's work, its brief mention of the film's "understatement," "disconcerting nonchalance," and escape from clichés by bringing murder "out in the sunshine" have been routinely repeated but have not been the basis of detailed appreciation or analysis (Truffaut 1984: 227).

The Return of *The Trouble with Harry*: Reviews and Critical Studies

After its initial release, *The Trouble with Harry* was rarely shown and then was pulled from circulation as part of a group of films (also including *Rope*, *Rear Window*, the remake of *The Man Who Knew Too Much*, and *Vertigo*) that became known as the "missing" or "lost" Hitchcocks. The highly publicized rerelease of these films in England beginning in late 1983 and in the USA in early 1984 led to a new round of reviews and reconsiderations of the individual films and of Hitchcock's entire career as a filmmaker.

The Trouble with Harry often suffers by comparison with the other films in the group. Rex Reed identifies it as the "most troublesome" of "these buried treasures" and then proceeds to bury the film in a pile of increasingly barbed epithets, calling its humor "odd and tedious" and concluding that it is a "creaky relic" betraying Hitchcock's "creeping senility" (*New York Post*, March 2, 1984, p. 18). Richard Corliss applauds the return of these films but notes that "anyone who expects to find a string of masterpieces will be disappointed. *The Trouble with Harry* is a desultory exercise in macabre whimsy and naturalistic acting at its most mannered" (*Time*, March 26, 1984, p. 77). But in the reviews there is also an effort to find something to praise in a Hitchcock film that is not *Rear Window* or *Vertigo*. As the reviewer for the *Boston Globe* notes, "It doesn't have the kind of virtuosic pacing or psychic drive of his best '50s movies. Yet within its narrower scope, it does offer a number of sly delights," ultimately reinforcing Hitchcock's "ultimate message" that "Nothing stands to reason" (March 2, 1984). The reviewer for *New York Native* similarly alerts us that this film is "not one of Hitchcock's masterpieces" but then illustrates how it is "a great deal more intricate" than the "extended gag" filled with British humor that it seems to present itself as and is in fact "something of a sex farce" with a comic message that is "vivid" and "exuberant" (March 1984, p. 37).[1] The rerelease of *The Trouble with Harry* gave Andrew Sarris a chance to reconsider it, and his second review is much more positive than the first, discussed above. His praise of the film is qualified, but meant to be precise rather than grudging: "Once one concedes the slightness of the movie, and the problematic nature of its squashed humor, it is very easy to enjoy it in a relaxed spirit of bemused acquiescence" (*Village Voice*, April 10, 1984, p. 41). Finally, the fullest review at this time of the rereleased films, David Kehr's "Hitch's Riddle," is also the most probing and broadly positive. He gives each of the films extensive attention, and his aim is to show how each illustrates the "extraordinary rush of creative power" during this part of Hitchcock's career (1984: 10). Kehr is particularly insightful in analyzing the reflexivity of *The Trouble with Harry*, noting that "Sam Marlowe's art is an idealized image of Hitchcock's own," but he also focuses extensively on the film as a thoughtful reflection on life and death, one characterized by a "glowing" that "radiates hope like the loveliest of fairy tales," and presents death and guilt as vehicles that "bring people together" (1984: 14), including at the end (see Fig. 16.2). His concluding comparison of the film to a Shakespearean comedy is high praise and shrewd critical judgment that later critics would explore in more detail.

There were few scholarly books on Hitchcock before the 1980s, and their coverage of *The Trouble with Harry* was sparse. As is well known, the first edition of Robin Wood's *Hitchcock's Films* in 1965 contributed enormously to the growing swell of attention to and appreciation of Hitchcock as a serious artist, but neither it nor later expanded editions comment substantively on *The Trouble with Harry*. Donald Spoto's *The Art of Alfred Hitchcock* summarizes this little-seen film usefully and offers an intriguing alternative to the French critics' emphasis on it as "a filmed parable on the death and resurrection of Christ" (1992: 238), which he says does a "disservice to Hitchcock's wit" (1992: 239). Spoto highlights

Figure 16.2 This image from near the end of the *The Trouble with Harry* showing the close group brought together during the course of the film was frequently used in advertisements and posters.

a provocative tension between a "Gnostic-Puritan ethic," embodied by the sheriff but also haunting everyone else, and a "Judeo-Christian optimism," and notes that these two ethics are "present[ed] … for balanced consideration" by a director who is a "moralist … but no homilist" (1992: 238, 239). Raymond Durgnat's few pages on *The Trouble with Harry* in *The Strange Case of Alfred Hitchcock* nicely capture how, despite its surface calm, the film revolves around a "disruption of complacency which can lead to nihilism, or religion or a double bed … alternatives through which [Hitchcock] evolves" (1974: 269). His notes are teasingly brief but usefully redirect our attention away from "too much stress on the deadness of Harry" and toward "the liveliness of the reactions which he provokes," heightening our sense of the film as a "field day for a series of freewheeling studies in individual character and neighborliness" (Durgnat 1974: 267).

The rerelease prompted increasing attention to *The Trouble with Harry* by scholars. To date it hasn't generated nearly the attention or attained the status of the small group of commonly acknowledged Hitchcock masterworks, but it has been recognized as a film very worthy of close analysis and that not only reinforces our understanding of what is Hitchcockian but contributes to expanding our sense of Hitchcock's range and depth. Slavoj Žižek uses *The Trouble with Harry* alongside *The Birds* to illustrate a fundamental dynamic in Hitchcock's films: the presentation of life as unresolvably but perhaps bearably paradoxical. Žižek sees the "understatement" and "nonchalance" of the film as a characteristically Hitchcockian response to a world that is "catastrophic but not yet really serious" (1986: 101). This links *The Trouble with Harry* with *Hamlet* and *Antigone*, other stories about a "Corpse that Wouldn't Die," but also Tom and Jerry cartoons and video games, in which death is a drama and a threat but not a finality.

One of the most persuasive and influential studies of *The Trouble with Harry* examines it as not a Shakespearean tragedy but as a Shakespearean comedy and especially a romance. Lesley Brill argues that it "sets forth with unequaled bluntness and economy the romantic vision of innocence and immortality that informs the greater part of Hitchcock's work" (1988: 283). Here death is generative, and the film dramatizes and celebrates rebirth, a triumph over the withering effects of time, and the joining of separate individuals into couples, married and otherwise, and a "reinvigorated and cohesive small society" (Brill 1988: 290), all this accomplished by nature and human effort, not religious design or intervention. As the other chapters in his book show, the "Hitchcock Romance" takes many forms, often tinged with irony, anxiety, and failure. But for Brill *The Trouble with Harry* is "unique" among Hitchcock's works, not because it is aberrant but because he "needed to make … only one parable of an unfallen world" (1988: 291). Hitchcock doesn't generally set his characters in such a world, but we need to recognize that he could envision one.

Thomas Leitch's few but densely packed and bountifully revealing pages on *The Trouble with Harry* pair up perfectly with Brill and further develop the way the film is playfully and positively Shakespearean, like *A Midsummer Night's Dream*, and charts a triumph over trauma and death and an escape from loneliness and isolation that is in fact facilitated by Harry's death, which, "unlike his life, has the power to unite the people around him into a community" (1991: 180). Leitch not only emphatically reinforces the uniqueness of the film thematically—"Nowhere else in Hitchcock's work … is the triumph of the community as complete, as unruffled, or as joyously celebratory" (1991: 183)—but stylistically as well. Mid and long shots are the norm, as well as two-shots rather than shot-reverse shots, establishing the primacy of interaction, connection, and "the framed group rather than the isolated individual as the fundamental social unit" (Leitch 1991: 182). Praise of the acting in the film was commonplace from the beginning, but Leitch focuses specifically on the subtlety of the major players and how "small changes of expression and gesture become disproportionately significant" (1991: 182). Similarly, he goes far beyond the usual praise of the natural setting, pointing out how recurrent shots of the landscape are used to introduce and rhythmically balance episodes of human activity, as in a film by Ozu, where so-called "pillow shots" set the characters in a broad "nonhuman environment" and establish a contemplative tonality and a "long view" of life.

While Leitch and Brill focus on how *The Trouble with Harry* ultimately releases sexual energy as a life force that counters the unavoidable presence of death, Ed Sikov praises it highly but interprets it as an unrelenting though finely wrought dramatization and examination of repression, representative of 1950s American culture. He sees the film as characterized by "morbid cartoonishness" (1994: 154), in part to associate Hitchcock appreciatively with the work of Ernie Kovacs and Charles Addams, but also to highlight that the characters in the film are presented without any psychological depth. There is basically only one dynamic at work in the film: failed sexuality. Harry's corpse, with its rigidity and especially its ever prominent feet "standing at priapic attention" (Sikov 1994: 160), suggests both perversely irrepressible sexuality and also immobility and permanently unfulfilled and troubling desire. Sikov recognizes Sam's energy as an artist and reshaper of others in the community but categorizes him as not so much a creative force as a "symbol manipulator" (1994: 170). He also acknowledges that by the end of the film, two couples have been formed, but this seems inconsequential. His conclusion is that the characters learn "that the finite quality of their lives virtually demands a conscious sexual resolution" (Sikov 1994: 171), but this is little solace if the resolution is impossible or imperfect, and that is what Sikov sees: "The sexual coupling at the film's end is troubled, uneasy," and there is "inherent instability in this new order" (1994: 172). The film is a brilliant critique of repression, but evidently unable to envision anything beyond a capitulation to it.

Robert Lightning also reads *The Trouble with Harry* as a disturbing reflection of postwar American culture and in particular as an illustration of "patriarchal oppression" and "male presumption" embodied in and supported by the institution of the family (1999: 110). Harry is the presiding symbol of all this, and while his death "signals a symbolic lull in patriarchal norms and, as a consequence, an opportunity for personal growth," no escape or lasting transformation ensues. The highpoint in the film is a brief moment when Jennifer gains a "phallic voice" (Lightning 1999: 111) and speaks freely and powerfully. But the pastoral setting is dominated by sinister characters, particularly Sam, whose unconventionality in some areas is totally undermined by his sexual totalitarianism: his "romantic idealism" marks him as another in the line of men in Hitchcock's films who aim to "remake" and control women. Understood for what it really is, the prospect of marriage is a consummation devoutly to be feared and avoided, and the gift of a double bed at the end foretells a future not to be celebrated. For Lightning, *The Trouble with Harry* has the veneer of a Shakespearean comedy but turns out to be a dark melodrama.

Ed Gallafent is fully aware of the darkness in *The Trouble with Harry*, signaled by the shift from summer in the original story to autumn, associated with tragedy. But his essay revolves around illustrating "why the film is not a tragedy" but a resourceful transcendence of and triumph over individual immobility, isolation, disconnection, and social fragmentation. Gallafent begins his examination of what he calls in his title "Matters of Proportion" by noting the significance of how the film plays with perspective and size, especially in sequences where various characters first come across Harry's body (see Fig. 16.3).

This approach in itself is an important new element in the study of the film: Gallafent and Leitch are rare among critics in showing how the effectiveness of the film's cinematography goes far beyond its rendering of the beauty of the landscape. For Gallafent, the play with perspective and size is not only visual but conceptual, and "bigness" turns out to be a measure of not only physical dimensions but

Figure 16.3 Size matters throughout *The Trouble with Harry*.

important character traits. What is at stake is not only the construction and maintenance of an integral self but the willingness and ability to enter into meaningful and, in particular, intimate relations with others. The latter especially requires personal adjustments: for example, "Sam must sacrifice part of his abstractness, and his sense of 'bigness,' just as the Captain must lose some of his childlike quality" (Gallafent 2006: 103). Gallafent presents the film as fundamentally reflexive, focused insistently on art, but perhaps most importantly not just the art of painting but the art of living, which requires above all else "imagination" (2006: 104). And in the film, the triumph of the art of living is marriage, envisioned not as compulsory and oppressive conventionality, as Lightning insists, but as "a fine form of human ease" (Gallafent 2006: 102), although "not without its problems or limitations" (2006: 104), which all the parties in the impending marriages in the film understand and accept. Although Gallafent doesn't make this specific reference, it may be worth noting that his interpretation alerts us that the New England setting of the film is ideological as well as spatial: *The Trouble with Harry* is anti-Puritan, although haunted by Puritanism, and in many ways deeply Emersonian.

The most substantive of the remaining critical studies of *The Trouble with Harry* cover an interesting miscellany of subjects. David Neumeyer's lengthy analysis of "Tonal Design and Narrative in Film Music" examines in great detail the complexity and subtlety of Bernard Herrmann's score, identifying the structure of the forty-two cues he composed, where they were used, and how they effectively express and provide a counterpart to what Royal S. Brown, another important commentator on the collaboration between Hitchcock and Herrmann, called Hitchcock's "perfect ambivalency" and "carefully elaborated visual structures" (1998: 120 and 122). Jack Sullivan's far less technical and much shorter but equally penetrating analysis of the significance of the music similarly calls attention to what is now routinely acknowledged as a critical part of the film but that, perhaps surprisingly, had been little commented on in previous reviews and commentaries. The score is still "far less celebrated than that composed for

Figure 16.4 Sam's artwork is important and valuable to him and others in the community, and to outsiders as well.

Vertigo, *North by Northwest*, or *Psycho*" (Sullivan 2006: 187), but Sullivan illustrates how it is "as original and inventive as any of these," sonically reinforcing the thoroughgoing duality of a film that is thematically and dramatically "ominous [and] merry" (2006: 189), dark and bright, serious and humorous.

Several essays focus on another art that is central to the film in a variety of ways: painting. Tom Gunning provides an extraordinarily comprehensive guide to understanding how painting and paintings have a radiating significance and power throughout Hitchcock's works. As objects, they are far from merely "decorative": "they project an influence into the world of character as conduits of guilt and desire" (Gunning 2007: 29) and prompt not only the spectator's experience of entering into a framed representation but also the "uncanny" experience of "the emergence of the subject from within the frame … into the space of the observer" (2007: 35). This is an accurate description of what often happens not only when we look at paintings but also, of course, when we look at films, and the provocative effects of this experience are compounded when we look at films like *The Trouble with Harry* that feature not only paintings but characters making and looking at paintings (see Fig. 16.4).

Gunning's discussion of the film is tantalizingly brief but illustrates how this "unfairly neglected and delightful" work is not only a major contribution to Hitchcock's ongoing consideration of visual art but a particularly intriguing statement about the value of abstract art, which often appears in his works as confusing and problematic (2007: 42). Gunning notes that it is "the modern artist," Sam, who "becomes the center of a newly formed Dickensian community set in a bucolic New England" (2007: 42). Hitchcock's films repeatedly dramatize the struggle between Eros and Thanatos, and in *The Trouble with Harry*, art is an essential part of "the victory of Eros over Thanatos." Consistent with Hitchcock's usual complexity and duality, the film includes moments where Sam and his art are, like everyone and everything else, laughed at, an aspect of the film emphasized to the exclusion of all else in a subsequent essay by John A. Calabrese, "How Hitchcock Lampoons Modern Art in *The Trouble with Harry*" (2017). A more balanced and detailed supplement to Gunning is Susan Felleman's "The World Gone Wiggy," which includes valuable information about John Ferren, whose art is featured in the film, including how he was quite literally involved in an instance where one of his paintings, as in the film, was hung upside down, and how overall his abstract works are used in the film as "indices of freedom, sensual experience, psyche, and spirit" (2014: 103), all positive values sought, endorsed by, and attained in the film.

The chapter on *The Trouble with Harry* in Steven DeRosa's *Writing with Hitchcock* (2001) is the shortest one in his consideration of the four films that screenwriter John Michael Hayes worked on with Hitchcock, and even the title of the chapter — "An Expensive Indulgence" — reinforces the common impression that it is the least important of the group. But DeRosa provides a very authoritative and informative introduction to and overview of the film, with many details about the production history and especially the script development, noting many differences between the novel and the film that highlight how what Hayes and Hitchcock ended up with is a creative adaptation of a work that they recognized from the very beginning was already quite Hitchcockian.

The most extended recent treatment of *The Trouble with Harry* focuses on a character always noticed but rarely discussed in detail: Arnie (see Fig. 16.5). Adrian Schober shows how Arnie illustrates the complexity of Hitchcock's conception of childhood as at least in this case a blend of innocence and experience, an "important corrective to a vision of the child and nature that might otherwise be termed romantic" (2014: 128). Schober is guided by Richard Allen's concept of "romantic irony" and sees Hitchcock as someone "who simultaneously creates and de-creates myths about childhood" (2014: 130). Mark Twain proves to be as useful a reference point as Wordsworth, and Arnie seems to be a "throwback … to the Good Bad Boy of American literary tradition" (Schober 2014: 145–146).

Figure 16.5 Arnie, with soon-to-be-father and dead rabbit.

But while it is of course significant that Arnie is a child, there is more at issue here than notions of childhood. For Schober, Arnie embodies Hitchcock's fundamental "multivalency," an attitude and quality that might just as well have been glossed by lines from another great nineteenth-century American author, Walt Whitman: "Do I contradict myself? / Very well then I contradict myself, / (I am large, I contain multitudes)" (*Song of Myself*, Section 51). Perhaps one of the myths that Hitchcock "de-creates" is an insistence on the differences between children and grown-ups that disregards what they share. If Arnie as a child is a human being in the making, so are we all: complex, paradoxical, idiosyncratic, evolving, always intriguing, and perhaps always inscrutable.

Finally, it is perhaps fitting that my brief overview of commentary on *The Trouble with Harry* ends on a very positive note: the latest extensive scholarly treatment of the film focuses on its unexpected but compelling combination of corpses and *joie de vivre*. Julie Michot compares *The Trouble with Harry* to Billy Wilder's *Avanti!*, emphasizing how in both films a constant confrontation with death helps the main characters to "live better" and become "reborn emotionally" (2021: 17). And while noting the presence of the many forces of life and celebration often noticed—sexuality, wit, song, playfulness, and artistic creativity—Michot adds another not often mentioned: food. Much commentary focuses on the way the film is a banquet for the eyes, but other senses are well served too, and the ever-expanding and regularly mentioned offerings—lemonade, blueberry muffins, coffee, bacon, wine, hot chocolate, fresh strawberries year-round—are key elements of the film's multidimensional groaning board of life, perhaps a figurative expression that Hitchcock himself would savor.

The Trouble with Harry Is Not Over

Near the end of his career, Hitchcock commented ruefully on the reception history of his films: "A constant pattern that occurs with my films is that they're criticized when they open—and then, a year later, they're hailed as classics. I don't understand it. Why can't they be hailed as classics immediately?" (Hall 1972).

This may fit *Vertigo*, but it isn't exactly the story told by the reception and critical history of *The Trouble with Harry*, which didn't need to be rescued from disrespect and disregard, and which time and renewed attention haven't transformed into a classic. An examination of the film through the years yields several valuable and positive lessons. First, we gain a clear sense of how extraordinarily accomplished the film is, technically, thematically, and tonally. There are, of course, dissenters to this view, but by and large the ongoing and collaborative effort of commentators has shown how ambitiously, resourcefully, and effectively *The Trouble with Harry* addresses many of the key subjects we think of as Hitchcockian. Looking backward on the critical history may also help us as we look forward, perhaps noting some things that have been missed and identifying fruitful areas for future work. For example, there's still more to be said about how the film explores numerous unconventional representations of and models for male and female behavior, lifestyles, family structures, and intimate relations premised on rather than destructive of individuality and freedom; and while the fairy-tale elements have often been noted, they have not been fully enough examined as part of a well-articulated illustration of what Bruno Bettelheim has so brilliantly presented as the therapueutic "uses of enchantment" (1976).

Finally, as important as it is to expand our interpretations of *The Trouble with Harry*, I think the key critical task and challenge is to integrate it more fully into our comprehensive appreciation and understanding of Hitchcock. It may not be in all ways the equal of, say, *Shadow of a Doubt*, *Rear Window*, *Psycho*, or *Vertigo*, but it stands up well alongside them as a useful, perhaps even necessary complement. If we want to get a full and true sense of his powerful and probing engagement with, to name a few of his main subjects, the challenges of living life close to others, the battle of the sexes, the burden of the past, the inevitability of trauma, the volatility of desire, and problematic male behavior, we must look closely at not only the "classics" mentioned above but also his somewhat different take on all those subjects in *The Trouble with Harry*. If we are to take Hitchcock seriously, we need to take *The Trouble with Harry* seriously.

Note

1. Unattributed, but a handwritten note on it in the New York Public Library clippings file identifies the author as Ed Sikov.

References

Alpert, H. (1955) "The Mechanics of Suspense," *Woman's Day*, January 12, pp. 102–103.
Bettelheim, B. (1976) *The Uses of Enchantment: The Meaning and Importance of Fairy Tales*, New York: Alfred A. Knopf.
Brill, L. (1988) "'Love's Not Time's Fool,'" in *The Hitchcock Romance: Love and Irony in Hitchcock's Films*, Princeton, NJ: Princeton University Press, pp. 283–291.
Calabrese, J. A. (2017) "The 'Art' of Alfred Hitchcock: How Hitchcock Lampoons Modern Art in *The Trouble with Harry*," *International Journal of the Image*, 8 (3): 35–39.
Demonsablon, P. (1956) "Tueurs à gags," *Cahiers du Cinéma*, 10 (58): 40.
DeRosa, S. (2001) *Writing with Hitchcock: The Collaboration of Alfred Hitchcock and John Michael Hayes*, London and New York: Faber & Faber.
Domarchi, J. (1956) "Humain, trop humain," *Cahiers du Cinéma*, 10 (58): 38–40.
Durgnat, R. (1974) *The Strange Case of Alfred Hitchcock, or The Plain Man's Hitchcock*, Cambridge, Mass.: MIT Press.
Felleman, S. (2014) "'The World Gone Wiggy': *The Trouble with Harry* (1955)," in *Real Objects in Unreal Situations: Modern Art in Fiction Films*, Chicago, Ill.: University of Chicago Press, pp. 89–105.
Gallafent, E. (2006) "Matters of Proportion: *The Trouble with Harry*," *Hitchcock Annual*, vol. 15, pp. 85–106.
Gunning, T. (2007) "In and Out of the Frame: Paintings in Hitchcock," in W. Schmenner and C. Granof (eds), *Casting a Shadow: Creating the Alfred Hitchcock Film*, Evanston, Ill.: Northwestern University Press, pp. 28–47.
Hall, W. O. (1972) "All about Terror," *San Francisco Sunday Examiner*, June 11.
Hitchcock, A. (1955) "Trouble with Vermont, It's Nice Place to Live or Die, Alfred Hitchcock Finds," *Cincinnati Inquirer*, September 4, section 3:4.
Kehr, D. (1984) "Hitch's Riddle," *Film Comment*, 20 (3): 9–18.
Leitch, T. M. (1991) *Find the Director and Other Hitchcock Games*, Athens, Ga.: University of Georgia Press.
Lightning, R. K. (1999) "A Domestic Trilogy," *CineAction*, 50: 103–119.
Michot, J. (2021) "When Someone's Death Makes Someone Else Blossom: How Hitchcock and Wilder Successfully Combine Corpses and Joie de Vivre in *The Trouble with Harry* and *Avanti!*" *Mise-en-Scène*, 6 (1): 16–27.
Neumeyer, D. (1998) "Tonal Design and Narrative in Film Music: Bernard Herrmann's *A Portrait of Hitch* and *The Trouble with Harry*," *Indiana Theory Review*, 19: 87–123.
Rivette, J. (1956) "Faut-il brûler Harry?" *Cahiers du Cinéma*, 10 (58): 41.
Rohmer, É. (1956) "Castigat ridendo," *Cahiers du Cinéma*, 10 (58): 36–38.
Rohmer, É., and C. Chabrol (1979) *Hitchcock: The First Forty-Four Films*, trans. Stanley Hochman, New York: Frederick Ungar.

Sarris, A. (1955) "The Trouble with Hitchcock," *Film Culture*, 1 (5–6): 31.
Sarris, A. (1984) "Films in Focus: Thoughts on Bresson and Hitchcock," *Village Voice*, 29, April 10, p. 41.
Schober, A. (2014) "Renegotiating Romanticism and the All-American Boy-Child: Alfred Hitchcock's *The Trouble with Harry* (1955)," in Debbie Olson (ed.), *Children in the Films of Alfred Hitchcock*, New York: Palgrave Macmillan, pp. 127–159.
Sikov, E. (1994) "Unrest in Peace: Hitchcock's Fifties Humor," in *Laughing Hysterically*: *American Screen Comedy of the 1950s*, New York: Columbia University Press, pp. 150–178.
Spoto, D. (1992) *The Art of Alfred Hitchcock*: *Fifty Years of His Motion Pictures*, 2nd edn, New York: Doubleday.
Sullivan, J. (2006) *Hitchcock's Music*, New Haven, Conn.: Yale University Press.
Truffaut, F., and C. Chabrol (2015) "Interview with Alfred Hitchcock," trans. James M. Vest, in *Hitchcock on Hitchcock*: *Selected Writings and Interviews*, vol. II, ed. Sidney Gottlieb, Berkeley, Calif.: University of California Press, pp. 191–200.
Truffaut, F., with H. G. Scott (1984) *Hitchcock*, rev. edn, New York: Simon & Schuster.
Vest, J. M. (2003) *Hitchcock and France*: *The Forging of an Auteur*, Westport, Conn.: Praeger.
Wood, R. (2004) *Hitchcock's Film's Revisited*, New York: Columbia University Press.
Žižek, S. (1986) "*The Trouble with Harry*: The Corpse that Wouldn't Die," *October*, 38: 99–111.

Chapter 17
More Blessed to Give
Tracking the Reception of Alfred Hitchcock's *Mr. & Mrs. Smith* (1941)

Elizabeth L. Bullock

As his lone "pure" screwball comedy, Alfred Hitchcock's *Mr. & Mrs. Smith* (1941) might seem distinct from his suspense-thrillers. Although early reviewers of the film receive it positively, its popularity subsequently declined as the screwball genre faded.

Alongside the growth of film studies as an academic discipline (Polan 2007), critics and historians reassess Hitchcock's apparent anomaly and find not only that it fits within his oeuvre but that it is an aesthetically and philosophically rich text. Gilles Deleuze even claims that the film allegorizes a turning point for Western culture's conception of cinematic imagery (2013a). This essay investigates the film's evolving reception by surveying popular and scholarly criticism, tracking the film's transformation from "mere" entertainment into a productive object of academic inquiry.

Mr. & Mrs. Smith follows an affluent childless Park Avenue couple whose three-year marriage is declared legally invalid due to an incorporation technicality. Each responds oppositely to the sudden annulment: David Smith's (Robert Montgomery) libido is piqued by the possibility of sex with his "unmarried" partner while Ann Smith (Carole Lombard) expects a proposal and reinstitution of marriage. Neither gets exactly what they claim to want. Ann kicks David out of their posh apartment, sending him to nurse his ego in the steam room of his men's club. He tries and fails to win her back, suffering a series of physical and emotional blows. Ann, resuming her maiden name, Krausheimer, soon begins dating David's law partner, Jefferson Custer (Gene Raymond), a Southern gentleman. Jeff's propriety prevents him from taking advantage of the situation, thus assuring the resumption of the Smiths' sexual relationship (if not their marriage contract) by the film's end.

Contemporaneous Criticism

Early American reception of *Mr. & Mrs. Smith* is primarily upbeat. Ivan Spear's review calls the film "virtually flawless entertainment in the lighter vein" (*Boxoffice*, January 25, 1941, p. 39). Jay Carmody's

Evening Star sneak peek recognizes "the Hitchcock touch" in the Smiths, who channel the director's "robust, hilarious innuendo […] as if it were as innocent as a nursery rhyme" (January 23, 1941, p. C4). The *Film Daily* calls Hitchcock a "master in the laugh field" (January 20, 1941, p. 5). William Boehnel's *New York World-Telegram* review finds the film a "frisky, scampish, gleeful comedy" (February 21, 1941). Kate Holliday claims Hitchcock "made you laugh" (1941: 19), while the *New York Herald Tribune* notes Hitch's "keen perception of how an American couple thinks and acts" (1941; quoted in Gehring 2003: 208).

Scores of reviewers delight in Lombard's return to screen comedy after she starred in a series of dramas. *American Cinematographer* finds she "looks better in this picture than she has in many another" (February 1, 1941, p. 65). Hollywood praises both Lombard and Montgomery (see Fig. 17.1), determining that the film's "double entendres [are] a good antidote for the country's current day war jitters" (1941: 72–73).

In both America and England, early criticism of *Mr. & Mrs. Smith* often blends disappointment with delight. By 1941, critics express fatigue with the screwball comedy genre, the principal style of romantic comedy since 1934. Bosley Crowther felt this weariness, but his *New York Times* review still praises Hitchcock's framing and the lead couple's performances (February 21, 1941, p. 16). Fan magazine *Modern Screen* hopes that the genre is over while condemning *Mr. & Mrs. Smith*'s pacing, which enables viewers to do (an apparently unwelcome amount) "of thinking through this one" (April 1941, p. 16).

Harrison's Reports calls the story flimsy and cautions that audiences expecting "thrilling melodramas" might be disappointed by this comedy featuring dialogue that's "a little too risqué for children" (February 1,

Figure 17.1 Conjugal compromise of the screwball sort.

1941, p. 19). *Motion Picture Magazine* excuses the film's thin story by extolling the compensatory virtues of Norman Krasna's "sparkling dialogue and screwy situations," brought to life by Hitchcock's "deft direction" (February 1941, p. 12). *Variety*'s reviewer believes any weakness in the plot is outweighed "by the general humorous melee," helped along by Hitchcock's "pacing at a steady gait" (January 22, 1941, p. 16).

The English reviewers exhibit similarly mixed appraisals. The *Hongkong Telegraph* dubs Hitchcock's film "sophisticated hilarity" featuring "excellent playing throughout" (April 19, 1941, p. 13). Crawford at *Film Bulletin* calls it "good entertainment" that "drags a little at times" but thinks recent screwball comedies are getting "brittle" (January 25, 1941, p. 6). The *Yorkshire Evening Post* calls the film "another good one" but ends by wishing for realism from Mr. Smith: "one could not help thinking that some men would have found a much easier way of going about the business" (March 8, 1941). Such speculation bespeaks a British sobriety that works against the glamorous intoxication central to screwball comedy.

In the highly negative category, the *Hollywood Reporter* criticizes Montgomery's evident boredom and calls Raymond miscast (February 16, 1941). *Motion Picture Reviews* finds the film's opening promising but the remainder derivative and "merely slapstick" (February 1941, p. 6). Otis Ferguson's *New Republic* review title tartly declares, "Not all to the good" (quoted in Sloan 1995: 359).

Despite the mixed reviews, the film performed well with general audiences, earning back its $750,000 budget twice over. Audiences were not burned out on screwball comedy quite yet, although the genre's denouement was on the horizon with America's entry into World War II.

By the end of the 1940s, popular criticism dwindles as *Mr. & Mrs. Smith* all but disappears from exhibition, especially in England. Writing for *Sequence*, a magazine he started at Oxford University, Lindsay Anderson reviews Hitchcock's artistry up to 1949 but offers only a passing mention of *Mr. & Mrs. Smith* by calling for a much-needed revival of the film (1949). This lack of familiarity seems to breed contempt, as unfavorable criticism of the film proliferates after 1950.

From 1950 Onward

The most provocative denigrations of *Mr. & Mrs. Smith* come from Hitchcock himself. His public ambivalence about the film begins as early as a 1950 interview with David Brady in the *New York Times*. Blaming the film's apparent inadequacy on audiences' expectations for thrillers, Hitchcock claims that "it wasn't a Hitchcock picture because it had no chase" (quoted in Gottlieb 1995: 131). Most famously, he dismisses the film in his 1962 interview with François Truffaut:

> The picture was done as a friendly gesture to Carole Lombard [...] and she asked whether I'd do a picture with her. In a weak moment I accepted, and I more or less followed Norman Krasna's screenplay. Since I really didn't understand the type of people who were portrayed in the film, all I did was to photograph the scenes as written.
>
> (Truffaut 1984: 139)

Still later, in a 1972 interview with Guy Flatley in the *New York Times*, Hitchcock fondly recalls Lombard's sense of humor in the same breath that he reiterates that he "had nothing to contribute" to the film (June 18, 1972, p. D13). Whether Hitchcock's disavowals indicate retrospective wisdom or a magician's "direction by indirection" (quoted in Spoto 1983: 240), critical distaste for the film snowballs thereafter.

Mr. & Mrs. Smith's eccentricity invites some pointed ire. For English author and biographer Charles Higham, the "insipid" *Mr. & Mrs. Smith* betrays Hitchcock as a "commercial-minded [philistine]" (1962: 11). American literary critic, Richard Gilman's *American Film* review of Donald Spoto's book, *The Art of Alfred Hitchcock*, argues that Hitchcock's fans are less of a critical force than an irrational cult, classifying both *Mr. & Mrs. Smith* and *Jamaica Inn* as "misfortunes" (1977; quoted in The Alfred Hitchcock Wiki).[1]

Academia

American scholars' engagement with Hitchcock begins with Robin Wood's seminal auteurist analysis, *Hitchcock's Films* (1965, revised 1989). Challenging the dichotomy between high and low culture, Wood premises that because Hitchcock's films display auteurist principles, critics may "take Hitchcock seriously" (1989: 55) and, by extension, popular movies. *Mr. & Mrs. Smith* appears briefly in Wood's taxonomy of plot motifs, identified as a "Story about a Marriage" (1989: 241). As Hitchcock's first film dealing with American culture, it is also filtered by and fitted to the conventions of the screwball genre, which, according to Wood, prevents Hitch from effectively criticizing capitalism, an art he would perfect in *Shadow of a Doubt* (1989: 240).

Concomitantly with auteur theory, the first Hitchcock biographies begin to appear. Originally published in France in 1957, Éric Rohmer and Claude Chabrol's *Hitchcock: The First Forty-Four Films* refers to *Mr. & Mrs. Smith* as an "uncertain success" (1979: 62) and inspires a series of such biographical surveys, particularly after publication of the English translation. British critic Raymond Durgnat authors *The Strange Case of Alfred Hitchcock* in 1974, in which he designates *Mr. & Mrs. Smith* as characteristic of Hollywood "sophisticated comedy," although for Durgnat it lacks the "individuality of the auteur" (1974: 175).

American biographer Donald Spoto, in his 1976 work, *The Art of Alfred Hitchcock*, writes that *Mr. & Mrs. Smith* "warrants only minimal discussion," but he also rebukes critics who "complain very loudly" about the film's exceptionality, countering that it exemplifies Hitchcock's democratic approach to filmmaking (1992: 98). Spoto's later offering, *The Dark Side of Genius*, includes more production context and cites the RKO archives when describing Lombard's onset playfulness and Hitchcock's excitement to direct "a typical comedy about typical Americans" (1983: 237). Spoto also reveals the permeable boundary between film text and biographical text, documenting Hitchcock's promise to take his wife, Alma, for a vacation in Saint Moritz that was delayed by filming. Hitchcock's apology is preserved in the cabin scene's dialog when comatose David mutters a promise to take Ann on vacation the first two weeks in December (1983: 238).

The English critic John Russell Taylor's 1978 biography, *Hitch: The Life and Times of Alfred Hitchcock*, balances historical-industrial context with personal details (1978). Hitchcock spent his early years in Hollywood learning the ropes of the studio system and figuring out how to avoid David O. Selznick's meddling. According to Taylor, Hitchcock mitigated those fraught years by returning favors to colleagues and acquaintances, including during production of *Mr. & Mrs. Smith* (1978: 53). Arriving for his blind date at the Florida Club, David is mortified to discover that the unknown woman is working-class. Played by Hitchcock's old friend, Betty Compson, "a hardworking utility actress" (1978: 53), Gertie is earthy and unselfconscious—personality traits of Compson's that Hitchcock appreciated when the two made silent pictures for Graham Cutts twenty years earlier—her jocularity satirizes David's pomposity. Taylor concludes by connecting the scene of Ann and Jeff's vertiginous ascent and entrapment atop a parachute ride with parallels in *Saboteur*, *Vertigo*, and *North by Northwest* (1978: 173).

Vital to *Mr. & Mrs. Smith*'s reassessment is the expansion of genre studies, although not all screwball comedy scholars analyze Hitchcock's film thoroughly. Ted Sennett's *Lunatics and Lovers* addresses the film only briefly, admiring Lombard and Montgomery's performances, while admonishing Raymond's, and lamenting Hitchcock's neglect of the "familiar techniques he used for suspense melodrama" (1971: 74–75). Sennett fails to recognize that this conflicting aesthetic execution warrants further consideration. Similarly brief, *Pursuits of Happiness*, Stanley Cavell's pivotal 1981 genre study of "comedies of remarriage," offers only a few words for *Mr. & Mrs. Smith*, writing that it "works brilliant variations within the genre" but that it doesn't fit with his transcendental utopian project due to "its somewhat cold comforts" (1981: 233).

Following Hitchcock's death in 1980, popular appreciation for *Mr. & Mrs. Smith* begins to grow alongside and influenced by expanding scholarship in film studies. Dave Kehr's review in the *Chicago Reader* begins, "Many 'minor' Hitchcocks turn out to be intriguing films once you forgive them for not being thrillers" (October 26, 1985). Kehr's caution against generic prejudice seems to address general audiences, film reviewers, and academic critics alike.

While mustering cinephiles to attend a 1992 Lombard retrospective at the Film Society of Lincoln Center, Vincent Canby offers a similar reevaluation of the film:

This is one of the most underrated comedies of its time, largely ignored by the critics and the public because Hitchcock was not expected to make a screwball comedy. Yet it's one of Lombard's best and, as is always the case in her successful films, she has a leading man who is her psychic match, Robert Montgomery.

(*New York Times*, August 21, 1992, p. C8)

Nevertheless, that same year, Carol Fleisher Kent's Brown University dissertation analyzes *Mr. & Mrs. Smith* as an example of what she calls "pure genre" (1992: 44) that avoids the doubling of Hitchcock's strongest films.

The American film theorist and critic William Rothman's *Hitchcock: The Murderous Gaze* aligns the traits of Cavell's "comedies of remarriage" with Hitchcock's entire body of work. Although he admires Hitchcock's "singular intelligence and sensibility" and recognizes that *Mr. & Mrs. Smith* "illuminates the conditions of the remarriage genre even as it illuminates the conditions of Hitchcock's authorship," he ultimately declares it "no more a major Hitchcock work than it is a major Hollywood comedy" (Rothman 1982: 178).

Decades later, Rothman refines his earlier criticisms by acknowledging the film's self-aware irony in *Must We Kill the Thing We Love?* Like other remarriage comedies, *Mr. & Mrs. Smith* questions the institutional foundation of monogamy but carries that question to its anarchic end, jettisoning honesty in favor of fighting (2014: 62–64). Finding the protagonists' flaws (David's snobbishness, Ann's irrationality) too unlikable, Rothman concludes that the film "falls flat as a romantic comedy" (2014: 68). Like Cavell, he wishes the film had more romantic "magic" (Rothman 2014: 68) and resentfully accuses the Smiths' (re)union of ironically mocking the sincerity of all screwball comedy (2014: 78).

American author Wes Gehring's biographical star study of Lombard (1986) takes *Mr. & Mrs. Smith* as evidence of her desire to return to comedic roles after a lukewarm reception of her dramas. Gehring dubs Krasna's original story "slight" but documents Lombard's intense interest as crucial to the script's development (1986: 206). She also enlisted her friend and tenant, Hitchcock, to direct.

In his later publication, *Hitchcock and Humor* (2019), Gehring credits Lombard's unpretentious star persona for most of *Mr. & Mrs. Smith*'s success. The marketing campaign during production emphasized Hitch and Lombard's onset playfulness, helping to establish the British filmmaker in his new homeland (2019: 133). *Mr. & Mrs. Smith* is, for Gehring, the first of Hitchcock's American pictures to use black humor to critique insanity, a series that includes *Shadow of a Doubt* (1943), *Rope* (1948), *Strangers on a Train* (1951), and *Psycho* (1960) (2019: 124–125). Similarly to Spoto, Gehring describes biographical intertexts that mark the film as Hitchcockian. Ann's reference to brandy as medicine reflects Hitchcock's heavy alcohol consumption, while Lake Placid echoes Saint Moritz (2019: 130–131). Finally, Gehring interprets the X-symbol formed by Ann's crossed skis in the film's final shot as a sign-off kiss or a crisscross indicating future darkness—if not for the Smiths, then certainly for Hitchcock's films (2019: 132).

Beyond the biographical and generic, Hitchcock films readily offer themselves up for philosophical engagement. In 1983's *Cinema I* and 1985's *Cinema II*, French philosopher Gilles Deleuze diagrams a historical-philosophical cinematic theory that pivots on a fundamental shift in the function of film images after World War II (2013a, 2013b). Building upon Henri Bergson's theories of movement, Deleuze identifies and describes cinematic concepts of motion, image, and time, and the contingent relational perspectives for understanding them in part or whole (2013a, 2013b). For Deleuze, Hitchcock's films harbinger the declining dominance of the movement-image and ascendance of the time-image, resulting from a breakdown of cause–effect relations rooted in a wider postwar sociocultural transformation.

Mr. & Mrs. Smith appears toward the end of *Cinema I*, as an example of Hitchcock's exteriorization of relations, or how Hitchcock conceives of and prioritizes the triangular cinematic relationship—a text(ure) woven between film, filmmaker, and audience (Deleuze 2013a: 224–225). For Deleuze, Hitchcock interrupts the flow between perception and action with a "mental image" (2013a: 222), a creation of the audience's mind distinct from perceptual comprehension of the action. Deleuze finds the Smiths appropriately Hitchcockian, writing that the film "belongs to Hitchcock's oeuvre, precisely because the couple learn all of a sudden that, their marriage not being legal, they have never been married" (2013a: 225). Deleuze translates his concept of the mental image via the Smiths' narrative predicament: the relationships in the film are also those that constitute the cinema, both now saturated with the existential possibility of never having been and, therefore, never being.

Working from Northrop Frye, American academic Lesley Brill's 1988 ethical-narrative study, *The Hitchcock Romance*, situates each Hitchcock film along a spectrum from romance to irony, positioning *Mr. & Mrs. Smith* at the highly ironic end. Lacking "real pathos" (Brill 1988: 176), the possessive sadomasochism of the Smiths' relationship parodies romance's utopian promise of "regeneration" (Brill 1988: 177). Resembling Hitchcock's thrillers and espionage stories, Brill suggests darker Hitchcock works are "comedies of remarriage without laughter" (1988: 177). The dissolution of the Smiths' marriage license is a juridical-conceptual adjustment, but that doesn't sincerely threaten their coupledom. Just as David finds no viable romantic partners, neither does Ann have suitable suitors. Brill describes Jeff's "sexless gentility" and the clear "lack of ardor in his decorous chivalry" (1988: 179). Brill's most promising inference is that because the Smiths resist evolution, "their lives lack transcendent meaning" (1988: 183), for it is just this that Deleuze appreciates of Hitchcock's work—a formal reflexivity that necessitates the transcendence to a new philosophical-spiritual cinematic era. Although Brill does not see it this way, the film is ironically ironic—to a reflexive degree that marks most, if not all, of Hitchcock's work—playing the screwball comedy game with one hand while puncturing its romance with the other.

American academic and film scholar Thomas Leitch's study of Hitchcock, *Find the Director, and Other Hitchcock Games*, follows Hitchcock's evolution in terms of games and play (1991). Leitch places *Mr. & Mrs. Smith* in "Hitchcock's Selznick period" (1991: 107), a transitional time during which the director was acclimating to America as his new home and learning the rules of the Hollywood filmmaking game. Calling the film "a comedy of homelessness" (1991: 123), Leitch tracks the migration of the Smiths from their Park Avenue apartment to various spaces around New York City and finally to Lake Placid (1991: 124). For Leitch, the film also exemplifies Hitchcock's transition toward depicting ambivalent maternal characters, citing David's repeated references to Ann as "Mother" as well as the perfidious name of the couple's nostalgic dinner spot, Momma Lucy's, now run by a grizzled, cigar-chewing man.

In "The Light Side of Genius," NYU professor and film scholar Dana Polan rebuts the "American optimism" of Cavell's remarriage project, refusing to accept comedy as ahistorical or immaterial (1991). Polan steers *Mr. & Mrs. Smith* through Continental philosophy with a political aim to uncover the reactionary ideological illusions of screwball comedy. Cavell's focus on remarriage reveals "the arbitrariness of any marriage: there can always be a fall from perfection that requires the whole process to start all over again" (Polan 1991: 134). By seeing *Mr. & Mrs. Smith* as a female gothic like the films that bookend it, *Rebecca* (1940) and *Suspicion* (1941), Polan upsets Cavell's idealistic definition of remarriage comedies by casting David's behavior in a darker light:

> The exonerative nature of the screwball comedy—a man violently knocks a woman off her pedestal, out of her principled pretentiousness, but does so because he really loves her, and his seeming cruelty is really an educating of her into the appropriate mode of love—can seem less pure if one reads the screwball as an alternate version of the Gothic.
>
> (Polan 1991: 139)

Hitchcock's generic suffusion reveals a malevolence underlaying fantasy, but insufficiently for Polan, who echoes Wood's observation that the film fails to critique capitalism (Polan 1991: 146). In fact, he finds *Mr. & Mrs. Smith* upholds bourgeois American ideology encapsulated by the commodification of sexuality by the representatives of patriarchal law, David Smith and Jefferson Custer.

Slovenian philosopher Slavoj Žižek psychoanalyzes Hitchcock's films, reading them as representations of Lacanian theory (1992). He locates *Mr. & Mrs. Smith* in Hitchcock's "modernist" period, finding the film tragicomic. Žižek explains that the tragic flaw, expressed as a mark of the symbolic order, is made comic when a subject is attached to it despite its contingent nature (1992: 76). "It is no accident that *Mr. & Mrs. Smith*, the Hitchcock film that exposes this constituent of his universe most clearly, is a comedy" (1992: 76). David's compulsions and Ann's absurd rules are practically mechanical and, therefore, humorous.

Despite an overall rise in appreciation for the film, some scholars remain skeptical. In *An Eye for Hitchcock*, Canadian film scholar Murray Pomerance finds Hitchcock's strongest American films critique consumer culture (2004: 38–39). Echoing Polan, Pomerance describes *Mr. & Mrs. Smith* as a tale "about the marriageable woman as product" (2004: 39). His later study, *Alfred Hitchcock's America*, diagnoses the Smiths' problem: "They are both too smart, too fast-thinking, too streamlined ciphers of modernism" (2013: 251). The Smiths may be perfect competitors, but for Pomerance, their modernized mechanization repels.

Dr. Ina Rae Hark, founder of the film and media studies major at the University of South Carolina, agrees that Hitchcock's early years in Hollywood allowed him to clarify his version of American

Figure 17.2 Jeff holds David's hand while Ann shaves her estranged husband.

masculinity, heavily influenced by the pop-cultural interest in Freudianism and momism's effect on men (2011: 302). Hark is one of the few critics who recognize that Jeff's behavior repeatedly "renders him positively effeminate," crystallized in Lake Placid when "David pretends to be delirious and mistakes Jeff for Ann, complete with handholding and caresses" (2011: 303; see Fig. 17.2).[2] Representations of queer male sexuality would bring Hitchcock later success, once he firmly characterized this shade of manhood as "neurotic or psychotic" (2011: 311).

Referring to Hark's work, American film scholar William Covey's interdisciplinary study concludes that the duplicitous characters and plot, and their discrepancies with other screwball comedies, work against the grain of those more optimistic films (2015). Ann's early rule that she and David never lie to one another becomes the film's structuring absence: "in terms of Hitchcock's aesthetic, it might be seen as the disappearance that everyone denies" (Covey 2015: 44). Covey describes the unhealthy tendencies of Hitch's hitched characters, determining that Ann and David "seem the least dysfunctional of Hitchcock's married couples" (2015: 48). Importantly, Covey finds Hitchcock's emphasis on lying as a necessary skill both in marriage and in American society.

Some of the most incisive recent academic work to consider *Mr. & Mrs. Smith* derives from visual and media cultures. NYU professor Alexander Galloway's essay, "The Bachelor's Fantasy: Autoimmunity in Theory" reviews the phenomenon of reflexivity in twenty-first-century life, finding it ubiquitous (2013: 103–107). Galloway considers *Mr. & Mrs. Smith* an allegory for discursive virtuality today and calls for further research into reflexivity's roots in modernism (2013: 108). Once radical, reflexivity has transformed into the very mode of production in the digital age (2013: 111). Using the Smiths as a cautionary tale, Galloway calls for radical honesty in criticism as a way to avoid the "bachelor's fantasy" enacted by David, who "wants to pursue his wife, but only because she is not his wife" (2013: 112). In this "emblematic figuration" (Polan 1991: 141), Ann takes the place of democratic capitalism while David is the political theorist who wants to reproduce the same system on slightly different terms.

American academic Casey McKittrick's *Hitchcock's Appetites* traces Hitchcock's personal embodiment, often painfully and publicly enacted, and occasionally infecting his film characters (2016). McKittrick identifies two regurgitative examples in *Mr. & Mrs. Smith*: Ann's forcing Jeff to over-imbibe while fondly reminiscing about David once throwing up on her and David's attempt to embarrass Ann by cheekily recalling her propensity for seasickness in front of Jeff's stodgy parents. McKittrick deems David's recollection a tender transtextual reference to Hitch's maritime marriage proposal to Alma despite her nautically induced nausea.

Taking a feminist viewpoint, American scholar Junha Jung reads *Mr. & Mrs. Smith* in terms of information asymmetry, a knowledge imbalance akin to dramatic irony, that enlightens the audience more than the characters while increasing the level of suspense (2017: 968). Jung finds the Smiths' marital information game exhibits a gendered inequality that forecloses the possibility of the characters' moral improvement and "explains the emotional callousness of the film's titular couple" (2017: 979–980). Like Cavell and Rothman, Jung ultimately laments the film's ambivalence.

Film historian Olympia Kiriakou's feminist star study *Becoming Carol Lombard* reviews Lombard's celebrity persona and its cruciality to her screen characters (2020: 118–134; see Fig. 17.3). Lombard

Figure 17.3 Carole Lombard directs Alfred Hitchcock's cameo appearance in *Mr. & Mrs. Smith* (1941).
© Warner Brothers

was a strong, sexually liberated feminist, but in 1940 she was also refashioning her star persona as she prepared to marry Clark Gable. These biographical details suggest a transtextual relationship between Lombard and Ann, preparing audiences for the performer's transformation into "Mrs." (Kiriakou 2020: 125–127).

Building upon Cavell's work, among others, French scholar Grégoire Halbout's genre study, *Hollywood Screwball Comedy: 1934–1945: Sex, Love, and Democratic Ideals* contextualizes the genre historically, identifying its semantic and syntactic elements as well as its ideological promise of American "happiness" in an "allegedly classless society" (2022: 1–2). Halbout rebuts critics who "attribute to a dominant ideology the Machiavellian goal of feeding the American middle class an illusory notion of marriage in order to safeguard the institution" (2022: 264). Rather, he sees the years leading up to World War II as ones where citizens learned to balance individual desire with social demands—enacting the cooperation necessary to healthy democracy. *Mr. & Mrs. Smith*, for Halbout, prioritizes "conjugal happiness" (2022: 255) and compromise over marriage and legality.

American academic Elizabeth Bullock's essay, "Naughts and Crosses," formally analyzes *Mr. & Mrs. Smith*, revealing the director's game. Hitchcock's ludic audiovisual matrix forms and formalizes a circuit of Xs and Os (see Fig. 17.4), or what Americans refer to as tic-tac-toe (2022).[3] Hitchcock plays this cyclically reflexive game with the audience from the opening credits to the final shot. Citing American scholar John Billheimer's *Hitchcock and the Censors* (2019), Bullock suggests that the Hitchcock game of images and sounds negatively incorporates the incorporeal elements sacrificed to the Production Code of America (PCA) censors. To Polan's point, *Mr. & Mrs. Smith* exhibits Hitchcock's engagement

Figure 17.4 Ann's skis crisscross suggestively in an X shape.

with America, Hollywood, and the PCA while maintaining his own established gamesman identity for which he was (and is) revered. In this way, *Mr. & Mrs. Smith* is a masterpiece of generic, industrial, and biographical reflexivity.

Over the past eighty-two years, *Mr. & Mrs. Smith* has proven a critically rich text. Sometimes overlooked and undervalued, the film's already rich critical history leaves room for further reassessment. In addition to the grounding method of neoformalism, remaining gaps in the literature offer future scholars promising avenues for further research.

Notes

1 https://the.hitchcock.zone/wiki/American_Film_(1977)_-_Books:_Cult_and_Puffery. In a subsequent rebuttal to Gilman, Elisabeth Karlin defends Spoto's "risky and interesting comparisons between Hitchcock and James, Dante, and Dostoevsky" (1977, qtd. in The Alfred Hitchcock Wiki). In doing so, Karlin prophesies the fecundity of literary comparisons for future scholarship.

2 Other queer behaviors include sitting beside David on his men's club bed discussing the Smiths' separation, being physically inserted between Ann and David while asking her to dinner, and asking Ann to leave the room for propriety's sake while undressing a seemingly unconscious David.

3 Maurice Yacowar's essay, "Hitchcock's Imagery and Art," identifies a recurring "X" symbol in Hitchcock's work (1986: 17). Later, Tom Cohen centralizes the transtextual X-motif, relating the metaphorical symbol to Hitchcock's version of Friedrich Nietzsche's eternal return, a "chiasmus" that functions as a "hermeneutic regime" indicating the self-negating semiotics of both philosophers (2009: 153). What Bullock neglects to note in 2022 is the similarity of that game to Deleuze's description of dream images in *Cinema II*, as a subtype of the mental image (2013b: 59).

References

Anderson, L. (1949) "Alfred Hitchcock," *Sequence*, 9 (autumn): 113–124.
Billheimer, J. (2019) *Hitchcock and the Censors*, Lexington, Ky.: University Press of Kentucky Press.
Brady, D. (1995) "Core of the Movie: The Chase," in S. Gottlieb (ed.), *Hitchcock on Hitchcock*, vol. I: *Selected Writings and Interviews*, Berkeley, Calif.: University of California Press, pp. 125–132.
Brill, L. (1988) *The Hitchcock Romance*: *Love and Irony in Hitchcock's Films*, Princeton, NJ: Princeton University Press.
Bullock, E. L. (2022) "Naughts and Crosses: Marital and Cinematic Gamesmanship in Alfred Hitchcock's *Mr. and Mrs. Smith*," *Hitchcock Annual*, vol. 25, pp. 93–120.
Cavell, S. (1981) *Pursuits of Happiness*: *The Hollywood Comedy of Remarriage*, Cambridge, Mass.: Harvard University Press.
Cohen, T. (2009) "Zarathustran Bird Wars: Hitchcock's 'Nietzsche' and the Teletechnic Loop," *Discourse*, 31 (1): 140–160.
Covey, W. (2015) "*Mr. and Mrs. Smith*: Alfred Hitchcock's Experiment in Screwball Comedy," *Interdisciplinary Humanities*, 32 (1): 42–52.
Deleuze, G. (2013a) *Cinema I*: *The Movement-Image*, trans. H. Tomlinson and B. Habberjam, London: Bloomsbury Academic.
Deleuze, G. (2013b) *Cinema II*: *The Time-Image*, trans. H. Tomlinson and R. Galeta, London: Bloomsbury Academic.
Durgnat, R. (1974) *The Strange Case of Alfred Hitchcock*: *Or, The Plain Man's Hitchcock*, London: Faber and Faber.
Galloway, A. R. (2013) "The Bachelor's Fantasy: Autoimmunity in Theory," *Camera Obscura*, 28 (1): 102–123.

Gehring, W. (1986) *Carole Lombard: The Hoosier Tornado*, Indianapolis, Ind.: Indiana Historical Society Press.
Gehring, W. (2003) *Screwball Comedy: A Genre of Madcap Romance*, New York: Greenwood Press.
Gehring, W. (2019) "*Mr. and Mrs. Smith* (1941)," in *Hitchcock and Humor: Modes of Comedy in Twelve Defining Films*, Jefferson, NC: McFarland, pp. 114–133.
Gilman, R. (1977) "Books: Cult and Puffery," *American Film*, 2 (4): 74–75.
Halbout, G. (2022) *Hollywood Screwball Comedy: 1934–1945: Sex, Love, and Democratic Ideals*, trans. Aliza Krefetz, New York: Bloomsbury Academic.
Hark, I. R. (2011) "Hitchcock Discovers America: The Selznick-Era Films," in T. Leitch and L. Poague (eds), *A Companion to Alfred Hitchcock*, Bognor Regis: Wiley-Blackwell, pp. 289–308.
Higham, C. (1962) "Hitchcock's World," *Film Quarterly*, 16 (2): 3–16.
Holliday, K. (1941) "Alfred Hitchcock says 'Actors are Cattle!'" *Hollywood Magazine*, 30 (9): 19 and 68.
Jung, J. (2017) "Games of Information Asymmetry in Alfred Hitchcock's *Mr. and Mrs. Smith* (1941)," *Journal of Popular Culture*, 50 (5): 968–982.
Karlin, E. (1977) "Pro-Hitchcock," *American Film*, 2 (6): 3.
Kiriakou, O. (2020) *Becoming Carole Lombard: Stardom, Comedy and Legacy*, New York: Bloomsbury Academic.
Leitch, T. M. (1991) *Find the Director, and Other Hitchcock Games*, Athens, Ga.: University of Georgia Press.
McKittrick, C. (2016) "The Pleasures and Pangs of Hitchcockian Consumption," in *Hitchcock's Appetites: The Corpulent Plots of Desire and Dread*, New York: Bloomsbury Academic, pp. 65–99.
Naremore, J. (2004) "Hitchcock and Humor," in R. Allen and S. Ishii-Gonzales (eds), *Hitchcock: Past and Future*, London and New York: Routledge.
Polan, D. (1991) "The Light Side of Genius: Hitchcock's *Mr. and Mrs. Smith* in the Screwball Tradition," in A. Horton (ed.), *Comedy/Cinema/Theory*, Berkeley, Calif.: University of California Press, pp. 131–152.
Polan, D. (2007) *Scenes of Instruction: The Beginnings of the US Study of Film*, Berkeley, Calif.: University of California Press.
Pomerance, M. (2004) *An Eye for Hitchcock*, New Brunswick, NJ: Rutgers University Press.
Pomerance, M. (2013) *Alfred Hitchcock's America*, Cambridge: Polity.
Rohmer, É., and C. Chabrol (1979) *Hitchcock: The First Forty-Four Films*, trans. Stanley Hochman, New York: F. Ungar.
Rothman, W. (1982) *Hitchcock: The Murderous Gaze*, Cambridge, Mass.: Harvard University Press.
Rothman, W. (2014) "Little Deaths," in *Must We Kill the Thing We Love? Emersonian Perfectionism and the Films of Alfred Hitchcock*, New York: Columbia University Press, pp. 58–72.
Sarris, A. (1999) "Notes on the 'Auteur' Theory in 1962," in L. Braudy and M. Cohen (eds), *Film Theory and Criticism*, 5th edn, New York: Oxford University Press, pp. 515–518.
Sennett, T. (1971) *Lunatics and Lovers*, New Rochelle, NY: Arlington House.
Sloan, J. (1995) *Alfred Hitchcock: The Definitive Filmography*. Berkeley, Calif.: University of California Press.
Spoto, D. (1983) *The Dark Side of Genius: The Life of Alfred Hitchcock*, Boston, Mass.: Little, Brown & Co.
Spoto, D. (1992) *The Art of Alfred Hitchcock: Fifty Years of His Motion Pictures*, 2nd edn, New York: Doubleday (Anchor Books).
Taylor, J. R. (1978) *Hitch: The Life and Times of Alfred Hitchcock*, New York: Pantheon Books.
Truffaut, F., with H. G. Scott (1984) *Hitchcock*, rev. edn, New York: Simon & Schuster.
Wood, R. (1989) *Hitchcock's Films Revisited*, New York: Columbia University Press.
Yacowar, M. (1986) "Hitchcock's Imagery and Art," in M. Deutelbaum and L. Poague (eds), *A Hitchcock Reader*, Ames, Iowa: Iowa State University Press, pp. 16–26.
Žižek, S. (1992) "How the Non-duped Err," in *Looking Awry: An Introduction to Jacques Lacan through Popular Culture*, Cambridge, Mass.: MIT Press, pp. 69–87.

Chapter 18

Criminal Indifference

The Strange Case of *The Wrong Man* (1956)

Jason P. Isralowitz and Robert E. Kapsis

Oscar-winning director Guillermo del Toro has studied the work of Alfred Hitchcock for more than forty years. But even though del Toro himself has made two of the most unsettling horror films of this century, he finds one Hitchcock picture too agonizing to revisit.

"The one I can't watch again is *The Wrong Man*," del Toro told Peter Bogdanovich in a podcast interview. "I suffer too much" (Stratten 2024).

Del Toro's comment points to one reason for the relative obscurity of *The Wrong Man*: it's not easy on the viewer. Based on a true story, the film stars Henry Fonda as Manny Balestrero, a New York nightclub musician who in 1953 was falsely arrested for armed robberies. It depicts Manny's disturbing odyssey through the criminal justice system and the resulting breakdown suffered by his wife, Rose (Vera Miles).

After premiering in December 1956, the film earned less than 1 million dollars in US domestic rentals the next year (*Variety*, January 8, 1958, p. 30). Audiences resisted its grim subject and tone, which ventured far from the escapism of Hitchcock's earlier mistaken-identity thrillers. In fact, James Naremore (2014: 146) has described *The Wrong Man* as "one of the bleakest movies ever produced in Hollywood."

The original critical reaction was not as bleak as the film. Many publications praised the director's foray into new territory. But several influential outlets disparaged the picture, erasing any hope that it might ride a critical consensus to popular acclaim or the award circuit.

The Wrong Man's failure to find an audience has persisted. So, too, has the sense that the film was a well-intentioned misfire. In 1991, London critic Alan Stanbrook observed that "[b]y common consent, *The Wrong Man* … is one of Alfred Hitchcock's few failures" (*Sunday Telegraph*, March 17, 1991, p. xxvii). Even the film's champions refer to it as "underrated" (Naremore 2014: 145), "undervalued" (Schickel 2015: 200), or "neglected" (Thomson 2012: 290).

But these adjectives mask a rise in *The Wrong Man*'s reputation. Seeded by rapturous reviews from France, this ascent has been fueled by increasing acclaim from film historians and critics, who credit Hitchcock for his uncompromising commitment to an uncommercial project, and close readings by scholars, who have brought the film's aesthetic and thematic richness into focus. *The Wrong Man* has also received the impassioned support of many renowned directors, which has raised its profile on the repertory scene. A case in point: even though del Toro cannot bear to watch the film again, he selected it for a 2023 series at New York's Museum of Modern Art.

This essay will examine the reception history of *The Wrong Man* and its prospects for future ascendance. One reason for its perceived failure—that it did not cater to popular expectations—has become a powerful source of its reappraisal. More than that, *The Wrong Man* taps into contemporary anxieties in its depiction of a reckless prosecution and the resulting family trauma. No other film in the Hitchcock canon speaks so powerfully to societal problems whose full dimensions have only recently come into public view.

The Film and Its Initial Reception

The Wrong Man sticks largely to the facts of the Balestrero case. In January 1953, Manny visited a Prudential insurance office in Queens to seek a loan. There he was misidentified as the man who had twice held up the office before. Police arrested Manny the next day. Within six weeks of the arrest, Rose suffered a breakdown and was moved to a sanitarium for mental-health care (*Life*, June 29, 1953, pp. 97–100, 132).

The case went to trial in April 1953. On the second day of testimony, an impatient juror brought on a mistrial when he declared "Your Honor, do we have to sit here and listen to this?" A week later, with a new trial looming, detectives arrested an unemployed plastics molder named Charles Daniell as he tried to rob an Astoria deli. Daniell confessed to the Prudential holdups, which in turn cleared Manny. But Rose remained institutionalized until September 1955 (Isralowitz 2023: 97–102, 118).

Given his "eternal fear of the police," Hitchcock was naturally drawn to the story and set out to authentically recreate it (Truffaut 1985: 205, 237). To that end, Maxwell Anderson consulted the court transcript while fellow cowriter Angus MacPhail and associate producer Herbert Coleman interviewed the participants in the case. Hitchcock also filmed many scenes at the locations where the events had taken place, including prisons, courtrooms, and the sanitarium (Isralowitz 2023: 132–136).

In place of his customary cameo, Hitchcock appears in silhouette at the film's start to announce that "every word of it" is true. While falling short of this standard, *The Wrong Man* reconstructs the case's details with striking fidelity (Isralowitz 2023: 138–141).[1] Hitchcock eschewed his signature action sequences and humor in favor of a spare, disturbing account of an innocent family devastated by false arrest.

It was a hard time to market such a film. To compete with television, studios were emphasizing spectacle and escapism. The highest-grossing movies in 1957 were lavish epics with starry casts: *The Ten Commandments*, *Around the World in 80 Days*, and *Giant* (*Variety*, January 8, 1958, p. 30). Hitchcock was not immune from this trend. His remake of *The Man Who Knew Too Much*, which debuted earlier in 1956, featured exotic locales and a thrilling assassination-attempt set piece.

The Wrong Man arrived in the shadow not only of this Technicolor adventure but also of Hitchcock's acclaimed television presence. *Alfred Hitchcock Presents*, then in its second season, was America's fourth-highest rated show (Kapsis 1992: 256, n. 28). Each episode mixed mystery, humor, and plot twists—along with Hitchcock's cheeky opening and closing comments.

Even without these ingredients, *The Wrong Man* drew praise from many US critics. *Variety* (January 2, 1957, p. 6) described it as a "gripping piece of realism," while the *Hollywood Reporter* (December 21, 1956, p. 3) called it a "most harrowing, pervading picture of almost disastrous consequence." *Newsweek* (January 7, 1957, p. 68) heralded "Hitchcock's success in filling the familiar with terror." These and other reviews belie the perception that the film was a critical flop (Kapsis 1992: 47–49).

But *The Wrong Man* left several influential critics cold. A. H. Weiler of the *New York Times* (December 24, 1956, p. 8) declared that "the story generates only a modicum of drama." Weiler found that "Hitchcock has done a fine and lucid job with the facts … but they have been made more important than the hearts and dramas of the people they affect." The *Los Angeles Times* (Scheuer, January 24, 1957, p. 79) lamented that "it proves again that life can be more interminable than fiction." Echoing these sentiments were the *Saturday Review* (Alpert, January 19, 1957, p. 49; Hitchcock "has shown more interest in the details of justice than in the emotions of his characters"), the *New Yorker* (McCarten, January 5, 1957, pp. 61–62; "simple realism is not enough"), and *Time* (January 14, 1957; "the drama … and near tragedy have been dissipated").

These reviews were especially damaging because *The Wrong Man* should have appealed to sophisticated audiences who in the postwar period had discovered foreign art films (Kapsis 1992: 48–49). In fact, Jonathan Rosenbaum (*Chicago Reader*, October 26, 1985) describes it as "the closest that Alfred Hitchcock ever came to making an art film." But arthouse patrons were more likely to read reviews appearing in the prestigious publications, which tilted toward the negative (Kapsis 1992: 49).

Mainstream audiences, meanwhile, likely resisted the film because it was so unlike Hitchcock's lighter thrillers. Even the favorable reviews came with this disclaimer. New York's *Daily News* (Hale, December 23, 1956) praised *The Wrong Man* as "a thought-provoking film" but cautioned that it is "not a typical Hitchcock picture, so don't expect excitement, humor and suspense." The *Philadelphia Inquirer* (Martin, January 13, 1957, pp. 15–16) conceded that this "virtuoso piece of work" lacked "the famed and familiar Hitchcock touch" and offered "nothing even remotely funny." Such reviews may have alienated filmgoers who attended Hitchcock films to be entertained, not to be challenged with a searing drama.

The Wrong Man also received mixed notices in England. In the *Sunday Times* (February 24, 1957), Dilys Powell praised its "ferociously circumstantial opening" but bemoaned its slow pacing. The *Manchester Guardian* (February 23, 1957, p. 5) declared that, after a suspenseful start, the film "wilts, simply because in the pursuit of truthfulness, the master can find no place for his old enthralling sleight-of-hand." Similar verdicts appeared in *Sight and Sound* (Houston 1957: 211; "the film's extreme slowness becomes an increasing dramatic liability") and the *Observer* (Lejeune, February 24, 1957; "a sterling effort" that "achieves dullness without conviction").

By contrast, French critics embraced Hitchcock's work with rhapsodic praise. Future director François Truffaut declared that *The Wrong Man* was "probably his best film." He praised the dissolve from Manny's face to the real culprit late in the film as "the most beautiful shot in Hitchcock's work" (1978: 86–87). Writing for *Cahiers du Cinéma* in 1957, Jean-Luc Godard highlighted many other elements that went ignored by US critics, including the structural innovation that "[e]ach crucial scene in *The Wrong Man* has … its 'double,' which justifies it on the narrative level while 'redoubling' its intensity on the dramatic level" (1972: 53).

That same year, two other *Cahiers du Cinéma* contributors, Éric Rohmer and Claude Chabrol, coauthored the first book devoted to Hitchcock's work. Unlike the critics who treated *The Wrong Man* as an anomaly, Rohmer and Chabrol wrote that the film "brings together the themes scattered throughout his work" and applauded Hitchcock for risking a "commercial failure" to "make the sort of film his heart was set on" (1979: 145).

An "Indifferent" Director?

The French critics laid the foundation for a reappraisal of *The Wrong Man*. In fact, the film was screened in a 1961 Manhattan series programmed by Bogdanovich that featured "critical failures in America" that

The Strange Case of *The Wrong Man* (1956)

had found favor in Europe (Davis 2017: 28). But Hitchcock himself slowed the film's momentum. In an interview published in 1963, he expressed regret over the narrative shift to Rose's breakdown: "I was disturbed by the fact that … we had to follow the wife's story, and [Manny's] story kind of collapsed." Hitchcock distinguished this section of the film from "the front part," which captured his "fear of the police" (Bogdanovich 1963: 38).

Two years later, in the groundbreaking *Hitchcock's Films*, Robin Wood echoed the director's views. Wood wrote that "[the film's] first half can stand comparison with anything Hitchcock has done" but concluded that "[t]he change of the focus of interest to Balestrero's wife … tends to dissipate the spectator's interest" (1989: 84).

A more significant blow to the film's standing came in 1967 with the publication of Truffaut's acclaimed book-length interview with Hitchcock. By this point, Truffaut had retreated from his adulation of *The Wrong Man*. He now claimed that Hitchcock's "stylized" aesthetic undermined his quest for authenticity. Truffaut contrasted the film's overall "trouble" with the success of a "specifically Hitchcockian scene" in which Manny's lawyer realizes that Rose is ill (see Fig. 18.1)—an episode that Truffaut characterized as a departure from "the real story." Hitchcock then responded (according to the book) by saying "Well, let's file *The Wrong Man* among the indifferent Hitchcocks" (Truffaut 1985: 240–243).

In the audio recording of this particular exchange with Truffaut, however, Hitchcock did not say "indifferent." Rather, after explaining that he made the film under an expired studio contract, he said "let's mark it down as a Warner Bros. production" (*Hitchcock Zone*, Part 21).[2] While Hitchcock added that "I don't feel that strongly about it," that phrase is not as freighted with apathy as the published version.

On top of that, the "Hitchcockian scene" that Truffaut praised was not an invented one. It was in fact the Balestreros' lawyer, Frank O'Connor, who realized at a meeting that Rose was "in a state of

Figure 18.1 A true Hitchcockian moment.
The Wrong Man, directed by Alfred Hitchcock. © Warner Bros. Pictures, Inc. 1956. All rights reserved.

shock" and told Manny to "seek competent medical advice" (Brean 1955: 55). Truffaut rightly praises the film's recreation of that meeting for setting up a counterpoint between visuals and dialogue. The cutting between O'Connor's worried expression and Rose's blank stare cues us to the lawyer's realization even as he professes his optimism about the case. But the scene is not the exception that proves Truffaut's case. It is instead one of many examples of how Hitchcock uses cinematic techniques to unsettle us without violating his commitment to fidelity. Still, the director failed to defend the film on these grounds. His apparent "indifference" encouraged its classification as an insignificant work (Powell 2016).

From "Indifferent" to Essential

Despite Hitchcock's ambivalence, *The Wrong Man* has won increasing attention and acclaim over the past forty years. Five years after Hitchcock's death, Robert Ray (1985: 140) observed that the film was "now regarded as important" even though it was seen as a "cult object" when released. Film historians have borne out Ray's assertion. Richard Schickel (2015: 200) finds that *The Wrong Man* is "without precedent or follow-up in Hitchcock's canon" and "is as great as anything he ever did." Scott Eyman (2017: 227) describes it as a "haunting picture that cuts deeper than most Hitchcock." Foster Hirsch (2023: 494) sees the film as his "most daring, or at least most uncompromising, achievement" during "a decade filled with experiment."

Scholars have brought a wide range of perspectives to the film. For example, David Sterritt (1993: 65–81) shows how *The Wrong Man* criticizes the isolation and loneliness underlying social structures in the 1950s. For Paula Marantz Cohen (1999: 155), the film marks a critical shift for Hitchcock away from Victorian cultural influences and toward "a postmodern American esthetic." Noa Steimatsky (2017: 153–171) explores how the framing of Manny's face against grid-like backgrounds evokes the way institutional apparatuses prematurely mark suspects as criminals. In a study of Hitchcock's actors, Dan Callahan (2020: 190–196) finds Fonda to be "unerring" and Miles "very touching" and includes the film among the "peak" Hitchcocks.

Several prominent critics have come to a similar conclusion. Rosenbaum (*Chicago Reader*, October 26, 1985) and Stanbrook (*Daily Telegraph*, December 1, 1989, p. 16) agree that *The Wrong Man* is one of the director's greatest works. Glenn Kenny (2016) argues that the film "is one of Hitchcock's most dread-filled but also one of his most compassionate." The *New Yorker*'s Richard Brody (2024) recently hailed it as one of the best "bio-pics" ever.

But *The Wrong Man* has gained an even bigger reputational boost from some of the world's most renowned filmmakers. Chief among them is Martin Scorsese, who selected it as a favorite for a series at 2002's Tribeca Film Festival (Fondazione Prada 2004: 71). For *Taxi Driver* (1976), Scorsese had drawn from Hitchcock's camera movements to create a mood of paranoia (Ebert 2008: 218–19). In 2019, Scorsese and screenwriter Jay Cocks chose *The Wrong Man* to open a double-feature series at New York's Film Forum. The venue was fitting since Scorsese's support of the film may be rivalled only by that of Film Forum's repertory artistic director, Bruce Goldstein, who has screened it many times over the past thirty years.

Among Scorsese's peers, Francis Ford Coppola has identified *The Wrong Man* as a favorite Hitchcock film (Rosen 1974: 44). Todd Haynes selected it for a series at San Francisco's Museum of Art in 2017. That same year, Christian Petzold made an admiring documentary short that features still images from the film (*Où en êtes-vous, Christian Petzold?*). An earlier documentary treatment came in Kent Jones's *Hitchcock/Truffaut* (2015), whose segment on the film features glowing comments by Scorsese and French director Arnaud Desplechin. And, following Scorsese's path, director Matt Reeves cited Hitchcock's subjective point of view shots as an inspiration for the camerawork in *The Batman* (O'Falt 2022).

As Reeves' tribute suggests, one divide between *The Wrong Man*'s detractors and admirers concerns its stylistic merit. Some of the original reviews complained that the film lacked the director's usual visual flair—a view that Pauline Kael (1991: 850) would echo in calling it "an unusually drab Hitchcock film." But both scholars and critics have made the contrary case. In Cohen's words (1995: 125), "the images are as artfully arranged … as any in the Hitchcock repertory." Brody (2024) argues that the film "depicts the mind-bending power of the police and the judicial system with the sort of hectic and harrowing visual compositions seen in his more sensational thrillers." Scorsese notes that in the scenes where the police display Manny before eyewitnesses (see Fig. 18.2), the camera movements are "so insidious and so incriminating" that we share the character's sense of guilt (Tribeca Talks 2004: 48).

An even more significant fault line is over the attention given to Rose's breakdown in the narrative's last third. Naysayers portrayed this shift as a "distraction" (Scheuer, *Los Angeles Times*, January 24, 1957, p. 79) that loses the viewer's interest (Houston 1957: 211). But more recent scholarship has vindicated Hitchcock's treatment of her descent. For example, Spoto (1992: 256–260) argues that Rose's retreat completes a "magnificently structured work—very close to true classical tragedy." For William Rothman (2014: 133), Rose is "the heart and soul of *The Wrong Man*." He finds in Rose's seeming "madness" not only a "clairvoyance" about the system's processing of Manny but also a recognition that Manny has failed to "take her ideas seriously" or see her as "a person in her own right" (Rothman 2014: 115, 119, 138).

Figure 18.2 An "incriminating" identification parade.

Edward White (2021: 163) concludes that Miles's turn as Rose provides "the emotional center of the film, the chilling awfulness of seeing a family unravel."

A Resonant Tale of Injustice

While *The Wrong Man* is not as undervalued as it once was, it remains underseen. One testament to its low profile lies in data from Letterboxd, a popular social network app where cinephiles rate films. As of December 2024, only about 40,000 of that platform's 15 million members had seen the film—compared to, for example, 374,000 for *North by Northwest*.

Even so, several factors point to the potential of the film to rise further in both profile and reputation. For one thing, the film has in its corner some of the world's most revered filmmakers. In September 2023, Steven Spielberg joined their ranks by selecting *The Wrong Man* as one of his five recommended films airing on Turner Classic Movies that month.

Another boon to *The Wrong Man*'s profile is its classification as a leading film noir. Commentators like Hirsch (1981: 178–179) and Eddie Muller (2021: 145) have highlighted the stylistic and thematic elements supporting this classification. In two recent surveys of the best noirs of all time, *The Wrong Man* ranked twenty-fifth (Paste 2023) and twenty-seventh (Slant 2019), respectively. Fans of noir remain among the most engaged cinephiles and have given the film a following independent of the deep well of Hitchcock fans.

But an even more potent source of the film's staying power—and its potential to engage future viewers—lies in its relevance to contemporary values. Hitchcock's critique of the criminal justice system, and his exploration of the trauma of the system's victims, resonate more today than they did in 1956.

A film's reception reflects the values of its era. At the time of *The Wrong Man*'s release, the issue of wrongful convictions had not dented the public consciousness. The few widely reported exonerations were treated as isolated anomalies rather than system failures. Authorities did not reckon with their role in imprisoning the innocent. Instead, in explaining cases like Manny's, the state deflected blame to "honest mistakes" by sincere eyewitnesses (Isralowitz 2023: 5–6).

This narrative seeped into the original reviews. The detectives who arrest Manny were seen as "hard and yet fair" (*Hollywood Reporter*, December 21, 1956, p. 30) and "dispassionate but understanding" (Weiler, *New York Times*, December 24, 1956, p. 8). The *Cincinnati Enquirer* (Radcliffe, January 17, 1957, p. 15) noted that the authorities "[a]ll work within the orderly framework of the law." According to the *Evening Star* (Carmody, January 18, 1957, p. 59), Hitchcock presented "an honest police mistake" and "circumstance is the villain." Even the left-leaning *Nation* opined that "the police show an understandable reluctance to let go of a suspect until he proves himself innocent" (Hatch, January 5, 1957, p. 27).

Ironically, some critics went so far as to question the story's plausibility. The *New York Herald Tribune* (Zinsser, December 24, 1956, p. 4) observed that "it is fantastic that a chain of errors could almost destroy an innocent citizen in this careful age of criminology." The *Boston Globe* (Adams, January 21, 1957, p. 22) declared that it "isn't a convincing story" because "[y]ou can't believe that an innocent man and devoted father and husband, could get into so much trouble." *Commonweal* (Hartung, January 25, 1957, p. 434) complained that "[e]ven with the truth, Director Hitchcock taxes our credulity and endurance."

These reviews presupposed a meticulous justice system and implied that only the most surreal of coincidences could land an innocent person in jail. They aligned with the reporting on the real case, which exonerated the state and attributed Manny's ordeal to his status as Daniell's "double"—a claim that does not survive scrutiny (Isralowitz 2023: 102–110).

Acceptance of the state's narrative excluded *The Wrong Man* from a cycle of successful "social problem" films in the postwar area. These films explored topical issues like the plight of returning veterans (*The Best Years of Our Lives*, 1945), antisemitism (*Gentleman's Agreement*, 1947), mental-health treatment (*The Snake Pit*, 1948), and union corruption (*On the Waterfront*, 1954) (Ray 1985: 144–145). Social problem films often earned big box-office receipts and Academy Award recognition (Cagle 2017: 1). But in 1956 false arrest was not seen as a problem requiring cinematic illumination or societal reform. And while the industry's self-censoring rules mandated the favorable portrayal of police (Mezey and Niles 2005: 137), the Production Code Administration found nothing threatening in Hitchcock's depiction of the justice system. Its report on the script identified the detectives, and the prosecutor, as "sympathetic" characters (PCA Report, 1956, "Portrayal of Professions")—a characterization that correctly anticipated the original critical reactions.

Do the Balestreros suffer because of fantastic coincidences and terrible luck, or because of the negligence of state officials? At first, the former reading prevailed. According to Godard (1972: 48), "chance" plays "the primordial role." Ray (1985: 157) argues that "Manny's troubles depended solely on absurd coincidences that piled up one after another." Hirsch (1988: 178) concludes that "the enemy" in the film "is a matter of purely blind chance, of dumb accident."

In light of the modern innocence movement, however, *The Wrong Man* lands differently. Since 1989, more than 3,400 Americans have been exonerated (National Registry of Exonerations, 2024a). News coverage transformed wrongful convictions "from a nonissue in 1990, to a matter of public interest by 2000, and to a major concern by 2010" (Zalman et al. 2013: 51). Annual exonerations in the USA hit a record high (251) in 2022 (National Registry of Exonerations, 2024b). A majority have come to believe that false convictions occur with sufficient regularity to warrant substantial reforms (Zalman et al. 2013: 59). So have many prosecutors, who have established wrongful conviction units to investigate innocence claims (*New York Times*, August 24, 2023). Meanwhile, advocacy groups like the Innocence Project have shown that wrongful convictions result from systemic problems, including unwarranted confidence in eyewitness testimony and suggestive police identification procedures (Brown and Neufeld 2021: 248–255).

In the UK, the "Post Office Scandal" recently brought national attention to the problem of false convictions. In a miscarriage of justice spanning 1999 to 2015, hundreds of sub-postmasters were wrongfully accused of financial crimes as a result of accounting software defects (see Castle, *New York Times*, January 10, 2024, p. A12). By December 2023, at least ninety-three people had been formally exonerated and an advisory board had recommended that all of the more than 900 convictions be vacated (*BBC*, December 15, 2023). The scandal, and especially its depiction in the ITV drama *Mr. Bates vs The Post Office* (2024), stirred public outrage (see Castle, *New York Times*, January 10, 2024, p. A12). Many victims—including those who, like Manny, were prosecuted but not convicted—experienced post-traumatic stress and depressive symptoms (Growns et al. 2023: 10).

In the wake of such miscarriages of justice, and the erosion of faith in law enforcement and the criminal justice system (Saad 2023), *The Wrong Man* gains extra resonance. Contemporary viewers will see in the Balestreros' ordeal not a case of ruinous bad luck but a reckless rush to judgment. They will see eyewitnesses whose testimony is tainted by anxiety and mob mentality. They will see detectives who presume Manny's guilt without even asking about his whereabouts on the dates of the crimes. They will see identification procedures that are prejudicial and unfair. They will see that the state's theory of

Manny's guilt is absurd because it requires the following conclusion: having robbed Prudential twice in 1952, Manny then returned to the office a month after the second holdup, accurately identified himself, presented his wife's policy, and asked for a loan.

In a pivotal scene before she is institutionalized, Rose tells Manny that "no matter how innocent you are, or how hard you try, they'll find you guilty." To a 1950s audience, this statement may have seemed no more than an expression of Rose's growing paranoia. But today it plays as an indictment of the state's blind deference to unreliable eyewitnesses—which in real life precluded an investigation of Manny's alibis and which is now understood to be a leading cause of wrongful convictions.

The likelihood of such reactions is borne out by more recent commentary on the film. John Orr (2005: 11–12) argues that Hitchcock's increasing willingness to criticize the law shows in scenes of "cheap corner-cutting and false accusation that leads to quick prosecution." Kenny (2016) notes that "the police are presented as surly, near-malevolent representatives of a system that wants to place Manny in captivity." And *Entertainment Weekly* (Stenzel 2023) finds that the film "highlight[s] the glaring flaws in the American justice system—in particular, the way that testimonies and actions based on fleeting memories can condemn people to a lifetime of punishment."

Hitchcock depicts these flaws in a singularly cinematic way but with so much restraint that the source of the film's power resisted discovery. Proof of his achievement continues to emerge from recent studies. In *Où en êtes-vous, Christian Petzold?*, for example, Petzold and fellow director Christoph Hochhäusler lay bare the brilliance of the scenes in which the police require Manny to parade before eyewitnesses. These scenes accurately present the "showup" procedure—the display of a suspect alone before eyewitnesses rather than in a group (a "lineup" or "identification parade"). While showups were routine in the 1950s, courts and legal commentators have criticized the procedure as inherently suggestive (Isralowitz 2023: 20, 196–197). Use of showups in the USA has led to the misidentification of many innocent people, including in several recent cases (Bazelon 2021; Isralowitz 2023: 199).

Petzold's documentary explores the inhumanity of this procedure, which the detectives first deploy after driving Manny to a liquor store that had been robbed. When they arrive at the store, Hitchcock positions the camera inside the vehicle to establish the opening of doors as a visual motif. Petzold notes that as Manny steps out of the car, he is walking into a "menacing reality," and his passage through each subsequent door is "a step toward perdition."

As they analyze images from the showups at the liquor store and a nearby deli, Petzold and Hochhäusler emphasize the destructive ways that the detectives force Manny to play the role of the criminal. Hochhäusler notes that the eyewitnesses treat Manny "like livestock, like someone who has already been condemned" (see Fig. 18.3). The situation is so inherently incriminating, and the stares of the onlookers are so judgmental, that "we are infected." Manny himself seems overcome by guilt. "We would all be guilty if we had to walk around the way he does," Petzold observes.

The camera movements in these scenes spike the film with a sense of unease. So does Fonda's performance, whose restraint upended audience expectations as much as Hitchcock's. Fonda suppresses his fiery resolve in favor of a haunted resignation. Under the gaze of the proprietors, he projects shame and fear with darting eyes, a tentative gait, and jittery, abrupt looks over his shoulder. His passivity subverts movie-star conventions, as does the startling moment later when, hinting at suicidal impulses, Manny declares that his family would be better off without him.[3]

Of course, Manny is not alone in suffering undeserved guilt. Rose blames herself for the arrest because her dental problems led to Manny's visit to the insurance office. While Hitchcock second-guessed his decision to follow her story, it was groundbreaking to show the devastation that false arrest wreaks on

Figure 18.3 Judgmental glares.

the accused's family members. "It was like tossing a hand grenade in an Easter dinner, where there is a house filled with people and it explodes," the Balestreros' younger son, Greg, said of the arrest. "There is absolutely no way to say it didn't impact everybody, down through first cousins" (Isralowitz 2023: 88). A similar spiral of tragedy came to the fore in the Post Office scandal as some victims suffered the disintegration of their marriages while others saw spouses or children afflicted by mental-health disorders (*New York Times*, January 10, 2024, p. A12; *The Guardian*, January 8, 2024, pp. 6–7).

Hitchcock's attention to the family trauma shows in visual echoes and transitions that fit within the "doubling" structure identified by Godard. A shot of the detectives taking Manny to their squad car is mirrored later by one of a doctor and nurse escorting Rose to her room—in each case, with eerily feigned smiles. A psychiatrist's questioning of Rose under the hot lights evokes Manny's police interrogation and ends with her false confession ("they know I'm guilty"). A shot outside the sanitarium gives way to one of the courtroom.

In a wrenching final scene, Manny finds that the news of his exoneration fails to snap Rose out of her condition. The absence of any cathartic restoration defied Hollywood conventions. As Imogen Sara Smith (2023: 16) has observed, "focusing on innocent men whose names are eventually cleared was a way to make movies under the Production Code that could have happy endings." But in *The Wrong Man*, Rose's confinement is a heartbreaking reminder that the Balestreros suffered even after the arrest of the right man.

Rose's storyline adds another element that many contemporary viewers can relate to: the harrowing effects of depression. In 2023, nearly four in ten adults worldwide reported that they either suffered from the condition or had a family member or close friend who did (Witters 2023). As the stigmatization of mental illness continues to recede, many will see in Rose's descent an experience that has touched their own lives. This is especially true because of Miles's quiet but piercing performance, which was informed by her meeting with her real-life counterpart and details secured from the treating psychiatrist (Isralowitz 2023: 133; Hitchcock 1956b).

Hitchcock, who was famously scarred as a child by a five-minute stint in a jail cell, extends the theme of family trauma to Manny's sons. An early scene reveals that both Bob (the older son) and Greg aspire to learn their father's craft. When Manny promises to give them music lessons before he goes to work, the boys react with delight. For the Balestreros, music is not only what Jack Sullivan (2006: 209) calls "a manifestation of love and connectedness", it's also a symbol of Manny's parental engagement.

But the arrest occurs on the very night Manny was to give the lessons. Hitchcock then makes a point of showing a failed attempt to shield the boys from the anxiety coursing through the household: after Rose's brother-in-law tells her of Manny's imprisonment, a cut reveals that the children have been peering through a crack in their bedroom door (see Fig. 18.4). Their expressions suggest that they have heard the entire conversation. It's a resonant image that conveys that a door has been opened to the horrors of the adult world.

Several other visualizations of that idea follow after Manny returns home on bail and retreats to his bed. As Bob passes by the bedroom, shadows cast by a banister pass over his back like prison bars (Fig. 18.5). Bob then looks back at the camera with an anguished expression (Fig. 18.6a)—an image that rhymes with multiple shots of Manny (Figs. 18.2, 18.6b). This suggestion of transferred trauma sets up an emotional scene in which Manny tells Bob that "I never knew what my boys meant to me till right now."

Even as that sentiment moves us, Hitchcock's framing underlines the double tragedy that the arrest has set in motion: Manny is in bed, seemingly powerless and looking up for support from his son, who has been prematurely thrust into an adult role (Fig. 18.7). The composition reverses the positioning of the characters in the earlier scene when Manny promises the lessons (Fig. 18.8). And with Manny flattened by the allegations against him, Bob is the one dispensing the advice: "You oughta get some sleep now," he tells his father. Just moments later, Bob is heard, offscreen, instructing Greg not to bother Manny: "He'll give us lessons as soon as he can, but not now." These words both poignantly express Bob's protective love for his father and encapsulate a profound interruption of his childhood. They are also the last words that either boy speaks in the film, which contributes to the sense of loss that lingers even after the exoneration.

Figure 18.4 Childhood interrupted.

Figure 18.5 Trauma marks the son.

The Strange Case of *The Wrong Man* (1956) 221

Figures 18.6a, 18.6b Rhyming gestures of distress.

Figure 18.7 Role reversal.

Figure 18.8 An earlier moment of family harmony.

Figure 18.9 Portrait of continued suffering.

Nowhere is that loss more devastating than in the final scene at the sanitarium. Manny once again finds himself looking up at a distraught family member (Fig. 18.9). While he insists that "we can start our lives all over again," Rose's impassive response suggests otherwise. The scene is painfully true to the experience of Manny and his sons, who found Rose to be unreachable during her extended confinement (Isralowitz 2023: 111).

Moments like these bear out del Toro's observation that the film offers "no rays for hope" (Stratten 2024). And, despite a controversial postscript relating that Rose was "completely cured" within two years, what stays with you is the sad reality that for the Balestreros and other victims of false accusation, the trauma is lasting.[4]

During the production of *The Wrong Man*, Hitchcock advised his team of one essential goal: "The film must breathe reality" (*Long Island Sunday Press*, April 22, 1956).

Almost seventy years later, in ways that remain all too timely, it still does.

Notes

1. For example, while accurately showing that two potential alibi witnesses died, the film omits that several others were prepared to testify for Manny. In another deviation, one of the arresting detectives plays a role in clearing Manny when in fact Daniell confessed to police in another precinct (Isralowitz 2023: 140, 176–177). Hitchcock acknowledged that he and MacPhail had "taken a real liberty" with this change (Hitchcock 1956c: 3).
2. Janet Bergstrom (2011: 387–404) has documented many substantial differences between the audio recordings of the interviews and the text of the book.

3   The screenplay makes the point explicit: "While [Manny] does not say, in so many words, that he contemplates taking his own life, yet it is quite obvious, from his tone, that this is uppermost in his mind" (*The Wrong Man*, screenplay, Anderson and MacPhail 1956: 157). Court records confirm that Manny was under psychiatric treatment during his trial (Balestrero Case, 1953: 106).

4   Articulating a recurring critique of the film, David Bordwell argued that the closing title card, which appears over a family of four walking under palm trees in Miami, is an "outrageously" pandering bid for a happy ending (1982: 5). Since Rose was in fact released from the sanitarium in 1955, however, Hitchcock defended the postscript on the ground that "we were just doing the true story" (Macklin 2015: 52). The title card's statement that Rose was "completely cured" may have been informed by her participation in the production, including one instance in which she relayed, "in a very lucid way," the details of a detective's visit to the Balestrero home (Hitchcock 1956a). But according to her son Greg, Rose remained forever "fragile" and never resolved her feelings of guilt over Manny's arrest (Isralowitz 2023: 206).

References

Anderson, M., and A. MacPhail (1956) *The Wrong Man* (unpublished screenplay), on file at The Morgan Library & Museum.

Balestrero Case (1953) Trial Transcript in *People v. Balestrero*, Indictment Number 271/53, Queens County, available in *The Wrong Man* files, Warner Bros. Archives at the USC School of Cinematic Arts.

Bazelon, E. (2021) "I Write about the Law. But Could I Really Help Free a Prisoner?" *New York Times Magazine*, June 30.

Bergstrom, J. (2011) "Lost in Translation? Listening to the Hitchcock–Truffaut Interview," in T. Leitch and L. Poague (eds), *A Companion to Alfred Hitchcock*, Malden, Mass.: Wiley-Blackwell, pp. 387–404.

Bogdanovich, P. (1963) *The Cinema of Alfred Hitchcock*, New York: The Museum of Modern Art Film Library.

Bordwell, D. (1982) "Happily Ever After, Part Two," *The Velvet Light Trap*, 19: 2, 5.

Brean, H. (1955) *A Case of Identity*: *The Balestrero Story* (Film Treatment), June 29, available in *The Wrong Man*—Script, File 1005, Margaret Herrick Library.

Brody, R. (2024) "The Best Bio-Pics Ever Made," *New Yorker*, March 19.

Brown, R., and P. Neufeld (2021) "Chimes of Freedom Flashing: For Each Unharmful Gentle Soul Misplaced Inside a Jail," *New York University Annual Survey of American Law*, 76 (2): 235–292.

Cagle, C. (2017) *Sociology on Film*: *Postwar Hollywood's Prestige Commodity*, New Brunswick: Rutgers University Press.

Callahan, D. (2020) *The Camera Lies*: *Acting for Hitchcock*, Oxford: Oxford University Press.

Cohen, P. M. (1995) *Alfred Hitchcock*: *The Legacy of Victorianism*, Lexington, Ky.: University Press of Kentucky.

Cohen, P. M. (1999) "Hitchcock's Revised American Vision: *The Wrong Man* and *Vertigo*," in Jonathan Freedman and Richard Millington (eds), *Hitchcock's America*, Oxford: Oxford University Press, pp. 155–172.

Davis, B. (2017) *Repertory Movie Theaters of New York City*: *Havens for Revivals*, *Indies and the Avant Garde*, *1960–1994*, Jefferson, NC: McFarland & Company, Inc.

Ebert, R. (2008) *Scorsese by Ebert*, Chicago, Ill.: University of Chicago Press.

Eyman, S. (2017) *Hank and Jim*: *The Fifty-Year Friendship of Henry Fonda and James Stewart*, New York: Simon & Schuster.

Fondazione Prada (2004) *Tribeca Talks*, Milan: Progetto Prada Arte.

Godard, J. (1972) "The Wrong Man," in J. Narboni and T. Milne (eds), *Godard on Godard*, Boston, Mass.: De Capo Press, pp. 48–55.

Growns, B., J. Kukucka, R. Moorhead, and R. Helm (2023) "The Post Office Scandal in the United Kingdom: Mental Health and Social Experiences of Wrongly Convicted and Wrongly Accused Individuals," *Legal and Criminological Psychology*, 29 (1): 17–31.

Hirsch, F. (1981) *The Dark Side of the Screen*: *Film Noir*, Boston, Mass.: Da Capo Press.

Hirsch, F. (2023) *Hollywood and the Movies of the Fifties*, New York: Knopf.

Hitchcock, A. (1956a) Letter to Maxwell Anderson, 29 February, in The Wrong Man – Script, 1955–56, File 1012, Margaret Herrick Library.

Hitchcock, A. (1956b) Letter to Maxwell Anderson, 15 March, in Maxwell Anderson Papers, Harry Ransom Humanities Research Center, University of Texas at Austin.

Hitchcock, A. (1956c) Letter to Maxwell Anderson, 20 March, in The Wrong Man – Script, 1955–56, File 1012, Margaret Herrick Library.

Hitchcock Zone, "Part 21: *The Wrong Man* through to *Vertigo*" (audio recordings of Francois Truffaut and Alfred Hitchcock broadcast on French Radio), available at https://the.hitchcock.zone/wiki/Alfred_Hitchcock_and_Fran%C3%A70is_Truffaut_(August 1962)

Houston, P. (1957) "The Wrong Man," *Sight and Sound*, 26 (4): 211

Isralowitz, J. (2023) *Nothing to Fear*: Alfred Hitchcock and the Wrong Men, Columbus, Ohio: Fayetteville Mafia Press.

Kael, P. (1991) *5001 Nights at the Movies*, New York: Henry Holt & Co.

Kapsis, R. (1992) *Hitchcock: The Making of a Reputation*, Chicago, Ill.: University of Chicago Press.

Kenny, G. (2016) "Hitchcock's Least 'Fun' Movie Is Also One of His Greatest," RogerEbert.com, February 17, https://www.rogerebert.com/features/the-wrong-man-hitchcocks-least-fun-movie-is-also-one-of-his-greatest

Macklin, A. (2015) "'It's the Manner of Telling': An Interview with Alfred Hitchcock (1976)," in S. Gottlieb (ed.), *Hitchcock on Hitchcock*, vol. II: *Selected Writings and Interviews*, Oakland, Calif.: University of California Press, pp. 49–57.

Mezey, N., and M. Niles (2005) "Screening the Law: Ideology and Law in American Popular Culture," *Columbia Journal of Law and the Arts*, 28 (2): 92–185.

Muller, E. (2021) *Dark City: The Lost World of Film Noir*, rev. edn, New York: Hachette.

Naremore, J. (2014) *An Invention without a Future: Essays on Cinema*, Berkeley, Calif.: University of California Press.

National Registry of Exonerations (2024a) "The National Registry of Exonerations," www.law.umich.edu/special/exoneration/Pages/about.aspx

National Registry of Exonerations (2024b) "Exonerations by Year: DNA and Non-DNA" (chart), www.law.umich.edu/special/exoneration/Pages/Exoneration-by-Year.aspx

O'Falt, C. (2022) "'The Batman': Director Matt Reeves," *IndieWire's Filmmaker Toolkit* [Podcast], March 6.

Orr, J. (2005) *Hitchcock and Twentieth Century Cinema*, London: Wallflower Press.

Paste (2023) "The 100 Best Film Noirs of All Time," November 3, www.pastemagazine.com/movies/film-noir/the-best-noirs-of-all-time

Powell, D. (2016) *Blu-Ray Review: The Wrong Man*, January 16, https://hitchcockmaster.wordpress.com/2016/01/16/blu-ray-review-the-wrong-man

Production Code Administration (1956) Report on *The Wrong Man*. Motion Picture Association of America. Production Code Administration records, Margaret Herrick Library.

Ray, R. (1985) *A Certain Tendency of the Hollywood Cinema*, Princeton, NJ: Princeton University Press.

Rohmer, É., and C. Chabrol (1979) *Hitchcock: The First Forty-Four Films*, trans. Stanley Hochman, New York: Frederick Ungar.

Rosen, M. (1974) "Francis Ford Coppola" (interview), *Film Comment*, July, pp. 43–48.

Rothman, W. (2014) *Must We Kill the Thing We Love? Emersonian Perfectionism and the Films of Alfred Hitchcock*, New York: Columbia University Press.

Saad, L. (2023) "Historically Low Faith in U.S. Institutions Continues," *Gallup*, https://news.gallup.com/poll/508169/historically-low-faith-institutions-continues.aspx

Scheuer, P. (1957) "Hitchcock 'Wrong Man' Lifelike but Plodding," *Los Angeles Times*, January 24, p. 79.

Schickel, R. (2015) *Keepers: The Greatest Films—and Personal Favorites—of a Moviegoing Lifetime*, New York: Vintage Books.

Slant (2019) "The 100 Best Film Noirs of All Time," April 12, www.slantmagazine.com/film/the-100-best-film-noirs-of-all-time

Smith, I. S. (2023) "The Naked Eye: Realism and the True Crime Aesthetic," *Noir City*, 38: 8–16.

Spoto, D. (1992) *The Art of Alfred Hitchcock: Fifty Years of His Motion Pictures*, 2nd edn, New York: Doubleday.

Steimatsky, N. (2017) *The Face on Film*, New York: Oxford University Press.

Stenzel, W. (2023) "Every Alfred Hitchcock Movie, Ranked," *Entertainment Weekly*, June 1, https://ew.com/movies/every-alfred-hitchcock-movie-ranked

Sterritt, D. (1993) *The Films of Alfred Hitchcock*, Cambridge: Cambridge University Press.

Stratten, L. (2024) "Guillermo del Toro and Alfred Hitchcock," *One Handshake Away: Peter Bogdanovich and the Icons of Cinema* [Podcast]. February 7.

Sullivan, J. (2006) *Hitchcock's Music*, New Haven, Conn.: Yale University Press.

Thomson, D. (2012) *The Big Screen: The Story of the Movies*, New York: Farrar, Straus & Giroux.

Truffaut, F. (1978) Review of *The Wrong Man*, in *The Films in My Life*, trans. L. Mayhew, New York: Simon & Schuster.

Truffaut, F. (1985) *Hitchcock*, rev. edn, New York: Simon & Schuster.

White, E. (2021) *The Twelve Lives of Alfred Hitchcock: An Anatomy of the Master of Suspense*, New York: W. W. Norton & Company.

Witters, D. (2023) "U.S. Depression Rate Reach New Highs," *Gallup*, May 17.

Wood, R. (1989) *Hitchcock's Films*, reprinted in *Hitchcock's Films Revisited*. New York: Columbia University Press.

Zalman, M., M. Larson, and B. Smith (2017) "Citizens' Attitudes toward Wrongful Convictions," *Criminal Justice Review*, 37 (1): 51–69.

PART FOUR

Four Reception Anomalies

Chapter 19
Hitchcock and His Critics
The Fall and Rise of *Strangers on a Train* (1951)

Robert E. Kapsis

When *Strangers on a Train* appeared in the summer of 1951, the critical establishment in Britain and the USA agreed: it was better than *Under Capricorn* (1949) and *Stage Fright* (1950) but still, as Dilys Powell put it, "not quite right" (*Sunday Times*, August 5, 1951). Richard Winnington's opening salvo for *Sight and Sound* was blistering: "When nearly ten years ago, Alfred Hitchcock broke away from his Daphne du Maurier phase with *Shadow of a Doubt*, there were premature congratulations." It got worse:

> The succeeding Hitchcock films, popular, adept and replete with useless trick effects, have been, however, peculiarly depressing in that their hollowness has derived from Hitchcock himself, and not … from Hollywood. Hitchcock, one has felt, no longer believes there's much point in making films, and satisfies a jaded urge mainly in the setting up and surmounting of pointless technical obstacles.
> (*Sight and Sound*, summer 1951; see also Anderson 1972)

Winnington echoed not only his co-patriot Lindsay Anderson's attack on Hitchcock but also that of his New York counterpart, Bosley Crowther, who complained,

> Just why is it that Mr. Hitchcock is watering his pictures down to the thinness of mere exhibitions of his known virtuosity—just why is it that he doesn't latch onto some good, meaty yarn that would make some significant contact with the world in which we live—eludes this unhappy observer. Certainly, the commerce of films needs today all of the substance that its artists can provide. Mr. Hitchcock would do well to ponder Nero, another corpulent man who applied his dexterity to mere fiddling at a time when the heat was on.
> (*New York Times*, July 4, 1951)

Ten years later, a new generation was more tolerant of the director's "exhibitions of his known virtuosity," and late-twentieth-century criticism and research has reexamined and celebrated his adaptation of Patricia Highsmith's novel from a variety of queer perspectives (see, e.g., Goldberg 2012 and Greven 2017). However, apart from Charles Barr's 2004–2005 study of how some negative British attitudes toward Hitchcock after he "deserted" for Hollywood in 1939 affected the reception of his 1940s films including *Notorious*—long considered among his five or six greatest achievements—none have explored how this contentious climate may have also affected the initial reception of other Hitchcock films from this period that have long been considered among his greatest works such as *Strangers on a Train* from 1951.[1]

In the past, critical studies of "classical Hollywood" film reception tended to privilege the usual suspects: a handful of New York or London papers and the boosterist industry trades (usually *Variety* and the *Hollywood Reporter*). These sources are very often preselected for scholars in archival clipping files and microfilm and become the template for truncated, establishment perspectives disconnected from rank-and-file ticket sales and more popular appraisals.

This essay will range more widely and systematically through the British and American press, and, where possible, more general contemporary public responses, not only to analyze critical judgments of *Strangers on a Train* but also, in the case of Great Britain, to also contextualize attitudes toward Hitchcock and Hollywood during World War II (1939–1945) and the postwar austerity period (1945–1951). This chapter also highlights how contrasting American and British views of Hitchcock and *Strangers on a Train* start to converge quite dramatically within ten years of the film's initial release in 1951.

Expatriate/Ex-patriot

Though *Strangers on a Train* was Hitchcock's fourteenth feature film since he immigrated to the USA in 1939, for many contemporary British critics, the director's Hollywood productions, lacking their national flavor and tarted up with lavish budgets and stars, would never be as good as *Blackmail*, *The 39 Steps*, or *The Lady Vanishes*. Dilys Powell dismissed *Rebecca* as "an overrated but interesting study in interior decoration" (*Sunday Times*, October 10, 1943, p. 2), and Winnington, writing for the *News Chronicle*, complained about the "empty polish" of *Spellbound* and *Notorious*'s "deadly slickness" and "dallying" closeups on beautiful stars (May 18, 1946; February 15, 1947). *Under Capricorn* and *Stage Fright* had some London critics "worried" that the master would be labeled "passé" if he didn't have another hit soon (Denis Duperley, *Kensington News and West London Times*, September 14, 1951). *Strangers on a Train*, set among Washington, DC's political and social elites, certainly had little in common with a warworn people still in the grip of rationing and reconstruction. But, consistent with Charles Barr's 2004–2005 essay, "Deserter or Honored Exile? Views of Hitchcock from Wartime Britain," British critics faced with the prospect of another Hitchcock film at their local theaters in September 1951 may have felt another, deeper kind of reservation (see Coda B).

While Hitchcock's frequent collaborator, English-born character actor Leo G. Carroll (Senator Morton in *Strangers on a Train*), had settled permanently in America as a supporting player in the early 1930s, Hitchcock signed his Hollywood contract on the brink of World War II and remained in southern California comfort while his ex-hometown endured the Blitz. The director's absence from the front line of wartime filmmaking was commented upon in the British press. Barr has suggested that, beginning in 1939,

Hitchcock was unfairly subjected to resentful coverage from key members of the filmmaking and journalistic establishment which may have colored the director's reputation and the critical reception of his films, among them *Strangers on a Train*. This film was not discussed by Barr in his 2004–2005 essay, but, in a memo to Kapsis dated March 22, 2022, he described how the film's critical reception in Britain had also been compromised by having to confront similar obstacles along the way.

British producer Michael Balcon, Hitchcock's former boss, is often targeted as the center of the anti-Hitchcock bias prevalent at that time, but he came late to the debate about the Hollywood British community that had been brewing in *Picturegoer* since the fall of 1939. Hitchcock scholars and fans will recognize Balcon from "Deserters," a *Sunday Express* article published in August 1940 and widely syndicated:

> I had a plump young junior technician in my studios whom I promoted from department to department. Today, one of our most famous directors, he is in Hollywood, while we who are left behind are trying to harness films to the great national effort. I do not give this man's name as I have decided not to mention any of the deserters by name.

But *Daily Telegraph* film critic Campbell Dixon had fewer scruples than Balcon and had named and shamed Hitchcock and producers Alexander Korda and Herbert Willcox back in April, urging them to return and make pictures in Britain (*Londonderry Sentinel*, April 25, 1940, p. 3).

Balcon only joined the public discussion in May, when interviewed by *Picturegoer*'s Herbert Cole. Appearing in print the day after the invasion of Belgium and Holland and the appointment of Winston Churchill as prime minister, Balcon remarked that he was "surprised and disgusted by the attitude of the British people at present in Hollywood" (*Picturegoer*, May 1940). Since Munich, there had been a steady stream of people "hurrying across the Atlantic" to lucrative contracts in Hollywood. "When things become tough here, they immediately desert the country and the British film industry and take cover in Hollywood." Cole, for his part, remarked, "I couldn't have argued with him if I had wanted to—and I didn't particularly want to" (*Picturegoer*, May 1940). But in addition to the producer and journalist agreeing on the issue, Malcolm Phillips' editorial "Are Our Stars Slacking?" ran on the opposite page (p. 11), endorsing Balcon's view, and issued an ultimatum: "Come home or give us a good reason for not doing so."

But Hitchcock and his Hollywood British peers were in hot water not only with the British establishment but with ordinary filmgoers as well. Cole received so many letters in response to his interview with Balcon that he had to stagger publishing some of them over two weeks in June. Many praised the substance of Balcon's interview, and Coles awarded a "first prize" to a Westminster-based reader who criticized the "specious excuses" some Hollywood Brits used to justify sitting out the war. A Liverpudlian also sided with Balcon, insinuating that those who put "careers before country" only cared about money. And one "R.A.F. Observer" from Cheltenham suggested that the British public should "boycott their films" (*Picturegoer*, June 8, 1940, p. 19). But *Picturegoer* also published opposing views from Hull and Chichester arguing the "deserters" shouldn't be "blackmailed for their possible objections to war" and that they were doing their bit, even by making films in Hollywood. Although a "specialist" magazine, *Picturegoer*'s letters to the editor point to a wider public interest in Hitchcock's patriotism and antagonism toward Hollywood that extended beyond the establishment world of filmmakers and journalists.

Hitchcock did not respond to *Picturegoer* but to the widely syndicated August article in the *Sunday Express*. Unfortunately, his response to Balcon's charges of desertion was not only angry and defensive; it was also a little pompous: "I have placed myself at the disposal of my government. It has only to ask." Was Mr. Churchill supposed to drop everything, including the threat of Nazi invasion, to ask Hitchcock personally to come home and make a film? Other former Hollywood Britons, such as David Niven and Leslie Howard, had dropped lucrative contracts to return to the British film industry in 1939. John Mills, Ralph Richardson, Alec Guinness, and Dirk Bogarde were in the armed forces. In other words, they volunteered rather than being drafted. Hitchcock dug himself an even deeper hole with an ill-chosen comment: "The whole thing has nothing to do with patriotism" (*Manchester Evening News*, August 26, 1940, p. 4). Others in Britain, including *Picturegoer*'s June readers, had already guessed what it did have to do with: Hollywood money.

Barr has argued that Hitchcock's second Hollywood film, the pro-British propaganda piece *Foreign Correspondent*, was an effective and timely retort to Balcon's criticisms (2004–2005: 5–9). The USA was still neutral, and Hitchcock joined several prominent filmmakers, including Hollywood's most famous resident Brit, Charlie Chaplin, in persuading the American public to fight the Nazis. London's *Daily Mirror* seemed to agree, stating that "Director Alfred Hitchcock is one of the few Britishers whose presence in Hollywood at this time is justified" (October 12, 1940, p. 9). London's *Daily Herald* called it "the most electrifying picture of the year" (October 11, 1940, p. 4), and the *Press and Journal* claimed that "Thousands are braving the Blitzkrieg in London every week to see *Foreign Correspondent*" (October 18, 1940, p. 4). But many other papers, including the *Liverpool Daily Post*, were furious about Hitchcock's imagination of London during the Blitz: "Nobody who has not been in England since the 'blitz' began can have any accurate notion of what it looks and feels like, and Mr. Hitchcock's notion is just slightly wrong all along the line." There was "a great film to be made" about 1939, but "not by Hitchcock in Hollywood," the journalist concluded (October 11, 1940, p. 4). Writing for *The Bystander*, contrarian George Campbell rejected the hero's final speech to America "Keep your lights going—they're the only lights left in the world" as "an appeal to America to join in", and dismissed the bulk of the film as senseless plot-juggling (October 23, 1940, p. 117). If Hitchcock had tried to make a message picture, James Agate wasn't buying it: "*Foreign Correspondent* won't make you think, but it will make you sit up and yell like a schoolboy at his first circus" (*Tatler*, October 23, 1940, p. 108).

Whatever the critics were saying, the British public seemed to like it: in 1941, *Kinematograph Weekly*, without listing any box-office numbers, claimed it was a runner-up to Hitchcock's *Rebecca* (January 9, 1941, p. 26), a romantic melodrama with nothing whatever to do with the war. Even so, listings like *Kinematograph*'s are tricky; it's impossible to say whether Hitchcock's American films topped the box office because nothing much else was at the local cinema or whether fans or critics, recognizing the familiar Hitchcock name, wanted to see what their former countryman was up to, regardless of genre.

If Hitchcock's intent was to make a film for the British war effort, the real public to persuade was American. In working with Walter Wanger, a producer known for his progressive, anti-Nazi views, Hitchcock had the ideal partnership for a message picture. Although it sold well in the USA, the film's high cost put Wanger several hundred thousand pounds in the red (Bernstein 2000: 440). Its ideological impact can be measured in part. In 1941, isolationist politicians in Washington launched an investigation into warmongering, anti-fascist filmmaking, singling out Warner Bros. (*Confessions of a Nazi Spy*), MGM (*Escape*) and British expatriate Alexander Korda (*That Hamilton Woman*) for special censure. Hollywood's most famous resident Brit, Charlie Chaplin, was at the center of press coverage, due to his parody of Hitler in *The Great Dictator*. But in the transcript of the US Congressional investigation into propagandizing in Hollywood, *Foreign Correspondent* was mentioned only in passing as "pro-British propaganda" (Propaganda in Motion Pictures, Hearings Before a Subcommittee of the Committee on Interstate Commerce, S. Res. 154, September 26, 1941, p. 172). The evaluation of the film by New York-based trade journal *Harrison's Reports* was included among the investigatory documents, but the review had concluded that though "the story has a significant political angle," it is "of secondary importance" (p. 182). Compared with the attention given to Chaplin and even Alexander Korda, Hitchcock's film made barely a ripple among the bigger box-office and political splashes of 1940–1941 (Birdwell 1999).

Among Hitchcock's many films of the 1940s, *Shadow of a Doubt* was a rare hit among British critics such as Dilys Powell and C. A. Lejeune (see also *The Sketch*, April 7, 1943, p. 176; *Kinematograph Weekly*, March 18, 1943, p. 29; *Newcastle Evening Chronicle*, March 27, 1943, p. 4). But *Shadow of a Doubt*'s more modest setting and cast of eccentrics are suggestive—throwbacks to the offbeat signatures in Hitchcock's earlier British films, from *The Lodger* to *The Lady Vanishes*, which cinephiles at *Sight and Sound* dwelt upon with nostalgia while slamming his star-studded melodramas with Ingrid Bergman (including *Notorious*) and, later, the elites of *Strangers on a Train*.[2]

Strangers on a Train in Austerity Britain

Set principally among wealthy Americans, perhaps *Strangers on a Train* was always doomed to fail with British critics in postwar Britain (rationing only ended July 4, 1954) though all indications are that it was a box-office bonanza in Britain—attracting more moviegoers than did many of Hitchcock's other films released in the ten-year period before *Stranger on a Train*'s initial run, including *Stage Fright* (1950), *Rope* (1948), *The Paradine Case* (1947), *Lifeboat* (1944), and *Shadow of a Doubt* (1943), and continues to be among Hitchcock's most commercially viable properties to this day (see Comprehensive Revenue Stream Data for the vast majority of Hitchcock post-1940 films, Hitchcock Family Trust Archives). *Picturegoer* noted that "After a couple of below-standard productions," the Master of Suspense had returned (August 4, 1951, p. 16). Though *Strangers on a Train* "may not quite be vintage Hitchcock," it was, as the *Daily Mail* wrote, "a good ordinaire" (August 3, 1951). In several reviews, critics deployed food and wine metaphors to convey *Strangers on a Train*'s appeal for audiences starved over the past few years by Hitchcock's poor film fare. However, Molly Hobman of the *Yorkshire Observer* likened Hitchcock's latest to an insubstantial meal "where they provide caviar and truffles, strawberries and champagne, but whisk away the main course before you get your teeth into it" (August 3, 1951, p. 4). Hollywood—the land of caviar and champagne—had eaten into their former countryman. "Embellishments," "tricks," "dazzling sleight-of-hand," "cleverness" and "contrivance"—these were the essence of a film that "must be seen" but wasn't "an experience in suspense" (*Middlesex Independent and West London Star*, September 14, 1951, p. 5). The *Kensington News and West London Times* argued that it did not possess "the dazzling vintage of his prewar films," but was "well worth seeing" (September 14, 1951, p. 3). The *Daily Telegraph*, never particularly warm toward Hitchcock, remarked that the merry-go-round scene was overdone but the film was "a half-warmed fish" (August 6, 1951). References to champagne and truffles may have been a swipe at insubstantial Hollywood glamor (in a time of British rationing), but, like food and wine, Hitchcock's films were to be consumed and forgotten. It was not flattering criticism.

Despite their considerable reservations, many, like Dilys Powell, were content to call *Strangers on a Train* "the best thing Hitchcock has done for a good many years." But a scattered few, such as the reviewer for the *Skegness News*, praised the director as "right on top of his form" in the "suspense-packed story" (December 26, 1951, p. 6). Derek Shephard of the *Staffordshire Evening Herald* claimed it was "The Most Exciting Film Drama since *The Third Man*" (August 4, 1951, p. 2), yet this comparison reminded filmgoers that Carol Reed's work was now the gold standard in Britain.

British journalists with more than a column of space paid scant attention to the dull Farley Granger and Ruth Roman's breathlessly well-bred girlfriend in her designer gowns. Instead, they were drawn to characters that Hitchcock had once put front and center in his British films: difficult women, eccentrics, and maniacs, played by Laura Elliott, Marion Lorne, the director's daughter Patricia, and Robert Walker, who Dilys Powell described as "a good actor long misused" by Hollywood (see Fig. 19.1). Granger's social-climbing tennis star with political aspirations, Roman's "colourlessly played" senator's daughter (Winnington, *Sight and Sound*, August 1, 1951, p. 21) were "dull." Elliott's abrasive first wife, Lorne's daffy if not quite psycho mother to Bruno, and Patricia Hitchcock's bespectacled imp earned praise for rendering more three-dimensional roles for women in Hollywood films, but the consensus, echoed from *Picturegoer* and *Sight and Sound* to *The Scotsman* (August 4, 1951, p. 9) was that Walker's "outstanding," "polished and chilling" Bruno "outshines" everyone. The actor had died from a combination of alcoholism and a broken marriage (wife Jennifer Jones had upgraded to producer David O. Selznick, ironically a little like Hitchcock had left Balcon in 1938). The praise for Walker had additional edge. Hollywood had wasted Walker's talent. He was another casualty of a system that threatened to destroy other national talents for decades, including Hitchcock. British critics who detested Hollywood's values and who may have still harbored resentment about Hitchcock's easy war could therefore praise Walker without reservation.

Figure 19.1 Bruno (Robert Walker) in hot pursuit of Guy's estranged and flirtatious wife (Laura Elliott).

Strangers on a Train, directed by Alfred Hitchcock © Warner Bros. Pictures Inc. 1951. All rights reserved.

The Initial Critical Reception of *Strangers on a Train* in the USA

US reception for *Strangers on a Train* was considerably more positive than in Britain.[3] The more middlebrow weekly magazines, such as *Time* (1951) and *Newsweek* (July 9, 1951), praised the film, with *Time*'s critic singling out the final scene on the merry-go-round that "goes wild like a pin wheel, and crashes in a gaudy blaze of explosions that no earthly carousel could touch off [see Fig. 19.2]. The movie itself is the same way: implausible but intriguing and great fun to ride" (July 16, 1951). The trade-paper reviews were even more positive, heralding *Strangers on a Train* as "by far the best of his recent pictures" (*Variety*, June 14, 1951) and proof of Hitchcock's "virtuosity" (*Hollywood Reporter*, June 14, 1951). The *Hollywood Reporter* argued that *Strangers on a Train* "is an admirable demonstration of [his] virtuosity in the area of suspense drama" because of Hitchcock's masterful use of "commonplace incidents and the long arm of coincidence as details by which he keeps the onlooker glued to his seat." And *Boxoffice* (June 16, 1951) declared *Strangers on a Train* a "murder thriller with such a wealth of plot, superb direction, fine acting and excellent photography that every type of adult audience should consider it an outstanding picture."[4]

The *Los Angeles Times* (June 30, 1951) proclaimed *Strangers on a Train* "one of his best" and expressed amazement over how "some of the [film's] most suspenseful scenes are at the same time the most genuinely laughable" (see Fig. 19.3). Also upbeat were many of the daily newspapers from the New York metropolitan area such as the *Daily News* and *Newsday* with a combined circulation of well over 3 million. Kate Cameron of the *Daily News* characterized *Strangers on a Train* as a "thriller of the first class," while applauding Hitchcock for regaining "the magic which he seemed to have lost in his last couple of films"—that unquantifiable quality that had "made him the outstanding director of thrillers in the business" (*Daily News*, July 4, 1951).

Strikingly, negative reviews appeared in the more prestigious review outlets. Most, apart from Richard Coe's pan in the *Washington Post* ("Hitchcock Messes Up a Real Chiller," July 5, 1951, p. 13), were

Figure 19.2 The out-of-control carousel.

Figure 19.3 Suspenseful while at the same time genuinely laughable.

based in New York City and included Crowther of the *New York Times*, Guernsey at the *New York Herald Tribune* (July 4, 1951), John McCarten at the *New Yorker* (July 14, 1951), and Manny Farber at *The Nation* (July 28, 1951).

Crowther's preeminence during the 1940s and 1950s as acknowledged dean of New York reviewers makes his views on Hitchcock and on *Strangers on a Train* of special interest. Crowther maintained that the essential requirement of any film was to entertain in the sense of holding and stimulating the audience. But, in addition, he believed a film should also have something "significant" to say (see Kapsis 1992). It is clear from his review of *Strangers on a Train* that he believed the film had failed as entertainment and as relevant content when Hollywood was "burning." (One might speculate that the blacklist and the threat of television were among the inflammatory contaminants Crowther had in mind.) In a follow-up piece a few days later, Crowther states unequivocally his belief that Hitchcock's films, especially the most recent ones, starting with *Rope*, in addition to lacking plausibility, also lack "significance" because of their failure to explore the actualities of daily life. And, as a "true fan" of Hitchcock, he longs for the time when Hitchcock will come to his senses and make films that are both entertaining and socially significant (*New York Times*, July 8, 1951).

Crowther's rebuke turned out to be one of the most consequential—among the half dozen or so reviews most frequently cited by film journalists and film scholars as evidence of *Strangers on a Train*'s poor showing among critics during the film's initial run in the USA (see, e.g., Wikipedia's *Strangers on a Train* entry and compare with Filmex's blurb on the film from 1978). In reality, as we have documented, this was only a minority opinion held by a handful of disgruntled New York–based film journalists writing for prestigious outlets such as the *New Yorker*, the *New York Times*, and the *New York Herald Tribune*.

Post-1951 Reassessment in Britain and the USA

In Great Britain since 1951, *Strangers on a Train* has been revived several times, inspiring many highly favorable reviews, which have improved the film's overall standing among the critics, while in the USA the reviews of more recent vintage—nearly all positive—have reaffirmed the film's already high regard among the vast majority of journalistic reviewers.

According to British reviewers who had seen the film prior to its 1961 rerelease, *Strangers on a Train* had remained, in their view, one of Hitchcock's better films and one that after ten years had held up extremely well. Here is a passage representative of the strong affirmation the film received from most of the critics covering its 1961 revival.

[Rereleased] after ten years, Alfred Hitchcock's *Strangers on a Train* now seems to belong more with the films he made in England before the war than with his American work—in which, too often, his real gifts as a raconteur have been sacrificed to show off and grandiloquence. Like the thirties' films, this one is a frank melodrama which depends simply and securely upon a good script by Raymond Chandler and Czenzi Ormonde and sheer narrative skill.

(David Robinson, *Financial Times*, April 21, 1961)[5]

During another major revival in 1999, part of a special series of screenings mounted to honor Hitchcock's 100th birthday, British reviewers speculated about how the film's "huge [commercial] success" during its initial run [especially in the USA] may have been instrumental in affecting the ebb and flow of Hitchcock's filmic career: "Made in 1951," writes Alexander Walker, "it followed four box-office flops (*The Paradine Case*, *Rope*, *Under Capricorn* and *Stage Fright*), and its huge success gave Hitch his confident second wind for the Fifties' masterpieces" (*Evening Standard*, August 12, 1999; cf. Scott, *Times*, October 16, 1993). As for the rest of the British reviews and commentaries I located in BFI's clipping file on *Strangers on a Train* for the year 1999 (there were twelve in all), the vast majority made similar points, with several using words like "classic thriller" or "masterpiece" or "one of those movies everyone should experience" to characterize the film, and "great genius" and "one of the supremely great artists of the 20th century" to characterize its director (see, e.g., Adam Mars-Jones, *The Times*, August 12, 1999; Nina Caplan, *Metro London*, August 13, 1999; Christopher Tookey, *Daily Mail*, August 13, 1999; Andrew O'Hagan, *Daily Telegraph*, August 13, 1999; Edward Porter, *Sunday Times*, August 15, 1999; Philip French, *Observer*, August 15, 1999; and Gilbert Adair, *Independent on Sunday*, August 15, 1999).

For both Great Britain and the USA, it took less than two decades before newly minted reviews were overwhelmingly ranking *Strangers on a Train* as among the ten greatest Hitchcock films (see Wood 1977; *Daily Telegraph*, May 19, 2006; Ross 2022; Collider 2023) or among the 100 best films noir of all time (see Rotten Tomatoes, n.d.; *Sight and Sound*, November 22, 2017) or the first and best (or among the best) of the film adaptations of a Patricia Highsmith novel (see *New York Times*, April 19, 2021; *Sight and Sound*, January 18, 2021).

Since the 1990s, and correlated with the rise of gay studies, much of the critical commentary on *Strangers on a Train* has focused on its gay subtext (one of the elements Crowther may have objected to without consciously realizing so at the time).[6] And yet we find in only a few rare instances the word "gay" showing up in the early discourse on *Strangers on a Train*. And, apparently, this was the case in both the UK and the USA.

It's extraordinary [recalled Alexander Walker in 1998] what the loss of innocence can do for a film … The innocence, [he asserted,] was, of course, ours. In 1951, when Hitchcock made [*Strangers on a Train*], hardly any reviewers in the popular press referred to the crypto-homosexual relationship between Robert Walker's psychotic playboy and Farley Granger's personable tennis champ, each of whom agrees to commit a murder on the other's behalf [Walker's father for Granger's wife]. Consider, for example, the tennis match that Granger has to win in double-quick time to save himself from

Walker's attempt to pin his wife's murder on him. [It] can now be "read" as a gay relationship that comes unstuck. Curiously, seen thus it rather resembles Hitchcock's film *Rope*, made three years earlier and also based on a union of two putatively gay killers, one of whom is again played by Granger.

(Walker, *Evening Standard*, December 5, 1998)

And, an eye-opener, reviewers were not the first viewers to have failed to pick up on the film's gay subtext. Before them were the censors, as reported in Goldberg:

The homoerotics of *Strangers on a Train* was apparently invisible to the censors. Various local boards, reviewing the film after its release, found nothing to object to on that account … Presumably, the minister at the end of the film did not finally look like a joke to [the censors]. It's safe to suppose that [they] never imagined the final scene with the minister on the train [Fig. 19.4] as another possible pickup since [they] hadn't registered it as such in the initial encounter [between Bruno and Guy that opens the film; Fig. 19.5].

(See Goldberg 2012: 346–381)

Summary and Closing Methodological Note

As for *Strangers on a Train*'s reception in Britain, our findings revealed that we were on the right track from the beginning, guided as we were by Barr's thesis that the negativity underlying much of the critical reception of Hitchcock's films in Britain during the 1940s also affected how an early post-1940s film like *Strangers on a Train* would be judged. On the other hand, what initially leads us astray—to misclassify *Strangers on a Train*'s reception trajectory in the USA as essentially a "rags to riches" saga—was a failure

Figure 19.4 Closing scene with the minister.

Figure 19.5 The initial encounter between Bruno (Robert Walker) and Guy (Farley Granger).

to question the accuracy of previously published summaries of how the first generation of US reviewers responded to the film (see, for example, Wikipedia's entry for *Strangers on a Train* and Filmex's capsule summary from March 24, 1979). In fact, much of the journalistic and online commentary on reception trends is, at best, misleading and, at worst, almost worthless—due primarily to relying too heavily on inferences drawn from extremely small samples of cherry-picked reviews. Methodological flaws of this kind also compromise recent calculations of *Strangers on a Train*'s currently high standing among major critics worldwide.[7] One such survey is the Metacritic poll, which collects reviews from "the world's top critics," assigns each review a score "based on its overall quality," and calculates a "summarized weighted average" that captures what Metacritic claims is "the essence of critical opinion."

But when we began sorting the cited reviews by geography and time period, we discovered that in reality the reviews selected had been cherry-picked to support both the claim of *Strangers on a Train*'s "universal acclaim" and the representativeness of the reviews pointing in that direction. There were fifteen reviews in all. The only "negative" one selected (misclassified as "mixed" in the Metacritic poll) was Crowther's notorious *New York Times* piece from 1951; all the rest were categorized as "positive." Of the fifteen reviews, ten were from the USA, three from Britain, one from Canada, and one "global" (*Timeout*)—hardly representative of the international film art world community. And of the ten from the USA, four were from 1951, while the three from British sources were post-2001. All fifteen reviews could easily be downloaded from a computer. A sample of convenience, indeed! Meanwhile, the review selected from the *New Yorker* was Pauline Kael's rave notice from circa 1995 ("It's intensely enjoyable—in some ways the best of Hitchcock's American films")—not John McCarten's zinger of a put-down from 1951 ("there's nothing boring about [Mr. Hitchcock's fancy shots] but the foolishness of the film's theme keeps obtruding until the spectator damned near loses patience with the whole affair"; *New Yorker*, July 14, 1951). The lesson to be drawn from such methodological shoddiness is clear: Film scholars and researchers should not shy away from implementing more methodologically rigorous approaches and strategies or, at the very least, become more knowledgeable of the potential usefulness of such approaches, for example, being respectful of the logic of random sampling and mindful of systematic biases in archival and online collections, while gathering the reviews and commentaries—the bedrock for any study examining the historical reception of a filmmaker's body of work.

Acknowledgment

I couldn't have carried out this assignment without the help of Jennifer Smyth, James Chapman, and Henry Miller.

Notes

1. "Little sleight of hand, no point of view, irrelevant sequences, gratuitous closeups and gloss—these now seem," writes Barr, "extraordinary comments to make on [*Notorious*] which stands up as well as any film, by Hitchcock or anyone else, to analysis as a model of tight, rigorous, organic construction. Whether you like the film or not, it seems perverse to criticize it in those terms, as being slack and rambling. Harcourt Smith's witticism at the expense of the long kissing scene is an accurate indication of his dilettantism, but Winnington was a critic of admirable care and seriousness whom Philip French, the longest-serving and most professional of his successors, has aptly compared with George Orwell (French, *Observer*, January 23, 1976). On the basis of these confidently scornful views of *Notorious*—Winnington the true enthusiast writing for a popular paper, Harcourt Smith the general arts man writing for a minority one, plus Anderson, voice of a new generation of cinéastes—it's easy to infer that in those days, in this British milieu, the critics just didn't get it: didn't begin to understand the new and productive directions that Hitchcock's work was taking, perhaps because they were too caught up in the euphoria of a new dawn for British cinema, and of the non-Hollywood aesthetic associated with it. Even when that new impetus petered out, neither Winnington nor Anderson would soften their severity towards the Hollywood Hitchcock" (Barr 2004–2005: 17).

2. Although William Schaefer's Warner Bros. box-office ledger reveals that audiences were still drawn to Hitchcock films with Ingrid Bergman, with *Under Capricorn* earning $1.46 million at the foreign box office, *Stage Fright* earned only $896,000 the following year (Warner Bros. Box Office Data for 1951).

3. American journalistic reviews and commentaries on *Strangers on a Train* are drawn primarily from the files of newspaper and magazine clippings of motion-picture criticism at the New York Public Library of the Performing Arts at Lincoln Center, New York City, and the Margaret Herrick Library, the Academy of Motion Picture Arts and Sciences, Beverly Hills California.

4. Audiences seemed to agree, as reflected in the film's boffo box-office performance not only in the USA but in Britain and other foreign markets as well. See *Variety*, January 2, 1952, p. 70; Warner Bros. Box Office Data for 1951, p. 31; and Hitchcock Family Trust Archives Comprehensive Revenue Stream Data for the bulk of Hitchcock's post-1940 films.

5. See also Dilys Powell, *Sunday Times*, April 23, 1961; Alexander Walker, *Evening Standard*, April 20, 1961; William Whitebait, *New Statesman*, April 21, 1961; and Penelope Gilliatt, *Observer*, April 23, 1961.

6. Not until the late 1980s and early 1990s did film journalists and scholars both in England and the USA begin approaching *Strangers on a Train* (and several of Hitchcock's other films as well) from a gay perspective and, in so doing, call attention to the film's gay subtext (see, e.g., Barton 1991; Desowitz 1992; Price 1992; Corber 1993; Wood 1995; and among the best and most comprehensive of the more recent entries, see Goldberg 2012; and Greven 2017).

7. See www.metacritic.com/movie/strangers-on-a-train/

References

Anderson, L. (1972) "Alfred Hitchcock," in Alfred LaValley (ed.), *Focus on Hitchcock*, New York: Prentice Hall.
Barr, C. (2004–2005) "Deserter or Honored Exile: Views of Hitchcock from Wartime Britain," *Hitchcock Annual*, vol. 13, pp. 1–24.
Barr, C. (2022) "Memo to Robert Kapsis," March 12.
Barton, S. (1991) "Criss-Cross Paranoia and Projection in *Strangers on a Train*," *Camera Obscura*, January 1.
Bernstein, M. (2000) *Walter Wanger, Hollywood Independent*, Minneapolis, Minn.: University of Minnesota Press.
Birdwell, M. E. (1999) *Celluloid Soldiers: Warner Bros.' Campaign against Nazism*, New York: New York University Press.
Collider (2023) "Collider's Ranking of Alfred Hitchcock's Best Movies Ever," December 10, https://collider.com/best-alfred-hitchcock-movies-ranked
Corber, R. J. (1993) *In the Name of National Security: Hitchcock, Homophobia, and the Political Construction of Gender in Postwar America*, Durham, NC: Duke University Press.
Desowitz, B. (1992) "Strangers on Which Train," *Film Comment*, May.
Goldberg, J. (2012) Strangers on a Train: *A Queer Film Classic*, Vancouver: Arsenal Pulp Press.
Greven, D. (2017) *Intimate Violence: Hitchcock, Sex, and Queer Theory*, New York: Oxford University Press.
Hitchcock Family Trust Archives, Comprehensive Revenue Stream Data for all Hitchcock Post-1940 Films, Compiled by Robert Kapsis, April 2022, San Francisco Calif.
Kapsis, R. (1992) *Hitchcock: The Making of a Reputation*, Chicago, Ill.: University of Chicago Press.
Price, T. (1992) *Hitchcock and Homosexuality: His 50-Year Obsession with Jack the Ripper and the Superbitch Prostitute—A Psychoanalytic View*, Metuchen, NJ: Scarecrow Press.
"Propaganda in Motion Pictures" (1941) Hearings before a Subcommittee of the Committee on Interstate Commerce, September 26, p. 172.
Ross, G. (2022) "Alfred Hitchcock's 20 Greatest Films from *Rebecca* to *The Birds*," *Independent*, August 26.
Rotten Tomatoes (n.d.) "100 Best Film Noir Movies Ranked by Tomatometer," https://editorial.rottentomatoes.com/guide/best-film-noirs
Warner Bros. Box Office Data for 1951, "The William Shaefer Ledger," Historical Journal of Film, Radio and Television, Vol. 15, 1995, Appendix 1, pp. 1–31.
Wood, R. (1977) *Hitchcock's Films*, 3rd edn, South Brunswick: A. S. Barnes.
Wood, R. (1995) *Hitchcock's Films Revisited*, New York: Columbia University Press.

Chapter 20
Frenzy (1972)
"Dark, Nasty, Full of Bile"… and a Masterpiece?

Tania Modleski

When *Frenzy* turned fifty, in 2022, a few assessments appeared that focused on the distastefulness and brutality of the work. Andrew Taylor (2022), for instance, wrote that *Frenzy* is a film that "grows more disturbing with time"; it is a misogynistic film filled with "crude extremes." Steph Green (2022) remarked, "*Frenzy* is Hitchcock at his most unrestrained—laying bare all his well-documented neuroses about how women should be punished on screen." Each echoed Thomas Leitch's (2002: 115) felicitous remark written a few years earlier that "If *Frenzy* is Hitchcock with the gloves off, it has made thousands of reviewers thankful for gloves." In fact, though, well into the twenty-first century, the film has had its champions. In 2012, the *Guardian* called it "a rich tapestry of suspense, and a masterpiece" (Jones 2012). In 2014, the *New Yorker*'s David Denby also dubbed it a "masterpiece." The filmmaker Guillermo del Toro (2016) tweeted: it is "a film I defend and think important in Hitchcock's career. Spiritually (not factually) his last film. One of my favorite Hitchcock's. Dark, nasty and full of bile." Finally, a full-length study of *Frenzy* by Raymond Foery (2017) was titled *Frenzy: The Last Masterpiece*.

But to begin at the beginning: Upon its release, *Frenzy* was met with much jubilation: "Still the Master" (*Time*, June 19, 1972); "The Master Proves He Hasn't Lost His Touch" (*Boston after Dark*, June 20, 1972, p. 4); "Return of the Master" (*Newsweek*, June 26, 1972, pp. 83–83a); "The Return of Alfred the Great" (*Life*, August 2, 1972) the headlines proclaimed. The relief was palpable. Having directed several flops following a particularly fertile period of artistic productivity, Hitchcock was thought to be washed up. Some critics dated his supposed decline as far back as *The Birds*. Although that film had its defenders, there was little doubt among critics of the time that *Marnie*, which followed it, had sounded the death knell of the aging director's career. *Torn Curtain* and *Topaz* had simply pounded more nails in the coffin. Then came *Frenzy*. In returning to London, Hitchcock had, it appeared, come alive. The recognizable style, the stunning camera work, the suspense, the "fanged" humor (Gilliat 1972: 52)—the glories of Hitchcockiana had returned, if tinged, according to some reviewers of the period (Sgammato 1973: 135), with a bitter tone that was not exactly new, perhaps, but somewhat more pronounced than hitherto.

Some critics rejoiced at the presence of favorite Hitchcock themes, most notably the theme of the wrong man—the pinning of guilt upon a nominally innocent person. This theme is closely allied with that of the transference of guilt identified by Rohmer and Chabrol back in 1957. The "innocent" man—a man wrongly accused of a crime—often has something to gain by a crime committed by another and hence may be innocent of the deed but not of the wish. Psychologically speaking, then, he might appear to share the guilt. This theme is introduced early in the film, which opens with a long take of the camera tracking over the Thames River. As we near the crowded shore, a politician is heard heralding the cleaning up of the city's and the river's pollution. His speech is disrupted by the sighting of a naked female corpse, with a man's tie around her neck, floating face down in the river. She is identified as a victim of a serial killer who rapes and then strangles his victims with a necktie. After one of the men in the crowd gathered on the banks of the Thames asks, "I say, that's not my club tie, is it?" there is a cut to a man, Richard Blaney (Jon Finch), putting on a tie in front of a mirror (Fig. 20.1). Soon revealing himself to be an unpleasant and self-pitying man down on his luck, various circumstances point to him as a prime candidate for the murder of his ex-wife Brenda (Barbara Leigh-Hunt), whom he resents and envies even as he takes advantage of her, when she turns out to be the next victim. The viewer at this point, however, already knows he is innocent as we are privy to the grisly scene of her rape/murder.

In *Frenzy*, however, Blaney is not alone in being the object of transferred guilt. The fact that he is introduced to the viewer directly following the onlooker's query about his tie suggests that Hitchcock is not simply transferring guilt to an individual but spreading it around to all the men, here implicating not only part-time bartender Blaney but a higher-class member of a gentlemen's club. The "lusts of men," the thought of which makes one minor character "want to heave," are hereby universalized. Here we have a possible answer to the question posed by Ian Cooper (2018: 63) as to why "as the Production Code faltered and restrictions were lifted so many talented filmmakers of the era dealt not with consensual sex but rather graphic rapes." Chalk it up to the lusts of men.

For indeed *Frenzy* was one of the films to take full advantage of the new freedom to show nudity, sexual activity, and sexual violence. It includes a lengthy and highly explicit rape and strangulation scene committed by Bob Rusk (Barry Foster), owner of a fruit market, a man who appears to befriend Blaney and later sets him up to take the blame. Commentators such as Donald Spoto (1983: 545) considered the sexually graphic *Frenzy* to be the picture Hitchcock always wanted to make: "Unable to realize a rape

Figure 20.1 Blaney putting on his tie.
Frenzy, directed by Alfred Hitchcock. © Universal Pictures Ltd. 1972. All rights reserved.

in *No Bail for the Judge* he hinted at it in *Psycho*, metaphorized it in *The Birds* and, against all advice, included it in *Marnie*. Now at last—encouraged by the new freedom in the movies—his imagination of this sordid crime could be more fully shown in all its horror" (quoted in Modleski 1988: 104). While at the time of the film's release some critics expressed dismay and found the rape scene to be off-putting ("Now Hitchcock has Gone Too Far" proclaimed Victor Davis in the *Daily Express* [May 6, 1972], to cite one example) most reviewers were not so bothered.[1] Gene Siskel (*Chicago Tribune*, July 14, 1972, p. b1) barely registered it and saw the film simply as "grand entertainment"—offering a "fascinating story" and possessing very little in the way of "meaning." Vincent Canby in the *New York Times* (July 2, 1972, p. D1) was also insistent on the film's lack of meaning, mocking scholars for "overanalyzing" Hitchcock's films. "Hitchcock's method is meaning," he asserted. Canby joined other critics as well as the director himself in focusing on method over meaning—what Hitchcock called "pure cinema": "I'm not concerned about issues but with pure cinema … and the critics seem to realize that that's what this film is about" (quoted in Foery 2012: 124).

If the film is not about "issues," if it lacks meaning, could it not be said that the entire film becomes a MacGuffin? As is well known, a MacGuffin is an object, device, or event that is necessary to the plot and the motivation of the characters but insignificant, unimportant, or irrelevant in itself. It seems especially perverse to invoke a notion of "pure" cinema in a film that deals so insistently with pollution—examples include the disgusting smell of Blaney after he spends the night in a flophouse, not realizing his ex-wife has slipped him some money; and the potato dust that eventually incriminates Rusk after he is forced on a midnight ride in a potato truck bearing away another dead body stuffed in a sack and gripping Rusk's tiepin. Mostly, of course, pollution is from the first linked with the female body, especially the dead body, like the nude female in the Thames floating up to shore in defiance of the official's proclamation that pollution is being conquered.

Freed from the ethical task of pursuing the film's meanings, Canby could allow himself, as it were, to get off on the film. He wrote with breathtaking insouciance,

> It is one of the oddities of the film that although Hitchcock treats us to one murder almost as brutal as the shower killing in *Psycho*, it isn't particularly brutalizing, principally, I think, because the presence of Hitchcock, the tall story teller, is never missed for a moment. There he is, just off camera, wearing a woeful expression that seems to ask us what this naughty fellow is likely to do next.

If Siskel and Canby were unmoved or even amused by the rape/murder and its "naughty" culprit, John Russell Taylor (*The Times*, May 23, 1972) was positively stimulated by it:

> Until we got to [the rape scene], Anthony Shaffer's script had been making heavy weather of some rather simple exposition … But once on to the slow strangulation, the dilated eyes, the hand clutching in vain for the telephone, Hitchcock is home and dry. The sequence is a model, shot silent and indeed very much like a silent film … and it really gets the film going with a bang.[2]

The fact that Hitchcock would deliberately and showily refrain from depicting the next rape—of Blaney's girlfriend Babs (Anna Massey)—seemed in the eyes of some critics to further exonerate Hitchcock from the charge of sexploitation. In a bravura piece of filmmaking, the camera follows Rusk and Blaney's girlfriend Babs, a plain-looking, warm-hearted barmaid, as they climb the stairs to his apartment. We expect to follow the pair into the apartment, but the camera backs off and slowly descends the stairs moving out to a scene of the uncaring world going about its business. Thus audiences aren't, as Albert Johnson (1972) noted, "permitted" the sight of yet another gruesome act. The use of the word "permitted" implies that viewers are hankering to see another ten minutes or so of sexual brutalization. Penelope Gilliat (1972: 53) even argued that "the violence shown [in the entire film] amounts to relatively little—the most upsetting murder isn't even shown." Steven Greenberg (1972) agreed: "In contrast to the earlier murder scene [the murder of Babs] seems much more tragic—traumatic even though it is wholly implied rather than shown." Gilliat and Greenberg never explained why the second, unseen act of sexual violence is the more disturbing one; one can only suppose they preferred the character of Babs to Brenda—and therefore didn't very much mind watching the latter being raped and strangled at length as she cites the 91st Psalm and tries desperately to cover up her nakedness.

Johnson's implicit suggestion that the viewer might want to be "permitted" a second scene of rape and murder brings up another tendency in Hitchcock's work: his habit of implicating viewers in the guilt of his characters—transferring guilt not just from one character to another but to the audience, universalizing, as I noted, "the lusts of men." Robin Wood's classic study *Hitchcock's Films*, published in 1965, continually referred to Hitchcock's tendency to draw viewers into close identification with the characters, both villains and victims. Many critics asserted that *Frenzy* turns its viewers into Rusk's guilty partners. "*Frenzy* makes misogynists of us all," wrote one critic (*Interview Magazine*, August 1972). *Newsweek*'s Paul Zimmerman (June 26, 1972, p. 83) claimed that the rape sequence "triggers our own latent excitement." It seems plausible, if at first glance counterintuitive, to argue that the critics who admit to being Rusk's "accomplices" are granting Hitchcock a sort of alibi for depicting the gruesome sexual violence that he does show. Hitchcock becomes the great moralist, indicting us for our sinful thoughts and desires. And viewers are allowed their mea culpas.

Before asking just whose "latent excitement" is triggered by the rape sequence, I can't resist pointing to one exceedingly misogynistic argument along the lines suggested somewhat more delicately by Zimmerman and others. In a 1973 discussion of *Frenzy* in *Sight and Sound*, Joseph Sgammato (1973: 136) noted that none of the film's women are the beautiful stars, like Ingrid Bergman and Grace Kelly, we are accustomed to seeing in Hitchcock's works. Therefore, he wrote, upon our sighting of the unglamorous businesswoman Brenda Blaney,

> our expectation of having a beautiful woman is "turned against us." Seeing Barbara Leigh-Hunt we see she is "ripe for seduction." Having this woman seem to serve as the romantic interest, the viewer is unquestionably disappointed by this candidate, neither goddess nor tigress. In movie terms, *this is tantamount to willing her destruction*. Hitchcock overcompensates for our disappointment: seduction becomes rape, physical plainness becomes grotesque distortion at a strangler's hands, unglamorous primness becomes grounds for murder. Just beneath the surface of OUR reaction to this scene is a subtly induced sense of connivance at its violence.[3]

While he was at it, Sgammato gratuitously disparaged other women in the film as well; of the silly-looking yet genial mother of Rusk who is seen at the window for all of ten seconds (Fig. 20.2) and whose only line is a smiling, "Pleased to meet you, I'm sure," Sgammato wrote, "The grotesque old cow with flaming hair who sticks her head out the window next to her son the Rapist, is a ludicrous exaggeration of the Portnoyan beast-mother"—"a Freudian Grendel and his dam"![4]

Figure 20.2 Rusk and his mother at the window.

A few weeks after the publication of Canby's pieces, Victoria Sullivan (1972) published a scathing response titled "Does *Frenzy* Degrade Women?" (*New York Times*, July 30, 1972, p. D9). Sullivan mocked Canby's notion that Hitchcock's films lack meaning by pointing out how, among other things, they mean to suggest that women are "natural victims," and, moreover, they mean to terrorize women. Sullivan was not alone in her belief that films like *Frenzy* have a performative function in that they actively contribute to women's fears, curtailing their freedom and encouraging their dependence on men: The National Organization for Women bestowed upon Hitchcock the "Keep Her in Her Place" award. In response to Canby's praise of Hitchcock's "'gift for implicating the audience in the most outrageous acts, which, as often as not, have us identifying with the killer'," Sullivan insisted that she did not identify with the rapist but with the victim.

While Sullivan did not support her claims by closely analyzing the film, such an analysis did appear some years later in the heyday of academic feminist film criticism. In her highly regarded article "The Representation of Violence to Women: Hitchcock's *Frenzy*," Jeanne Thomas Allen (1985: 35) came to the opposite conclusion of Sullivan's. Allen argued that, regardless of gender, we identify not with the victim but with the violator, even if against our will. Noting that in the beginning of the rape sequence, point-of-view shots are divided between the two characters, by the end of it Rusk is in control of point of view. We are presented with "the objectification of a particularly pathological but culturally logical male subjectivity in patriarchy, and the film spectator, male or female, is unambiguously forced to share it" (Allen 1985: 35). But are we "forced" (a word Allen uses twice) to share Rusk's erotic excitement? Isn't the abject fear on the woman's face as Rusk stares down on her likely to cause some viewers, especially female viewers, to share her terror, and, moreover, to be repelled by the sight of the sweaty, panting, maniac doing the deed? Surely for some of us, women in particular, for whom sexual violence is an ever-present threat, what is activated is not our "latent" sexual "excitement" but our empathy.

To support my argument that viewers are by no means forced to share the masculine perspective, I refer to the opinion of a man whom one might expect to be the least likely person to have claimed sympathy for the victim: Sam Peckinpah, whose *Straw Dogs*, which appeared one year before *Frenzy*, has frequently been viewed as an over-the-top misogynistic depiction of sexual violence against women. According to

Peckinpah (1974), a fellow recipient of the "Keep Her in Her Place" award, "the murder … in *Frenzy* is just as remarkable [as the one in *Torn Curtain*] because Hitchcock really causes us to feel the intensity of the suffering of a person who decomposes under our very eyes." He went on to note, "I am not a Hitchcock fanatic, but all the same one has to admit that he knows how to render tangible … human suffering."[5]

In his 2018 book on *Frenzy*, Ian Cooper remarked that the viewer's response to the rape/murder no doubt "depends to some extent on gender" (2018: 69). Yet one would hope that there would be more men who share the view that Brenda's suffering is cause for sorrow, not glee (Cooper 2018: 69). In an article that appeared close to the time of this writing, Ismail Ben-Youssef (2024: 15) provided an interesting explanation of why the scene ought not to be perceived as erotic:

> [It] reinserts the fetishized female body into a linear temporality that runs counter to the erotic instinct and thus focuses attention on how a fetishizing look typically works to violently rip its object from the environment. Hitchcock's real-time depiction of sexual violence frames the anguish when a woman is thus ripped from the temporality of the living and thrust into the timeless sphere of the dead.[6]

Of course, people who believe they are watching snuff films may find themselves aroused so it is certainly not the case that the sight of women "ripped from the temporality of the living" is necessarily a turnoff for everyone.

That Hitchcock would proceed in *Frenzy* to create incidents that are meant to be humorous indicates his own aloofness from the suffering he depicts, even as he might want to implicate everyone else. So we come to his treatment of Babs, whom many view as the most sympathetic character in the film. For all those who believed and still believe that Hitchcock was doing the audience a favor and showing restraint by not depicting her murder, the director in fact reserves Babs for a different, ugly and more bizarre, fate.[7] No longer is it about the violation of a living woman, but the desecration of a corpse. Realizing that he has lost his tiepin and that it is no doubt in the victim's hand, Rusk runs out to the potato truck to retrieve it from the body he has stuffed in a sack there. The truck starts to move, and Rusk desperately scrabbles around, at a couple of points being kicked in the face by the corpse which has been placed head first into the sack (Fig. 20.3). Eventually he finds the pin clutched in a hand in rigor mortis. He must snap the fingers one by one to retrieve the pin. Mark Goble (2015: 216) pithily remarks, "Here, all the violence that Hitchcock did not show us when Babs was murdered is just as bad when it is rendered the second time as farce."

After Rusk leaves the truck, which has stopped briefly at a "pull-in," it starts to move, and the body falls out. The police pull the bag off Babs's head, and, to quote Goble again, her "horrifying rictus is, at least in part, a knowing gesture … since Anna Massey had played the tortured love interest of the serial killer in [Michael] Powell's *Peeping Tom*" (2015: 216). There is no doubt that this scene is played for laughs, emphasized and made even more ghoulishly humorous when the inspector's wife, discussing the murder with her husband, snaps breadsticks in two and munches on them as she mulls over the truck episode. Many critics have chuckled over this scene, but not all have been amused. In his excellent essay "Hitchcock and Humor," James Naremore (2014: 138) argued that late Hitchcock, beginning with *The Birds*, lost his ability to perfectly balance humor and horror: Various acts of horrific violence, like the rape–murder in *Frenzy* (1972), "tend to overpower the respective conventions of the screwball comedy, the romantic melodrama, the spy story, and the 'wrong-man' thriller. Hitchcock's aloof irony remains, but violence ruptures the glamorous surface to such a degree that the humor dies or grows sour."

The scenes between Inspector Oxford (Alec McCowen) and his wife (Vivien Merchant) are one of the high points of the film for most critics, who generally find the couple endearing, and the scenes funny, although the husband suffers mightily at the hands of his wife who is experimenting with Continental

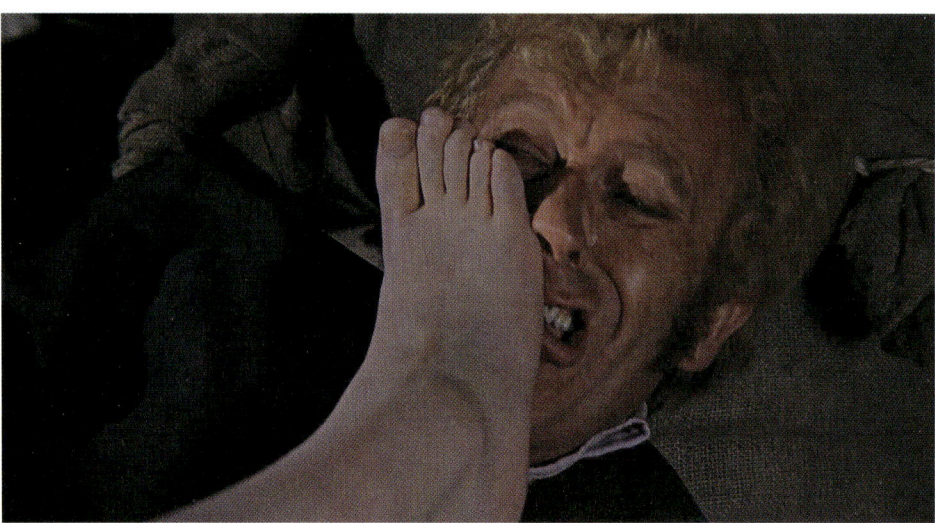
Figure 20.3 Rusk being kicked in the face by a corpse.

cuisine and feeding him unappetizing food, knowing full well he'd prefer "steak and a baked potato." She is the one who believes the inspector has the wrong man because the murder seems to have been a "*crime passionelle*," and she says that Blaney and his wife were married long enough that that seems unlikely. "Look at me we've been married ten years and you can hardly keep your eyes open at night." While Leslie Brill (1988: 141) saw the relationship between this couple as redemptive—"loving, orderly, and stable, [contrasting] reassuringly with the darkness and chaos that envelop the main plot"—Robin Wood (1988: 247), with his usual acumen, agreed only up to a point. He detected "a central opposition between the Blaney marriage and the Oxford's, the former, disordered, violent, broken, the latter ordered and permanent, built upon a willed mutual forbearance, ironically counterpointed by pervasive signs that the couple detest each other." Denby (2014) is perceptive on this point as well: "*Frenzy*, with its piles of peaches and lettuces, its constant drinking, is a masterpiece devoted to appetite in all its varieties—but it is most seriously devoted to the perversion of sexual happiness in murder and to the absence of sexual happiness in 'normal' life."

In the end, Mrs. Oxford's disgusting meals may be a way of avenging herself for her unfulfilled (sexual) appetites.

Janet Maslin (Review of *Frenzy*, *Boston after Dark*, June 20, 1972, p. 4), pointed out early on that in *Frenzy* "Food serves as a surrogate for sexual appetite, with the wife cooking parts that are as clearly flesh as food."[8] Humorous as these scenes may be, then, they open onto the theme of cannibalism that has been taken up by a couple of critics (see Lefebvre 2005–2006). I myself (Modleski 1988) had occasion to note the theme of cannibalism (e.g., the scene with the breadsticks). The motif of cannibalism—the symbolic partaking of the dead woman's flesh—and that of pollution come together in *Frenzy*, I claimed. Drawing on Julia Kristeva and Claude Lévi-Strauss, I argued that the corpse of the dead female, whose body parts are symbolically served up in Mrs. Oxford's dinners—the pigs trotters that remind us of Babs's feet in the potato truck—is the most impure, most polluted, of objects. It is not insignificant that these concerns came to the fore in the early 1970s. Via Kristeva, I referred to the work of anthropologist Mary Douglas (1966: 142) who observed that "sex is likely to be pollution free in a society where sex roles are secure and enforced directly."[9] In a society in which sex roles are threatened, "ideas about sex pollution are likely to thrive" (Douglas 1966: 142). Because *Frenzy* was made when women had begun successfully challenging male dominance (note, for instance, that Brenda Blaney, in running a marital agency, has taken over the role usually assigned to men—the exchange of women), the emphasis on society's pollution was strong. When I initially wrote about the film, it seemed important to historicize Hitchcock instead of bowing down to the master or psychologizing him on an individual level. And I stand by much of what I said in 1988. I'm pleased that I was able to persuade some critics.[10] Is there anything I would change, writing now? Perhaps in my eagerness to suggest that for all his attempts to kill off women (and keep killing them when they, like the eponymous Rebecca, seem to rise from the ashes), they remain unassimilable in patriarchy. I'd like to think that's true in large part, but perhaps at times I overreached. Here's Vlad Dima (2011: 176), discussing my analysis of the rape scene:

> [Brenda] accepts her weakness, and surrenders to Bob's brute force, which is marked by the fact that she is willing to take her dress off. This is in fact the only small victory she pulls off in the precarious situation. Bob had said that she "was his type," which means that he wanted her to put up a fight ("I like you to struggle," he tells her). Her capitulation becomes a refusal because in the end she does not struggle, and as Modleski suggests, the women's "capitulation to male desires and expectations is never complete." However, this seems like a very small victory in the grand scheme of the scene.

Indeed, it does! And yet, if Brenda's "victory" is Pyrrhic, to say the least, I stand by my position that the viewer is not "forced" to capitulate to patriarchal views of women or to turn against women in the throes of their agonies depicted so vividly on the screen. In the end, as I argued, we do best to see *Frenzy* as a defense against the women's movement which was gaining ground at the time it was made. In its own peculiar way, *Frenzy* attests to the fact that hope for women was alive. Let us try to keep it that way.

Figure 20.4 Detective terrified by wife's cooking.

Notes

1. For another example, see Alexander Walker, *Evening Standard* (April 25, 1972): "They [the murders] are crude beyond belief without the saving grace of wit, irony surprise, or even sheer shock." Or another from the *Guardian* (February 25, 1972): "The whole thing amounts to little more than a rather cynical and not very psychologically sound jape constructed out of virtually nothing by a master craftsman with nowhere much to go."
2. Kapsis (1992) notes that there were in fact critics who, under the influence of auteurism, which was coming into its own, found plenty of meaning in the film. Perhaps not surprisingly the meanings (e.g., "the failures of friendship") mostly had little to do with violence against women (Kapsis 1992: 110–113). Kapsis is quoting from a *Newsweek* review (June 26, 1972).
3. Italics in original, but if they hadn't been I would have added them myself.
4. The actress, Rita Webb, a character actress who appeared in sitcoms and some movies, would have been well known to English audiences of the time.
5. English-language transcript of interview published in Quebec newspaper *Le Devoir*, 1974. Quoted in Sklar (2006: 22), who quotes it from Prince (1998: 238).
6. See Sklar's useful summary of the various positions taken on questions of spectator identification with regard to the depiction of sexual violence, particularly in *Frenzy* (2006).
7. "Indeed, there is nothing else in the film as brutal as Brenda's murder—in fact that later murder of Babs is quite ingenious in its use of restraint" (Allison 2022). Allen, however, makes a compelling point about this so-called restraint: "Furthermore, might not the camera's gesture of withdrawal be experienced as much as brandishing the threat of repeated violence or promise of conquest, triggering cues so that the previous sequence can be rerun in the mind (a haunting), as well as an instigator of self-examination and motivation? It is as a sort of musical 'rest' in the continual onslaught of graphic violence to women that Hitchcock's occasional reflexivity must be viewed. Self-reflexivity implies no judgment of voyeurism; no moral position is implied." Finally, Blevins (*Herald Examiner*, 1972) is one of the only critics I have come across to note that we do see flashes of the rape and murder of Babs, as they occur in Rusk's mind soon after.
8. One critic actually refers to the "afterbirth-like concoctions of continental cuisine"! (Greenberg 1972: 12).
9. Quoted in Modleski (1988: 113).
10. See Goble (2015: 223) and Sklar (2006: 226–227), although the latter gives more a summary of my argument than an actual endorsement. In his book on the film, which is largely devoted to the shooting of the film, Foery (2012) briefly discusses the film's reception and agrees with my analysis of the treatment of women in the film. His is a very odd discussion of this "topic," however. He has a section on responses to the film from the academy and a separate section on women critics of the film, as if we were not an integral part of the academy and as if the woman question can be treated separately from the film as a whole. Even stranger, Foery spends most of the section talking about Hitchcock's positive relationships with many women—as if that proved anything! (Foery 2012: 136–143)

References

Allen, J. T. (1985) "The Representation of Violence to Women: Hitchcock's *Frenzy*," *Film Quarterly*, 8 (3): 30–38.
Allison, M. (2022) "*Frenzy* at 50: The Most Violent Film Hitchcock Ever Made," BBC, July 4, www.bbc.com/culture/article/20220704-frenzy-at-50-the-most-violent-film-hitchcock-ever-made
Ben-Youssef, I. (2024) "Uncanny Reflections: *Frenzy* as Hitchcock's Kaleidoscope," *Quarterly Review of Film Studies*, February 2, pp. 1–31.
Brill, L. (1988) *The Hitchcock Romance: Love and Irony in Hitchcock's Films*, Princeton, NJ: Princeton University Press.

Cooper, I. (2018) *Frenzy*, Liverpool: Liverpool University Press.
Denby, D. (2014) " In a *Frenzy*," *New Yorker*, March 24, www.newyorker.com/magazine/2014/03/31/in-a-frenzy
Dima, V. (2011) "Strangers No More: The Initial Hitchcock Murder," *Cinema Journal*, special issue, 1: 171–178.
Douglas, M. (1966) *Purity and Danger: An Analysis of the Concepts of Pollution and Taboo*, New York: Praeger.
Foery, R. (2012) *Alfred Hitchcock's* Frenzy*: The Last Masterpiece*, Lanham, Md.: Rowman & Littlefield.
Gilliat, P. (1972) "Dear, What's a Pull-In? Or, the Sausages-and-Mash Drama," *New Yorker*, June 16, pp. 52–54.
Goble, M. (2015) " Live Nude Hitchcock: Final Frenzies," in J. Freedman (ed.), *The Cambridge Companion to Alfred Hitchcock*, Cambridge: Cambridge University Press, pp. 207–228.
Green, S. (2022) "50 Years of *Frenzy*: Hitchcock's Brazen British Homecoming Film," June 21, www.bfi.org.uk/features/alfred-hitchcock-frenzy
Greenberg, S. (1972) "*Frenzy*: An Appreciation," Pan USC Cinema, September 9. In clippings at Margaret Herrick Library.
Johnson, A. (1972) Review of *Frenzy*, *Film Quarterly*, 26 (1): 58–60.
Jones, N. (2012) "My Favorite Hitchcock Film: *Frenzy*," August 17, www.theguardian.com/film/filmblog/2012/aug/17/my-favourite-hitchcock-frenzy
Kapsis, R. E. (1992) *Hitchcock: The Making of a Reputation*, Chicago, Ill.: University of Chicago Press.
Lefebvre, M. (2005–2006) "Conspicuous Consumption: The Figure of the Serial Killer as Cannibal in the Age of Capitalism," *Theory, Culture & Society*, 13 (1): 43–62.
Leitch, T. (2002), *The Encyclopedia of Alfred Hitchcock*, New York: Checkmark.
Modleski, T. (1988) *The Women Who Knew Too Much: Hitchcock and Feminist Theory*, London and New York: Routledge.
Naremore, J. (2014) "Hitchcock and Humor," in *An Invention without a Future: Essays on Cinema*, Berkeley, Calif.: University of California Press, pp. 124–138.
Prince, S. (1998) *Savage Cinema: Sam Peckinpah and the Rise of Ultraviolent Movies*, Austin, Tex.: University of Texas Press.
Sgammato, J. (1973) "The Discreet Qualms of the Bourgeoisie: Hitchcock's *Frenzy*," *Sight and Sound*, 42 (3): 134–137.
Sklar, R. (2006) "Death at Work," in D. Boyd and R. Barton Palmer (eds), *After Hitchcock: Influence, Imitation and Intertextuality*, Austin, Tex.: University of Texas Press, pp. 217–234.
Spoto, D. (1983) *The Dark Side of Genius: The Life of Alfred Hitchcock*, New York: Ballantine.
Taylor, A. (2022) "Hitchcock's *Frenzy* Only Grows More Disturbing with Time," *Collider*, June 18.
Wood, R. (1966) *Hitchcock's Films*, South Brunswick and New York: A. S. Barnes and Tantivy.
Wood, R. (1988) *Hitchcock's Films Revisited*, New York: Columbia University Press.

Chapter 21
Topaz (1969)
"One of the Most Uneven Films in the History of Cinema"

James Chapman

In the 1977 "Retrospective" to *Hitchcock's Films*, Robin Wood remarked, "*Topaz* must surely be one of the most uneven films in the history of the cinema, in which something approaching Hitchcock's best rubs shoulders with his very worst: the relationship of good to bad in the film is very revealing" (Wood 1991: 222). *Topaz* polarized critical opinion: It received some of the worst reviews of Hitchcock's late career but paradoxically also some of the best. These polarized views have persisted since its original release. While the majority view remains that *Topaz* was an artistic and commercial failure, there are some critics who claim it as a misunderstood achievement.

Topaz had been a troubled film: Its mixed reception was to some extent a reflection of the compromises and missteps taken during its production. Universal had acquired the rights to Leon Uris's novel, which spent fifty-two weeks on the *New York Times* bestseller list, as a potential project for Hitchcock. Following the postponement of *Frenzy*, *Topaz* was announced as Hitchcock's next film in May 1968: Uris was paid $125,000 for the rights and another $125,000 to write the screenplay (*Motion Picture Exhibitor*, May 15, 1968, p. 5). Uris delivered an incomplete first draft in July 1968 which streamlined his labyrinthine narrative. Samuel Taylor, who had written the final draft of *Vertigo*, was brought in to finish *Topaz*: Taylor had to work quickly as the location shooting in Copenhagen and Paris was scheduled for September 1968. Following *Torn Curtain* (1966), where he felt constrained by the casting of name stars in Paul Newman and Julie Andrews at the studio's insistence, Hitchcock deliberately avoided major stars for *Topaz*, feeling that, as the film was based on a real spy story against the background of the Cuban Missile Crisis of 1962, actors without an established persona would be better suited (*Variety*, May 8, 1968, p. 32). However, this strategy may have backfired: One of the recurring criticisms of *Topaz* in contemporary reviews would be the undistinguished cast.

The main problem that affected the making of *Topaz* was uncertainty over the ending. At a script conference in August 1968, Hitchcock remarked, "Well, to sum up, gentlemen, we have no ending to our picture. We have to devise some other way to unmask Columbine … At least we don't have in the picture a character called R" (Hitchcock 1968a). This was a reference to the secret-service chief "R"

("As in 'Aargh'?"; "No, as in rhododendron") in *Secret Agent* (1936) and might perhaps be read as an indication that Hitchcock was keen to differentiate *Topaz* from the James Bond films which had recurring characters known as "M" and "Q".[1] *Topaz* started shooting without a finished script: this was unusual for Hitchcock but not unprecedented (*Torn Curtain* being another example). What was unusual, however, is that halfway into the shooting period Hitchcock had still not determined the final act:

> We are in the last quarter of our picture. At the "Safe House" in Virginia, we send André Devereaux off as a man with an urgent mission and 2 or 3 days in which to accomplish it … This would indicate that there should be, first and foremost, an urgency about these scenes in which Devereaux must be shown as the instigator.
>
> (Hitchcock 1968b)

Hitchcock was never able to work out a satisfactory conclusion to the film. First, it was intended to have been a formal pistol duel between André Devereaux (Frederick Stafford) and Jacques Granville (Michel Piccoli) at the Roland Garros Stadium where Granville is shot by a KGB sniper concealed in the empty stands. However, a test screening of *Topaz* in San Francisco, at which the duel was described variously as "unnecessary," "anticlimactic," and an "anachronism," prompted Hitchcock and Universal to shoot another ending in which Deveraux and his wife, boarding a flight for Washington, are wished a cheery "Bon voyage" by Granville as he takes a plane to Moscow. Hitchcock felt that allowing Granville to get away at the end was "the correct ending. In every case, whether it be Philby, Burgess [or] McLean, they've all gotten away with it and they've gone back to Russia" (Auiler 1999: 538). The uncertainty over the ending continued until the release of *Topaz*. A third version—in which Granville enters his house and a gunshot is heard indicating that he has committed suicide—was used in North America and France. That version was shown to critics in Britain, but the final release had the airport scene instead.

Unusually, *Topaz* was released in Britain six weeks before it was seen in North America. It had the sort of reception generally described as "mixed." The national critics were largely united in their disappointment with the film, despite some characteristically "Hitchcockian" touches (the opening sequence of the defection was mentioned in most reviews). For Penelope Mortimer, "While there are splendid moments, the picture as a whole weighs heavy as lead. It is not helped by an undistinguished cast and a story that cries out for a frivolous touch of the James Bonds" (*Observer*, November 9, 1969, p. 32). Richard Roud agreed that "there are great sequences, like the opening one I described … But it is just such successful scenes as these that point up the low voltage of the rest" (*Guardian*, November 5, 1969, p. 8). David Robinson felt that "*Topaz* is excessively long and tedious" and had ended up a "sub-Hitchcock spy story that practically anyone else could have made and even (given more responsive players than Hitchcock has chosen) made better" (*Financial Times*, November 7, 1969, p. 3). Hitchcock's future biographer John Russell Taylor thought *Topaz* the director's worst: "Hitchcock, like all major directors, has made his share of bad films. But never, I think, one which was so generally flat, undistinguished, and lacking in any sign of positive interest or involvement on his part" (*The Times*, November 6, 1969, p. 8). The popular press were a little more favorably disposed. Dick Richards felt it was lacking humor but otherwise was up to par: "*Topaz* has all the tricks of the Maestro of Menace … You are duly puzzled, teased and absorbed. But compared with many of Hitchcock's more chilling entertainments, *Topaz* seems to me to lack fun" (*Daily Mirror*, November 7, 1969, p. 25). And Ernest Betts thought it in the best tradition of the director's work: "Alfred Hitchcock still has plenty of the old wizardry. He does a lot to restore the somewhat tarnished image of the spy-thriller in *Topaz* … The complicated story tied me in knots, but it's intelligent, exciting, and good to look at it" (*The People*, November 9, 1969, p. 12).

The British Film Institute's two film magazines—catering for a cine-literate readership and reflecting the intellectual film culture of the time with its preference for European auteur directors and a barely concealed disdain for commercial genre cinema—had rather different positions on *Topaz*. On the one hand, John Gillett (*Sight and Sound*) was underwhelmed:

> It is not difficult to analyse why the latest Hitchcock is a disappointment, but less easy to establish why he was apparently unable to do anything about it … To be fair, the treatment of the Cuban characters (all looking like Castro, of course) is not entirely without wit or sympathy—John Vernon's Rico states his country's case in bold closeups, yet seems somewhat absentminded when it comes to guarding valuable papers. Neither Hitchcock nor his scriptwriter can make much of the cardboard romance between Juanita and Frederick Stafford's stolid, lifeless André; and, in any case, Hitchcock's political moralising is not exactly profound, as we know from *Torn Curtain*.
>
> (Gillett 1969: 261)

On the other hand, Philip Strick (*Sight and Sound*), while accepting that "we will never, surely, be able to rate it as highly as *North by Northwest* among Hitchcock's collection of spy films, or as *Vertigo* or *Marnie* among his psychological thrillers," nevertheless found much to like in *Topaz*:

> Above all, most of its sequences are spellbindingly well made. While flamboyant tracking shots are evidently a thing of the past, the style of *Topaz* is nothing less than perfect for such scenes as the "silent" longshot in which a brash little spy (beautifully played in the Martin Balsam manner by Roscoe Lee Browne) talks his way into the Cuban stronghold in Harlem [Fig. 21.1], the cold tension of a sidelong camera prowl as a woman stares into the eyes of the man who is about to kill her, the numerous low-angle shots of characters pacing like caged animals and the final tour-de-force—the unmasking of the master spy in the conference chamber by a single shot that strolls from closeup to the far end of the enormous room and back again is as good as anything in Hitchcock since *Under Capricorn*.
>
> (Strick 1969: 49)

Strick's emphasis on the stylistic flourishes of *Topaz* rather than its narrative or characterizations set the tone for some of the later critical reevaluations of the film.

Topaz was released in the USA on December 19, 1969: It was no doubt intended for the lucrative Christmas holiday market, although its "M" rating deterred its booking at showcase theatres such as Radio City Music Hall in New York. The trade reviews were mixed. For *Variety*: "This latest Hitchcock suspenser—a spy yarn—came out at 125 minutes at the press showing and felt like it … [The] picture seems to move predictably and lacks the fun and surprise bloodcurdling moments that can lift his thrillers to the skies with breathtaking excitement" (November 12, 1969, p. 21). The *Hollywood Reporter* thought it "one of the season's major disappointments from a veteran film director … After two hours, the film simply stops, reaching an arbitrary conclusion that is neither inevitable nor satisfying, as if there had never been a completed script to guide it" (December 9, 1969, p. 3). Boxoffice found it "rather pale Hitchcock by the Master's usual standards of suspense" and that "it somehow falls short of the mark" (January 12, 1970, p. 11). However, the *Motion Picture Exhibitor* found it "a delightfully polished piece of

Topaz (1969): "One of the Most Uneven Films in the History of Cinema" 255

Figure 21.1 Dubois (Roscoe Lee Browne) infiltrates the Cuban headquarters in Harlem in an extended "Hitchcockian" suspense sequence from *Topaz*.

Topaz, directed by Alfred Hitchcock. © Universal Pictures 1969. All rights reserved.

entertainment whose whole is somewhat less than the sum of its parts." It added — presciently, as it turned out: "Though it remains to be seen how the general public will receive this bizarre 'campy' film, film buffs will probably applaud Hitchcock's continuing trend away from realism and towards abstraction" (*Motion Picture Exhibitor*, December 17, 1969, p. 6). The *Independent Film Journal* felt it was an improvement on Hitchcock's previous two pictures:

> There will undoubtedly be those movie buffs who will argue that Alfred Hitchcock's *Topaz* is an echo chamber — that everything in it has been done before by the Master, and better. But after the malnutritious *Marnie* and *Torn Curtain*, it is a pleasure to find the director working with a densely plotted storyline … The film is a thoroughly absorbing work, but an abrupt ending, meant probably to be ironic, has the effect of pulling the carpet out from under the viewer. As a commercial entry, the boxoffice potential is very strong; the Hitchcock name, alone, would be a crowd-puller, but this time he is also working with a presold property; the Leon Uris novel his film is based on was an international bestseller.
>
> (*Independent Film Journal*, December 9, 1969, p. 1153)

A Chicago exhibitor who had seen a trade show predicted that the film would be a popular success:

> Although we haven't had *Topaz* (Univ.) … at our theatre yet, I saw the film and any exhibitor who wants to have a really prestigious run can book *Topaz*. Hitchcock is at the height of his powers; the director has the look of a young man with new ideas, not a man who has been entertaining the public for over thirty years.
>
> (*Boxoffice*, January 29, 1970, p. 3)

The major weekly magazines were all disappointed with *Topaz*: Their recurring complaint was that it was too old-fashioned a film. *Time* felt that "Hitchcock seems suddenly to have forgotten his own recipe. *Topaz* contains no chills, no fever—and most disappointing, no entertainment" (January 19, 1970). Other critics were even less charitable: several suggested that Hitchcock was out of touch with popular film culture. Pauline Kael averred that *Topaz* "is the same damned spy picture he's been making since the thirties, and it's getting longer, slower and duller" (*New Yorker*, December 27, 1969, p. 49). *Cue* echoed Kael: "The old-fashioned variety of espionage is hopelessly outdated, and this in turn makes old-fashioned spy films an anachronism. Alfred Hitchcock's latest effort at suspense is not only incredible on its face, it is also boring most of the time" (December 13, 1969). For Hollis Alpert, *Topaz* "seems a relentless effort to prove that cinematic times have not changed" (*Saturday Review,* December 27, 1969). And Paul Zimmerman compared it to another disappointing late film from a great filmmaker: "*Topaz* moves with an arthritic quality reminiscent of Chaplin's *A Countess from Hong Kong* … And the Hitchcock style, always so fluent and straightforward, seems here oddly old-fashioned" (*Newsweek*, December 29, 1969). The entertainment monthly *After Dark* felt that the film had failed to make the same impact as the book:

> Publicity for *Topaz* involves reproductions of news articles concerning international spy scares created by Leon Uris's novel when it came out in 1963. But Alfred Hitchcock's film version, unfortunately, could not create controversy if the entire cast appeared in the nude throughout. What *Topaz* is is bad—shameful, for Hitchcock—out of date and practically without interest.
>
> (Robin 1970: 59)

While more positive responses were in a minority, there were some reviewers who found much to admire in the film. Vincent Canby, who had replaced Bosley Crowther (following a brief stint by Renata Adler) as senior film critic of the *New York Times*, was fulsome in his praise:

> *Topaz* is … quite pure Hitchcock, a movie of beautifully composed sequences, full of surface tensions, ironies, absurdities (some hungry seagulls blow the cover of some Allied agents), as well as odd references to things such as Michelangelo's Picta … *Topaz* is not only most entertaining. It is, like so many Hitchcock films, a cautionary fable by one of the most moral cynics of our time.
>
> (December 20, 1969, p. 36)

Kevin Thomas was slightly less fulsome but found more to like than not: *Topaz* was "one of those pictures in which the whole is not greater than the sum of its parts, yet some of those parts are indeed pretty great" and included "bravura displays of the fabled Hitchcock technique, replete with dazzling camera movements and acute imagery" (*Los Angeles Times*, December 19, 1969, p. D1).

Robert Kapsis has argued that the reception of *Topaz* needs to be understood in the context of a changing film culture in the USA: the three and a half years since the release of *Torn Curtain* had seen publication of Andrew Sarris's *The American Cinema* (1968), the establishment of the first film studies programs in American universities, and the honoring of Hitchcock by the Academy of Motion Picture Arts and Sciences, which, having neglected ever to award him the Oscar for best director, presented Hitchcock with the prestigious Irving G. Thalberg Award in 1968 "for the most consistent high level of achievement by an individual producer" (Kapsis 1992: 100–103). It was also the historical moment of the emergence of what came to be identified as "New Hollywood" or the "American film renaissance" with films oriented more directly towards a young adult market—including *The Graduate* (1967), *Bonnie and Clyde* (1967), *Night of the Living Dead* (1968), *Easy Rider* (1969), and *Midnight Cowboy* (1969)—whose directors identified with the idea of the auteur. As Peter Biskind puts it, "New Hollywood directors … were unembarrassed—in many cases rightly so—to assume the mantle of the artist, nor did they shrink from developing personal styles that distinguished their work from that of other directors" (Biskind 1998: 15).

A key tenet of the auteur theory—at least the version of auteur theory promoted by Sarris—was "that the worst film of a great director may be more interesting though less successful than the best film of a fair to middling director" (Sarris 1968: 17). *Topaz*, a lesser film by a great director, became a test case for the auteur theory. There is a broad correlation between the reviews of *Topaz* and where the critic concerned stood on the auteur debate. Nat Freedland, for example, wrote that "*Topaz*, the newest Hitchcock thriller, doesn't succeed at much of anything except in helping disprove the auteur theory and in demonstrating that Alfred Hitchcock's suspense gimmicks are most likely passé" (*Entertainment World*, December 12, 1969, p. 18). And it is no surprise that Pauline Kael did not like *Topaz*: Kael was an outspoken opponent of the auteur theory, which she said in her review amounted to uncritical admiration for "the directors who go on making the same kind of picture in the same way year after year" (*New Yorker*, December 27, 1969, p. 49). On the other hand, the most laudatory review was by John Belton, a self-professed "auteur man," for whom "*Topaz* is Hitchcock's best composed, framed and cut film since *Vertigo*, his classic 50s masterpiece." Belton admired the film's "profoundly disturbing ambiguity" and concluded that "*Topaz* is a cinematic parade. The variety of shooting styles, filters, colors, lighting and focal lengths not only illustrate Hitchcock's technical tour de force, but reflect, cinematically, the director's thematic concerns" (*B.A.D.*, February 4, 1970, p. 31).

Perhaps the most measured assessment of *Topaz* came from Richard Corliss in an article for *Film Quarterly*. Corliss admired the films of Hollywood's classical directors without ever fully being a convert to the auteur theory. His article began with a balanced critical assessment of its limitations when presented with a director's late work:

There's an auteur proposition that the best American directors keep improving throughout their careers until, in their sixties and seventies, these artists deliver their film testaments. But this romantic formulation doesn't hold up if you take a long, painful look at the final movies of Andrew Sarris's Pantheon directors: Charles Chaplin's *The Countess from Hong Kong*, a sadder and more misdirected jape than his *Monsieur Verdoux*, without even that film's saving venom; John Ford's *Seven Women*, in which the director tries to camouflage a limp, *Painted-Veil* woman's story with scenes of gratuitous violence; D. W. Griffith's *The Struggle*, a strongly felt but ineptly made antidrink tract, powerfully pathetic in its directness; Howard Hawks's *El Dorado*, a relaxed and superficial restatement of Rio Bravo; Fritz Lang's *The Thousand Eyes of Dr Mabuse*, an aimless, commissioned repetition of his early classic; Ernst Lubitsch's *Cluny Brown*, an impeccable trifle (well, no theory can be all wrong); Josef von Sternberg's *Anatahan*, personal and pure, but as dull as his wartime documentaries; and, until the recent release of *Topaz*, Alfred Hitchcock's *Torn Curtain*, the Master of Suspense's fiftieth completed feature, as slick, manipulating and lifeless as a vibrator.

(Corliss 1970: 41)

Turning to *Topaz*, Corliss navigated between the wholly negative and the uncritically adulatory opinions, regarding the film as a mixture of the awful and the sublime: "*Topaz*, inept and ineffable, poorly acted and well acted, shoddily shot and exquisitely shot, mediocre and transcendent, should be borne in mind before we send 'Hitchcock' to the Pantheon or to critical perdition" (1970: 78). Corliss was one of the few critics to focus on Hitchcock as a genre director rather than just an auteur:

> The film is Hitchcock's twenty-eighth in America and his twelfth in the spy genre … Hitchcock's best spy films seem to transcend their maker's intentions—whether by a witty script (like the one by Charles Bennett, Joan Harrison, James Hilton, and Robert Benchley for *Foreign Correspondent*) or by an actor's extra, usually independent effort (Michael Redgrave)—while, in his worst, Hitchcock's concentration on technique seems empty when there's an absence of dense detail (as in *Notorious*) or involving, living characters (as in *Torn Curtain*).
>
> (Corliss 1970: 44)

Corliss concluded with a corrective to the polemical excesses of the auteur theory in his assertion that:

> any film … is the result of a number of stimuli, controlled perhaps by the director, but created by actors, writers and technicians. Beneath the mythical Hitchcock who is the author of everything grand in his oeuvre is a partly creative, mostly collaborative craftsman who must rely on the crucial contributions of his coworkers.
>
> (Corliss 1970: 44)

Hitchcock always maintained that the box office was the real test of a film's success rather than the views of critics: in this regard, *Topaz*, which after a year had earned domestic rentals of only $3,839,363 and was outside the top thirty (*Variety* had it as thirty-fifth in 1970), must be regarded as a failure (*Variety*, January 6, 1971, p. 9). To put this in context, the biggest-grossing films in the North American market in 1970—all released between January and April—were *Airport* ($37,650,794), *M*A*S*H* ($22 million), and *Patton* ($21 million), while other films released in the same month as *Topaz* were *Bob & Carol & Ted & Alice* ($13.9 million), *On Her Majesty's Secret Service* ($9 million), *Z* ($6.5 million) and *They Shoot Horses, Don't They?* ($6.5 million). The popular success of *Airport* and *Patton* demonstrates that traditional commercial genre films continued during the era of New Hollywood. The fact that *Topaz* fared less well than either Costa-Gavras's political thriller *Z* or the Bond adventure *On Her Majesty's Secret Service* might suggest that Hitchcock's film was somewhat betwixt and between: It was neither a political tract for the times—Hitchcock himself averred that Uris's novel had been intentionally "depoliticized" and that "No political films have ever been commercially successful" (Hitchcock 1968a: 32)—nor was it an out-and-out adventure thriller in the style of the Bond picture.

It would probably be fair to say that, overall, the critical reputation of *Topaz* has not been significantly enhanced following its initial release. Neil Sinyard's dismissive verdict that it is "quite the dreariest picture the Master ever made" is not untypical (Sinyard 1986: 133). However, there have been some voices who, while in a minority, have sought to make sense of a film that fits uneasily into Hitchcock's oeuvre. The first indications of a limited revisionism came following the release of Hitchcock's next film *Frenzy* (1972), which was generally seen as a return to form in the serial-killer realm of previous pictures including *The Lodger* (1926), *Shadow of a Doubt* (1943), and *Psycho* (1960). A discourse emerged that the critical and commercial failure of *Topaz* was due to it not being typical Hitchcock. One "George Kaplan" made this point in *Film Comment*: "*Topaz* is, in obvious ways, atypical. No-one seriously regards it as a fully realized masterpiece. It is a startlingly uneven film, and its success and its losses, and the relationship

Figure 21.2 The overhead shot of the death of Juanita (Karin Dor) was one of the few moments of *Topaz* universally admired by critics.

between them, seem to me very revealing" (Kaplan 1972: 46). "Kaplan," it turned out, was Robin Wood (pseudonyms seem to have been a feature of Hitchcock criticism around this time), and the article anticipates his later verdict that *Topaz* was "one of the most uneven films in the history of the cinema" (Wood 1991: 223–240). Wood highlights "three superb sequences"—the defection of Kusenov (Per-Axel Arosenius), the Hotel Teresa scene, and the death of Juanita (Karin Dor; see Fig. 21.2)—as standout moments of "pure cinema," while contending that "[the] badness of other parts of *Topaz*—badly written, badly acted, and shot any old way—can doubtless be attributed to the fact that the material doesn't lend itself easily to 'pure cinema,' only to 'photographs of people talking'" (Wood 1991: 223–240).

Donald Spoto similarly accepts that *Topaz* is "flawed," but argues that it was misunderstood and should be seen as an experiment in film form that did not quite work:

> The wholly negative response is a shallow one. *Topaz* is surely a demanding film, complex and often prolix. It is a significant departure from Hitchcock's previous work. Let there be no mistake—it is flawed. But it is also far from a disaster. It should be regarded as one of Hitchcock's few consciously experimental films. It is a film whose angles and colors tell the story, and whose dialogue is much less important than in comparable movies about the cold war. But it is, after all, perhaps too subtle, too obscure for the mass audience which Hitchcock usually reaches.
>
> (Spoto 1979: 423)

And for Justin Busch, *Topaz* is a challenging film because it deals in moral and ideological ambiguities rather than presenting the Cold War in Manichean terms:

> *Topaz*, properly understood, deserves considerably more respect than it has hitherto enjoyed. *Topaz* operates, as befits its subject, on several sequential yet overlapping levels; to take any one of the levels as that of the film as a whole is to misrepresent (in effect to betray) the overall concept and

structure of the film. What makes *Topaz* so unsettling, and so easily misunderstood and unfairly criticized, is precisely that it has no moral center.

(Busch 2005: 29–30)

In this context, it is notable that what might be considered Hitchcock's more existential spy pictures—the others were *Secret Agent* and *Sabotage* (1936)—have generally been more problematic for critics than the more adventure-oriented films such as *The 39 Steps* and *North by Northwest* (1959); the two versions of *The Man Who Knew Too Much* (1934, 1956) also highlight this.

Slavoj Žižek, nominating *Topaz* as one of his "guilty pleasures," offers a reflection on the reasons why certain Hitchcock films are subject to critical revisionism:

One of the standard exercises of Higher Hitchcockian Criticism is to pick the master's "failure" and proclaim it his great masterpiece: in France, there is a whole school of thought that claims *Under Capricorn*, the ridiculous historical melodrama set in Australia, fulfills the role; Fredric Jameson's choice (from the same period) is *Stage Fright*; and so on. As far as I am aware, nobody has dared to consider *Topaz*, the anti-Communist spy story generally dismissed as Hitchcock's worst film (at least after World War II). Although critics usually praise some scenes, they dismiss *Topaz* as a clumsy, overlong mixture of rehashed Hitchcock motifs and anti-Communist clichés. However, what if we reperceive *Topaz* as a European art film—with its complex love triangles, "cold" marriages where affairs are tolerated, echoes of the old camaraderie of the Resistance, chamber-drama atmosphere, and strangely twisted nonlinear narrative? This shift allows us to appreciate the film's qualities properly.

(Žižek 2006: 12–13)

It seems to me there is some substance to this argument: the "cold" marriage and presence of Michel Piccoli both suggest parallels with Buñuel's *Belle de Jour* (1967)—a film that Hitchcock admired—and there is some evidence to suggest that Hitchcock and Catherine Deneuve wanted to work together. Hitchcock met Deneuve in Paris during the shooting of *Topaz*, after which she wrote, "I was very please [sic] to see you the other day for lunch, and I am sure you know how much I would like to work with you" (Deneuve 1968). Their subsequent correspondence suggests that Hitchcock was thinking of Deneuve for the role of Carla in *The Short Night*.

My own "take" on *Topaz* is that while it is far from being an unrecognized masterpiece, it is a film that fascinates because of its flaws rather than despite them. It is essentially a film of three acts—Copenhagen/New York, Cuba, and Paris—and only the final act is subpar Hitchcock. It is the only one of Hitchcock's American spy films that was not reworking (or in the case of *The Man Who Knew Too Much*, remaking) aspects of his British spy pictures of the 1930s. At the age of seventy, Hitchcock should be credited for attempting to vary the formula rather than resting on his laurels: *Topaz* did not (quite) come off, but its existence was probably necessary for the emergence of a cycle of ideologically ambiguous Hitchcock-influenced conspiracy thrillers during the next decade including *The Parallax View* (1974), *Three Days of the Condor* (1975) and *All the President's Men* (1976), the last of which bears certain parallels, in content and form, to Hitchcock's film.

Note

1   The first director of the Secret Service Bureau, Sir Mansfield Smith-Cumming, had signed correspondence as "C." Ian Fleming's James Bond novels had "M" as Head of the British Secret Service. "M" (played by Bernard Lee) had appeared in the Bond films since the first, *Dr No* (1962), while "Q" (played by Desmond Llewelyn)—for Quartermaster—had been present since *From Russia with Love* (1963).

References

Auiler, D. (1999) *Hitchcock's Secret Notebooks*, London: Bloomsbury.
Biskind, P. (1998) *Easy Riders, Raging Bulls: How the Sex'n'Drugs'n'Rock'n'Roll Generation Saved Hollywood*, London: Bloomsbury.
Busch, J. E. A. (2005) "The Centre Cannot Hold: Betrayals in Alfred Hitchcock's *Topaz*," *CineAction*, 66: 29–41.
Corliss, R. (1970) "*Topaz*," *Film Quarterly*, 23 (3): 41–46.
Deneuve, C. (1968) Letter to Alfred Hitchcock, November 14, Alfred Hitchcock Collection, folder 1215, Margaret Herrick Library, Academy of Motion Picture Arts and Sciences.
Durgnat, R. (1974) *The Strange Case of Alfred Hitchcock; or, The Plain Man's Hitchcock*, London: Faber & Faber.
Gillett, J. (1969) "*Topaz*," *Sight and Sound*, 36 (420): 261.
Hitchcock, A. (1968a) "August 27th Story Conference in Mr Hitchcock's Office," transcript of tape recording, Alfred Hitchcock Collection, folder 679, Margaret Herrick Library, Academy of Motion Picture Arts and Sciences.
Hitchcock, A. (1968b) Letter to Samuel Taylor, December 11, Alfred Hitchcock Collection, folder 695, Margaret Herrick Library, Academy of Motion Picture Arts and Sciences.
Kaplan, G. (1972) "Alfred Hitchcock: Lost in the Wood," *Film Comment*, 8 (4): 46–54.
Kapsis, R. E. (1992) *Hitchcock: The Making of a Reputation*, Chicago, Ill.: University of Chicago Press.
Robin, S. (1970) "*Topaz*," *After Dark: The Magazine of Entertainment*, 11 (10): 60.
Sarris, A. (1968) *The American Cinema: Directors and Directions, 1929–68*, New York: Da Capo Press.
Sinyard, N. (1986) *The Films of Alfred Hitchcock*, London: Admiral.
Spoto, D. (1979) *The Art of Alfred Hitchcock: Fifty Years of His Motion Pictures*, Garden City, NY: Dolphin Books.
Strick, P. (1969) "*Topaz*," *Sight and Sound*, 39 (1): 49.
Wood, R. (1991) *Hitchcock's Films Revisited*, London: Faber & Faber.
Žižek, S. (2006) "Guilty Pleasures," *Film Comment*, 42 (1): 12–13.

Chapter 22

What the Two Versions of *The Man Who Knew Too Much* Reveal about Film Criticism in the USA and Britain

Robert E. Kapsis

Of the five Hitchcock films reissued in the mid 1980s, the one that generated the most unexpected response among reviewers in the USA was the 1956 *The Man Who Knew Too Much*. Long regarded by Anglo-American reviewers and scholars alike as "minor" Hitchcock, this film came to be viewed by American reviewers as one of the major "revelations" of the Hitchcock "revival." A review of the history of critical response to this film in the USA and England will launch a more general discussion about the possible cultural variations in the diffusion of Hitchcock's artistic reputation and of those stellar or canonized works behind that reputation. Differences in the perception of "Hitchcock" in the USA and England also shed light on the connection between Hitchcock's improved stature as a filmmaker in America during the 1960s and 1970s and the reputation of the thriller genre (circa 1992).

When first released in 1956, *The Man Who Knew Too Much* received generally positive reviews in the USA, especially among reviewers writing for the average filmgoer. For those most favorably disposed to the film, the 1956 version contained an effective blending of the various elements that had recently come to be associated with the Hitchcock Hollywood thriller—spine-tingling suspense, relief through humor, exotic locations, box-office stars—all shot in color and displayed on a wide screen. On the other hand, the critics for more sophisticated publications such as the *New Yorker* or the *Saturday Review*, who typically compared the film to the earlier British version, tended to be more critical of the remake, preferring the quickness of pace and surface realism of the original to the slowness and greater subjectivity of the remake (see, e.g., Alpert, *Saturday Review*, May 26, 1956). In England, by contrast, the vast majority of critics, regardless of type of publication, compared the new version unfavorably to the 1934 original. For them, the remake violated all the rules governing their model of perfection—the British thriller form (see, e.g., Lejeune, *Observer*, June 24, 1956; *The Times*, June 24, 1956; *Evening Standard*, June 21, 1956; Houston 1956). C. A. Lejeune, who had reviewed the original when it first came out, put it this way: "the first *The Man Who Knew Too Much* was stronger in every way" (*Observer*, June 24, 1956). During the 1950s, America's more intellectual critics shared with most British reviewers the view that Hitchcock's American films were inferior to his British output (especially when compared to the six "classic" espionage thrillers, including the original *The Man Who Knew Too Much*, he made for Gaumont between 1934 and 1939). In contrast to the Anglo-American critics, who, as a whole, viewed the American version as "minor" Hitchcock, were the French critics of the *Cahiers du Cinéma*, especially Jean-Luc Godard, Claude Chabrol, and Éric Rohmer, who became early champions of the film. In their 1956 book, *Hitchcock: The First Forty-Four Films*, Rohmer and Chabrol characterized the 1956 version as vastly superior to the 1934 film, singling it out as "one in which the Hitchcockian mythology finds its purest, if not its most obvious expression" (Rohmer and Chabrol 1979). For the French, the Hitchcockian mythology referred to the film's metaphysical trappings of a world where "salvation can only be obtained through the combined interplay of Fate (but isn't it rather Providence?) and Free Will" (Rohmer and Chabrol 1979: 141; see also Godard 1956).

While American reviewers and critics would have few opportunities to write publicly about *The Man Who Knew Too Much* until after its posthumous rerelease almost thirty years later in 1984, English critics had occasion to remain outspoken about the film. In championing Hitchcock, the French auteur critics had argued that Hitchcock's Hollywood films, especially those made during the 1950s, were better made than his British ones. For the English critics, especially those connected with the British Film Institute (BFI) publication, *Sight and Sound*, the two versions of *The Man Who Knew Too Much* became central to their debate with the French auteurists over the relative stature of Hitchcock's British and American films. For many British critics, the 1934 version of *The Man Who Knew Too Much* held a special place in their hearts, representing not only a major turning point in Hitchcock's career (which indeed it was) but also an important new direction for British cinema. With this film, said Peter John Dyer in a 1961 *Sight and Sound* article, Hitchcock broke away from his reputation, as "a model of compliance" and as a "critic's director," to make thrillers for "the unsophisticated"—a viewing echoing C. A. Lejeune's much-quoted review of the film when it first came out:

> Now at last he has thrown critics and intellectuals overboard with one of his incomparable rude gestures, and gone in for making pictures for the people … For my own part, I am very happy about *The Man Who Knew Too Much*. It seems to me, because of its very recklessness, its blank refusal to indulge in subtleties, to be the most promising work that Hitchcock has produced since *Blackmail*, and quite possibly the best picture he has ever made.
>
> (*Observer*, December 29, 1934)

In addition, Lejeune had hoped that the film would encourage English filmmakers to be less pretentious and make more movies with "quick action and robust playing" or in the tradition of the Hollywood genre film with its easily recognizable types. Twenty years later, on the eve of a special screening of the 1934 film, an English critic commented on how this version, in addition to being one of the yardsticks by which critics have measured Hitchcock's subsequent work, also "blueprints the British comedy-thriller so long the standby of our studio" (*News Chronicle*, April 25, 1953).

Not surprisingly, Ian Cameron, the editor of *Movie*, the English magazine that spoke for the French auteur view, defended the Hollywood version on the occasion of its reissue in 1962. In response to earlier complaints that the 1956 version was slow-moving, Cameron explained that Hitchcock had done that on purpose so that audiences could get to "like the couple whose child is kidnapped. Hitchcock knows better than his critics and he sets out to use our liking for the couple to help break down our resistance to suspense. It is a measure of his astounding skill that one is still thrilled when one knows what is going to happen" (*Spectator*, September 4, 1962; see also Cameron 1962, 1963). Not so, according to more traditional critics such as *Sight and Sound* editor Penelope Houston (1963: 162) who, in responding to Cameron, argued that Hitchcock had broadened or loosened the film for commercial considerations. ("I can't but feel that this long introduction is precisely what one might have expected at that moment in Hollywood history, when the pressure was on to exploit both stars and locations.") Judged as a thriller, the original, according to Houston, was a superior film. But that, said Houston, is not how the remake was being judged. Rather, several critics (mostly French but also a growing band of English renegades as well) had judged the Hollywood version to be superior precisely because it transcended the lowly thriller form. As Houston sarcastically put it, "But can't we see, we may be asked, that [the Hollywood version is] so much more than a thriller" (1963: 162). Seventeen years later, Houston hadn't modified her view of the film, although by then she conceded that a number of Hitchcock's other Hollywood films such as *Strangers on a Train*, *Rear Window*, *Vertigo*, *North by Northwest*, and *Psycho* were at least as good as anything he had ever made in England (Houston 1980).

The 1934 version of *The Man Who Knew Too Much* remained an important yardstick for a majority of English reviewers when the Hollywood remake was reissued in 1984. This time, the British reaction to the American film was more varied than it had been in 1956. A sizable minority of London movie reviewers wrote favorably if not enthusiastically about the film. Although not one of Hitchcock's masterpieces, the 1956 Hollywood version, they thought, was clearly superior to contemporary thrillers such as *Indiana Jones and the Temple of Doom* and *Friday the 13th* (see, e.g., *Guardian*, June 14, 1984; *Financial Times*, June 15, 1984). That is, for movie reviewers who compared *The Man Who Knew Too Much* to other thrillers then in circulation, Hitchcock's was the best available at that time. Still, a majority of British reviewers remained highly critical of the film, especially those who professed some familiarity with the original.

Typical of the majority position was Philip French's commentary in the *Observer* (June 17, 1984), echoing Houston's perennial reservations about the film. According to French, a frequent contributor to *Sight and Sound*, the problem with the remake was that, unlike the original, the 1956 version was simply not a well-designed thriller. The unattractiveness of the American couple, argued French, was what made the remake so "heavy and oppressive." By contrast, "the balance between character and dramatic incident in the economic, unpretentious earlier film," said French, "makes for a far better thriller." The real heavy in French's indictment of the 1956 remake was Doris Day, whose "querulous, pouting homemaker who pops pills and saves her son by sitting down at the piano to sing a doleful pop tune," "Que será, será," is no match for the international crack shot played by Edna Best who saves her daughter with a well-aimed bullet in the 1934 version. Judging the remake against the benchmark of the classic British thriller, French and other English critics (e.g., *Sunday Telegraph*, June 17, 1984; *What's On*, June 14, 1984) concluded that the 1956 version was no match for the 1934 original—that prototype of the thriller form.

On the other hand, the American reviewers who saw the 1956 *The Man Who Knew Too Much* as much more than a thriller were also much more enthusiastic about the reissued film. While aware of its long-standing reputation among Anglo-American critics as a "minor" work from Hitchcock, several American reviewers, under the influence of auteur criticism, now asserted that the remake was actually one of Hitchcock's greatest artistic triumphs. A key promoter of this revised view of the film was Andrew Sarris, who wrote:

> Alfred Hitchcock's *The Man Who Knew Too Much* (1956) is, along with *Vertigo* and *Rear Window*, one of the major revelations of the current Hitchcock series. (*The Trouble with Harry* and *Rope* emerge

as comparatively minor.) Don't miss it just because of any lingering prejudice against Doris Day. I shall analyze it in greater detail, as well as compare it with Hitch's 1935 original, when I am sure that I cannot "spoil" it for anyone by giving away the plot, which I have to do in order to redeem its reputation from its persistent detractors.

(*Village Voice*, spring 1984)

In his follow-up reflections on the two films, Sarris (*Village Voice*, June 12, 1984) argued that along with the "genre conventions of guns and chases" there coexisted in both versions "a very lucidly realized world of family feelings." In the 1956 remake, however, Hitchcock's relationship with his players was "less intimate and more ironic," enabling him to explore the darker side of his not-so-wholesome All American couple, while moving beyond the thriller form.

Whereas the British critics had tended to regard the Hollywood remake as far less than a great film because it was not a fully realized thriller, the American critics, heavily influenced by the principles of auteur criticism, tended to view the remake as a superior film precisely because, if one took the trouble to dig beneath the film's thriller surface, one would discover something more than a mere thriller. As a critic for the *Philadelphia Inquirer* put it:

Here, beneath the masterfully handled suspense, is an extraordinary richness of theme and a serving of Hitchcock's dolorous view of the world. In this story of an American family in Morocco that becomes unwittingly involved in an assassination attempt against an international leader, Hitchcock found many elements that engaged him on a profound level.

It is possible, as a result, to enjoy *The Man Who Knew Too Much* as a drama of excruciating superficial tension. It is also a movie, like *Rear Window* and *Vertigo*, that offers great rewards to those prepared to look beneath the surface.

(June 25, 1984; see also *Boston Globe*, April 20, 1984; *Boston Phoenix*, May 8, 1984; *New York Magazine*, April 30, 1984)

To increase the credibility of their own favorable reassessments of the 1956 remake of *The Man Who Knew Too Much*, a number of US critics (e.g., Michael Blowen, *Boston Globe*, April 20, 1984) invoked Hitchcock's now famous remark to Truffaut about the differences between the 1934 original and the 1956 remake: "the first version is the work of a talented amateur, and the second was made by a professional" (Truffaut 1984: 94). This view of Hitchcock as a serious auteur which, as we have seen, Hitchcock himself came to embrace, had been the dominant perspective among American journalistic reviewers since *Frenzy* in the early 1970s and has continued right up to the present. By contrast, the vast majority of England's mainstream reviewers, at least through the 1980s, had not yet adopted the view of Hitchcock as a serious artist. Rather, they continued to feel more comfortable with the Hitchcock who made those entertaining "little British comedy thrillers" back in the 1930s. Symptomatic of this bias was their assessment (at the time) of Hitchcock's last two films: *Frenzy* and *Family Plot*. American reviewers generally agreed that *Frenzy* was an important and substantial film, while *Family Plot* was entertaining but lacked depth. The British reviewers sharply disagreed with the Americans, overwhelmingly preferring *Family Plot* to *Frenzy* precisely because the former was more entertaining than the latter.

Frenzy had made the British critics uncomfortable because of its unflattering portrayal of the English as well as its artistic flourishes, which were perceived as pretentious. *The Listener*'s critic complained,

"What is so curious about this effort is that while it freely, and offensively, takes advantage of recent permissiveness, it also portrays the English as stifled by sexual inhibition. An unmarried couple has to bribe the desk clerk at the Coburg Hotel, Bayswater, to hire a double room" (*Listener*, June 1, 1972). The film, in other words, reflects bad taste and unnecessary nastiness. On the other hand, the reviewer for the *New Statesman* was made uneasy by the film's overtly artistic flourishes, most notably the long virtuoso camera movement "out of a room, down some stairs, out of the front door, to pull back and look blankly at a house front"—which this critic found only "tricky," lacking any deeper purpose (*New Statesman*, June 2, 1972).

By contrast, when *Family Plot* was released four years later, the English critics proclaimed it the triumphant return of Hitchcock's magical touch, which, in their eyes, had made him a great entertainer but not an important artist. Typical is the following excerpt from a review that appeared in the *Daily Mail*:

> For all its neatly engineered tensions, his latest film is primarily a comedy rather reminiscent of his underrated *The Trouble with Harry* ... After the mixed-up *Frenzy*, which tried to combine a modern permissiveness with vintage Hitchcock style, *Family Plot* is a delightful return to form ... "Hitch" himself has never quite understood the fussing idolatry he has provoked in his old age. He marveled to me, for instance, at the subtle nuances Truffaut and Claude Chabrol found in his films ... All he is concerned with is giving the customer a good night out at the movies ... Hitchcock is still the best screen entertainer in the business.
>
> (August 18, 1976)

As the English auteur critic Ian Cameron astutely put it (1976), the fact that *Family Plot* has been unanimously praised by the English critics "signals" that it must be a "lightweight work."

This English view of Hitchcock as essentially a "lightweight" persisted, leading British reviewers in 1984 to include different works on their list of preferred Hitchcock films. While *Rear Window* was favored among the reissued films, *Vertigo* ran a distant third with many critics viewing it as highly overrated. In contrast to their American counterparts, British reviewers who liked *Vertigo* tended to concentrate on matters relating to plot construction and the building of suspense rather than on thematic concerns or mise-en-scène. That is, the British were more interested in reassessing *Vertigo*'s effectiveness as a thriller than in exploring the implications of its probings into psychopathology and its indictment of romantic love. When *Vertigo* was first released in 1959, England's premiere critic, C. A. Lejeune, had attacked Hitchcock for prematurely revealing the murder plot to audiences. In the 1980s, English critics applauded Hitchcock for doing this. By sharing information about the conspiracy with audiences, Hitchcock was being perfectly consistent with his much publicized views on how to make a successful thriller. Applying Hitchcock's distinction between suspense and surprise, a London *Times* reviewer explained that "the audience knows more than Stewart and the spectator's interest in the final part of the film is that much greater, following Stewart's gradual realization of the truth, than if the information had been held back" (March 3, 1984, p. 17). Not surprisingly, a number of British reviewers preferred *The Trouble with Harry*—a film Hitchcock had often described as characteristically English—to *Vertigo* and *The Man Who Knew Too Much*. (The unusual reception history of *The Trouble with Harry* in Britain is dealt with more fully in Chapter 16 of this volume.) American critics, on the other hand, continued to assess *The Trouble with Harry* as a relatively minor Hitchcock film (see, e.g., Sarris, *Village Voice*, spring 1984).

In sum, British critics, at least through the 1980s, continued to assess Hitchcock's work against the high standard, they claim, he set with his early British thrillers. By contrast, American reviewers, because they had been more inclined to embrace auteurism than their British counterparts, had already come to view Hitchcock less as a thriller director and more as a serious artist whose work, they believed, often transcended the thriller form.

There are signs that film culture in the USA and Great Britain are more in synch today, at least in their assessment of Hitchcock, than they were at any time during the latter half of the twentieth century. BFI's sponsorship of Canadian scholar Murray Pomerance's 2016 monograph on the 1956 remake of *The Man Who Knew Too Much* is in and of itself prima-facie evidence for this viewpoint when you consider that at the very outset of his study, Pomerance unabashedly declares,

> I intentionally make almost no mention of the first (1934) version of the story, which Hitchcock himself considered weaker. It seems to me that a man of his intelligence and capacity would seek to remake a film only if the early version had no persisting value for him; but more, he in fact told his screenwriter, John Michael Hayes, not to watch the original film or engage with it in any way.
>
> (Pomerance 2016: 8)

Additional signs of this convergence are reported elsewhere in this volume, for example, in the following passage, abridged from Chapter 12 on *Vertigo* and *Marnie*:

> Starting in the early to mid 1990s, evidence starts to build of a profound shift in attitude about *Vertigo* occurring among British critics following the film's dizzying successes in *Sight and Sound* magazine's influential "Greatest Films of All Times" poll—climbing from fourth in 1992 to second in 2002, and then, most dramatically of all, in 2012, replacing *Citizen Kane* in the coveted number 1 spot, which, according to Nick James, editor of *Sight and Sound*, reflected a dramatic transformation in the "culture of film criticism" to a new kind of criticism "not so much about films that strive to be great art, such as *Citizen Kane*, and that use cinema's entire arsenal of effects to make a grand statement, but more about works that have personal meaning to the critic" (quoted in the *Independent*, August 3, 2012). But perhaps even more significantly, according to the *Guardian*'s arts correspondent, Mark Brown, *Vertigo*'s rise to the top "reflects the remarkable change in fortune Hitchcock has had with critics, some of whom [including critics and other spokespersons for BFI's own *Sight and Sound* magazine] once looked down on him as little more than a Hollywood thriller director." These days, continues Brown, "the BFI, which is currently showing a retrospective of the director's films, believes Hitchcock should be studied in schools alongside Shakespeare and Dickens."
>
> (*Guardian*, August 1, 2012)

Acknowledgment

An earlier version of this essay appeared in Kapsis 1992: 149–157.

References

Cameron, I. (1962) "The Mechanics of Suspense," *Movie*, 3, October, pp. 5–7.
Cameron, I. (1963) "Suspense and Meaning," *Movie*, 6: 8–12.
Godard, J.-L. (1956) Review of *The Man Who Knew Too Much*, *Cahiers du Cinéma*, 64 (November).

Houston, P. (1956) Review of *The Man Who Knew Too Much*, *Sight and Sound*, 26 (1): 31.
Houston, P. (1963) "The Figure in the Carpet," *Sight and Sound*, 34 (4): 159–164.
Houston, P. (1980) "Alfred Hitchcock," in R. Roud (ed.), *Cinema: A Critical History—The Major Film-Makers*, New York: Viking, pp. 487–501.
Kapsis, R. (1992) *Hitchcock: The Making of a Reputation*, Chicago, Ill.: University of Chicago Press.
Pomerance, M. (2016) *The Man Who Knew Too Much*, London: British Film Institute.
Rohmer, É., and C. Chabrol (1979) *Hitchcock: The First Forty-Four Films*, trans. S. Hochman, New York: Frederick Ungar.
Truffaut, F. (1984) *Hitchcock*, rev. edn, New York: Simon & Schuster.

PART FIVE

Hitchcock's Television Series

Chapter 23
The Final Frontier
Hitchcock's Television Work

Thomas Leitch

Even as aspiring feature-film directors like William Friedkin, Robert Altman, and Sydney Pollack were cutting their teeth on television, Alfred Hitchcock, encouraged by the suggestion of his former agent, MCA president Lew Wasserman, that "we ought to put Hitch on the air" (Taylor 1978: 228) became "The first major Hollywood director to venture into the world of series television" (Erickson, n.d.). For the next ten years, Hitchcock repeatedly filled in the breaks between his feature projects by directing episodes of *Alfred Hitchcock Presents* (1955–1962) and its successor, *The Alfred Hitchcock Hour* (1962–1965) (Fig. 23.1). From a commercial point of view, the project could hardly have been more successful. The Neilsen Company rated *Alfred Hitchcock Presents*, the half-hour series that premiered on October 2, 1955, with "Revenge," one of four episodes Hitchcock directed during its first season, the sixth most popular television program in America in 1956–1957, with an estimated 13 million viewers (Classic TV Guide, n.d.). Even though the number of viewers it attracted gradually declined over the next few years, it had a far more important and lasting benefit for Hitchcock's career, establishing him as the American filmmaker most widely and instantly recognized for his image, his voice, and his gravely playful persona. More powerfully even than the fifty-three feature films Hitchcock directed, *Alfred Hitchcock Presents*, which ran for seven seasons, and *The Alfred Hitchcock Hour*, the expanded version that succeeded it between 1962 and 1965, made Hitchcock a household name.

Sixty years after their initial run ended, the two series remain remarkably popular with fans. Both *Alfred Hitchcock Presents* and *The Alfred Hitchcock Hour* have earned a rating of 8.5 out of 10 on the Internet Movie Database, a rating equaled only by *Rear Window* and *Psycho* among all the director's feature films. And when an Australian package collecting all seven seasons of *Alfred Hitchcock Presents* on DVD, including several episodes unavailable on streaming services because they had been withdrawn from syndication, was made available through Amazon in 2023, purchasers rated them an average of 4.6 out of 5 stars, nearly equaling the 4.7 stars they had given the complete DVD set of *The Alfred Hitchcock Hour*. Both series continue to be available on Amazon Prime, Peacock, and Roku.

But despite its evergreen popularity and its indispensable role in shaping and spreading the director's persona, Hitchcock's television work has attracted remarkably little critical attention—more attention

Figure 23.1 Critics have long neglected Hitchcock's television work despite its pivotal importance in establishing its director as an iconic presence.

Alfred Hitchcock Presents, created by Alfred Hitchcock. © Shamley Productions 1955–1965. All rights reserved.

than *Bon voyage* and *Aventure Malgache*, the two short French-language films in which Hitchcock directed the Molière Players in 1944, or the wartime propaganda shorts *The Fighting Generation* (1944) and *Watchtower over Tomorrow* (1945), but less than virtually any of Hitchcock's feature films. Jane E. Sloan's monumental 1993 *Alfred Hitchcock: A Guide to References and Resources* lists all twenty television episodes Hitchcock directed: seventeen 25-minute episodes of *Alfred Hitchcock Presents*; "I Saw the Whole Thing," the single 50-minute episode he directed for *The Alfred Hitchcock Hour*; "Four O'Clock," the premiere 50-minute episode of the anthology series *Suspicion* (1957–1958); and "Incident at a Corner," a 50-minute episode he directed for *Ford Startime* (1959–1961) in 1960—along with their cast credits and original air dates but departs from Sloan's handling of feature films by omitting summaries of them and citations of critical writing about them. Although countless viewers have seen and loved different episodes of the programs or returned repeatedly to their entire run, virtually no one has written about them. For Hitchcock scholars, as opposed to Hitchcock fans, they have long remained the final frontier.

Since Sloan's bibliography appeared, more scholars have turned their attention to Hitchcock's television work. But this modest upsurge cannot compare to the torrent of analyses of contemporaneous features like *Vertigo* (1958), *Psycho* (1960), and *The Birds* (1963). There are several reasons for this neglect. In the years before streaming services became ubiquitous, Hitchcock's teleplays were largely unavailable to general audiences. Two VHS videotapes each containing four episodes from *Alfred Hitchcock Presents*, the half-hour series that ran from 1955 to 1962—the first including "Revenge" (1955), "Breakdown" (1955), "The Perfect Crime" (1957), and "The Crystal Trench" (1959). The second, including "Dip in the Pool" (1958), "Man from the South" (1960, directed by Norman Lloyd), "Mrs. Bixby and the Colonel's Coat" (1960), and "The Horseplayer" (1961), did not appear until 1995, fifteen years after the director's death. Universal released four DVDs containing twelve episodes of *Alfred Hitchcock Presents*—the first including "The Case of Mr. Pelham" (1955), "Back for Christmas" (1956), "Lamb to the Slaughter" (1958), and "Banquo's Chair" (1959); the second including "Revenge," "Breakdown," "Wet Saturday" (1956), and "Mr. Blanchard's Secret" (1956); the third including "One More Mile to Go" (1957), "The Perfect Crime," "Dip in the Pool," and "Poison" (1958); and the fourth including "Arthur" (1959), "The Crystal Trench," "Mrs. Bixby and the Colonel's Coat," "The Horseplayer," and "Bang! You're Dead" (1961)—in 1999. The studio released all 268 episodes of *Alfred Hitchcock Presents* between 2005 and 2012, and Fabulous Films followed in 2016 with a set that included all seven seasons of *Alfred Hitchcock Presents* and all three seasons of *The Alfred Hitchcock Hour* (1962–1965). New opportunities to see these episodes have inspired online plaudits like "8 Reasons Why 'Alfred Hitchcock Presents' Might Be the Greatest TV Show Ever." But "Four O'Clock" and "Incident at a Corner" have never been released on video in the USA, though they can both be found online.

Another reason for the critical neglect of Hitchcock's work for television is that for many years it seemed less the product of the auteur of *Vertigo* and *Psycho* than of the journeyman who filmed each television episode on a two- or three-day schedule and issued oracularly, often ghoulishly amusing comments on all the others scripted by ghostwriter James B. Allardice, who both imitated and further developed Hitchcock's public persona. He appeared onscreen to introduce and conclude every episode of *Alfred Hitchcock Presents* and *The Alfred Hitchcock Hour*. Even so, Hitchcock directed only seventeen of the 268 episodes of *Alfred Hitchcock Presents*, only one of the 93 episodes of *The Alfred Hitchcock Hour*, and only two other television episodes. So his television work has generally been regarded as Hitchcock-adjacent rather than Hitchcock-central. The most prominent of his early critics—Éric Rohmer and Claude Chabrol, Robin Wood, and Raymond Durgnat—agreed in defining him as an auteur whose ascendant brand was merely promoted by these collaborative spin-offs. Virtually all the commentary on Hitchcock's television work takes off from the question of whether and how it should be discussed in the light of Hitchcock's formidable reputation as a cinematic auteur.

The earliest examinations of Hitchcock's television work include two brief essays that adopt strikingly different views toward it. John Crosby's "Macabre Merriment," a column in the *New York Herald Tribune*, which salutes the "magnificently irrelevant" (November 16, 1955, p. 138) introductions Hitchcock supplies for "Breakdown" and "Premonition," the first two episodes of *Alfred Hitchcock Presents*, waives questions of authorship to accept Hitchcock frankly as an entertainer. In contrast, Jack Edmund Nolan's "Hitchcock's TV Films," which first appeared in *Film Fan Monthly* (June 1968), introduces its index of writing and cast credits and sentence-long plot summaries for each of the twenty television episodes Hitchcock directed by arguing along auteurist lines that these Hitchcock-directed segments deserve special consideration because "they tend to utilize his favorite stars from his feature films" and because "typical Hitchcock thematic material (the exchange of guilt, friendship between disparate types, the woman at bay) obtrudes in those segments which he directed" (Nolan 1972: 140). Gene D. Phillips, taking his cue from Nolan, concentrates on pointing out echoes or previsions of Hitchcock's feature films in the television segments he directed, from the theme of "a man becoming infected with evil in his effort to overcome it" in *Strangers on a Train* and "Revenge" to the paranoia induced by repeated images of a police officer in apparent pursuit of the protagonists of "One More Mile to Go" and *Psycho* (Phillips 1982: 74).

Both the standard reference volumes on Hitchcock's television work chart a middle course between these two positions by treating every episode of *Alfred Hitchcock Presents* and *The Alfred Hitchcock Hour* as equally Hitchcockian and therefore equally worth taking seriously whether or not Hitchcock happens to have directed it. John McCarty and Brian Kelleher observe that the "twist endings" most people consider the most distinctive features of Hitchcock are "not representative of Hitchcock's film career" but "the very signature of his extensive and very visible" television work (McCarty and Kelleher 1985: 3). They expand Nolan's list to include writing, direction, and cast credits and paragraph-length summaries for all 268 episodes of *Alfred Hitchcock Presents* and all ninety-three episodes of *The Alfred Hitchcock Hour*. And they add a substantial introduction focusing on the series' genesis, principal contributors, and most characteristic devices of plot and presentation and an appendix providing similar information for "Incident at a Corner" and all ten episodes of *Suspicion*, and a bibliography that balances its scholarly sources with listings of *TV Guide* columns on the series. Martin Grams, Jr. and Patrik Wikstrom accurately note that "[m]ost writers who have bothered to deal at all with Alfred Hitchcock's television work have focused exclusively on the shows which he himself directed" (Grams and Wikstrom 2001: 9). This tendency has continued with a few notable exceptions to the present. Grams and Wikstrom expand most of McCarty and Kelleher's sections. They kick off with a closely printed hundred-page introduction. They present more detailed writing, directing, and cast credits and longer summaries, and provide verbatim transcriptions of Hitchcock's opening and closing remarks for each episode. And they add similarly detailed treatments of *Alfred Hitchcock Presents: The Movie*, a television compendium of four remade episodes broadcast on May 5, 1985, and the twenty-two remade television episodes that followed during the 1985–1986 season, for which Hitchcock's trademark introductions and conclusions were colorized and repurposed. In place of McCarty and Kelleher's more scholarly bibliography, they append a complete list of suspense collections and Alfred Hitchcock and the Three Investigators stories for young adults issued under Hitchcock's byline between 1945 and 1994.

A number of essays offer more sustained analyses of Hitchcock's television work from an auteurist perspective that assumes an essential continuity between the television episodes he directed and his feature films. Ulrich Rüdel's "Cinema en miniature: The Telefilms of Alfred Hitchcock," an essay embedded in Grams and Wikstrom's volume, examines several recurring tropes—suspended motion, black humor, the frozen gaze—in the light of Hitchcock's own remarks on the conditions and pleasures of working for television in support of its contention that "Hitchcock's television work should be evaluated on its own merits, as an essential chapter of his career" (Rüdel 2001: 97). "TV Episodes," an appendix to Michael Walker's comprehensive 2005 volume *Hitchcock's Motifs*, introduces its much briefer survey of the leading motifs Hitchcock's television work shares with his feature films—bed scenes, children, confined spaces, the corpse, doubles, food and murder/endings and the police, and lights—with the forthright announcement that "The most frequently recurring motif in the *Alfred Hitchcock Presents* episodes is corpse disposal" (Walker 2005: 401). Brad Stevens offers what seems to be a contrary proposition: that "taken as a group, [Hitchcock's television episodes] also have their own logic which distinguishes them from those films intended for theatrical release, in which crimes were usually punished" (Stevens 2014: 83). Stevens's examination of each individual episode emphasizes the homosexual panic that leads so many of his male leads, from Mr. Princey (Cedric Hardwicke) in "Wet Saturday" to Arthur Williams (Laurence

Harvey) in "Arthur," who are "wrestling with repressed homosexual impulses" (Stevens 2014: 93), to react violently when they think their masculinity has been threatened. But Stevens's frequent comparisons of these patterns in Hitchcock's television episodes to analogous patterns in feature films like *Vertigo*, *North by Northwest*, and *Psycho* (Stevens 2014: 84, 89, 104, 112, 113, 121), ends up subordinating his argument that the films constitute "a sub-oeuvre, one with its own trajectory and structure" (2014: 83) to a close analysis of them as mini-features that employ many of the same themes and techniques as Hitchcock's feature films.

In the meantime, the gradual yielding of auteurism to more collaborative theories of cinematic authorship paved the way for a reconsideration of Hitchcock's television work that did not force it to decide between focusing on the twenty segments Hitchcock had directed himself and the more general focus on Hitchcock as presenter. Neill Potts caps his detailed account of the premiere episode's manipulation of the audience's sympathies (see Fig. 23.2) by considering the advantages and disadvantages of approaching Hitchcock's television work from an auteurist perspective "which concentrates exclusively on the thematic and stylistic links between 'Revenge' (and the other nineteen programs) and his cinema films" and from an industrial perspective that considers "issues pertinent to the narratives' televisuality: narrative form, television aesthetics, censorship, and so on," and recommends an approach that "considers its television origins as well as its director's influence" (Potts 2000–2001: 161).

My own essay on Hitchcock's television work examines the ways Hitchcock's participation in the series, both as occasional director and as incessant commentator, develops a dialectical relationship between "Hitchcock the creator" and "Hitchcock the impresario," whereby each of these apparently distinct Hitchcocks reinforces the other (Leitch 1999: 69). Andrew A. Erish focuses on five episodes

Figure 23.2 "Revenge," the inaugural episode of *Alfred Hitchcock Presents*, closes with a two-shot of its avenging husband (Ralph Meeker) and the wife (Vera Miles) whose assault he has sought to avenge, to indicate just how grim some episodes of the program would be.

"Revenge," directed by Alfred Hitchcock © Shamley Productions 1955. All rights reserved.

Hitchcock directed—"The Case of Mr. Pelham," "Breakdown," "Lamb to the Slaughter," "The Perfect Crime," and "Back for Christmas"—in order "to examine how episodes by Hitchcock both compliment [sic] and depart from his motion picture work; the importance of Hitchcock's wraparound comments on the individual narratives; and how the program contributed to his status as an auteur," before acknowledging, "We'll probably never know with any certainty the degree to which the television episodes Alfred Hitchcock directed reflect his own personal struggles" (Erish 2008–2009: 385, 391). As if in response to this conclusion, which he does not cite explicitly, Jan Olsson supports his overarching argument that "the enduring success of the Hitchcock franchise hinged on embodiment in all senses of the term" and that Hitchcock treated his corporeal body, in a Bakhtinian sense, as being "in a perpetual act of becoming, never completed, constantly reauthored and refashioned" by means of an extended chapter on Hitchcock's television appearances and persona, punctuated by briefer analyses of two 1959 episodes of *Alfred Hitchcock Presents*: "The Specialty of the House," which Hitchcock did not direct, and "Arthur," which he did, giving them equal thematic, performative, and metafictional weight (Olsson 2015: 3, 37).

Two recent essays indicate the increasingly wide range of approaches recent commentators on Hitchcock's television work have adopted. Nadine Seligmann examines Hitchcock's "intros and outros" as paratexts that challenge Gérard Genette's rule that "the paratextual element is always subordinate to 'its' text" because they not only provide a trademark element that is "essential to the success of the show" but "play an even more important role than the episodes themselves" in establishing Hitchcock as a recognizable star (Seligmann 2017: 131; see Genette 1997: 12). And Mark Jacovich, sidestepping questions about authorship entirely to focus on the historical and industrial contexts of the horror genre, takes off from Hitchcock's well-known remark that television "has brought back murder into the home—where it belongs" to "demonstrate the ways in which the series presented horror and domesticity as not only compatible but intimately connected" (Jacovich 2017: 37, 41. For Hitchcock's remark, see *Observer*, December 19, 1965, p. 9).

It is ironic to see the ways in which the reception history of Hitchcock's television work has echoed the first years in the reception history of the feature films that made his reputation by placing him at the heart of long-running debates about the nature and status of cinematic auteurism and authorship. The earliest responses are those of reviewers who either make a sharp division between the episodes Hitchcock did and did not direct or waive that distinction entirely in the interest of celebrating the pleasures these episodes provide. The critics who follow divide their analyses in more complicated but closely related ways between those that stick to canonical episodes directed by Hitchcock, those that accept Hitchcock's implicit authorship of every episode in both *Alfred Hitchcock Presents* and *The Alfred Hitchcock Hour* in extending a Hitchcock universe that remains thematically and rhetorically coherent, those that take the knotty questions about auteurism and professional identity the two series raise as their subject (see Fig. 23.3), and those that consider these questions irrelevant to the entertainment both series continue to provide.

Although all four of these approaches have unquestionable merits, the first three of them inevitably neglect "Four O'Clock" and "Incident at a Corner," the two segments Hitchcock directed for series whose role in shaping his persona remains marginalized and largely unexamined because neither series was labeled with his name, featured introductions or commentary by him, or bore the weighty stamp of his physical presence. Years after Hitchcock's work for the two television series most closely associated with him began to attract critical attention, the theoretical movement away from auteurism and the debates it inspires has left behind a teasing question: Will it be a new critical approach yet unimagined or the tireless

Figure 23.3 Commentators on Hitchcock's television work have continued to debate its status as urgently as the tailpiece to "The Case of Mr. Pelham" contested the identities of the two Alfred Hitchcocks it presented, one of whom ended up being carried away by the authorities.

"The Case of Mr. Pelham," directed by Alfred Hitchcock. © Shamley Productions 1955. All rights reserved.

appreciations of enthusiastic fans of the director that further illuminate these two fugitive episodes that remain for now Hitchcock's final frontier?

References

Classic TV Guide (n.d.) https://classictvguide.com/tvratings/1956.htm
Erickson, H. (n.d.) "*Alfred Hitchcock Presents* (1955)," AllMovie, www.allmovie.com/movie/alfred-hitchcock-presents-vm518229
Erish, A. A. (2008–2009) "Reclaiming *Alfred Hitchcock Presents*," *Quarterly Review of Film and Video*, 26 (5): 385–392.
Genette, G. (1997) *Paratexts*: *Thresholds of Interpretation*, trans. Jane E. Lewin, Cambridge: Cambridge University Press.
Grams, M. Jr., and P. Wikstrom (2001) *The* Alfred Hitchcock Presents *Companion*, Churchville, Md.: O T R Publishing.
Jacovich, M. (2017) "'Where It Belongs': Television Horror, Domesticity, and *Alfred Hitchcock Presents*," in L. Belau and K. Jackson (eds), *Horror Television in the Age of Consumption*: *Binging on Fear*, London and New York: Routledge, pp. 29–44.
Leitch, T. (1999) "The Outer Circle: Hitchcock on Television," in R. Allen and S. Ishii-Gonzalès (eds), *Alfred Hitchcock*: *Centenary Essays*, London: British Film Institute, pp. 59–71.

McCarty, J., and B. Kelleher (1985) Alfred Hitchcock Presents: *An Illustrated Guide to the Ten-Year Television Career of the Master of Suspense*, New York: St. Martin's Press.

Nolan, J. E. (1972) "Hitchcock's TV Films," in A. J. LaValley (ed.), *Focus on Hitchcock*, Englewood Cliffs, NJ: Prentice Hall, pp. 140–144.

Olsson, J. (2015) *Hitchcock à la Carte*, Durham, Md.: Duke University Press.

Phillips, G. D. (1982) "Hitchcock's Forgotten Films: The Twenty Teleplays," *Journal of Popular Film and Television*, 10 (2): 73–76.

Potts, N. (2000–2001) "'Revenge': Hitchcock's Sweet Little Story," *Hitchcock Annual*, vol. 9, pp. 145–162.

Rüdel, U. (2001) "Cinema en miniature: The Telefilms of Alfred Hitchcock," in M. Grams Jr. and P. Wikstrom (eds), *The* Alfred Hitchcock Presents *Companion*, Churchville, Md.: O T R Publishing, pp. 97–108.

Seligmann, N. (2017) "'If I Won't Be Myself, Who Will?' The Making of a Star Persona in *Alfred Hitchcock Presents* and *The Alfred Hitchcock Hour*," in W. Schwanebeck (ed.), *Reassessing the Hitchcock Touch*: Industry, Collaboration, and Filmmaking, Cham: Palgrave Macmillan, pp. 113–135.

Sloan, J. (1993) *Alfred Hitchcock*: A Guide to References and Resources, New York: G. K. Hall.

Stevens, B. (2014) "Troubled Bodies: Notes on Hitchcock's Television Work," *Hitchcock Annual*, vol. 19, pp. 82–130.

Taylor, J. R. (1978) *Hitch*: The Life and Times of Alfred Hitchcock, New York: Pantheon.

Walker, M. (2005) "Appendix I: TV Episodes," in *Hitchcock's Motifs*, Amsterdam: Amsterdam University Press, pp. 401–415.

Chapter 24

Toward a New Appreciation of *Alfred Hitchcock Presents*, *The Alfred Hitchcock Hour*, and Shamley Productions

Christina Lane

Of all the questions surrounding Hitchcock's creative output, one of the most vexing might be the relative paucity of scholarship on *Alfred Hitchcock Presents* (1955–1962) and its expanded successor, *The Alfred Hitchcock Hour* (1962–1965). The apparent lack of interest is startling when one stops to consider the series premiered more than sixty-five years ago and yielded 361 total episodes. In Thomas Leitch's examination of scholarly approaches (Chapter 23), he reflects on several reasons why Hitchcock's films have received substantially greater attention than his small-screen output (which also includes episodes for the anthology series *Suspicion* and an episode of *Ford Startime*).[1] One key contributor to this disparity, the firm grip of auteurism, took hold following François Truffaut's interviews with Hitchcock in 1962 (Truffaut 1985). Indeed, the asymmetric critical attention to Hitchcock's television career might well be the most obvious indicator of the prevailing auteurist bias within critical discourses on Hitchcock.

The success of the television series in the mid 1950s meant that the cult of the director arrived earlier for Hitchcock than for some others. The show made him, according to Robert Kapsis, "one of the best known film directors around the world … a star, a celebrity" and enabled Hitchcock to take what today would be termed his brand to audiences who previously had been unfamiliar with him, reaching markets that even he likely could not have foreseen (Kapsis 1992: 34). The series has continued to be closely linked with the director for decades owing to the Hitchcock estate's tight control both over the distribution rights and the licensing of his image, as Kapsis adeptly demonstrates in Chapter 25 of this volume.

Subsequently, the scholarship on *Alfred Hitchcock Presents* and *The Alfred Hitchcock Hour* exhibits a strong tendency to focus on the eighteen episodes directed by Hitchcock, the implicit bias being that the Hitchcock-directed episodes are the most representative of the series.[2] These installments embody pure Hitchcock, many scholars and critics would have us believe, while the other 300-plus episodes are merely residual, excess, or at best supporting material. From this perspective, *Alfred Hitchcock Presents* and *The Alfred Hitchcock Hour* are (mis)taken for Alfred Hitchcock television movies.³ This is precisely the view expressed in a 1971 *Cinema* article, titled "The Television Films of Alfred Hitchcock" (Mamber 1971).

While there are notable examples of scholarship that consider the television series in complex ways, such as work by Brad Stevens or Mark Jancovich (and others cited by Leitch not to mention Leitch's "The Outer Circle: Hitchcock on Television"), it is striking how frequently even recent analysis continues to view Hitchcock's influence on *Alfred Hitchcock Presents* through an auteurist framework in ways that go unpacked (Leitch 1999). For example, Curt Hersey centralizes the director in his *Quarterly Review of*

Figure 24.1 *Alfred Hitchcock Presents*, created by Alfred Hitchcock © Shamley Productions 1955–1965. All rights reserved. Image courtesy CBS and Photofest.

Film and Video article which examines how "the stylistic flourishes and narrative drives of Hitchcock the film director became rearticulated for the small screen, especially in relation to domestic space" (Hersey 2014: 723). Similarly, Andrew A. Erish endeavors to cement the relationship between episodes that Hitchcock directed and his cinematic productions (Erish 2009: 385–392).

To seek out the "Hitchcock" in *Alfred Hitchcock Presents* is to miss the mark, however (see Fig. 24.1). Such scholarship addresses a tiny portion of a vast body of work; after all, Hitchcock directed only roughly 5 percent of the series. Perhaps more crucially, research on the series' production indicates that Hitchcock's involvement was minimal, a point made even at the time the program ran (*New York Times*, November 1, 1960, p. 48). His contribution consisted primarily of several stages of approval (including two stages of the script, rough cut of the show, and final cut) and his performance as host.

Ultimately, *Alfred Hitchcock Presents* and *The Alfred Hitchcock Hour* are best considered not through a filmic lens but as groundbreaking television produced independently by Shamley Productions, a nascent production company that attempted to forge autonomy and creative freedom for writers and other contributors in ways that other companies did not (Letter from Slesar to Bowie, 1996; Letter from Elfman to Bowie, 1996). These contextual factors are particularly critical given that the show was conceived and produced at MCA's Television Limited, presided over by Lew Wasserman (who, not coincidentally, was Hitchcock's agent). Yet they have largely gone undertheorized.

There is mounting evidence that women working behind the scenes were empowered in specific ways that fueled the series' feminist possibilities. This essay seeks to better understand the dynamics that have so narrowly determined the critical reception of Hitchcock's "small screen" and to bolster the feminist discursive readings that may have been foreclosed as a result. In doing so, I intend to offer new ways of conceiving the *Alfred Hitchcock Presents* series, pointing the way toward theoretical alternatives to the auteurist paradigm. In what ways might the lens of media industry studies help explain how and why auteur frameworks have endured over time? What are the underlying historical and cultural determinants at work that perpetually sustain the allure of Hitch-centrism? How might missed cues from the past point toward new directions for scholars looking to reconceive ways to approach Hitchcock's work?

Situating Shamley Productions

From the start, *Alfred Hitchcock Presents* was conceived as a format that would maximize Hitchcock's image and style while minimizing his day-to-day participation and creative responsibility as much as possible (Grams and Wikstrom 2001: 26). The biggest role he played was to supervise story selection—with authority to approve initial story pitch and final script draft—while the bulk of the executive and operational work was conducted by a very small number of experienced individuals from the film industry. The concept for the show was hatched by the director's trusted friend, and super-agent, Lew Wasserman, president of Music Corporation of America (MCA), who hoped that, with Hitchcock as host, the series would become a preeminent vehicle for MCA's efforts to secure an ascendant position in film and television production. (MCA was the largest employer of entertainment talent in the industry and, by the late 1950s, would aggressively acquire Paramount's film library and stage the sale of Universal-International, while retaining its 360-acre lot, Revue Productions, later named Revue Studios.)

Though the market for anthology series was highly competitive, the rationale for competing in that space was that the Hitchcock hook—his weekly presence as host—would separate this product from all others. Wasserman fervently hoped that, by having Hitchcock as both an emissary and creative figurehead, other MCA talent would follow suit (McCarty and Kelleher 1985: 10; Rebello 2013: 43). The deal offered a shrewd step toward solving the problem—shared by the media industry and commercial sponsors—of film stars continuing to shy away from television appearances. Central to the enterprise was a promise from Wasserman that Hitchcock's steady flow of moviemaking would not be interrupted. It was contractually agreed upon that his participation would be "peripheral" (Grams and Wikstrom 2001: 19).

For these reasons, the principals who presided over and facilitated *Alfred Hitchcock Presents* were vitally important, making the inattention to them by scholars particularly disconcerting. The significant role of lead producer Joan Harrison is difficult to overstate. An associate of Hitchcock's since 1933 and a producer in her own right, Harrison had been responsible for cowriting and coproducing (in some instances uncredited) eight Hitchcock films, including *Jamaica Inn* (1938), *Rebecca* (1940), *Foreign Correspondent* (1940), and *Suspicion* (1941), before embarking on a solo producing career that included the noir classics *Phantom Lady* (1944) and *Ride the Pink Horse* (1947). Harrison's duties on the *Alfred Hitchcock Presents* series, as I have demonstrated in previous work, ranged from selecting stories to securing legal rights, casting, finding locations, supervising writers, working closely with art directors, editors, and costume designers, and overseeing production on the set (Lane 2020: 248).

One of Harrison's most important functions was to guarantee the Hitchcock quotient of each show. Because she had worked so closely with Hitchcock, no one was more capable of ensuring adherence to the director's signature style and tongue-in-cheek tone. It is the "idea" of his presence—"the idea of Hitchcock as the creative and almost supernatural force behind the program," in the words of Howard Prouty—that Harrison could preserve more successfully than anyone else (Prouty 1984: xiv, cited in Kapsis 1992: 31).

Harrison was, without question, the show's most significant creative voice. She was central to the formation of the production's fundamental textual practices. When the one-hour mystery anthology series *Suspicion* (1957–1958) was added to Revue Studios' slate (with Hitchcock executive producing half the season), Harrison joined the team as well. (She was credited as associate producer.) This made her the first to produce television programs for two networks (CBS and NBC) at the same time.

While for the first two seasons of *Alfred Hitchcock Presents* Harrison served as sole producer, in fall 1957, Norman Lloyd was hired as associate producer. The addition of Lloyd, who had acted in the Hitchcock films *Saboteur* (1942) and *Spellbound* (1945) (as well as the "Nightmare in 4-D" episode of *Alfred Hitchcock Presents*), was intended to support Harrison and ease the production's workflow, allowing Harrison to focus more on development and business for both series.[4] Gordon Hessler joined the producing team in fall 1962 (with the start of *The Alfred Hitchcock Hour*), bringing a background in documentaries and editing and bolstering Lloyd's efforts on the artistic side.

With Harrison, Lloyd, and eventually Hessler forming the series' core producing team, Harrison's consequential role as an early showrunner often goes unnoted. Even while asserting the collaborative nature of television, it is crucial to account for her feminist contributions and the explicit feminism of the show. By the middle 2000s, the industry would more commonly use the term "showrunner" to describe the head of production on certain television series, particularly those who were seen as authors of "legitimate" or "elevated" programming. While the designation is not regularly used in show credits, it is the case—especially so with "aestheticized television" (series such as *Breaking Bad*, *Mad Men*, or *Twin Peaks*)—that the showrunner is seen as "potentially an auteur: an artist of unique vision whose experiences and personality are expressed through storytelling craft, and whose presence in cultural discourses functions to produce authority for" the medium, according to Michael Z. Newman and Elana Levine (Newman and Levine 2012: 38).

For Women, By Women

In this showrunner role, Harrison consciously generated domestic suspense and horror for primarily female audiences. As Annie Berke claims in *Their Own Best Creations: Women Writers in Postwar Television*, "television demands to be reread as not only for women in the postwar era, but also by them, even if the credited author is male" (2022: 154). Harrison cultivated numerous women writers, creating pipelines for seasoned and budding talent alike. By acquiring and adapting their source material for the series, she incorporated a wide array of established writers, including Adela Rogers St. Johns, Gina Kaus, Margaret Manners, Marie Belloc Lowndes, Dorothy L. Sayers, Margaret Cousins, Lillian de la Torre, Patricia Highsmith, Margery Vosper, and Ann Bridge (aka Mary Ann Dolling).

Harrison also ushered into television new or struggling writers such as Emily Neff and Helen Nielsen. In the instance of Marian B. Cockrell (who wrote individual episodes and additionally partnered with her husband Frances Cockrell), Harrison helped support the transition of writers from studio-era film production to television.[5] Among Cockrell's many contributions is the crucial first-season episode "Into Thin Air," an adaptation of the vanishing-lady tale, which features Hitchcock's daughter Patricia and pays homage to *The Lady Vanishes* (1938; see Fig. 24.2). In ways that were career-sustaining, she assigned teleplay writing on a recurring basis to pros like Charlotte Armstrong, Kathleen Hite, and Sarett Rudley (whom Harrison would hire for a total of four series across two decades). In *Alfred Hitchcock Presents*' sixth season, Harrison recruited independent filmmaker Ida Lupino—the only woman at that time who was writing, directing, and producing films—to direct two episodes (see Fig. 24.3). In Season 1 of *The Alfred Hitchcock Hour*, Harrison produced the episode "The Lonely Hours," which featured a women-only cast, a decision determined by the story's intense treatment of motherhood (Grams and Wikstrom 2001: 413). To review the series, then, is to more fully comprehend Shamley Productions as a female-led enterprise that deliberately created pipelines for women in the industry.

More than a mere propensity of Harrison's, the cultivation of women writers and female talent functioned as an industrial norm for the series. This was notably the case in the first few years but persisted because associate producer Lloyd (who was promoted to producer in 1962) proved to be well aligned with Harrison's approach.[6] It was Harrison whom—through long battles over quiet back channels—orchestrated the hiring of Lloyd, enabling him to return to the industry from a decade-long studio blacklist (Lane 2020: 257). In numerous instances, she leveraged her powerful position (while often invoking Hitchcock's preeminence) to revitalize the careers of directors, writers, and actors who had been blacklisted or "graylisted" during the McCarthy era.[7]

Although women's contributions of the series are often rendered practically invisible by the emphasis on Hitchcock as auteur, it is crucial to note that this did not happen with full force until the late 1960s and early 1970s, when auteur theory gained traction through film retrospectives, revivals, and the burgeoning of campus cinemas and academic courses. Only then was Hitchcock's importance to *Alfred Hitchcock Presents* strongly asserted (Kapsis 1992: 111). In contrast to feature articles and interviews in the trade and popular press during the show's initial run, which paid specific attention to the producers and co-collaborators who shaped the production, subsequent critical essays and fan reviews largely posited *Alfred Hitchcock Presents* as a series of Hitchcock television films, a point underscored through phrases such as "Hitchcock's TV films" and "the television films of Alfred Hitchcock" (*Time*, December 26, 1955, p. 46; *Variety*, February 23, 1955, p. 2; *TV Guide*, March 8, 1958, pp. 17–19; *New York Times*, November 1, 1960, p. 48; Nolan 1968; Mamber 1971). This locked conversation, which hinged

Figure 24.2 Marian B. Cockrell wrote the episode "Into Thin Air," featuring Patricia Hitchcock as Diana Winthrop in the Vanishing Lady tale.

"Into Thin Air," directed by Don Medford. © Shamley Productions 1955. All rights reserved. Still courtesy of Photofest.

Figure 24.3 Joan Harrison and Ida Lupino on the set of "Sybilla."

Directed by Ida Lupino. © Shamley Productions 1960. All rights reserved. © Courtesy Imago images/ Everett.

so centrally on Hitchcock as film director, notably was unfolding in the last decade of his career, with the release of *Frenzy* (1972) and *Family Plot* (1976). *Frenzy*'s premiere in particular, as Kapsis demonstrates, provided an occasion for Hitchcock's artistic stature to be reasserted and rearticulated, specifically by a new generation of reviewers (e.g., Richard Schickel, Vincent Canby, and Janet Maslin) who were simultaneously invested in making a case for the American film industry as a place where artistry could thrive (Kapsis 1992: 114).

Reviving the Past

The television series was revived by NBC in 1985 as *The New Alfred Hitchcock Presents*. Following the May 5 airing of *Alfred Hitchcock Presents: The Movie*, a two-hour omnibus that contained four reworked episodes, twenty-two episodes were commissioned for the 1985–1986 season. (Hitchcock's opening and closing sequences were colorized and incorporated in each episode.) Tellingly, NBC marketed *The New Alfred Hitchcock Presents* alongside the premiere of its much-hyped anthology series produced by Steven Spielberg, *Amazing Stories*. Because the two shows were programmed back to back in prime positions on Sunday evenings, Hitchcock was rebranded as an auteur for contemporary audiences through a campaign that capitalized on Spielberg's status as a "boy wonder" and blockbuster director.

The heavy auteur discourse around *Amazing Stories* dramatically shaped critical reception of *The New Alfred Hitchcock Presents*. Aside from an "unprecedented commitment" of budget, the network kept a virtual blackout on information about Spielberg's series (Mitchell 1985: 63). In the absence of details on its premise or storylines, the sole emphasis leading up to the season premiere was on *Amazing Stories*' roster of recognized (or "hotshot") directors. At the time, Elvis Mitchell commented, "The list, which includes Spielberg, Martin Scorsese, Clint Eastwood, Thomas Carter, Burt Reynolds, Irvin Kershner, Paul Bartel, Bob Clark, Peter Hyams, reads like some 'Happy Holidays from the DGA [Directors Guild of America]' advertisement that one would find on the pages of *Daily Variety*" (Mitchell 1985: 63).[8] *The New Alfred Hitchcock Presents* was produced and marketed similarly, spotlighting both rising and esteemed directors, such as Frank Pierson, Tim Burton, and Brian De Palma (who would ultimately not helm an episode). In this way, *The New Alfred Hitchcock Presents* and *Amazing Stories* reflected together a shared romance with the auteur. Moreover, NBC's pairing of the shows yoked a classic past to "unprecedented" works of present visionaries.

The paradox of such preoccupation with the male director's mystique—left over from the show's first iteration in the 1950s and 1960s—is that *The New Alfred Hitchcock Presents* series was premiering during an era of fervent activity for independent and emerging women film directors. Filmmakers such as Martha Coolidge, Claudia Weill, Kathleen Collins, Donna Deitch, Penelope Spheeris, and Amy Heckerling were making great gains at festivals. In 1982, Susan Seidelman's *Smithereens* became the first feature by any American director to be screened in competition at Cannes. Many female directors were making their second feature films, even though women comprised only 0.5 percent of the DGA in 1985 (Rickey 2017).[9]

The fact that Joan Tewksbury and DGA- and Emmy-nominated Randa Haines directed episodes for *The New Alfred Hitchcock Presents* in the first season suggests that women certainly participated. However, their lack of mention in the publicity and the overall gender disparity (two women out of twenty-five directors) illustrate how the perpetuation of auteur logic led to their marginalization. At a time when women's flourishing careers might have been mobilized creatively toward a recalibration of the Hitchcock series, they were relegated to the background.

Bearing in mind that television has always been a writers' medium, women writers were not highly prioritized in the 1980s reboot, either. As with directors, only two of twenty-five writers were women in *The New Alfred Hitchcock Presents*' first season (one of whom was Tewksbury on a different episode than she directed). Without question, many more women wrote for *Alfred Hitchcock Presents* and *The Alfred Hitchcock Hour* in the 1950s and 1960s. In effect, due to the industry conditions in the 1980s, numerous opportunities to reenvision the series outside of the conventional trope of the (male) genius were missed and the way was paved for critical discourse around the new series to reassert Hitchcock's centrality. This perspective is helpful in recognizing that the conception and marketing of *The New Alfred Hitchcock Presents* might have taken a different path; however, certain auteurist narratives won out over other viable frameworks.

Over the past several decades, a few factors have opened possibilities for understanding *Alfred Hitchcock Presents* in fresh ways. Even as it appears that many scholars and critics are prone toward auteurism—and even as they frequently privilege the Hitchcock-directed episodes of the original series—the stage is set for critical reception to reframe *Alfred Hitchcock Presents* through multiple lenses. Having found much wider release—through airings that began on Nick at Nite and TV Land in the 1990s and remain prevalent today via outlets such as MeTV, Cozi TV, Hulu, and YouTube—the series has engaged many audiences, galvanizing a proliferation of readings, fan communities, and a plethora of voices. Furthermore, with the media landscape having changed considerably and women of many diverse backgrounds having assumed roles as television writers, directors, executives, and showrunners, cultural alternatives to the auteur father figure or boy wonder have been unharnessed. Through these contexts, scholars might productively reimagine fresh motifs, vocabularies, tools, and imagery to apprehend authorship in relation to *Alfred Hitchcock Presents*.

Moreover, work by scholars such as Erin Hill, J. E. Smyth, Annie Berke, and Jennifer Clarke has provided an array of feminist interventions into industry studies and production histories, charting a course for approaching Hitchcock studies differently (Hill 2016; Smyth 2018; Berke 2022; Clarke 2024). Contributing to this research have been the annual reports by the Center for Study of Women in Television and Film (initiated at San Diego State University in 1998), which have provided much-needed data on gender formations in media industries.

I would point to an often-ignored watershed moment that catalyzed many scholars to rethink previous notions regarding the way Hitchcock authorship has been historicized and theorized: the Hitchcock Centennial Conference hosted by the Department of Cinema Studies at New York University in October 1999. Bringing together scholars, critics, curators, and archivists with writers, actors, and other collaborators who had worked with Hitchcock, the "largest conference ever devoted" to the director turned out to offer a unique forum in which many women's contributions came to light in unexpected ways and were connected in a manner that would foster unprecedented inroads in media theory and history (*New York Times*, October 12, 1999, p. E1; Allen 2002; Raubicheck 2002; Poague 2011). These overlapping dialogues not only gave rise to women chronicling their experiences but also generated more complex understandings of the methods that inform the work of Hitchcock and his collaborators (to say nothing of the scholarly methodologies that might be required to further grasp such practices).

Considering the accrual of new forms of knowledge about *Alfred Hitchcock Presents* and *The Alfred Hitchcock Hour*, and in the context of methodologies recently shaped by media studies informed by feminist methods, racial inquiry, and queer theory, this is a particularly inviting moment to examine Hitchcock's television work. The partiality that we have seen by scholars toward analyzing the

Hitchcock-directed episodes has left much of the series unexplored, and vast ground remains open. Shamley Productions' unique production practices and configurations of power supply numerous lines for critical inquiry. With exciting scholarship to build on, this space is anything but a small screen for those seeking to take up the challenge. The analysis put forward here, reconsidering the series through the perspective of female authorship, offers but one example of many potential avenues. Just as they are ripe for feminist analysis, *Alfred Hitchcock Presents* and *The Alfred Hitchcock Hour* furnish a multitude of intriguing possibilities.

Acknowledgments

I express deep gratitude to Stephen Bowie for generously sharing with me his primary research on the *Alfred Hitchcock Presents* and *The Alfred Hitchcock Hour* series, which has informed the assertions made here. These contain correspondence and interviews, which Bowie conducted over several years in the 1990s. Specific materials are cited here. I also thank Jennifer Pena, doctoral student in communication at the University of Miami, for research assistance.

Notes

1. *Suspicion* ran for forty-two episodes from 1957 to 1958. Hitchcock directed "Incident at a Corner" for *Ford Startime*, which aired on April 5, 1960.
2. Hitchcock directed seventeen episodes for *Alfred Hitchcock Presents* and "I Saw the Whole Thing" in Season 1 of *The Alfred Hitchcock Hour*.
3. Throughout this essay, for stylistic reasons, I refer to the series as a whole when referencing any portion or all of *Alfred Hitchcock Presents* or *The Alfred Hitchcock Hour*. This is not meant to collapse differences between the two.
4. The addition of Lloyd was also meant to support the production of *Suspicion*. The first (and only) season would alternate twenty-two filmed episodes generated by Revue in Los Angeles with twenty live episodes broadcast from the East Coast by S. Mark Smith and Mort Abrahams.
5. Harrison shared screen credit as cowriter with Marian B. Cockrell on *Dark Waters* (1943). It is often assumed that they worked together on *Dark Waters*. However, due to the production circumstances, in which Harrison played more of an uncredited producer role, the script was first drafted by Cockrell and then revised by Harrison, with little collaboration between the two (Lane 2020: 164–165).
6. In a prominent example, Lloyd hired Leigh Brackett to write two teleplays for *The Alfred Hitchcock Hour*. Brackett was an influential writer of science fiction and highly respected for her contributions to such screenplays as *The Big Sleep* (1946) and *Rio Bravo* (1959).
7. Paul Henreid (Harrison's longtime friend and colleague) is perhaps the best example of the way that Harrison strategically used the platform of *Alfred Hitchcock Presents* and *The Alfred Hitchcock Hour* to resuscitate the careers of exiled filmmakers; having been cut off from the major studios, Henreid regained his footing by helming forty-eight episodes of *Alfred Hitchcock Presents* and *The Alfred Hitchcock Hour*, going on to direct for numerous television series. See Lane 2020: 257.
8. Burt Reynolds, who would direct "Guilt Trip" for *Amazing Stories*, also directed "Method Actor" for *The New Alfred Hitchcock Presents* (November 10, 1985) and had starred in "Escape to Sonoita" in Season 5 (June 26, 1960) of *Alfred Hitchcock Presents*.
9. Some of women's progress has been attributed to the 1983 class-action lawsuit filed against the DGA on behalf of the Original Six (the founding members of the Women's Steering Committee of the Directors Guild of

America). An enormous legal setback occurred in spring 1985—in fact, only two months prior to the broadcast of *Alfred Hitchcock Presents: The Movie*—when the judge dismissed the case, sending a clear signal that women directors were not supported in their quest for equal employment.

References

Allen, R. (2002) "An Interview with Jay Presson Allen, in C. Brookhouse and S. Gottlieb (eds), *Framing Hitchcock: Selected Essays from the Hitchcock Annual*, Detroit, Mich.: Wayne State University Press, pp. 206–218.

Anderson, C. (2013) *Hollywood TV: The Studio System in the Fifties*, Austin, Tex.: University of Texas Press.

Bagni-Dubov, G. (1997) Letter to Stephen Bowie, June 20.

Berke, A. (2022) *Their Own Best Creations: Women Writers in Postwar Television*, Berkeley, Calif.: University of California Press.

Clark, J. S. (2024) *Producing Feminism: Television Work in the Age of Women's Liberation*, Berkeley, Calif.: University of California Press.

Cockrell, M. B. (c. 1996) Letter to Stephen Bowie, n.d.

Elfman, I. (1996) Letter to Stephen Bowie, February 21.

Erish, A. (2009) "Reclaiming *Alfred Hitchcock Presents*," *Quarterly Review of Film and Video*, 26 (5): 385–392.

Grams, M., and P. Wikstrom (2001) *The Alfred Hitchcock Presents Companion*, Churchville, Md.: OTR Publishing.

Hersey, C. (2014) "The Televisual Hitchcockian Object and Domestic Space in *Alfred Hitchcock Presents*," *Quarterly Review of Film and Video*, 31 (8): 723–733.

Hessler, G. (1997) Interview with Stephen Bowie, July 29.

Hill, E. (2016) *Never Done: A History of Women's Work in Media Production*, New Brunswick, NJ: Rutgers University Press.

Kapsis, R. (1992) *Hitchcock: The Making of a Reputation*, Chicago, Ill.: University of Chicago Press.

Lane, C. (2020) *Phantom Lady: Joan Harrison, Hollywood Producer—The Forgotten Woman behind Hitchcock*, Chicago, Ill.: Chicago Review Press.

Leitch, T. (1999) "The Outer Circle: Hitchcock on Television," in R. Allen and S. Ishii Gonzales (eds), *Alfred Hitchcock: Centenary Essays*, London: British Film Institute, pp. 59–71.

Mamber, S. (1971) "The Television Films of Alfred Hitchcock," *Cinema*, 7 (1): 2–7.

McCarty, J., and B. Kelleher (1985) Alfred Hitchcock Presents*: An Illustrated Guide to the Ten-Year Television Career of the Master of Suspense*, New York: St. Martin's Press.

Mitchell, E. (1985) "Amazing Anthologies," *Film Comment*, 21 (5): 63–65, 80.

Newman, M., and E. Levine (2012) *Legitimating Television: Media Convergence and Cultural Status*, London and New York: Routledge.

Nolan, J. E. (1968) "Hitchcock's TV Films," *Film Fan Monthly*, June, pp. 3–6.

Poague, L. (2011) "'Tell Me the Story So Far': Hitchcock and His Writers," in L. Poague and T. Leitch (eds), *A Companion to Alfred Hitchcock*, Malden, Mass.: Wiley-Blackwell, pp. 141–161.

Prouty, H. (1984) The Alfred Hitchcock Teleguide. Unpublished reference draft, West Hollywood, Calif.

Raubicheck, W. (2002) "Working with Hitchcock: A Collaborators' Forum with Patricia Hitchcock, Janet Leigh, Teresa Wright, and Eva Marie Saint," *Hitchcock Annual*, vol. 11, pp. 32–66.

Rebello, S. (2013) *Alfred Hitchcock and the Making of Psycho*, New York: Soft Skull.

Rickey, C. (2017) "What Happened to the Female Directors of Hollywood?" *Truthdig*, March 17, www.truthdig.com/articles/what-happened-to-the-female-directors-of-hollywood-part-4

Schatz, T. (2010) *The Genius of the System: Hollywood Filmmaking in the Studio Era*, Minneapolis, Minn.: University of Minnesota Press.

Slesar, H. (1996) Letter to Stephen Bowie, February 20.

Smyth, J. E. (2018) *Nobody's Girl Friday: The Women Who Ran Hollywood*, New York: Oxford University Press.

Truffaut, F. (1954) "Une certaine tendance du cinéma français," *Cahiers du Cinéma*, 31 (1): 15–28.

Truffaut, F. (1985) *Hitchcock*, rev. edn, New York: Simon & Schuster.

Chapter 25

Life after Death

Preserving and Promoting Hitchcock's TV Persona

Robert E. Kapsis

This chapter focuses on "small-screen Hitchcock" by exploring and assessing the role of Alfred Hitchcock's family and advisers in preserving and promoting his legacy and by documenting the extent to which the family's investment in Hitchcock's legacy has been an effective strategy for influencing the ongoing reception of his work in the present day. The major thrust of the present essay is to call attention to the Hitchcock family's investment in preserving and extending Hitchcock's TV work—particularly by keeping alive his TV persona—and to provide documentation of the family's considerable success in doing so, not only in the USA but globally. Much of the documentation points to several key distribution deals carved out since Hitchcock's death in 1980 that revolved around Hitchcock's television series from the 1950s and 1960s as well as plans introduced at different points in time, to develop a new series or property inspired by the original. Other findings reported here and in Chapter 12 (especially in connection with the critical reception of *Marnie*) suggest the importance of factors external to the family (such as the depth of Hitchcock's international fan base), which have also contributed substantially to the longevity and elasticity of Hitchcock's posthumous reputation.

The cornerstone of this chapter is unprecedented access to archives from the Hitchcock Family Trust, a heretofore-unexamined collection that will shed new light on the forces that have shaped Hitchcock's posthumous reputation. Through the estate's chief executor, the Hitchcock family has granted me access to this untapped resource. Materials especially relevant for this chapter include:

- distribution deals involving Hitchcock's television series from the 1950s and 1960s and plans to develop a new series or related projects;
- all movie distribution agreements executed since 1980 (the year of Hitchcock's death) as well as records of the negotiations leading up to them;
- documentation of efforts to prevent name infringement;
- development and maintenance of the official Hitchcock website;

- requests to license Hitchcock's image for advertising campaigns involving the sale of cameras, condominiums, T-shirts and other wearing apparel, and the use of the Hitchcock brand in the heart of record albums (e.g., Eminem's 2020 rap album *Music to Be Murdered By*) as well as in video games, puzzles, and board games;
- requests for use of Hitchcock-related materials for museum exhibitions, documentaries, scholarly books, and articles; and
- requests for producing feature films and TV shows based on Hitchcock's "unrealized projects" (especially *Kaleidoscope* [1964–1967], *Mary Rose* [circa 1964], and *The Short Night* [1976–1979]).

Having access to such a broad range of requests for use of Hitchcock-related materials makes it possible to determine which "Hitchcock" or combination of "Hitchcocks" dominate these various requests, e.g., "Hitchcock the serious film artist" (and innovator) versus "Hitchcock the popular entertainer" versus "Hitchcock the TV personality" and to be able to do so country by country.

Pat Hitchcock and the Legacy of Her Parents

Patricia Hitchcock O'Connell, the only child of famed filmmaker Alfred Hitchcock and [who] championed his work in the decades following his death, has died at age 93. "She was always really good at protecting the legacy of my grandparents and making sure they were always remembered," said [Tere] Carrubba, one of her three daughters.

(*Los Angeles Times*, August 11, 2021)

My mother [Alma Reville Hitchcock] had much more to do with the films than she has ever been given credit for—he depended on her for everything, absolutely everything.

(Rose 1999)

Sociologists Kurt Lang and Gladys Engel Lang have suggested several reasons to account for the durability of a reputation, including "the availability of others who, after the artist's death, have a stake in preserving or giving a boost to that reputation [and] the artist's own efforts, in his lifetime, to protect or project his reputation" (Lang and Lang 1988: 86). For almost forty years, Hitchcock's daughter Patricia Hitchcock O'Connell (1928–2021) was actively engaged in advancing and protecting the legacy of both her father and mother. Today, this responsibility is largely in the hands of her three daughters.

Focusing on how Pat Hitchcock and other caretakers of the estate approached the 1999 celebration of Hitchcock's 100th anniversary is instructive. Multiple events worldwide, especially in the USA and England, heralded this milestone, yet when I asked Leland Faust, the estate's chief trustee, to comment on the family's involvement in the anniversary, his response surprised me: "The family really didn't actually have to do that much preparation because there were so many others eager to get involved," he said (Faust 2021). Still, for the caretakers of the Hitchcock Family Trust, preparations for Hitchcock's 100th did pose a major challenge: how to enhance Hitchcock's reputation as a serious artist while, at the same time, not diminishing or trivializing his persona as a popular entertainer nor reducing the monetary value of the Hitchcock brand. The family's imprimatur of *Multimedia Hitchcock*—an interactive kiosk I developed for

New York's Museum of Modern Art and other nonprofit institutions celebrating the Hitchcock Centennial in 1999—seemed to bear this out (Fig. 25.1). While preparing *Multimedia Hitchcock* for the centennial, it soon became apparent to me that my early characterization of it as a "showcase for the enduring genius of Hitchcock as artist, entertainer, and self-publicist" had quite accurately encapsulated what had attracted the Hitchcock family to my project in the first place.[1] Moreover, his daughter, Pat Hitchcock, had understood that while there were numerous others who could and would make the case for viewing Hitchcock as a major artist, her talking points during interviews conducted around this time, were shrewdly strategized, reminding those privy to these interviews (viewers/readers) of her famous father's extraordinary skills as a popular entertainer and TV host. In doing so, she essentially downplayed his auteur status as a major artist by calling attention to her mother's own trailblazing career as a skilled filmmaker and as collaborator, in varying degrees, on all of her husband's films—"[having] had much more to do with [the success of her husband's] films than she had ever been given credit for" (Rose 1999).

We see this strategy playing out in a number of Pat Hitchcock's interviews recorded in 1999 around the time of the centennial. Consider, for example, her appearance on Charlie Rose's late-night interview program on public television where she left it to Rose's other guests that evening—filmmaker Peter Bogdanovich and MoMA's senior curator Larry Kardish—to make the case that her father was a major artist:

Figure 25.1 Installation view of the exhibition "Alfred Hitchcock Centenary," April 15–August 17, 1999.

Photographic Archive, The Museum of Modern Art Archives, New York, IN1831.5. Photograph by Thomas Griesel. Digital Image © The Museum of Modern Art/Licensed by SCALA.

Charlie Rose: Did he consider himself—to use a bad word—[an] "auteur"... [or] did he consider himself simply a storyteller who made movies of a suspense nature? Or did he know and feel and define himself as this kind of film auteur?

Pat Hitchcock O'Connell: No. He was a man who told a story. He wanted to tell that story in the best way he could.

Charlie Rose: Did he think he was an artist, rather than just [a storyteller]?

Pat Hitchcock O'Connell: I don't think ... he did ... It was amazing, once he had made a picture and then gone out to sell that picture, he [would forget] all about that picture [and] go on to the next one.

Laurence Kardish: But we [at MoMA] regard [Hitchcock] as an artist. And Peter was one of the ... first in this country to do so. He did the first [Hitchcock] retrospective at the Museum of Modern Art in 1963. And I think that [our first film] curator, Iris Barry, certainly considered him an artist as early as the late '20s.

Another of her talking points was that after the success of his television show had brought him even greater fame worldwide, Hitchcock started worrying about how this might adversely impact on the reception of his feature films. As Pat explained it to Rose, her father felt that he would now have to factor in the possibility that his new celebrity status could become a distraction for his increasing fan base. Take, for example, his cameo appearances. Hitchcock thought now that it might make sense for him to start programming his "little walk-ons" earlier in his films—well before jump-starting the film's major plotline because of his concern that audiences might be distracted by the thought of when in the film he would be making his cameo appearance, and yet, at the same time, he wouldn't want to deny them from being able to say, "There he is. There he is." In other words, Hitchcock reasoned that by planting his cameo appearances earlier and earlier in his films, his fans would be less likely to be distracted from experiencing the full power of his films.[2] Another of her talking points was that his hosting of the TV show had been the key to its success and that the taping of his TV appearances—especially the zany monologues ghostwritten for him to recite, was something he really got a kick out of doing (Rose 1999; see also Kapsis 1992: 29–34).[3]

Retooling Hitchcock's TV Persona

Twenty years before the Hitchcock centennial and only a short time after Hitchcock's death in 1980, a distribution deal inspired by Hitchcock's television series from the 1950s and 1960s gained momentum, having benefitted significantly from the commercial and critical success of the rerelease, a few years earlier, of his five so-called "lost" Hitchcock films—*Rope*, *Rear Window*, *The Trouble with Harry*, *The Man Who Knew Too Much*, and *Vertigo*, which had been taken out of circulation by Hitchcock during the early 1970s. Their success had motivated Universal's television division to develop the idea of remaking four episodes from Hitchcock's suspense series that originally aired in the early 1960s for a two-hour anthology movie titled *Alfred Hitchcock Presents* that would include colorized versions of Hitchcock's original opening and closing remarks made to match the new material. And, as would be expected, the Hitchcock estate was quick to come on board in support of the project.

When they first came up with the idea for the television movie, Universal and NBC entered into lengthy negotiations with the Hitchcock estate. "It was a complicated negotiation," said Tom Thayer, a Universal vice president.

We had the remake rights to some of the episodes, while the estate had rights to others. In any case, they had all rights to Hitchcock's likeness and the use of his name. So we spent a lot of time talking to the lawyers. Hitchcock's daughter also had to give her approval. They were all very cooperative, and once they approved the overall concept, they did not insist on approving each individual script.

(*New York Times*, January 29, 1985, p. 16)

The two-hour anthology movie first aired in late spring of 1985 before morphing into a weekly anthology series, which ran for two seasons. Coincidentally, around this time I was teaching an undergraduate Hitchcock course, and several of my students who had watched episodes from the new series went into shock when I told them that Hitchcock had died in 1980. Life after death, indeed.

Turning ahead to 2016, we learn of a similar project first announced in the *Hollywood Reporter* that the Hitchcock estate had "inked a deal" with Universal Cable Productions (UCP) to "develop an anthology series called *Welcome to Hitchcock* based on the filmmaker's most popular movies including *The Birds* and *Psycho* and television series, *Alfred Hitchcock Presents*." According to the article, the new show would focus on "a single season long mystery or crime in the vein of Hitchcock's classic style." The article then quotes Dawn Olmsted, UCP's executive vice president of development, adding, "Long after his death, Alfred Hitchcock continues to be one of the most celebrated directors and visionaries in the world, a master manipulator of the macabre … We're honored that the Hitchcock Estate has put its trust in our studio to pay homage to his work." The article ends with one of Hitchcock's granddaughters getting the last word: "Our grandfather always collaborated with the best and the brightest to help shape his vision … We're confident that Universal Cable Productions will take great care in helping us to continue preserving his legacy" (*Hollywood Reporter*, September 28, 2016).

But, as of September 2022, there were few signs that *Welcome to Hitchcock* would ever see the light of day, while a more recent project, *Alfred Hitchcock Presents: The Musical*, was on the uptick—with expectations running high that the show would eventually make it to Broadway.[4]

There had been signs of trouble brewing predating the July 2016 contractual agreement worked out between the Hitchcock estate, Universal's cable division, and the production company handling the project.[5] Early on in the negotiations, an attorney representing the production company argued that his clients were entitled to a larger cut of the royalties than was the Hitchcock estate. A compromise was soon reached.[6] Another stumbling block that would prove fatal to the proposed series was the poor quality of the script for its one-hour pilot (Script, *Welcome to Hitchcock*, 2016). Early attempts to redress this problem included digging up drafts of several of Hitchcock's unrealized film projects for ideas, among them, *Kaleidoscope* (1964–1967), *Mary Rose* (circa 1964), and *The Short Night* (1976–1979). A far simpler solution and one that never occurred to the production team would have been to add a few lines here and there for a small-screen Hitchcock look-alike to recite—a Hitchcock-like narrator of sorts who on occasion might comment on the action—a role which, much to my amazement, was missing from all the versions of the script I reviewed. Meanwhile, Universal's cable division was rapidly losing interest in *Welcome to Hitchcock* as other, more promising Hitchcock-inspired projects emerged such as a TV series based on *Rear Window*, the prospect (alas, short-lived) of Martin Scorsese and Leonardo DiCaprio collaborating on a remake of *Vertigo*, and a made-for-TV movie loosely based on *Rope* minus the original film's gay subtext.[7]

More innovative was the script for *Alfred Hitchcock Presents: The Musical* (dated July 13, 2018) which opens with a short prologue that ends dramatically with "A husky, British-accented voice that chimes in with two simple words: 'Good Evening.' We know that voice. We recognize that cadence. It's none other than SIR ALFRED HITCHCOCK, here to welcome us to this evening's entertainment …" Next in the script is the title of the show: "ALFRED HITCHCOCK PRESENTS: The Musical." After that, we learn that the Alfred Hitchcock look-alike will be hosting the musical and serving as the show's narrator—similar to his predecessor's role on the original TV series, and, in that role, he will sing a song appropriately titled "Good Evening," which opens with the following lyrics: "After all, knives and saws and bullets don't kill people. Petty resentments, unfulfilled desires, coveting things one should not covet—those are the things that kill people" (see Fig. 25.2).

Another interesting aspect of the script is that it incorporates easily recognizable characters drawn from several of the most famous episodes from "Alfred Hitchcock Presents" (e.g., Mary Maloney, the estranged wife from "Lamb to the Slaughter"), who are placed in stories predating the events described in the original or postdating the episodes they originally appeared in. By 2021, the production had already secured significant financial backing from Universal and other investors, which increased the odds that this Hitchcock-inspired musical would eventually see the light of day. In the fall of 2023, a "developmental reading" of the show involving prospective cast members took place at a venue in New York City with Hitchcock family members present. And in the spring of 2025, "Hitchcock Presents: The Musical" had its world premiere in Bath, England.

Next, I turn to what many might consider to be the most unusual and unexpected pitch for honoring small-screen Hitchcock to date—one conceived by the brilliant rapper and showman Eminem. The first phase of his tribute was launched in early 2020, and, over the course of the year, it would take on

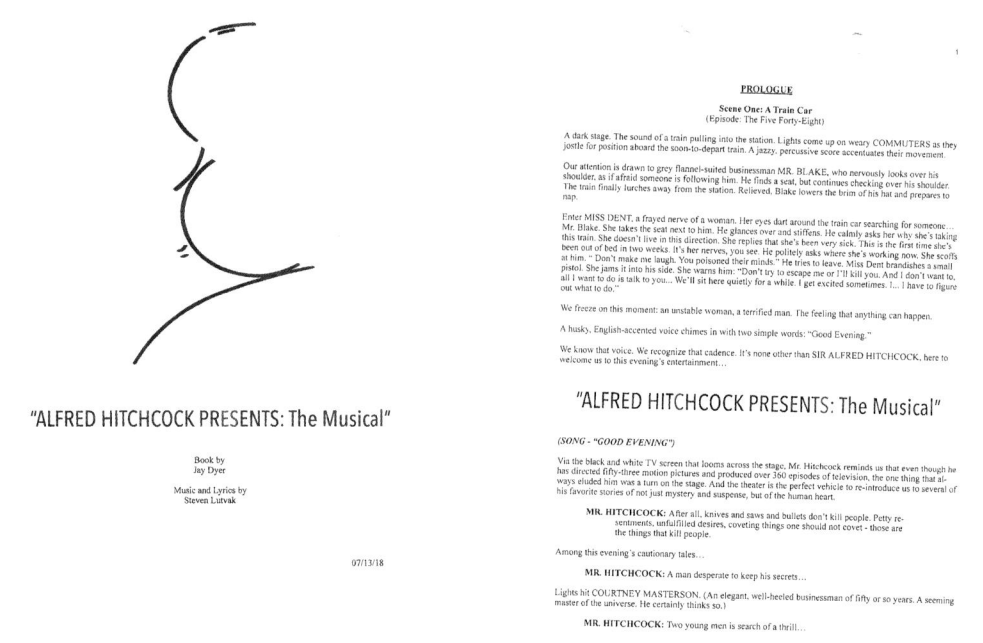

Figure 25.2 Script for *Alfred Hitchcock Presents: The Musical* (2018), July 13.
Courtesy the Hitchcock Family Trust.

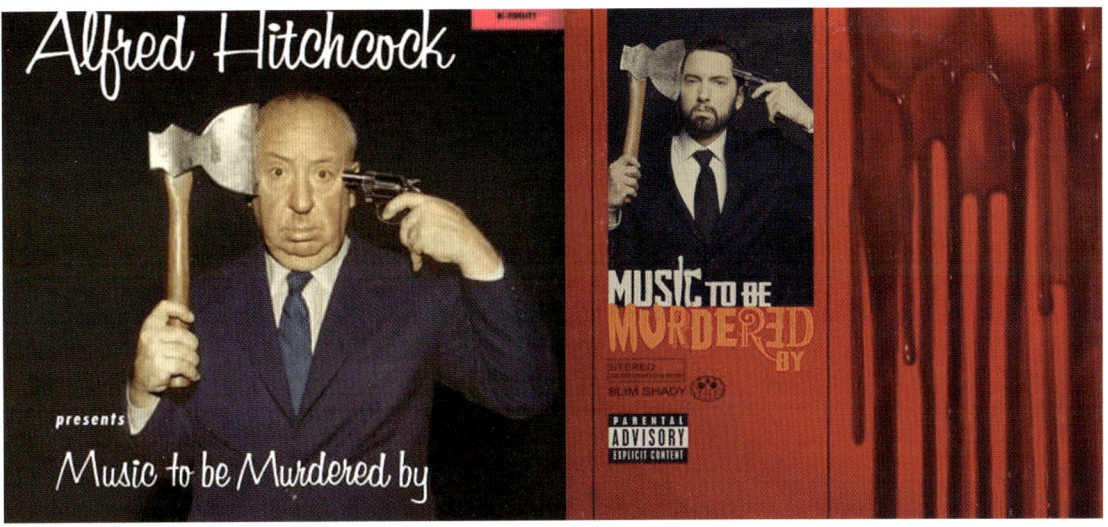

Figure 25.3 *Variety* (2020) "Eminem Pays Homage to Alfred Hitchcock with 'Murdered' Album Cover and Title Album," January 16. Courtesy of the Alfred Hitchcock Trust

different shapes and forms. Here is how *Variety* characterized the public unveiling (without any prior warning) of Eminem's surprise tribute to small-screen Hitchcock:

> Eminem may not be the Master of Suspense: He just dropped his new album, "Music to Be Murdered By," Thursday at midnight, without even milking it with any prior warning. But he appears to be a fan of Alfred Hitchcock anyway. The new set shares its title and cover concept with the one and only album Hitchcock ever released, a 1958 collection that had the legendary director dropping bits of his trademark dry and macabre humor between easy listening-style instrumental arrangements of songs with ironically appropriate titles, like "I'll Never Smile Again" and "I Don't Stand a Ghost of a Chance with You." As Hitchcock did, Eminem poses holding both a hatchet and pistol to his head [see Fig. 25.3].
>
> The album also uses portions of Hitchcock's spoken-word contributions to the '58 album, in interludes titled "Alfred" and "Alfred (Outro)." Eminem's album ends just as Hitchcock's did: with the filmmaker saying, "If you haven't been murdered, I can only say better luck next time. If you have been, goodnight, wherever you are."
>
> (*Variety*, January 16, 2020)

Released in mid January 2020, this album turned out to be just the warm-up to Eminem's yearlong homage to Hitchcock. Eleven months later, he released a second album—a sequel to the first one in the form of a deluxe edition of the original—and followed that a few months later with a cleverly conceived music video featuring an animated version of Eminem's likeness rapping his heart out while in the background one can discern throughout the video's eight-minute duration the theme song from Hitchcock's original series—a tune originally conceived in the mid-nineteenth century by French composer Charles Gounod for his opera *Faust* (see Fig. 25.4).

Figure 25.4 The image from Eminem's animated short, featuring him at the keyboard serenading Hitchcock is a loving homage to Hitchcock's cameo appearance in *Rear Window*.

The details of the licensing agreement for the second album, and all the potential publicity surrounding it, had been approved only a few weeks before the expanded album was released. Below are the relevant passages from the licensing arrangement between Eminem's production company and the Hitchcock Family Trust that reveal the scope and complexity of a deal worked out within such a short time frame.

This nonexclusive license and release is for the purpose of the album embodying the musical performances of the recording artist professionally known as "Eminem" ("Artist") entitled "Music To Be Murdered By" Deluxe Edition The B-Sides with additional album artwork as depicted in Exhibit A (the "Eminem Album") which additional album artwork and title was based upon and/or inspired by the Alfred Hitchcock album entitled "Music To Be Murdered By" ("AH Album") and other Alfred Hitchcock works with respect to the depiction of a bird and graveyard as shown in Exhibit A ("Other References"), and other uses of the foregoing as expressly set forth herein … In consideration of payment … [the estate of Alfred Hitchcock] hereby consents, licenses and grants to [Eminem's production company] its licensees, designees, and assigns, including without limitation, Interscope Records ("Licensee"), the nonexclusive right, license, and permission to use and exploit throughout the universe, in perpetuity any and all rights that the [Hitchcock Estate] may have, on a quit claim basis, in the title and album artwork of the "AH Album" and "Other References" for the exploitation of the Eminem Album, including the right to use the title and additional album artwork as depicted in Exhibit A for the manufacture and distribution of phonograph records in all audio and audiovisual configurations and formats and in all media … now known or hereinafter devised.
(Licensing Arrangement with Eminem, December 2020)

Closing the Eminem deal had meant a lot to the Hitchcock family. For here at long last, according to Leland Faust, was a project whose appeal extended to three generations of Hitchcock's—his daughter Pat, her three children, and her children's children—and a project that might help inspire a new generation of Hitchcock fans and aficionados. As one fan of both Hitchcock and Eminem perceptively put it:

Been thinking, it would have been really cool if they hyped the album up as Eminem versus Hitchcock and used his samples more throughout the album … The Em demographic might not know it, but in his day Hitchcock was as big and controversial as Eminem. In the 60's hearing somebody talk so casually about murder would have been the equivalent of Em's lines about mass-shootings, people were like "You can't say that!" even then.
(Alfred Hitchcock LLC. Alfred Hitchcock, 2020)

In fact, it was Pat Hitchcock, not her father, who, on April 1, 1958, and incognito, had signed off on the original record deal for the album *Music to be Murdered By* which until now had been attributed to her dad alone. Perhaps astute businesswoman should be added to Pat Hitchcock's credits.[8]

Global Hitchcock: Requests from Countries around the World

The more routine kinds of requests for Hitchcock materials requiring approval from the Hitchcock Family Trust come from all over the globe. For the project previously mentioned, I have been examining in depth the dynamic or interplay of Hitchcock's various incarnations—e.g., "Hitchcock the TV entertainer" versus

"Hitchcock the artist" in those territories where such requests for Hitchcock materials are commonplace, especially Japan, France, Italy, Germany, Australia, Spain, Brazil, and Canada. One of my research goals is to determine the extent to which the caretakers of the Hitchcock Family Trust have themselves been proactive in trying to nurture, maintain and preserve the economic potency of "Hitchcock." My findings for Japan are instructive and will serve here as both a closer to this chapter and a teaser for this other research, which is ongoing.[9]

Japanese advertisers often seek permission from the Hitchcock estate to use images of Hitchcock to sell such things as toys, alcoholic beverages, condos, automobiles, and, yes, even feature films (based on a review of Hitchcock Family Trust archival materials collected April 2022). A *New York Times* piece from 1994 reports that it is commonplace for Japanese advertisers to use photos of foreign celebrities (especially dead ones) "to entertain, set a mood, grab attention" (February 20, 1994, p. 4). To illustrate this, a newspaper ad is reproduced displaying a humorous photo of Alfred Hitchcock along with a caption of Hitchcock saying, "As you can see, I'm not very good at scary things." The ad then displays a photo of a Toyota vehicle with a caption describing the vehicle as "safe and reliable." This ad, unusually direct, uses what I have been characterizing throughout this chapter as Hitchcock's small-screen persona to call attention to the car. "Television commercials," continues the piece, "also use images of Mr. Hitchcock, dubbing a voice that sounds like his—in Japanese" (*New York Times*, February 20, 1994, p. 4).

But, perhaps, the penultimate Japanese retooling of small-screen Hitchcock was the one displayed in a movie trailer from 2013 promoting the release in Japan of *Hitchcock*, the controversial Fox Searchlight film reenacting Hitchcock's life and career around the time of the making of *Psycho* (see Fig. 25.6). Here, as one reviewer astutely observed,

Figure 25.5 Two images from a Toyota TV commercial from the 1990s that reference Hitchcock's *The Birds* (1963).

two Japanese actors give their rendition of [Hitchcock's] long and varied résumé and personal history. And it's wonderful. No matter what language you speak, the comedy in the duo's performance is loud and clear. As the first actor maintains a deadpan stature throughout the sketch as Hitchcock himself, his partner goes ape as the variety of characters leading the film maker's movies.[10]

I would only add to this perceptive review that the "Hitchcock" lovingly parodied here is none other than the one repeatedly referred to in this chapter as "small-screen Hitchcock."

Figure 25.6 Two images from a Japanese movie trailer spoofing Hitchcock's *Rear Window*.
Hitchcock, directed by Sacha Gervasi © Fox Searchlight Pictures 2012. All rights reserved. Promotional video courtesy シネマトゥデイ (Cinema Today).

Still frequent but not nearly as common in Japan as the requests paying tribute to "TV Hitchcock" are those soliciting the use of film clips, movie posters, trailers, etc., at venues honoring Hitchcock, the auteur. Over the years, a number of Japanese arts organizations have made such requests, as indeed was the case during the period of the Hitchcock centennial (see, e.g., Fig. 25.7). But, overall, my sense is that Hitchcock the popular TV entertainer (or brand name) is much more of a presence or selling point in Japanese society than is Hitchcock the serious film artist.

As mentioned earlier, I have been examining this dynamic or interplay of reputations in other territories as well, especially where such requests are fairly common, and I am engaged in assessing the extent to which the caretakers of the Hitchcock Family Trust have themselves been proactive in trying to nurture, maintain, and preserve the economic potency of "Hitchcock the brand," "Hitchcock the persona," "Hitchcock the trademark," "Hitchcock the aura," "Hitchcock the TV entertainer." Consider, for example, Hitchcock's "official webpage" at www.alfredhitchcock.com and the hyperbolic content of its call or solicitation for partnerships with other brands (see Fig 25.8): "Hitchcock's global recognizability and unparalleled creativity continue to make him popular with audiences and a logical choice for brands seeking to align themselves with attributes like innovation, genius, artistry, and greatness."[11]

And the Hitchcock Trust has the contracts and other paperwork to justify such rhetorical flourishes. Globally, the Hitchcock TV persona appears to be very much alive and well.

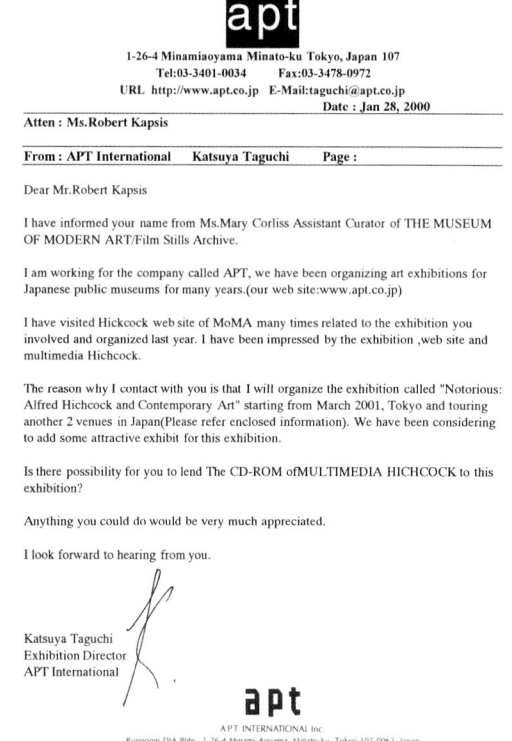

Figure 25.7 A request from Japan to honor Hitchcock, the auteur.

Courtesy of the Alfred Hitchcock Trust.

Figure 25.8 Apple simultaneously extolling and aligning themselves to the image of Hitchcock as a one-of-a-kind innovator and artistic genius—just as they did with other figures in their "Think Different" campaign, including Pablo Picasso, John Lennon and Albert Einstein.

"Think Different" Advert Campaign. © Apple. Courtesy of the Alfred Hitchcock Trust.

Notes

1. See www.moma.org/interactives/exhibitions/1999/hitchcock/multimedia_kiosk.html
2. Hitchcock's "walk ons" in *North by Northwest*, *Psycho*, and *The Birds* all occur within the first five minutes of the film.
3. In an interview published in the *Guardian* (August 27, 1999), Pat Hitchcock O'Connell makes many of the same points she had made four months earlier during her conversation with Charlie Rose (1999).
4. These projections are based on my onsite review of archival records during April 2022 and February 2024 and from numerous conversations during this period with Leland Faust—chief executor of the Hitchcock Family Trust.
5. Actually, the idea for this project originated with the production company, Vermillion Entertainment. Here's how the *Hollywood Reporter* (September 28, 2016) described the arrangement: "Vermilion Entertainment and 1492 Pictures/Ocean Blue Entertainment will produce *Welcome to Hitchcock* with UCP. The anthology marks Vermilion's first scripted television project. The Exec producers are Chris Columbus, Michael Bamathan, Timmy Thompson and Todd Thompson, who will all work alongside the Hitchcock family. Columbus will also direct the pilot. Casey Tebo will serve as coproducer."
6. Archival correspondence files.
7. A remake of *Vertigo* is still in the works. Robert Downey Jr. and his production team recently signed on to remake *Vertigo*, with Downey taking over the lead role made famous by James Stewart.
8. For more revelations about her business acumen, see *Life after Death: Preserving, Protecting, and Promoting the Legacy of Alfred Hitchcock*, unpublished manuscript.

9   Germany is another interesting case, as documented in a letter from Random House to the trustees of the Hitchcock Family Estate: "As you probably know, we are the publishers of a line of children's detective novels called the Alfred Hitchcock and the Three Investigators Series. Our license agreement with Mr. Hitchcock is worded in such a way that we are not permitted to use his name on titles added to the series after his death … The series is managing to grow in this country without Mr. Hitchcock, but the foreign publishers of the books are greatly distressed by the loss of Mr. Hitchcock's name. The German publisher, in particular, feels that the whole series will stop selling in Germany unless new titles bearing Mr. Hitchcock's name are added to it regularly.… As you may have noticed on the recent royalty statements, the bulk of the Estate's income from the Three Investigators series is now earned abroad, especially in Germany and the sums are quite substantial. We would therefore like to accommodate the foreign publishers who want to put Mr. Hitchcock's name on the series titles published after his death. To do so would require an amendment to the license agreement. Would you be willing to grant us such an amendment?" (March 5, 1982).

10 "Two Japanese Guys Reenact Alfred Hitchcock's Entire Career in Introductory 'Hitchcock' Trailer," 2013, www.hollywood.com/movies/japanese-hitchcock-trailer-57157420.

11 See www.alfredhitchcock.com/hitchcock-brand (Note: The content of Hitchcock's "official webpage" is in constant flux.)

References

Artist Agreement for the Original *Music to be Murdered By* Record (1958), April 1.
Dyer, J., and S. Lutvak (2018) Script for *Alfred Hitchcock Presents: The Musical*, July 13.
Faust, L. (2021) Interview, August 15.
Kapsis, R. (1992) *Hitchcock: The Making of a Reputation*, Chicago, Ill.: University of Chicago Press.
Kapsis, R. (n.d.) *Life after Death: Preserving and Promoting the Legacy of Alfred Hitchcock*, unpublished manuscript.
Lang, K., and G. E. Lang (1988) "Recognition and Renown: The Survival of Artistic Reputation," *American Journal of Sociology*, 94 (1): 79–109.
Licensing Arrangement with Eminem (2020), Hitchcock Archive, December 1.
Rose, C. (1999) "Conversation with Pat Hitchcock, Peter Bogdanovich, and Larry Kardish," *Charlie Rose Show*, PBS, May 5.
Script for *Welcome to Hitchcock*, received by Hitchcock Family Trust in 2016.

Chapter 26
Travels in Hitchcock's Multiverse

Joel Gunz

If word count is anything to go by, a newcomer to film studies could conclude that the twenty teleplays that Alfred Hitchcock directed don't merit sustained critical consideration. Title for title, these episodes make up over a quarter of his total directorial output, yet they've only received a tiny fraction of critical commentary when compared to his fifty-four movies. True, they are smaller in every way—from screen size to the episodes' length (23 minutes, including his bookending monologues) to their compressed production timelines of days, compared to the months and even years he put into his films—yet, as various scholars have argued, they are worthy of close viewing. Twenty-five years ago, Thomas Leitch drew attention to this deficit and called for critical reevaluation; since then, the needle has moved only slightly (Leitch 1999: 59–71).

A second gulf separates Hitchcock's own "playlets" (his word, from the intro monologue to "Revenge") from the other 340 episodes of *Alfred Hitchcock Presents* and *The Alfred Hitchcock Hour* that he did not direct. So little has been written about them that one could think that there's practically nothing there of Hitchcock to see, that they are his in name (and paycheck) only. Hitchcock criticism could thus be sorted into three hierarchal categories: his prestige work (the feature films), his minor work (the teleplays he directed), and his purportedly in-name-only projects.

However, that categorization isn't so fixed or clear-cut. For example, owing to his battles over creative control with David O. Selznick during the making of *Rebecca* (1940)—conflicts that Selznick won—Hitchcock himself maintained that it was "not a Hitchcock picture" (Truffaut 1984: 230). Which category does that one go under? The director might have dropped it into the third group. On the other hand, his involvement with the television episodes that he did not personally direct ran deeper than some have supposed. As the owner of Shamley Productions, the company responsible for the show, Hitchcock's leadership was unmistakable. Recalled *Psycho* author Robert Bloch, who scripted twelve episodes, "Hitchcock himself was generally absent in the all-too-solid flesh, but he was nonetheless a palpable presence. When the script decisions were made, there was always a reference to his taste and standards—will Hitch like this, would he disagree with that?" (McCarty and Kelleher 1985: xii).

Hitchcock concurred: "I do insist on approval on all the writers' scripts. I read every last one and make whatever suggestions I can think of" (Gottlieb 2015: 233). This was far from a mere formality, as he stressed in a television interview: "I definitely go into the stories very thoroughly with an indication as to how they should be treated" (Markle 1964). For a director who claimed that script development was the most interesting part of making a film, to put his mark on them from his desk and never set foot in the studio must have been a dream come true.

Hitchcock's duties thus dispatched on paper, he left the show in producer Joan Harrison's hands. In Chapter 24, Christina Lane likens her to what we today would call a showrunner: "Harrison was, without question, the show's most significant creative voice. She was central to the formation of the production's fundamental textual practices."

Still, home audiences expected an Alfred Hitchcock mini-movie each week, and Shamley Productions delivered. As Leitch points out, Hitchcock's persona as host and impresario exerted power over the show's creation:

> [He] is the putative controlling force stipulated by the series' actual producers, the *deus abscondida* of the program who does nothing himself but whose presumed preferences are essential to the success of the enterprise … whenever we attempt to look behind Hitchcock the impresario, we find Hitchcock the creator, and vice versa.
>
> (Leitch 1999: 69)

Hitchcock may not have been personally present in the show's day-to-day production, but he was present virtually as the "protean creator who is the true power behind the screen" (Leitch 1999: 69).

If Hitchcock was the invisible creative force behind the series—its daemonic muse—Harrison was his channel. She was uniquely up to the task. Beautiful, brilliant and independent—and a feminist before the term had common currency—she was a real-life Hitchcock blonde. A member of Alfred and Alma Hitchcock's inner circle since the early 1930s, she was practically family and, for several years, contributed to his films as a writer and producer. It's likely that some of her personality rubbed off on Hitchcock. Observes Elizabeth Karlin, "the films of Alfred Hitchcock are abounding with some of the most active and dynamic female characters to be found in 20th century cinema" (Karlin 2021: 32). Conceivably, some of the credit for this can go to Harrison's influence. Without question, they were kindred spirits—and she was his first choice to head his television enterprise. In her biography of Harrison, Lane writes, "[C]rucially, as someone who had helped Hitchcock build the bridge between his persona and his work from a very early stage, Joan was an authority like almost no other on how to produce 'Hitchcock'" (Lane 2020: 251).

All of which is to say, to relegate the vast bulk of Hitchcock's television productions to in-name-only status would sell him and his show short. On the other hand, much of the actual production was handled by others—mainly Harrison. Therefore, I propose avoiding categorical divisions and instead would envision his works along a single continuum. As objects of critical commentary, they're all fair game.

Inspired by such entertainment franchises as the Marvel Comics Multiverse, which makes room for a variety of media as well as contradictory storylines—alternate universes—I propose calling this the Hitchcockian multiverse. What can we include therein? We'd have to start with the seven germinal short stories that he wrote for the *Henley Telegraph* as a youth. As already suggested, we should include the 400+ movies and teleplays made by or under his name. There's also room for the *Alfred Hitchcock Mystery Magazine*, along with the short-story anthologies—ventures bearing his name and designed to supply a pipeline of potential candidates for screen adaptation. Twelve-year-old me would insist on the inclusion of the Alfred Hitchcock and the Three Investigators series. His unrealized work—from deleted scenes to entire pictures that were planned but not produced—occupies a virtual place in the multiverse that, like dark matter, invisibly influences his completed canon.

This Hitchcockian multiverse orbits the central universe of his feature films, each "planet" perturbing the gravity fields of the others based on proximity and the extent of Hitchcock's involvement—and are distinguished from each other by their respective physical, narrative, aesthetic, and censorship laws.

In this multiverse, stories interpenetrate in fascinating and complex ways. Hitchcock fans and scholars are already tuned into the characters and storylines that hop from one movie to the next so frequently that Hitchcock's fifty-three extant movies could be described as One Big Film. These narratives also stretch into his television series. Welcome to the Hitchcock multiverse, where it's all One Honking Huge Film.

Let's start at that blazing quasar, arguably situated at the center of Hitchcock's vast domain: *Vertigo* (1958). Specifically, the apartment of Midge Wood (Barbara Bel Geddes), which, of all the film's locations, exerts the strongest gravitational pull: her ex-fiancé, Scottie Ferguson (James Stewart), spends more of his screen time there than at his own home (see Fig. 26.1). After a prologue, the film starts there, and, in the alternate universe of its European release, it also ends there.

With its expansive corner view atop San Francisco's Russian Hill, Midge's place functions as an observatory from which to take note of Scottie's comings and goings, as well as the goings-on in the city. It's a study in white: bone-pale houses cling to a dramatic hillside penciled into a purgatorial sky socked in with clouds and fog whose doleful miasma seems to drain even the color from the flowers and artwork on her windowsill. This panorama compares favorably with El Greco's *View and Plan of Toledo* (1608)—an early hint at past glory in a film haunted by memories of the Spanish conquest of California, whose ghosts linger as Catholic missions. (They're also literalized as the apparently real ghost of Carlotta Valdes.) The artist's tribute to colonial expansion quivers with freedom, power, color, and excitement. By

Figure 26.1 Midge's apartment and view of Russian Hill. Inset: *View and Plan of Toledo*.

Vertigo, directed by Alfred Hitchcock. © Alfred J. Hitchcock Productions 1958. All rights reserved. *Plan of Toledo* by El Greco, 1595–1600. The Metropolitan Museum of Art, New York.

contrast, the city seen from Midge's apartment depicts a city whose *siècle* has come to its *fin*, making visible the complaint made by Gavin Elster (Tom Helmore) that "the things that spell San Francisco to me [i.e., those four quivering attributes] are disappearing fast." *Vertigo* exceeds its own frame, reaching beyond its filmic borders spatially (through the window, possibly to Toledo), temporally (to the Age of Conquest) and, as we'll see, transtextually (into other Hitchcockian narratives).

An artist freelancing as a fashion illustrator, Midge's space is cluttered with books, modernist paintings and *objets d'art* befitting a rich and fertile inner life that contrasts with her reproductive inactivity. "There's only one man in the world for me, Johnny-o," she says, to the only man in the world for her. "I'm still available. Available Ferguson," Scottie replies, to the one woman to whom he's not available. She's past ready to settle down, get married, and start a family. We know whose children she wants to raise: those fathered by the once future chief of police of San Francisco. Instead, she ends up mothering him, clinging to an unrequited love that resigns her to a future of dinner, then dishes, then bed—alone. If Madeleine—Midge's rival for Scottie's affection—symbolizes the eternal feminine, Midge serves as its archetype of the unfulfilled maternal feminine (see Fig. 26.2). Yet both share affinities with Carlotta: Madeleine, in her seeming possession by the ghost, and Midge, by being spurned in love and deprived of children.

Bel Geddes, like Joseph Cotten and several other prominent actors, appeared both in Hitchcock's films and in his TV shows. Of such crossovers, Lane writes: "One effect of this dynamic was to create the sense that Hitchcock's films and his television series … had an almost seamless relationship" (2020: 261). Viewing the film and the four *Alfred Hitchcock Presents* episodes that Bel Geddes appears in sequentially—two of them dropped in the weeks preceding the release of *Vertigo*, and two came a while after—reveals an intertextual conversation between them, bringing into relief an accumulation of uncanny parallels and recurring themes (see Fig. 26.3). In fact, Bel Geddes' four characters closely mirror her role in *Vertigo*, so I will here treat them as variations of an archetype, referred to as "Midge." Together, they coalesce into a picture of a woman cycling as if on a wheel of samsara into a new life again and again, seeking true love as she progresses toward self-actualization.

Figure 26.2 Midge cradles Scottie in a maternal pose suggestive of the *Pietà*.

Figure 26.3 In her travels across the Hitchcockian multiverse, "Midge" (Barbara Bel Geddes) is often associated with flowers, especially a nosegay arrangement. Clockwise from top left: Midge and Carlotta Valdes, *Vertigo* (1958); Lucia, "The Foghorn" (*Alfred Hitchcock Presents*, 1958); Mary Maloney, "Lamb to the Slaughter" (*Alfred Hitchcock Presents*, 1958); Helen Brewster, "Morning of the Bride" (*Alfred Hitchcock Presents*, 1959); Sybilla, "Sybilla" (*Alfred Hitchcock Presents*, 1960).

We can begin with the first installment of this cycle, broadcast on March 16, 1958, two months before *Vertigo*'s May 15 premiere.

"The Foghorn"

Based on a 1934 short story of the same name by Gertrude Atherton, "The Foghorn" (1958) was not directed by Hitchcock—that credit goes to Robert Stevens—yet it is a boon companion-piece to *Vertigo*. The episode opens with the intoning, described in the source story, of a "long-drawn-out, almost human moan of the foghorn" (Atherton 1970: 8)—a signal that also figures in *Vertigo*. It accompanies this surreal image: a still photo of a woman in a Breton stripe navy shirt, her wet hair and surf-spattered face superimposed on a churning sea whose horizon is obscured by a wall of fog (Fig. 26.4). Ophelia in a sailor suit. Has she drowned? Is this an out-of-body experience? As if to reassure herself as much as the audience, a hushed voice wells up: "I'm dreaming … I'm dreaming … It's that dream." This is the first view we have of Barbara Bel Geddes as Lucia Clay. She knows she's dreaming and can shape what

Figure 26.4 Lucia's (Barbara Bel Geddes) dreams of a near-death echo Madeleine's plunge into the very same waters of San Francisco Bay.

"The Foghorn," directed by Robert Stevens © Shamley Productions 1958. All rights reserved.

might otherwise be a recurring nightmare: her name is echoic of this form of lucid dreaming. Turning away from that eldritch mood, she adds, "You're the happiest girl in the world," and drops anchor on a happier memory—"the first night I met Allen." A flashback nested within a dream and dwelling in the hypnagogic zone between dreaming and wakefulness, it evokes the eerie liminality and melancholy mood that suffuses *Vertigo*. Further affinities abound.

Set in fog-enshrouded, antebellum San Francisco, Lucia comes across at first as a time-traveling Midge, caught up in an unrequited love, this time with a prosperous businessman: Allen Bliss (Michael Rennie). Their desire to marry is frustrated by his current wife's refusal to grant a divorce. Then, one day, while out boating in the Bay, they hatch a plan to "sail off to the fortunate isles" near China. At that very moment, a fogbank rolls in. Disoriented and enveloped in mist, their little sailboat is struck by a ship. Bliss is lost.

Lucia survives, though her mind cracks under a pain too heavy to bear, and she represses her memory of Bliss's death. She grows old, waiting for her lover to return from the sea and make good on their plan to run off to "the fortunate isles." This island paradise, a motif that recurs in a number of Hitchcock films, invokes J. M. Barrie's play *Mary Rose: The Island that Likes to Be Visited.* The director tried for decades to bring it to the cinema screen; in 1964, he commissioned Jay Presson Allen to write a screenplay, which envisions the island as "lonely, sun-speckled yet mist-dim, somehow unsubstantial." Like the title character of that play, figures in the television drama also appear and disappear into the fog. And, in both works, key personages are trapped in a time-suspended neverland.

Aspects of Atherton's story that didn't make it into the TV episode do appear in *Vertigo*—and they offer details provided by neither *D'Entre les morts*—*Vertigo*'s source novel by Pierre Boileau and Thomas Narcejac—nor Georges Rodenbach's *Bruges-la-Morte*, the presumed inspiration behind the French novel. For example, her tale is redolent with an atmosphere of classical antiquity. The lovers attend a lecture at the University of California, Berkeley's Greek Theater, where they find it "easy to imagine themselves in Greece of the fifth century b.c., alone in that vast gray amphitheater" (Atherton 1970: 12). In *Vertigo*, those neoclassical colonnades find expression in the Palace of the Legion of Honor in San Francisco. Atherton's lovers can also be found "admiring the 'ruins' of a Roman temple"—most likely the faux ruins of the Palace of Fine Arts, which also appear in the film (Atherton 1970: 13).

In another scene, Atherton's lovers "wandered off the terrace," into

> dim aisles of redwoods, born when the earth was young, whose long trunks never swayed, whose high branches rarely sang in the wind—unfriendly trees, but protective, sentinel-like, shutting out the modern world; reminiscent were those closely planted aisles of ancient races ... forgotten races ... godlike races, perhaps.
>
> (Atherton 1970: 14)

The passage reads like a description of *Vertigo*'s wanderers, Scottie and Madeleine, who, finding themselves in a redwood forest, are overcome by its primeval grandeur. Scottie supplies a poetic flourish to what would otherwise be a simple statement of fact when he describes the trees as "Sequoia Sempervirens: always green, ever-living ... the oldest living things." To the list of proposed source material for *Vertigo*, we can add Atherton's "The Foghorn."

Reciprocally, minor details that show up in *Vertigo* find fuller expression in the teleplay. For example, San Francisco's "gay old bohemian days," merely alluded to in the movie, are here brought to life. Lucia's city by the bay is populated with fresh-minted millionaires who are as at home on the rough streets of Chinatown as they are in a ritzy restaurant: while the lovers' favorite hideaway is a Chinese teahouse, the ballroom where they first meet could pass for the Venetian Room at the Fairmont Hotel—a haunt apparently favored by *Vertigo*'s Scottie and Madeleine. According to Alec Coppel and Samuel Taylor's shooting script, Elster has "cool, watchful eyes. He is beautifully tailored and gives the sense of a man who relishes money and knows how to use it" (Coppel and Taylor 1957). The same could be said of Bliss, whose cultivated manners and lean physique bear a clear resemblance to those of Gavin Elster. Elster is a shipbuilder, and Bliss is a banker with ties to the shipping industry—yet both find their respective businesses as dull as they find their wives. There is one key difference: while both men want to dispose of their mates, Elster wants to do so from, shall we say, a great height; Bliss simply wants to buy off unhappiness with an alimony check.

Changes made in adapting the story for the small screen anticipate motifs that appear in *Vertigo*. In a scene that doesn't appear in the story, the pair go browsing in a bookshop, where Lucia reads from Elizabeth Barrett Browning's "Sonnet 1":

> ... Straightway I was 'ware,
> So weeping, how a mystic Shape did move
> Behind me, and drew me backward by the hair;
> And a voice said in mastery, while I strove,

"Guess now who holds thee?"—"Death," I said, But, there,
The silver answer rang—"Not Death, but Love."

(BARRETT BROWNING 1967: 7)

While the setting evokes the film's Argosy Book Shop, the poem infuses the teleplay with a Liebestod theme that is richly developed in *Vertigo*.

Like Midge, Lucia—whose name, like Bliss's, is not revealed in the story—has ties to *Vertigo*'s Carlotta Valdes. Given Spanish names, both women lived in the same era—around the end of the nineteenth century—and, tragically deprived of their lovers, are consigned to wander in a fog of madness. They're also involved in the revealing of a truth by way of a piece of jewelry: when Scottie sees Carlotta's necklace on Judy, who he'd remade to look like Madeleine, he realizes that she had already once been Madeleine; when Lucia gazes at a wishing ring Bliss had given her, it breaks her spell, and she remembers that he died and that she's grown old vegetating in a hospital bed. The shock kills her, and, as with the end of *Vertigo*, the episode concludes with a nun performing the Last Rites with hasty reverence.

"The Foghorn" can be read as something of a prologue to *Vertigo*. By contrast, "Lamb to the Slaughter," directed by Hitchcock, takes certain ingredients from that film and reenvisions them in a parallel universe.

"Lamb to the Slaughter"

"Lamb to the Slaughter" fades in on Mary (Bel Geddes) tidying up about the house, an anxious housekeeper fumbling a handful of cigarettes into a tabletop box. In this alternate universe, "Midge's" diligence seems to have paid off: she's married and will soon bear what Midge wanted most—a baby. But, as with her other incarnations so far, her love is doomed (Fig 26.5). Her husband, police chief Patrick Maloney (Allan Lane), comes home from work and announces that he's divorcing her so that he can marry another woman. But she isn't the divorcing type. Shocked and in a fugue state, Mary remembers that she has a little lamb—in the pantry. Numbly announcing that she's making dinner, she raises its frozen leg and smashes Patrick's head in. To get rid of the murder weapon, she roasts it up and feeds it to a squad of investigating policemen.

Airing one month after "The Foghorn," on April 13, 1958, this teleplay is also connected to the release of *Vertigo*. Like Hitchcock's big-screen masterpiece, it is replete with Catholic themes and motifs. The connections start with its title: an allusion to Isaiah 53:7, which prophesied that the Messiah would be led to his crucifixion like a Passover lamb. The lead character shares a name with Christianity's preeminent mother, and the family religion is proclaimed by a picture that hangs near the kitchen door: a print of "His Madonna," which depicts a teenage boy carving a wooden statue of the Blessed Virgin (see Fig. 26.6). Finally, the investigating police reenact the Passover when they crowd around her kitchen table, devouring the murder weapon like it's their Last Supper.

Mary is a lot like Midge: bright, efficient, pretty enough—a tad mousy, perhaps—and eager to please, with a strong maternal instinct. Her marriage to the chief of police—a position that Scottie had aspired to, but not achieved—links her to her character in *Vertigo*, making Maloney a fellow traveler in this multiverse. His reputation as a philanderer also recalls Scottie: in *Vertigo*, the retired detective doesn't think twice about plunging into an affair with Madeleine Elster, whom he believes to be married, not to mention mentally ill. It prompts one to imagine a Midge–Scottie marriage suffering from similar headaches.

Figure 26.5 A flock of birds—two prints and one print reflected in a mirror—surrounds Mary as she makes a telephone call, expressionistically evoking her fluttering, chaotic mental state. It also points forward to similar imagery in *Psycho*.

"Lamb to the Slaughter," directed by Alfred Hitchcock. © Shamley Productions 1958. All rights reserved.

Figure 26.6 Scene from "Lamb to the Slaughter," with *His Madonna* by Toby Edward Rosenthal (1916). With her arms raised as if to bless the young artist for his piety, the Holy Mother seems to come to life as the boy sculpts her into being. The depiction resonates with *Vertigo*'s *Pygmalion* themes.

In this black-and-white parallel universe, "Midge" got what she wished for. Nevertheless, she was definitely better off forlorn but free in her Russian Hill apartment rather than guilty of murder and facing prison time, as Hitchcock implies in his closing monologue.

"The Morning of the Bride"

So far on her journey, "Midge" has been restless and increasingly impatient in her search of a happy ending. How does she fare in "The Morning of the Bride" (1959)?

In this episode, directed by Arthur Hiller, Helen Brewster (Bel Geddes) waits to tie the knot with her fiancé, Philip Pryor (Dan Dubbins). He keeps her on the hook for years, on the grounds that his elderly mother is ill and that caring for her takes priority over their marriage. Finally, Helen delivers an ultimatum: marry her or call off the engagement. He succumbs to the pressure. The morning after the wedding, she learns, to her horror, why he'd been putting her off: his mother has been dead for years. Ensnared in a labyrinth of psychotic delusion, he's been caring for the dead woman as if she were alive.

As in "The Foghorn," the story begins with Bel Geddes in bed, as if declaring herself the "happiest girl in the world": she's got a bridal bouquet on her nightstand, a new wedding ring on her finger and a glowing smile on her face. The rest of the story is told through a flashback that catches us up to her current situation, where we see Helen flitting about her home, preparing for dinner and straightening up around the house. Channeling Mary Maloney, she is earnest and attentive—and even checks the cigarette box. Like Midge, she assumes a motherly, infantilizing, relationship with her sweetheart, saying to her roommate, "It bothers me a little, me being older than Philip. Sometimes he seems just like a little boy. I guess he needs me."

When Philip returns from the Korean War, he takes up employment as a junior editor at a publishing house, where he has a bright future. They slip back into their established mother–son roles as he renders an account of his experiences overseas:

> PHILIP: I feel like a kid with a good report card. I want my head patted.
> HELEN: [*Rubbing his head*] You mean like this?
> PHILIP: Just like that.
> HELEN: I have a whole box of gold stars waiting for you when you become vice president or something.

The episode also compares uncannily to *Psycho*, released the following year. Like Norman Bates, Philip uses every excuse he can to avoid introducing his mother to his friend—and, therefore, the audience—while at the same time keeping her alive and present in Helen's (and our) mind. A photograph of his mother serves to concretize her existence, just as "Mother's" silhouette does in the window of the Bates mansion.

Patricia Hitchcock crosses the Hitchcockian multiverse to play Helen's saucy, truth-telling roommate, Pat (Fig. 26.7); later that year, she'll be playing a strikingly similar character in *Psycho* as Marion's coworker Caroline. She says of Philip, "He's all his mother's got." Then, all but scowling prophetically at Norman, she adds, "Listen, I'm all for mothers, but there's a special breed of women with only sons that lingers on for years."

Figure 26.7 Patricia Hitchcock as Helen's roommate, Pat, in "Morning of the Bride."
"Morning of the Bride," directed by Arthur Hiller. © Shamley Productions 1959. All rights reserved.

At the end of the episode, we arrive where we started in the prologue. Helen, a new bride, intent on meeting her new mother-in-law, enters Mrs. Pryor's room and finds a musty chamber dominated by a huge carved bed and filled with antique bric-a-brac—a foretaste of Mrs. Bates's bedroom. Exploring the space, she pieces together half stories about the occupant's life in much the same way that Lila Crane does in *Psycho*. She finds an old newspaper clipping with an obituary for Mrs. Langley Pryor, who died many years before. Then Philip enters the room, his eyes fixed in a psychotic trance. Placing a shawl around the shoulders of a woman that only he can see, he says, "You never remember to keep warm, Mother. You'll get another chill if I don't watch over you every minute." Philip, whose mother lives on in his fractured imagination, is a multiverse-hopping "Norman Bates."

The very week that "Morning of the Bride" aired—February 15, 1959—galleys of Robert Bloch's as-yet-unreleased novel, *Psycho*, were circulating the studio. The timing precludes any conjecture that the film influenced the teleplay. However, the opposite is possible: that summer, screenwriter Joseph Stefano joined Hitchcock to begin story conferences for the film (Rebello 1990: 13, 37). Still, the coincidence is uncanny.

"Sybilla"

So far, "Midge" is zero for three in finding a happy home in Hitchcock's multiverse, but things finally take a turn for the better in "Sybilla" (1960, directed by Ida Lupino). In her last *Alfred Hitchcock Presents* appearance, Bel Geddes returns approximately to the time in which "The Foghorn" is set as the mysterious title character in a poignant tale of self-sacrificing love. In the opening scene, she has recently died, and her bereaved husband reflects on the strange turn his life took when she came into it. "How did I come to marry Sybilla?" he wonders. "I really cannot remember very clearly. For a determined bachelor of forty to have suddenly found himself married to Sybilla was as incredible as finding himself on the moon." We're advised to take the hyperbole at face value.

After that prologue, we return in flashback to the new couple's postnuptial home. In spite of Horace's egocentric demands and disturbing misogyny, Sybilla promises to be an almost too-perfect wife, serenely promising, "I don't want to make any mistakes, never. You must always tell me just how you prefer everything. I only want to please you." She's going to make this marriage work if it kills her, and it almost does. Her attentiveness eventually incites "his castration fears" (Lightning 2017: 125), and he attempts to dispose of her with a glass of wine spiked with a deadly dose of sleeping serum. (The camera follows him up the stairs to her bedroom, keeping the tray and its lethal beverage in closeup. Was this homage to the milk scene in *Suspicion* (1942) one of Hitchcock's script suggestions or did Lupino come up with it on her own?) The plan fails. Whether it was clairvoyant foreknowledge that allowed her to thwart his plan, or—as she claims—a chance substitution of the liquid that did so inadvertently, is difficult to say. Viewers can choose what to believe.

Later, Sybilla tells Horace about the plot of a crime novel she's reading wherein, upon learning of an adversary's plan to kill him, the would-be victim secretly makes a copy of the would-be killer's diary that includes details of his machinations. After handing the copy to his lawyer for safekeeping with instructions that he turn the incriminating document over to the district attorney upon his death, he then informs his foe of this arrangement—thus restraining him from going through with the scheme. Since Horace, too, had journaled about his homicidal plans, he concludes that Sybilla read his diary and took similar precautions. Fearing the consequences that would blow back on him if any harm were to befall her, he does an about-face, going to extraordinary lengths to keep her safe and comfortable.

Sybilla has the patience of a saint, and maybe that is what she is—if not his guardian angel. Enigmatically, she abides Horace's domineering treatment with that indomitable Barbara Bel Geddes smile—yet, she's no victim. From the moment she enters the home, she takes control in subtle ways, and before long the tables turn, and her husband "wants only to please" her.

Eight years go by, and then Sybilla dies an untimely—and natural—death. Horace goes to her attorney to obtain the copy of his diary, but in the twist ending, it's revealed that the firm never received such papers. He'll never know how much his wife knew about his evil machinations. After she's gone, Horace realizes that he had come to love her, and that she had taught him how to love. His unwitting penance yielded redemption and a change of heart—a real awakening.

This is not a story about female subversion, as some have argued. Sybilla's equanimity leaves no room for rivalry. The wisdom of this teleplay lies in its implicit understanding that victories in the battle of the sexes only perpetuate the conflict, instead offering a profound rejoinder to sitcoms like *I Love Lucy*, which trafficked in such marital contentiousness. It is Sybilla's quiet determination, free of guile or self-interest, that underpins her otherworldly quality. She was indeed a sybil—an oracle—come to impart a lesson.

"Sybilla" stands out as a prime example of Joan Harrison's unique contribution to the series. A nuanced portrait of a woman successfully using her wits and charm to successfully navigate a male-dominated environment, it's a story that mirrors Harrison's Hollywood career—and that of Lupino. Perhaps it was on the strength of the story that the latter turned down a $5,000 offer to star in this episode in exchange for $1,250 to direct it (Grisham and Grossman 2017: 135). Among the series' many strong women characters, Sybilla is one of the strongest, if also the strangest. Based on a short story by Margaret Manners and scripted by Charlotte Armstrong—two female writers whose professional relationship Harrison cultivated, it stands out as an example of women-made, feminist television in the 1950s. It also demonstrates how the Hitchcockian multiverse makes ample room for other voices while staying true to its "deus abscondida."

Transcending the Wheel

Perhaps ancient religions' "many lives" theory is not all that different from the science-based "many worlds" theory: according to Hindu tradition, souls reincarnate across time; in the multiverse, events reiterate across space. A series of purifying trials spanning five narrative worlds have taught Midge, variously manifested, to let go of her dearest desires: first, of fantasies of escape to "the fortunate isles," then of her dream of a picture-perfect marriage to the chief of police, which turns into a nightmare. Her overzealous mothering instinct is taken to its logical end when she marries a man with extreme mother issues. Finally, she empties herself and finds strength and—in a sublime twist ending—gets the devoted husband she'd wanted all along.

Conceptualizing Hitchcock's multifarious productions as a multiverse brings their seamless interconnectedness more clearly into focus; works produced in one medium can shed light on those produced in another. Besides, it more accurately reflects the nature of the creative team that was Shamley Productions—old friends who sometimes gathered in a conference room and sometimes around the dinner table to come up with new ways to tell old stories.

Hitchcock's films never really end. His characters live on in "icebox conversations," where audience members can muse on what's next for them after the house lights come up. The Hitchcockian multiverse imagines infinite possibilities for Midge. And yet, perhaps I've been talking about the wrong heroine. *Vertigo* is haunted by another heartweary wanderer, a bereaved mother, the ghost of Carlotta Valdes. Midge's empathetic connection to her is telling. At the Argosy Book Shop, she's visibly touched as Pop Leibel tells the tale of Carlotta's loss in love and her subsequent peregrinations. Moved by her plight, Midge whispers, "Poor thing." Her later self-portrait in Carlotta's image forces the identification, as if to confront Scottie and the audience with the question, "How am I not like her?" Rejected by her onetime lover, Midge is doomed, as if possessed by the spirit of Carlotta, to wander alone and melancholy right out of the movie. The archetypal quality previously attributed to her fits Carlotta better: she already exists purely in the realm of the imaginal. In fact, something of Carlotta's spirit dwells in each of the women discussed here, driving them desperately forward in the quest for love and family, a soul turning and returning in a woeful samsara of love and loss. At long last, liberated from desire, our peripatetic heroine escapes the karmic cycle. Carlotta transcends.

References

Atherton, G. (1970) "The Foghorn," in *The Foghorn and Other Stories*, Freeport, NY: Books for Libraries Press, pp. 3–24.

Barrett Browning, E. B. (1967) *Sonnets from the Portuguese*. Kansas City, Miss.: Hallmark Cards, Inc.

Coppel, A., and S. Taylor (1957) *Vertigo*. Unpublished. https://the.hitchcock.zone/wiki/Scripts:_Vertigo_(12/Sep/1957)

Gottlieb, S. (2015) *Hitchcock on Hitchcock*: *Selected Writings and Interviews*, vol. 2, Oakland, Calif.: University of California Press.

GramsM Jr., and P. Wikstrom, (2001) *The* Alfred Hitchcock Presents *Companion*, Churchville, Md.: O T R Publishing.

Grisham, T., and J. Grossman (2017) *Ida Lupino, Director: Her Art and Resilience in Times of Transition*, New Brunswick, NJ: Rutgers University Press.

Karlin, E. (2021) "Beyond the Blonde: The Dynamic Heroines of Hitchcock," *The Hitchcock Annual*, ed. Sidney Gottlieb, pp. 32–55.

Lane, C. (2020) *Phantom Lady: Hollywood Producer*, *Joan Harrison—The Forgotten Woman behind Hitchcock*, Chicago, Ill.: Chicago Review Press.

Leitch, T. (1999) "The Outer Circle: Hitchcock on Television," in R. Allen and S. Ishii-Gonzales (eds), *Alfred Hitchcock Centenary Essays*, London: British Film Institute, pp. 59–71.

Lightning, R. K. (2017) "Alfred Hitchcock Presents 'Sybilla'," *Film International*, 15 (4): 120–130.

Markle, F. (1964) *Telescope: A Talk with Hitchcock*, CBC.

McCarty, J., and B. Kelleher (1985) Alfred Hitchcock Presents: *An Illustrated Guide to the Ten-Year Television Career of the Master of Suspense*, New York: St. Martin's Press.

Perry, D. R. (2003) *Hitchcock and Poe: The Legacy of Delight and Terror*, Lanham, Md.: The Scarecrow Press.

Presson Allen, J. (1964) *Mary Rose*. Unpublished. www.stevenderosa.com/writingwithhitchcock/scripts/mary_rose.pdf

Rebello, S. (1990) *Alfred Hitchcock and the Making of Psycho*, New York: Red Dembner Enterprise Corp.

Stam, R. (1991) "Hitchcock and Buñuel: Authority, Desire, and the Absurd," in W. Raubicheck and W. Srebnick (eds), *Hitchcock's Rereleased Films: From Rope to Vertigo*, Detroit, Mich.: Wayne University Press, pp. 116–146.

Truffaut, F. (1984) *Hitchcock*, rev. edn, New York: Simon & Schuster.

PART SIX

Global Hitchcock: Beyond the USA and the UK

Chapter 27

Hitchcock and *L'Écran français*

At the Roots of the *Politique des auteurs*?

Tifenn Brisset

Editor's Note

Many of the texts in this volume comment on the significance of Hitchcock's connection to France. His early reception there initiated the *Politique des auteurs* ["Politics of authorship"] through the film journal *Cahiers du Cinéma*, as well as the writings of Jean-Luc Godard, Éric Rohmer, Claude Chabrol, Jean Domarchi, Jean Douchet, and François Truffaut. Throughout this book, there are frequent references to Hitchcock's reception in France, indicating that the French were often among the first to write seriously about specific Hitchcock films (see, for example, the chapters on *Rope*, *The Wrong Man*, and *The Trouble with Harry*). In the current chapter, the focus is on the emergence of the auteurist vision as articulated in *L'Écran français*. This little-known magazine predates *Cahiers du Cinéma* but is essential for understanding the evolution of the French defense of Hitchcock's cinema.

An Introduction to *L'Écran français*

Hitchcock is well known as the most enlightening example of the *Politique des auteurs*. The British-born director was at the heart of a passionate controversy between his supporters and those who thought he had gone downhill since moving to Hollywood and claimed there was a lack of depth in his recent subjects. The name *Politique des auteurs* was invented by François Truffaut, although the concept surely existed beforehand in various parts of the world.[1] But in the 1950s, the tendency to defend with force a director considered as an outsider and to assign to him the sole paternity of the film was a provocation. The names of these pro-Hitchcock critics have become internationally famous: Éric Rohmer, Claude Chabrol, François Truffaut, and others like Jean Domarchi or, *inter alia*, Alexandre Astruc. Hitchcock's genius was revealed in extended essays, through interviews that exposed his techniques and working methods, and also in formal scrutiny of the films by critics. His suspense films were described as highly spiritual and metaphysical, and every Hitchcock film enclosed a secret; the role of the critic was to discover its profound and hidden meaning. Hitchcock had created a universe, filled with symbols and variations, and his genius was indisputable. Without any doubt, Hitchcock was an author. Starting in 1952, in the notorious issue number 39 of *Cahiers du cinéma* (October 1954), these French critics laid the foundation for the appraisal and celebration of Hitchcock's genius, which spread across the Atlantic through the important work of writers such as Bill Krohn, William Rothman, Robin Wood, and others.

However, the narrative of Hitchcock as an author may have started a few years before, in a French magazine called *L'Écran français* (see Fig. 27.1). The American scholar James Vest wrote two major studies on the director's reception in France in the 1950s (2003, 2011). As his analysis really starts in 1950, *L'Écran français* is not the object of his close attention. He accurately evokes a background of negative assessments among which André Bazin's (Vest 2011: 367, 369), but a closer look at the different articles from 1945 onwards reveals that there is much more. Antoine de Baecque, French historian and film critic, explains the importance of these more supportive reviews in an essential book about French cinephilia (de Baecque 2003). He sheds light on the dynamism of the young critics at *L'Écran français* who wanted to "break through the wall of contempt and easy prejudice" about Hitchcock (de Baecque 2003: 97), who was until then mainly seen as a good technician and a

Figure 27.1 Front cover of *L'Écran français*, December 26, 1949.

moneymaker. This essay will analyze in more detail the writings in this quite unfairly forgotten journal that anticipated the positive reception of Hitchcock that we normally associate with the *Cahiers* critics.

L'Écran français was born in secret during the Nazi occupation, as a part of *Les Lettres françaises*, a literary publication of the French Resistance. The first official issue came out in July 1945. Many great writers and thinkers such as Jean-Paul Sartre, Georges Sadoul, Albert Camus, Jacques Becker, and Henri Langlois were part of its sponsorship committee. After the war, *L'Écran français* was "the most reactive and lively film weekly of the time," and, along with *La Revue du cinéma* "the only truly stimulating periodical of the late 1940s" (de Baecque 2003: 99). In May 1946, the Blum–Byrnes agreement had led to a dramatic increase in the number of American films entering the French market. For instance, in 1949, twenty-three American films and only five French films were screened in Paris (Néry 1949). Against this imbalance, a part of *L'Écran français*'s team clearly came to the defense of French cinema. This controversy also took the form of the creation of a radical new vision of cinema. In 1948, Alexandre Astruc shaped the concept of *caméra-stylo* (1948). The goal of this essay was clear: to assert that cinema is the equivalent of any other art form. The director's camera is as meaningful and expressive as the writer's pen: "Cinema is, simply, becoming a means of expression, like what every other art was before. Little by little, cinema becomes a language, a means of expression as subtle as written language" (Astruc 1948). With the concept of camera as a pen, Astruc articulates a new theory. A director is as much responsible for his films as the writer is responsible for his book: "the author writes with his camera, just as a writer writes with his pen" (Astruc 1948). In this clash, two groups formed. One gathered around André Bazin in support of Hollywood cinema (André Bazin, Jean-Charles Tacchella, Roger Thérond). The pro-Hollywood critics, following the path of Alexandre Astruc, spoke in the name of the form of the films and virtuosity of the writing initiated by Orson Welles' *Citizen Kane*, William Wyler's *Viper*, and, as we shall see, Hitchcock's *Rope*. Another group attempted to resist America (André Vermorel, Georges Sadoul, Louis Daquin), defending a cinema of significant themes rather than formalism. Therefore, Hitchcock's defense took place in a tense political and ideological context.[2]

Hitchcock, Bazin, and *L'Écran français*

The first comments about Hitchcock's films in *L'Écran français* are to be found as early as 1945 and 1946, under Bazin's name. He had just seen *Shadow of a Doubt*, which was released in France on September 26, 1945. His opinion about one of Hitchcock's favorite films is lukewarm at best: "A crime movie like so many, a crime movie which doesn't avoid any of the commonplaces that the average American spectator likes to see in his moving pictures" (Bazin 1945). Bazin values the content: films must have a strong subject; they must say something about the world, about society, about humanity. That's what great art can achieve. To him, Hitchcock's Hollywood films are often shallow, and *Shadow of a Doubt* is no exception:

> The screenwriter and the director obviously didn't have the courage to follow through with their subject. If cinema so rarely achieves the quality of great American literature, it is not because the power of expression of the screen is inferior to that of the book, but rather because cinema shies away from the normal exigencies of art.
>
> (Bazin 1945: 6)

As Bazin's critical comments reveal, the battle to defend Hitchcock was also a battle to finally place Hollywood cinema on a par with great literature. This will be the strategy of the *Politique des auteurs*.

In October 1946, Bazin writes only a few words about *Notorious*, which was in competition during the first Cannes Film Festival. He notes that Ingrid Bergman is "the most beautiful, the most sensual, the purest, the most surreal, the most carnal, but the most alive and the most intelligent actress in contemporary cinema" (1946a). Bazin quotes the director Pierre Laroche, who praises Hitchcock's art as "disturbing by his intelligence and his sensuality."

Bazin discovers *Suspicion* in 1946 and seems to relish its suspense: "Hitchcock manages to make us walk a tightrope above an abyss until the last image, nudging us left, then right, in only to catch us at the precise moment when we think we are going to fall" (1946b). But, once again, the master's tremendous technique doesn't seem to give rise to seriousness: "Will this technician of suspicion ever give us something other than the mere shadow of an authentic tragedy of doubt?" (Bazin 1946b).

In 1948, he writes another few lines about *Notorious*. His ambivalence about Hitchcock's work is obvious here. He comes back to *Shadow of a Doubt*, which he now considers a masterpiece. Hitchcock's formalism has become more acceptable to him, but content is more essential:

> Hitchcock's rhetoric is certainly the most brilliant worldwide. We know now that he has no equal in spiral tracking shots and in expressing the most secret movements of anxiety and doubt. […] Subjective camera is as well and good, but it is even more important to have a subject!
>
> (Bazin 1948: 13)

These lines are the last he wrote about Hitchcock in *L'Écran français*. He will pursue his comments in *Cahiers du Cinéma*, arguing about the same topics with the so-called "young Turks," who will defend their idol Hitchcock at all cost. It is certainly interesting to note that Bazin's lukewarm appreciation of Hitchcock was contested by two other young critics as early as 1949.[3]

The Turning Point of "Hitchcock se confie"

Rope premiered in August 1948 in the USA and in February 1950 in Paris.[4] The starting point of the French critical debate was a series of three provocative articles published as early as May 1948, September 1948, and January 1949. Quite short, the first one mainly praises the rapidity of the filming, which took only ten days. Each one of the long takes in the film covers an average of eleven pages of script. This innovation leads the (unknown) writer to state that "for some technicians, this new conception is as revolutionary as the invention of the closeup" in the history of cinema techniques ("Hitchcock a tourné en dix jours son premier film en couleurs [Hitchcock shot his first film in color in ten days]" 1948). A few months later, a laudatory half page is dedicated to the same film by Claude Elsen. The journalist compares it to *Lifeboat* (1944), a masterpiece of technical skills since the camera leaves the survival craft for only a single shot. In *Rope*, Hitchcock goes even further. Here, he "obeys the three unities rule: place, time and action" (Elsen 1948). In order to do so and to achieve his long-take shots, Hitchcock seems to have used a mobile stage (Elsen got some production information about this precise point.) For his first Technicolor film, the director used color not only for its artistic value but also for its dramatic value. Thus, the whole film is a technical feat (because the camera never leaves the characters) and also a dramatic one, due to the psychological thoroughness of the murder story.

The third in the series, "Hitchcock se confie [Hitchcock confides]," is an extensive article written by Jean-Charles Tacchella and Roger-Marie Thérond, published on January 25, 1949. This article led to a rich controversy about Hitchcock and cinema modernity that lasted between January and April 1949. "Hitchcock se confie" is historically very important and quite daring: *Cahiers du cinéma* had not yet been founded, and Hitchcock was not critically appreciated despite his commercial success. Therefore, it was the first defense of a Hitchcock film of that kind. The text is long, filled with quotes from the director. It contains sharp and provocative analysis, showing the superiority of this outsider over classical French directors. The length of the article is as innovative as its writers' profound desire for Hitchcock to be recognized. Their enthusiasm is such that they don't shy away from bold pronouncements, saying that Hitchcock is already a "legend" of cinema. Hitchcock and William Wyler are the only directors at the apex of their careers, and Hitchcock has never once disappointed during his twenty-year career. How provocative this statement must have been in 1949! And to back up these opinions, they go as far as to call *Rope* "a masterpiece of prefabricated film." The concept of "prefabricated" or "prefab" was very much in vogue after the war, in reference to "prefabricated" architectural elements that limited costs and speeded up the reconstruction of towns destroyed by bombing (Jean-Loup Bourget, personal conversation). That is why "the most astonishing thing, in this article, lies in the choice of the film put forward, *Rope*, seen as a vulgar and anecdotical stylistic exercise" (de Baecque 2003: 98).

For Thérond and Tacchella, this so-called "prefabricated film" is created by a genuine mastermind. Its virtuosity is technical, of course: "it is the most innovative film directed since *Citizen Kane*. And still. *Citizen Kane* was a concentrate. *Rope* is a leap forward" (1949: 3). It is a well-known fact that Orson Welles' film was used as a model of the avant-garde for Alexandre Astruc and the pro-Hollywood critics of *L'Écran français* (de Baecque 2003: 100). But Tacchella and Thérond push it into the background in order to put *Rope* into the spotlight. Their defense of Hitchcock's methods already started with *Spellbound* (1945), when Hitchcock tried new techniques to cut costs, namely by cutting shooting time. The film was shot in forty-eight days instead of the fifty-seven that were scheduled, saving the director ten percent on his budget. A few years later, Hitchcock produced *Rope*, a masterpiece of economy. It was shot in thirty-six days and necessitated only twenty-six takes, "a record for a Technicolor film" (Tacchella and Thérond 1949: 3). He could have stopped there, but right after *Rope* he made a costume film with virtuosic camera movements in only fifty-five days, with the same long-take technique. This film is, of course, *Under Capricorn* (1949).

Tacchella and Thérond ask how Hitchcock could achieve such an accelerated shooting schedule. In order to answer this, they refer to an article published a few months earlier in the British film technicians' trade-union publication, *The Cine-Technician* (Hitchcock 1948). This article was written after a lecture Hitchcock gave at the British Kinematograph Society (initially titled "Methods of Film Direction") in September 1948. After reading it, Tacchella and Thérond say that "Hitchcock confides. He delivers his secrets with the simplicity of an artisan" (1949: 3). A director sharing secrets would also be a key characteristic of the *Politique des auteurs*. It is worth remembering that when François Truffaut planned to interview the master for his book *Hitchcock/Truffaut*, he wanted to exhibit Hitchcock as an inventor of forms. In order to do so, he undertook "very precise and meticulous work around the master's words talking about his technique, revealing his secrets" (de Baecque 2003: 123).

Thérond and Tacchella use a great deal of the *Cine-Technician* article, claiming that the real "secret" of Hitchcock lies in his art of editing: "here is his secret: TO PLAN EVERYTHING IN ADVANCE" (1949: 3). Even if Hitchcock affirms that every director at least tries, Thérond and Tacchella think that he is the first one to do it "in such a complete and definitive way" (1949: 3). So, unlike the way films are usually made, he has the editor work directly on the script: "The cuts should be made in the script itself, before a camera rolls, and after the cameras have stopped rolling," says Hitchcock in *Cine-Technician*. These techniques are only possible because the director has a global vision of his film and because he anticipates everything with perfection. The end goal is to banish any useless shots, and to film only what is necessary to avoid extra costs. Hitchcock is described as a master of organization: the film is already complete in his mind, and he will refuse to make a single change (and won't need to) — he could even not turn up on the set for the shooting.

Tacchella and Thérond assume that, having removed most of the cuts, Hitchcock "doesn't shoot pieces of film that he will then have to be put together with his editor, he takes on the responsibility himself" (1949: 3). Hitchcock directs a film that is already a whole in his mind. Therefore, he is responsible for everything: the script, the cutting, the shooting. The prime advantage is financial because it forces the director to plan everything in advance and to stop hiding (even unconsciously) behind the convenience of editing. This may be the prefabricated part of *Rope*. But Hitchcock brilliantly manages to make it an artistic gesture, a condensed and purified style. Here, the defense of a director as the real producer of his film is obvious, and, although the word "author" is not used, the soon-to-be philosophy of the *Politique des auteurs* is already noticeable. With this method of making a movie, the director "finally embraces his work in its entirety" and directs all aspects; "the total sum is his film" (Tacchella and Thérond 1949: 3). Astruc's theory of the *caméra-stylo*, at the heart of auteurism, seems to be acutely illustrated here.[5]

Thanks to his new way of filming — fast, economical, well prepared, no editing ornament, cinema "moves very fast" and is ahead. Ahead of what? The critics don't state this point precisely. One may assume that cinema is ahead of television, a medium that appeared a decade before and still used old cinema techniques and shot films like theater. For its part, cinema has always needed to move forward. It is an art of modernity. In that respect, *Rope*'s revolutionary long shots may "renew the art of telling stories" (Tacchella and Thérond 1949: 3) and may even contribute to the realization of cinema as a modern art.

But Hitchcock is critical about the technique for its own sake: "The making of a picture is nothing but the telling of a story, and the story — it goes without saying — must be a good one" (Hitchcock 1948). Everything is dependent on maintaining the attention of the spectator. Technical skills are not a goal per se, but, as he says himself, they must fit and serve the story: "The motion picture is not an arena for a display of techniques. It is, rather, a method of telling a story in which techniques, beauty, the virtuosity of the camera, everything must be sacrificed or compromised when it gets in the way of the story itself." This statement leads Thérond and Tacchella to conclude that "the era of pure image is behind us" (1949: 3).

It is worth noting that in *Cine Technician*, Hitchcock never mentions *Rope* nor the long cutting techniques. He speaks like a craftsman about his work, and the French critics do their job as critics, replacing his work in the history of cinema. But they also do their jobs as pro-Hitchcockians: they speak extremely highly of him in a very innovative way. Their colleagues at *Cahiers du cinéma* would do the same a few years later.

The Controversy about Hitchcock in *L'Écran français* (February–May 1949)

"Hitchcock se confie" did not go unnoticed. One month later, Claude Vermorel wrote "Le cinéma, art clandestin [Cinema, a clandestine art]" (Vermorel 1949). For him, cinema is an underground and courageous art, Hitchcock is dismissed as a commercial filmmaker, and the so-called revolutionary long-shot techniques are merely filmed theater.

Louis Daquin was one of the most fervent defenders of French cinema in *L'Écran français* and had always despised Hitchcock (see Brisset 2022). Therefore, he unsurprisingly drove his message home a few weeks later in "Remarques déplacées [Inappropriate comments]" (Daquin 1949). In this article he is very incisive about the new generation's formalist approach and derides the hollowness of analyzing a film shot by shot instead of thinking about its production conditions:

> What can I do about the incomprehension with which I greet this technical, aesthetic and philosophical language so dear to some of our young critics, and which is not without displeasure for some film creators? […] Will Hitchcock and Wyler's work methods revolutionize cinema? Do we care about this question, gentlemen, when our best directors are reduced to unemployment or to sporadic activity?

Daquin brings a political dimension to the debate and strongly rejects the use of the term avant-garde to describe Hitchcock (Barrot 1979: 277–279). After this trenchant response, Thérond and Tacchella (who were the new generation targeted by Vermorel and Daquin) invited several French filmmakers to give their opinion about Hitchcock in three articles called "Autour de Hitchcock [Around Hitchcock]." Jean Delannoy is very negative, whereas René Clément seems more indulgent: "All those who search must be praised, and in America, Hitchcock is one of the few real explorers. He can only be congratulated." But Clément values the random nature of the filming over the extreme preparation: "On set, one must try to transcend oneself. Beauty comes from an unpredictability which transports us" (Clément and Delannoy 1949: 3).

Maurice Tourneur (Jacques Tourneur's father) and Henri Decoin lay out their clashing viewpoints. Tourneur defends Hitchcock ("For me, Hitchcock is the one who's right" [1949: 10]) while Decoin considers him as an excellent technician and a master handyman but as skilled as any other and no real inventor. Decoin adds a few lines to defend French cinema against the hegemony of the slick, overproduced Hollywood movies:

> Technique has no soul. For us French men, our strength is our poverty. We work best in misery. We try to make do with what we have in hand. We invent, we create, we falsify, we discover, we rack our brain all day long, we complain […], we think about this fat boy Hitchcock who suddenly wants to play the tramp because he's ashamed of his wealth.
>
> (Decoin 1949)

And last, let's hear Jean Dreville's words about the controversy:

> When M. Hitchcock states that technique must be at the service of the subject, I'd be tempted to follow his lead. […] Only one shot per reel is all very nice, but doesn't it mean trampling underfoot the wonderful possibilities of selection that cinema can offer? […] Stop harassing us with crazy questions: you won't know why I filmed this scene with a long shot or this one with a low angle shot, and this is for one good reason: I have no idea myself.
>
> (Dreville 1949)

After these exchanges, other films were reviewed in the columns of the magazine. Some of the opinions were rather enthusiastic, such as Roger Thérond, of course, in his review of *The Paradine*

Case (1947). He notes that Hitchcock's assurance and expertise "make him, along with Wyler, the current master of American cinema" even though the script of the film is rather unsatisfactory. Thérond regrets the fact that "he is so mysteriously neglected, and even despised, by most French filmmakers" (1949: 11).

But the other reviews are more severe. For instance, Roland Violet recognizes that the trial of *The Paradine Case* is meticulously reconstructed "but the soul is not always there" (1949: 25). Robert Pilati forcibly denigrates *Saboteur* (1942), entitling his review "taillée en plein navet" (a *navet* is a turnip, and also a slang word to describe a very bad piece of art). The whole story is a tissue of implausibilities, and Pilati wonders, with irony, if Hitchcock made the film simply because he needed money. The last review of *Rope* is written by François Timmory and is extremely harsh. The critic pays attention to the content of the story and draws a parallel with recent history. But the references to the darkest hours of Nazism seem to be shocking and inexcusable. François Timmory goes as far as writing: "Don't even think about why Hitchcock chose to bring this sludge to the screen; it's because this 'great' director doubles up as a dangerous maniac" (1950: 11). The chronological proximity of the film with the war may explain the fierce rejection of the Nietzschean theory used by the two characters to justify their ugly murder. Even the final speech of James Stewart only brings to mind the shameful explanations of Nazis used in courts after the war.

Lastly, Jean-Pierre Darre regrets the incessant, overstudied camera movements, the long useless speeches and the awkward use of color of *Under Capricorn* (Darre 1950).[6]

Conclusion

To conclude, this study of Hitchcock in *L'Écran français* reveals the genesis of many elements soon to be found in *Cahiers du cinéma*: the enthusiasm and youth of the critics, the heritage of the concept of *caméra-stylo* by Alexandre Astruc, the defense of a Hollywood filmmaker seen only as a good technician, the revolutionary techniques which are more than simple technical curiosities, the genius of a director who not only knows the whole film in his mind before the shooting but who entirely controls it, the defense of a film usually seen as minor, the revelation of the director's secrets, and a strong controversy. In both *L'Écran français* and *Cahiers du cinéma*, Hitchcock has been the focal point of a crucial debate about politics, ideology, and conception of cinema. *L'Écran français* was the first to take Hitchcock so seriously in over twenty articles written between 1945 and 1952, and the journal's history deserves to be better known for it.

Acknowledgments

Our warm thanks to the Cinémathèque de Grenoble, Tillyan Bourdon, James Bogdanski, Jean-Loup Bourget, Sidney Gottlieb, Robert Kapsis, Conor Short, and Géraldine Tixier.

Notes

1   François Truffaut, "Ali Baba et la 'Politique des Auteurs'," *Cahiers du cinéma*, 44, February 1955. See also Ciment 2012. All translations from the original French are mine.
2   See De Baecque 2003: 99–106.

3   Some Hitchcock films are reviewed by other critics. For instance, Roger Régent says about *Spellbound* that "it is not the first time that cinema has exploited the dramatic resources and surprise effects of psychoanalytical investigation: but it doesn't seem that it has ever done so incisively!" Hitchcock and his camera operator Georges Barnes take the suspense so far that the spectator is "thrown into this vertiginous descent." On the other hand, Hitchcock has taken the easy way out when it came to three love scenes. Ingrid Bergman is fabulous and dominates the casting (Régent 1948). Throughout a whole page, Gilbert Robin analyzes *Spellbound*'s medical implausibilities (Robin 1948). Finally, Jean Queval dismisses *Foreign Correspondent* for its heavy cutting and the silliness of its premise, whereas *Jamaica Inn* is seen as a work of quality (Queval 1948).

4   This is contrary to Antoine de Baecque's statement that the film premiered in January 1949 (de Baecque 2003: 97). Source: "1949: Toutes les données chiffrées du cinéma: le box office de Paris/France [1949: All the figures on cinema: the box office in Paris/France]", *Centre National de la Cinématographie*. https://www.cnc.fr/professionnels/etudes-et-rapports/box-office/boxoffice-1949_1079590.

5   Astruc wrote the first article of the issue 39 of *Cahiers du cinéma*, comparing Hitchcock to Dostoevsky and Faulkner: "When a man has been telling more or less the same story for thirty years, through 5 films—that of a soul in the grip of evil—and maintains the same style along this single line, essentially an exemplary way of stripping down the characters and plunging them into the abstract world of their passion, I find it hard not to admit that for once we are faced with what is after all the rarest thing in this industry: an author of films" (Astruc 1954: 5).

6   *L'Écran français* 340, January 16, 1952, is missing in this study.

References

Astruc, A. (1948) "Naissance d'une nouvelle avant-garde: la caméra-stylo," *L'Écran français*, 44, March 30, p. 5.
Astruc, A. (1954) "'Quand un homme…'," *Cahiers du cinéma*, 39, October, p. 5.
Barrot, O. (1979) *L'Écran français 1943–1953: histoire d'un journal et d'une époque*, Paris: Les Éditeurs français réunis.
Bazin, A. (1945) "L'Ombre d'un doute," *L'Écran français*, 14, October 3, p. 6.
Bazin, A. (1946a) "Cannes 1946: Les Enchaînés," *L'Écran français*, 6, October 2, p. 12.
Bazin, A. (1946b) "Soupçons," *L'Écran français*, 70, October 29, p. 6.
Bazin, A. (1948) "Les Enchaînés," *L'Écran français*, 142, March 16, p. 13.
Brisset, T. (2022) "Poussah, tricheur, mineur! La réception critique d'Hitchcock dans la revue *Positif* (1952–1989)," in Frédéric Cavé (ed.), *(D')Après Hitchcock: Reprises, théories, lectures*, Paris: Éditions The Searcher, pp. 296–322.
Ciment, M. (2012) "Éditorial," *Positif*, 617–618, July, p. 1.
Clément, R., and J. Delannoy (1949) "Autour de Hitchcock," *L'Écran français*, 195, March 22, p. 3.
Daquin, L. (1949) "Remarques déplacées," *L'Écran français*, 193, March 8, p. 3.
Darre, J. P. (1950) "Les Amants du Capricorne," *L'Écran français*, 272, September 25, p. 10.
De Baecque, A. (2003) *La Cinéphilie: Invention d'un regard, histoire d'une culture 1944–1968*, Paris: Fayard.
Decoin, H. (1949) "Autour de Hitchcock," *L'Écran français*, 196, March 29, p. 10.
Dreville, J. (1949) "Autour de Hitchcock," *L'Écran français*, 199, April 19, p. 12.
Elsen, C. (1948) "Alfred Hitchcock," *L'Écran français*, 168, September 14, p. 2.
Hitchcock, A. (1948) "Production Methods Compared," *The Cine-Technician*, 14 (7): 170–174.
"Hitchcock a tourné en dix jours son premier film en couleurs," *L'Écran français*, 151, May 18, 1948, p. 4.
Néry, J. (1949) "Le Cinéma en quête d'écran," *L'Écran français*, 190, February 15, p. 8.
Pilati, R. (1950) "Cinquième colonne, taillée en plein navet," *L'Écran français*, 235, January 2, p. 12.
Queval, Jean (1948) "Correspondant 17," *L'Écran français*, 176, November 9, p. 12.
Régent, R. (1948) "La Maison du Docteur Edwards," *L'Écran français*, 143, March 23, p. 13.
Robin, G. (1948) "La Maison du Docteur Edwards," *L'Écran français*, 146, April 13, p. 3.

Tacchella, J. C., and R. M. Thérond (1949) "Hitchcock se confie," *L'Écran français*, 187, January 25, p. 3.

Thérond, R. (1949) "Le Procès Paradine," *L'Écran français*, 234, December 26, p. 11.

Timmory, F. (1950) "La Corde: Hitchcock, le vénéneux," *L'Écran français*, 243, February 27, p. 11.

Tourneur, M. (1949) "Autour de Hitchcock," *L'Écran français*, 196, March 29, p. 10.

Vermorel, C. (1949) "Le cinéma, art clandestin," *L'Écran français*, 189, February 8, p. 3.

Vest, J. (2003) *Hitchcock and France: The Forging of an Auteur*, Westport, Conn.: Praeger.

Vest, J. (2011) "French Hitchcock, 1945–55," in T. Leitch and L. Poague (eds), *A Companion to Alfred Hitchcock*, Chichester: Wiley-Blackwell, pp. 371–386.

Violet, R. (1949) "Le Procès Paradine," *L'Écran français*, 233, December 19, p. 25.

Chapter 28

Hitchcock in Germany—A Germanic Hitchcock?

Transnational Genre, Art Cinema, and Auteurism in 1970s/1980s *Filmkritik* and in the Work of Harun Farocki and Christian Petzold

Jaimey Fisher

Stefan Reinecke: Were you thinking of Hitchcock's Vertigo *when creating the scene [in Wolfsburg] in which Nina Hoss falls into the river and is saved by Benno Führmann? Christian Petzold: Well, I basically always think of* Vertigo *[laughs]."*

(REINECKE AND PETZOLD 2023: 44)

While the story of Hitchcock's influence on the French New Wave is well known and often told, this essay explores another case of Hitchcock's considerable influence in Europe, namely, on the (later) New German Cinema via Harun Farocki and then on the Berlin School's most influential director, Christian Petzold. If New German Cinema were one of the key European "new waves," then the Berlin School is one of the most important European art cinema movements to have emerged post-2000 (Nowell-Smith 2013; Abel 2013). In a way underattended to in both Hitchcock studies and German film studies, Hitchcock exerted hitherto-underexamined influence on the work of a filmmaker—Farocki—whose stock continues to rise, and on another who is one of the few German directors, Christian Petzold, to have attained an international profile since 2000. Although many would associate New German Cinema and the Berlin School with the classic, "slow" art cinema of Bresson and Godard (see Jaffe 2014), this strain of German cinema—made under the star of Hitchcock—highlights the strong streak of auteurist genre moviemaking by some of Germany's most recognized filmmakers (this is the argument of Fisher 2013, cf. Abel and Petzold 2008). In a way also parallel to the French (and *Cahiers du Cinéma*) case, this filmmaking influence was first routed through the high-profile, published reception of Hitchcock that I shall discuss herein. This essay will focus on Farocki's critical interest in Hitchcock in the most important German-language journal of the New German Cinema era, *Filmkritik*, and on Farocki's subsequent, surprise realization of a conspicuously Hitchcockian thriller in the single feature film Farocki made (*Betrayed*, 1985)—and his passing this noirish project on to Petzold.

Such a critical engagement with Hitchcock, and influence by him, is very clear in the work of both Farocki and Petzold, but it is also fitting, given that Hitchcock seems to have been indelibly marked by his early-career time in Germany and the proto-noir thrillers of a filmmaker like Fritz Lang (Gottlieb 1999; Hitchcock 1973). Hitchcock, of course, made two of his first three features in Germany at the same time Lang was working there, and he famously recounts what an impression Lang's work made on him: Hitchcock praised, for example, Lang's enormous and intricate sets for *Siegfried* (1924)—a telling foreshadow of the Austrian's sheer monumental scale for *Metropolis* (1927) (Thomas and Hitchcock 1973). Such articulated admiration anticipates Hitchcock's interest in elaborate set designs, for example, in his single-set films, particularly with the enormous structure for, say, *Rear Window* (Jacobs 2007). Likewise, famously, Hitchcock was clear about the general influence of the German films of the 1920s, under whose Expressionist and proto-noirish influence he made his breakthrough *The Lodger* (1926) and then, of course, would deploy throughout his career. Beyond the general notion of a visual language, Lang and Hitchcock shared a number of key themes and core interests: meticulous construction of unstable systems of looking (and gazing); of subtle surveillance saturating the city; of human seriality and replaceability in modernity; of the malleability and transferability of guilt; and of any normal person's potential for criminality—and the criminality of normalcy. If we take Hitchcock at his word and his images at face value—the undercutting of both, of course, a further theme of Lang and Hitchcock—it seems that Hitchcock's career has long been entwined with his Weimar experience, especially that era's cultural pessimism and dimly lit themes and techniques.

A good late case in Langian point was Hitchcock's 1972 *Frenzy*, which many regarded a return to thriller form for the aging master. Hitchcock's last film to be shot in the UK seems, in retrospect, an amalgamation of *Blow-Up*'s spectacularized London and *M*'s social degeneration—and it is tonally similar to Lang's classic in its surprisingly humorous entertainment about an urban serial killer embodying the overdetermined deviances of his age. Made just six years after Antonioni's global phenomenon, which had delivered London's high-fashion and glamorous superficiality to art cinema, *Frenzy*—also more in the mode of *M*—explored the seedier corners of the great city (late Hitchcock's postwar London vs. *M*'s prewar Berlin), with the former's dripping produce markets, packed pubs convening divergent English classes, and cavernous Salvation Army hostels full of postwar men, and masculinities, set adrift—the last another great theme of the Weimar era. *Frenzy*'s abiding male bonding amid the humiliations of unemployment could be right out of Lang's anarchic *Testament of Dr. Mabuse* (1933). *Frenzy* also appears to update Hitchcock with the fashion for England's angry young men: Richard "Dick" Blaney (Jon Finch) is angry at his employment lot, angry at his business-minded ex-wife, and ultimately angry at the hapless police who fall for an obvious framing by war-camaraderie-faking Bob Rusk (Barry Foster).

Given its overlap with Lang-style noir, *Frenzy* was also of interest to the journal on which I am focusing herein, *Filmkritik*. The journal ran an entire section on *Frenzy* in December 1972 that highlights the lefty journal's interest in certain aspects of Hitchcock's work. Even before Farocki's extensive work on *Vertigo*, *Filmkritik* was foregrounding how Hitchcock's films—and despite and even through its genre mechanisms—could be viewed as socially critical. For example, rather than focusing on *Frenzy*'s clear continuities with *Psycho*—sexually frustrated killer with curious attachment to his mother, imaged in complex murder and cleanup sequences—Wolf-Eckart Bühler underscores how much new urban and social territory the 1972 thriller covered. Bühler highlights *Frenzy*'s more urban and economically critical aspects: thus, rather than a return to form, a viewer can see immediately, pace Bühler, that "things have changed since *The Wrong Man*" (Bühler 1972: 627 ff.).

Bühler's piece also offers a long series of exegetical interpretations of *Frenzy*'s various scenes that highlight how Hitchcock managed a more overt entwinement of the thriller plot with money and economy than is typical in his work. For example, the contrast between wrong-man Dick Blaney and his doppelgänger Bob Rusk is that between a man, Blaney, whose wartime heroism has been rendered obsolete, and Rusk, who seems to have mastered the new economies that have, not coincidentally, rendered Blaney obsolete. Rusk runs a successful produce business in the busy Covent Garden market in and around which most of the film is set. Shot on location, the bustling business of the market helps viewers comprehend how confused Blaney has ended up in his attempts to navigate and negotiate postwar society and economy. Both his ex-wife Brenda (Barbara Leigh-Hunt) and former underling Rusk are now outperforming the former squadron leader economically, and, indeed, by some distance. The film, in fact, opens with Blaney's firing from a pub, setting him adrift in modern London and leaving him to rely on the kindness of his various exes: the ex-wife who divorced him and the ex-underling who cheerfully frames him. Bühler points out that Blaney is barely able to control his fury that his wife is able to make a handsome living from matchmaking while having failed at actual love, underscoring the blithe monetization of everything, no matter how tenuous, in the postwar economy.

Filmkritik's Vertigo Obsession

A rather amazing endorsement of Hitchcock's growing stature in Germany came in the shape of a *Filmkritik* special issue in June 1980 (Fig. 28.1). Despite that year's belonging to the era of high New German Cinema (the year that saw the premieres of now classics like R. W. Fassbinder's sprawling *Berlin Alexanderplatz* and Helma Sanders-Brahms' piercing *Germany, Pale Mother*), Germany's most important film journal dedicated an entire issue to a Hitchcock work that was released twenty-one years before.

Vertigo was well received upon its 1959 West German release, but many reviews nonetheless tempered their enthusiasm with caveats about what they found was an unconvincing ending—in short, they don't adopt the adoration that *Filmkritik* articulated by 1980 (Ev. 1959; Th. K. 1959). The issue furthermore included a wide variety of pieces on the film, by many of its top editors and major writers, including Hartmut Bitomsky, Jürgen Ebert, and Farocki (as well as a translation of Godard's Hitchcock obituary, to affirm the influence of *Cahiers du Cinéma*). Such a commitment of an entire issue of *Filmkritik* to *Vertigo* confirms, to my mind, an undersold countercurrent in the era of New German Cinema, one dedicated to a genre-driven auteurism rather than a merely art-cinema *Autorenkino* (author's cinema). This engagement with a US classic made by a British émigré emphasizes how this New German Cinema era was thoroughly a transnational one, despite the movement's usual association with national cinema (the German past, German politics at the present, revisiting Weimar cinema, adapting German literary classics, etc.; see Rentschler 1980: 154, Prinzler 2019: 13). Here, too, genre became the means to relate to films from abroad—as with Fassbinder's melodramas or Wenders' road movies. With Farocki, it would be socially critical crime thrillers, confirming Hitchcock's Germanic inclinations as well as the genre's broad, transnational appeal.

The title page of the *Vertigo* special issue explains why they were dedicating the issue now: it was due not only to Hitchcock's death earlier that year (in April) but also to the checkered distribution history of his

Figure 28.1 Front cover of *Filmkritik*, June 1980.

1950s work. Released in West Germany in February 1959 (the US premiere had been May 1958), *Vertigo* had the usual five- or six-year run in theaters there, but after that had disappeared. Even a Hitchcock retrospective at the Austrian Filmmuseum in 1977 had not been able to screen the film, one of the reasons the special issue offers a detailed summary of the film by Bitomsky and then a closer recounting of a number of key scenes by Ebert, Bitomsky, and Heinrichs ("Sequenzbeschreibungen," by Ebert 1980b, Bitomsky 1980, Heinrichs 1980)—all amounting to a level of plot and visual specificity in the journal that Petzold, in discussing the importance of *Filmkritik* for his generation, still remembered years later as an inspiration (Osteried and Petzold 2023). This engagement with *Vertigo* long after its release highlights a telling belatedness (what one would term, in German, its *Nachträglichkeit*) in its reception that rendered it even more influential for *Filmkritik* and Farocki. This sort of belatedness in reception and impact recalls the delayed discovery and deferred influence of the films noirs in France: due to the Nazi occupation, US films had been banned in much of Continental Europe in the early to mid 1940s, so this noirish ensemble of darkly shot, and toned, crime thrillers struck audiences and critics all the more powerfully after Germany's unconditional surrender in 1945 and Hollywood's subsequent block exports in the late 1940s. This belatedness lent a coherence, and even culturally pessimistic *Weltanschauung*, to the movie miscellany.

In one of the most substantive essays in the *Filmkritik* issue, Jürgen Ebert explores, in a *Screen*-like, psychoanalytical mode essay, the function of the fetish in and via *Vertigo* (Ebert 1980a). Ebert's piece investigates both the staging of fetishism within the film (in contrast to *Rear Window*'s diegetic focus on the vagaries of voyeurism), but, moreover, the function of the fetish of the film itself for its viewers (Ebert 1980a). Entitled "The Basis of the Makeup" ("Die Basis des Make-Up," with "Make-up" left in English), Ebert's piece highlights how both the foundations of the film's approach (the eponymous "basis") and Madeleine/Judy's literal and metaphorical makeup are all entwined in fetishistic mechanisms at multiple levels. Building on the film's curious narrative repetitions—especially the plot's doubling back on itself after the crime is ostensibly solved and its protagonist apparently broken—Ebert concludes that *Vertigo* unfolds psychological, really psychosexual, processes much more intensively than Hitchcock's other films. This includes arguing that affixing to Hitchcock's famous *Vertigo* shots the label "subjective" does not do justice to the director's micro-examination of the psychology of filmic images and of sexual perversity. In a close reading of Scottie's initial encounter with his eventual, metamorphosizing object of desire—at Ernie's, the memorably wallpapered restaurant, and then in the dazzlingly fecund flower shop—Ebert shows that Hitchcock dismantles the usual system of shot/reverse shot to subject the psychology of desire to new rigors and challenges.

The Inter- and/or Ex-change of Women in Farocki's *Vertigo*

Rounding out the Hitchcock material in the special issue on *Vertigo*, Farcoki's essay "Vertauschte Frauen" ("Mistakenly Interchanged Women") has continued to have an important impact, particularly in its remarkable afterlife via Farocki's erstwhile student and longtime collaborator, Christian Petzold. Petzold is probably the only director of German-language films to have gained an international profile since 2000, with multiple awards at major festivals and multiple films getting theatrical distribution in, for example, the USA, which has been almost unheard for German-language films since the heady days of the New German Cinema. I shall return to Petzold's Hitchcock-inflected work below, but I would argue that "Vertauschte Frauen" underscores how influential Farocki's work and teaching—he was Petzold's professor at the Berlin film academy DFFB before becoming an official collaborator—have been for Petzold's approach. As Petzold has observed about his teacher's essay in an interview (Osteried and Petzold 2023), the "Vertauschte Frauen" piece was "fantastic … it was an important text for me"—highlighting how unusual it is to have a student quote an essay by a professor decades later. In terms of the *Filmkritik* essay in the *Vertigo* special issue, it is also remarkable because the essay details the approach of the single feature film Farocki directed himself: *Vertigo* was, as I discuss below, the point of departure for the single feature film made by a director whose stock continues to rise. "Vertauschte Frauen" revealingly makes *Vertigo* its telos—the last two and a half pages of the six total pages of the essay are spent on Hitchcock's film, but, before then, Farocki carefully traces a number of other somewhat pulpy examples of *vertauschte Frauen* in French and US film and literature that help contextualize and frame Boileau-Narcejac and Hitchcock's approach in what became the film classic.

One should begin with the essay's title, which *Filmkritik* pairs with the cover image of the novel on which the film was based, Boileau-Narcejac's *From among the Dead* (*D'entre les morts*, 1954).

In German, the term "vertauschte" is tricky to translate, with "exchanged" or "interchanged" probably closest, although the *ver-* prefix has something mistaken or unintended and usually more negative about it ("tauschen" is to exchange). That adds an interesting level of ambiguity: on the one hand, it subjects women, via passive participle, to the actions done by another ("interchanged") but also offers the sense that something went or is going awry with the process of exchange undertaken by another. Perhaps more importantly for Farocki's purposes, "vertauschte" has the clear resonance of an economic relationship, and in the essay, Farocki catalogues a series of "exchanged women" whose stories are inextricably interwoven with money. Although he never cites Marx explicitly, it is hard to imagine that Farocki would not have been familiar with Marx's definition of money itself in the famed 1844 Manuscripts as the "the general confounding and confusing of all things" ("die allgemeine *Verwechslung* und *Vertauschung* aller Dinge"—emphasis in original). The examples of the exchange of women he subsequently offers in the essay all pertain not only to clear monetary incentives but also to foundational aspects of modern capitalism, key themes of his nonfiction work. The essay opens by citing Agnès Varda's disconcerting *Le Bonheur* (1965), in which a man takes a new wife who resembles his old wife, who kills herself at his infidelity, and the story ends happily or at least in an overdetermined and symbolic happiness, per its title. But even this putative happiness at the interchanged woman, declares Farocki, is highly unusual: most stories of inadvertently interchanged women—and there are quite a few of them—end unhappily for the participants, for the man and/or women who engineer the exchange. The examples he chooses that lead up, and ultimately frame, his approach to *Vertigo*, highlight an important aspect of his work: the way that modern world, especially in its economics and the mobility/social forms they require, provides fertile grounds for the seriality of people, the loss of self, and the subsequent degradation of society.

After his prologue with *Le Bonheur*, Farocki offers two examples in which the interchange of women is initially possible due to the distortions of colonialism—especially the distance of colonies from the metropole. Colonialism and its exploitative systems as well as its inherent violence were all key themes of Farocki's nonfiction work (see Alter 2024). Here, interestingly, both examples are French and based on the French Indian-Ocean colony of Réunion (island). The distances from the metropole make possible the unlikely game of replacing a relatively unknown dead woman with a living one—such distance, as well as the economics of colonialism, play a foundational and framing role in creating the conditions for the inadvertent interchange of women. In one, *The Secret of the Fake Bride* (Truffaut's *La Sirène du Mississippi*, 1969, with Jean-Paul Belmondo), a new bride arriving all the way from France to Réunion can be substituted by another because, of course, at that distance and cultural remove, identities are hard to confirm and easy to manipulate. In the other, *When a Dead Woman Loves Two Men* (like *Vertigo*'s source material, by Boileau-Narcejac), a plane flying from Réunion to France crashes, allowing the passengers to replace a wealthy woman who perished in the crash with another passenger who survived and targets the dead woman's money.

Two further examples—before Farocki arrives at perhaps the penultimate and most telling one before *Vertigo*—are interwoven with modern capitalism and the social forms it secretes. The first, also French, is similarly based on modern mobility and, in this case, tourism: as Kristin Ross has argued, cars and car-based tourism were uniquely powerful emblems for French modernity in the 1950s and 1960s (Ross 1996). After dropping her corporate boss off at the airport in a large automobile, a female assistant decides to tour the Riviera in the car, only to discover everyone thinks they know her already, a car-bred confusion on the Côte d'Azur that turns out, again, to be a deliberate manipulation of identities. Another, later example anticipates *Vertigo* even more directly: in *Phantom Lady*, the sheer scale of the modern US city renders a woman effectively anonymous and interchangeable amid the metropolis, such that she can conveniently disappear when a man accused of murder needs her for an alibi. In *Phantom Lady*, Farocki implies, the mistaken interchange of women plays upon male gullibility and manipulability amid the modern metropolis, particularly amid its ever-shifting rootless masses and objects of desire—a tidy foreshadow, indeed, of *Vertigo*.

After the Criticism: Specters of *Vertigo* in Farocki's *Betrayed* (*Betrogen* 1985)

In the course of time since the essay's appearance, the many examples from "Vertauschte Frauen" have proven more than merely academic or critical—it turns out that they would come to form the basis for the feature-film project that Farocki abruptly initiated in the early 1980s. Farocki's surprise feature project, as Nora Alter has detailed, signaled a sea change for his career: Alter reports that in November 1983—some three after years after his "Vertauschte Frauen" essay—Farocki wrote to "friends, colleagues and staff at *Filmkritik*" to inform them of his decision to depart the journal that he had edited for ten years and throughout its highest profile period. Along with his likewise surprising, even shocking, decision to part with his long-term production team from his many nonfiction films, Farocki seems to have initiated a deep rethinking and reorientation in his productivity. His interest—obsession?—with a *Vertigo*-like news story, detailed as the penultimate example in "Vertauschte Frauen," would take over his career for a couple of years.

After exploring the above, pulpy fictional examples of novels or films substituting one woman for another cited above—and before concluding with *Vertigo*—"Vertauschte Frauen" details a newspaper story that Farocki carried around with him for a long time. Set in another colonial context—this time in Singapore—the report recounts how a British soldier stationed there murdered his wife, returned to the UK, secretly substituting the murdered spouse with her own sister in the existing marriage (vs. the more obvious option of just marrying the sister). The newly minted, substitute wife played the role, apparently successfully, of her own murdered sister, with one notable challenge: the substitute already had a family, with four (!) children, that she (really their own mother) now had to adopt in her new role as their aunt. The labyrinth of galvanizing desire, unhappy marriage, and shocking familial seriality proved fertile fuel for a film to Farocki: although he does not say so in the 1980 essay in the *Vertigo* special issue, it clearly forms the basis of his sole feature, *Betrayed*, which would relocate the colonial-metropole topography of the newspaper story to wealthy West Germany of the 1980s.

Betrayed follows Jens Baumann (Roland Schäfer), a plumber turned HVAC specialist, who meets Anna (Katja Rupé), a sometimes escort, in a nightclub, marries her but then cannot maintain her interest in the domestic life that he, in his newly found wealth, is committed to cultivating. His commitment to a good middle-class family in his new apartment apparently arises from his having become much wealthier via HVAC work on the many new buildings sprouting up in the wealthy West-German 1980s. Both Farocki's and Petzold's films are filled with the upwardly social mobile and the disconcerting dizziness (one might say *Vertigo*) they feel as they scale up the social heights. Although Anna agrees to the well-heeled household he has promised her, Anna grows increasingly frustrated and bored and returns to her earlier life. Inadvertently or not—his intentions are kept intriguingly vague—he ends up killing her, hides her corpse, and then substitutes her with her sister Edith (Nina Hoger), who is desperate to keep her children after legal problems with the local authorities. Edith figures she can do so by taking on the identity of her now-dead sister and then adopting her own children, pace the "Vertauschte Frauen" essay's news report.

Beyond these plot similarities of an exchanged woman as wife, *Betrayed*'s themes also dovetail with those in *Vertigo*, including the suspect nature of male desire. *Betrayed* introduces viewers to a protagonist, here Jens, whom it quickly renders an obsessive observer and then dogged desirer, someone who waits and watches a woman unwaveringly—rather like a moviegoer. Jens sees and falls for Anna, whom he will eventually kill, and then starts to observe her from afar—watching, waiting, increasingly wanting. Like *Vertigo*, *Betrayed* explores, and creatively exploits, the boundaries between casual looking, surveillance, and a gaze-like look overdetermined by interwoven (sexual) desire and (middle-class) ideology.

With these logics of movie-made desire—and recalling *Filmkritik*'s interest in *Frenzy* detailed above—Farocki also tracks a terrain of class in Jens's Scottie-like pursuit of this newly found object of desire. Parallel to *Vertigo*'s Scottie, Jens's decision to betray his more working-class vocation—and the social context it represents—yields his murderous nightmare. *Vertigo*'s Scottie, after all, decides against his better judgment to take an assignment from a wealthy friend and is quickly pulled away from modest

Midge into a world of the finest fashions, expensive restaurants, baroque jewelry—all of which only seem to intensify his desire for Madeleine. In *Betrayed*, Jens, whose family name literally means construction worker ("Baumann"), has decided he needs the romantic and familial accouterments of the middle-class to accompany his newly found wealth. His car designates him a simple plumber, but increasingly lucrative jobs in the burgeoning HVAC industry have delivered him wealth that surprises even him. But the nightclub he subsequently visits with this new money—like *Vertigo*'s lewd reds in contrast to the muted grays of work life—enters him in a game that he is not prepared to play. In fact, Jens's taking this nightclub game of flirtatious play too seriously, instead of just playing within its rules, leads to his proposal to, and then murderous frustration with, Anna.

Jens's killing of Anna is highly ambiguous in the film, highlighting the contiguity of everyday life with criminal malice, the thin line between the normal person and the murderer—all familiar, of course, from Hitchcock's world and *Vertigo*'s ending in particular. After Jens has convinced his now-wife Anna to leave her regular club again and to return home, the camera hues close to his point of view, particularly as she suddenly elects to flee the car rather than return to the bubble of domestic unhappiness. In this moment of greatest plot tension, and sticking close to Jens's point of view in a Hitchcock mode, viewers see her flee and then pans over to her handbag on the passenger seat of the car. In that moment, as Jens grabs the bag, the car lurches toward his unsuspecting wife, rendering ambiguous his intention to cut her down with his car. It is notable that this same inadvertent distraction to apparent unintentional vehicular fatality is duplicated in a Petzold film on whose script Farocki collaborated, namely, *Wolfsburg*. As in *Wolfsburg*, even if the protagonist's vehicular homicide were itself unintentional and/or unconscious, the afterlife of the ambiguous act requires a subsequent level of shocking criminality from a character who had seemed completely normal until that plot point: here, a shocked Jens fails to get his wife medical attention, effectively leaving her to die.

Besides these narrative and thematic parallels between the films—e.g., the association of the desiring with the surveilling male, the waiting lover with the observing detective—other sequences reveal Farocki's not merely thematic but also visual mining of *Vertigo*'s vein of cinematic ore (see Fig. 28.2). After Anna begins to flee the marriage sphere in which Jens has tried to domesticate her, he is left searching for, and surveilling, her once again. The montage of this search highlights the garish topography of West Germany's late economic-miracle (*Wirtschaftswunder*): closeups of Jens's literally well-heeled feet dissolve to another bar and then to another nightclub bathed in red light, the darkness illuminated primarily by neon signs that *Vertigo* also deploys to blur reality and the stuttering fantasies of its diminished protagonist. Intriguingly, Petzold has also said the images of Scottie's tracking and chasing of Madeleine through the city made a great impression on him: "The chase scenes in *Vertigo* with James Stewart and Kim Novak left a deep mark on me, even on my bodily memory, with their somnambulistic slowness" (Gansera and Petzold 2023: 38).

The urban topography of both films intensifies the class dynamics that noirish thrillers often intensify. In *Vertigo*, Scottie's following and observing of Madeleine is overdetermined by an upper-middle-class lifeworld that viewers never see Scottie otherwise indulge: Ernie's garishly lavish restaurant, Madeleine's handsome apartment building adorning the summit of Nob Hill, the Legion of Honor Museum, as well as (allegedly) Madeleine's keeping a secret room in a hotel, perhaps for assignations. Scottie, an early-retirement city detective, admires not only the woman he is following but also lingers over these trappings of an upper-class lifestyle enjoyed by his wealthy friend (and eventual doppelgänger), Gavin. In *Betrayed*, Jens's pursuit of a wife to go with his surprise wealth and nice new seaside apartment is also one overdetermined by similar class distinctions and his commitment to ascending the socioeconomic

Figure 28.2 *Betrayed* (1985) and *Vertigo* (1958). Chasing ghosts on foot: Both are chasing their lost love objects across their respective cities. *Betrayed*: left column; *Vertigo*: right column.

Vertigo, directed by Alfred Hitchcock. © Alfred J. Hitchcock Productions 1958. All rights reserved. *Betrogen*, directed by Harun Farocki. © Bayerischer Rundfunk (BR) 1985. All rights reserved.

ladder. He, for instance, has to watch Anna, his object of desire, in the club company of wealthier patrons, from whom Jens imagines he is rescuing the much younger Anna via a similar monetary upside.

The reviews of *Betrayed* were mixed, and many criticized the acting's consistent artificiality and conspicuous coldness (Müller 1990; Glomb 1990). It is true throughout the film that the actors play their characters coolly, likely emphasizing the social roles they represent, a remnant of Farocki's interest in Brecht: the notion of a Brechtian gestus (a socially conditioned and revealing bodily gesture) is something of which Farocki often wrote, as Nora Alter has convincingly shown in her recent book on Farocki (Alter 2024). But this coldness is also something that Farocki could well have mined directly from *Vertigo*. *Vertigo*, of course, turns Scottie shockingly, and terrifyingly, cold toward Judy in those moments one might have hoped for the warmth of relieved recognition. Instead, Scottie's arc seems to stretch from the warmth that he shows Midge, then heat to Madeleine, to the kind of cold cruelty that he offers remade Madeleine–Judy in the final, fatal climb up the tower. Jimmy Stewart was the warmest, aw-shucks actor in the USA by the late 1950s, but he had been differently cast earlier in his career, and Hitchcock's joke in *Vertigo* appears to have been turning America's good guy back into a murderous villain, here willing to risk a woman so he can get (it) up the tower. Here and for Farocki and later Petzold, desire runs cold, particularly owing to its amalgamated character, a mix of personal and sexual neuroses with collective, especially social forces.

"Alles Theater!" Performativity within the Interchange

In an ill-advised effort to interest Anna early in the film, Jens declares to her (an ambiguous sort of escort rather than prostitute): "I find whores more honest [than you]. Here the women act as if the men have a chance, as if [the women] might be in love." To this unusual come-on, Anna coldly replies, "Men know women will act in love with them if the men spend money on them. That is what they are paying for. You still go to the cinema even though you know the actors don't actually die." Anna invokes here a deceptive kind of performance, a suspect sort of cinema, and the mechanisms of serial desire—and, she suggests, the entwinement of all three of these phenomena. All three are central and recurring themes of Hitchcock (and Lang), especially in the former's *Vertigo*. Such performative themes are sustained through the late stages of Farocki's *Betrayed* as well, after Edith has replaced her sister Anna. A city employee comes to check the newly minted family before signing off on the adoption of Edith's children by the new Anna–Edith.

As she inspects the house and them, this city employee abruptly declares the carefully cleaned apartment, stiffly formal clothes, and meticulously prepared coffee and cake: "Alles Theater [it's all a performance]!" For a moment, viewers think this inspector might actually unmask these criminal performers. But she, instead, offers that she only wants to get to know the couple for real. Jens and Anna–Edith obligingly act more casual, but, of course, merely continue to feign fake Anna, a fake marriage, and act as a fakely parenting couple. The performativity of everyday—particularly deceptive performances by the interchanged women—abides.

Another key theme of these performances of the interchanged woman is that she starts to take on, inadvertently, sundry attributes of whomever she is playing. In this Langian modernity, in which every interaction demands a persuasive performance of economic skills and/or social station, one quickly loses one's own personhood and starts to become another—especially, as in all these cases, if the other's life affords something one desires (usually illicit monies). In *Vertigo*'s second half, Judy quickly calculates that knowing and being herself—in good Socratic, classical-humanistic fashion—will not interest Scottie in the least. She subsequently adjusts her personhood accordingly: her Madeleine performance soon overwhelms her Judy self, right up, and off, the climactic tower. In Farocki's film, the substitute sister Edith, after she has taken on the role of her deceased sister Anna, acts increasingly like the latter, not least because she can rely on Jens to watch her now adopted children. She goes so far as donning Anna's much more provocative clothing, visiting Anna's old club haunts, and even cavorting with Anna's former clients—though the newly minted Anna–Edith could have easily deflected their attentions by invoking her new status as a good middle-class housewife. Of course, a deflection of seedy, sniveling male attentions interests neither Anna nor Edith: strategic diversion rather than outright deflection is the goal of the gendered game that Farocki depicts. Edith's overly effective acting in the role of Anna—including the latter's seductive manner and sensuous indulgences—soon yields tensions between new Anna–Edith and Jens. Indeed, it is unclear how long the marriage would have lasted anyway before they are unmasked by one of the denizens of the nightclub in which the new Anna–Edith insists on hanging out.

These self-submerging perils of performance grow ever clearer in the collaborations of Farocki and Petzold, a peril whenever one undertakes a performance for love and, much more often the case in their work, for money. The performances, in fact, often confuse the entwinement of erotic and pecuniary incentives, a theme throughout *Vertigo*, *Betrayed*, and then especially in Petzold's earlier films (see Landry 2018). Revealingly, Farocki gave up fictional filmmaking after the tepid reception of *Betrayed* but began to collaborate, as cowriter or "dramaturge," with his onetime student Petzold on the latter's increasingly successfully feature films. It would certainly seem that *Vertigo* was a central aspect of this pedagogical and professional passing of the baton: Petzold has been clear that *Vertigo* occasioned his first ruminations on taking cinema seriously (Gansera 2002). And *Vertigo*-esque performances' remaking of their performers, intentionally and not, proves one of Farocki's and Petzold's perennial themes: Jens tries to remake Anna, and Edith remakes herself in Anna's mold, shocking Jens at her ability to take on a

Figure 28.3 *Toter Mann*, directed by Christian Petzold.
© teamWorx Television and Film GmbH 2001. All rights reserved.

new self. Also a great Brechtian theme (see his underrated *Mann ist Mann*), the shocking malleability of personhood runs through Petzold's early and midcareer, that is, those films on which Farocki worked. In those films, from *Pilots* (*Pilotinnen*, 1994) through *Cuba Libre* (1995) and *The Sex Thief* (*Beischlafdiebin*, 1998), women remake themselves via performances to navigate a largely man's world. By the time of 2001 TV film *Toter Mann* (dir. Christian Petzold, "dramaturgy" by Farocki), the quotations of *Vertigo* become even more overt (Fig. 28.3).

In this award-winning film, a woman deceives a man by playing someone she is not, but then she changes abruptly midway through, to the shock of the assorted men around her. The title refers, first, to death generally—notably, the title of *Vertigo* in Germany was "From the Realm of the Dead" (*Aus dem Reich der Toten*)—but also to a *Vertigo*-echoing plunge into the water, in which one pretends to be the dead person hitting the waves obliviously. Although, in English, such an aquatic maneuver is known as a "cannonball" (a more forward-leaning metaphorical expression), in German the phrase suggests a corpse hitting the water unawares, underscoring the liminality of life in and around water—perhaps the key moment of Scottie's love for Madeleine and, here, yet another moment of influence of the British émigré on luminaries of New German Cinema and the Berlin School.

References

Abel, M. (2013) *The Counter-Cinema of the Berlin School*, Rochester, NY: Camden House.
Abel, M., A. Bademsoy, and J. Fisher (eds) (2023) *Christian Petzold: Interviews*, Jackson, Miss.: University of Mississippi Press.
Abel, M., and C. Petzold (2008) "The Cinema of Identification Gets on My Nerves: An Interview with Christian Petzold," *Cineaste online*, 33 (3). www.cineaste.com/articles/an-interview-with-christian-petzold.htm
Alter, N. (2024) *Harun Farocki: Forms of Intelligence*, New York: Columbia University Press.
Bitomsky, H. (1980) "Sequenzbeschreibung: Die Verführung," *Filmkritik*, 24 (6): 271–273.
Bühler, W. (1972) "Alfred Hitchcocks *Frenzy*: Materialien und Notizen," *Filmkritik*, 16 (4): 626–637.
Ebert, J. (1980a) "Die Basis des Make-Ups," *Filmkritik*, 24 (6): 248–260.
Ebert, J. (1980b) "Sequenzbeschreibung: Die Begegnung," *Filmkritik*, 24 (6): 261–263.
Ev. (1959) "Aus dem Reich der Toten," *Film-Dienst*, 12 (8): film #7835.
Farocki, H. (1980) "Vertauschte Frauen," *Filmkritik*, 24 (6): 274–279.
Fisher, J. (2013) *Christian Petzold*, Champaign, Ill.: University of Illinois Press.
Gansera, R., and C. Petzold (2023) "Dead Man, What Now? A Frontrunner for the Television Prize—Christian Petzold between Andersen and *Vertigo*," in M. Abel, A. Bademsoy, and J. Fisher (eds), *Christian Petzold: Interviews*, Jackson, Miss.: University of Mississippi Press, pp. 37–39.
Glomb, R. (1990) "Betrogen," *Volksblatt*, February 15.
Gottlieb, S. (1999) "Early Hitchcock: The German Influence," *Hitchcock Annual*, vol. 8, pp. 100–130.
Heinrichs, K. (1980) "Sequenzbeschreibung: Das Scharnier," *Filmkritik*, 24 (6): 272–273.
Jacobs, S. (2007) *The Wrong House: The Architecture of Alfred Hitchcock*, Rotterdam: 010 Publishers.
Jaffe, I. (2014) *Slow Movies: Countering the Cinema of Action*, New York: Columbia University Press.
Jaffe, I. (2018) "No Place Is Home: Christian Petzold, the Berlin School and Nuri Bilge Ceylan," in M. Abel and J. Fisher (eds), *Berlin School and Its Global Contexts: A Transnational Art Cinema*, Detroit, Mich.: Wayne State University Press, pp. 135–153.
Kaes, A. (1989) *From Heimat to Hitler: The Return of History to Film*, Cambridge: Cambridge University Press.
Landry, O. (2018) *Movement and Performance in Berlin School Cinema*, Bloomington, Ind.: University of Indiana Press.
Müller, K. B. (1990) "Betrogen," *Die Tageszeitung*, February 15.
Nowell-Smith, G. (2013) *Making Waves: New Cinemas of the 1960s*, London: Bloomsbury.

Osteried, P., and C. Petzold (2023) "Interview with Christian Petzold about Phoenix," in M. Abel, A. Bademsoy, and J. Fisher (eds), *Christian Petzold: Interviews*, Jackson, Miss.: University of Mississippi Press, pp. 158–162.

Prinzler, H. H. (2019) "Was damals geschah," in B. Presser (ed.), *Aufbruch ins Jetzt: Der Neue Deutsche Film*, Berlin: Edition Achsensprung, pp. 10–21.

Reinecke, S., and C. Petzold (2003) "The Cinema as Experimental Setup: A Workshop Conversation with Director Christian Petzold," in M. Abel, A. Bademsoy, and J. Fisher (eds), *Christian Petzold: Interviews*, Jackson, Miss.: University of Mississippi Press, pp. 42–45.

Rentschler, E. (1980) "Introduction: Critical Junctures since Oberhausen—West German Film in the Course of Time," *Quarterly Review of Film and Video*, 5 (2): 141–156.

Ross, K. (1996) *Fast Cars, Clean Bodies: Decolonization and the Reordering of French Culture*, Cambridge, Mass.: MIT Press.

Th K. (1959) "Aus dem Reich der Toten," *Filmkritik*, 3 (3): 77–80.

Thomas, B., and A. Hitchcock (1973) "Alfred Hitchcock: The German Years," *Action* 8, January/February, pp. 23–25.

Chapter 29
Alfred Hitchcock and Italian Film Criticism
"A Good Second-Rate Director"

Francesca Cantore and Andrea Minuz

Hitchcock, Italy, and the *Cahiers du Cinéma*

"In Italy, we are all more or less guilty, compared to France, of having underestimated the Maestro for many years" (*Corriere della Sera*, August 9, 1999). Recalling Alfred Hitchcock on the occasion of his centenary, the Italian film critic Tullio Kezich openly confessed Italian criticism's delay, compared to the critics of the *Cahiers du Cinéma*. "If someone finally undertook a documented analysis of the critical success and adversity of Hitchcock from our parts," he continued, "he would discover that his films have always been spoken of with a certain consideration, but as if they did not concern the Seventh Art, and instead fell, even with all the trappings of spectacular quality, within the context of pure entertainment" (*Corriere della Sera*, August 9, 1999). Indeed, much of Hitchcock's critical reception in Italy is based around the rigid contrast between art and entertainment. However, there are many elements to take into account in trying to reconstruct such a complex and nuanced affair.[1]

The innovative scope of *Cahiers du Cinéma*'s Hitchcockian readings, capable of "putting emphasis on that which was least acceptable for the cultural establishment of the time" (Costa 2021: 8), is obviously indisputable. It must be said, however, that Hitchcock was also appreciated by many critics in Italy. The difference, compared to France, is that he was never used as a pawn in a theoretical battle to demonstrate that one could also be an author in Hollywood or to reiterate that the industrial and spectacular dimension of cinema did not exclude the search for a refined artistic and personal language. While the Hitchcock of *Cahiers* shattered the distinctions between author and genre, individual creativity, and the Hollywood system, the Hitchcock of Italian criticism remained "a good second-rate director" (Fava 1981: 47), the creator of astute films, which were captivating from a technically spectacular point of view, yet which had little to do with art and the dominant idea of cinema in Italian critical discourse. His films were looked upon with great interest. But the fact that in Hitchcock's work there were formal motifs, visual ideas, obsessions, themes, and recurring characters—as Rohmer and Chabrol would demonstrate in their famous study—was not taken much into consideration.

The critic Morando Morandini, for example, explained how beyond the hostility of *Cinema Nuovo* (a leftist and Marxist Italian film magazine, most consistently contemptuous of Hitchcockian cinema) or the idolatry of *Cahiers du Cinéma*, there was an alternative. Reviewing *The Man Who Knew Too Much* in 1957, which he also described as "artificial" and "banal," Morandini wrote: "As an entertainer, Alfred Hitchcock is a master. Far from both certain Frenchmen who consider him a genius and our own certain Marxist puritans who despise him as a hack, we are modestly grateful to him for being what he is without taking him too seriously" (Morandini 1981: 153). In the mid 1980s, the director Carlo Lizzani laid claim to a primacy of Italian criticism over the French: "We loved Pudovkin, but also Réné Clair, King Vidor. And already in 1943, the first positive criticism of Hitchcock appeared in the magazine *Cinema*: we didn't have to wait for the *Cahiérs du Cinema* in the 1950s" (Francione 2004: 172). Lizzani was referring to *Rebecca*, which, like *Notorious*, was generally well received in Italy both by the public and a large number of the critics, without however inspiring any authorial readings of Hitchcock. Although exaggerating a bit, Lizzani suggested that the situation was more nuanced and complex than it appeared at first glance. The fact that there was an ignored or misunderstood Hitchcock, as if due to a deficit of critical acumen as well as a forced hypothesis, does not take into account the contexts, the cultural battles, the very different interpretive schemes that regulated the Italian and French debate, as well as the various distribution factors at play. Many Hitchcockian titles arrived haphazardly in theatres after the war and during the 1950s, without a specific order. Five titles in particular from the mid 1960s disappeared from screens due to problems related to rights, at least until 1984, when Patricia Hitchcock, daughter of the director, sold the rights to Universal for 6 million dollars. The agreement put the films back in circulation, making them known to new generations: this process cannot be ignored in analyzing the construction of the cultural value of Hitchcock's cinema.

Overall, the Italian reception of Hitchcock (here understood exclusively in his Hollywood period) unfolds along three main phases. During the first phase, between the 1940s and 1950s, there was a strong rejection of a cinema that appeared truly distant from the themes, needs, and obsessions of Italian criticism of the time, is marked by the head-on clash between two ideological blocs: the defenders of a realism with a social backdrop and an aestheticizing criticism, which sought to defend some sort of artistic purity in cinema. Recalling, in general terms, the perception of Hitchcock's cinema in the 1950s, Claudio G. Fava observed:

> It was a decisive decade for more than one reason. On the one hand, a good part of the Italian critics had independently decided, once and for all, that Hitchcock was a good second rate director, specializing in giallos (detective fiction), with a certain mocking chill, and notable above all for his habit of appearing in person, fleetingly, in his own films: subliminal apparitions that the fans (led by Truffaut), as it is known, always anticipated, and then used against him, almost as if it were a shameful coquetry. On the other hand, we continued to hear that behind that second-rate director there was not only a first-rate craftsman, but behind that first-rate craftsman, that proponent of crime novels which often overturned all the rhetorical trends of the giallo—since they didn't involve the search for an unknown murderer but the description of a known murderer, or the image of the fear in a childhood dream, all coloured black, all inexplicably "evil" and badly arranged—there was something else.
>
> (Fava 1981: 47)

A second phase, which began in the mid 1960s, saw interpretive French influences shaping a new perspective on Hitchcock. Though Truffaut's interview was translated into Italian only in 1977 (and Rohmer and Chabrol's book in 1986), the cultural fracture triggered by 1968 brought greater attention to the analytical models of semiotics, psychoanalysis, and structuralism—fields that instantly reveal themselves to be particularly effective for overinterpretive forays between the hidden meanings and the "latencies" of Hitchcock's works. With his death, we finally enter the third phase: that of unanimous consecration, enabled also by the new circulation of his films. The disappearance of Hitchcock, in fact, coincides in Italy with the surge in private television and the possibility to rewatch titles like *Rear Window* or *Vertigo*, which had long been absent from screens due to legal issues. On the occasion of the director's centenary, the beatification of Hitchcock's work can be said to have been fully realized, in Italy too.

In this contribution, we will try to provide an overall picture of the encounter between Hitchcock and Italian culture, to better understand the reasons for the distrust and reluctance, beyond the very hasty ways in which the matter is archived by film historians. We address the period between the 1940s and 1960s, taking into consideration, in addition to the review of magazines and newspapers, various articles that appeared in the Italian press on the occasion of the director's death in 1980. In particular, we will focus on the films *Rear Window*, *North by Northwest*, *Psycho*, and *The Birds*, a choice partly dictated by the notoriety and importance of these titles within Hitchcock's filmography and partly linked to the fact that, as Callisto Cosulich recalled, it was with *Rear Window* (presented at the Venice Film Festival in 1954), that the delay of Italian criticism towards that of the French began (Cosulich 1991).

Rear Window, *North by Northwest*, *Psycho*, *The Birds*

"They were showing an American film, in which a reporter discovers, through a window, that a husband is cutting his wife into pieces." Thus, the writer Italo Calvino, at the time a correspondent from Venice for *Cinema Nuovo*, dismissed the opening film of the 15th Venice International Film Festival, barely even mentioning it (Calvino 1954: 127). However, his was not a voice out of the chorus, as *Rear Window* at the time was generally classified as a "commercial film of good quality, but not suitable for an art exhibit" (Ojetti 1954: 36). Defined by critics as "a stupid idea" (Weinberg 1954: 483), "rushed and sloppy" (Ghelli 1954: 24), a "doughnut without a hole" (Castello 1954: 523), with "ridiculous and superficial dialogue" (Chiarini 1954: 38), the film was also received with detachment by the festival audience, so much so that Ugo Casiraghi recounted "loud laughter in the theatre during moments of tension" (*L'Unità*, August 24, 1954).

The most aggressive attack, however, came from *Cinema Nuovo*, led by Guido Aristarco. In an article that attempted to take stock of the event that has just concluded, the critic took a position against what he defined as the "open door policy" adopted by the festival, according to which cinematographic works were exceptionally admitted, for particular technical and artistic requirements. *Rear Window* would be among the films chosen "out of quota" by the Association of American Producers (Aristarco 1954: 130). As Callisto Cosulich would say years later, the hostile attitude of Italian critics toward American cinema was such that "if a Hitchcock film ended up in a festival's program, it was obvious that it had been imposed by the omnipotence of the Major which had it in the catalogue" (Cosulich 1991: 43).

The deception of the technique, the "imprisonment of the formula" that critics talk about, goes hand in hand with the search for a human dimension of the characters, as the title of Herman G. Weinberg's review for *Cinema emblematically summarizes:* "Technical Perfection and the Absence of Humanity." For Luigi Chiarini, the color effects in the blinding scene with the flash are even "horrific" and "without any dramatic functionality," while for Ernesto G. Laura, "the starting point [of the story] could give rise to the discovery of a small community, those tenants who always see each other and yet barely know each other: however, this human interest is absent" (Laura 1954: 8). Therefore, if sometimes the criticism of Hitchcock's "craft" is to be understood in a strictly technological sense (the use of color, sound, the use of aesthetic virtuosity, etc.), other times it concerns the "clockwork" dramaturgical construction typical of much Hitchcockian cinema. Whether it has to do with visual or narrative aspects, his technique is perceived to the total detriment of the psychological depth of the characters, to the extent that critics talk of stories experienced "by puppets and not by human beings" (Terzi, in *Avanti!*, August 24, 1954).

When faced with particularly intricate plots, the question of technique leads to accusations of improbability. Criticism of the logic and plausibility of Hitchcockian plots recur, read in the name of realism they are often seen as bizarre, improbable, artificial. For example, regarding *North by Northwest* (1959), if a minority of Italian critics identify its strong point precisely in the dramaturgical development of the film, so much so that in *La Stampa* they speak of the "art of cinematographic muddling" (October 30, 1959), Roger Thornhill's misadventures don't agree with everyone. For example, they worry a critic like Morandini who defines Ernest Lehman's screenplay as "one of the most farfetched and illogical stories that has ever been brought to the screen" (Morandini 1959: 125). According to his reading, the first to disbelieve would be the director himself "who this time, more than the others, simply wanted to entertain himself and others" (Morandini 1959: 125). Starting from the question of technique, the most anti-American of objections evidently inserts itself, that of direction at the service of entertainment which ends up perpetually flattening any discussion around Hitchcockian cinema on the art/entertainment dualism, leaving out the other decisive component, namely style. Hence, the imaginative efforts attributed to the director are the most varied names, far from the orbit of artistic recognition: "craftsman," "artisan," "master of the thriller," "hidden persuader," "skilled mathematician," "chemist," "great cook," "effects artist/sensationalist."

We are at the turning point of the 1960s, and the arguments of Italian criticism are still crystallized around rigid neorealist parameters. In this sense, the comparison made by Guido Fink in *Cinema Nuovo* between the stabs inflicted by Simone on Nadia in *Rocco and His Brothers* (1960) and those delivered by Norman on Marion in *Psycho* (1960), in addition to not being surprising, goes exactly in the direction of highlighting how not only narrative but also visual devices (the detail of the eye, for example) are used for a purely attractive function, without there being a real ethical-theatrical necessity:

Only biased or clueless individuals can consider the stabs inflicted by Simone on Nadia in *Rocco and His Brothers* as "immoral" and allow those of Norman on Marion Crane to pass: the tragic dimension and the expressive violence are functional, in Visconti, for the purposes of a clear condemnation, while Hitchcock entertains and enjoys himself, slides from sexual to necrophilic complacency, goes beyond the very limits of good taste (the tracking shot that starts from the detail of a wide open eye of the dead girl, following the detail of the blood dripping into the drain) and above all calls the public to enjoy, in a state of unconscious complicity, a long anticipated act.

(Fink 1961: 58)

Furthermore, the Italian critical landscape is characterized by an attitude that pays so little attention to the film's promotional strategy that it only partially respects Hitchcock's instructions regarding the secrecy of the plot. Although the ending is somehow preserved, articles unhesitatingly reveal Marion's premature death, speaking of her narrative storyline as a "trick story" (*La Stampa*, November 18, 1960). Similarly, the other big innovation introduced by *Psycho*, preventing late admission into the cinema, does not seem to be followed up in Italy, where the invitation to respect the screening times and not reveal the ending is left solely to advertising campaigns.

The other issue raised across the board by critics regarding Hitchcock's filmography is the attention to "content." In a 1991 contribution recalling the climate of disagreement between the two French journals *Cahiers du cinéma* and *Positif* on Hitchcock's work and attempting to compare with the ambiance of Italian criticism, Callisto Cosulich would say:

> There was a substantial difference between the attitude of *Positif* and that of the majority of Italian critics. Seguin contested Hitchcock's vision of the world, the "messages," direct or transversal, that shone through his films. In other words, he took it seriously. Italian critics, however, denied that Hitchcock's films were bearers of "messages" that expressed a vision of the world: they were "frivolous entertainment," period; they remained "bullshit," even when they were presented in a clever way.
>
> (Cosulich 1991: 40)

In this sense, the film that is most suited to being read from this perspective is *The Birds* (1963). Together with the ever-pressing search for narrative logic, which for example pushes Alberico Sala to wonder why no one in Bodega Bay owns a shotgun (*Corriere della Sera*, May 10–11, 1963), the issue of the "message" seems to be the dominant question. The search for an allegorical meaning to attribute to this "vivid spectacle of ornithology in a Freudian key" (Pestelli, in *La Stampa*, October 31, 1963) clearly derives from the open ending of the film. Thus, for example, Guglielmo Biraghi in *Il Messaggero* writes:

> The director doesn't explain to us why all that pandemonium is happening; he does not humanly denounce faults that justify it, nor does he bother to give some explanation of the events, if not logical, then at least moral. Indeed, he reaches the point of malice of not even giving an answer to a question that, little-by-little, makes its way into the mind of the spectator: that is, whether some symbolic meaning is not haphazardly to be found in a pair of inseparable budgies who […] remain calmly in a cage all the time, without even showing signs of rebelling against their masters.
>
> (*Il Messaggero*, May 10, 1963)

The need to explain an event that finds no scientific evidence in the plot leads critics to the most adventurous interpretations: "What on earth do these devastating and murderous birds that fill Hitchcock's latest film represent?" asks *La Stampa* (November 1, 1963). From the condemnation of hunting, to the threat of nuclear weapons and flying saucers, passing through the gloomy prospects of a mass civilization, the hypotheses are pursued rather haphazardly in the columns of the Italian press. The most complex interpretative operations instead come from *Filmcritica*'s analyses. The editorial staff of the magazine, which not by chance will promote the first Italian conference after Hitchcock's death, in the wake of their French colleagues, identifies in the "plasticity of the theme" such a "significant potential" and a "particular originality, to be reproduced, visually, effectively, even the most impossible relationships between the individual and the environment in which he lives" (Martelli 1963: 635). That same plasticity, for Giovanni Grazzini, and we would say for the majority of Italian critics, is nothing other than the result of a "commercial machine too exposed for the 'Birds' to take on the meaning of a warning: those black bunches on the wires, the roofs, the antennas, those outstretched beak assaults are an end in themselves, they do not become figurative elements of a universal flood" (*Corriere della Sera*, May 10, 1963).

The Public Image of Alfred Hitchcock

The attention to style, formal elegance, and technique, so specific to Hitchcock's cinema, are aspects of his films that soon begin to overlap with his figure as a bourgeois and *bon vivant*, lover of gourmet cuisine, French wines, films made as if they were "slices of cake" (*tranches de gâteau*), rather than "slices of life" (*tranches de vie*), according to one of his well-known aphorisms. By the end of the 1940s, reviews of Hitchcock's films made constant reference to the director's image. His trips to Italy always found great coverage in the newspapers. The Italian press and critics indulged themselves, using various names: "ruddy gentleman," "plump," "chubby," as if to underline the contrast between Hitchcock's bourgeois and good-natured appearance and the creator of anxiety and macabre murders. Reviewing *Shadow of a Doubt* in *Star*, the critic Antonio Pietrangeli defines him as a "talented craftsman" and "a hardhead brooding over dramatic subjects and thrills offered to the simple palate of all spectators" (a recurring term in the Italian press, "craftsman" indicates the prevalence of craft, of technical ability, of a knowledge of cinema condemned to remain separate from the universe of art, aesthetics, and authorship).

The renowned work by Robert Kapsis (1992) has shown how Hitchcock personally pursued the construction of his artistic reputation through careful control of his public image, but these mechanisms were also viewed with suspicion and traced back to the broader prejudice toward the industrial nature of cinema and its logic of communication. Unlike Fellini or Bergman, for example, whose image was considered a direct emanation of an expressive intimacy, that of Hitchcock was seen as a clever publicity stunt, a further element that reiterated the commercial, not artistic, nature of his films. In this sense, the mythology that is built upon the arrival in Italy of the *Alfred Hitchcock Presents* series is significant. Its broadcasting began in January 1959, four years after its American release on CBS, and Rai included it in the schedule every Saturday evening after the prime-time musical show. The acquisition of the TV series was initially hailed as an excellent business as well as a way to diversify the television schedule, pave the way for the importation of foreign serial products, and give a boost to the production of indigenous crime dramas (for example, the series *Giallo Club* with Lieutenant Sheridan aired from a few months later). The press, however, reported the disorientation of Italian spectators who, faced with those "small, rather modest consumer products," asked themselves "Where is this Hitchcock?" (Buzzolan, in *La Stampa*, July 9, 1980). Of the over 200 episodes, only a small percentage actually featured the director. The idea that Hitchcock had to physically manifest himself in his own TV series also arose from the public's affection for the famous cameos that the director had collected in his films. And the disapproval of the Italian public was largely due to the difficulty of imagining and thinking of the author as a "brand," which Hitchcock already was, at the end of the 1950s.

Years later, Hitchcock's death would also become the occasion for a general assessment of the complicated relationship between Italian critics and the English director. "There was a time when our critics allowed themselves to ignore Hitchcock," wrote the critic Ruggero Guarini in *Il Messaggero*, "a skilled hack or something like that. This was how he was defined by a bunch of provincials who preferred the worst byproducts of local neorealism to his splendid films" (April 30, 1980). "By mythologizing the separation between the artist and the public," wrote Giovanni Grazzini, critic for the *Corriere della Sera*, the Italian historiography of cinema was not able to recognize "the greatness of his high craftsmanship, a creator of forms immediately perceivable by the universal audience, but not therefore devoid of a content rich in meaning" (May 1, 1980). It is, above all, around this term "craftsman/crafts" that the various editorials dedicated to Hitchcock's death take their position. The contrast between cinema as art (linked to spirit and subjectivity) and cinema as craftsmanship (linked to technique, to industrial products, to serial production, to public taste)—the nodal point of an idealist film criticism which, in Italy, so powerfully brought together the Catholics and Marxists—was now read within the synthesis offered by the Hitchcock case. Thus, for example, as Oreste Del Buono wrote: "Hitchcock was a craftsman and, at a certain point, craftsmanship borders on art. But Hitchcock was something more, indeed much more: he was an artist who did not take himself seriously as such in the slightest, because he wanted above all to be a craftsman" (*Corriere della Sera*, April 30, 1980). The critic Paolo Mereghetti invoked Leonardo da Vinci and the "Renaissance spirit of the prodigious, skillful Hitchcockian technique" (*Corriere della Sera*, April 30, 1980). In a long article in *La Stampa*, the director Dario Argento disputed the use of the term "craftsman," due to the contemptuous and "reductive" way of approaching Hitchcock's work: "I don't get angry when so many critics (today turncoats, all you need to do is read their crocodile tears in the newspapers) considered Hitchcock's cinema artisanal, but when there was condescension and irony in this definition" (*La Stampa*, May 1, 1980). In this way, Hitchcock inspired a reexamination of the complicated relationship of Italian culture with genre forms, industry, and the popular vocation of cinematographic imagery. More than a missed opportunity, Hitchcock was the complete demonstration of the limits of an entire cinematographic system, the Italian one, which at the end of the 1970s was showing signs of an increasingly irreversible crisis. *L'Unità*, the Communist Party's newspaper, spoke of "a recently appreciated, rediscovered, and reevaluated 'genre' director," specifying, first of all, that Hitchcock "loved expressionism" (April 30, 1980). The newspaper therefore hosted the comments of various directors: Marco Bellocchio, Bernardo Bertolucci, Luigi Comencini, and Dario Argento. While recognizing the genius of Hitchcock's direction, Bellocchio considered Hitchcock "the faithful servant of a certain type of traditional spectacle," author of films which more recently had become "poor and reactionary in content": "Hitchcock is the best," Bellocchio concluded, but it is "the best of a certain type of levelling logic, and in this sense, for us European directors his experience is worth little" (*L'Unità*, April 30, 1980). In short, even in death, Hitchcock struggled to enter the pantheon from a Marxist perspective, still obsessed with anti-Americanism and the rejection of Hollywood rules. Perhaps it is worth concluding this rapid overview of Hitchcock's passing in the Italian daily press with the most refined and precise article, written not by chance by the two writers, Fruttero and Lucentini, both intellectuals (and giallo writers) who were distant and detached from the harsh cinephile controversies of those days and therefore more capable of inserting Hitchcock into the pantheon of the "last great era of bourgeois civilization," as well as of cinema: "A Soviet Bergman, a Cambodian Rossellini is conceivable: but there cannot be a second Hitchcock, who belonged to the last great era of bourgeois civilization. To replicate it, he would need to have around him Fred Astaire, Cocteau, Aldous Huxley, Coco Chanel, Ravel, Pirandello" (*La Stampa*, May 4, 1980).

Acknowledgment

This essay is the result of a joint collaboration. The section *Rear Window*, *North by Northwest*, *Psycho*, *The Birds* was written by Francesca Cantore, the section The Public Image of Alfred Hitchcock was written by Andrea Minuz, while the introductory paragraph, Hitchcock, Italy, and the *Cahiers du Cinéma*, was written by both authors. Special thanks to Giuliano Tomarchio for his crucial help in archival research and the examination of magazines and newspapers.

Note

1. In this sense, we would like to signal Fabio Francione's essay, "Hitchcock e la critica italiana" (Francione 2004); and the volume edited by Marina Fabbri, *Hitchcock: il maestro negato* (1991). Published for the occasion of the Noir in Festival, the volume edited by Fabbri contains an essay by Callisto Cosulich that addresses the relationship with Italian criticism as a whole and contains a selection of exerpts from magazine and newspaper reviews, edited by Leonardo Gandini.

References

Aristarco, G. (1954) "I veri vincitori," *Cinema Nuovo*, 42 (3): 130–132.
Calvino, I. (1954) "L'inaugurazione," *Cinema Nuovo*, 42 (3): 127–129.
Castello, G. C. (1954) "I film della XV^a Mostra," *Cinema*, 141 (7): 512–532.
Chiarini, L. (1954) "La Mostra di Venezia: Cronaca e appunti," *La Rivista del cinematografo*, 3 (8–9): 35–58.
Costa, A. (2001) "Rohmer e Chabrol interpretano Hitchcock," in É. Rohmer and C. Chabrol, *Hitchcock*, Venice: Marsilio.
Cosulich, C. (1991) "Hitchcock e le 'colonne infami' della critica italiana," in M. Fabbri (ed.), *Hitchcock il maestro negato*, Molfetta: La Meridiana.
Fabbri, M. (1991) *Hitchcock: il maestro negato*, Rome: Meridiana.
Fava, C. G. (1981) "Le opere e lo stile: Annotazioni di un critico," in R. Salvadori (ed.), *Alfred Hitchcock. La critica, il pubblico, le fonti letterarie*, Florence: La Casa Husher.
Fink, G. (1961) "*Psyco*," *Cinema nuovo*, 149 (10): 57–58.
Francione, F. (2004) "Hitchcock e la critica italiana," in D. D'Alto, R. Lasagna, and S. Zumbo (eds), *La congiura degli hitchcockiani*, Rome: Falsopiano, pp. 172–187.
Ghelli, N. (1954) "I film in concorso," *Bianco e Nero*, 15 (8): 32–35.
Kapsis, R. (1992) *Hitchcock: The Making of a Reputation*, Chicago, Ill.: Chicago University Press.
Laura, E. G. (1954) "L'Italia unica alternativa alla decadenza di Hollywood," *Rassegna del film*, 24 (3): 3–11.
Martelli, L. (1963) "Gli uccelli," *Filmcritica*, 138 (14): 633–636.
Morandini, M. (1959) "Intrigo internazionale," *Il nuovo spettatore cinematografico*, 1 (5): 125.
Morandini, M. (1981) "Confessioni di un critico hitchcockiano a scoppio ritardato," in E. Bruno (ed.), *Per Alfred Hitchcock*, Montepulciano: Editori del Grido.
Ojetti, P. (1954) "Rapporto sul Festival," *La Rivista del cinematografo*, 27 (9–10): 36.
Weinberg, H. G. (1954) "Perfezione tecnica e assenza di umanità," *Cinema*, 7 (140): 483–485.

Chapter 30
Alfred Hitchcock's Cinema in the USSR and Post-Soviet Russia
Loud Absence

Sergei Kapterev

The history of the exhibition and appreciation of Alfred Hitchcock's work in the former Soviet Union and, less so, in the new, post-Soviet Russia is replete with lacunas, legends, misunderstandings, and near-mysteries. During the Soviet period, which started several years before the start of Hitchcock's career in cinema and ended in 1991, no Hitchcock films gained national commercial distribution. The only exception to this phenomenon was the purchase and distribution—despite the absence of diplomatic and economic relations between the Soviet Union and the United Kingdom in 1927–1929—of *The Ring* by the All-Ukrainian Photo Cinema Administration (VUFKU) in the Ukrainian market under the title *A Strong Man's Love*. VUFKU, which ceased to exist in 1930 after eight years of successful activities in different sectors of film economy, not least because of the Soviet center's displeasure with the Ukrainian cinema's independence, had its own system of contacts with foreign countries, which allowed it to distribute Ukrainian films abroad and purchase foreign films for distribution in Ukraine.

The Stalinist 1930s spelled the end for the mass distribution of foreign films in the USSR typical of the 1920s. And, although the program of the first (and last) Soviet Film Festival, held in Moscow in 1935, included several British entries and could potentially lead to the acceleration of film exchanges with other countries, the worsening of the political situation in the second half of the 1930s meant that only a limited number of films shown at the festival were distributed in the USSR. That is, the British period of Hitchcock's career was not represented in Soviet cinemas until later times, when his films from the 1930s began to pour into the main Soviet film archive, Gosfilmofond, via "friendly" archival collections (primarily those located in the socialist bloc countries). Later, in the 1990s, Russian audiences were able to see these films on TV; probably, this was the most important public appearance of Hitchcock's work in the history of its irregular appearances within Soviet/Russian film culture.

However, as it often happened in Soviet history, small, privileged groups of people were probably able to see films unavailable to wider audiences. Thus, the atmosphere in *Engineer Kochin's Error*, a Soviet spy film released at the end of 1939, sometimes uncannily resembles—in spite of the ideological differences (the Soviet film showed the state's struggle with "enemies of the people")—the quirky mood of *The Lady Vanishes*, which opened one year earlier, as well as Hitchcock's other British thrillers. Aleksandr Macheret, who directed the Soviet thriller, could possibly see Hitchcock's masterpiece at the British Embassy in Moscow; we know that, for example, the US Embassy held regular screenings of American films (screenings attended by, among others, Sergei Eisenstein), and the British Embassy could also screen *The Lady Vanishes* for Soviet guests.

At some point (probably during World War II or soon after it), Hitchcock's last British film, *Jamaica Inn*, received Russian subtitles—that is, it was to be shown to general Soviet audiences. However, for some reason (likely, due to copyright problems: during and immediately after the war some form of film exchange was being negotiated with the British side), its mass distribution did not materialize. The subtitled print was exhibited only to specialized audiences—for instance, to those film fans who attended screenings at the Moscow-based, Gosfilmofond-affiliated theater Illyuzion.

World War II created new opportunities for the exhibition of American and British films in the USSR, and it seemed that Hitchcock's works, with their entertaining anti-Nazi statements, had a good chance of being shown to the Allied Soviet audience. However, this did not happen. The Soviet side preferred more straightforward anti-Nazi (and pro-Soviet) propaganda or more old-fashioned types of film entertainment (such as fairy tales and operetta-like musical films).

The beginning of the Cold War meant that "bourgeois" Western films were effectively banned from Soviet screens. However, the new ideological pressures did not prevent the Soviet authorities from the all-national exhibition of films made in Hollywood before or during the war. Again, Hitchcock's works were not among the so-called "trophy" films, which included films imported from German archives as well as films that had been bought from the US under wartime agreements.

Hitchcock's wartime and early postwar American work appeared in the Soviet Union later, in the 1950s and 1960s, when prints of such films as *Rebecca*, *Foreign Correspondent*, *The Shadow of a Doubt*, *Spellbound* and *Strangers on a Train* were obtained by Gosfilmofond. Usually, it is not easy to get any reliable information about these prints' sources, but one may assume that they came, as it has been already mentioned, via archival contacts and exchanges, without negotiations with film studios or other copyright holders.

For reasons of secrecy, prints of such films were shown to limited audiences—often as incentives for cinema-related transactions or as perks for people of importance. Gosfilmofond arranged special screenings at its base near Moscow, at the Illyuzion theater (the general public could also see a number of Hitchcock films there, beginning with *The Lodger* and the sound version of *Blackmail*) or at places elsewhere convenient for important audiences. Possibly the most famous—and typical—of such screenings was the unannounced Illyuzion exhibition of a Polish release print of *Vertigo* on March 5, 1975. (In Poland, the film opened much earlier, in September 1963.) Later, in the post-Soviet period, the Gosfilmofond collection of Hitchcock films was augmented by entries from the BFI National Archive.

The rating of Hitchcock's films as fruits forbidden by Soviet ideologues provided additional thrills: even people who did not have a chance to see Hitchcock's films knew Hitchcock's name and were aware of his reputation as "the king of horror." "The king of horror"—rather than "the king of suspense"—was how Soviet cultural ideologues presented Alfred Hitchcock to Soviet audiences, predominantly unfamiliar with Hitchcock's work but eager to embrace Western cultural products. Hitchcock as filmmaker was mostly absent from Soviet society; as an ideological object, he was more than present: progressively, he was becoming one of the main culprits in the cultural struggle waged with the West during the Cold War.

Probably, Hitchcock's name, unusual for Russian speakers, contributed to the process of his demonization. Also contributing were the real or invented connections of his themes and images with Freudian psychoanalysis (ostracized in the USSR since the late 1920s but especially unpopular there since its enthusiastic embrace by American theoreticians, practitioners, and artists with the beginning of the Cold War). On the other hand, Soviet excursions into "classical" genre cinema were rare and often unsuccessful. The traditions of radical Russian intelligentsia, inherited by Soviet Marxism, treated entertainment as something below understanding and evaluating. This combination of political conformism and cultural radicalism was a major obstacle on Hitchcock's way to Soviet spectators' eyes, ears, and minds.

It would be an overstatement to say that Hitchcock's name was treated as a symbol of shameless commercialism from the very beginning. References to Hitchcock's work in Britain remained rather neutral. For example, his thrillers of the British period were characterized as "adventure detective stories" in the 1961 edition of *Children's Encyclopedia* (p. 636)—by none other than the famous filmmaker Mark Donskoy—and were analyzed in a generally positive manner in the 1970 *History of International Cinema*: Hitchcock "succeeded in imparting detective films with a particular sharpness and to fill them with the breath of real life"—in spite of his "permeating the audience with the thoughts about the world's hostility to human beings, the thought that they are mere toys in the hands of dark forces and blind fortuity" (Kolodiazhnaia and Trutko 1970: 214, 218). As for Hitchcock's post–World War II American films, they were dealt with superficially—in connection with ideologically correct descriptions of the decadent situation in Western cinema—as contributions to the Cold War struggle.

A major step towards the "intelligent" demonization of Hitchcock was made in March 1963 in the journal *Iskusstvo kino* (*The Art of Film*), when *Psycho* was subjected to criticism by Aleksandr Aleksandrov, who in 1962–1966 was the head of Gosfilmofond's foreign department and had a reputation of relative tolerance towards Western cinema. Aleksandrov described "Hitchcockian mystifications" as "hollow products," and in *Psycho* he saw an especially vile mystification leading "into the world of macabre psychosis" and "inflating—in a virtuoso performance—a pathological incident into a universal problem" (Aleksandrov 1963: 139–140). There was nothing new in this statement from the viewpoint of Soviet ideology; however, the fact that this viewpoint was presented in detail by an expert in cinema signified an important stage in the Soviet criticism of Hitchcock's work.

Hitchcock's position within Soviet cultural criticism was further aggravated by the release of *Torn Curtain* and *Topaz*: from now on, he was not only a contributor to the cultural excesses of the Cold War but also an open Cold Warrior.

The end of the Soviet period preceded by the reformist "perestroika" and "glasnost" rehabilitated many Western cultural products, including Hitchcock's American films. However, among the Western productions abundantly shown on Soviet screens at the end of the 1980s and the early 1990s, there were no Hitchcock films. The dissemination of VHS players and recorders—first within narrow groups of those who could afford them and then within a broad circuit of public exhibition points—in the USSR in the second part of the 1980s profoundly changed Soviet film culture. The resultant flow of foreign films (of very variable quality but unusual and provocative by traditional Soviet standards) included those Hitchcock films that had been inaccessible to those Soviet citizens who were not connected to the political and cultural elite and had very few opportunities to see such films abroad. VHS audiences were mostly attracted by the explorations of pathologies in *Psycho* and *Frenzy*, as well as the anti-Communist messages of *Torn Curtain* and *Topaz*. And when they saw those films by Hitchcock they wanted to see, their attention switched to more "modern," more violent and sexually explicit thrillers. Thus, one may say that Hitchcock appeared in the USSR too late and was eventually appreciated by a rather small section of newly formed Soviet and post-Soviet film fandom.

After the demise of the Soviet Union, Hitchcock films began to be screened mostly as art-house products aimed at connoisseurs who had heard so much about the director's thematic and stylistic achievements and now got a chance to watch those of his works which had not been available during the Soviet era.

To assist the "true" film lovers, a Russian translation of Truffaut's interviews with Hitchcock was published in 1996—by the Eisensteinian Center of Film Culture Studies! The 2010s saw translations of *Alfred Hitchcock and the Making of Psycho* by Stephen Rebello and *Alfred Hitchcock* by Peter Ackroyd. And Hitchcock's 120th anniversary produced several original commentaries from Russian film scholars and filmmakers whose praise for Hitchcock further defined him as a filmmaker for those who truly understand cinema.[1]

This elitist approach, formed since the 1990s, seemed to be partially undermined in 2005, when the Moscow International Film Festival showed *North by Northwest* for a more mixed audience as part of a program titled "Around the World." In 2012, the same festival showed *The Birds* and *Torn Curtain* as part of the program "Universal Pictures: Golden Collection." And 2014 saw a Moscow retrospective of earliest Hitchcock films "Hitchcock: Nine Unknown Films" organized by the BFI with the assistance of several Moscow organizations. (This event, of course, was aimed at a more "refined" audience, but it allowed Russian spectators to see and appreciate the origins of Hitchcock's more familiar and more famous work.)

Also, several years ago, *Rear Window* got a limited distribution in Russia, giving hope that all these theatrical releases—together with the release of "collector's editions" of several Hitchcock classics in the Blu-ray format—will return, albeit belatedly, the genius of Alfred Hitchcock and his body of work from the realm of limited connoisseurship to broader Russian audiences, including young people. After all, the psychological traditions of Russian literature have a lot in common with Hitchcock's brilliant explorations of the intricacies of human behavior, and, on the other hand, the sometimes disappointing inattention of Russian writers to plot construction could be overcome through the study of his narrative skills.

Note

1   Thus, screenwriter Yuri Arabov (who frequently collaborated with Aleksandr Sokurov) believed that Hitchcock "filled his films with Christian philosophy … with stories about how love helps a person get out from the web of crime" (*Izvestiia*, August 13, 2019).

References

Aleksandrov, A. (1963) "'Psycho' (USA)," *Iskusstvo kino*, 6: 139–140.
Detskaia Entsiklopediia, vol. x: *Literatura i Iskusstvo* (1961) Moscow: Russian Federation Academy of Pedagogical Sciences Publishing House.
Kolodiazhnaia, V., and I. Trutko (1970) *Istoriia zarubezhnogo kino*, vol. II: *1929–1945*, Moscow: Iskusstvo.

Chapter 31
Tracing Hitchcock in South Korea
From *I Confess* to *Decision to Leave*

Hye Seung Chung

The first Alfred Hitchcock film that was theatrically released in South Korea is *I Confess* (1953), which was introduced to Korean audiences in 1956. Although the film is considered Hitchcock's minor work in Western auteur criticism, it was enthusiastically received in South Korea due in part to the star power of Montgomery Clift whose performance as a younger Italian lover for a married American woman in Vittorio De Sica's *Indiscretion of an American Wife* (1954) had enamored sentimental Korean audiences drawn to tragic love stories and melodramas. According to film critic Park Yu-hui, Clift's character in *I Confess*, Father Michael William Logan, caught in a hopeless "no way out situation" (wherein the only way to clear himself of the false murder charge is to betray the inviolable sacramental seal of penance), was a cross-cultural object of empathy and identification for Korean theatergoers coping with the devastating aftermath of the Korean War (1950–1953) (*Farmers Newspaper*, July 1, 2013). As a unique local canon, Hitchcock's *I Confess* influenced a number of 1950s Korean films about court proceedings and confessions including *A College Woman's Confession* (*Eoneu yeodaesaeng-ui gobaeg*, 1958). When *Dial M for Murder* (1954) was released in 1957, Hitchcock's name was promoted as "the director of *I Confess*" in Korean newspaper and film-magazine reviews. The second Hitchcock film in Korea was another hit and sparked imitative slogans such as "Dial 113 [national counterespionage line] and Catch Spies" and "Dial [radio station] 900." Legendary Golden Age director Lee Man-hee made the Hitchcockian thriller *Dial 112* (*Daieol 112reul dollyeora*, 1962), about the cat-and-mouse game between a wealthy heiress and three men who are after her fortune (under her ex-husband's machination), in an apparent homage to *Dial M for Murder*.

A Late Arrival: Hitchcock *Yeonggam* ("Old Man") Goes to Korea in the 1960s

It appears that *North by Northwest* (1959) is the first Hitchcock film that received more serious inquiries from Korean critics as an example of auteur cinema. This in-depth review of Hitchcock's auteur signatures in a local fan magazine attests to his growing popularity and influence among Korean cinephiles four years after *I Confess* debuted in Korean theaters. For example, writing for the October 1960 issue of the monthly magazine *International Film* (*Gukje Yeonghwa*), O. Sang-sun observes,

> Hitchcock's pride in detective films lies in suspense. It is the trademark of his productions to maximize spectatorial psychological effects through uneasy scenes. If a motion picture is far removed from its audience, regardless of artistic merits, its vitality is lost. In order to enhance spectatorial identification, Hitchcock presents interesting settings which are conducive to effective arousal of fears. In addition, he always makes appearances somewhere in little corners of his films to comic effects. Another trait of his cinema is the use of convertible props made of mixed materials that characterize Hitchcock's attitude toward enterprises and progress. For example, *North by Northwest* incorporates a small Buddha sculpture with a hidden microphone. The original statue found in an antique store was made prior to Columbus's discovery of America and its historical significance cannot be overestimated.
>
> (*International Film*, October 1960, p. 64)

When *Psycho* (1960) was released in 1962, divisive reviews ran in the Korean press. An anonymous reviewer *of International Film* extolled Hitchcock as an "enthusiastically acclaimed" filmmaker who generates sensations film after film. The review talks up Hitchcock's coming attraction as his most "ambitious work" whose title and content remained confidential during production on the Paramount set. The reviewer concludes, "Although Hitchcock's films have always supplied thrills and excitement to his audiences, [this level of secrecy] is unprecedented in the history of cinema" (*International Film*, May 1962, p. 131). Another reviewer writing for *Kyunghyang Sinmun*, a daily newspaper, was unimpressed despite the noisy ballyhoo leading up to *Psycho*'s summer release. Comparing Hitchcock's split-personality film unfavorably to Hollywood adaptations of Robert Louis Stevenson's 1886 gothic novella *Strange Case of Dr. Jekyll and Mr. Hyde*, the reviewer faults the much-criticized exposition in the final scene wherein a psychiatrist offers a lengthy medical explanation for Norman Bates's (Anthony Perkins') recreation of his dead mother as an alternative personality in his psychotic mind. The reviewer further dismisses *Psycho* as a film with "cliché narrative events and complacent closure" which is less suspenseful than *Rear Window* (1954) and *The Man Who Knew Too Much* (1956). However, the critic begrudgingly approves the "old man's [yeonggam's] age-appropriate" camerawork without showy or deceptive tricks used in Hitchcock's earlier works (*Kyunghyang Sinmun*, July 1962, p. 4). The irreverent use of the colloquial expression *yeonggam* for the then sixty-three-year-old master of Hollywood's finest thrillers thinly veils the condescension on the part of the presumably younger writer. This implied agism is more explicitly demonstrated in a *Chosun Ilbo* newspaper article that contrasts the youthfulness of Korean and French filmmakers (for example, both Lee Man-hee and Jean-Luc Godard were in their early thirties) with the advanced age of major Hollywood directors such as Howard Hawks, John Ford, and Alfred Hitchcock all in their sixties (*Chosun Ilbo*, December 6, 1962, p. 8).

Throughout the 1960s, Korean audiences were able to see Hitchcock's new films such as *The Birds* (1963), *Marnie* (1964), *Torn Curtain* (1966), and *Topaz* (1969) in theaters, and, throughout the 1970s and 1980s, they caught up with his British films (*The 39 Steps* [1935], *The Lady Vanishes* [1938]) and studio system-era collaborations with David O. Selznick (*Rebecca* [1940], *Spellbound* [1945], *Notorious* [1946], and *The Paradine Case* [1947]) on television. The Korean press compared to Hitchcock local directors such as Kim Su-dong, Jeong Jin-woo, and Kim Soo-yong who made cameo appearances in their own films. Korean newspapers occasionally reported on Hitchcock's commentaries on the Hollywood industry and his filmmaking philosophy. For example, the June 19, 1964 edition of *Chosun Ilbo* reports Hitchcock's interview in Paris where the master of suspense explained the shift of his narrative focus from chases between detectives and criminals to "psychological pursuits" (p. 4). In its report on the decline of the Hollywood industry on August 14, 1970, *Chosun Ilbo* quotes Hitchcock who reportedly cited *Psycho* and *The Birds* as evidence that famous stars were no longer needed to make box-office hits (June 19, 1964, p. 6). A clue as to why Hitchcock failed to receive the same critical reevaluations in South Korea as he did in Western academia of the 1970s (when, according to Robert E. Kapsis, "the auteur theory … has strengthened Hitchcock's reputation as a great 'film artist'" [1992: 122]) can be found in an August 20, 1974 report in *Kyunghyang Sinmun* on Hitchcock's seventy-fifth birthday. According to the Korean daily, the British-born director identified the film business as "an industry, not art" and himself as "not a genuine artist" (i.e., he would not be starving if his movies did not sell) (*Kyunghyang Sinmun*, August 20, 1974, p. 8). This (self-)labeling of Hitchcock as a commercially minded craftsman of popular Hollywood entertainment is most likely attributable to his lower standing in the canons of world cinema among Korean cinephiles and intellectuals.

As Robin Wood laments in his 1965 introduction to *Hitchcock's Films*,

> The cinema—especially the Hollywood cinema—is a commercial medium. Hitchcock's films are—usually—popular: indeed, some of his best films (*Rear Window*, *Psycho*) are among his most popular. From this arises a widespread assumption that, however "clever," "technically brilliant," "amusing," "gripping," etc., they may be, they can't be taken seriously as we take, say, the films of Bergman or Antonioni seriously.
>
> (Wood 1989: 57)

This artistic preference for European cinema was particularly true in postwar Korea where major auteurs such as Yu Hyun-mok and Ha Kil-jong were inspired by European art cinema movements, particularly Italian neorealist classics (in the case of Yu) and the modernist films of Pier Paolo Pasolini (in the case of Ha). Moreover, Hitchcock's films became widely publicized in South Korea starting in the 1960s when the French New Wave films of Jean-Luc Godard and François Truffaut provided more attractive alternatives to Hollywood in the eyes of youth audiences. In terms of unique Korean canons of classical Hollywood cinema, as I argued elsewhere,

> According to the Korean Broadcasting System (KBS)'s nationwide survey of "100 Films That Audiences Want to See Again" (conducted in 1996), the ten most requested films were, in order of preference: *Roman Holiday* (1952), *Gone with the Wind* (1939), *Romeo and Juliet* (1968), *The Sound of Music* (1965), *Breakfast at Tiffany's* (1961), *Ben-Hur* (1959), *Waterloo Bridge* (1940), *Doctor Zhivago* (1965), *The King and I* (1956), and *Casablanca* (1942) … South Korean audiences generally flock to star vehicles in lieu of auteur films. Remarkably, yet tellingly, not a single Hitchcock, Ford, or Welles film broke into the KBS one hundred list, whereas four romantic comedies starring Audrey Hepburn (*Roman Holiday* [no. 1], *Breakfast at Tiffany's* [no. 6], *Sabrina* [no. 16], and *My Fair Lady* [no. 33]) were included in the top fifty.
>
> (Chung and Diffrient 2015: 25, 28)

With the rise of what Andrew David Jackson terms "the late and post dictatorship cinephilia boom" and noncommercial art-house exhibition between 1985 and 1997, Hitchcock met new audiences associated with the "cinematheque" or "videotheque" movement of aspiring filmmaker collectives whose leaders opened makeshift film libraries and screening/discussion/education spaces in rented offices (Jackson 2024: 68–69).[1] Film Space 1895, the first videotheque, founded in 1988, organized a monthlong marathon of twenty-six Hitchcock films (from *The Lodger* [1926] to *Frenzy* [1972]) from January 3 to 27, 1991. Supplementing daily evening screenings of two films were four public lectures by local film critics on Saturdays. The Seoul School of Culture, another cinematheque, hosted a smaller scale retrospective of nine Hitchcock films (*The Lady Vanishes*, *Sabotage* [1936], *Rope* [1948], *I Confess*, *Rear Window*, *The Man Who Knew Too Much*, *Vertigo* [1958], *Psycho*, and *The Birds*) from December 5 to 14, 1994. As film critic turned festival programmer Kim Young-jin recalls in his interview with Jackson, Film Space 1895 and other private cinemas were the only exhibition venues where movie buffs (mostly college students or recent graduates) could access canonical masterpieces of world cinema such as "(Italian) Neo-Realism, (French) Nouvelle Vague, New American Cinema, Hitchcock, or (Ingmar) Bergman" (Jackson 2024: 70). Although the late conglomeration of the Korean film industry (including the emergence of blockbuster-oriented multiplex theaters) in the late 1990s killed underground cinematheque culture, this movement was instrumental to unofficial film education for up-and-coming cinephiles such as Bong Joon-ho and Park Chan-wook who would gain worldwide fame as award-winning celebrity directors years later.

"I Have Hitchcock's Blood in Me": Resurrecting *Vertigo* (1958) in Park Chan-wook's *Decision to Leave* (2022)

Under the Korean title *Hwangsang* (translated as "Fantasy"), Hitchcock's *Vertigo* opened in Korean theaters in February 1959 to lukewarm reception. Korean reviewers agreed with their stateside counterparts who described its contrived plot as "farfetched," "unbelievable," and "illogical" upon the film's original US release (*Harrison's Reports*, May 17, 1958, p. 79). In a review published in *International Film*, a local critic dismissed the film on two accounts. First, the Korean reviewer found it implausible for the killer Gavin Elster (Tom Helmore) to manipulate his detective friend John "Scottie" Ferguson (James Stewart) to fall in love with his wife Madeleine (or, rather, her impersonator Judy Barton [Kim Novak]) so that he can serve as an acrophobic, temporarily incapacitated witness to a staged suicide of the (already dead) woman. Second, the character of Judy (Elster's accomplice and girlfriend who genuinely falls for Scottie) is too weak and underdeveloped to support the romance plot (*International Film*, February 1959, p. 96). A different reviewer (for *Chosun Ilbo*) grumbled about the film's unbalanced split diegesis, stating, "Compared with the speedy tempo of the first part, the climax loses its driving force after the flawed flashback of Judy hastily exposes the mystery in the final third of narrative" (February 10, 1962, p. 4). There are no traces of *Vertigo* between the 1960s and the 1980s in the largest Korean historical newspaper database Naver News Library. More than three decades after its theatrical release in February 1959, the next newspaper article referencing the film was published in *Kyunghyang Sinmun* on December 30, 1992. *Vertigo* is mentioned in a short announcement by cinematheque SA/se (formerly Film Space 1895) about forthcoming screenings of the top 10 greatest films in the 1982 *Sight and Sound* critics poll. While Hitchcock's film similarly vanished from public circulation in the West until its theatrical rerelease in 1983 (followed by home video release the following year), as Kriss Ravetto-Biagioli and Martine Beugnet point out, it continued to "haunt" a number of Hitchcockian films made in Europe and the USA, "from Chris

Marker's *La Jetée* [1962] and *Sans Soleil* [1983], to Brian De Palma's *Obsession* [1976], Paul Verhoeven's *Basic Instinct* [1992], Nicole Garcia's *Place Vendôme* [1997], and David Lynch's *Mulholland Dr.* [1999]" (2019: 229). In South Korea, outside of small-group cinematheque screenings, *Vertigo* did not resurface until 1995 when it was finally released on video as part of the Hitchcock masterpiece collection.[2] The film's extended unavailability (for another full decade after its resurrection in the Western home video market) appears to be the primary reason for its obscurity and lower critical standing in South Korea.

Approximately six months after SA/se screened *Vertigo* as part of the *Sight and Sound* 1982 poll of the top 10 greatest films of all time, Park Chan-wook, then a little-known director (who had just debuted with *The Moon Is … the Sun's Dream* [*Dareun … haega kkuneun kkum*, 1992], a box-office flop), was interviewed for *Chosun Ilbo* in which he criticized limited access of Hitchcock's films in the Korean home video market. A twenty-nine-year-old film critic turned director who had watched an average of thirty to forty films per month (more than 10,000 films in total by 1993), Park lamented, "In world film history, Alfred Hitchcock is considered the greatest director. However, out of 50-odd feature films he made, only *North by Northwest* is currently available on video in South Korea. This demonstrates how shallow our video market is despite its explosion in size" (*Chosun Ilbo*, June 16, 1993, p. 16). Identifying himself as an advocate for "undervalued masterpieces," the young director went on to name *Vertigo*, an obscure Hitchcock in his home country, as the greatest film of all time. As widely reported by Korean print media, Park decided to become a film director after watching *Vertigo* as a student of Sogang University, a Jesuit school. Park's alumnus and film critic Kim Young-jin recalled,

> Through a special exhibition of Alfred Hitchcock movies shown on video for members of the student film club at Sogang, [Park Chan-wook] made the decision that he would live his life as a film director … He stated that through repeated viewings of Hitchcock's *Vertigo*, he gained a sense of what really drove directorial talent for creating screen images. The Park Chan-wook of that time joked, "So James Stewart and Kim Novak are kissing, and in the background the waves on the sea are rolling. Of course it's a process shot, but I was thinking … Hitchcock says 'The waves must crash,' and even the waves move like that for him."
>
> (Kim 2007: 3)

The connection between these two directors is not intuitive. Unlike other Hitchcockian auteurs such as Brian De Palma and Dario Argento, Park Chan-wook does not specialize in suspense and horror films. Murders do happen in his celebrated "Vengeance Trilogy" (consisting of *Sympathy for Mr. Vengeance* [*Boksuneun naui geot*, 2002], *Oldboy* [2003], and *Lady Vengeance* [*Chinjeolhan Geumja-ssi*, 2005]), but they are tools of revenge on the part of bereaved parents who have been wronged by their children's kidnappers or an incestuous brother who lashes out on a gossiper who has defiled his departed sister/lover's deified memory. These wrathful yet tragic avengers are a far cry from Hitchcock's cold-blooded, premediating murderers such as Uncle Charlie (Joseph Cotten) of *Shadow of a Doubt* (1943) and Gavin Elster of *Vertigo*. While Hitchcock's films were instrumental to the formation of feminist film theory due to their voyeuristic and fetishistic uses of interchangeable cool blondes (Grace Kelly, Kim Novak, Tippi Hedren, etc.), Park's films were approached from diverse cultural studies perspectives on such contemporary societal issues as national division (*Joint Security Area* [*Gongdonggyeongbiguyeok*, 2000]), class warfare (*Sympathy for Mr. Vengeance*, *Oldboy*), child abuse (*Sympathy for Mr. Vengeance*, *Lady Vengeance*), incarceration (*Oldboy*, *Lady Vengeance*), disability or mental illness (*Joint Security Area*, *I'm a Cyborg, but That's Okay* [*Ssaibogeujiman gwaebchana*, 2006], *Thirst* [*Bakjwi*, 2009]), homosexuality (*The Handmaiden* [*Agassi*, 2016]), and immigration (*Thirst*, *Decision to Leave* [*Heeojil gyeolsim*, 2022]).

Despite national, linguistic, and generational differences between these two film artists, however, both Hitchcock and Park were born and raised as Catholics and received Jesuit education. Regardless of genres and subject matters, their films share a common Catholic vision of human nature, which, according to Marina Elena de las Carreras Kuntz, "is weakened by original sin but capable of redemption through the exercise of the free will" (2002: 130). In the archetypal Hitchcock narrative, as Kuntz observes, "an ordinary man or woman" faces "an out-of-the-ordinary situation … caused by some manifestation of evil [and] good triumphs over evil and the moral balance is restored, but not without the providential intervention of chance" (2002: 130). Extending and complicating this moral vision of classical Hollywood Hitchcock, Park Chan-wook's oeuvre is preoccupied with the gentler possibility, if not actualization, of forgiveness and atonement for transferred guilt among morally ambiguous characters. Despite his predilection for flashy postmodern aesthetics and stylized violence, Park is more than a cult auteur of global "extreme cinema," and his cinema is deeply spiritual. In an interview with Kim Young-jin, Park admitted to an affinity for deeper religious themes, elaborating, "I'm … opposed to the opinion that sees the themes of sin and redemption or guilt and obsession as Western concepts. These concepts are already exceedingly well established as routine in our [Korean] lives as well. I feel that perhaps the time has come to show them in our own way" (Kim 2007: 115–116).

Comparing Park's English-language psychological thriller *Stoker* (2013), starring Nicole Kidman and distributed by Fox Searchlight Pictures, to Hitchcock's classics, Korean-born German philosopher Byung-Chul Han commented, "Had Hitchcock been alive in our age, he would have made films like Park Chan-wook's because today is much more violent than his times" (*Hankyoreh Sinmun*, March 25, 2014). Since *Vertigo*-like sensual murder mystery *Decision to Leave* premiered at the 2022 Cannes International Film Festival, this cross-cultural analogy (Park as the Korean Hitchcock) was commonly made by numerous critics, journalists, and bloggers both in and outside of South Korea. Responding to this reception in the Korean press conference for *Decision to Leave*, Park stated,

> This film resembles David Lean's *Brief Encounter* (1945), another patient love story between mature adults … But when it was shown at Cannes, many people thought it was like a Hitchcock film. [This evaluation] made me smile and realize that I have Hitchcock's blood in me. It made sense as I studied his works like film textbooks when I was young.
>
> (*Chosun Ilbo*, June 22, 2022)

In an interview with Carlos Aguilar in the *Los Angeles Times*, the Korean master further articulated intertextual influences, "*Vertigo* is the film that made me want to become a filmmaker. As someone who didn't go to film school, Hitchcock was my film school. That influence definitely does exist, but I didn't think of *Vertigo* when I was writing *Decision to Leave*" (October 14, 2022).

Park's denial of *Decision to Leave* as an explicit homage to *Vertigo* is reminiscent of Judy Barton's rebuttal to Scottie Ferguson upon being accidentally spotted on the streets of San Francisco. The necrophiliac detective follows the young woman, who looks almost identical to his dead lover, to her hotel room. Judy feigns antagonism and ignorance, trying to convince Scottie that she is a salesgirl from Salina, Kansas, who moved to the Bay Area three years ago. Although the lovelorn detective takes the brunette look-alike out on dates, he is unable to accept Judy as she is and obsesses about transforming her into the spitting image of the ideal blonde (forcing her to dye her hair, style it up, and dress in

Madeleine's iconic grey suit). Through their critical detective work, commentators of *Decision to Leave*, which bears an uncanny resemblance to Hitchcock's midcentury masterpiece, followed Scottie's suit and resurrected *Vertigo* in the popular discourse regardless of cowriter/director Park's auteur intentions. For example, Aguilar's interview with Park in the *Los Angeles Times* is catchily titled "How a Master Filmmaker Channeled Hitchcock with 'the James Stewart of Korea.'" Although actor Park Hae-il played a sinister murder suspect in Bong Joon-ho's *Memories of Murder* (*Salinui chuoek*, 2003), the article (mis)identifies him as the "Korean Jimmy Stewart" in an apparent attempt to draw parallels between Park's character Jang Hae-joon, a Busan police officer, and Stewart's Scottie, a retired detective from the San Francisco police (*Los Angeles Times*, October 14, 2022). Naming *Decision to Leave* as the eighth "best movie of 2022," *New York Times* film critics Manohla Dargis and A. O. Scott reason,

> One of the dizzying pleasures of this labyrinthine movie is that it's a delirious riff on *Vertigo*, Alfred Hitchcock's aching 1958 drama about a male detective's obsession with a mystery woman … Yet as *Decision to Leave* unfolds and settles into its own distinctively kinked groove, the movie's emotional focus progressively shifts from the obsessed lover to the object of his relentless, uncomprehending gaze, and Park's clever homage turns into a poignant rejoinder.
>
> (*New York Times*, December 6, 2022)

Across the Atlantic, the *Guardian* critic Peter Bradshaw puts Park's "gorgeous Hitchcockian thriller" at the number ten spot of "best films of 2022 in the UK" (December 12, 2022). Echoing his stateside counterparts, the British reviewer observes, "There is something very Hitchcockian … in the film's tension, its intrigue, its showstopping emotional confrontations, its ingenious use of the mobile phone technology that is so often a narrative stumbling block in thrillers, and its setpieces, including a rooftop chase" (*Guardian*, December 12, 2022) (see Fig. 31.1). Notably, on January 15, 2023, the American Cinematheque hosted double-bill screenings of *Decision to Leave* and *Vertigo* with Park Chan-wook in presence for a question-and-answer session and an introduction to Hitchcock's film (thus explicitly linking the Korean filmmaker to Hollywood's master of suspense).

Figure 31.1 The rooftop chase between the detective hero and a criminal in Park Chan-wook's *Decision to Leave* is reminiscent of the opening sequence of Alfred Hitchcock's *Vertigo*.

Despite *Vertigo*'s relative obscurity in South Korea, Korean reviewers and critics almost unanimously supported the Western critical evaluation of *Decision to Leave* as a Hitchcockian thriller/romance. For example, in his review for *Le Monde*, Kim Gyeong-uk compares the story development and characterizations of the two films, pointing out many similarities. In particular, the Korean critic identifies both stories as a "fantasy" (or *hwangsang*, the Korean release title for *Vertigo*) of romance wherein the "narcissistic" hero falls in love with a phantom woman who does not exist (*Le Monde*, September 13, 2022). Scottie is obsessed with a counterfeit "Madeleine" (puppet-mastered by another man unbeknownst to him) and unable to start a happy life with Judy, an unsophisticated working-class woman with tacky taste in fashion and makeup. He can consummate his passion with her only after turning the real woman into a replica of the ghostly original (an aristocratic, graceful beauty that Elster has created for him). Not unlike Scottie (who is hired by Elster to spy on his wife allegedly possessed by the ghost of her great grandmother Carlotta Valdes), Hae-joon falls in love with the object of his professional investigation: Song Seo-rae (Tang Wei), a migrant bride from China whose older, abusive husband is found dead after a suspicious fall from a mountain peak. Despite subtle clues that suggest the griefless widow's involvement in his death (including her awkward police statement that she feared her husband might die "at last [*machimnae*]"), the politically correct detective is sympathetic toward the foreign woman whom he idealizes as a resilient victim of (xenophobic) domestic violence and angelic caregiver/home nurse for elderly patients. After closing her husband's case as an accident, Hae-joon, a married man, develops a platonic romance with the cleared suspect only to find the evidence of her guilt in her dementia-struck patient's apartment (the switched iPhone which Seo-rae carried on the day she killed her husband after leaving her own in the workplace as an alibi). The awful truth shatters the proud lawman who "decides to break up" (the Korean title of the film) with the guilty woman after implicating himself in the cover-up of incriminating evidence (see Fig. 31.2). The ending of both films leaves its action hero in suspension, helplessly gazing, knowingly or not, at the abyss of death (on the top of the bell tower from where Judy has accidentally fallen or on the deserted coastline where Seo-rae has buried herself in the sand grave as ebbing tides approach).

Figure 31.2 In *Decision to Leave*, detective Jang Hae-joon (Park Hae-il) breaks up with Song Seo-rae (Tang Wei) after telling her that he is "shattered" by her guilt.

To borrow a famous Korean saying, *Decision to Leave* is a derivative text that proves that "blue is extracted from indigo but is bluer than the plant it comes from" (i.e., pupils surpass masters). It is arguably a more mature work that corrects *Vertigo*'s regressive ideology from a contemporary perspective. In Hitchcock's film, Scottie espouses classist values by openly displaying disdain for Judy's working-class wardrobe and hairdo which are counterpoised to the idealized high-class image of Madeleine, a blonde heiress of a shipping fortune. As Virginia Wright Wexman puts it, "the figure of Madeleine" is repeatedly associated with Europe and "the old-world idea of aristocracy" (1986: 38). After the demise of this symbolic ideal for white femininity, Scottie has a nightmare in which Elster is seen with a darker Madeleine who looks like the portrait of her Hispanic ancestor Carlotta (who committed suicide after being abandoned by a white lover). As Wexman interprets, "Carlotta represents what ultimately terrorizes Scottie, and the fears Carlotta arouses in him are more culturally specific than either Hitchcock or his feminist critics are in a position to acknowledge" (1986: 38). Park's film does the exact opposite as far as ethnic difference and foreign representation are concerned. Referring to Chinese actress Tang Wei's accented articulation of Korean dialogue with awkward expressions, the Korean writer-director commented,

> Seo-rae's Korean pronunciation is imperfect … but the more and more you hear it, you realize that her Korean is more accurate than it sounds, more elegant. So a [native-speaker] viewer might end up feeling a bit sorry, or a bit awkward, about having thought her speech was funny earlier.
>
> (Robinson 2022)

Furthermore, Park Chan-woo has transformed passive Judy—an accessory to murder who refuses to accept responsibility and is desperate to win back Scottie's affection in her final hour—to active Seo-rae who chooses "her method of liberation and to attain freedom for herself" (Wang 2022) from the moral responsibility of killing three individuals (including her terminally ill mother and her first husband, a wife-beater and corrupt immigration official). In that sense, as Park explains, Seo-rae's suicide, unlike Judy's accidental death, is a "sacred act" (Robinson 2022) despite its ostensible incompatibility with the Catholic doctrine (see Fig. 31.3). As Korean film scholar Park So-hyeon observes, *Decision to Leave* is

Figure 31.3 Park Chan-wook describes Seo-rae's suicide as a "sacred act" of taking responsibility for her sin.

a composite Hitchcockian text that contains palimpsests of several iconic images such as a handcuffed couple in *The 39 Steps* (1935), binocular spying in *Rear Window*, and a lone man dwarfed by a vast landscape in *North by Northwest* (2023: 130). However, Park Chan-wook's film does not offer normative closure as at the ending of *Vertigo* wherein male impotency (Scottie's acrophobia) is cured by female punishment (Judy's fatal fall). Rather, insomnia-afflicted Hae-joon faces a cruel fate of eternal damnation as described by Park: "Seo-rae must forever remain an unresolved case to Hae-joon, Seo-rae wanted Hae-joon to spend sleepless nights looking at a photo of her and thinking about her" (Wang 2022). This exquisitely haunting ending might be one of the many reasons why *Decision to Leave* will continue to capture the hearts and minds of cinephiles around the world who take delight in seeing *Vertigo* resurrected in modern sensibilities and technologies.

Notes

1   Cinematheque managers collected videos and laser discs of unreleased art films from Japan and Europe through personal connections.
2   The other films in the collection include *Rope* (1948), *Rear Window*, *The Man Who Knew Too Much*, *Vertigo*, *The Birds*, *Marnie*, *Torn Curtain*, *Topaz* (1969), and *Frenzy*.

References

Chung, H., and D. Diffrient (2015) *Movie Migrations: Transnational Genre Flows and South Korean Cinema*, New Brunswick, NJ: Rutgers University Press.
Jackson, A. (2024) *The Late and Post-Dictatorship Cinephilia Boom and Art Houses in South Korea*, Edinburgh: Edinburgh University Press.
Kapsis, R. (1992) *Hitchcock: The Making of a Reputation*, Chicago, Ill.: University of Chicago Press.
Kim, Y. (2007) *Park Chan-wook*, Seoul: Korean Film Council.
Kuntz, M. (2002) "The Catholic Vision in Hollywood: Ford, Capra, Borzage, and Hitchcock," *Film History*, 14 (2): 121–135.
Park, S. (2023) "About Unintentional Hitchcockian Elements in *Decision to Leave* [Heeojil gyeolsimui uidohaji aneun Hitchcockjeogime daehayeo]," *Decision to Leave* Special, *Prism Of*, pp. 129–133.
Ravetto-Biagioli, K., and M. Beugnet (2019) "Vertiginous Hauntings: The Ghosts of *Vertigo*," *Film-Philosophy*, 23 (3): 227–246.
Robinson, T. (2022) "Park Chan-wook Explains *Decision to Leave*'s 'Sacred' Ending and Small, Crucial Details," *Polygon*, November 8.
Wang, J. (2022) "Park Chan-wook Invented *Decision to Leave*'s Tragic Ending Decades Ago," *Entertainment Weekly*, October 14.
Wexman, V. (1986) "The Critic as Consumer: Film Study in the University, *Vertigo*, and the Film Canon," *Film Quarterly*, 39 (3): 32–41.
Wood, R. (1989) "Introduction (1965)," in *Hitchcock's Films Revisited*, New York: Columbia University Press.

Chapter 32
Hitchcock in Japan
Invisibility and Hypervisibility

Daisuke Miyao

Introduction

Alfred Hitchcock was a filmmaker who was obsessed with the sense of vision. Many of his films are focused on the notion of gaze and the tension between visibility and invisibility by way of cinematographic and editing techniques. In Japan, the visibility and invisibility of Hitchcock as a filmmaker played a unique role from the period of the Sino-Japanese War in the 1930s to that of television in the 1960s, especially concerning the geopolitics of the time. In particular, Hitchcock's films as the representative of the thriller genre were utilized by critics who tried to define what a national cinema in Japan would be. This chapter critically traces the discursive history of Hitchcock's films in Japanese film criticism.

The Man Who Was Not Known Too Much, 1930s–1945

Only three Hitchcock films were released in Japan in the 1930s: *The Man Who Knew Too Much* (1934), *The 39 Steps* (1935), and *Secret Agent* (1936). The release dates were, respectively, December 12, 1935, March 5, 1936, and March 10, 1938. As the delay of release dates, especially that of *Secret Agent* indicated, his films were not particularly well received except by "not very many" enthusiasts (Uekusa 1976: 30). Compared to Hollywood, where the director was invited as an acclaimed filmmaker in 1939 by David O. Selznick, Hitchcock was not famous in Japan. He was an invisible figure. While Hitchcock's arrival in the USA on the *Queen Mary* was publicized with photographs in nationally circulated magazines, including *Time* and *People*, and made him a visible figure, none of his portraits were published in Japan until World War II ended so that his well-known cameo appearances in his films were not even recognized by Japanese audiences (Uekusa 1954: 47). After the attack on Pearl

Harbor in December 1941, American films were not screened in Japan until the end of the war. While Hitchcock secured his unshakable status in Hollywood after the success of *Rebecca* (1940), his films were unviewable in Japan during the absence of American films.

Without knowing Hitchcock too much, though, those enthusiastic Japanese critics highly valued Hitchcock's films as the alternative to Hollywood cinema from a nationalist perspective, especially in the historical context of the outbreak of the Sino-Japanese War in 1937 and the start of the so-called Total National Spiritual Mobilization Movement in Japan. As Hideaki Fujiki argues, "[C]inema was seen as a powerful medium through which to cultivate individuals to form a redefined 'national populace'" (2022). "There was a view," continues Fujiki, "that film should promote the individual's conception of 'the national populace' as a people who share a common 'culture' that encompasses both everyday life and the arts" and "cinema first and foremost should contribute to the formation of 'the national populace' as an identity" (Fujiki 2022). There was an assumption, according to Fujiki, about "the homogeneity of 'the West' and 'Western films' and attempts to differentiate Japanese film from the West and associate it with 'the national populace' instead" (Fujiki 2022). What these critics had in mind, in particular, was how to make a national cinema competitive with the dominance of Hollywood. I would thus rephrase Fujiki's "West" to Hollywood because some critics made distinctions among "Western" films so that Japanese films could learn from some of them. For instance, Iijima Tadashi, one of the leading critics at that time, wrote, "To watch a film is to reflect on ourselves as the national populace" in 1943 (Iijima 1943: 3). He claimed in his March 1938 review of *Secret Agent*:

> Thriller films are what Hitchcock is specialized in and arguably the most British film genre. While other British directors are trying to make films with the American style, only Hitchcock seems to be making purely British thriller masterpieces without having any artistic ambitions. In this sense, Hitchcock's films have an interesting characteristic in addition to their values in themselves as films. British films should find their representative values in these films as British thriller novels occupy an incomparable place in the world.
>
> (Iijima 1938: 53)

He was thus trying to think of films to reflect a national culture and regarded the thriller genre as the representative of British national cinema. For him, Hitchcock was the leading figure of British cinema in this regard. Iijima did not define the thriller genre clearly but introduced Hitchcock's own words, "Thriller films make the freest cinematic expressions possible." As for "cinematic expressions," Iijima considered Hitchcock's films to be "full of techniques of silent cinema, which were visually oriented" (1938: 53).

It was another critic, Sugiyama Heiichi, who went into details of Hitchcock's cinematic techniques that Iijima referred to. Sugiyama shared Iijima's idea that Britain was expertized in "mysteries" (Sugiyama did not use the term "thrillers," but they meant almost the same genre). Sugiyama wrote in his May 1938 review of *Secret Agent*:

> Recently as the films of Britain, the best place of mysteries, came into Japan, we have begun to recognize how the genre of mysteries is fully utilized in the work of Alfred Hitchcock. The genre of detective novels, or if I use the poet Sato Haruo's phrases, "the branch of a tree of rich Romanticism, the fruit of grotesque mysteries, and the mystifying cut of a jewel of multifaced poem," is freely flourishing in his films. In the images within the frame as well as in their edited structure, a unique

cinematic atmosphere is created. It is the same attraction as the thrill of speed and development of deduction in detective novels.

(Sugiyama 1938: 66)

Sugiyama then tried to define what he meant by "the unique cinematic atmosphere" that Iijima connected to the visuality of silent cinema by analyzing the film's cinematography. His argument is particularly noteworthy in terms of the nationalist tendency of the time. Sugiyama wrote:

Barnard Knowles' cinematography is rough and dirty, compared to *The 39 Steps*. White is too white. However, this harsh tone between black and white seems to be utilized by the author. The pitch-black tone of blackness is effective in creating the mysterious atmosphere of the entire film. This is clearly what Hitchcock intended to do. For example, in the scene in which the protagonist writes a letter of resignation, the heroine cuts the letter into a spiral after he goes out. The camera shows her feet standing in the dark. The black frame is intruded by the shining white paper spinning down round and round. This is the beauty of monochrome, like a "photogram." Such extraordinary blackness plays a significant role in the film's atmosphere.

(Sugiyama 1938: 67)

Sugiyama's appreciation of blackness should be understood in the context of the so-called aesthetics of shadow that developed as a thriving discourse on lighting among critics and cinematographers in Japan in the late 1930s in the context of imperialist war efforts. Shadows in Japanese art and architecture were appreciated in opposition to electricity and bright lighting that represented modern Western culture. *In Praise of Shadows* (*Inei raisan*, 1933–1934), by the renowned novelist Tanizaki Jun'ichiro, was a cornerstone of the emerging aesthetics of shadow. In a section in which he discusses Japanese architecture, Tanizaki writes, "Ultimately, it is the magic of shadows. Were the shadows to be banished from the corners, the alcove [in a Japanese room] would in that instant revert to mere void. This was the genius of our [Japanese] ancestors" (Tanizaki 2001: 32–33). In 1940, quoting Tanizaki extensively, Midorikawa Michio, the head of the Nipponese Society for Cinematographers, argued, "In cinema, there is 'architecture based on lights.' … Therefore, we should observe the beauty of shadows, which appears gracefully in the harmony of [Japanese] architecture and lights" (Midorikawa 1940: 65). As I have demonstrated in *The Aesthetics of Shadow: Lighting and Japanese Cinema* (2013), the aesthetics of shadow was not simply a nationalist project but a discourse that emerged as an amalgamation of multiple desires: adoration of Hollywood cinema and desperation for material conditions in Japanese filmmaking, among others. Some Japanese cinematographers adored the low-key lighting in Hollywood cinema, exemplified by Josef von Sternberg's films with Marlene Dietrich. When Japanese cinematographers realized that it would be difficult to achieve such low-key cinematography under the deplorable conditions of wartime Japan, they turned to one aspect of Japanese art: the use of shadows, which was easily available. They justified their newly adopted aesthetic practices in the name of Japanese tradition. In other words, they strategically connected the aesthetics of shadow to a nationalist discourse. Sugiyama's review of *Secret Agent* extended the discourse to the thriller genre of Britain not only to justify the aesthetics but also to relinquish the binarism between East and West. He insisted there was a British filmmaker who adopted the aesthetics of shadow to present an alternative to Hollywood even though he was not resorting to "Japanese" tradition but a genre that

Britain specialized in. In sum, Japanese film critics in the late 1930s utilized Hitchcock's British films to define, or even justify, what Japanese national cinema should be as an alternative to dominant Hollywood cinema.

The Hitchcock Case, 1946–1950s

As widely known, critics contributing to *Cahiers du cinéma* were ambivalent about how to evaluate the films of Alfred Hitchcock in the 1950s. While the future French New Wave filmmakers, including Éric Rohmer, Claude Chabrol, and François Truffaut, were enthusiastic supporters of Hitchcock, especially of his style, or mise-en-scène, other critiques went against them by insisting on the significance of subjects in films. André Bazin, the leader of *Cahiers*, who had combined the mise-en-scène with the subject as the critical method to evaluate films, was hesitant to value Hitchcock's work. The debate of mise-en-scène versus subject was, according to Ogawara Aya, often based on different political viewpoints: "socialism versus bourgeois capitalism (or Catholicism)" (Ogawara 2015: 226). Rohmer and Chabrol insisted that Hitchcock was an auteur who expressed his worldview, "the conflict between two orders, including human and nature, material and spirit, etc." via mise-en-scène (Ogawara 2015: 229). Yet even Bazin, while supportive of the New Wave critics, was not fully convinced (Bazin 1954: 25–32). The debate was later called "le cas Hitchcock" (the Hitchcock case) or "l'affaire Hitchcock," especially after *Cahiers* published a special issue on Hitchcock in October 1954.

The discussion on Hitchcock's films among Japanese critics was similarly ambivalent, but the focus was more geopolitically oriented. To be more exact, the Japanese response to Hitchcock's Hollywood films was heavily influenced by the US Cold War international politics, especially during the period that followed the end of World War II and the subsequent Allied Occupation of Japan between 1945 and 1953.

> Hitchcock's fame and invisibility of his films formed "something like Hitchcock legend" in postwar Japan even before any of his Hollywood films were released (Nakahara and Watanabe 1971: 98). As an example of the preformed "Hitchcock legend," Iijima Tadashi, who had praised Hitchcock in the 1930s, wrote in January 1947: "Everybody who reads news from America in newspapers and magazines must know that thriller films are very popular in America now, that Alfred Hitchcock is responsible for the popularity of the genre, and that the success of his film *Rebecca* was the main reason, etc."
>
> (Iijima 1947: 11)

On December 17, 1946, *Shadow of a Doubt* (1943), Hitchcock's wartime Hollywood production, was released in Japan. Then, on February 11, 1947, only two months later, *Suspicion* (1941) opened. *Shadow of a Doubt* and *Suspicion* were received "in an extraordinary manner," recalled Nakahara Yumihiko (the pseudonym of Kobayashi Nobuhiko), the editor-in-chief of Japanese *Hitchcock Magazine*, which started in June 1959, as the Japanese edition of *Alfred Hitchcock's Mystery Magazine* (1956–present) (Nakahara and Watanabe 1971: 98). By choosing the word "extraordinary," Nakahara indicated a certain complication. First, Hitchcock's fame and the popularity of the thriller genre had attracted particular attention from critics and filmgoers. Second, such attention was entirely favorable.

While Nakahara briefly talked about the second issue by saying, "critics thought that Hitchcock did not have philosophy" (Nakahara and Watanabe 1971: 100), filmmaker Kurosawa Akira was much more eloquent. In his 1947 essay on the thriller genre, he wrote:

> Sometimes thrillers are good, but it is not very valuable if they are made one after another like these days. The best thriller movie could only be equal to the novels by Georges Simenon if compared to literature. But if we regard authentic novels as breads and meats, Simnon's light realism has only values comparable to whisky and soda. The same is true for authentic drama films and thrillers … Hitchcockian thrillers are easy to make and easy to sell. Indeed, they've been sold well. But frankly speaking, thrillers only appeal to peripheral nerves. Nothing different from sword-fighting flics. Yet, excellent film viewers cannot help praising Hitchcock's work as if they were first-class films. I have to say that Hitchcock uses mysterious magic.
>
> (Kurosawa 2009: 310–311)

Kurosawa rephrased the "mysterious magic" of Hitchcock's filmmaking as his "theory of absolutism in continuity," which made it possible to complete films efficiently and on a lower budget. Kurosawa argued that Hitchcock's theory "goes extremely well with the commercialism of American cinema" (Kurosawa 2009: 311). Kurosawa thus valued Hitchcock's editing techniques that led to the commercial success of his films but at the same time, as Hiyama Sachiko points out, he questioned the "sensationalist aspect" of his techniques that easily appealed to "the mass" (Hiyama 2018: 2). Critic Uekusa Jinichi also used in his 1951 review of *Rebecca* the phrase "Hitchcock's consciousness of mass appeal" when he directed the film "for the American audience" (Uekusa 1976: 61). Uekusa concluded his review by saying, "Hitchcock is no longer the British Hitchcock after he moved to Hollywood. I still have a faith in him, but at the same time I feel sad somehow" (1976: 65).

Iijima Tadashi, who had been a Hitchcock enthusiast since the 1930s, questioned the sensationalism of thriller films more clearly than Kurosawa did. Bearing Hitchcock in mind, Iijima defined the thriller genre as first and foremost films about crimes, and crimes were regarded as "evil" in society. "It is not necessary to explain why thrillers are sensational and popular to the masses. Crimes have such characteristics in nature" (Iijima 1947: 14). "The author has a grave responsibility," continues Iijima, "to make crimes either a vehicle of art or dangerous madness to draw vulgar interests." Iijima hoped that thrillers could become "a study of evil" that "explores humanism" but was also concerned that the topic of crimes could lead to sensationalist entertainment (1947: 15).

The issue of sensationalism in crimes was a sensitive topic in postwar Japan. The goal of the Allied Occupation led by the USA was to abolish the militarism and ultranationalism that had prevailed in Japanese politics and culture before and during the war and to educate Japanese people about American-style liberalism and democracy. Under the Cold War conditions, the US government needed to complete the reconstruction of the Japanese political and economic system as soon as possible so that Japan could become the shield against Communism in Asia. Douglas MacArthur, the Supreme Commander for the Allied Powers (SCAP), tried to use Japanese films to promote democratization under strict censorship led by the Civil Censorship Detachment (CCD) and the Civil Information and Education Division (CIE). Crimes including "suicide, gambling, murder, black marketing, prostitution," were "inappropriate topics in films" by the occupation censorship because of their sensationalism (Hirano 1998: 124). Hiroshi Kitamura argues that film criticism was also placed under occupational censorship to publicize the spirit of American democracy (Kitamura 2014: 165–166). The CIE gathered notable film critics in 1948 and explained that the ethical and moral standard of occupational censorship was equivalent to that of the Production Code in Hollywood (Hiyama 2018: 3). The ambivalence toward thrillers typified by Hitchcock demonstrated in film criticism was based on such a historical context of rebuilding Japanese nation using cinema.

Another unique aspect of criticism of Hitchcock's films in Japan was its relation to the labor movement in the Japanese film industry. The ambivalence between artistic techniques and sensationalist commercialism demonstrated in the criticism of Hitchcock's thrillers was enhanced in the labor struggle at Toho studio, where Kurosawa was contracted, which was directly connected to Cold War geopolitics. Following the SCAP's endorsement of the labor movement, each Japanese film company including Toho started establishing its union as early as November 1945. Toho was the company that supported the militarist government most ardently during the war. Even though most workers at Toho engaged in the production of the so-called national policy films, only the company executives were prosecuted by the SCAP as war criminals. In other words, as critic Sato Tadao argues, the employees of Toho considered that the SCAP did not acknowledge the "autonomy" or "subjectivity" (*shutaisei*) of filmmakers during the war and also worried that they continued to do so after the war ended. When Toho established its union in February 1946, the union requested not only to improve labor conditions but also to approve the participation of union members in "managing the company and proposing plans" (Sato 2006: 194–195). The negotiation broke down in March, which resulted in the so-called Toho Labor Dispute that lasted until 1948. Tsumura Hideo, the film critic who had supported Toho films during the war, responded to the dispute and asked to "explore transparency of the current business system and the company's financial management" in order not to make Japanese film producers of "entertainment films that only target the vulgar mass who cannot appreciate foreign films" (Tsumura 1947: 22). During the second round of disputes, Toho approved to include labor members at the planning stage. As a result, according to Sato, the quality of Toho films greatly improved (Sato 2006: 200). Critics selected six Toho films in the influential film journal *Kinema Junpo*'s best ten of the year. Yet, the number of produced films by Toho decreased drastically especially when 450 skilled workers left the company during the dispute. Those workers included both experienced directors and young filmmakers who could produce films efficiently and on lower budgets. Concerned about the quantity of productions, Toho decided to exclude the union members from the management of the company again. To oppose the company's decision, the union started its third strike. Hiyama argues that the second dispute questioned Toho's "inclination to commercialism" (*goraku-sei*) and the third one criticized the company's "overemphasis on artistic quality" (*geijutsu-sei*) (Hiyama 2018: 4). The reception of Hitchcock in Japan was caught in this debate between commercialism and art within the film industry. Some critics valued Hitchcock's autonomy and subjectivity as an artist in Hollywood while others questioned it from the perspective of commercialism. Such a debate was not limited to the issue of artistic independence, which seemed to be the core of French film criticism, but was also strongly connected to the question of Japanese political independence from the control of the US occupation under the Cold War condition.

Alfred Hitchcock Is Presented, 1960s–Present

As a result of the geopolitical controversy, Hitchcock had never been received wholeheartedly in Japan as a creative artist, or an auteur. His films did not do very well at the box office. Kobayashi Nobuhiko, the editor-in-chief of *Hitchcock Magazine*, wrote in his diary on August 28, 1959, "Hitchcock is lowly valued in Japan so that it is difficult to publish the magazine [bearing his name]" (Kobayashi 1985: 18). Indeed, the TV series *Alfred Hitchcock Presents* was broadcast in Japan from 1957 but was suspended in 1959 "for a financial reason" (Uekusa 1976: 158). Kisoyama Koji, who was in charge of the program at Nippon Television (NTV) recalled that the resumed series in December 1960 also "had a difficult time"—the program needed to switch schedules multiple times, and the sponsor changed from Nikka Whiskey to Crown Lighter amid the run (a PR person at Nikka was demoted according to a rumor) (Kisoyama 1975: 233).

However, beyond the geopolitical controversy in film criticism, thanks to his undoubtedly recognizable look as a TV program host as well as his legend as a Hollywood celebrity, his presence itself was more than welcomed in Japanese media in the 1960s, especially after he visited there in person in 1960. The timing was perfect. The year 1960 arrived during the rapid rise of television as the main form of mass entertainment, replacing the film industry (whose audience peaked in 1958). The continuous live events, from Prince Akihito's wedding in 1959 to the Tokyo Olympics in 1964, kept drawing the attention of the Japanese populace, who were eager to purchase TV sets.

Hitchcock arrived in Yokohama, Japan, by the ship *President Cleveland* on April 17, 1960, for the promotion of the film *Psycho*.[1] While *Psycho* was not received in Japan as well as expected (Kobayashi 1985: 16), his eight-day stay in Japan was a battle with the paparazzi. Even though he spent most of his time appearing in news media conferences, live TV interviews, and receptions one after another, the Japanese fans did not leave him and his wife Alma alone (see Fig. 32.1). For instance, on the afternoon

Figure 32.1 Publicity stills of Hitchcock during his promotional tour for *The Trouble with Harry*. Images courtesy *Geijutsu Shincho*. February 1956.

of April 20th, the couple took off on a short vacation to a hot spring inn in Hakone, a few hours' train ride from Tokyo. But, according to a report by Hosogoe Rintaro, "More than twenty paparazzi from weekly entertainment magazines got on the train and shot the couple with flashes as if they were on the *Vulcan Express* (the Japanese title of *The Lady Vanishes*) taking the direction of north by northwest, they did not have time to rest." Once they arrived at the Fujiya Inn in Hakone, "newspaper people were waiting for them there, and they had to cancel their plan to enjoy the open-air bath privately." On the following day, the paparazzi were still there, and Hitchcock, who came out to a garden of the inn, was "followed to everywhere as if he were a movie star." The couple moved to Kyoto by train, and "fans and media people were waiting at the platform of every station that the Shinkansen bullet train stopped, including Shizuoka and Nagoya, and gave them flower bouquets. How tough!" On the following morning, their drive from the hotel to the Heian Shrine where the couple was scheduled to visit was followed by more than a dozen cars, which looked "like a parade of a state guest" (Hosogoe 2001: 76). It looked like the whole country wanted to see Hitchcock on TV shows and in newspapers and magazines in 1960. Hitchcock thus became a hypervisible figure who came to represent the postwar economic miracle of Japan, which was, ironically, made possible by the US procurement. Eventually in the 1990s, Hitchcock as the celebrity of Japanese commercialism reached its peak when he appeared in a TV commercial for Toyota Mark II automobiles (see Fig. 32.2).

As film studies started to develop in Japan in the 1980s, scholars started to follow British, French, and US academia to examine the films of Hitchcock from various perspectives: ideological criticism, linguistics, psychoanalysis, gender studies, etc.[2] The most prominent method that was adopted was the so-called "surface criticism" (*hyoso hihyo*), coined by Hasumi Shigehiko, arguably the most influential film critic in Japan at that time. Separating his work from a dominant type of film criticism in Japan,

Figure 32.2 Toyota Mark II advert.
© Toyota Motor Corporation. Released in Japan, 1960. All rights reserved.

i.e., the impressionist reading in which educated critics thematically and subjectively express their ways of reception, Hasumi proposed to pay attention only to what was visible on the surface of the screen. Hasumi's 1983 book *Kantoku Ozu Yasujiro* [*Director Ozu Yasujiro*] was the perfect example of his "surface criticism." Focusing on not only stylistic but also visible details on the screen, Hasumi argued that Ozu was conscious of the capabilities and limits of cinema as a medium. Hasumi's examples of Ozu's consciousness about the limits of cinema included the peculiar eyeline matches that would refuse the illusion of looking while his examples of Ozu's belief in the capabilities of cinema included various "themes" (*shudai*) or fragments (*danpen*), such as eating, changing clothes, or looking, that Ozu consistently adopted in his films but exceeded the linearity of the narrative or the intellectual reading. This was his version of *la politique des auteurs*. Yet Hasumi's approach enhanced the problematically apolitical view toward history, including Japan's imperial past and the Cold War geopolitics in which the Japanese film culture existed without a doubt. As he rejected any political, historical, or categorical reading of Ozu, Hasumi showed little interest in the political or historical dimensions of the directors he praised, including Hitchcock. Aaron Gerow criticizes Hasumi's apolitical approach by arguing, "It would be tempting to historicize Hasumi's work in relation both to Japanese postmodern, bubble culture, and to the rise of Asia in Japan as a consumer object from that period, where his transnational consumption of cinema paralleled consumerist appropriations of Asia" (Gerow 2018: 56). While analyzing textual details meticulously, Hasumi's approach did not question why Hitchcock became hypervisible in Japanese commercialism while not all of his films were received well.

Hitchcock in Japan remains ambivalent. Like a torn curtain, he is the auteur filmmaker in academia on one hand and the celebrity icon in popular media on the other. As the opposition movement against the continued US military presence in Japan is now long gone (except for the ongoing anti-US military base movement in Okinawa), the geopolitical debate between auteurism and commercialism exists no longer. However, the Hitchcock case in Japan is not yet closed.

Notes

1. It was Hitchcock's second visit to Japan. The first one was in December 1955 to publicize *The Trouble with Harry* (1955). He stayed four days in Tokyo. *Screen* magazine already included eight photographs of him in its two-page special report titled, "Hicchicokku shi ga honshi no tame ni netsuen shita surira kihon kozu" [Mr. Hitchcock Enthusiastically Played the Basic Compositions of Thrillers for Us], *Screen*, 11 (3) (1956): 50–51.

2. For instance, Raymond Bellour's "Le Blocage symbolique," *Communications*, 23 (1975); Steven Heath's "Narrative Space," *Screen*, 17 (3) (1976); and Geoffrey H. Hartman's "Plenty of Nothing: Hitchcock's 'North by Northwest'," *The Yale Review*, 71 (1) (1981) were translated into Japanese and introduced in *Cinéaste 1: Hitchcock*, edited by Shimizu Yasuo, Tokyo: Seido sha, 1985. (Heath's essay was translated from its French version to Japanese.)

References

Bazin, A. (1954) " Hitchcock contre Hitchcock," *Cahiers du cinéma*, 39: 25–32.
Fujiki, H. (2022) *Making Audience: A Social History of Japanese Cinema and Media*, New York: Oxford University Press.
Gerow, A. (2018) "Ozu to Asia via Hasumi," in J. Choi (ed.), *Reorienting Ozu: A Master and His Influence*, New York: Oxford University Press, pp. 45–58.

Hasumi, S. (1983) *Kantoku Ozu Yasujiro* [Director Ozu Yasujiro], Tokyo: Chikuma shobo.

Hirano, K. (1998) *Tenno to seppun: Amerika senryoka no Nihon eiga kenetsu* [The Emperor and the Kiss: Japanese Film Censorship under the Occupation], Tokyo: Soshi sha.

Hiyama, S. (2018) "The Birth of Japan-made Thriller Film and Music in the History of the Postwar Japanese Film: The Role of Counterpoint in 'A Stray-Dog,'" *Kobe Daigaku Daigakuin Ningen Hattatsu Kankyo Gaku Kenkyu-ka Kenkyu Kiyo*, 11 (2): 1–12.

Hosogoe, R. (2001) "Hitchcock in Japan," *GQ Japan*, 95 (January): 74–76.

Iijima, T. (1938) "Kancho saigo no hi" [Secret Agent], *Kinema Junpo*, 638 (March 1): 53.

Iijima, T. (1943) *Eiga no mikata* [How to Watch Films], Tokyo: Bunsho sha.

Iijima, T. (1947) "Surira ni tsuite" [About Thrillers], *Eiga Hyoron*, 4 (5): 11–15.

Kisoyama, K. (1975) "Ichinen rokkagetsugo ni sai sutato" [Restart after One Year and Six Months], in Kofujita C. (ed.), *Sekai no eiga sakka 12: Arufureddo Hicchikokku hen* [The World Filmmakers 12: Alfred Hitchcock], Tokyo: Kinema Junpo sha, pp. 229–233.

Kitamura, H. (2014) *Haisen to Hariuddo: Senryoka Nihon no bunka saiken* [Defeat and Hollywood: Cultural Reconstruction in Occupied Japan], Nagoya: Nagoya Daigaku Shuppan kai.

Kobayashi, N. (1985) *Kobayashi Nobuhiko 60 nendai nikki: 1959–1970* [Kobayashi Nobuhiko's Diary in the 1960s], Tokyo: Byakuya shobo.

Kurosawa, A. (2009) "Surira ni tsuite" [About Thrillers], in Hamano Y. (ed.), *Taikei: Kurosawa Akira* [Compendium], Tokyo: Kodan sha, pp. 310–311.

Midorikawa, M. (1940) "Kameraman no seikatsu to kyoyo" [Cameraman's Life and Culture], in Tane S. (ed.), *Eiga satsueigaku dokuhon: Jo kan* [Cinematography Reader: Volume 1], Tokyo: Dainihon eiga kyokai, pp. 46–83.

Miyao, D. (2013) *The Aesthetics of Shadow: Lighting and Japanese Cinema*, Durham, NC: Duke University Press.

Nakahara, Y., and Watanabe T. (1975) "Taidan: Sengo mita Hicchikokku eiga" [Dialogue: Hitchcock Films that We Watched after the War], in Kofujita C. (ed.), *Sekai no eiga sakka 12: Arufureddo Hicchikokku hen* [The World Filmmakers 12: Alfred Hitchcock], Tokyo: Kinema Junpo sha, pp. 98–100.

Ogawara, A. (2015) "Hicchikokku, aratana nami: Romeru & Shaburoru Hicchikokku no seiritsu jokyo to sono eikyo" [Hitchcock, the New Wave: The Situation around Rohmer and Chabrol's Hitchcock and Its Influence], in É. Rohmer and C. Chabrol, *Hitchcock*, trans. Kimura T. and Ogawara A., Tokyo: Inscript, pp. 223–248.

Sato, T. (2006) *Nihon eiga shi 2* [History of Japanese Film 2], Tokyo: Iwanami shoten.

Sugiyama, H. (1938) "Kancho saigo no hi" [Secret Agent], *Nihon Eiga*, 8 (5): 65–67.

Tanizaki, J. (2001) *In Praise of Shadows*, trans. T. J. Harper and E. G. Seidensticker, London: Vintage.

Tsumura, H. (1947) "Sengo no kaiso: Showa 21 nendo no eigakai" [Recalling Postwar: The Film World in 1946], *Eiga Geijutsu*, 7 (March): 21–23.

Uekusa, J. (1954) "Hicchikokku shutsuen eiga ni kansuru kosatsu" [Thoughts on the Films in Which Hitchcock Appeared], *Screen*, 9 (10): 46–47.

Uekusa, J. (1976) *Hicchikokku banzai!* Tokyo: Shobun sha.

Chapter 33

Introducing Hitchcock to Communist China

Two Decades of Reception and Popularization

Sun Yi

The year 1976 marked the US release of Alfred Hitchcock's last film. Simultaneously, on the other side of the Pacific, China was about to awaken from the nightmare of the Cultural Revolution, which had cut the country almost completely off from Western cultures and cultural products for an entire decade. The Communist authorities' official antagonism toward the West and especially the USA had appeared as early as 1950 when China entered the Korean War. As a consequence in the cultural sphere, only a handful of US (and Western European) films were shown in Chinese theaters from the early 1950s to mid 1970s, with most Western films and filmmakers becoming taboo. This was in sharp contrast to the Republic era (1912–1949), when Western films, especially Hollywood features, dominated the Chinese market. During this period, a number of Hitchcock's works were imported shortly after their release in the UK or the USA. In the People's Republic of China (PRC) era, likewise, soon after the film industry stepped out of the shadow of the Cultural Revolution in the early 1980s and could afford to catch up on the latest fads in international cinema, new foreign releases constituted the majority of imports. The work of a recently deceased foreign filmmaker would thus stand only a limited chance of having widespread influence. However, Hitchcock would become famous once again in China. Chinese film scholars and critics discussed how Hitchcock might inform the future direction of local cinema, and his work played a part in the transition and development of Chinese film criticism.

    Following a roughly chronological order, this chapter charts the initial reception of Hitchcock in the PRC spanning from the late 1970s to the turn of the century. These two decades witnessed the establishment and consolidation of Hitchcock's reputation in the country, during a period when the Chinese film industry was being normalized and commercialized and Chinese film criticism was liberalized and developed. This chapter probes into this history through an archival study, exploring materials ranging from scholarly journals and popular periodicals to relevant books. It reveals Hitchcock's multifaceted role in Chinese culture, as a window to Western film culture, industry icon, and inspiration for Chinese filmmakers, as well as a popular legend in public discourse. The early reception of Hitchcock represented and served the Chinese film community's aspirations to reconnect to the West and to redirect local cinema toward commercial filmmaking in a period of profound change.

A Window into Western Film Culture

During the Cultural Revolution, while Western films were off limits to the populace, foreign "films for internal reference" were nonetheless screened for the ruling members of the Communist Party. Among these was Hitchcock's *Notorious* (1946), but its extremely limited exhibition made no contribution to the director's public visibility. Not until the end of the Cultural Revolution and the beginning of the period of economic reform did Hitchcock's name reach a wider audience. Nevertheless, for the two decades that followed, only a few of his films, including *Rebecca* (1940), *Spellbound* (1945), *The Lady Vanishes* (1938), *Blackmail* (1929), and *North by Northwest* (1959), received theatrical distribution in China, most of them during the brief window between the end of the Cultural Revolution in the late 1970s and the normalization of film importing in the late 1980s, a period in which China Film Corporation's budget was too tight for new foreign releases (see Li 2010: 40). While these screenings did help spread Hitchcock's name, the effect should not be overstated. More instrumental in the establishment of his reputation were local film scholars, a translator-turned-theorist named Shao Mujun in particular.

In 1978, prior to the public screening of any Hitchcock films in the PRC, an essay titled "A Talk on Film Directing" appeared in *Collection of Film Art Translations* (renamed *World Cinema* in 1981), a scholarly journal devoted primarily to publishing translations of foreign film-theoretical works. Comprised of translations of Hitchcock's own remarks on filmmaking and a concise introduction, both by Shao, the essay marked the first effort to introduce Hitchcock to Communist China. Longtime editor-in-chief of the journal in its post-Cultural Revolution era and one of China's most distinguished film theorists, Shao was arguably the most important figure in reintroducing Hitchcock to the country. Shao began his career translating foreign film-theoretical texts for the China Film Administration. Unlike most of his colleagues, who specialized in Russian and film theories from the Soviet Union, he studied English, alongside French, German, and Italian, which determined his interest in and affinity with Anglo-American and Continental European film theories. As soon as the end of the Cultural Revolution allowed discussion of non-Soviet foreign films and film theories, the nonpartisan translator became an advocate of Western films and film theories and a "spokesman for the Hollywood system" (Hu 2005: 241), disclosing his genuine theoretical position and especially his preference for commercial and genre cinema. It was within these personal and cultural-political contexts that the Hitchcock essay appeared.

Shao (1978: 93) made two general comments in his introduction. First, Hitchcock specializes in thrillers that are generally bold and sophisticated in artistic terms; second, his films are commercially successful, but increasing commercial consideration renders his later works less artistically creative than the earlier ones. Shao's conclusion was that Hitchcock's approaches and techniques are worth learning, though a critical eye needs to be kept on the prioritization of style over substance suggested in some of the director's remarks (1978: 94). While being careful not to challenge the official ideology's remaining aversion to capitalism and formalism, Shao's discussion of Hitchcock in effect hinted at a new path for Chinese cinema: commercial genre filmmaking.

Shao's essay appeared in the first issue of *World Cinema* after its post-Cultural Revolution resurrection. Consisting of a first half of essays on Soviet art- and cinema-related subjects and a second half of essays on American, European, and Japanese cinema, it epitomized China's changing cultural-political position. Shao's Hitchcock piece was the first one in the section on non-Soviet subjects and can thus be described as the very first essay on Western film in post-Cultural Revolution China. As one of the first Western filmmakers introduced by this landmark publication, Hitchcock became a window through which China reconnected with the outside cultural world.

Another key film journal, *Film Art*, resurrected in the following year, publishing Shao's "On the History and Present of American Film Directors" in its first year. In this essay, Shao provided an overview of filmmaking in the USA and mentioned a series of filmmakers, including Hitchcock. Later, in his 1982 book *An Introduction to Western Film History*, the first of its kind published in the PRC, Shao divided Western film history into two traditions—technicalism and realism—and treated Hitchcock's works as genre films (crime films in his categorization), which, according to him, belong to the tradition of technicalism. He acclaimed Hitchcock's stylistic and narrative strategies and noted the director's significant role in the development of the Hollywood crime film (1982: 48–49). During these immediate post-Cultural Revolution years, Shao used Hitchcock as an exemplar of Western film culture, writing about him from the perspective of a film scholar and for the implicit purpose of urging a change in the direction of Chinese cinema.

Shao's *World Cinema* piece was followed by a string of translations of critical writings on Hitchcock. In 1980, *Film Art* published an omnibus article about the director comprised of translations from various sources. China Film Press embarked on a "Foreign Cinema Series" in the same year, a series of books comprised of translations of foreign film scripts and critical essays. The commencing volume included three translated essays on Hitchcock's films. The volume was divided into six sections—"Film Scripts," "Overviews of Scriptwriters, Directors, and Actors," "Creative Techniques," "Film Schools and Genres," "Cinematography and Art Direction," and "Overviews of Foreign Cinema"—and the three essays on Hitchcock constituted the entire "Creative Techniques" section. This arrangement was in accord with Shao's classification of Hitchcock in the tradition of technicalism and reflected the general opinion of Chinese film scholars during these early days.[1]

The critical sensitivity of translators and scholars was in contrast to that of most local reviewers (and audiences) at the time. After *Rebecca* became the first Hitchcock film screened in the PRC in 1980, a handful of reviews appeared in film- or culture-related periodicals such as *Film Art*, *Film Culture*, *Movie Review*, and *Wen Hui Monthly*. However, most reviews—or, rather, sketchy viewing responses instead of in-depth film analyses or criticisms—mentioned Hitchcock's name perfunctorily or not at all, focusing mainly on the film's plot and main characters. Only two reviews displayed some knowledge about the director: one noted David Selznick's acquisition of the rights to the original novel for Hitchcock (Chen 1980: 70); the other discussed Hitchcock's working methods (Hou 1980: 38). Generally speaking, as a 1982 article summarized, "the audience in this country are unfamiliar with the name Alfred Hitchcock" (Zhou 1982: 14).[2]

However, article-length studies by Chinese critics did begin to emerge. In 1981, *New Films* published an article titled "On Hitchcock's Art of Direction and Techniques," revolving around how Hitchcock builds suspense by means of narrative devices and cinematographic-sonic techniques. It ended with the verdict that "for us, many of his films are worthy to be examined and learned from" (Fang 1981: 87), echoing Shao's trailblazing essay. Similar statements appeared in subsequent years (see, e.g., Chen 1983: 68; Qian 1983: 54; Wang 1984: 104; Wang 1986: 13), as critical essays on Hitchcock increased after the 1983 screenings of *Spellbound* and *The Lady Vanishes* as well as that of *Blackmail* as part of the touring "British Film Retrospective" in 1984.[3] At the same time, brief portrayals of the director appeared in anthologies on foreign cinema: Hitchcock was the subject of the first chapter of a 1982 book edited by a China Film Association member, *Sketches of Foreign Cinema*, which was the first anthology on foreign cinema post-Cultural Revolution; a chapter on Hitchcock was also included in the 1983 *Anecdotes about Chinese and Foreign Cinema*. By 1984, an editorial epilogue in *New Films* was able to assert that, "the Chinese audience are [no longer] unfamiliar with Hitchcock's work" ("Editorial Epilogue," 1984: 112). Chinese critics unanimously regarded him as a master whose storytelling and stylistic techniques should provide inspiration for local filmmakers, especially concerning the realm of genre filmmaking.

An Industry Icon in Two Debates

While *World Cinema*'s translation and publication of foreign film-theoretical texts marked the piecemeal beginning of the introduction of Western film theories into the PRC, a series of lectures by Western film scholars sponsored by China Film Association and the China Import and Export Corporation during 1984–1988 was considered "the Chinese film community's first systematic engagement with modern film theories" (Hu 2005: 248). In 1986, the only key lecture in the series that focused on an individual director, Bill Nichols' "Hitchcock: Problems of Interpretation," enhanced Chinese filmmakers' and researchers' understanding of the director and further cemented his reputation. The event also led to a surge of dedicated journal sections and other publications.

In 1986, *Popular Cinema* took the lead by publishing a "Master of Suspense: Hitchcock" section, containing translations and original essays, over three consecutive issues. The journal commissioned an introductory commentary from Shao for the entire series. The thrust of Shao's (1986: 5) commentary was that although Hitchcock's works are "one hundred percent entertainment films," the director showcased superb artistry in his commercial productions. Shao's dialectic comments need to be read in the context of the ongoing vigorous debate on and destigmatization of the "entertainment film" during the mid to late 1980s. Whereas the term—set in contradistinction to films with didactic purposes—had been laden with derogatory connotations in film criticism until the end of the Cultural Revolution, it gained increasing critical currency and became a neutral label for commercial and especially genre films in the late 1980s (see Sui 2021: 38–54). Shao was among the first to endorse the "entertainment film" both as a concept and as a type of cinema (see, for example, Shao 1980: 17) and saw the emergence of local entertainment films as "a point of departure for Chinese cinema's growth into maturity" (Wang 1989: 53). His description of Hitchcock's films at this moment functioned to provide Chinese filmmakers and critics with a worthy example or template of the "entertainment film."

The next year, an issue of *World Cinema* featured a section on Hitchcock that included a series of translations of critical essays and a film script; *Contemporary Cinema* published translations of critical essays on him and scripts of his films across three consecutive issues. *West Films: Monthly Magazine of Film Literature* devoted almost an entire issue to him (Fig. 33.1), including translations of film scripts, his filmography and potted biography, and two original essays that were both broader in scope and more in-depth than most previous publications. One essay was a direct result of Nichols' lecture: instead of reviewing Hitchcock's films or analyzing his techniques, it delineated the various theoretical approaches to his films (see Xiao 1987). The other can be seen as an elaborated version of Shao's commentary in *Popular Cinema*: it argued for the artistry and value of the "entertainment film" and commercial filmmaking through appraisals of Hitchcock's skills and imagination (see Chen 1987). Soon, in 1988, the first Chinese translation of a book on Hitchcock was published: François Truffaut's *Hitchcock: The Definitive Study of Alfred Hitchcock*.[4]

Figure 33.1 An issue of *West Films: Monthly Magazine of Film Literature* (May 1987) devoted to Hitchcock.
Xi'an Film Studio 1987. All rights reserved.

Although most publications that appeared during this period were still translations, they illustrated a marked increase in both general interest in Hitchcock's work and critical attention to Hitchcock scholarship. General audiences seemed well acquainted with the Hitchcockian style, to the extent that a 1989 review in a general-interest newspaper mistakenly identified *Charade* (dir. Stanley Donen, 1963) as a Hitchcock film (*Hangzhou Daily*, May 21, 1989). Original writings by critics provided little criticism but much lavish acclaim, idolizing Hitchcock as a potential mentor to Chinese directors. In fact, varied perspectives on the development of Hitchcock's reputation, such as Robert E. Kapsis's argument for the significance of self-promotion in that process, had been introduced in China, but local critics downplayed such knowledge while idealizing the image of Hitchcock by suggesting that his success rested solely on his artistic creativity.[5]

In 1989, at the peak of the critical debate on the "entertainment film," *North by Northwest* became the last Hitchcock film shown in Chinese theaters. One review was written as a direct response to the debate, its opening paragraph stating that,

The debate on the entertainment film is fermenting. In my opinion, instead of discussing the role and function of the entertainment film at a macro level, it is more beneficial to examine the aesthetic characteristics and narrative structures of entertainment films from a micro, technical perspective, in order to diagnose the causes of local entertainment films' commercial failures. Concretely, this essay takes Hitchcock's recently screened *North by Northwest* as an example to analyze the thriller film, which is the main constituent of the entertainment film.

(Mao 1989)

Similarly, in the book *Road to Reform: Film Practice and Criticism from 1977 to 1986*, published in the same year, the author took Hitchcock (alongside Steven Spielberg) as a counterexample to the assertion that entertainment films lack artistic quality (Li 1989: 139). Additionally, a 1990 essay characterized the examination of Hitchcock's work as conducive to improving "the quality of [Chinese] entertainment films" (Shi 1990: 47). As illustrated by these materials, the reception of Hitchcock played an integral part in the destigmatization of the "entertainment film" in China in the 1980s and early 1990s, the goal of which was a fundamental change in the orientation of local film production.

The debate on the "entertainment film" went hand in hand with another wide and more specific "debate on the thriller film." Following the relatively systematic introduction of Western genre theories through translations published in *World Cinema* in 1984, the concept of genre was brought into unprecedented focus, with the thriller film receiving more attention than any other genre. A symposium on the thriller film held by *Popular Cinema* and Yantai Film Studio and a symposium held by Changchun Film Studio, both in 1984, the greatly influential weeklong symposium held by *Film Art* in 1985, a feature section in an issue of *August 1st Film* (1987), a symposium held by *Popular Cinema* in 1988, a feature section in *China Film News* in 1989, and a slightly distant ripple of *World Cinema*'s extended translations of book chapters on the thriller genre and Hitchcock in 1992, among others, were a testimony to the widespread enthusiasm. Hitchcock as a subject became an organic part of most of these events and documents. Most of the articles generated by the most famous *Film Art* symposium, for example, mentioned him (see, e.g., Chang 1985: 18; Chen 1985: 37; Meng 1985: 42; Xiao 1985: 39; Yu 1985: 45). Discussion of Hitchcock and his work also constituted the major part of an article on the history and status quo of foreign thrillers (see Yan 1984), demonstrating that he served as a primary point of reference for this far-reaching debate in the Chinese film community.

Eager to prove that genre films can meet with both commercial and critical success, Chinese critics used Hitchcock's accomplishment to suggest a promising prospect for local filmmakers working in the genre. While reviews and critical essays in the early 1980s focused primarily on Hitchcock's specific styles and techniques or perceived him as an artist, the discussions within the "debate on the thriller film" tended to define him more as a successful model of genre filmmaking. The debate in effect brought his renown to another level. For some Chinese critics, he was more than simply one master of cinema among others; rather, his name represented an industry icon and, perhaps less explicitly in the documents but equally crucially, an auteur brand. Several essays appeared around the mid 1980s expressing disappointment in local thrillers, for example, one was titled "Hopefully China Will Have Its Own Hitchcock" (Tong 1985: 12; Meng 1985: 42; "'The Thriller Film …'" 1987: 3). At that juncture, "Chinese Hitchcock" became a catchword in Chinese film criticism, encapsulating the local film community's (as well as the entire Chinese intelligentsia's) strong desire to learn from the West again as Chinese cinema commercialized.

As suggested earlier, the initial spread of Hitchcock's fame in post-Cultural Revolution China was largely a critical matter. Only a small number of his films were screened in theaters, and these received a limited number of reviews. Film scholars and critics played a key part in inscribing the name Hitchcock into the collective memory of the Chinese audience. Most notably, it was the two debates on the "entertainment film" and the thriller genre that considerably increased both the visibility of the director in the Chinese film community and the significance of his legacy for Chinese cinema. Because of these two debates and the broader context of the normalization of the Chinese film industry, Hitchcock and his work were inextricably woven into the history of Chinese film criticism and the narrative of the reorientation of Chinese cinema. It can be summarized that the second half of the 1980s saw the substantive consolidation of Hitchcock's reputation in China.

A Popular Legend Belonging to the World

As the debates settled and Hitchcock films ceased to be shown in theaters, the number of journal articles on him decreased through much of the 1990s, with new articles tending to repeat the ideas put forward in previous ones. However, book publications increased. In the early 1990s, John Russell Taylor's *Hitch: The Life and Work of Alfred Hitchcock* and Patrick Humphries' *The Films of Alfred Hitchcock* were translated into Chinese. Most remarkably, the early 1990s saw the publication of the first monograph on Hitchcock by a Chinese scholar. Written by Wang Xinyu, a Beijing Film Academy professor who taught courses on Hitchcock, *Hitchcock and Suspense* came out in 1993 as an in-house textbook.[6] Aimed at a readership of future film practitioners, it both provided a general introduction to Hitchcock and his work and conducted detailed analyses of how he builds suspense. A milestone in Chinese-language Hitchcock scholarship, an expanded edition of the book was finally published in 1999 (see Fig. 33.2), broadening its readership from film professionals to the masses. In the late 1990s, a biography

Figure 33.2 *Hitchcock and Suspense* by Wang Xinyu, the first Chinese-language book on Hitchcock.

Published by China Radio and Television Press 1999. Cover by Guo Yunjuan. All rights reserved.

of Hitchcock written in Chinese for a popular readership served as further evidence of the spread of the director's fame to Chinese mass audiences.

In celebration of Hitchcock's 100th birthday, a new translation of Taylor's *Hitch* was released, and a range of Chinese periodicals arranged special sections or articles. On the more scholarly side of the film journal spectrum, *World Cinema* and *Home Drama* both published translated essays as a tribute; Wang, the author of *Hitchcock and Suspense*, wrote a commemorative article for *Film Art* that was "a result of years of research" (Wang 1999a: 38). On the more popular side, *Popular Cinema* devoted a feature to the director, with the title of the keynote article proclaiming that "[Hitchcock] Belongs Not Only to the UK and the US but to the World" (see Dai 1999: 18; see Fig. 33.3). In addition to acknowledging his legacy for world cinema, these tributes from Chinese critics showed the Chinese film community's increasing consciousness of participating in worldwide Hitchcock discourse.

More remarkably, some non-film-related venues partook in the celebration as well. Commemorative essays were found in magazines of various sorts, such as *World Vision*, *Portrait*, and *Shanghai Philately*, and in newspapers, such as *China Reading Weekly*. Most of the essays were of a biographical and anecdotal rather than critical nature, functioning to popularize Hitchcock rather than advance scholarly understanding. From an object of study in film journals and special symposiums to a celebrity in non-film periodicals, the image of Hitchcock multiplied and slightly changed in the 1990s: he was relieved of his role as an urgently-needed mentor to Chinese filmmakers, and, apart from being a cinematic artist and a film-industry icon, he was now a cultural legend in a general sense.

Younger Chinese audiences might have missed the chance to watch Hitchcock's films on the big screen, but they had easier access both to the films on television, VHS, VCD, or DVD and to his life story and anecdotes in different types of publications.[7] Over more than twenty years of radical change

Figure 33.3 "Belongs Not Only to the UK and the US but to the World," the keynote article in *Popular Cinema* in celebration of Hitchcock's 100th birthday.

Popular Cinema, 1999. China Film Assosciation. All rights reserved.

in China's attitude toward the West and capitalism, Hitchcock and his work became a common part of the cultural experience of the local people, who, in the meantime, were accustomed to films of diverse genres and to the profit-making and entertaining nature of cinema. In retrospect, the early reception and popularization of Hitchcock represents a microcosm not only of the development of Chinese film criticism and the reorientation of Chinese cinema but of one of the most intellectually liberal and open periods in Chinese history.

Notes

1. On the more biographical and anecdotal side, *Film Art* posted news on both Hitchcock's reception of a knighthood and his death in 1980. In 1982, a piece of translation on the last months in Hitchcock's life appeared in *Shijie dianying Dongtai* [World Cinema News].
2. All translations in this chapter are my own.
3. This was the first large-scale foreign-film retrospective taking place in the PRC. See Tan 2014: 79.
4. Much content from the book had been translated into Chinese and published in film periodicals previously.
5. Kapsis's article "Alfred Hitchcock: Auteur or Hack? How the Filmmaker Reshaped His Reputation among the Critics" was translated into Chinese in 1986, and an excerpt reappeared in 1987.
6. Another Beijing Film Academy textbook published in the same year, *To the Pantheon of Cinema: Textbook for the Film Analysis Course at Beijing Film Academy*, included Hitchcock's *Rear Window* (1954), among other international and national classics.
7. In the 1990s, Hitchcock films were at times shown on television. On the occasion of the 100th anniversary of his birth, some television stations launched two-month-long feature programs to show a couple of his films every week.

References

"Bian hou" [Editorial Epilogue] (1984) *Dianying xin zuo* [New Films], 5: 112.
Chang, Y. (1985) "Wei jingxian yangshi yingpian nahan" [Salute to the Thriller Film], *Dianying yishu* [Film Art], 3: 18–19.
Chen, M. (1980) "Xiaoshuo li bei ka yu yingpian hudie meng" [Rebecca: Novel and Film], *Shijie dianying yicong* [World Cinema Collection of Film Art Translations], 1: 69–79.
Chen, Y. T. (1983) "Xi qu ke ke de xuannian yishu" [Hitchcock's Art of Suspense], *Dianying xin shidai* [New Age of Cinema], 1: 66.
Chen, Y. T. (1985) "Jingxian pian chuangzuo ying zhuiqiu shenmei jiazhi: jingxian dianying de yishu texing ji qi jixing hua wenti" [Thrillers Should Pursue Aesthetic Values: The Artistic Characteristics and Problems of the Thriller Film], *Dianying yishu* [Film Art], 8: 36–41.
Chen, Y. T. (1987) "Shuo bu jin de xi qu ke ke" [The Untold Greatness of Hitchcock], *Xibu dianying* [West Films: Monthly Magazine of Film Literature], 45: 47–52.
Dai, H. Y. (1999) "Shi ying mei de, geng shi shijie de" [Belongs Not Only to the UK and the US But to the World], *Dazhong dianying* [Popular Cinema], 1: 18–20.
Fang, Y. (1981) "Mantan xi qu ke ke de daoyan yishu he jiqiao" [On Hitchcock's Art of Direction and Techniques], *Dianying xin zuo* [New Films], 6: 87, 99–100.
Hou, L. J. (1980) "Xi qu ke ke de moli" [Hitchcock's Magic], *Dianying yishu* [Film Art], 5: 37–38.
Hu, K. (2005) *Zhongguo dianying lilun shiping* [History of Chinese Film Theories], Beijing: China Film Press.
"'Jingxian pian': xie zai dianying jie mianqian de jingtan hao" ["The Thriller Film": An Exclamation Mark to the Film Industry] (1987) *Ba yi dianying* [August First Film], 3: 3.

Li, J. (2010) "Xin shiqi tizhi yanbian zhong de dianying jinkou yanjiu" [Research on Film Imports amid Institutional Evolution in the New Era], Ph.D. thesis, Shandong University.

Li, X. Y. (1989) *Fuxing zhi lu: 1977 nian zhi 1987 nian dianying chuangzuo yu lilun piping* [Road to Reform: Film Practice and Criticism from 1977 to 1986], Beijing: China Film Press.

Liu, W. M (ed.) (1983) *Zhong wai yingtan yishi* [Anecdotes about Chinese and Foreign Cinema], Nanning: Guangxi People's Press.

Mao, S. A. (1989) "Ciji yu xuannian: jingxian pian de dongli: cong xi qu ke ke de die hai yiyun shuo qi" [Suspense and Thrill: The Driving Force of the Thriller Film—Hitchcock's North by Northwest as a Point of Departure], *Wen hui dianying shibao* [Wen Hui Film Times], February 25.

Meng, L. Y. (1985) "Jingxian pian de gexing yu yishu de gongxing" [The Specificities of the Thriller Film and The Generalities of Art], *Dianying yishu* [Film Art], 4: 41–44.

Qian, S. L. (1983) "Chongfen fahui 'hejin' de zuoyong" [The Effects of the Fusion of Artistic Elements], *Dianying yishu* [Film Art], 9: 54.

Shao, M. J. (1978) "Mantan dianying daoyan" [A Talk on Film Directing], *Shijie dianying yicong* [World Cinema Collection of Film Art Translations], 1: 93–114.

Shao, M. J. (1980) "Zai wenming shijie de li ceng: riben yingpian renzheng guan hou" [The Inner Side of Civilization: Review of Japanese Film Proof of the Man], *Dazhong dianying* [Popular Cinema], 2: 17.

Shao, M. J. (1982) *Xifang dianying shi gailun* [An Introduction to Western Film History], Beijing: China Film Press.

Shao, M. J. (1986) "Wo kan xi qu ke ke" [My Take on Hitchcock], *Dazhong dianying* [Popular Cinema], 10: 4–5.

Shi, Y. S. (1990) "Leixing pian de fei leixing hua biaoxian: guanyu xi qu ke ke de yishu gexing" [Non-Generic Expression in Genre Films: Hitchcock's Artistic Idiosyncrasy], *Ying ju yuebao* [Drama and Film Journal], 6: 47–49.

Sui, Z. Q. (2021) "20 shiji 80 niandai zhongguo yule pian yanjiu: yi gainian shi wei shijiao" [Research on Chinese Entertainment Films in the 1980s: From the Perspective of Conceptual History], Ph.D. thesis, Shandong Normal University.

Tan, H. (2014) *Zhongguo yizhi dianying shi* [A History of Dubbed Films in China], Beijing: China Film Press.

Tong, M. Z. (1985) "Xiwang you zhongguo de xi qu ke ke: xiao yi ba si nian jingxian pian" [Hopefully China Will Have Its Own Hitchcock: On Thrillers of 1984], *Dianying pingjie* [Movie Review], 6: 12.

Wang, C. L. (1984) "Xi qu ke ke zhangwo guanzhong qingxu de yishu" [Hitchcock's Evocation of Audience Emotions], *Dianying xin zuo* [New Films], 5: 103–104.

Wang, D. (ed.) (1993) *Tongxiang dianying shengdian: Beijing dianying xueyuan yingpian fenxi ke jiaocai* [To the Pantheon of Cinema: Textbook for the Film Analysis Course at Beijing Film Academy], Beijing: China Film Press.

Wang, X. Y. (1993) *Xi qu ke ke yu xuannian* [Hitchcock and Suspense], Beijing: Beijing Film Academy.

Wang, X. Y. (1999a) "Lun xi qu ke ke dianying de shangye xing yu xianfeng xing: xiangei xi qu ke ke bainian huadan" [On the Commercial and the Avant-Garde in Hitchcock's Films: A Tribute to the 100th Anniversary of Hitchcock's Birth], *Dianying yishu* [Film Art], 2: 37–44.

Wang, X. Y. (1999b) *Xi qu ke ke yu xuannian* [Hitchcock and Suspense], Beijing: China Radio and Television Press.

Wang, Y. M. (1986) "Richang shenghuo de xi qu ke ke hua" [Hitchcockization of Everyday Life], *Dazhong dianying* [Popular Cinema], 12: 12–13.

Wang, Y. Z. (1989) "Zhou chuanji Shao mujun tan zhongguo dianying yu haolaiwu" [Zhou Chuanji and Shao Mujun on Chinese Cinema and Hollywood], *Dianying yishu* [Film Art], 1: 43–53.

Xiao, F. (1987) "Zenyang pingshuo xi qu ke ke" [How to Discuss Hitchcock], *Xibu dianying* [West Films: Monthly Magazine of Film Literature], 45: 52–54.

Xiao, Y. X. (1985) "Jingxian pian bixu tichang xin guannian" [Thrillers Must Engage with New Ideas], *Dianying yishu* [Film Art], 4: 39–41.

Yan, M. (1984) "Waiguo jingxian dianying de lishi he xianzhuang" [The History and Status Quo of Foreign Thrillers], *Dianying xin shidai* [New Age of Cinema], 2: 72–73.

Yang, J. F. (ed.) (1982) *Haiwai yin tan jianying* [Sketches of Foreign Cinema], Guangdong: Flower City Press.

Yu, S. (1985) "Jingxian yangshi tansuo er ti" [Two Issues in the Development of the Thriller Genre], *Dianying yishu* [Film Art], 4: 45–48.

Zhou, J. J. (1982) "Xuannian dashi xi qu ke ke" [Hitchcock the Master of Suspense], *Yingshi shijie* [Screen World], 2: 14–16.

Chapter 34
Hitchcock in Spain

Dona M. Kercher

Highlighting key elements of Hitchcock's filmography, this essay traces his evolving reception in Spain and his importance for the Spanish film industry. We begin by discussing his relationship to and reception in Spain. Concentrating on the lessons three post-Franco directors learned from the master, we signal how their films attracted a transnational audience. We address whether Hitchcock remains a point of reference in their mature careers. The last section elaborates the recent efforts of a singular female Hitchcock.

The Initial Reception of Hitchcock as Auteur

Hitchcock's relationship with Spain is long and enduring. In the early 1920s, he scouted locations in Spain for the silent film *The Spanish Jade* when he worked for Famous Players-Lasky. Beginning with *De mujer a mujer* (*Woman to Woman*) in 1927, a steady stream of Hitchcock movies opened in Madrid. Carlos Fernández Cuenca's *El cine británico de Hitchcock* leaves no doubt that Hitchcock was viewed positively as an auteur in Spain, especially after *The Man Who Knew Too Much* (1935).

As Spanish law mandated from the 1930s onwards, all of Hitchcock's sound films were dubbed into Spanish for their initial exhibition. This delayed their openings for approximately a year from initial English releases. Dubbing of course made foreign films like Hitchcock's accessible to a wider, more popular audience. In general the censors were less strict with foreign material than with national movies, though in Hitchcock's case they exacted substantial cuts to *Lifeboat* (1947) and *Psycho* (1961), probably due to the depiction of suicide in the first case and marital infidelity and violence in the second.

Humor, glamor, aesthetic innovation, and a moral tone reflective of Hitchcock's Catholic background all factored into the initial public response. Significantly during the Franco era, *Rebecca* and *Spellbound* impacted cultural politics, especially emanating from Barcelona, where they served as a rallying cry for a new type of cinematic aesthetics that departed from the patriotic or folkloric state-sanctioned fare. At times, Hitchcock did fit the Nationalist paradigm, as *The Wrong Man* opened the International Festival of Religious Cinema in Valladolid in 1959.

Within Spain, *Spellbound* has a special place due to Hitchcock's difficult, and ultimately unhappy, collaboration with Salvador Dalí for the dream sequence. Hitchcock rejected most of what Dalí proposed. Dalí, nonetheless, continued to be associated with Hitchcock. Dalí was called upon to judge a Kim Novak look-alike contest to promote *Vertigo*. In 2005, the Spanish opened an exhibition of the original Dalí backdrops for *Spellbound*.

At the height of Hitchcock's career, in the late 1950s, the most prominent Hitchcock reception took place at the San Sebastián Film Festival. The festival was newly conceived but immediately recognized as a major global event on par with Cannes and Venice. *Vertigo* had its first screening ever there in 1958. Hitchcock's press conference was far better reviewed than the film, which received a lukewarm response and the second prize of the Silver Shell. In 1959, Hitchcock returned to San Sebastián to premiere *North by Northwest*, which was better received, in no small regard due to the film's sexual innuendos. It garnered a Best Actress award for Eva Marie Saint, though no recognition for Hitchcock himself. Hitchcock's two visits to San Sebastián were well documented in photographs. They formed the basis of an exhibition "Welcome, Hitchcock!" at the 2016 festival. Hitchcock had worked his marketing magic for the camera. He posed in settings associated with his filmography: in a cemetery and a church, by a staircase, in a shop window, and on the street with a nun in full habit (see Fig. 34.1).

Figure 34.1 Hitchcock in front of the Basilica of Santa María del Coro, San Sebastián, 1958.

© Courtesy of Fondo Marín-Kutxa Fototeka. Photo by Paco Marí, 1958. All rights reserved.

Figure 34.2 Hitchcock teasingly imitating an ice-cream vendor, Basque Country tour, 1958.
© Courtesy of Fondo Marín-Kutxa Fototeka. Photo by Paco Marí, 1958. All rights reserved.

He also played up his conflictive relation to food, as he was captured next to a menu board, and teasing a female ice-cream vendor (see Fig. 34.2).

Subsequent generations of spectators and filmmakers encountered Hitchcock's movies at cine clubs, on videos and DVDs, but especially on television. Despite limited broadcast channels, Spanish television has a rich history of regularly showing film classics, often with accompanying commentary. The family of Alex de la Iglesia, a filmmaker whose work in the 1990s we will discuss later, gathered together for obligatory family viewings of international cinema from his earliest childhood on. Spanish state TV continues to promote Hitchcock. In 2023, RTVE offered the documentary *Yo soy Alfred Hitchcock* for streaming.

Spanish Cinema after Franco: Pedro Almodóvar and a New Aesthetic

Even before Franco's death in 1975, Spanish cinema was changing. Metaphorical critiques of the repressive Francoist regime and its social isolation were common in highly original movies of this period, such as *El espiritu de la colmena*, *Furtivos*, *El corazón del bosque*, and *Cría cuervos*. Yet many Spaniards held the national cinema in low regard. Young Spaniards in particular found the rehashing of the Spanish Civil War boring and frequented American movies instead. Again, Hitchcock came to the fore, as aesthetic inspiration and as a model of a filmmaker who successfully moved from a national cinema to Hollywood and transnational recognition. What follows illustrates key borrowings of narrative structure, images, and aesthetic techniques, as well as humor to underscore how Spanish cinema translated Hitchcock at a moment of transition. The combination of these elements contributed greatly to the international commercial success of Hitchcock's Spanish inheritors. Significantly these directors got his humor, which marks and distinguishes their borrowings.

The new aesthetic movement, based in Madrid, was called La Movida, literally young Spaniards on the move partaking of everything that had been forbidden: sex, drugs, and punk-rock club culture. Pedro Almodóvar, the foremost innovator of the new Spanish cinema of this era, depicted the frenetic pace of the times both in his first film *Pepi, Luci, Bom* (1980), and subsequently in *Women on the Verge of a Nervous Breakdown* (1988). Eschewing film school, Almodóvar was a cinematic autodidact. While working a day job at the national telephone company in Madrid, he read about cinema and saw classic Hollywood cinema at the Filmoteca. From Hitchcock he learned how to make sophisticated dramas with modest budgets, aimed at older audiences mostly ignored by Hollywood.

While Almodóvar's debt to Hitchcock permeates his filmography, as I indicate in my book *Latin Hitchcock*, he found his narrative stride in his 1984 film *What Have I Done to Deserve This?*, the first to receive distribution in France, by re-situating Hitchcock's well-known teleplay "Lamb to the Slaughter." Almodóvar's film tells the story of an overworked cleaning lady Gloria (Carmen Maura) who kills her cabdriver husband Antonio with a ham bone, like Hitchcock's long-suffering Mrs. Maloney, who used a lamb bone. In both cases, detectives investigate the murders. The evidence is already being cooked up in a dish. In the teleplay, while the detectives eat, Mrs. Maloney sits in an adjoining room and smiles, acknowledging that she has gotten away with her crime. She is framed in a frontal medium shot against a 1950s wallpaper pattern. Almodóvar steals the motif and puts it in motion.

Symbolically turning over a new leaf, Gloria is about to repaper her kitchen. She finds out that the child Vanessa, whom she has agreed to babysit, has magical powers. Vanessa repapers the kitchen telepathically. A brush moves over the wallpaper like the sorcerer's apprentice/Mickey's mop in Disney's *Fantasia*. Gloria's smile, shown against a backdrop of vintage wallpaper, reiterates Mrs. Maloney's sense of satisfaction. The viewer is in on the joke and sympathizes with the women as they achieve freedom in the domestic realm. The use of special effects, which are rare in Spanish cinema of the 1980s but a fundamental element of international mass culture of the time, underscores Almodóvar's claim to originality vis-à-vis Hitchcock's work.

With the immensely successful screwball comedy *Women on the Verge of a Nervous Breakdown*, Almodóvar appealed to a more general audience. As many critics have noted (see Kercher 2015: 82–88), the film references Hitchcock in genre and aesthetics. Moreover, it is the first film for which Almodóvar storyboarded, a technique closely associated with Hitchcock. In the film, the harried Pepa (Carmen Maura) is depressed because she has been jilted by her lover. Numerous scenes show her distress by framing her through objects. When she faints, we see her through her eyeglasses on the floor, a shot that recalls the vision of Miriam's last breath seen though enlarged eyeglasses in *Strangers on a Train*. In another scene, Almodóvar captures her through the spectacles-like bobbins of an answering machine's cassette. Almodóvar observed to Frédéric Strauss that he was inspired in this latter shot by how Hitchcock enlarged and positioned the teacup that contains the poison that sickens Alicia in *Notorious*.

Another moment alludes to *Rear Window*, specifically Miss Torso's dance, as Pepa voyeuristically spies on people in windows of an elegant Madrid building as she sits on a street bench below.

Both directors shared a cinematic obsession with women. Although Almodóvar wrote disparagingly of the real-life Hitchcock's treatment of women, using swear words, he never let go of his fascination with *Vertigo* and, seeing himself as a director of women, refashioned his actresses as Scottie tried to transform Judy. This fixation fully surfaces in Almodóvar's 2014 film *The Skin I Live In*, a complex transgender reinterpretation and critique of *Vertigo*. His introduction to the script is revelatory. The film tells the story of Dr. Robert Ledgard, who, through his experiments with artificial skin, transforms Vicente into Vera in the image of his dead wife Gal. Whereas in *Vertigo* Judy reluctantly allows herself to be transformed into Madeleine, Dr. Ledgard transforms Vicente into Vera in captivity and under great duress. To console herself in imprisonment, Vera makes art reminiscent of Louis Bourgeois's sculptures. Their spirals evoke Saul Bass's spiral images of *Vertigo*'s opening sequence. Vera eventually escapes by killing Ledgard. The bodily change of gender does not, however, affect Vicente/Vera's identity. In a final scene, a clerk recognizes Vicente, now as Vera, as their former self by renewing talk of a Dolce and Gabbana dress they had discussed years before in their mother's dress shop. Still drawing inspiration from Hitchcock, Almodóvar "redresses" Hitchcock's gender politics.

Two years later, evoking not only *Strangers on a Train* but also *Rebecca* and *The Lady Vanishes*, *Julieta* recuperates a more serious, empathetic version of the mature woman/mother who was so often caricatured in Hitchcock. A sexual encounter on a train introduces the film's complex dual structure of young versus old versions of the protagonist Juliet. While neither *Julieta* nor *The Skin I Live In* achieved the box-office success of many of Almodóvar's earlier movies, they secured the place of Spanish cinema in a transnational industry through transformations of Hitchcockian narrative and aesthetics.

Alex de la Iglesia and Hitchcock's Scenes on Monuments

Alex de la Iglesia is a self-taught filmmaker who, like Almodóvar, learned from Hitchcock. As he recounts, he received "an electric shock to the neurons" when he attended a film series in Bilbao, Spain, called "Essential Hitchcock" while in high school (Angulo 2012: 102). He incorporated what he saw into his nascent filmmaking. Not surprisingly, Almodóvar recognized De la Iglesia's talent. The first film produced by Almodóvar's company El Deseo was De la Iglesia's debut feature film *Mutant Action*, a black comedy about crazy space pirates who kidnap an executive. The story resonates with the Basque separatist group's (ETA) kidnappings of that era. Unlike De la Iglesia's second feature, *Day of the Beast*, which drew a huge young, hipper audience to the theaters and then swept the Goyas, the Spanish equivalent of the Oscars, *Mutant Action* met with limited commercial success. The difference was the full-blown presence of aesthetic and narrative elements traceable to Hitchcock's films in the latter.

Day of the Beast tells the story of Angel Berriatúa, a Basque priest who discovers a prediction of the Apocalypse. On December 25, 1995, the Devil will appear and kill a baby. The priest can only avert catastrophe by committing evil deeds on purpose. The priest, together with a clerk from a heavy-metal store, kidnap a well-known television personality, a professor with a program on the occult, to force him to teach them how to summon the Devil. When the Devil finally appears in the professor's apartment, they all escape out the window onto the façade of the Capitol building, a landmark movie theater in Madrid. They dangle off a Schweppes advertising sign like Fry dangling from Miss Liberty's upraised hand in

Saboteur. While the humor comes from the absurd situations, the mise-en-scène marks the movie. Spaniards saw their urban environment anew, with great irony, but also as a European audience. In the film the Kio or Gate of Europe leaning office towers symbolize the Devil since they resemble a cloven hoof. By linking movie theater and office towers, the film slyly comments on the flow of transnational capital and art.

De la Iglesia repeats the Hitchcockian leitmotif of a chase that ends in danger at great heights in many other movies. In *Common Wealth*, a chase across the monumental statues of what was the Madrid BBVA bank evokes the Mount Rushmore sequence of *North by Northwest*. A fall from those heights ends in a flowerlike image of death that recalls Juanita's death in *Topaz*. More monumental chases on high take place on a Ferris wheel in *Ferpect Crime*, on the rooftops in *The Oxford Murders*, and, most spectacularly, in *The Last Circus* in the Valley of the Fallen, the gigantic monument synonymous with Franco.

De la Iglesia is himself acutely aware that he repeats his formulas that foreground mise-en-scène and in turn references Hitchcock as a director who remakes the same movie over and over. About his monumental location sequences, he explains, "When you take the characters to the Heights, it's as if you raised them up to Olympus, as if you perfected them. Unconsciously the spectator also feels that sensation and believes that when on high the person is telling the truth and can't lie" (Angulo 2012: 156).

As did Hitchcock regarding television, a newer medium in his day, De la Iglesia has turned to television, and now streaming, in his later career. After the global success of the Spanish thriller caper *Money Heist*, set again in an iconic location, the Bank of Spain in Madrid, his earlier explorations of this medium, such as *Dying of Laughter*, in which the rivalry between two TV personalities plays out against the *coup d'état* invasion of the Spanish Congress, have only recently been appreciated as an important part of his filmography. Most notably De la Iglesia has picked up where *Day of the Beast* left off for his HBO hit series *30 Monedas* (*Thirty Coins*, 2020–2023), which he wrote and directed. In it, the world is again threatened by the Apocalypse, symbolized by a now monstrous baby. A priest possesses a special coin, one of those paid to Judas for betraying Jesus, that implicates an international conspiracy. Not forgetting his Hitchcockian beginning, De la Iglesia has gained exceptional prominence with the series' global streaming.

Alejandro Amenábar's Early Hitchcockian Triptych

Though far from the monumental settings so loved by De la Iglesia, location was still key in the 1990s to the success of Alejandro Amenábar, another Spanish filmmaker who looked to Hitchcock. Amenábar set his debut film, the thriller *Thesis* (1996), in the university. He chose this setting for its global appeal to a younger audience, not for any specific connection to Spanish culture. In *Thesis*, Prof. Castro explains, echoing Amenábar's opinion, that contemporary Spanish cinema is not commercial enough and sees Hitchcock, who was so often criticized for being too commercial, as a way out of this dilemma.

The film tells the story of Angela, a student writing a thesis on audiovisual violence, who discovers evidence of a real snuff film. As a result, Bosco, a psychopathic killer, pursues her throughout the university. For this chase, Amenábar storyboarded a heart-stopping sequence in which Bosco finally surprises Angela from behind. The sequence took two days to shoot. The veteran cameraman Hans Burman, who shot *Thesis*, observed that the high number of shots per sequence, for which *Psycho*'s shower sequence was the gold standard, was exceptional for a Spanish film of its time. Likewise evoking the *Psycho* soundtrack, *Thesis* broke new ground in Spanish terror films through its reliance on strings and piano to the exclusion of brass instruments.

Aware that horror continues to be a reliable performer, Amenábar filmed the dark entrance to a fellow student Chema's apartment to resemble a chamber of horrors. Bound mannequins are suspended upside down from the ceiling, as if they were Norman Bates's taxidermy. Furthermore, the student's offhand comments about Angela refusing an offer of food humorously reprise Norman Bates's compliments to Marion for "eating like a bird."

Just as Norman Bates spied on Marion through a peephole in his office wall, Bosco installs a spy camera in Angela's bedroom to keep her under surveillance. In a nightmarish sequence, the red "on" light blinks in the corner of the frame as Angela lies in bed. She later discovers tapes of herself in Chema's camera. In the film's epilogue, hospital patients crane their necks to see violent snuff images on the television despite the anchor warning them of their violent content. Ironically, the film portrays Chema and Angela as "good" spectators, walking away from the spectacle on television. The scene thus affirms a generational break: the younger generation can discard the television violence that mesmerizes their elders because they understand how visual culture works and can act on it even when they are its protagonists.

Whereas Amenábar built his debut around *Psycho* to enormous acclaim, his much anticipated second film *Abre los ojos* (*Open Your Eyes*, 1997) overtly remade *Vertigo* in a Spanish contemporary setting and "corrected" Hitchcock's errors. *Open Your Eyes* tells the story of César (Eduardo Noriega), a handsome, wealthy womanizer. Every morning, an alarm clock wakes him with an insistent recording of the title line, "Open your eyes." César falls in love with Sofía (Penélope Cruz), an aspiring actress, who his best friend Pelayo brings as his date to a lavish birthday party at César's apartment. At the party's conclusion, César leaves with Sofía and spends the night at her apartment. They talk, he sketches her, but they do not have sex. When his current, soon former, steady girlfriend Nuria, who was shunned at the party, comes by to pick him up the next morning at Sofia's, she drives the car into a wall in an angry attempted murder/suicide. César survives the crash, but his face is horribly disfigured, so much so that he has to wear a mask. The film moves in and out of César's subjective world, in flashbacks and dreams, as he tries to make sense of his life and his attraction to these two women, especially to Sofía, the love of his life, for whom Nuria doubles visually in his dreams.

In the film's final scene on a skyscraper rooftop, which brings together the film's overarching themes of life and death, César confronts all the major characters from the film. The cryogenic executive Duvenois reveals that the characters are only figments of César's imagination, for when he despaired at never having his face reconstructed, he committed suicide and was then frozen until 2045, which is supposedly the current moment. Duvenois tells César that he has been living a nightmare of his own creation, but that he can choose a different dream if he commits suicide again. After a brief hesitation on the precipice to observe that he suffers vertigo, César jumps off the building.

Despite Amenábar's claims of revision, *Open Your Eyes* nonetheless repeats key images of *Vertigo*. A hazy shot of Sofía coming through a door recalls the apparition of Judy entering a hotel room as the made-over blonde Madeleine. Similarly, Sofía and César's lovemaking to a symphonic soundtrack echoes the rotating kiss, also staged in the hotel room, accompanied by romantic theme music associated with Scottie's vision of Madeleine in the mission stable. Unlike Hitchcock, Amenábar does not let the spectator into the ruse of Judy playing Madeleine; rather, he keeps the women's identities a mystery by maintaining the subjective viewpoint of the main character César throughout most of the film.

Open Your Eyes is a uniquely Spanish interpretation of *Vertigo*, rooted in Spanish cultural history of urban architecture, home design, and, especially, the modern paintings of Antonio López García. Conveying the complexity of his subjective confusion, César at one moment finds himself on the Gran Vía, a boulevard of Madrid, totally devoid of people, exactly as López García depicted this space at dawn in his much-lauded realistic painting *La Gran Vía, 1974–1981*. Still, the maddeningly dense *Open Your Eyes* flummoxed most spectators, disappointed critics, and underperformed in prizes. Nonetheless, it captured the attention of Tom Cruise, who bought the film rights and remade it as *Vanilla Sky* (2001), transforming the Gran Vía into Times Square, thereby continuing the recirculation of Hitchcockian motifs.

Amenábar made his own journey into English-language cinema with his third thriller, *The Others* (2001), which starred Nicole Kidman, then married to Cruise, who produced the film. The film tells the story of children who cannot leave a haunted house due to light sensitivity. Kidman plays their mother. Filmed in a mansion in Santander, Spain, the movie's setting and mood recall the Manderley estate of Hitchcock's *Rebecca*. *The Others* marked a closure to a stage of Amenábar's career, built through Hitchcockian thrillers. He changed directions generically with the Oscar-winning drama *The Sea Inside* (2004), based on a real-life case of euthanasia. Subsequently, he probed other political and intellectual controversies in two historical dramas from widely ranging periods in *Agora* (2009), about the Greek philosopher and mathematician Hypatia, who was murdered by Christian zealots in Roman Egypt, and *While at War* (2019), about the writer and philosopher Miguel de Unamuno during the first years of the Spanish Civil War.

The Spanish Thriller Trend Continues

Hitchcock's impact remains strong in Spain in the twenty-first century, serving as a consistent model for building a career. The thriller-driven films of the writing-directing duo of Rodrigo Sorogoyen and Isabel Peña, *El reino* (*The Candidate*, 2018) and *Que Dios Nos Perdone* (*May God Save Us*, 2016), or J. A. Bayona's career start of *The Orphanage* (2007), can be considered in this vein. Hitchcockian motifs abound in Alberto Rodríguez's *Marshland* (2014), a trend magnified in his subsequent films, *Smoke and Mirrors* (2016), and *Prison 77* (2022). The latter has a magnificent prison scene atop a panopticon that recalls Hitchcock's finale in *Blackmail* atop the library dome of the British Museum. Until recently, few women filmmakers in Spain would have made their careers via Hitchcockian aesthetics. This should not be surprising due to the lack of parity in the industry. Yet the sparse representation of Spanish women directors, detailed by Annette Scholz in *Cineastas emergentes: mujeres en el cine del siglo XXI* (2018), has been changing slowly, as evidenced in the gender-identity report of the 71st San Sebastián Festival (2023). Even within this challenging cinematic landscape, one Spanish woman filmmaker, Carlota Pereda, is a major exception as she has taken a Hitchcockian career path. Her 2022 debut *Piggy*, a horror film, features Hitchcockian motifs and genre mix. Besides a successful commercial run, the film received numerous Goya nominations and a Best New Actress Award for Laura Galán.

Piggy centers on Sara, an overweight teenager, daughter of the town butcher. The cool-girl crowd bullies her at her family's shop and especially at the town pool. When Sara witnesses a stranger kidnap her tormentors, she faces the dilemma of whether to help rescue them or to exact revenge by staying silent. The man continues to attack villagers, including Sara's overbearing parents. The film's climax occurs at the killer's lair, an abandoned slaughterhouse. Sara discovers the girls strung up by their hands like meat on an overhead conveyor, in homage to Hitchcock's hanging scenes. With perfect shotgun aim honed from hunting game, she severs the ropes tying them up.

The Hitchcockian motif of hanging is foreshadowed from the film's title sequence that first shows how sausage is made through a montage of close-ups. A huge slab of meat is jammed onto a meat hook, blood is poured over a mixture, a huge butcher knife cuts meat, which is then stuffed into the casing. This gory sequence creates a sense of taboo which is carried over to the next montage that reveals the chubby Sara through a series of extreme close-ups of her hands, her pink-clad feet, and then her head of curly hair crowned with a pair of pink headphones. The final shot frames her head with sausages hanging behind her as if she were one of them (see Fig. 34.3). By emphasizing the visual in these montages, Pereda follows Hitchcock's concept of "pure cinema."

Although *Piggy* mainly exploits horror genre tropes, it is the genre mix, adding a touch of romance and humor, so characteristic of Hitchcock's best films, that gives the film realistic depth. The spectator connects with the plot and its main characters. In one funny scene, the town bad boy Carlos, who wants information about one of the missing girls with whom he is in a relationship, hands Sara her first smoke. When she coughs and makes faces, they laugh together. It foreshadows a rom-com pair shift, realized in the film's ending when they ride off together into the sunset on a motorcycle.

Even more significant to the spectatorship bond, as well as Sara's ethical quandary, is how the serial killer befriends Sara throughout the film. As a fellow outcast, he shows he understands the dynamics of bullying. Just as Norman Bates showed sympathy to Marion's plight, so does the mysterious stranger.

Figure 34.3 Sara (Laura Galán) watches from her perch in the butcher shop in *Piggy* directed by Carlota Pereda.
© Morena Films 2022. All rights reserved.

Sara first meets him after the cool girls steal her clothes while she is swimming and she is forced to walk home in her bikini. Taking a side path, she comes upon a van with the girls, beaten up and bloody, pleading to her through the back window. The stranger opens the door, stares her down, and then throws out a towel. In this shot/reverse shot they bond for the first time. Sara runs back home to shower. As she showers, she imagines hearing the kidnapped girls' screaming. Her conscience bothers her as Marion's did driving to the Bates Motel. Still, she does not disclose the girls' abduction. An intervening sequence shows the danger, as the killer slits the throat of a woman in her house then leaves a gift of a candy on Sara's balcony. Later, the killer returns to her house and beats up Sara's parents. When her little brother, who is on the toilet, calls out for Sara to replenish the toilet paper, Sara silently pleads to the killer for him to spare her innocent brother. The killer does, and they leave the house together. The scene follows Hitchcock's rule, only broken in *Sabotage*, to his regret, that children are not to be harmed in the movies.

For Pereda to focus on a less-than-perfect female body, on fatness, affirms her indebtedness to Hitchcock, whose weight struggle figured into his public reputation. Piggy's unflinching depiction of Sara's almost naked body, shown jiggling with scars and all, as she flees the cruel assaults of the town boys who stop their car to grope her, is not about body positivity but about empathy toward women victimized by sexual assault. The unique comprehension of humanity that underlies Hitchcock's movies, and seen in *Piggy* as well as in other examples of Spanish films we have explored, continues to nurture Spanish cinema today. It remains to be seen what direction Pereda takes in her second film and if others will follow Hitchcock's trajectory in Spain.

References

Angulo, J., and A. Santamarina (2012) *Alex de la Iglesia*: *La pasión de rodar*, San Sebastián: Filmoteca Vasca.
Kercher, D. (2015) *Latin Hitchcock: How Almodóvar, Amenábar, De la Iglesia, Del Toro and Campenella Became Notorious*, New York: Columbia University Press.
Strauss, F. (1995) *Pedro Almodóvar*: *Un cine visceral, conversaciones con Frédéric Strauss*, Madrid: Ediciones Aguilar.

Chapter 35
Hitchcock's Audiences in Mexico
From Movie Theaters to TV

Ana Rosas Mantecón

The most perfect criminal Hitch ever created was himself: Hitchcock, the reliable monster of the neighbourhood who, unlike other subversive auteurs, was always accessible and popularly acclaimed ... He committed the perfect crime ... 53 times: He poisoned our souls with the liquor of cinema. He invited us to look into the abyss ... And the abyss looked at us in turn ...

GUILLERMO DEL TORO (1990: 25)

Hitchcock is recognized in Mexico as an essential auteur. But his appreciation, not only as a commercially successful filmmaker but also as an exceptional creator, was not a linear process, nor did it depend solely on movie showings. Hitchcock's popularity is complex and multifaceted, across locations and media. His work established a dialogue at different times with multiple audiences and through different media: first- and second-run theaters, art cinemas, TV, video, pirated versions, streaming platforms, movie scripts, and various publications and popular literature that sprung from his films and TV series.

Over the decades, opposing viewpoints on Hitchcock by film critics, as well as differences of opinion between them and nonspecialized audiences can be seen. These viewpoints were influenced by various international and national publications that valued his work, his rereleases in art cinemas, film associations, and universities, and, since the late 1970s, recognition from the Cineteca Nacional and other national cultural institutions.

Two authors have paved the way for studying Hitchcock's reception in Mexico. Dona Kercher (2015) analyzed the changing recognition of his work from the 1930s to the 1960s, drawing on two national newspapers and some other publications. Raúl Miranda (2018) explored the transit of his films through theaters and TV and the changing appreciation of his audiences and critics. Taking into account their research progress, this chapter is based on a fourfold exploration. First, a record of theaters in which Hitchcock's films were premiered and then rereleased in Mexico City, as well as other media outlets through which they became known. Second, the reception of his work by film critics and Mexican film directors, as seen in books, film reviews, and articles in literary, popular, and film periodicals from the 1930s onwards. Third, interviews with film critics and scholars and a man who sells bootleg films. Finally, an exploration of the varied dissemination of his work through the Cineteca Nacional.

Early Audiences

Just over half of Hitchcock's films were not released theatrically in Mexico at the time they were produced (twenty-one from his British period and two from his Hollywood period). Only three were never made available for viewing. The rest later appeared through art-house cinemas, TV, video, or bootleg copies. *Champaña* (*Champagne*, 1929) was the first of Hitchcock's films to be screened in the country. It "did not receive any significant reviews." It was overshadowed by news of the release of the first feature film produced in the USA dubbed into Spanish: *Shadows of Glory*, 1930 (Kercher 2015: 240–241). The absence of several early Hitchcock films from Mexican film circuits "is partly explained by the fragmentation of the English production houses that produced his films: Gainsborough Pictures, Associated British Corporation, Gaumont and British Films, among others." From *39 escalones* (*The 39 Steps*, 1935) onwards, Hitchcock's films in Mexican cinemas became commonplace, thanks to Mexican film distributor Camus y compañía (Miranda 2018).

Some opened in large theaters, such as the Cosmos with *Agonía de amor* (*The Paradine Case*, 1947) and the Cine de las Américas with *Mi secreto me condena* (*I Confess*, 1953). As can be seen in Table 35.1, a good number of premieres lasted two to four weeks of showings, some for five weeks: *Tuyo es*

Table 35.1 Films released in Mexico City.

Year	Original title	Title in Mexico	Release date	Premiere venue(s)	Time on billboard
1928	*Champagne*	*Champaña*	April 4, 1930	San Juan de Letrán	At least two days, after which there was no publicity
1935	*The Thirty-nine Steps*	*Treinta y nueve escalones*	November 14, 1935	Palacio	One week*
1936	*Sabotage*	*Sabotaje*	February 11, 1937	Palacio	One week*
1936	*Secret Agent*	*Cuatro de espionaje, Agente Secreto*	September 18, 1936	Rex	Twelve days*
1938	*The Lady Vanishes*	*La dama desaparece*	July 16, 1942	Rex	One week*
1939	*Jamaica Inn*	*La posada maldita*	May 2, 1940	Alameda	One week*
1940	*Rebecca*	*Rebeca*	August 1, 1940	Alameda	Four weeks*

Year	Original title	Title in Mexico	Release date	Premiere venue(s)	Time on billboard
1940	*Foreign Correspondent*	*Corresponsal extranjero*	October 23, 1940	Alameda	Two weeks*
1941	*Mr. & Mrs. Smith*	*Casados y descasados*	April 12, 1941	Magerit	Two weeks*
1940	*Suspicion*	*Sospecha*	December 25, 1941	Olympia	Two weeks*
1942	*Saboteur*	*Saboteador*	August 4, 1942	Teresa	Two weeks*
1943	*Shadow of a Doubt*	*La sombra de una duda*	April 8, 1943	Alameda	Two weeks*
1944	*Lifeboat*	*Náufragos*	January 4, 1945	Alameda	Two weeks*
1945	*Spellbound*	*Cuéntame tu vida*	June 13, 1946	Alameda	Four weeks*
1946	*Notorious*	*Tuyo es mi corazón*	February 12, 1947	Alameda	Five weeks*
1947	*The Paradine Case*	*Agonía de amor*	June 24, 1948	Cosmos y Orfeón	Five weeks‡
1948	*Rope*	*La soga*	May 19, 1949	Palacio Chino	Two weeks‡
1949	*Under Capricorn*	*Bajo el signo de capricornio*	January 19, 1950	Alameda	Three weeks*
1950	*Stage Fright*	*Desesperación*	December 25, 1951	Alameda	One week†
1951	*Strangers on a Train*	*Pacto siniestro*	December 7, 1951	Alameda	Two weeks‡
1953	*I Confess*	*Mi secreto me condena*	December 30, 1953	Las Américas	Three weeks‡
1954	*Dial M for Murder*	*Con M de muerte*	November 11, 1954	Alameda	Three weeks‡
1954	*Rear Window*	*La ventana indiscreta*	May 5, 1955	Chapultepec	Five weeks‡
1955	*To Catch a Thief*	*Para atrapar al ladrón*	December 22, 1955	Chapultepec	Four weeks‡
1955	*The Trouble with Harry*	*El Tercer Tiro*	April 25, 1957	Chapultepec	Two weeks‡
1956	*The Man Who Knew Too Much*	*En manos del destino*	November 8, 1956	Chapultepec	Three weeks‡

Year	Original title	Title in Mexico	Release date	Premiere venue(s)	Time on billboard
1956	*The Wrong Man*	*El Hombre Equivocado*	April 25, 1957	Las Américas	Two weeks[‡]
1958	*Vertigo*	*Vértigo (de entre los muertos)*	March 5, 1959	Alameda y Polanco	Seven weeks[†]
1959	*North by Northwest*	*Intriga internacional*	October 10, 1959	Roble, Ariel y Roble	Three weeks[‡]
1960	*Psycho*	*Psicosis*	March 29, 1962	Chapultepec	Eleven weeks[‡]
1963	*The Birds*	*Los pájaros*	July 18, 1963	Chapultepec	Nine weeks[‡]
1964	*Marnie*	*Marnie, la ladrona*	January 28, 1965	Latino y Continental	Four weeks[‡]
1966	*Torn Curtain*	*Cortina rasgada*	February 2, 1967	Chapultepec	Five weeks[‡]
1969	*Topaz*	*Topaz*	September 15, 1970	Tlatelolco	Five weeks[‡]
1972	*Frenzy*	*Frenesí*	September 14, 1972	Pecime	Three weeks[‡]
1976	*Family Plot*	*Trama macabra*	May 5, 1977	Pecime, Polanco, Las Américas, Cinema Uno, Villa Coapa[§]	Five weeks[‡]

Sources:
Release dates and cinemas are from Amador and Ayala Blanco (1999, 1986, 1985, 1982 and 1980) unless otherwise specified.
Notes: * *Excélsior*; [†] *El Universal Gráfico*; [‡] Nelson Carro (personal communication); [§] Miranda 2018.

mi corazón (*Notorious*, 1946), *Agonía de amor*, and *La Ventana indiscreta* (*Rear Window*, 1954). His biggest hits were *Vértigo* (*Vertigo*, 1958), *Psicosis* (*Psycho*, 1960), and *Los pájaros* (*The Birds*, 1963), which had seven, eleven, and nine weeks respectively. Even films that were poorly rated by international critics were well attended: *Marnie, la ladrona* (*Marnie*, 1964), *Cortina rasgada* (*Torn Curtain*, 1966), *Topaz* (1969), and *Trama macabra* (*Family Plot*, 1976), with four weeks of showings for the former and five for the rest of them.

How can we evaluate time spent in cinemas?[1] It's a complex matter because we only have information about weeks of release. So, we don't know how they were distributed to the rest of the theater circuits to which these spaces were integrated, mostly because not all theaters advertised in the press. However, thanks to interviews, we know that in the 1950s, 1960s, and 1970s, "many people went to see Hitchcock films, not at the first-run cinemas … they went to second-run theaters which featured two Hitchcock films" (Raúl Miranda, interview, December 10, 2023).

Hitchcock as a Star

Hitchcock aimed to attract audiences via his visibility as a unique figure, the creator of a style, a genre, guaranteed entertainment. However, a review of his films' publicity offers a glimpse of how hard it was to be recognized as an auteur when actors' success was determined by the star system. Hitchcock's career began in classic Hollywood industrial cinema, which was genre-based and where a star system sought to nurture idealized images (Bordwell et al. 1997). Stars became myths for audiences and reference points for critics. As Edgar Morin (2005) has shown, they largely constituted the basis of the collective imaginary of that time.

Hitchcock's name first appears in ads for *Sabotaje* (*Sabotage*, 1936). It was reviewed in the English section of the *Excélsior* newspaper, which described Hitchcock as having "that master's touch in bringing to the screen real people with appropriate sets and surroundings" (Kercher 2015: 245). Until then, his films were promoted only through actors who appeared in them. Fascination with film stars was shared even by critics: Xavier Villaurrutia highlights "about the film *Sabotage* (1936) the great performance by Sylvia Sidney in a whole paragraph; on the other hand, Hitchcock merits a solitary sentence: 'Masterfully directed'" (Miranda 2018).[2]

A few years later, Hitchcock moved to Hollywood. His first American film, *Rebecca* (*Rebecca*, 1940), had its release extended by four weeks, a first for him. Curiously, the film was not reviewed in Mexican newspapers, nor was his name mentioned, but publicity described it as "the best film of the year," a "wonder of wonders" (Excélsior, October 31, 1940). A few months later, *Corresponsal extranjero* (*Foreign Correspondent*, 1940) was released. Ads highlighted Hitchcock as "the magician who directed *Rebecca* and *39 Steps*" (*Excélsior*, October 23, 1940), linking the two periods of the director and using these productions as bait for viewers—a strategy that would be repeated again and again. Film critics gradually gave him more weight in their reviews. Xavier Villaurrutia "became the pioneer of 'Hitchcockian' criticism." Villaurrutia recognized in *Foreign Correspondent*, "his mastery in conducting and sustaining scenes that create suspense in the viewer's mood ... taking his work to something more than mere entertainment" (Miranda 2018). *El Duende Filmo* "admitted he had not yet seen *Shadow of a Doubt* 1943, but he recommended it 'SHOULD BE SEEN because the director is Alfred Hitchcock, creator of *Rebecca* and *Suspicion*' (*El Universal*, April 8, 1943)" (Kercher 2015: 253).

How did this continental shift transform perceptions of Hitchcock? The link with producer David O. Selznick made it easier for him to not only "adapt to the peculiar (and financially strict) 'Hollywood industrial system' of production, but also to make himself known in the United States, where he was only appreciated as the creator of small English thrillers" (Del Toro 1990: 16). In addition to his collaboration with Selznick on three films—*Rebeca* (*Rebecca*, 1940), *Cuéntame tu vida* (*Spellbound*, 1945), and *Agonía de amor* (*The Paradine Case*, 1947)—he worked with Warner Bros., Paramount, Universal, 20th Century Fox, Metro Goldwyn Mayer, and RKO. This led to consolidated regular exhibition of his productions in Mexico (except for his documentaries *Bon voyage* and *Aventure Malgache*, 1944). He quickly went from being perceived as an British director to a Hollywood one, as evidenced by the fact that *Casados y descasados* (*Mr. & Mrs. Smith*, 1941) was chosen for its premiere at the Magerit cinema as part of celebrations for the inauguration of a flight between Mexico City and Los Angeles. Three Pan Am Airlines planes arrived full of Hollywood stars for the occasion (Kercher 2015: 250–251; see also *Novedades*, April 12, 1941).

It was becoming increasingly common in advertising to recognize Hitchcock as a "magician," a "master of emotion," and a "guarantee for the viewer," except for those films featuring big-name stars, such as

Ingrid Bergman. Her presence in *Spellbound* (1945) "was exploited way beyond the star discourse for his films in Mexico." Unusual for serious newspapers at the time, there were full-page fashion spreads for local stores that promoted the film and Bergman's image as "appropriate for Mexican women". Kercher considers that celebrity fashion was important because of how it allowed for the Mexican woman to see a new vision of herself at the time, while still underscoring the family (Kercher 2015: 255).

This was also the case with Hitchcock's films starring Grace Kelly, whose fame was promoted in advertising, minimizing the reference to Hitchcock. *Con M de muerte* (*Dial M for Murder*, 1954), *La ventana indiscreta* (*Rear Window*, 1954) and *Para atrapar al ladrón* (*To Catch a Thief*, 1955) were successful (between three and five weeks of release), and El Universal Gráfico's ads contain stills, protagonists' names, some even the production company, but no mention of the director (November 11, 1954; December 22, 1955; and May 5, 1944).[3] In *Excélsior*, the image and name of James Stewart take up half the ad for *Rear Window*, while Hitchcock is mentioned in small print as "the master of suspense" (May 5, 1955). Significantly, in its remastered screening in 2000, the director's face dominates advertising.[4] In the ad for *En manos del destino* (*The Man Who Knew Too Much*, 1956), Hitchcock was touted not only as the latest in technology, for Vistavision and Technicolor, but also recommended as family entertainment (Kercher 2015: 258).

By the 1960s, a wide range of Mexican audiences could not only pick out Hitchcock's cameos in his films but also flocked to see his latest movies. *Psicosis* (*Psycho*, 1960) and *Los pájaros* (*The Birds*, 1963) broke all attendance records in Mexico City (eleven and nine weeks). Ads for both films were written in first person: For *Psycho*, the director warned that "latecomers would not be admitted to theatres ... You don't begin a book at the end, or dinner with dessert and *Psycho* is a genuine banquet of emotions. My aim is, naturally, to help you to deeply enjoy this movie. See it from the beginning!" (Kercher 2015: 259). In the case of the second film, cinemas were flooded with an image of Hitchcock with birds. Underneath the photograph, his name appeared in large print along with the caption "This could very well be the most terrifying film I've ever made" (*El Universal*, July 16, 1963, p. 20). "I still remember the lines to see *Psycho*, they were amazing" (Cuervo Cruz, interviewed on February 3, 2024).

Television was one of the keys to Hitchcock's success with mass audiences as Alarcón's sketch sharply suggests (Fig. 35.1). It did so both through the successful screening of series he produced as well as films, documentaries about him, and interviews. The series *Alfred Hitchcock Presenta* (*Alfred Hitchcock Presents*, 1955–1962) and *La hora de Alfred Hitchcock* (*The Alfred Hitchcock Hour*, 1962–1965) remained on the air for almost ten years in their first run (the average time for a "successful" programme was two years) and were intermittently rerun thereafter. The director became part of the "public domain, integrated into common language and everyday life" (Del Toro 1990: 16 and 20).

Newspapers—such as *Novedades*, *El Nacional*, *Excélsior*, *El Universal*, and *Esto*—and magazines—such as *Premiere*, *Cinemanía*, and *24 por Segundo*, among others—announced and commented on his television and cinema programming, further reinforcing his integration into Mexican daily life.

The globalized slogan "the master/magician/master of suspense" undoubtedly made Hitchcock accessible and identifiable.[5] "In general people went to the cinema to see famous stars ... Hitchcock was one of the first who became known for the kind of films he made, that is, his name was identified with a certain kind of cinema: thriller or suspense" (Leonardo Garcia Tsao, interview, February 7, 2024). Both the nickname he created and promoted for himself (Hitch) and his caricature, "which he himself drew with a few lines and which became famous as a product logo representing the 'wizard of suspense' ... were intended to simplify an intricate and convoluted personality and artistic work, perhaps partly as a publicity strategy" (Del Toro 1990: 20–21).

Figure 35.1 Juan Alarcón's sketch of Hitchcock for *El Financiero*, August 12, 1999.

Film Criticism

Very early in his career, Hitchcock caught the attention of Mexican film critics. Kercher's study shows the transformation of film critics' perception of his movies: as experimental cinema, comedies, spy films, and intrigue in the pre–World War II era; as melodramas in the golden age of Mexican cinema; and as suspense movies after the success of his television programs. They were praised for their humor and technical improvements in sound or color, as well as for their ability to entertain (Kercher 2015: 257).

The exile caused by the Spanish Civil War affected film culture, including criticism, where it started a time of renewal (Palomero 2013: 92). Consider Antonio Perucho, a Valencian writer exiled in 1939, who became a pioneer of film journalism. Early in his career, Perucho began to write about Hitchcock. In a review of *Somewhere in the Night* (dir. Joseph L. Mankiewicz, 1946), he said that it brought "to mind a masterpiece of that style—*39 escalones* (*The 39 Steps*, 1935)—the extraordinary film that Hitchcock directed in England many years ago" (*El Nacional*, April 2, 1947, p. 1). But for *Pacto siniestro* (*Strangers on a Train*, 1951), with a more critical eye, he claimed to observe "in Hitchcock two parallel processes, which develop in the opposite direction: as his technique becomes more refined and prodigiously superior, declines the quality of the topics chosen for his films" (*El Nacional*, January 6, 1952, p. 1).

And, regarding the lukewarm reception that *Mi secreto me condena* (*I Confess*, 1953) received, Perucho admitted that

> he knows how to create distressing situations that keep the spectator's soul in suspense. This characteristic is hardly noticeable in *I Confess* because he gives the key to the mystery at the beginning of the film instead of at the end … This time, then, the "suspense" fails entirely.
>
> (*El Nacional*, January 10, 1954, p. 15)

Para atrapar al ladrón (*To Catch a Thief*, 1955) also surprised him: "The obese British director, famous for his deft handling of 'suspense,' seems to be taking a new direction in his filmmaking. In this film, humor prevails over emotion ... Hitchcock is one of the great directors of our time" (*El Nacional*, January 15, 1956, p. 15).

The early 1960s saw a second key moment in the development of Mexican film criticism. A new generation of filmmakers, scholars, analysts, and film associations emerged. Inspired by André Bazin, they set out to renew Mexican cinema and film research. In 1961, they formed the Nuevo Cine Group: José de la Colina, Emilio García Riera, and Carlos Monsiváis, among others. Publications such as *Nuevo Cine* (1961–1962), the bulletin *Cine Club* (1955), and columns multiplied in *Revista de la Universidad*, inter alia.

This vibrant film culture was also fed by magazines geared towards more commercial offerings (Aranzubia 2011; Miquel 2016; Kercher 2015). Efforts to build audiences also extended to TV: a show with López Moctezuma on Channel 5 showing silent films at 11 p.m., another of film criticism hosted by García Riera on Channels 11 and 13, *Tiempo de cine* (Cuervo Cruz, interviewed February 3, 2024; Leonardo García Tsao, interviewed February 7, 2024). Emilio García Riera, who left Spain as a child with his family because of the Civil War, became a famous film critic, historian, and writer. He boosted research at Universidad Nacional Autónoma de México's Filmoteca, the Centro Universitario de Estudios Cinematográficos, and the Universidad de Guadalajara Centro de Investigaciones y Enseñanza Cinematográfica. He wrote the multivolume *Historia documental del cine mexicano*, first published in 1966 but added to over decades, considered the most complete work of its kind due to its exhaustive and comprehensive documentation.

Television had opened the doors of popularity, financial gain, and worldwide celebrity for Hitchcock. "This success and popularity, the American and European critics were going to make him pay for it by examining his work with condescension, denigrating one film after another" (Truffaut 1974: 9). Rowing against the current, French critics since the end of the 1950s recognized him as a seminal author and devoted several books to his films and a special issue of *Cahiers du Cinéma* that analyzed and praised his career. The renowned volume *Hitchcock/Truffaut* had great impact in Spanish-speaking countries. Once it was published in Spain by Alianza Editorial in 1974 (*El cine según Hitchcock*), articles about it multiplied in the press, magazines, and in various books and research projects (Miranda 2018).

Two other books marked Hitchcock's positive imprint in Mexico: *Hitchcock's Films*, by Robin Wood (translated by publishing house ERA in 1968) and *Alfred Hitchcock* by film director Guillermo del Toro— published in 1990 by the Universidad de Guadalajara in its collection "Grandes cineastas" and later republished by the Cineteca Nacional. Both are out of print and considered collectors' items (Miranda 2018).

Some film critics in Mexico in the 1950s and 1960s, in close contact with the discussions of the time, recognized Hitchcock for his filmmaking mastery, but other prominent analysts—particularly some members of the Nuevo Cine Group—viewed him with suspicion and reproached him for his quest for commercial success. This was the case of the critic and historian Emilio García Riera, who wrote the first review of *Hitchcock/Truffaut* in Mexico. He was fascinated: it is "the film book that most resembles a film because it allows us to penetrate the intimacy of cinema in a way that neither a treatise on film technique nor a film script can achieve." But he took a much more critical distance from the English director: "our appreciation of Hitchcock's films takes a back seat to indisputable evidence: Hitchcock is ... a man who guides our attention where he wants and makes us react as he wants, independently of the a posteriori judgment we make about his films" (García Riera 1967: xv).

The seven volumes of the magazine *Nuevo Cine* (1961–1962) applied the label of "new" cinema to various European and North American directors, the Japanese Kurosawa, and, of course, the Mexicanized

Spaniard, Luis Buñuel. The few references to Hitchcock are all judgmental in tone. In his article "El Western," Emilio García Riera pronounces himself "against cinema that places itself above or below the human being, whether based on a metaphysical conception of the world (Hitchcock, for example) or on a pseudo-liberal and pseudoprogressive petit-bourgeois piety such as that of neorealism" (García Riera 1962a). During the magazine's run, *Psycho* was the only Hitchcock film to be released. While *El Universal* considered it "the best film directed by the master of suspense" (Miranda 2018), García Riera tore it to shreds, distancing himself from *Cahiers du Cinéma*:

> With *Psycho*, Hitchcock has tried to make a film entirely in keeping with what the public expects of him. That is to say, a film of suspense and not the moralistic one discovered by the French critics, by the author of *The Wrong Man*, which seemed to have been commissioned by the *Cahiers du Cinéma* … In truth, *Psycho* is disappointing … The trick, the needs of suspense, leads the director to the renunciation of any attempt to study, cinematographically speaking, the character. But Hitchcock plays dirty, not because he has no choice, but because he does not know how to play otherwise. It is here, then, that in *Psycho* we discover a weak and impotent Hitchcock, prisoner of the sacrosanct necessities of the script … Let's face it: deep down, Hitchcock is of little interest to us. Even if he sometimes amuses us.
>
> (García Riera 1962b)

That skepticism was shared in part by Tomás Pérez Turrent, a researcher, writer, and film critic. In 1970, he wrote the column "Nuestra Gran Cartelera" in the *Sucesos para todos* magazine. Pérez Turrent recognized that Hitchcock

> is one of the few—if not the only one—capable of making people form queues at the incantation of his name. Along with this public success, he has also had great fortune with serious critics … who have found in his pure style, in the ease offered by appearances, the perfect terrain for the investigation of all possible depths.
>
> (Pérez Turrent 1970)

However, he distanced himself from the French critics:

> Acknowledging his great skill as a manipulator, we have never shared such enthusiasms. If anything, we are interested in some of his films from his very early British period … and a few others from his American period … The latter, *Marnie, la ladrona* (*Marnie*, 1964) and *Cortina rasgada* (*Torn Curtain*, 1966), have begun to make clear what the real Hitchcock is … The truth is that the overuse of a style has obliterated his earlier mastery … we found that appearances had no depth.
>
> (Pérez Turrent 1970)

That critical view was not shared by everyone in the New Cinema Group. José de la Colina, another émigré from the Spanish Civil War, wrote a review of the book *Hitchcock/Truffaut* in *Excélsior*, where he stated that "What is interesting is to see how the need for constant finetuning … led the director to produce more complex works than simple gimmicky instruments, and sometimes to achieve 'something more': psychological and dramatic depth, and poetic vision … an imposing filmography in numbers and in masterpieces" (*Excélsior*, July 22, 1975).

The Consolidation of a Reputation: Film Societies and the Cineteca Nacional

Hitchcock was accessible to very different audiences because of his work's wide circulation through multiple cinema circuits and channels. Thanks to a reader of *Nuevo Cine*, we confirm that at the Teatro del Pueblo, a film association in a working-class area, *Strangers on a Train*, *Under Capricorn*, and *The Trouble with Harry* were shown for 1 peso, as was the case at the IFAL film society (Guerrero 1961). The movie buff referred to the Cine Club de México, linked to the French Institute of Latin America (IFAL), which emerged in 1948, supported by the French government, and was crucial to the founding of *Nuevo Cine* in 1961 (Lafranchi et al. 1999: 205–215; De la Vega 1999: 571–582).

Although with a long history, film associations of the 1960s and 1970s, which grew under the umbrella of trade unions, public-sector organizations, political parties, embassies, and universities, were part of this renewed world cinema scene in Mexico. New magazines and cultural supplements in newspapers offered specialized film criticism, information on foreign aesthetic innovations and auteur cinema, and promoted independent productions and film associations and art cinemas. The Universidad Nacional Autónoma de México also experienced a real boom in the creation of film clubs during these years (González Casanova 1961). In addition to the programming of these spaces, there were also art cinemas run by associations or the private sector, such as the Regis, Electra or Bella época, which were very popular for film revivals. All of these spaces screened Hitchcock movies.

In the mid 1970s, the Cineteca Nacional, a national film archive, library and cinematheque, was launched. With a program focused on directors, film trends, country of origin, and genres, it steadily increased its screenings, capacity, and audiences (*Memorias de la Cineteca Nacional*, 1974–2007). Early on, the Cineteca spread Hitchcock's work. In 1978, it hosted the Retrospectiva Alfred Hitchcock film season. In 1980, after Hitchcock's death, a posthumous season was held at the Bella Época cinema. Six years later, another was presented at the Centro Cultural Universitario at the UNAM (Miranda 2018). In subsequent years, the Cineteca Nacional offered three more: in 1990, Una década sin Hitchcock (A Decade without Hitchcock), along with the publication of a booklet with photographs and memorable phrases by the director, and in 2013, El primer Hitchcock (The First Hitchcock). In 2018, accompanying the Hitchcock: más allá del suspenso (Hitchcock: Beyond Suspense) exhibition, sponsored by the Fundación Telefónica, the Cineteca screened thirty-five films, hosted conferences, and launched publications (one was a collection of essays about Hitchcock's work and another a reprint of del Toro's book). The work of the Cineteca Nacional in the dissemination of Hitchcock's work has been extensive and varied. It has also included seminars given by critics and film directors.

Afterword

Hitchcock's most severe critic radically changed his mind some time later. Almost forty years after his review of *Psycho*, Emilio García Riera recalled in an interview his favorite directors, whose films really interested him: "Of course Luis Buñuel, who was a Mexican filmmaker although he was born in Spain; John Ford, and Alfred Hitchcock" (*El Informador*, March 14, 1999, p. 2F).

While it is true that García Riera never failed to recognize Hitchcock's cinematographic skills, it seems that his critical opinions had to do with content, something Perucho shared. Something similar happened to Tomás Pérez Turrent. A quarter of century after he accused Hitchcock of being "shallow" in the column "Nuestra Gran Cartelera," he refers to him as the "master of modern universal cinema and particularly of American cinema" (Pérez Turrent 1970 and 1995).

These previous critical views—far from the French film critics' perspectives—had been something particular to the Mexican film critics' reception, in contrast to the wide acceptance that the French revaluation of Hitchcock's work was worldwide. What Leonardo Garcia Tsao said about García Riera applies to a certain extent to the three of them: "Emilio … was always looking for films to manifest leftwing ideas, something he obviously wasn't going to find in Hitchcock … When he got older, he was already a great admirer of him" (Leonardo Garcia Tsao, interview, February 7 2024). Perucho and García Riera—from different generations—had exiled from the Spanish Civil War. Pérez Turrent was Mexican and, along with García Riera, was part of the New Cinema Group, which sympathized with legitimate causes (the 1968 movement, independent trade unionism, etc.). None of them were militant in any political party, and, with the exception of Carlos Monsiváis, they did not express themselves much politically, but they could be considered left-wing. This could lead them to decry Hitchcock's "commercialism" in his early years as critics. It is also possible that all the admiration of different audiences, and the work of public and private institutions, forced them later to recognize Hitchcock as a great director-author, hence finally achieving what *Cahiers du Cinéma* and its critics tried to do more than half a century earlier.

Acknowledgments

I am grateful for Yucli Cervantes and Angélica Del Toro's research assistance and Julia Tuñón's advice and access to her library. Dona Kercher made suggestive comments to a first version of this text, and Liliana Valenzuela proofread the style.

Interviews

Cuervo Cruz, seller of bootleg art movies (February 3, 2024). Born in 1951 in México.
Leonardo Garcia Tsao, film critic and former director of Cineteca Nacional de México's Programación (February 7, 2024). Born in 1954 in Mexico.
Nelson Carro Rodríguez, Director of Cineteca Nacional de México's Difusión y Programación (January 23, 2024). Born in 1952 in Uruguay.
Raúl Miranda, Vice principal of Cineteca Nacional de México's Centro de Documentación (December 10, 2023). Born in 1959 in Mexico.

Notes

1   So far, the longest running feature film in Mexico City is the musical *The Sound of Music*, starring Julie Andrews, which ran for sixty-five weeks. https://www.eluniversal.com.mx/articulo/espectaculos/cine/2016/08/1/100-anos-de-cartelera-mexicana/.

2   In her analysis of Mexican film criticism of Argentine films from the 1930s to the 1950s, Julia Tuñón finds that while they value the role of the director, they give a lot of attention to the actors and actresses (Tuñón 2017: 357).

3   On p. 9 of *El Nacional*, on May 10, 1955, it was mentioned that *Rear Window* had been the highest grossing film of the past weekend.

4 Digital remastering (2000) Cinema International Corporation publicity sheet, UnoMásUno, Espectáculos section, September 8, 2000.
5 In a newspaper article announcing that Marlene Dietrich would star in a Hitchcock film, Hitchcock is referred to as "the magician of uncertainty" (*El Nacional*, April 17, 1949). In Mexico, it was in 1954—during the promotion of *Dial M for Murder*—that Hitchcock was first advertised as "the magician of suspense" (*El Universal*, November 10 and 11, 1954, first section, pp. 24 and 29).

References

Aranzubia, A. (2011) "Nuevo Cine (1961–1962) y el nacimiento de la cultura cinematográfica mexicana moderna," *Dimensión Antropológica*, 52 (May–August): 101–121.
Bordwell, D., J. Staiger, and K. Thompson (1997) *El cine clásico de Hollywood: Estilo cinematográfico y modo de producción hasta 1960*, Barcelona: Paidós.
Cineteca Nacional (1979) *Memorias de la Cineteca Nacional 1978*, Mexico City: Cineteca Nacional.
De la Colina, J. (1975) "Quinientos golpes al maestro con cariño," *Excélsior*, July 22.
De la Vega Alfaro, E. (1999) "El cine club del IFAL: un testimonio de Emilio García Riera," Congreso de Cine Clubes, Mexico City: Universidad Nacional Autónoma de Mexico, pp. 571–582.
Del Toro, G. (1990) *Alfred Hitchcock*, Guadalajara: Universidad de Guadalajara.
García Riera, E. (1962a) "El western," *Nuevo Cine*, 7 (August): 12.
García Riera, E. (1962b) "*Psicosis*," *Nuevo Cine*, 7 (August): 27–28.
García Riera, E. (1967) "Hitchcock por Truffaut, el más apasionado documento sobre cine," *La Cultura en México, Revista Siempre!* October 11, p. X.
González Casanova, M. (1961) *¿Qué es un cineclub?* Mexico City: Universidad Nacional Autonóma de México.
Kercher, D. (2015) "Latin American Openings of Hitchcock's Films: The Reception History from Mexico City," *Latin Hitchcock: How Almodóvar, Amenábar, De la Iglesia, Del Toro, and Campanella Became Notorious*, London and New York: Wallflower Press Book and Columbia University Press, pp. 235–265.
Lafranchi, H. (1999) "Primer auge de los cineclubes en México," Congreso de Cine Clubes, Mexico City: Universidad Nacional Autónoma de México, pp. 205–215.
Miller, T. (2001) *Global Hollywood*, London: British Film Institute.
Miquel, A. (2016) "Orígenes y consolidación del periodismo cinematográfico en México," *Miradas al cine mexicano*, vol. I, Mexico City: Instituto Mexicano de Cinematografía, pp. 161–174.
Miranda, R. (2018) "Cómo nos volvimos hitchcockianos en México," RevistaIconica.com, December 4.
Monsiváis, C. (1990) "El matrimonio de la butaca y la pantalla," *Artes de México*, 10: 36–39.
Morín, E. (2005) *The Stars*, Minneapolis, Minn.: University of Minnesota Press.
Palomero, J. (2013) "Vida y obra de Arturo Perucho," *Laberintos: revista de estudios sobre los exilios culturales españoles*, Valencia, pp. 71–100.
Peredo Castro, F. (2012) "Las Intervenciones gubernamentales como estrategia de crecimiento y supervivencia durante la segunda guerra mundial y la posguerra (1940–1952)," in *El estado y la imagen en movimiento: Reflexiones sobre las políticas públicas y el cine mexicano*, Mexico City: Instituto Mexicano de Cinematografía, pp. 75–107.
Pérez Turrent, T. (1970) "Nuestra gran cartelera," *Sucesos para todos*, November 21, pp. 28–30.
Pérez Turrent, T. (1992) "Cinecrítica," *El Informador*, June 25, p. 13-E.
Rosas Mantecón, A. (2017) *Ir al cine: Antropología de los públicos, la ciudad y las pantallas*, México: Gedisa and Universidad Autónoma Metropolitana Iztapalapa.
Truffaut, F. (1974) *El cine según Hitchcock*, Madrid: Alianza.
Tuñón, J. (2017) "La crítica como espejo: el cine argentino en la mira de la prensa mexicana (años treinta a cincuenta)," *Pantallas transnacionales: El cine argentino y mexicano del periodo clásico*, Buenos Aires: Cineteca Nacional de México and Imago Mundi, pp. 339–363.
Wood, R. (1968) *El cine de Hitchcock*, México: Era.

Chapter 36

Hitchcock in Argentina

Some Preliminary Findings

Dona M. Kercher

From the few accessible sources, the obsessions, compulsions, and technical prowess that shaped the extraordinary movies of Alfred Hitchcock were recognized and celebrated in Argentina. Beginning with his silent films, they were noteworthy if not always acclaimed. Given how vital and prescient they are today about desire, violence, greed, and the corporeal, as when they first graced Argentine screens, they continue to impact Argentine filmmaking. This essay traces first the history and reception of Hitchcock's films and then their contemporary cinematic impact. Among the various options, we concentrate on two recent films that highlight taxidermy: *The Aura* (2005) and *Rojo* (2018). Although *Psycho* is their obvious source, the filmmakers reposition the imagery to stress the hidden violence in the art of taxidermy, exploring the dead/alive bodily intermingling and the ensuing questions of greed and justice. In so doing they anticipate and validate Subarna Mondal's recent *Alfred Hitchcock's "Psycho" and Taxidermy: Fashioning Corpses* of this practice as metaphor that recurs and structures many of Hitchcock's major films.

Hitchcock in Buenos Aires: History and Reception

As Ross Melnick observes in *Hollywood's Embassies*, "Argentina was the preeminent market in silent-era Latin America" (Melnick 2023: 149). By deciphering the press of the 1920s, we can note a strong and early presence of Hitchcock's films, although he is seldom mentioned by name. The Argentine cinema journal *Excélsior: Correo cinematográfico sudamericano* (*Excélsior: South American Cinematographic News*, December 29, 1927) lists among the openings for the month of January 1928 a Piccadilly Pictures drama in ten acts, entitled *Los Misterios de Londres* (*Mysteries of London*) starring Ivor Novello, Marie Ault, Charles Chesmey, Malcolm Keen, and June Elvidge.

A subsequent issue for January 19, 1928, under the heading of "Corporación A. A. de Cine," that is, Anglo-American Films, gives the date as Saturday, January 21, whereas on the main page of January listings for the December 29, 1927 issue, the date is January 22. Since January 22 is mentioned in the movie magazine *La Película*, which we will discuss shortly too, it can be assumed to be the correct date of the opening.

The name of Ivor Novello among the cast is enough to reveal that this is indeed Hitchcock's early silent film *The Lodger*. Neither Hitchcock's name, nor that of any other director, accompanies any of the announcements. The movie theater is not specified either.

The issue of *Excélsior* that includes the information on *The Mysteries of London* features a drawing of Betty Compson and Theodore Kosloff in *La Bailarina y el Impostor* on its cover, most likely the film *New Lives for Old*, a Famous Players-Lasky Corporation Production directed by Clarence G. Badger in which these two actors costarred. *Excélsior* notes it was distributed by Paramount in Argentina in 1927. Paramount was the usual distributor of Famous Players-Lasky. From this evidence we can be certain that *The Lodger* was released in Buenos Aires in 1928.[1] Moreover, the movie was received well there.

A review succinctly titled "The Premiere of The Mysteries of London Receives the Good Reception It Deserves" in *Excélsior* (January 26, 1928, p. 8) praises the film as a potent drama with emotive acting by Novello:

> It is based on that murderous ghost that brought death to the neighborhoods of London and that recently reappeared in a German city. This is how "The Mysteries of London" begins, a powerful drama, with a strong story and flawless acting. Ivor Novello is the protagonist and he performs with true emotional fiber. Marie Ault, Arthur Chesney, Malcon Ken, June Elvidge form the supporting cast.[2]

A subsequent column in *Excélsior*, February 2, 1928, comments that the film's run continued successfully. Another journal, *La Película*, also announced the opening and discussed the film's plot in detail, underscoring the victims as blondes, which would become Hitchcock's trademark:

> It is a mysterious plot with a police case cleverly woven together and whose emotional content continually builds. It is based on that murderous ghost that brought death to the neighborhoods of London and that recently repeated the same in a German city. He dedicated himself, as is known, to injuring, killing or making women faint, especially blondes.
>
> (*La Película*, January 19, 1928)

Another positive review, entitled "'The Mysteries of London' is a film filled with emotion" followed in *La Película* (January 26, 1928, p. 9).

The earliest image I could find of Hitchcock as a director was in a supplement published by the Anglo-American Corporation, distributing British International Pictures, at the end of 1928, entitled "Some of the Directors and Scriptwriters of this Great Brand." The supplement, appended to various film magazines of that year, features a prominent portrait of Hitchcock in the upper-left corner. In this same issue, another Argentine distributor, Terra, announced two of Hitchcock's other silent movies, *The Ring* (1927) and *Champagne* (1928), among their coming attractions for 1928.

Hitchcock's Movies (1935–1984) as Reviewed in the *Cinematic Herald*

Heraldo del cinematográfico (*Cinematic Herald*, 1931–1988) is an excellent source through which to trace the initial reception of Hitchcock's films in Argentina. Movie theater managers throughout Argentina consulted this widely available publication for programming. The general public could refer to it for reviews as well. Besides the dates and theater location for the Buenos Aires premiere, each entry included an assessment of the film, according to three categories: commercial potential, artistic value, and plot or narrative coherency. These were given a numerical rating on a five-point scale at the top of the entry. Also, two brief adjectives noted the film's genre and its general "category" or quality, which ranged from "average" for *The Secret Agent* (August 5, 1936) to "special" or "extraordinary" for virtually all of Hitchcock's movies after that. An age rating was first included for *Rope* (October 9, 1951), "prohibited to those under 18," and appeared regularly thereafter.

The numbers ratings show a few idiosyncrasies. *Strangers on a Train* rated a low 2½ for its plot, even though it was one of Hitchcock's most inventive. The review doesn't explain why, although it does classify the film as a "melodrama." *The Birds* is also found to be subpar for its plot, rated 3½: "The movie's weakness is its plot that lacks interest overall, and scarcely manages to link the situations with the birds. What is especially strange for the king of suspense is that the film lacks an effective ending" (*Cinematic Herald*, §145-163). Only *Notorious* (*Cinematic Herald*, February 5, 1947) received the full endorsement of three 5s. From today's viewpoint, it seems a little harsh to mark *Vertigo* down to a 4 for artistic value, saying, "as usually happens in movies where supernatural elements appear to come into play, a certain disillusionment ensues, but that doesn't invalidate the fact that the entire film is greatly entertaining" (*Cinematic Herald*, §43-59), especially seeing that *Torn Curtain* later scored higher: 5 and 4½. Of all the films, *To Catch a Thief* received the most enthusiastic review in terms of commercial potential: "it should be a smash hit" (*Cinematic Herald*, April 12, 1956). The review begins, "Seldom does a film open under more auspicious circumstances. Besides the novelty that the presentation of the new VistaVision system means for the audience of the capital, there is the sensational and extraordinary circulation of Grace Kelly's name due to her upcoming marriage to the Prince of Monaco" (§77-56).

Two-thirds of Hitchcock's films opened in Buenos Aires within a year of their US premieres. *The Paradine Case* was the film with the longest delay (opening on January 12, 1955, almost eight years later). The reason may well have been the film's reediting as the version that opened in Buenos Aires was twenty-six minutes shorter than the original. Other films with openings delayed more than a year were *Jamaica Inn*, *The Lady Vanishes*, *Suspicion*, *Rope*, *Under Capricorn*, *Strangers on a Train*, *I Confess*, *Rear Window*, *Dial M for Murder*, and *The Trouble with Harry*. *Rear Window*'s surprising delay may have been due to the shift to color film and the need for different equipment.

All of the films were shown in Buenos Aires in English with Spanish subtitles. Regarding *Suspicion* (January 20, 1942), the quality of the translation was praised. Perhaps because he was already well known from the silent era, Hitchcock was not identified as a British director in any entry. A playbill for *The 39 Steps*, on the other hand, features Hitchcock's name alongside a blurb praising British directors (see Fig. 36.1).

Nor was Hitchcock's move to Hollywood mentioned, although the US box-office reception was frequently noted, especially regarding *Rebecca* (June 28, 1940):

The dialogue contains the suggestiveness that envelops the film overall, and even if its artistic quality doesn't reach the exceptional level. The plot creates so much interest, despite its incursions in melodrama, that it ensures its unquestionable commercial value justifiying the extraordinary success it has achieved in the USA, where it stayed for six weeks on the Radio City Music Hall bill in New York.

For the thirty-seven films for which I have found entries, from *The Man Who Knew Too Much* (1935) to *Family Plot* (1977), a few trends stand out. First, Hitchcock was recognized as an auteur early on. His

Figure 36.1 1936 Buenos Aires playbill, lower right: "39 Steps shows that the British continue to be the masters of the crime genre."

Advertisement for *The 39 Steps*, directed by Alfred Hitchcock. © Gaumont-British Picture Corporation 1935. All rights reserved.

name as director was included in the program publicity, a short blurb at the end of every entry, from the first film recorded, and continued for all the others. His technical assurance and aesthetic innovations were consistently commented on, as well as the excellence of the music in many films. The first mention of the "master of suspense" is for *Saboteur* (1942).

Secondly, humor is a criterion of judgment, consistently noted and commented on and not always positively. *The Man Who Knew Too Much* received the most negative critique: "The comic situations fail due to excessively local British humor and less than interesting acting" (§1035-35). On the other hand, *The 39 Steps*, the next film reviewed, is praised for its situational humor: "A film of a dramatic nature, it is nuanced, however, with abundant humorous situations. Even the more serious parts dissolve into amusing scenes" (§1152-35). Likewise, *Lifeboat* is praised for its humor: "In spite of its dramatics, humorous touches abound" (§75-46). *Rope*, however, is deemed weak because "there is no romance and touches of humor are scarce."

Thirdly, major literary or artistic antecedents are noted in the entries: John Steinbeck for *Lifeboat*, Salvador Dalí for *Spellbound*, Joseph Conrad for *Sabotage*, and Daphne du Maurier for *The Birds*. This reflects a wider cultural bias. Characteristically prioritizing high culture, Jorge Luis Borges, who wrote film criticism for the journal *Sur*, critiqued Hitchcock by negatively comparing his work to Conrad's *Heart of Darkness*.

Fourthly, psychoanalysis and psychological profiling are prominently mentioned. The entry for *Spellbound* begins, "The specialist in 'suspense' films delves into psychoanalysis and does it seriously. He manages to do so in unexpected ways by skillfully calibrating the element of surprise through repeated abrupt cuts during moments of greatest intensity and by masterfully using sound to produce effective shocks" (§75-46). Interestingly, *Rope* is judged deficient because it does not psychoanalyze: "Nor does the film go into any depth in the psychological description of the protagonists, consequently resulting in a long and cold story, although it can be partially defended as entertainment because of the unusual 'case' it deals with. 'Touches' of Hitchcockian suspense appear in isolation" (§252-51). These four characteristics will mark the films of his followers in Argentina.

Contemporary Auteurs, Hitchcockian Adaptations: *Psycho*'s Taxidermy Motif in Two Thrillers

Hitchcock's sway on contemporary Argentine filmmakers is pervasive and merits an extensive study. They include both women—Lucía Puenzo (*XXY* [2007] and *Electrophilia* [2023]), Lucrecia Martel (*The Headless Woman* [2008] and *Zama* [2017])—as well as men—J. J. Campanella (*Secret in Their Eyes* [2015]), Santiago Mitre (*The Summit* [2017] and *15 Ways to Kill Your Neighbor* [2022]). We will now turn to two highly successful thrillers, *The Aura* (2005) and *Rojo* (2018), by Fabián Bielinsky and Benjamín Naishtat respectively. Both films foreground the motif of taxidermy, fundamentally linked to *Psycho*, as well as other aspects of Hitchcock's aesthetics and narrative structure (see Fig. 36.2).

Bielinsky built his career, cut short by an early death, by wisely studying the master. His only two films, *Nine Queens* (2000) and *The Aura*, both heist movies, are profoundly Hitchcockian in plot and aesthetics. Both star Ricardo Darín. *The Aura* tells the story of Esteban Espósito, a taxidermist who suffers from epilepsy. His attacks are preceded by an aura, described as a moment in which all the senses are intense and when past and present coincide. The aura sequences are filmed with the camera rotating around the protagonist before he falls to the ground. This technique recalls how camera movements depict the psychological distress of Manny Balestrero (Henry Fonda) in a prison cell in *The Wrong Man*, after he has

Figure 36.2 Dining with Marion: Norman (Anthony Hopkins) is defiantly placed among his taxidermy birds in *Psycho*.

been arrested for being mistaken for a robber. Like "the wrong man" Manny, Esteban is blameless for these episodes, which occur at moments of great stress but have major consequences.

Esteban's art of taxidermy, his profession, bookends the film. In the credit sequence, he mounts a fox, and in the final sequence, a reptile (see Fig. 36.3).

Although he carefully attends to the details of the carcasses, Esteban assiduously and ethically avoids hunting until, distraught from the discovery that his wife has left him, he accepts an invitation to a hunting trip from a fellow taxidermist. In the deep woods, Esteban mistakes Dietrich, the owner of the hunting camp, for a buck he has been tracking, shoots from a distance and kills the man but is able to hide the deed. Through observation and clever lies, Esteban then takes over the plot that Dietrich was masterminding, the heist of an armored car containing the take from a casino.

In terms of narrative, Bielinsky's movie, like his previous heist film, is a self-contained system, which is a characteristic of many Hitchcockian plots. To recall *Shadow of a Doubt*, Young Charlie does not reveal to the town that her Uncle Charlie was a serial killer. We as spectators know the truth, which we judge justifiable within the circumstances of the movie, but external authorities never find out. Likewise with Esteban. He returns to his taxidermy without any living being, except Dietrich's dog, knowing that he has killed someone and assumed their identity. When he absconds with the casino cash, he enacts his profession's intermingling of dead and alive bodies. Through taxidermy, he achieves the wholeness and stability that the aura jeopardizes. Moreover, justice is carried out, for he saves Dietrich's wife from an abusive husband.

Like Bielinsky, Benjamín Naishtat developed a thriller vocabulary in his early films, especially *The History of Fear* (2014), which leaned heavily on the visual (Hitchcockian "pure cinema") and sound design. Reminiscent of Lucrecia Martel's satire of the bourgeoisie, *The Swamp* (2001), Naishtat's movie, set in a

Figure 36.3 Esteban in his workshop preparing a fox for a museum diorama in *The Aura*, directed by Fabián Bielinsky.

© Aura Films 2005. All rights reserved.

steamy summer locale, follows the daily activities of a few country-club families and those who work for them in a series of vignettes. Noises create suspense but are then revealed to be mundane occurrences.

His subsequent endeavor, *Rojo*, is set in 1975–1976, in the early years of the Dirty War when clandestine actions to reassert order and "disappear" dissidents began. The imminent coup of General Videla of March 24, 1976, that overthrew President Isabel Perón, looms over the whole film and is announced at a dance recital in the film's final scene. The color red of the film's title repeats throughout the film as a warning, in instances as varied as the taillights of a car at night, bloodstains from assault, references to menstruation, and the red sky of an eclipse. Likewise, within the film's code, taxidermy represents a hidden, yet visible, violence.

The movie opens with multiple people, none dressed as movers, removing furniture and a television out the front door of an expensive house. It is gradually revealed that the house's owners fled, or more likely were taken away due to their political beliefs. In the meantime, apparently innocent encounters hide or escalate into violence, beginning with an altercation between our protagonist, a well-respected lawyer Dr. Claudio Morán, and a fellow diner at a restaurant who complains to the waiter that Claudio should not be able to occupy a table if he is not eating. Though Claudio cedes his place to the man, he taunts the diner and calls him "uneducated," a devastating insult. The confrontation escalates. Outside on the street, the enraged man pulls a gun, but rather than attacking Claudio he pummels his own face and shoots himself in the head. Claudio loads the madman's still-breathing body into the back seat of his car. Instead of taking the injured to a hospital, Claudio leaves him in the desert to die.

Subsequently, Claudio is drawn into his friend Vivas's scheme to illegally take possession of the abandoned house seen in the film's opening. For his services, he will earn a substantial fee. When Claudio tours the house, he notes bloodstains on the staircase wall. Undeterred, he finds a trustworthy but unconnected third person to attest that Vivas is the house's owner.

The turning point comes in the next scene at a gallery event. Vivas's wife Mabel has a breakdown, shouts, and overturns a waiter's tray. While she is being calmed down, Claudio and Vivas retreat to an adjoining room with multiple plinths covered with sheets. As they talk, Claudio lifts the sheets one by one to reveal taxidermy specimens. The first is a raven, the Hitchcockian archetype of his only true horror film, *The Birds* (see Fig. 36.4).

As specimens are revealed, including a snarling bobcat, Claudio's identity is threatened. Vivas informs Claudio that Mabel is upset because her brother Diego, who has been involved in revolutionary actions, has gone underground, that is, he has or has been disappeared. On seeing Vivas's snapshot of the brother, Claudio recognizes the man he left for dead. Furthermore, Vivas has hired the famous Chilean detective Sinclair to solve the mystery. Ominously, Sinclair appears in the room in a predatory position over Claudio's shoulder. By manipulating Claudio to take him on a "tourist" visit to the desert, Sinclair manages to get Claudio to confess to his role in Diego's death. Yet, surprisingly, after triggering this confession, Sinclair tells Claudio he will return to Buenos Aires without taking any further action. Despite multiple references by Sinclair to God's laws, the circuit of evil deeds is kept secret, as were many actions at that time. Diego is just one more disappeared. Having solved the crime, the Chilean detective is now complicit in the cover-up. It is not too farfetched to see Sinclair as an archetype of multiple right-wing Chileans who collaborated closely with the Argentine military in Operation Condor.

Both *The Aura* and *Rojo* repurpose the taxidermy motif through their closed thriller narratives to subtly interpret economic and political issues of Argentina. They enhance a sense of secrecy, which informed experiences of the Argentine public. Both films define the world in terms of victim and predator, hunted and hunter, in which the hunter always wins. *Rojo* gives this dynamic an ominous political overlay.

Figure 36.4 Claudio (Dario Grandinetti) uncovers a taxidermy raven while talking to Vivas (Claudio Martínez Bel) in *Rojo*, directed by Benjamín Naishtat.
© Pucará Cine 2018. All rights reserved.

Claudio, a right-wing collaborator, is not on the side of justice like Esteban. He uncovers and then again covers up the taxidermy he peruses just as many deaths were purposely left unsolved in those decades. These gestures to Hitchcock's legacy contributed to box-office success. As we have seen, Hitchcockian aesthetics and narrative structure effectively serve to underpin significant Argentinean cinematic undertakings.

Acknowledgments

I want to thank Adrián Muoyo, head librarian, and Lucio Mafud, assistant, at INCAA ENERC, the library of the Argentine national film school, for their exceptional guidance during my research there in 2017.

Notes

1. *The Lodger*'s US release date, according to Jane E. Sloan, in *Alfred Hitchcock: A Definitive Filmography*, was September 1926. Sloan does not list *The Mysteries of London* as an alternate title.
2. All translations are mine.

References

Melnick, R. (2022) *Hollywood's Embassies: How Movie Theaters Projected American Power around the World*, New York: Columbia University Press.
Mondal, S. (2024) *Alfred Hitchcock's "Psycho" and Taxidermy: Fashioning Corpses*, New York: Bloomsbury.

Coda A

A "Signature Pattern"

The Importance of Music in Hitchcock's Films

Jack Sullivan

Music is essential to Hitchcock and has boosted the reception of all his films, especially *Blackmail* and the following other case studies. As Terry Teachout pointed out in a *Commentary* piece from 2007, critics' reception of Hitchcock's films is closely linked to commentary on the music, especially the Herrmann scores, because the music endows the films "with an emotional depth they would not otherwise possess" (Teachout 2007). For Teachout and others, this achievement is singular:

> There was only one director who employed music with such unfailing sensitivity that the quality of the scores accompanying his films became one of his trademarks ... Though Hitchcock was notorious for his reluctance to share credit, he himself admitted that Herrmann's music was central to the appeal of these remarkable films.
>
> (Teachout 2007)

Teachout points out that because of this essential linkage, the films with the highest reputation are the ones with the greatest scores, but music boosted the status of lesser movies as well: Franz Waxman's score for *Rebecca* was so highly regarded that it was turned into a concert suite to boost the movie's reception—a novel practice for the 1940s that changed the way music was used to market films; the grandiose cantata so important to the plot of *The Man Who Knew Too Much* was central to that movie's reputation in both versions. The most dramatic example is *Vertigo*, the acclaimed score of which gave the film status even when the movie vanished for decades. Since 1958, numerous *New York Times* critics have pointed out the critical role of Herrmann's music in its reception, most notably Alex Ross, who twice in the 1990s cited the music as the cinema's greatest score and used it as a reason to celebrate the film yet again: "It is the music as much as the lighting and the filters that gives those scenes their eerie shimmer ... *Vertigo* is a symphony for film and orchestra" (*New York Times* 1996).

Blackmail

From its release in 1929, *Blackmail*, which Hitchcock called his "silent talkie," has captivated critics, from the initial reviewers in *The Times* and *Bioscope* to recent critics such as Tom Ryall, Elisabeth Weis, and Tania Modleski. Its stock has always been high and continues to soar. *Blackmail* arouses a special enthusiasm among those who fixate on the film's revolutionary use of music and sound. In *Blackmail*, music becomes not only a mood-setter but an interior narrator, inaugurating what John Williams (in an interview with me) called a "signature pattern." Just as Hitchcock learned the art of visuals from German expressionists in the 1920s, he picked up musical traits from the same aesthetic: looming shadows, tilted angles, sinister staircases, high-contrast lighting, and anxious close-ups are paralleled by discordant harmonies, astringent orchestration, anxious silences, sudden dynamic contrasts, obsessive chord repetitions, and ghostly *pizzicato*. Expressionist modernism is powerfully present in chromatic ascending scales that take us up a nightmarish Hitchcockian staircase; in a tremulous high pedal as the landlady who discovers the body frantically calls the police; in the quivering organ that slinks with the heroine into her bed after the crime; in the repetitions of the main title theme during the "Wanted" poster montage and the chase up the dome of the British Museum. This soundscape, created before Max Steiner's groundbreaking score for *King Kong* and before the establishment of movie-music clichés, became a template for Hitchcock's musical experiments through the next five decades. Scholars have consistently marveled at how many characteristic touches—the witty cameo, the "Hitchcock blonde," the transfer of guilt, the wrong-man theme, the young female point of view, the conflict between love and duty, the climactic chase on a public monument—indeed, the whole Hitchcockian world of sex and suspense—were already present in *Blackmail*. The same wonder holds for music. Aside from explicitly expressionist elements, *Blackmail* unveils an array of Hitchcockian signatures, including musical irony, vertiginous arpeggios, fateful chimes, popular song as a narrative device, and a dreamlike merging of "real" music with the "invisible" score. The opening combination of imagery and music, a hubcap spinning with tense discords, establishes a design Hitchcock would use in the police van wheels in *The Wrong Man* and the spirals and arpeggios of *Vertigo*. Already, in his first talkie sequence, dialogue and music counterpoint what we see on the screen rather than imitating it. The most provocative example is Cyril Ritchard singing "Miss Up to Date" on the piano to a young woman he is about to assault. The heroine defends herself with a knife as music turns into silence—another technique Hitchcock would continue to use—then comes back as an orchestral variation during the unforgettable image of the traumatized heroine staggering in slow motion with the knife. Equally acclaimed is the "knife montage" breakfast scene, where a sound becomes a kind of psychological "music." This early experiment in sound was an avant-garde musical concept that anticipated by two years the symphony of noises in Mamoulian's *Love Me Tonight*, not to mention the scoreless "music" for the train scenes in *The Lady Vanishes*, the factory sequence in *The Secret Agent*, and the entirety of *The Birds*.

In an early piece of Hitchcockian musical symmetry, the dizzying arpeggios that spin the movie into motion during the chase-arrest scene also wind it down. The vicious circle in Hitchcock, a Poe-like musical design depicting a mental maelstrom, would continue to spiral into the collapsing waltz in *Young and Innocent*, the "Merry Widow" dancers in *Shadow of a Doubt*, the repeating theremin in *Spellbound*, the convoluted "love" theme in *Strangers on a Train*, and the lost highway in *Psycho*. The human psyche spinning its wheels was set in motion by Hitchcock's music in 1929.

The Man Who Knew Too Much

The Man Who Knew Too Much, Hitchcock's first symphonic thriller, presents a daring musical conceit: a grandiose cantata cuing an assassination during a concert in which a member of the audience must decide between saving her kidnapped daughter and preventing the murder. The new cantata provides spectacular concert music—surely the most ambitious in any film prior to 1934—linked with Hitchcock's most sustained suspense montage.

Much has been made of Hitchcock's statement that the first *Man Who Knew Too Much* was the work of an amateur, the second that of a professional. But the context is important: he made the remark to Truffaut after the latter belittled the original and praised the remake for having more drama and irony. The critics also demurred, but only for a short while; by the 1970s, they had inverted Truffaut's verdict, finding the first version brilliant and quirky, the second overstuffed and glitzy (a microcosm of opinion regarding British versus American Hitchcock among those who prefer the former).

As a result of the surging popularity of Bernard Herrmann and a melting of the prejudice against the remake, in the late twentieth century opinions shifted regarding the relative merits of the two films. The sequel wasn't as slick and superficial as critics had thought, said revisionists, who began discovering all sorts of subtleties in the remake, especially the music. Actually, both versions offer unique pleasures: the first is scruffier and more energetic, the second sleeker, yet more compassionate. The two have radically different métiers, atmospheres, settings, characters, and musical values. The more complicated remake involves symphonic music versus pop, music as an instrument of violence versus healing; the original is a showcase for musical irony and the power of source music. Both explore a key Hitchcock theme: public versus private duty—an idea that reverberates through *Saboteur*, *Notorious*, *North by Northwest*, and other films. In both versions, the *Storm Clouds Cantata* provides the vehicle for the heroine's moment of decision.

The grainy black-and-white version lacks the glamour of Technicolor and the elaborate ballet movements of the 1955 improvement, where the camera cuts rhythmically back and forth between the heroine moving through the hall, her husband dashing from box to box, and the maestro sweeping his arms in broad gestures, as if he is directing a much bigger show than the one on stage. Still, this is far from the work of a "talented amateur." As John Russell Taylor points out, it is one of Hitchcock's great storyboards: "Considering that the film was made on a very restricted budget, it looks surprisingly elaborate, especially in the Albert Hall sequence … Here, Hitch's detailed preplanning helped enormously. He decided in advance exactly how he was going to shoot the sequence, from eight distinct viewpoints" (Sullivan 2006: 36).

Rebecca

Franz Waxman's score for *Rebecca* is a landmark in the history of film music, a lavish yet deeply interior work that changed the way movies were marketed and received, anticipating Bernard Herrmann's more celebrated music for Hitchcock films in its ability to act as an inner narrator.

Waxman faced a daunting challenge, as he revealed in a 1940 speech to the Hollywood Women's Club Federation: "The really dominant character in the story is dead … yet the entire drama revolves around her … Whenever a scene involving Rebecca appeared on the screen, it was up to the music to give Rebecca's character life and presence" (Sullivan 2006: 76). The idea of film music as a "presence" capable of revealing the character of someone living or dead became a Hitchcock signature, but it went against the prevailing notion that film music should be unnoticed and unnoticeable. In Waxman's view, this precept was absurd: "A motion picture score should be noticed just as much as you notice the other elements" (Sullivan 2006: 77).

Waxman's complex tapestry of moods and character motifs envelops the movie from beginning to end: The haunted hero and heroine float through Manderley in a sonic dreamscape enhanced by Waxman's pioneering use of the novachord, an electronic keyboard anticipating the eerie theremin in Hitchcock's *Spellbound*. The most original cues unveil a music of the subconscious, as in the menacing string glissandos that trouble the heroine's dreams even before she knows what the nightmares are about, or the descending two-note siren call tempting her to commit suicide.

Rebecca marked the first time Hitchcock had access to a big Hollywood score, and he used it to maximum effect. Counting Alfred Newman's Selznick "Trademark" overture, the dense three and a half page cue sheet lists seventy-one items. As in *Suspicion*, *Shadow of a Doubt*, and *Waltzes from Vienna* (a rare Hitchcock musical depicting the life of the Strauss family), Hitchcock used waltzes as a veneer covering impending disaster, including Waxman's languid waltz for the catastrophic masked ball and the discordant waltz during Mrs. Danvers's fiery immolation (complete with spectacular outtakes from the burning of Atlanta in *Gone with the Wind*).

Written under near-impossible circumstances, the score was at the center of behind-the-scenes battles. David O. Selznick had lured Hitchcock to Hollywood and was making *Gone with the Wind* across the street, hiring Waxman as an "insurance composer" in case Max Steiner failed to complete his assignment. The detailed music notes reveal a close working relationship between Hitchcock and Waxman as they struggled against Selznick's numerous interferences and attempts to rush or water down the score.

Hitchcock and Waxman were both European emigrés, the latter having fled the Nazis. The storyline of *Rebecca* fits the emigré pattern. Like Hitchcock and Waxman, its nameless heroine is a stranger in a bizarre but glamorous new world. Manderley is a stand-in for Hollywood, a wondrous but artificial place full of seductive wealth and great peril. Hitchcock had chosen to come to America, but Waxman, who left Germany for Paris and then America after being attacked on a Berlin street by Nazis, could never go back; for him, the Old World was lost forever. It is not surprising that the music of *Rebecca*, despite its silken veneer, has a bleak undertone, nor that its most celebrated cues resurrect a dead past. Yet *Rebecca* thrust Waxman into a promising present. It came out just as he became an American citizen, which he called "the happiest day of my life" (Sullivan, 73).

The score was so highly regarded when the film was released that Waxman was commissioned to turn it into a concert suite to help sell the picture—a not uncommon practice today, but novel in 1940. *The Rebecca Suite*—the predecessor of his popular suites for *Sunset Boulevard* and *A Place in the Sun*, not to mention the numerous concert suites of Bernard Herrmann and Waxman's student, John Williams—immediately raised his personal cachet as well as that of the film. Waxman's masterpiece became a Hollywood game changer.

Some Hitchcockians distrust *Rebecca* because of its Selznickian linearity and lack of quirky eccentricity. The public, perhaps a better judge, has always loved it. Truffaut had it right in the 1960s when he commented that the music leaves a "haunting impression," one that lingers long after Rebecca's R has gone up in smoke.

Vertigo

Vertigo opens with triplets spiraling in contrary motion, plunging the audience into the cinema's most beautiful nightmare (see Fig. A.1). Obsession, the film's theme, receives its definitive sound in Bernard Herrmann's endless circlings, recirclings, and suspensions. By the time the haunted prelude becomes the furious whirrings launching the terrifying rooftop chase, we are already hooked. For the next two hours, Scottie Ferguson's obsession becomes ours.

The gigantic, terrified eye from which Saul Bass's geometrical circles spin herald some of the cinema's most hypnotic images. Bass might have designed an ear as well. Unlike *Notorious*, *Rear Window*, and other films in which sound and silence exist in tense counterpoint, *Vertigo* is driven by music practically from beginning to end, with enough ideas for three or four movies. Herrmann's sounds constitute an independent force, a dangerous fever enveloping the audience as well as characters. Critics have used musical terminology to describe the film even when not discussing music. In his excellent study, David Sterritt calls *Vertigo* "a symphony of attraction-repulsion feelings projected by Hitchcock onto his characters" (quoted in Sullivan 2006: 222). This is one movie that is impossible to imagine without its music.

The Cinema's Most Beautiful Nightmare

Vertigo's soundtrack opens with spiraling triplets and sinister suspensions, plunging the audience into the cinema's most beautiful nightmare. Herrmann's Prelude establishes the design of the film, in everything from Hitchcock's circling camera to the curl in the heroine's hair. In the words of Herrmann's friend and colleague John Williams, the score "spins along this relentless path that gives a sense of timelessness … of the unstoppability of a destiny." By the time the hypnotic Prelude becomes the furious *Allegro con brio*, launching the rooftop chase, we are hooked.

While Hitchcock used more kinds of music than any director in history, from jazz and cabaret to pop and complex symphonic scores, *Vertigo*'s soundtrack has a unique range and complexity. The modernist sections include the traumatic tower cues, the terrifying "Vertigo" chord as the camera pulls back and zooms in, the gurgling dissonance as Madeleine jumps into the bay, the chilling clusters in the Sequoia forest and on the staircase with the shadowy nun at the end (an angel of death if ever there was one.) The Wagnerian eroticism of the love music is equally memorable, especially the dreamlike hotel sequence, a crescendo of trembling lyricism, when a deranged Scottie tries to resurrect the memory of his lost lover by dressing his new one exactly like her. Hitchcock removed all other sounds, telling Herrmann, "We'll just have the camera and you."

This is one of many dialogue-free cues where Hitchcock had just the camera and Herrmann, examples of what he called pure cinema. They include the restless rhythms colored by bass clarinet as Scottie circles through twisting San Francisco streets in pursuit of Madeleine, the lyrical "Park" cue, and the "Dawn" and "Farewell" panoramas. Some of these undergo constant transformation, especially "Carlotta's Theme," a Ravelian habanera that glides mysteriously through the art museum, screams with terror during Scottie's nightmare, and erupts with jolting clarity in the great mirror-necklace epiphany. In all these, no words are necessary: Bernard Herrmann is the narrator.

Two moments in Vertigo, from top: a haunted James Stewart, and Stewart with Kim Novak, the object of his obsession

Figure A.1 Extract of Jack Sullivan's essay on *Vertigo*'s soundtrack. Produced for the programme of the New York Philharmonic's "The Art of the Score" (2024).

Martin Scorsese states that the "tragically beautiful score by Bernard Herrmann is absolutely essential to the spirit, the functioning, and the power of *Vertigo*" (quoted in Auiler 1998: xiii). Indeed, it is hard to think of any movie more dependent upon the seductiveness of its score. The violent sections alone—the "vertigo" chord and its many offshoots, the nightmare dissonance hurling James Stewart's Scottie into an open grave—are sensational enough to give the score permanent notoriety. Were there nothing else, this score would be groundbreaking. But the melancholy elegance of the love music, if anything, is even more gripping and obsessive, repealing forever two conventions: the notion of movie music as background and the standard view of Bernard Herrmann as exclusively a manipulator of tiny motifs who assiduously avoided melody, a myth he himself helped perpetuate. In *Vertigo*, Hermann's signature scraps and fragments do appear but in counterpoint with a sensuous lyricism unique to film music: the "Scene d'Amour," the luscious "Beach" and "Park" cues, the "Dawn" and "Farewell" panoramas, and many other moments. This music is modern, to be sure, but it is also unabashedly Romantic, the most Wagnerian score in the movies.

The reputation of Herrmann's score has been steadily building. It was in *Vertigo*, said Donald Spoto in the 1970s, that the Herrmann–Hitchcock "emotional landscape was most perfectly realized" (1980: 12). The dreamlike haze of *Vertigo*, unique even for Hitchcock, was credited by Spoto and others as largely Herrmann's. In *Vertigo*, as in *Psycho* two years later, the music was inextricably linked to the central idea of the movie. By the 1990s, the generalizations were far broader. Joseph Horowitz, a writer for the *New York Times*, told me that the *Vertigo* score was a greater achievement than that of many composers seeking to write the Great American Symphony; Alex Ross compared the petrified-forest sequence to the avant-garde dreamscapes of Morton Feldman and declared there is no greater film score than *Vertigo*.

An extreme generalization, perhaps, but one hard to counter, especially given the adulation this movie, initially a box-office failure, has recently received. *Vertigo* is now not just a movie but a cult, an object of fetishism much like its subject, a status enhanced since its dramatic rereleases in 1983 and 1996 and fueled by its long absence from the movie scene. Vanishings and resurrections are exactly what *Vertigo* is about, and the strange permutations of its music since 1958—homages, pastiches, symphonic renderings, installations, and much else—are part of its Proustian allure.

Vertigo: Postscript by Robert Kapsis

More recently we see *Vertigo*'s allure play out in a March 2023 *New York Times* article where four of its classical-music critics were assigned to highlight programming events from the New York Philharmonic's upcoming 2023–2024 season. Their published selections included performances of monumental symphonic works such as Mahler's 2nd Symphony and Mozart's *Requiem* but also the playing of film scores live alongside screenings of three movies: *West Side Story*, *Black Panther*, and *Vertigo*. Of the three, Bernard Herrmann's score for *Vertigo* is the one Zachary Woolf, the *Times*' chief classical music critic, singled out for special treatment:

> Playing film scores live alongside screenings has become a booming business for orchestras struggling with attendance, but the fare is usually blockbusters: the "Harry Potter" series, *Jurassic Park*, *Raiders of the Lost Ark*. Not when the Philharmonic performs Bernard Herrmann's lush, ominous music for Hitchcock's *Vertigo* [January 23–26] as audiences watch that strange, hypnotizing study in erotic

obsession. Next season also brings *West Side Story* (September 12–17)—Spielberg's 2021 version, which featured the Philharmonic on its soundtrack—and *Black Panther* (December 20–23).

It is important to be mindful that from the beginning, going back to the time of the film's initial release in 1958, the *New York Times* has assigned critics to write about *Vertigo* who, with few exceptions, have all been outspoken advocates of the film and of the critical role of Herrmann's music in both the shaping and reception of the film. In 1996, on the occasion of the theatrical release of a painstakingly restored 70-mm, digital sound version of *Vertigo*, a then youngish Alex Ross, who later that year would become the chief music critic of the *New Yorker*, had this to say about the film's latest reincarnation:

It would be heresy to suggest that the greatness of *Vertigo* is owed to anyone but Hitchcock, whose fingerprints cover every aspect of the production. But there is a second genius at work in *Vertigo*, and his voice will be heard more clearly in the restoration. [The restorers] refurbished not just the images but also the sound, bringing digital technology to bear on the Bernard Herrmann score, whose original tape turned up in a vault nearly intact … Herrmann was an absolute master of the strange art of film scoring, and in a career that stretched from *Citizen Kane* to *Taxi Driver*, the 1958 *Vertigo* was probably his peak. How much, indeed, of this film's famous atmosphere is owed to Herrmann? Close your eyes and think of one sequence, and you may well remember Kim Novak's somnambulistic tour of San Francisco, from a chapel to a graveyard to a picture gallery. It is the music as much as the lighting and the filters that gives those scenes their eerie shimmer. None of which is to detract from Hitchcock's glory; he knew the nature of the talent he had engaged, and he created extraordinary opportunities for Herrmann to make his mark. *Vertigo* is a symphony for film and orchestra.

(*New York Times*, October 6, 1996, H17)

References

Auier, D. (1998) *Vertigo: The Making of a Hitchcock Classic*, New York: St. Martin's Press.
Spoto, D. (1980) "Sound and Silence in the Films of Alfred Hitchcock," *Keynote Magazine*, April.
Sullivan, Jack (2006) *Hitchcock's Music*, New Haven, Conn.: Yale University Press.
Teachout, T. (2007) "Hitchcock's Music Man," *Commentary*, February.

Coda B
Deserter or Honored Exile?
Views of Hitchcock from Wartime Britain

Charles Barr

Hitchcock was nearly forty, and had directed more than twenty British films, when he moved to America in March 1939 to take up a contract with David O. Selznick. When war broke out in Europe six months later, on September 3, he was on the point of shooting his first Hollywood film, *Rebecca*, and he remained from then on, a Hollywood director. Since the USA did not join the war until December 1941, he was based for more than two years in a neutral country while his own was at war. Although he subsequently came back to visit Britain from time to time, he never again made his home there, and when, occasionally, he filmed there, it was as a visitor from Hollywood who stayed in luxury London hotels.

There were those who saw his move out of Britain, at that particular time, or at least his failure to return home after the war started, as a form of betrayal. He had let his country down by leaving it at a time when it was clearly moving toward war. The most pointed attack on him in these terms came from the veteran actor Sir Seymour Hicks, who in 1922 had given Hitchcock his very first commission as a director. Moreover, he had let his friends down: his colleagues in the British film industry which had nurtured him, and which needed him at this time of extreme crisis and challenge. The man who articulated this attack most persistently was Michael Balcon, now head of Ealing Studios, who had produced many of Hitchcock's best British films.[1] And, not least, he had let himself down: cut himself off from his cultural roots, betrayed his distinctive talents, sold out to the sheltered opulence of America. The classic statement of this view came at the end of the decade from the critic, later filmmaker, Lindsay Anderson, in an article in *Sequence* that made a lasting impact (1949, reprinted in Anderson 1972).

Patrick McGilligan's biography of the director makes two main points about this view of Hitchcock from 1940s Britain. He refers to the attacks on Hitchcock made by Balcon early in the war for staying in Hollywood, and dismisses them as hasty and misguided; and he quotes Lindsay Anderson's 1949 account of the decline in Hitchcock's work after he went to America, and treats it as being typical:

> In England the director's reputation had [as of 1943] predictably declined, with a general feeling among critics that Hollywood had not only robbed England of Hitchcock, but Hitchcock of his individuality … Lindsay Anderson, like other English critics, embraced little of what Hitchcock did after he left home.
> (McGilligan 2003: 326 and 327)

This is probably the impression of Hitchcock's status in 1940s Britain that most people have: the impression that there was some initial resentment of Hitchcock's absence, but that it was quickly shown up as being misguided, and that most serious British critics of the time were less than enthusiastic about the actual films that Hitchcock made in his first decade in Hollywood (see Barr 1999: 207–210 for some discussion of the first of the two issues).

On both issues, however, the reality is rather more complicated. The decade of the 1940s was easily the most turbulent and eventful one in the intertwined histories of British film production and British film culture, and the contested public image of Hitchcock and of his films not surprisingly reflects this (see Barr 2004). The reception of two films in particular, with topical war themes, will help to illustrate the contentiousness of this debate over Hitchcock's public image—*Foreign Correspondent*, made between the start of the war and America's entry into it, and released in August 1940, and the other made at the end of the war, *Notorious*, released in America in 1946 and in England early in 1947.

Wartime Britain, 1940–1947

The main attacks on Hitchcock and other so-called deserters came in the spring and summer of 1940—a period that spanned the fall of France, the superseding of Chamberlain by Churchill as prime minister, and the airborne Battle of Britain. The attack by Seymour Hicks was published in May 1940, and included the proposal that Hitchcock should direct Charles Laughton, and other Hollywood-British actors in a film entitled "Gone with the Wind Up." The weekly fan magazine, *Picturegoer*, had already, from the start of the war, been discussing the issue of what the Hollywood British should do, presenting both sides of the argument. On October 7, 1939, the magazine's editor, Malcolm Phillips, reported on the urgent campaign to, in the words of his headline, "Keep The Home Cameras Turning," and approved the action of those who were coming back to assist this. While their Hollywood correspondent W. H. Mooring was broadly sympathetic to those who stayed, Maurice Cowan took a less friendly line. In a two-page spread on January 27, 1940, "Call Up for Hollywood," he sardonically invited them to come back and work for military rates of pay: among the illustrations is one of Hitchcock with the caption "Here's Alfred Hitchcock as he'd look as a major-general. Pay £4 10s 6d a day plus allowances" (see Annakin 1992: 5).[2]

On May 11, the same month as the Hicks article, came Michael Balcon's first main intervention, in a *Picturegoer* interview published under the heading "Call Up the Hollywood Britons." Hitchcock is unmentioned but is implicitly contrasted with another filmmaker who had returned after starring in two films produced by Selznick immediately prior to *Rebecca*: "Leslie Howard, for instance, has come back to work here, and immediately the money is forthcoming for him to produce pictures."[3]

Though outspoken, this piece is less prominent and less violent than the full-page article, "Deserters," published as the main feature article in the *Sunday Dispatch* on August 25, 1940. Here, the central text by Balcon is backed up by inserts from four others with film connections: the comedy star George Formby, the actors Owen Nares and Sir Seymour Hicks, and the writer J. B. Priestley. A variety of points are made, ranging from hysterical to thoughtful, but one passage from Balcon stands out:

> I had a plump young junior technician in my studios whom I promoted from department to department. Today, one of our most famous directors, he is in Hollywood, while we who are left behind are trying to harness films to the great national effort. I do not give this man's name as I have decided not to mention any of the deserters by name.

The name was hardly needed, and Hitchcock was provoked into a sharp reply, published two days later. He hit back at Balcon, accusing him of jealousy and insisting that "The British government has only to call upon me for my services. The manner in which I am helping my country is not Mr. Balcon's business" (*New York World-Telegram*, August 27, 1940, quoted by Spoto 1983: 235–236).

Hitchcock's second Hollywood film, *Foreign Correspondent*, opened in America on the very day of his reply to Balcon, and in early October it reached Britain. It supplied the most vivid and timely illustration of the way in which Hitchcock had chosen to "'help his country,'" in that it mounted, in the format of a suspense thriller, a stirring attack on American isolationism and could thus be seen as doing an important propaganda job. Joel McCrea plays an American reporter in Europe, Huntley Haverstock, who moves from naïve disinterest to commitment during the countdown to war; the main action ends with his return to America on the eve of war, but a tacked-on coda shows him a year later in London, broadcasting to America from a BBC studio while the bombs fall. Like Chaplin's *The Great Dictator*, released early in 1941, the film ends with a set-piece speech directed in effect at the audience, and specifically the American one, as Hitchcock and his writers construct from 6,000 miles away the experience of a blitz that was still in the future as they filmed it, but was very real to the first British audiences who viewed it:

> I can't read the rest of the speech I had because all the lights have gone out — so I'll just have to talk off the cuff. All that noise you hear isn't static. It's death coming to London. Yes, they're coming here now. You can hear the bombs falling on the streets and the homes. Don't tune me out. Hang on a while, this is a big story — and you're part of it. It's too late to do anything here now except stand in the dark and let them come. It's as if the lights are out everywhere — except in America. Keep those lights burning there. Cover them with steel — ring them with guns. Build a canopy of battleships and bombing planes around them. Hello, America! Hang onto your lights. They're the only lights left in the world!

An intense debate about the film and about this climactic speech is played out in the columns of the polemical film magazine of the time, *Documentary Newsletter*, whose title speaks for itself, though it covers wider issues than actual documentary production.[4] The film is reviewed by a committed long-term member of the British documentary movement, Basil Wright, codirector of the classic *Night Mail* (1936). If anyone, at that time, can be said to have been dedicated to the realist aesthetic and to the support of indigenous production close to the daily realities of British wartime life, this is the man. The journalistic output of Wright and his close associates is filled with references to the importance of getting ordinary people and their struggles and their aspirations onto the screen. And yet he is also a champion of Hitchcock's Hollywood work, right from the start:

> In *Rebecca* Alfred Hitchcock showed that Hollywood had supplied for him two essentials which had been markedly lacking in his long and successful career in British studios. The first was full and unstinted filmmaking facilities. The second was good producership. *Rebecca*, for all its faults, had qualities both of technique and imagination which transcended anything Hitchcock had achieved over here. Apparently, the long traditions of Hollywood really do mean something.
>
> Certainly, in *Foreign Correspondent* this always talented director has made his best film; and it is no detraction from Hitchcock's own qualities to emphasize the fact that it was made under the

producership of Walter Wanger, one of the most enlightened and talented of the younger school of Hollywood tycoons.

(*Documentary News Letter*, November 1940)[5]

So, Wright is not just opposing Balcon's already well-publicized line on Hitchcock's exile, he is suggesting that Hitchcock was held back in Britain by the low quality of his producers, of whom the dominant one had, of course, been Balcon himself. He goes on to praise the robust propaganda value of the film, and especially its ending. A letter appears in the next issue from an equally prominent member of the documentary movement, Paul Rotha, who, like Wright, was a critic as well as a filmmaker.[6] He places on record his "deep resentment" of the final speech and of the magazine's support of it. "The lights over here are still burning; the sequence could only have been made by people who didn't understand British democracy and British morale." And the letter is endorsed by a total of seven other journalists and filmmakers, including Michael Balcon and the Brazilian-born director Alberto Cavalcanti.[7]

Meanwhile, British audiences flocked to this film almost as eagerly as they would do two years later to MGM's *Mrs. Miniver*. On October 15, at the height of the German bombing of London, the *Evening Standard* noted:

> Queues were seen at West End cinemas for the first time for a month. People lined up to see Hitchcock's *Foreign Correspondent* at the Gaumont. Takings on Sunday were only £50 below *Rebecca* on a similar day six weeks ago. Customers will face the Blitz if the cinemas will give them the right films.

Moreover, as it turned out, these controversies scarcely seemed to impinge on those who reviewed films week by week in newspapers and magazines. Rarely do they even refer to the attacks on Hitchcock for making films in Hollywood rather than in Britain. His move is soon taken as a *fait accompli*, and most reviewers refer to his films with a degree of respect, affection, and pride, even if they have mixed feelings about the success of some of them. They especially welcome *Shadow of a Doubt* in 1943: Dilys Powell of the *Sunday Times* speaks for many in finding it "delightful," in that it marks a full return, in his new environment, to the assurance of *The Lady Vanishes* (*Sunday Times*, March 28, 1943).

His next film, *Lifeboat*, makes the headlines in advance: a front-page story in the *Sunday Chronicle*, "Film Angers America," is linked to the syndicated weekly column by the American journalist Dorothy Thompson, who protests that:

> it shows a typical Nazi as a superman, and a cross-section of American society as morons … A lot of Americans are asking whether Hitchcock would have dared, in the middle of the war, to have presented a cross-section of British society in the same light.

(*Sunday Chronicle*, February 13, 1944)

One of those who defends Hitchcock most vigorously, when the film opens in Britain, is Richard Winnington, film critic of the daily *News Chronicle*:

> Wild complaints that [the Nazi's] superior competence and resourcefulness cast a slur on democracy strike me as foolish … As a portrait of the Nazi makeup it is a relief after the succession of swaggering imbeciles we are accustomed to. I find this good and timely propaganda. The film is a virile, polished, and workmanlike job.

(*News Chronicle*, March 19, 1944)

And yet, when he next reviews a Hitchcock film, *Spellbound*, in 1946, Winnington's line has changed: "Year after year we go on expecting things from Alfred Hitchcock through a deep-rooted gratitude for his 'early' and 'middle' British periods. And year after year we see him becoming more and more dedicated to that empty polish which is the standard achievement of the Hollywood director" (*News Chronicle*, May 18, 1946).

This line is very close to that of Anderson in the 1949 *Sequence* article and may even have influenced him. Winnington was, of all British critics, the one most respected by the "young Turks" who founded the magazine in 1947, a respect that he reciprocated. Here he has in effect repudiated his praise for *Lifeboat*, without admitting it. I see this not as dishonesty but as a response to what had been happening in the intervening period — he may well have forgotten what he wrote two years earlier. Those years from 1944 to 1946 were momentous ones for British cinema, with a whole string of films seeming to establish both a distinctive British film aesthetic, based primarily on restraint and realism, and a more promising basis for commercial prosperity than ever before. In his survey of 1945, Winnington called it "Britain's most dazzling year of filmmaking," and detected a shift in the power relations of Britain and Hollywood:

> British films have taken an unprecedented leap forward in the last year both in entertainment value and in techniques … Considering the relative sizes of the two industries and the appalling restrictions of space, apparatus and personnel that still afflict her studios, Britain's achievement is nothing less than epic. The British cinema has been truly born.
>
> (*News Chronicle*, December 29, 1945)

This is not the place for further elaboration of these developments, destined to be short-lived, but the context does help to explain this critic's change of attitude to a Hitchcock who had by now fully committed himself to Hollywood and its ways. *Notorious* follows in early 1947, opening in London in the same week as the rerelease of a celebrated Duvivier film of the 1930s, and Winnington's verdict on it begins thus:

> If *Poil de Carotte* sparkles, *Notorious* can be said to glitter with a deadly slickness. Alfred Hitchcock has gone out, at all costs, for polish, at the price of originality and suspense and story … He seems bent on refuting his previous theories of condensation by dallying with closeups and irrelevant sequences.

Compare the socialist political weekly *Tribune*: their critic, Simon Harcourt Smith, reviews *Notorious* alongside another momentous film of that year, *The Best Years of Our Lives*, characterizing the pair of them as:

> a couple of large, glossy, slightly self-important pictures from Hollywood … The one has been directed by Alfred Hitchcock, the other by William Wyler. Both provide uninspired but quite competent entertainment.
>
> *Notorious* is perhaps the worse film of the two because of what we used to expect from Hitchcock. Looking back, I am inclined to think we expected too much … No Hitchcock film has any point of view to give it substance; and when the quickness of his hand no longer takes us in, there is very little to do but doze. Certainly, there is little sleight of hand in this new Hitchcock picture … Nevertheless, the film is just worth seeing if only for the hearty appetite with which Miss Bergman eats Mr. Grant in one of the earlier sequences.
>
> (*Tribune*, circa early 1947)[8]

Little sleight of hand, no point of view, irrelevant sequences, gratuitous close-ups and gloss—these now seem extraordinary comments to make on a film which stands up as well as any film, by Hitchcock or anyone else, to analysis as a model of tight, rigorous, organic construction. Whether you like the film or not, it seems perverse to criticize it in those terms, as being slack and rambling. Harcourt Smith's witticism at the expense of the long kissing scene is an accurate indication of his dilettantism, but Winnington was a critic of admirable care and seriousness whom Philip French, the longest-serving and most professional of his successors, has aptly compared with George Orwell (French, *The Observer*, January 23, 1976).[9] On the basis of these confidently scornful views of *Notorious*—Winnington, the true enthusiast, writing for a popular paper; Harcourt Smith, the general arts man, writing for a minority one; plus Anderson, voice of a new generation of cineastes—it's easy to infer that in those days, in this British milieu, the critics just didn't get it, didn't begin to understand the new and productive directions that Hitchcock's work was taking, perhaps because they were too caught up in the euphoria of a new dawn for British cinema, and of the non-Hollywood aesthetic associated with it. Even when that new impetus petered out, neither Winnington nor Anderson would soften their severity towards the Hollywood Hitchcock.

Acknowledgment

Abridged from Charles Barr, "Deserter or Honored Exile? Views of Hitchcock from Wartime Britain," *Hitchcock Annual*, 2004–2005, pp. 1–24.

Notes

1. Balcon had employed Hitchcock at Gainsborough, promoted him to director in 1925 and—after his departure in 1927 to BIP for a higher salary—welcomed him back to Gaumont British in 1934 to make *The Man Who Knew Too Much* and its four successors, the series of thrillers that decisively established his international reputation.

2. This is f4.52p in decimal coinage, or around $18 at 1940 rates of exchange. The director Ken Annakin recalls, in an interview, his work on a recruiting film in 1942, "with important actresses like Flora Robson working for f5 a day"—a precise index of the financial sacrifice they were ready to make for the war effort.

3. Howard had starred with Ingrid Bergman in *Intermezzo* and played Ashley Wilkes in *Gone with the Wind*; these were his last two Hollywood films, both released in 1939. His first and best British war film, as star and director, was *Pimpernel Smith* (1941), released in the USA as *Mister V.* Leslie Howard died in a plane crash in 1943.

4. *Documentary News Letter* was the successor to two earlier voices of the minority film culture centered on the documentary movement founded by John Grierson: *Cinema Quarterly* (1932–1935) and *World Film News* (1936–1938). It published sixty issues between January 1940 and December 1947, and continued for a time as *Documentary Film News* before ending in 1949.

5. The review is, following the magazine's normal practice, unsigned, but its closeness to the argument and phraseology of Wright's signed review of the same film, in the political weekly, *The Spectator* (October 18, 1940), establishes the authorship beyond any doubt. Wright was a long-term member of the *Documentary News Letter* editorial board.

6. Rotha was well known as the author of a wide-ranging history of the medium, *The Film Till Now* (1930), reissued with updates several times in the following decades. He later published *Documentary Film* (1936) and had begun a career as a documentary producer and director, which he continued throughout the war.

7   The other five are Dilys Powell, film critic of the *Sunday Times*; Aubrey Flanagan, of the *Motion Picture Herald*; and three prominent journalists who were not film specialists: Ritchie Calder, Michael Foot, and Alexander Werth.
8   *Tribune*, undated cutting from early 1947, included on the microfiche on *Notorious* held by the British Film Institute's library.
9   Philip French, review of the collection edited by Paul Rotha (1975). French was the film critic of *The Observer* between 1978 and 2015.

References

Anderson, L. (1972) "Alfred Hitchcock," in A. LaValley (ed.), *Focus on Hitchcock*, New York: Prentice-Hall.
Annakin, K. (1992) in B. McFarlane (ed.), *Sixty Voices*, London: BFI Publishing.
Barr, C. (1999) *English Hitchcock*, Moffat: Cameron & Hollis.
Barr, C. (2004/2005) "Deserter or Honored Exile: Views of Hitchcock from Wartime Britain," *Hitchcock Annual*, vol. 13, pp. 1–24.
McGilligan, P. (2003) *Alfred Hitchcock*: *A Life in Darkness and Light*, Chichester: John Wiley.
Spoto, D. (1983) *The Life of Alfred Hitchcock*: *The Dark Side of Genius*, London: Collins.

Index

15 Ways to Kill Your Neighbor (2022) 410
20th Century Fox 58, 74, 398
24 por Segundo 399
30 Monedas (*Thirty Coins*, 2020–2023) 389
The 39 Steps (1935) 2, 19, 25, 31–42, 80–1, 93–6
    in Argentina 408–9
    and auteurism 62
    British critical reception 98–9
    expatriate/ex-patriot 230
    in Japan 364, 366
    in Mexico 395, 398, 400
    in South Korea 355, 362–3
"*39 Steps* Stars Pained by Realism" (1935) 34
1492 Pictures 301n5
2001: A Space Odyssey (1968) 152

Abre los ojos (*Open Your Eyes*, 1997) 390–1
absolutism in continuity 368
abstraction, abstractness 155, 191–4, 254–5
abuse allegations against Hitchcock 39, 128–33, 136–8, 149, 154–5
academic film criticism
    Mr. & Mrs. Smith 198, 201–8
    The Trouble with Harry 188–95
    Vertigo and *Marnie* 144–8
Academy Awards 55, 58, 110, 217
    see also Oscars
Academy of Motion Picture Arts and Sciences 7, 141, 240n3, 256
Ackroyd, Peter 353
"aestheticized television" 282
aesthetics of shadow 366–7
"l'affaire Hitchcock" (the Hitchcock case), Japan, 1946–1950s 367–9
After Dark 256
After Hours (1985) 70
Agora (2009) 391
Aguilar, Carlos 359–60
AIDS epidemic 116
Airport (1970) 258

Akihito (Prince) 370
Akira, Kurosawa 368
Aleksandrov, Aleksandr 352
Alfred Hitchcock: A Definitive Filmography (Sloan) 413n1
Alfred Hitchcock: A Guide to References and Resources (Sloan) 272
"Alfred Hitchcock: Auteur or Hack? How the Filmmaker Reshaped His Reputation among the Critics" (Kapsis) 382n5
Alfred Hitchcock: The Legacy of Victorianism (Cohen) 113
Alfred Hitchcock (Ackroyd) 353
Alfred Hitchcock and the British Cinema (Ryall) 18
Alfred Hitchcock (del Toro) 401, 403
The Alfred Hitchcock Hour (1962–1965) 271–88, 303, 399
Alfred Hitchcock and the Making of Psycho (Rebello) 353
Alfred Hitchcock Presents: The Movie 274, 285, 288n9
Alfred Hitchcock Presents: The Musical 293–4
Alfred Hitchcock Presents (1955–1962) 73, 78, 113, 211, 271–88
    Hitchcock's public image in Italy 347
    Italian film criticism 347
    in Japan 369–70
    in Mexico 399
    preserving/promoting Hitchcock's TV persona 292–4
    travels in Hitchcock's multiverse 303, 306–7, 314
Alfred Hitchcock's America (Pomerance) 204
Alfred Hitchcock's Mystery Magazine (1956–present) 5, 304, 367
Alianza Editorial 401
All the President's Men (1976) 260
All-Ukrainian Photo Cinema Administration (VUFKU) 350
Allardice, James B. 273
Allen, Jay Presson 39
Allen, Jeanne Thomas 72, 246, 250n7
Allen, Richard 3–4, 18, 83, 155, 175–81, 194

Almodóvar, Pedro 6–7, 386–8
Alpert, Hollis 183, 211–12, 256, 262
Amazing Stories 285, 287n8
Amenábar, Alejandro 389–91
The American Cinema (Sarris) 256–7
American Cinematographer 160, 199, 256, 406
American critical reception, *Strangers on a Train* 236–8
American criticial reception
    Shadow of a Doubt 54–8
    Strangers on a Train 235–8
    The Trouble with Harry 182–4
American culture and *The Man Who Knew Too Much* 106–14
American democracy 368–9
American Film Institute 149, 376
American Film magazine 150, 201, 208n1
American film renaissance 256–7
American Graffiti (1973) 70
"Anal *Rope*" (Miller) 122, 126n3, 161, 165
Anatahan (1953) 257
Anderson, Lindsay 17–18, 40
    and auteurism 61–3
    Mr. & Mrs. Smith 200
    Strangers on a Train 229
    and wartime Britain 421–2, 425–6
Anecdotes about Chinese and Foreign Cinema 376–7
Anglo-American Corporation 407
Anglo-American Films 406–7
Anschluss (March 12–13, 1938) 35
anti-Nazi policy 232, 351
anti-representation and representation 86
antisemitism 217
    see also Jewish undertones; Nazism
anti-Stalinism 72
"apocalyptic poem" 134–5
Arabov, Yuri 353n1
"Are Our Stars Slacking?" (Phillips) 231
Argentina 8, 406–13
    1935–1984, and the *Cinematic Herald* 407–10
    auteurism, adaptation, and *Psycho* 410–13
    history and reception, Buenos Aires 406–7
Argento, Dario 348, 358
aristocracy 48, 50, 362
    see also bourgeoisie
Around the World in 80 Days (1956) 211
"Around the World" (Moscow International Film Festival) 353
Arsenic and Old Lace (1944) 185
The Art of Alfred Hitchcock: Fifty Years of His Motion Pictures (Spoto) 149, 189–90, 201
The Art of Alfred Hitchcock (Spoto) 189–90, 200–1
art cinema 329–41

The Art of Pure Cinema: Hitchcock and His Imitators (Isaac) 83
"Arthur" (1959) 273–6
Arzner, Dorothy 45–6
Ashenden (Maugham) 93, 98
Associated British Corporation 395
Association of American Producers 344
Astruc, Alexandre 319, 321, 323–4, 326, 327n5
Atherton, Gertrude 307, 309
Atkinson, G. A. 14–15, 17, 170, 172–3
August 1st Film (1987) 379
The Aura (2005) 410–11, 412–13
austerity 230, 233–4
Australia 271, 298
Austrian Filmmuseum 331–2
auteurism 48, 61–6
    in Argentina 410–13
    in Communist China 379
    in Germany 329–41
    Hitchcock at the Source: The Auteur as Adapter by Boyd & Palmer 83, 93
    Hitchcock's television work 276–7
    "Notes on the Auteur theory" by Sarris 63, 95
    and Patricia Hitchcock 291–2
    Politique des auteurs 63, 319–28, 372
    preserving/promoting Hitchcock's TV persona 300
    reception in Spain 384–6
    in South Korea 356, 359–60
    in Spain 384–6
    travels in Hitchcock's multiverse 303
authorship 41n7, 44, 286–7
    and *L'Écran français* 319
    gendered reception of *Rebecca* 51–2
    Hitchcock and wartime Britain 426n5
    Hitchcock's television work 273, 275–6
    and Italian film criticism 347
    and *Mr. & Mrs. Smith* 202
    and *Rear Window* 69–71
autonomy 369
Autorenkino (author's cinema) 331
Avanti! (1972) 195
Aventure Malgache (1944) 271–2, 398

"The Bachelor's Fantasy: Autoimmunity in Theory" (Galloway) 205–6
"Back for Christmas" (1956) 273, 275–6
B.A.D. magazine 257
Bailin, Rebecca 146
Balcon, Michael 173, 231–2, 234, 421–4, 426n1
"Bang! You're Dead" (1961) 273
"Banquo's Chair" (1959) 273

Barr, Charles 2
   39 Steps 32
   and auteurism 61–2
   Blackmail 22, 26–7
   Downhill 169
   English Hitchcock 19, 22, 26–7, 169
   Hitchcock's earliest literary influences 19
   Sabotage 101–3
   Strangers on a Train 230–2
   Under Capricorn 175
   Vertigo and *Marnie* 142
   and wartime Britain 61, 421–7
   and women's roles in film 31
Barrie, J. M. 186, 290, 293, 308–9
Barry, Iris 14–15, 17, 96, 170, 172, 292
Basic Instinct (1992) 357–8
"The Basis of the Makeup" ("Die Basis des Make-Ups") 332–3
Bazin, André 320, 321–2, 367, 401
Becoming Carol Lombard (Kiriakou) 206–7
Bectu (Broadcasting, Entertainment, Communications and Theatre Union) 41n6
Beijing Film Academy 382n6
Beischlafdiebin (*The Sex Thief*, 1998) 339–40
Belfast News Letter 100
Belfast Post 100
Bella Época cinema 403
Belle de Jour (1967) 260
Bellocchio, Marco 348
Bellour, Raymond 86–8, 117, 119, 130–1, 372n2
Belton, John 69–70, 73, 257
Ben-Hur (1925) 16
Ben-Hur (1959) 356
Benjamin, Arthur 110
Bennett, Charles 28–9, 32–4, 97, 103–4, 258
Bergman, Ingmar 357
Bergman, Ingrid 31, 58–61, 233, 245
   and auteurism 63, 66
   Notorious 233, 322
   reception in Mexico 398–9
   Under Capricorn 175–6, 178
Berlin Alexanderplatz (1980) 331
Berlin School 329–30, 340
Best New Actress Award 391
the *Best Years of Our Lives* (1945) 217
Betrayed (1985) 7, 329–30, 334–40
Betrayed (*Betrogen*, 1985) 334–40
"Beyond the Gaze" (Brent) 18
BFI *see* British Film Institute
Bible 29, 179
Bielinsky, Fabián 410–11
The Big Sleep (1946) 65, 287

bildungsroman 85
Bioscope 170, 415
BIP *see* British International Pictures
Biraghi, Guglielmo 346
The Birds (1963) 3, 31, 144, 242–4
   in Argentina 408, 409, 412
   and auteurism 63
   following Hitchcock's death, 1980 153–4
   Hitchcock and Italian film criticism 344–7
   Hitchcock's "walk-ons" 5–6, 292, 301n2
   #MeToo movement, assault allegations 128–39
   in Mexico 395, 397, 399
   preserving/promoting Hitchcock's TV persona 293
   in South Korea 355–7, 363n2
   television work 272–3
   USSR and post-Soviet Russia 353
Birmingham Post 16
Bitomsky, Hartmut 7, 331–2
Black Panther 419–20
blacklisting 283
Blackmail (1929) 2, 8, 17–19, 21–30, 230
   and Communist China 375
   in Communist China 376–7
   music in Hitchcock's films 414, 415
   in Spain 391
   USSR and post-Soviet Russia 351
Blitz of London 230–1, 232
"Le Blocage symbolique" (Bellour) 372n2
Blow Out (1981) 75
Blow-Up (1966) 75, 330
Bogdanovich, Peter 18, 70–1, 210, 212–13, 291
Boileau-Narcejac, Pierre 309, 333, 334
Bolton, Matthew 108
Bon voyage (1944) 271–2, 398
Le Bonheur (1965) 334
Bonnie and Clyde (1967) 256–7
Bordwell, David 70, 224n4
Boston after Dark 242, 248
Boston Globe 188, 216, 265
Boston Mercury 104n1
Boston Phoenix 150, 265
bourgeoisie 66, 204, 347–8, 351, 367, 388, 402, 411–12
Boxoffice 43, 198–9, 235, 254–5
boycotts 231
Boyd, David 83, 93
Bradshaw, Peter 360
Braudy, Leo 121
Brave Smiles 49–50
Brazil 298
   preserving/promoting Hitchcock's TV persona 271
"Breakdown" (1955) 272–3, 275–6

Breakfast at Tiffany's (1961) 356
Breaking Bad (2008) 282
Brecht, Bertolt 338, 339–40
Brent, Jessica 18
Brien, Alan 185
Brill, Leslie
   Frenzy 248
   The Hitchcock Romance 18
   Mr. & Mrs. Smith 203
   North by Northwest 84–8
   The Trouble with Harry 190–1
   Under Capricorn 176, 179
Britain post-1951, reassessment, *Strangers on a Train* 236–8
British austerity 230, 233–4
British colonialism *see* colonialism
British critical reception
   Sabotage 93–105
   Shadow of a Doubt 54–8
   The Trouble with Harry 184–6
British democracy 424
British Film Institute (BFI) 109–13
   BFI Classics series 44, 131, 138n2
   BFI National Archive 22–6, 41n7, 95, 351
   BFI Reuben Library 88
   "Hitchcock: Nine Unknown Films" 353
   The Man Who Knew Too Much 110–13, 263, 267
   Marnie 154
   Monthly Film Bulletin 101
   Strangers on a Train 236–8
   Vertigo 143, 151
   see also Sight and Sound magazine
"British Film Retrospective" (1984) 376–7
British International Pictures (BIP) 14, 29–30, 169, 407, 426n1
British Kinematograph Society 323
British National 169
   see also British International Pictures
British New Wave of the 1960s 61–2
British Romanticism 131–2
Brody, Richard 154–5, 214–15
Brown, Mark 151, 267
Brown, Royal S. 121, 192
Browning, Elizabeth Barrett 309–10
Bruges-la-Morte (Rodenbach) 309
bubble culture 372
Buchanan, Ian 129, 134
Buenos Aires 406–9, 412
Bühler, Wolf-Eckart 330–1
Bullock, Elizabeth L. 3–4, 198–209
Burgess, Islay 122, 124, 253

Busch, Justin 259–60
Buzzolan, Ugo 347
The Bystander magazine 96, 232

Cahiers du cinéma 3, 104, 319–26, 326n1, 327n5
   and auteurism 63
   Bazin, André 320, 321–2, 367, 401
   "le cas Hitchcock", 1946–1950s 367
   early queer theory 121
   and Germany's *Filmkritik* 331
   Hitchcock and Italian film criticism 342–4, 346
   and *The Lodger* 18
   and *The Man Who Knew Too Much* 107, 262–3
   and *North by Northwest* 83
   and *Rear Window* 73
   reception in Germany 329–30, 331
   reception in Italy 342–3, 346, 348–9
   reception in Japan 367
   reception in Mexico 401–2, 404
   and *The Trouble with Harry* 187–8
   and *Under Capricorn* 176
   and *The Wrong Man* 212
Callahan, Dan 214
Calvin, Italo 344
caméra-stylo 321, 324, 326
   see also Astruc, Alexandre
Cameron, Ian 263–4, 266
Cameron, Kate 235
Campbell, George 96, 232
Camus y compañia 395
Canada 250n5, 298
   preserving/promoting Hitchcock's TV persona 271
capitalism, commercialism 8, 201, 204–6, 333–4, 367–82
   see also bourgeoisie
Carroll, Leo G. 85, 230–1
Carroll, Madeleine 32–4
Carroll, Sydney 95–7
Carrubba, Tere 290
cars and car-based tourism 334
"le cas Hitchcock" (the Hitchcock case), Japan, 1946–1950s 367–9
Casablanca (1942) 58, 356
"The Case of Mr. Pelham" (1955) 273, 275–7
Castle (2013) 75
Castle, William 125
Catholicism
   Downhill 173
   Italian film criticism 348
   in Japan 367
   in South Korea 359, 362–3

in Spain (auteurism) 384
    travels in Hitchcock's multiverse 305–6, 310
    The Trouble with Harry 184, 187
Caught (1949) 51
Cavell, Stanley 85, 88, 202, 204, 206–7
CBS Network 280, 282, 347
CCD *see* Civil Censorship Detachment
The Celluloid Closet (Russo) 116
censorship 368–9
    see also propaganda
Center for Study of Women in Television and Film 286
Centro Cultural Universitario at the UNAM 403
Centro Universitario de Estudios Cinematográficos 401
Cermorel, Claude 324–5
Chabrol, Claude 6–7, 69
    academia, *Mr. & Mrs. Smith* 201
    and auteurism 63
    Blackmail 22
    Downhill 173
    Frenzy 242–3
    and *L'Écran français* 319
    The Man Who Knew Too Much 263, 266
    narrative and narrational tactics 69
    North by Northwest 88
    reception in Italy 342–4
    reception in Japan 367
    Rope 160
    Sabotage 94
    television work 273
    The Trouble with Harry in France 187–8
    Under Capricorn 179–80
    The Wrong Man 212
Champage (1928) 30, 88
Champagne (1928) 395
Changchun Film Studio 379
Chaplin, Charlie 85, 129, 185, 232–3, 256–7, 423
Chapman, James 3, 84, 93–105, 240, 252–61
Chester Chronicle 99, 101
child abuse 358–9
Children's Encyclopedia (1961) 352
The Children's Hour (1934–1936) 49
China 8, 374–83
    and Hitchcock's legend 380–2
    industry icons, debate 377–80
    and Western film culture 375–7
China Film Association 376–7
China Film Corporation 375
China Film Press 376
China Import and Export Corporation 377
China Reading Weekly 381
"Chinese Hitchcock" 379
"Les Choses sérieuses" (Chabrol) 69

Chosun Ilbo newspaper 355–9
Christianity 175–81, 189–90
CIE *see* Civil Information and Education Division
Cincinnati Inquirer 183, 216
El cine británico de Hitchcock 384
Cine Club (1955) 401
Cineastas emergentes: mujeres en el cine del siglo XXI (Scholz) 391
Cinéaste 1: Hitchcock 372n2
Cinema: Technical Perfection and the Absence of Humanity 344–5
"Cinema en miniature: The Telefilms of Alfred Hitchcock" (Rüdel) 274
Cinema I (1983) and *Cinema II* (1985) 203
Cinema magazine 279–80, 343
Cinema Nuovo 343, 345
Cinema Quarterly (1932–1935) 426n4
Cinemanía magazine 399
cinematheque/videotheque movement 326, 356–60, 363n1, 403
Cineteca Nacional 394–5, 401, 403
The Cine-Technician 323–4
Citizen Kane (1941) 56, 151–2, 267, 321, 323, 420
Civil Censorship Detachment (CCD) 368–9
Civil Information and Education Division (CIE) 368–9
The Civil and Military Gazette 96
Civil War, Spain 386–7, 391, 400–2
class systems 339–40
    and *Blackmail* 27–8
    Germany, and Farocki's *Betrayed* 335–7
    and injustice 177, 179
    and *The Lady Vanishes* 32–3, 40n1
    and Park Chan-wook 358–9
    see also bourgeoisie
Classic TV Guide 271
classical cinema 44, 64, 230, 352, 356–9
Clément, René 325
Close Up magazine 22
Clover, Carol 119–20
Cluny Brown (1946) 257
Cohen, Tom 87, 208n3
Cold War
    and Japanese cinema 367–9, 372
    The Man Who Knew Too Much 108
    North by Northwest 84
    Rear Window 72
    Rope 165
    Topaz 259–60
    see also Communism
Collection of Film Art Translations 375
    see also World Cinema

A College Woman's Confession (*Eoneu yeodaesaeng-ui gobaeg*, 1958) 354
colonialism 33–4, 49, 117–18, 305–6, 334–5
comedies 184–6, 202
    satire 68, 73–5, 201, 411–12
Common Wealth (2000) 389
Commonweal (Hartung) 69, 216
Communism
    in China 374–83
        McCarthyism 283
        USSR and post-Soviet Russia 350–3
Confessions of a Nazi Spy (1939) 232
Conrad, Joseph 93–4, 96–103, 409
Contemporary Cinema 377
The Conversation (1974) 75
Cooper, Ian 243, 247
Coppola, Francis Ford 214–15
El corazón del bosque 386–7
Corliss, Richard 188, 257–8
Cosmos Theatre 395
Cosulich, Callisto 344, 346, 349n1
    Rear Window and the Association of American Producers 344
A Countess from Hong Kong (1967) 129, 256–7
Cozi TV 286
craftsman/crafts 84, 249n1, 324, 343–8, 356
    see also "master/magician of suspense"
Cría cuervos 386–7
crime 368–9
Crime and Punishment (Dostoyevsky) 93–6
critical reception 2, 93–166
    anomalies 229–68
        Frenzy 242–51
        Strangers on a Train 229–41
        Topaz 252–61
        two versions of *The Man Who Knew Too Much* 262–8
    British critics and *Sabotage* 93–105
    changing receptions 3
        The Birds and #MeToo allegations 128–39
        The Man Who Knew Too Much and American culture 106–14
        Psycho and queer theory 115–27
        Rope 158–66
        Sabotage 93–105
        Vertigo and *Marnie* 140–57
    gender, *Rebecca* 43–53
    #MeToo movement, assault allegations 128–39
    Mr. & Mrs. Smith 198–209
    Notorious (1946) 58–61
    Rebecca 50–2
    Shadow of a Doubt 54–8

    The Trouble with Harry 182–6
    The Wrong Man 211–12
    see also globalization
critical studies
    The Trouble with Harry 188–95
    see also academic film criticism
crossdressing and cross-gender identification 124, 126n5
Crowther, Bosley
    and auteurism 62
    The Man Who Knew Too Much 107, 113
    Mr. & Mrs. Smith 199
    narrative and narrational tactics 68–9
    Notorious 59–60
    Rope 160
    Shadow of a Doubt 57, 62
    Strangers on a Train 229, 235–40
    Topaz 256
    The Trouble with Harry 183
    Vertigo and *Marnie* 141–2
"The Crystal Trench" (1959) 272–3
Cubra Libre (1995) 339–40
Cultural Revolution of China 8, 374–7
    see also post-Cultural Revolution China

Daily Express 14–15, 17, 172–3, 244
Daily Film Renter 185
Daily Herald 60, 97, 101, 232
Daily Mail
    and *Downhill* 170, 172
    and *The Lodger* 14–15, 17, 20n2
    and *The Man Who Knew Too Much* 266
    and *Strangers on a Train* 233, 237
    and *The Trouble with Harry* 185–6
Daily Mirror 25–6, 232, 253
Daily Telegraph 60–1, 66, 214, 231, 233, 237
Dalí, Salvador 385, 409
Daquin, Louis 321, 325
Dargis, Manohla 360
"The Dark Side of Blondeness: *Vertigo* and Race" (Greven) 156n3
The Dark Side of Genius: The Life of Alfred Hitchcock (Spoto) 149, 201
Dark Waters (1943) 287n5
Day of the Beast (1995) 388–9
Day, Doris 107–13, 264–5
de Baecque, Antoine 320–1, 323, 326n2, 327n4
De la Iglesia, Alex 386, 388–9
de Lauretis, Teresa 48, 72
De Palma, Brian 75, 143, 149–50, 285, 357–8
De Sica, Vittorio 354
de Unamuno, Miguel 391

Una década sin Hitchcock (A Decade without Hitchcock) 403
Decision to Leave 7–8, 354, 357–63
Decision to Leave (2022) 7–8, 357–63
Decision to Leave (Heeojil gyeolsim, 2022) 7–8, 354, 357–63
Decoin, Henri 325
del Toro, Guillermo 4
   Frenzy 242
      reception in Mexico 394, 398–9, 401, 403
   The Wrong Man 210, 224
Delannoy, Jean 325
Deleuze, Gilles 134, 198, 203, 208n3
Demme, Jonathan 122
democracy 8, 207, 368–9, 424
   see also capitalism, commercialism
Demonsablon, Philippe 187
Deneuve, Catherine 260
DeRosa, Steven 184, 194
"Deserter or Exile? Views of Hitchcock from Wartime Britain" (Barr) 61, 230, 421–7
"Desire in Narrative" (de Lauretis) 48
Desplechin, Arnaud 214–15
Le Devoir 250n5
DFFB Berlin film academy 333
DGA see Director's Guild of America
Diabolique (1955) 141–3, 156n2
Dial 112 (*Daieol 112reul dollyeora*, 1962) 354
Dial M for Murder (1954) 354, 396, 399, 405n5, 408
Dima, Vlad 249
"Dip in the Pool" (1958) 272–3
Director's Guild of America (DGA) 285–6, 288n9
Dirty War, Argentina (1955) 412
disability 358–9
Disney 387
Disturbia (2007) 75
Dixon, Campbell 60, 231
Doctor Zhivago (1965) 356
Documentary Film News 426n4
"Does *Frenzy* Degrade Women?" (Sullivan) 246
Domarchi, Jean 187, 319
The Donna Reed Show (1958) 113
Donskoy, Mark 352
El Dorado (1966) 257
Dostoyevsky, Fyodor 93–6, 208n1, 327n5
Doty, Alexander 48, 119, 120, 122, 126n2
Double Feature (Logan) 129
Double Indemnity (1944) 65
"doubling" structures 219
Douchet, Jean 71–3, 319
Downey Jr., Robert 301n1
Downhill (1927) 3–4, 17–18, 169–74

Dr No (1962) 261n1
drama see melodrama
Dreville, Jean 325
du Maurier, Daphne 43, 46–7, 51–2
Duke and Duchess of York 26
Durgnat, Raymond
   academia, *Mr. & Mrs. Smith* 201
   Downhill 173–4
   early queer theory 121
   The Man Who Knew Too Much 107–8
   North by Northwest 85
   queer theory, *Psycho* 121, 124
   Rear Window 70–1
   Sabotage 93, 102–3
   The Strange Case of Alfred Hitchcock 121, 173–4, 189–90, 201
   television work 273
   The Trouble with Harry 189–90
Dying of Laughter (1999) 389

East Kent Times 104n1
Easy Rider (1969) 256–7
Easy Virtue 169, 172
Ebert, Jürgen 331–3
L'Écran français 319–28
   Andr(')e Bazin 320, 321–2
   controversy 324–6
   "Hitchcock se confie" 322–4
   introduction to 321
   see also Cahiers du cinéma
Edelmnan, Lee 72, 122, 126n3, 133
Eisensteinian Center of Film Culture Studies 353
El Deseo 388
El Duende Filmo 398
El Greco 305–6
Electra cinema 403
Electrophilia (2023) 410
ellipses 70
Elsen, Claude 322
Elstree studios 25–6, 169
Elvey, Maurice 16
émigré(s) 331, 340, 402, 417
Eminem 290, 294–8
Engineer Kochin's Error 350–1
English Hitchcock (Barr) 19, 22, 26–7, 40n1, 169
"entertainment film" in China 377–80
Entertainment Weekly 218
D'entre les morts (*From among the Dead*, 1954) 309, 333
The Era magazine 36, 40, 97
eroticism 49–50, 130–2, 137–8, 145, 170, 246–7
   homoeroticism 238
   male gaze 31, 40, 64–5, 107, 122, 137–8

music in Hitchcock's films 419–20
New German Cinema 339
see also sexuality
Escape (1940) 232
El espiritu de la colmena 386–7
"Essential Hitchcock" (2012) 388
Esto newspaper 399
eternal feminine 306
Evans, Ray 110
Evening News 14–15, 171–2, 185
Evening Standard
    and *Downhill* 170
    and *Frenzy* 249n1
    Hitchcock and wartime Britain 424
    and *The Lodger* 14, 17
    and *The Man Who Knew Too Much* 262
    and *North by Northwest* 80
    and *Strangers on a Train* 237–8, 240n5
    and *The Trouble with Harry* 185
Evening Star 198–9, 216
Everyman Cinema 21
Excélsior (newspaper/journal) 395–9, 402, 406–7
exonerations 216, 217, 219, 224
expressionism 23, 29, 70, 171, 311, 330, 348, 415
    see also modernism
An Eye for Hitchcock (Pomerance) 88, 204
Eyman, Scott 214

Fabbri, Marina 349n1
failed sexuality 191
"fallen women" *see* melodrama
Family Guy (2017) 75
Family Plot (1976) 265–7, 283, 285, 395, 397, 408–9
Famous Music Corporation 420n1
Famous Players-Lasky Corporation 384, 407
"fantasy" (*hwangsang*) 357–63
Far Out magazine 80–1, 83
Farber, Manny 122, 235–6
Farmers Newspaper 354
Farocki, Harun 7, 329–41
Fassbinder, R. W. 331
Father Knows Best (1954) 113
Faust (1926) 16, 295
Faust, Leland 290, 297–8, 301n4
Fava, Claudio G. 343
Felleman, Susan 194
Fellini, Federico 134–5
female spectator 49, 51, 72, 145
"Female Spectator, Lesbian Specter" (White) 49
feminism 2–3
    "Desire in Narrative" by de Lauretis 48
    feminist film theory 3, 64–5, 358

    gendered reception of *Rebecca* 43–53
    ideological criticism of *Rear Window* 72
    Marnie 146
    #MeToo movement, assault allegations 128–39
    Mr. & Mrs. Smith 206–7
    and Park Chan-wook 358–9
    post-Suffrage era 33–7
    and *Rebecca* 45, 48, 50, 51
    Scarlett's Women by Taylor 50
    and Shamley Productions 281, 282, 286–7
    travels in Hitchcock's multiverse 304
    The Women Who Knew Too Much by Modleski 45, 51, 64–5, 83, 119, 145–6
    see also individual feminist scholars & publications…
The Feminist Mystique (Friedan) 132–3
femmes fatales 131
    see also heroines
Fernández Cuenca, Carlos 384
Ferpect Crime (2004) 389
fetishism 124, 126n5, 358–9
    see also voyeurism
The Fighting Generation (1944) 271–2
Film Art journal 376, 379, 381, 382n1
"film artist" 144, 290, 300, 356, 359
Film Bulletin 200
Film Comment 65, 153–4, 258–9
Film Culture journal 63, 143, 376
Film Daily journal 45–6, 56–9, 143, 199
film festivals
    "Around the World" 353
    Berlin Film Festival 149
    Cannes Film Festival 7–8, 128, 285, 322, 359, 385
    International Festival of Religious Cinema 384
    Moscow Film Festival 350, 353
    Odessa Film Festival 22–3
    San Sebastián Festival 385, 391
    Venice Film Festival 344, 385
Film Quarterly journal 143, 257
Film Society of Lincoln Center 202
Film Space 1895 356–8
The Film Till Now (Rotha) 17–18, 95, 426n6
Film Weekly magazine 93
Filmcritica 346
Filmkritik 7, 329–36
The Films of Alfred Hitchcock (Humphries) 380
The Films of Alfred Hitchcock (Sterritt) 83
Financial Times 185, 237, 253, 264
El Financiero 399–400
Find the Director, and Other Hitchcock Games (Leitch) 204
Fink, Guido 345
Finler, Joel W. 107–8

The First True Hitchcock (Miller) 19
Five Lesbian Brothers 49–50
Fleming, Ian 261n1
    see also James Bond films
The Flintstones (1961) 75
Focus on Hitchcock (LaValley) 145, 173
"The Foghorn" (1958) 307–10, 314
Fontaine, Joan 47–52, 55
food and sexuality 248–9
For Whom the Bell Tolls (1943) 58
Ford Startime (1959–1961) 272, 279, 287n1
"Foreign Cinema Series" (China Film Press, 1980) 376
Foreign Correspondent (1940) 8, 47, 55–6, 84, 232–3, 423–4
    in Mexico 396, 398
    and Shamley Productions 282
    USSR and post-Soviet Russia 351
"Four O'Clock" 272–3, 276, 287n2
Fox Searchlight 298–9, 359
Framing Hitchcock: Selected Essays from the Hitchcock Annual (Gottlieb & Brookhouse) 83
Francione, Fabio 343, 349n1
Franco, Francisco 384–8
Franks, Robert 158
Free Cinema documentary movement of the 1950s 61–2
French Institute of Latin America (IFAL) 403
French New Wave 62, 329, 356, 367
    see also Cahiers du cinéma
French Nouvelle Vague 357
French, Philip 40, 240n1, 264, 426, 427n9
French reception 298
    The Trouble with Harry 187–8
    see also L'Écran français
Frenchman's Creek 51
Frenzy: the Last Masterpiece (Foery) 242
Frenzy (1972) 4–5, 7, 242–51, 252, 265
    in Germany 330–1
    in Mexico 397
    and Shamley Productions 283, 285
    in South Korea 357, 363n2
    USSR and post-Soviet Russia 352–3
Freud, Sigmund 36, 40, 48, 50, 130–1, 204–6
Friday the 13th (1980) 264
"From the Realm of the Dead" (*Aus dem Reich der Toten*) 340
From Russia with Love (1963) 261n1
The Front Page (1931) 21
Fruttero, Carlo 348
Fujiki, Hideaki 365
Fundación Telefónica 403
Furtivos 386–7

Gaiety Theatre 16
Gainsborough Pictures 13–15, 19, 37–9, 169–71, 395, 426n1
Galán, Laura 391–2
Gallafent, Ed 177, 191–2
García, López 391
Gaslight (1944) 58
Gaumont-British Picture Corporation 33, 81, 94–6, 99, 101, 262–3
    audiences in Mexico 395
    Hitchcock in Argentina 409
    and wartime Britain 424, 426n1
"gay" 237–8
gay-affirming 116
    see also queer-affirming
Gehring, Wes 199, 202–3
Gentleman's Agreement (1947) 217
George VI 26
Germany 302n9, 329–41
    bildungsroman 85
    Farocki's *Betrayed* (1985) 334–40
    Filmkritik 7, 329–36
    performativity 338–40
    "Vertauschte Frauen" ("Mistakenly Interchanged Women") by Farocki 333–4
    Weimar era 37–8, 330–1
    see also Nazism
Germany, Pale Mother (1980) 331
Gerow, Aaron 372
Get Smart (1969) 75
Giallo Club 347
giallo writers 343–4, 348
Giant (1956) 211
Gielgud, John 39
Gillett, John 254
Gilliat, Sidney 34–40, 41n6
The Girl (2012) 129
glasnost 352–3
Glen or Glenda (1953) 125
globalization 298–301, 319–413
    Argentina 406–13
    Communist China 374–83
    L'Écran français 319–28
    Hitchcock and Italian film criticism 342–9
    Japan 364–73
    Mexico 394–405
    New German Cinema 329–41
    South Korea 354–63
    Spain 384–93
    USSR and post-Soviet Russia 350–3
Gloucester Citizen 160
Gnostic-Puritanism 189–90

Godard, Jean-Luc
    and auteurism 81–2
    Berlin School and "slow" art cinema 329
    Filmkritik and the film *Vertigo* 331
    The Man Who Knew Too Much 262–3
    reception in France 319
    The Wrong Man 212, 217, 219
    Yeonggam in South Korea 355–6
The Godfather (1972) 152
Goldberg, Jonathan 230, 238, 240n6
Goldfinger (1964) 83–4
Goldstein, Bruce 214
Gone with the Wind (1939) 2, 43–7, 50, 356, 417, 426n3
Gosfilmofond film archive 350–2
Gottlieb, Sidney 3–4, 83, 151, 182–97
Gounod, Charles 16, 295
Goya nominations 388, 391
the Graduate (1967) 256–7
La Gran Vía, 1974–1981 (García) 391
"Grandes cineastas" (Universidad de Guadalajara) 401
Gray, James 152–5
graylisting 283
Grazzini, Giovanni 346–8
The Great Dictator (1940) 232–3, 423
Greene, Graham 97–8, 100, 173
Greven, David
    The Birds 113
    The Man Who Knew Too Much 108
    North by Northwest 87–8
    queer theory, *Psycho* 115–27
    Rear Window 72
    Rope 165
    Vertigo and *Marnie* 154, 156n3
Grierson on Documentary (1946) 16–17
Grierson, John 16–17, 94, 97, 101
Griffith, Richard 18, 184–5
The Guardian
    and *Frenzy* 242, 249n1
    and *The Lodger* 16
    and *The Man Who Knew Too Much* 264, 267
    and *North by Northwest* 80
    and Park Chan-wook 360
    preserving/promoting Hitchcock's TV persona 301n3
    and *Sabotage* 104n1
    and *Topaz* 253
    and *Vertigo* and *Marnie* 151
    and *The Wrong Man* 219
Guarini, Ruggero 347–8
Guernsey, Otis 235–6
Gunning, Tom 193–4
Gunz, Joan 303–16
Gyeong-uk, Kim 361

Ha Kil-jong 356
Haines, Randa 285–6
Halberstam, Jack 133–4
Halbout, Grégoire 207
Hamilton, Patrick 158–9
Hamlet (Shakespeare) 36–7, 85, 87, 190
Han, Byung-Chul 359
The Handmaiden (*Agassi*, 2016) 358–9
Hangzhous Daily 378
The Happiest Days of Your Life (1950) 38–9
Hark, Ina Rae 107, 204–5
Harrison, Joan 282–4, 287n5–7, 304, 315
    The Lady Vanishes 39
    Rebecca 44–8, 51–2
    and television 5
    Topaz 258
Harrison's Report 59, 199–200, 233, 357
"Harry Potter" series 419–20
Hartung, P.T. 69, 216
Hasumi Shigehiko 371–2
Hay, Ian 32, 34, 97–8, 103–4
Haynes, Todd 214–15
HBO 389
The Headless Woman (2008) 410
Heart of Darkness (Conrad) 94, 409
Hedren, Tippi 39, 138n3
    The Birds 128–33, 136–8
    Marnie 31, 137–8, 149, 154–5
    reception in South Korea 358
    sexual abuse allegations 39, 128–33, 136–8, 149, 154–5
hegemony 109, 325
Heiichi, Sugiyama 365
Henley Telegraph 304
Hepworth, John 122, 126n2
Heraldo del cinematográfico (*Cinematic Herald*, 1931–1988) 407–10
heroines
    39 Steps 32
    The Birds 132
    Blackmail 415
    in Japan 366
    karmic cycles 315
    The Lady Vanishes 32, 34, 36
    The Man Who Knew Too Much 416
    Marnie 154
    Notorious 59–60
    Psycho 122
    Rear Window 31
    Rebecca 47–52, 417
    Sabotage 99
    Under Capricorn 176

Hessler, Gordon 282
"Hicchicokku shi ga honshi no tame ni netsuen shita surira kihon kozu" 372n1
Hidden Hitchcock (Miller) 165
high and low culture 201, 409
Hindle Wakes (Elvey) 16
Hinduism 315
Hirsch, Foster 214, 216, 217
Historia documental del cine mexicano 401
The History of Fear (2014) 411
History of International Cinema (1970) 352
Hitch: the Life and Times of Alfred Hitchcock (Taylor) 201, 380
Hitch: The Life and Work of Alfred Hitchcock (Taylor) 201, 380
Hitchcock: il maestro negato 349n1
Hitchcock: más allá del suspenso (Hitchcock: Beyond Suspense) exhibition 403
Hitchcock: The Murderous Gaze (Rothman) 18, 202
"Hitchcock: Nine Unknown Films" (2014) 353
"Hitchcock: Nine Unknown Films" (BFI) 353
"Hitchcock: Problems of Interpretation" (Nichols) 377
Hitchcock: The Definitive Study of Alfred Hitchcock (Truffaut) 377
Hitchcock: The First Forty-Four Films (Chabrol & Rohmer) 22, 188, 201, 263
Hitchcock: The Murderous Gaze (Rothman) 18, 202
Hitchcock (2012) 298–9
Hitchcock à la Carte (Olsson) 5
Hitchcock and Adaptation (Osteen) 93
Hitchcock aka (*Hitchcock/Truffaut*) 63, 149–50, 214–15, 323, 401–2
Hitchcock, Alma Reville 14, 33, 39, 41n4, 44–5
    and Joan Harrison 304
    maritime marriage proposal 206
    Mycroft and *Downhill* 170
    reception in Japan 370–1
    Sabotage 103–4
    vacation in Saint Moritz and *Mr. & Mrs. Smith* 201
    Vertigo and *Marnie* 149
Hitchcock Annual 83–4, 173, 180–1, 426
Hitchcock at the Source: The Auteur as Adapter (Boyd & Palmer) 83, 93
Hitchcock and the Censors (Billheimer) 207–8
Hitchcock Centennial Conference 286, 290–1, 300
Hitchcock in Context (Duckett) 83
"Hitchcock e la critica italiana" (Francione) 343, 349n1
Hitchcock Family Trust & Estate 141, 152, 233, 289–93, 294, 297–8, 300n4, 302n9
Hitchcock and Humor (Gehring) 247
"Hitchcock and Humor" (Naremore) 247
Hitchcock Magazine 367

Hitchcock, Patricia (O'Connell) 290–2, 301n3
The Hitchcock Romance (Brill) 18, 84, 87–8, 190, 203
"Hitchcock se confie" 322–4
"Hitchcock se confie" (Tacchella) 322–5
"Hitchcock se fonie" 322–4
Hitchcock and the Spy Film (Chapman) 84
Hitchcock and Suspense (Wang) 380–1
Hitchcock (Truffaut) 2, 6
Hitchcock and the Twentieth Century (Orr) 83
"Hitchcockian Bird-Event" 135
Hitchcock's Appetites (McKittrick) 206
Hitchcock's British Films (Yacowar) 18, 104
Hitchcock's Cryptonomies (Cohen) 87
Hitchcock's Films Revisited (Wood) 45, 63, 66, 107, 112–13
    and *Frenzy* 245
    Hitchcock in Mexico 401
    Hitchcock in South Korea 356
    Mr. & Mrs. Smith 201
    Pyscho and queer theory 121
    and *Rope* 160–1
    and *Topaz* 252
    The Trouble with Harry 189
    and *Vertigo* and *Marnie* 145
    and *The Wrong Man* 213
"Hitchcock's Homophobia" (Hepworth) 122, 126n2
"Hitchcock's Imagery and Art" (Yacowar) 208n3
"Hitchcock's Modernism" (Trotter) 18
Hitchcock's Motifs (Walker) 274
HMV 30
Hochhäusler, Christoph 218
Hollywood Costume exhibition at the Victoria & Albert Museum (2012) 129
The Hollywood Reporter
    and *Mr. and Mrs. Smith* 200
    and *North by Northwest* 79
    preserving/promoting Hitchcock's TV persona 293, 301n5
    and *Strangers on a Train* 230, 235
    and *The Trouble with Harry* 183
    and *The Wrong Man* 211, 216
    and *Topaz* 254
    and *Vertigo* and *Marnie* 143, 149–50
Hollywood Screwball Comedy: 1934–1945: Sex, Love, and Democratic Ideals (Halbout) 207
Hollywood's Embassies (Melnick) 406
Home Drama 381
homophobia 49–50, 108, 118, 122–5, 126n2, 160–5
homosexuality 87–8, 160–1, 237–8, 240n6
    "Anal *Rope*" by Miller 122, 126n3, 161, 165
    homoeroticism 238
    lesbianism 49–50

and Park Chan-wook 358–9
"*Rear Window*'s Glasshole" by Edelman 72, 122, 126n3
travels in Hitchcock's multiverse 305–9
see also queer theory
Hongkong Telegraph 200
Horowitz, Margaret 131
horror genre 210, 243–7, 276, 351, 391–3
slasher-horror films 115–16, 119–20
see also individual horror films…
Horsbrugh, Florence 33–4
"The Horseplayer" (1961) 272–3
Hosogoe Rintaro 370–1
"How Hitchcock Lampoons Modern Art in *The Trouble with Harry*" (Calabrese) 193
"How Queer Is My *Psycho*?" (Doty) 122
Hulu 286
Huston, Penelope 184–5
Hwangsang ("Fantasy", or *Vertigo*) 357–63
Hypatia 391

I Confess (1953) 188, 354–63, 395–7, 400, 408
I Lost My Girlish Laughter comic novel (1938) 46
"I Saw the Whole Thing" 272, 287n2
icebox conversations 315
idealism 48, 191, 204, 348, 359–62, 378, 398
ideological criticism 2–3, 65–6, 68, 70–2, 371–2
"Ideology, Genre, Auteur" (Wood) 65–6
IFAL film society 403
Iijima Tadashi 365–8
Illyuzion theater 351
I'm a Cyborg, but That's Okay (*Ssaibogeujiman gwaebchana*, 2006) 358–9
immigration 358–9
see also émigré(s)
"imprisonment of the formula" 344–5
"In Northcliffe Jail: Iris Barry, Film Journalist" (Miller) 20n2
In a Northwesterly Direction 84–5
see also North by Northwest
In Praise of Shadows (*Inei raisan*, 1933–1934) 366
incarceration in film 358–9
"Incident on a Corner" 272–4, 276, 287n1
The Independent 80–1, 151, 267
Independent Film Journal 255
Independent on Sunday 237
Indiana Jones 264, 419–20
Indiscretion of an American Wife (1954) 354
"The Inscription of Femininity as Absence" (Doane) 51
inter- and /or ex-change of women in New German Cinema 329–41

International Festival of Religious Cinema, Valladolid (1959) 384
International Film (*Gukje Yeonghwa*) 354–5, 357
Internet Movie Database 271
Interview Magazine 245
Intimate Violence: Hitchcock, Sex, and Queer theory (Greven) 122, 165
"Into Thin Air" (1955) 283, 284
An Introduction to Western Film History (Shao) 376
The Irish Independent 16
Irving G. Thalberg Award 256
Isaiah 53:7 310
Iskusstvo kino (*The Art of Film*) journal 352
Isralowitz, Jason P. 3–4, 210–26
It Happened One Night (1934) 35
Italian Neo-Realism 347–8, 356–7
Italy 342–9
Cahiers du cinéma 342–4
Hitchcock's public image 347–8
preserving/promoting Hitchcock's TV persona 298
Rear Window, *Vertigo*, *Psycho*, *The Birds* 344–7
It's A Wonderful Life (1946) 65
Ivor Novello: Screen Idol (2003) 18

Jacovich, Mark 276
Jamaica Inn (1938) 32, 46–7, 93, 201, 282, 327n3, 351, 395, 408
in Argentina 408
in Mexico 395
and Shamley Productions 282
James Bond films 83–4, 88, 252–3, 261n1
James, Nick 151, 267
Jancovich, Mark 280–1
Jane Eyre (Brontë) 49, 51
Japan 8, 364–73
1930s–1945 364–7
1960s–present 369–72
"le cas Hitchcock", 1946–1950s 367–9
preserving/promoting Hitchcock's TV persona 298
Jeanne Dielman 23 quai du Commerce, 1080 Bruxelles (1975) 152
La Jetée (1962) 357–8
Jewish undertones 49
Jinichi, Uekusa 368
Joint Security Area (*Gongdonggyeongbiguyeok*, 2000) 358–9
Jones, Kent 214–15
Jordan, Neil 6–7
Judeo-Christian optimism 189–90
Julieta (2016) 388
Jun'ichiro, Tanizaki 366
Jurassic Park (1993) 419–20

Kael, Pauline 215, 239–41, 255–7
Kaleidoscope (1964–1967) 290, 293
Kann, Red 59
Kantoku Ozu Yasujiro (*Director Ozu Yasujiro*) by Hasumi 371–2
Kapsis, Robert E. 1–9, 249n2, 382n5
   Alfred Hitchcock Hour 279
   and Hitchcock's public image 347
   The Man Who Knew Too Much 106–8, 262–8
   narrative and narrational tactics 69
   North by Northwest 83
   preserving Hitchcock's legacy 289–302
   reception in Communist China 378
   Strangers on a Train 229–41
   Topaz 256–7
   Vertigo and *Marnie* 140–57, 419–20
   and women in television 283, 285
   The Wrong Man 210–26
   Yeonggam in South Korea 356
Kapterev, Sergei 7, 350–3
Kardish, Larry 291–2
karmic cycles 315
Kauffman, Stanley 40
KBS *see* Korean Broadcasting System
Keane, Marian 85, 88
"Keep Her in Her Place" award 246
Keeper of Fiction Film (BFI) 22
Kehr, Dave 66, 150, 189, 202
Kelly, Grace 31, 71, 128, 245
   reception in Argentina 408
   reception in Mexico 399
   reception in South Korea 358
Kenny, Glenn 214, 218
Kensington News and West London Times 230, 233
Kercher, Dona M. 6–7
   reception in Argentina 406–13
   reception in Mexico 8, 394, 395, 398–401, 404
   reception in Spain 384–93
Kimi (2022) 75
Kind Hearts and Coronets (1949) 185
Kinema Junpo 369
Kinematograph Weekly 94, 170, 232–3
The King and I (1956) 356
Kinsey, Alfred 124, 126n5
Kiriakou, Olympia 206–7
Kitamura, Hiroshi 368–9
Kitty (1929) 30
Knight, Arthur 69
Korean Broadcasting System (KBS) 356
Korean War (1950–1953) 312, 354, 374
Krohn, Bill 319–20
Kyunghyang Sinmun 355–7

La Movida, new aesthetic movement 386–8
Lacan 130
   Lacanization 131
   Lacanian 133, 204
The Lady Vanishes (1938) 2, 31–42, 84, 93, 230, 233
   in Argentina 408
   and auteurism 62
   and Communist China 375
   in Communist China 376–7
   in Japan 370–1
   in Mexico 395
   music in Hitchcock's films 415
   and Shamley Productions 283
   in South Korea 355, 357
   in Spain 388
   USSR and post-Soviet Russia 350–1
Lady Vengeance (*Chinjeolhan Geumja-ssi*, 2005) 358–9
The Ladykillers (1955) 185
"Lamb to the Slaughter" (1958) 273, 275–6, 294, 307, 310–11, 312, 387
Lane, Christina 5, 46–7, 279–88, 304, 306
Lang, Fritz 95–6, 257, 330–1, 338–9
Lang, Kurt & Gladys Engel 148, 290
The Last Circus (2010) 389
Launder, Frank 34–40
Launder and Gilliat 34–6, 40
Laura (1944) 65
Leave It to Beaver (1957) 113
Leff, Leonard J. 45, 84–5
Legion of Honor Museum 336
Leitch, Thomas 303–4
   North by Northwest 3, 78–9
   television work 5, 271–81
   The Trouble with Harry 190–2
   Vertigo and *Marnie* 154
Lejeune, C. A.
   Downhill 171
   The Lodger 16–17
   The Man Who Knew Too Much 262–3, 266
   North by Northwest 80
   Sabotage 96, 99–100
   Shadow of a Doubt 56
   Strangers on a Train 233
   The Trouble with Harry 185
Leominster Picture News 98–9
Leopold, Nathan 158
"Les Choses sérieuses" (Chabrol) 69
lesbian readings 49–50
lesbianism 49–50
Lessard, Burno 135–6
liberalism 368–9

Life Achievement Award 149
Life after Death: Preserving, Protecting, and Promoting the Legacy of Alfred Hitchcock (Kapsis) 289–302
Life magazine 68, 211, 242
Lifeboat (1944) 8, 58, 233, 322
    in Argentina 409
    in Mexico 396
    in Spain 384
"Light, Looks, and *The Lodger*" (Pomerance) 18
"The Light Side of Genius" (Polan) 204
Lightning, Robert 191–2, 314
Lincoln Center 202, 240n3
"liquefied library" 87
The Listener 265–6
The Little Foxes (1941) 66n2
Liverpool Daily Post 232
Livingston, Jay 110
Lizzani, Carlo 343
Lloyd, Norman 282
Lockwood, Margaret 2, 34–40, 41n7
The Lodger (1926) 1, 13–20, 27–8, 30, 39, 169–70, 172, 233
    in Argentina 406–7, 413n1
    in Germany 330
    in South Korea 357
    USSR and post-Soviet Russia 351
"The Lodger and Hitchcock's Aesthetic" (2001–2002) 18
Loeb, Richard 158
London 102, 330
    and the German Blitz 230–1, 232
    Los Misterios de Londres 406–7, 413n1
London Observer 140
London's Evening News 144
"The Lonely Hours" (1965) 283
A Long Hard Look at Psycho (2002) 121
Lord Jim (Conrad) 94
Los Angeles Examiner 140–1
Los Angeles Times 142, 235
    and Park Chan-wook 360
Love Lies 26, 415
Love Me Tonight (1932) 415
Lowdness, Marie Belloc 39
Lucentini, Franco 348
Lucky Star (Lockwood) 39–40
Lunatics and Lovers (Sennett) 202
Lupino, Ida 283–4, 314–15
Lurie, Susan 131

"Macabre Merriment" column 273
Macarthur, Douglas 368–9
McCarten, John 68–9, 142–3, 156n2, 184, 235–6, 239

McCarthyism 283
McCombe, John P. 131
Mad Men (2007) 282
The Mad Miss Manton (1937) 35
Maedchen in Uniform (1931) 49
The Magnificent Ambersons (1942) 56
Majdalany, Fred 185–6
male gaze 31, 40, 64–5, 107, 122, 137–8
male spectators 34, 71–2, 145
"Man from the South" (1960) 272–3
The Man Who Knew Too Much (1956) 3, 5, 17–18, 32, 81, 93, 140, 188, 211, 260
    and American culture 106–14
    in Argentina 408–9
    and auteurism 62
    British critical reception 97–9
    following Hitchcock's death, 1980 148–9
    and Graham Greene 97–8
    Hitchcock and Italian film criticism 343
    in Japan 364–7
    in Mexico 396, 399
    "missing" or "lost" Hitchcocks 188, 292
    music in Hitchcock's films 414, 416
    preserving/promoting Hitchcock's TV persona 292
    in South Korea 355, 357, 363n2
    in Spain 384
    two versions and British/USA criticism 262–8
Manchester Evening Chronicle 16
Manchester Evening News 232
Manchester Guardian 15–17, 96–7, 171, 185, 212
manhood, masculinity 71–2, 204–6
    see also queer theory; sexuality
Manichean, Manicheism 180, 259–60
Mann ist Mann (Brecht) 339–40
Mannock, P. L. 60, 97, 101
The Manxman (1929) 17–18, 30
"many lives" theory 315
Marble Arch Pavillion 14–15
Margaret Herrick Library 7, 240n3
Markiewicz, Constance 41n5
Marnie (1964) 3, 31, 39, 137–8, 140–57, 242–4
    and academic film criticism, 1970s and 80s 144–8
    and auteurism 63
    following Hitchcock's death, 1980 148–55
    #MeToo movement, assault allegations 128
    in Mexico 395, 397
    and queer theory 122
    reactions during its initial run, 1964 143–4
    in South Korea 355, 363n2
Marshland (2014) 391
Martel, Lucrecia 410
Marvel Comics Multiverse 304

Marxism, Karl Marx 97–8, 107, 146, 333–5, 348, 352
    Cinema Nuovo 343, 344, 345
Mary (Queen) 26
Mary Rose: The Island that Likes to Be Visited (Barrie) 186, 290, 293, 308–9
Mary Rose (circa 1964) 290, 293
masculinization of film authorship 41n7
Maslin, Janet 248, 285
Mason, Carol 72
"Master of Suspense: Hitchcock" (*Popular Cinema*) 377
"master/magician of suspense" 31, 80, 88, 233, 242, 257, 294–5
    in Argentina 408–10
    in Communist China 377
    in Mexico 399, 402, 405n5, 408–10
    in USSR and post-Soviet Russia 351
maternal feminine 306
"mature period" 63
    see also *The Birds*; *Marnie*; *North by Northwest*; *Psycho*; *Rear Window*; *Strangers on a Train*; *Torn Curtain*
Maugham, W. Somerset 93, 98
May, Derwint 69
MCA *see* Music Corporation of America
Melnick, Ross 406
melodramas 84, 175–81, 199–200, 408
Memorias de la Cineteca Nacional, 1974–2007 403
Memories of Murder (*Salinui chuoek*, 2003) 360
mental illness 217, 358–9
Il Messaggero 346, 347–8
metafiction 73–5, 276
metaphor *see* symbolism
#MeToo movement 128–39
    see also abuse allegations
Metro Goldwyn-Mayer 79, 398
Metropolis (1927) 330
MeTV 286
Mexico 8, 394–405
    celebrity culture 398–400
    early audiences 395–7
    film criticism 400–2
    film societies and the Cineteca Nacional 394–5, 401, 403
    Mexico City 8, 394–9, 404n1
Meyerowitz, Joanne 124, 126n5
MGM 46, 84–5, 232–3, 424
Michot, Julie 195
The Middlesex Independent 233
Midnight Cowboy (1969) 256–7
A Midsummer Night's Dream (Shakespeare) 190–1
militarism 368

Miller, D. A. 122
Miller, Henry 240
Miller, Hildy 132
Miller, Toby 6, 32
Millington 85
Millions Like Us (1943) 38–9
Miranda, Raúl 394–5, 397, 398, 401–3
mise-en-scène 47, 50, 70, 150–1, 266, 367, 388–9
misogyny 31–42, 72, 118, 133, 242, 245–7, 314
    see also abuse allegations
"Miss Up to Date" 26, 415
"missing" or "lost" Hitchcocks 188, 292
Los Misterios de Londres (*Mysteries of London*) 406–7, 413n1
model of scenario construction 63
Modern Screen 199
modernism 4, 69–75, 180, 204–6, 356–7, 415
    "Hitchcock's Modernism" by Trotter 18
    Joseph Conrad 93–4, 96–103, 409
    Pier Paolo Pasolini 356
    sapphic, lesbianism 49
Modleski, Tanya 4–5
    and auteurism 64–5
    Frenzy 242–51
    ideological criticism, *Rear Window* 72
    The Man Who Knew Too Much 107–8
    music in Hitchcock's films, *Blackmail* 415
    North by Northwest 83
    queer theory, *Psycho* 119, 122
    Rebecca 45, 48, 51
    Vertigo and *Marnie* 145–6, 154
Molière Players 271–2
momisms *see* Oedipus/Oedipal complex
Mona Lisa (1986) 70
Mondal, Subarna 406
Le Monde 361
Money Heist 389
monographs 380–1
Monsieur Verdoux (1947) 185
Montagu, Ivor 13, 18, 23
Monthly Film Bulletin 101
Monthly Film Bulletin (BFI) 101
monumental location sequences 388–9
The Moon Is… the Sun's Dream (*Dareun… haega kkuneun kkum*, 1992) 358
Morandini, Morando 343, 345
Morin, Edgar 398
"The Morning of the Bride" (1959) 307, 312–13
Morris, Christopher D. 87
Motion Picture Daily 58
Motion Picture Exhibitor 252, 254–5
Motion Picture Herald 56–7, 59, 427n7

Motion Picture Magazine 199–200
Motion Picture Reviews 200
Mount Rushmore 78, 80–5, 389
The Mountain Eagle 169
Movie magazine 160, 263
Movie Review 376
Mr. & Mrs. Smith (1941) 3–4, 55, 198–209
    academic film criticism 198, 201–8
    contemporaneous criticism 200–1
    from 1950 onward 200–1
    in Mexico 396, 398
"Mr. Blanchard's Secret" (1956) 73, 75, 273
"Mrs. Bixby and the Colonel's Coat" (1960) 272–3
Mrs. Miniver (1942) 66n2
De mujer a mujer (Woman to Woman, 1927) 384
Mullholland (1999) 357–8
Multimedia Hitchcock 290–1
multivalency 195
Mulvey, Laura
    and auteurism 63–5
    Hitchcock scholarship 101
    ideological criticism, *Rear Window* 71–2
    male gaze 136–7
    The Man Who Knew Too Much 107
    queer theory, *Psycho* 122
    "to-be-looked-at-ness" 48
    "Visual Pleasure and Narrative Cinema" 51, 145
Munich Agreement (September 30, 1938) 35
Museum of Modern Art (MoMA) 18, 210, 290–2
Museum of Transgender History & Art (MOTHA) 122, 123
music 50, 414–20
    music in Hitchcock's films 192–3
Music Corporation of America (MCA) 271, 281–2
    see also Television Limited
Music To Be Murdered By (2020) 290, 294–8
Must We Kill the Thing We Love (Rothman) 202
Mutant Action (1993) 388
My Fair Lady (1964) 356
Mycroft, Walter 14, 17, 170–1, 173
mythologizing 86, 347–8

Nachträglichkeit 332
El Nacional newspaper 399–401, 404n3, 405n5
Naishtat, Benjamín 410–12
Naremore, James 70, 85, 88, 210, 247
narrative and narrational tactics 68–71
"Narrative Space" (Heath) 372n2
The Nation 107, 142–3, 216, 235–6
National Organization for Women 246
National Registry of Exonerations 217
nationalism 21, 368
    see also globalization; ultranationalism

"Naughts and Crosses" (Bullock) 207–8
Nazism 37, 332, 351, 417, 424
    anti-Nazi policy 232, 351
    and *L'Écran français* 321, 326
    London Blitz 230–1, 232
    and *Notorious* 58–60
    and *Strangers on a Train* 232–3
NBC Network 282, 285, 292
Neilsen Company 271
neorealism 345, 347–8, 356–7, 402
Neumeyer, David 192
"Never to Be 36 Years Old: *Rebecca* as Female Oedipal Drama" (Modleski) 51
new aesthetic movement 386–8
The New Alfred Hitchcock Presents 285–6, 287n8
New American Cinema 357
"The New Border War? An Intergenerational Exchange on Bad Trans Horror Objects" 122
New Films 376–7
New German Cinema 7, 329–41
New Hollywood 256–7
New Lives for Old (1925) 407
"new" Mexican cinema 401–2
New Statesmen 56, 240n5, 266
New Wave critics 367
New York Herald Tribune 160, 183, 199, 216, 235–6, 273
New York Magazine 265
New York Native 188–9
New York Public Library of the Performing Arts at Lincoln Center 240n3
New York Times
    and *Frenzy* 244, 246
    Hitchcock in South Korea 360
    and *The Man Who Knew Too Much* 107, 113
    and *Mr. & Mrs. Smith* 199–200, 202
    music in Hitchcock's films 414, 419–20
    and *North by Northwest* 79
    and *Notorious* 59
    and Park Chan-wook 360
    preserving/promoting Hitchcock's TV persona 292–3, 298
    and *Rear Window* 68–9
    and *Rebecca* 43
    and *Rope* 160
    and *Shadow of a Doubt* 57
    and Shamley Productions 281, 283, 286
    and *Strangers on a Train* 229, 235–7, 239
    and *Topaz* 252, 256
    and *The Trouble with Harry* 183
    and *Vertigo* and *Marnie* 140–4
    and *The Wrong Man* 211–12, 216–17, 219

New Yorker 142–3
    and *Frenzy* 242
    and *The Man Who Knew Too Much* 107, 262
    music in Hitchcock's films 420
    and *North by Northwest* 79
    and *Rear Window* 68–9
    and *Strangers on a Train* 235–6, 239
    and *Topaz* 256–7
    and *The Trouble with Harry* 184
    and *Vertigo* and *Marnie* 142, 154–5, 156n2
    and *The Wrong Man* 212, 214
New York-World Telegram 199, 423
Newcastle Evening Chronicle 97, 233
Newman, Kim 134–5
News Chronicle 18, 61, 230, 263, 424–5
Newsday 235
Newsweek 68, 142–3, 211, 235, 242, 245, 249n2, 256
Nichols, Bill 377
Nick at Nite 286
Nietzsche, Friedrich 158, 208n3, 326
Night of the Living Dead (1968) 256–7
Night Train to Munich (1940) 38–9
Nightmail (1936) 29
"Nightmare in 4-D" 282
Nightmare Movies (Newman) 134–5
nihilism 134, 190
Nine Queens (2000) 410–11
Nipponese Society for Cinematographers 366, 369–70
Nobody's Girl Friday: The Women Who Ran Hollywood (Smythe) 45–6
Nobuhiko, Kobayashi 367–70
noir cinema
    and auteurism 63–5
    in Germany 329–32, 336–8
    Notorious 58, 63–5
    and Shamley Productions 282
    Strangers on a Train 237
    The Wrong Man 216
Noir et Blanc 138n1
North by Northwest (1959) 3, 31, 78–89, 144, 192–3, 201, 216, 264
    and auteurism 63
    and Communist China 375, 378–9
    Hitchcock's television work 274–5
    Hitchcock's "walk-ons" 5–6, 292, 301n2
    in Mexico 397
    in South Korea 354–5, 358, 362–3
    in Spain 385, 389
    USSR and post-Soviet Russia 353
Northern Whig 100
Nostromo (Conrad) 94

"Notes on the Auteur Theory" (Sarris) 63, 95
Notorious (1946) 31, 51, 54–67, 84, 142, 230, 418
    in Argentina 408
    and auteurism 62, 63–5
    in Communist China 375
    critical reception 58–61
    and *L'Écran français* 322
    Hitchcock and Italian film criticism 343
    in Mexico 395–7
    in South Korea 355
    in Spain 387
Nouvelle Vague 357
Novedades newspaper 399
Novello, Ivor 16, 18–19, 169–71, 406–7
Nuevo Cine (1961–1962) 401–2, 403

obscenity laws 49
The Observer
    Hitchcock and wartime Britain 426, 427n9
    Hitchcock's television work 276
    and *The Lodger* 13, 15
    and *The Man Who Knew Too Much* 262–4
    and *North by Northwest* 80
    and *Rear Window* 69
    and *Sabotage* 99
    and *Shadow of a Doubt* 56
    and *Strangers on a Train* 237, 240n1, 240n5
    and *Topaz* 253
    and *The Trouble with Harry* 185
    and *The Wrong Man* 212
Obsession (1976) 149–50, 357–8
Ocean Blue Entertainment 301n5
O'Connell, Patricia Hitchcock 290–2, 301n3
Oedipus/Oedipal complex 36, 48, 51, 72, 87
    The Birds 128–34
    The Man Who Knew Too Much 108
    Mr. & Mrs. Smith 204–6
    Vertigo and *Marnie* 146
    see also Psycho
Ogawara, Aya 367
Old Vic company 39
Oldboy (2003) 358–9
Olsson, Jan 5, 276
Olsson, Mats Helge 6–7
On Her Majesty's Secret Service (1969) 258
"On the History and Present of American Film Directors" (Shao) 376
"On Hitchcock's Art of Direction and Techniques" (*New Films*) 376
On the Waterfront (1954) 217
Ophuls, Max 51
Orientalism (Said) 109

Original Six 288n9
The Orphanage (2007) 391
Orwell, George 173–4, 174n1, 240n1, 426
Oscars 2, 43–4, 47, 49, 54–6, 58, 66n2
    Guillermo del Toro 210
    and Sarris' *The American Cinema* 256
    The Sea Inside (2004) 391
    see also Goya nominations
Osteen, Mark 93, 103
The Others (2001) 391
Où en êtes-vous, Christian Petzold? 214–15, 218
Our Town (Wilder) 55–6, 63, 66
Out in Culture: Gay, Lesbian and Queer Essays on Popular Culture 126n2
"The Outer Circle: Hitchcock on Television" (Leitch) 280–1
overlapping dialogue 56, 286
The Oxford Murders (2008) 389
Oxford-educated critics 40n2, 200

Pact of Steel (May 22, 1939) 35
Paglia, Camille 131–5, 138n2
Palace of the Legion of Honor, San Francisco 309
Palmer, R. Barton 73–5, 83, 93
Parade magazine 80–1
The Paradine Case (1947) 62, 158, 233, 237
    in Argentina 408
    L'Écran français 325–6
    in Mexico 395–8
    in South Korea 355
Parallax View (1974) 260
Paramount 3, 62, 74, 83, 109, 140–1, 171
    Hitchcock in Argentina 407
    Hitchcock in South Korea 355
    Mexican celebrity culture 398
    music in Hitchcock's films 420n1
    situating Shamley Productions 281
    see also Technicolor
Paramount Showmanship Manual (1955) 182
Paramount World 184
Park Chan-wook 7–8, 357–63
Park So-hyeon 362–3
Park Yu-Hui 354
parody 68, 73–5
    see also satire
Pasolini, Pier Paolo 356
patriarchy 32, 36, 40, 64–5, 72
    The Birds 131–2, 137–8
    Frenzy 246, 248–9
    The Man Who Knew Too Much 106–8
    Mr. & Mrs. Smith 204
    Pyscho and queer theory 117, 119, 122
    Rear Window 72
    The Trouble with Harry 191
    Under Capricorn 177, 180
    Vertigo and *Marnie* 155
patriotism 230–3
Patton (1970) 258
PCA *see* Production Code of America
Pearson, Roberta 73
La Película magazine/journal 406–7
Peña, Isabel 391
People magazine 253–4, 364–5
People's Republic of China (PRC) 374–83
Pepi, Luci, Born (1980) 387
Pereda, Carlota 391–3
perestroika 352–3
"perfect ambivalency" 192–3
"The Perfect Crime" (1957) 272–3, 275–6
Perkins, V. F. 160–1
Perón, Isabel 412
Perucho, Antonio 400, 403–4
Peterborough Standard 104n1
Petzold, Christian 7, 214–15, 218, 329–41
phallic feminine 117–18, 125–6n1
phallic imagery 117–18
Phantom Lady: Hollywood Producer Joan Harrison, the Forgotten Woman Behind Hitchcock (Lane) 46, 304, 334
Phantom Lady (1944) 234, 282, 334
Philadelphia Inquirer 212, 265
Piccadilly Pictures 406
The Picture of Dorian Gray (Wilde) 175
Picturegoer 34, 39, 94, 231–4, 422
Pietà 306
Pietrangeli, Antonio 347
Piggy (2022) 391–3
Pilati, Robert 326
Pilots (*Pilotinnen*, 1994) 339–40
Piso, Michelo 146
Place Vendôme (1997) 357–8
The Pleasure Garden (1926) 13, 14, 23, 24, 169
"Plenty of Nothing: Hitchcock's North by Northwest" (Hartman) 372n2
Poague, Leland 154
Polan, Dana 204, 207–8
Politique des auteurs 63, 319–28, 372
Pomerance, Murray 18, 88, 108–13, 154, 204, 267
Popular Cinema 377, 379, 381
Popular Photography 159
Portrait magazine 381
Positif journal 346
postcolonial criticism 108–9

post-Cultural Revolution China 375–7, 379–80
postmodernism 372
post-Suffrage era 33–7
postwar austerity period (1945–1951) 230, 233–4
Powell, Dilys 2, 18, 32, 40, 240n5
   North by Northwest 80
   Rear Window 69
   Sabotage 96
   Shadow of a Doubt 56
   Strangers on a Train 229, 230, 233–4
   The Trouble with Harry 185–6
   and wartime Britain 424
   The Wrong Man 212
PRC *see* People's Republic of China
Premiere magazine 399
Press and Journal 232
The Pride of the Yankees (1942) 66n2
"El primer Hitchcock" booklet (The First Hitchcock, 2013) 403
Prison 77 (2022) 391
Production Code of America (PCA) 59–61, 118, 158, 207–8, 217, 219, 243, 368–9
propaganda 232–3, 271–2, 351, 423–4
proto-noir cinema 330
Prouty, Howard 282
Psycho (1960) 3, 31, 83, 144, 192–3, 195–6, 203, 243–4, 264
   in Argentina 410–13
   and auteurism 62, 63
   in Germany 330–1
   globalization 298
   Hitchcock and Italian film criticism 344–7
   Hitchcock's "walk-ons" 5–6, 292, 301n2
   in Japan 370–1
   in Mexico 395, 397, 399, 403
   music in Hitchcock's films 415
   preserving/promoting Hitchcock's TV persona 293
   and queer theory 115–27
   in South Korea 355–6, 357
   in Spain 384, 389–90
   television work 271–3
   travels in Hitchcock's multiverse 312–13
   USSR and post-Soviet Russia 352–3
psychoanalysis 48, 332–3, 335, 409–10
   Sigmund Freud 36, 40, 48, 50, 130–1, 204–6
   see also Oedipus/Oedipal complex
psychoanalytic theory 63–4
Puenzo, Lucía 410
'pure' cinema 83, 116, 244, 259, 392, 411–12
Pursuits of Happiness: The Hollywood Comedy of Remarriage (Cavell) 85, 202

Quarterly Review of Film and Video 280–1
Que Dios Nos Perdone (*May God Save Us*, 2016) 391
queer male sexuality 204–6
   see also homosexuality
queer readings 49–50
queer theory 48, 87–8, 115–27, 208n2, 237–8
   Braudy and Durgnat, early stages 121
   homophobia, queer-affirming and transphobia 122–5
   Intimate Violence by Greven 122, 165
   phallic mothers, vulture mothers 117–18
   Strangers on a Train 230
   women and acting 118–21
queer-affirming 116, 122–5
Quéval, Jean 326–7n3
Quigly, Isabel 80
quotation 68, 73–5

Radio City Music Hall 78–9, 254, 408
Random House 302n9
Ray, Robert 214, 217
RCA sound equipment 25–6
realism 34, 57, 62
   and Italian criticism 343, 345
   and Japanese cinema 376
   The Man Who Knew Too Much 262
   Mr. & Mrs. Smith 200
   neorealism 345, 347–8, 356–7, 402
   North by Northwest 84
   Rear Window 69–75
   Sabotage 101
   surrealism 70
   Topaz 254–5
   and wartime Britain 423, 425
   The Wrong Man 211
Rear Window (1954) 2–3, 31, 68–77, 83, 140, 144, 188, 195–6, 264–5
   in Argentina 408
   and auteurism 62, 63
   British critical reception 103
   in Communist China 382n6
   following Hitchcock's death, 1980 148–51
   in Germany 330
   and Germany's *Filmkritik* 332–3
   globalization 298–9
   Hitchcock and Italian film criticism 344–7
   ideological criticism 71–2
   in Mexico 395, 396, 397, 399
   "missing" or "lost" Hitchcocks 188, 292
   music in Hitchcock's films 418
   narrative and narrational tactics 68–71

preserving/promoting Hitchcock's TV persona 292
referentiality, quotation, parody, satire 73–5
in South Korea 355–7, 362–3, 363n2
in Spain 388
television work 271
USSR and post-Soviet Russia 353
"*Rear Window*'s Glasshole" (Edelman) 72, 122, 126n3
Rebecca (1940) 2, 8, 31, 43–53, 55, 158
and Communist China 375
film text 47–50
Hitchcock and Italian film criticism 343
in Japan 364–5, 368
in Mexico 395, 398
music in Hitchcock's films 414, 416–17
production 44–7
and queer theory 122
reception 50–2
and Shamley Productions 282
in South Korea 355
in Spain 384, 388, 391
travels in Hitchcock's multiverse 303
USSR and post-Soviet Russia 351
Rebello, Stephen 353
receptions *see* critical reception
Redgrave, Michael 39
Reed, Carol 156n2, 234
Reed, Rex 188
Reeves, Matt 214–15
referentiality 68, 73–5
Regis cinema 403
reincarnation 315
Reinecke, Stefan 329
El reino (*The Candidate*, 2018) 391
religion 175–81, 190, 310, 315, 362–3
"many lives" theory 315
Spanish festivals and auteurism 384
see also Catholicism
La Remplaçante de Marilyn… et celle de Grace Kelly (Anon.) 138n1
"Reseeing *Blackmail*" (Watt) 29
"Revenge" (1955) 271–3, 275, 303
reviews
The Trouble with Harry 188–95
see also academic film criticism
Reville, Alma 14, 32–3, 39, 41n4, 44–8, 51–2, 103–4, 170
revisionism 107, 150, 258–60, 416
Revista de la Universidad 401
La Revue du cinéma 321
Revue Studios (formerly Revue Productions) 281, 282
Reynolds, Burt 285, 287n8
Rich and Strange (1931) 16–17

Richard II (Shakespeare) 36–7
Ride the Pink Horse (1947) 282
Riera, Emilio García 401–4
right to vote 36–7
The Ring (1927) 24–5, 169, 350
Rio Bravo (1959) 287
Ritchard, Cyril 26, 415
RKO 58, 60, 201, 398
Road to Reform: Film Practice and Criticism from 1977 to 1986 (Li) 379
Roar (2016) 137
Robinson, T. 362–3
Robinson, David 237, 253
Roc, Patricia 38–9
Rocco and His Brothers (1960) 345
Rohmer, Éric
academia, *Mr. & Mrs. Smith* 201
and auteurism 63
Blackmail 22
Downhill 173
Frenzy 242–3
and *L'Écran français* 319
The Man Who Knew Too Much 263
North by Northwest 88
reception in Italy 342–4
reception in Japan 367
Rope 160
Sabotage 94
television work 273
The Trouble with Harry in France 187–8
Under Capricorn 179–80
The Wrong Man 212
Rojo (2018) 410, 412–13
Roman Holiday (1952) 356
romantic idealism 191
romantic irony 194
Romanticism 131–2, 365–6
Romeo and Juliet (1968) 356
Rope (1949) 3, 158–66, 188, 203, 236–7, 264–5
"Anal *Rope*" by Miller 122, 126n3
in Argentina 408, 409–10
and auteurism 62
and British austerity 233
and *L'Écran français* 319, 321, 322–4
following Hitchcock's death, 1980 148–9
in Mexico 396
"missing" or "lost" Hitchcocks 188, 292
preserving/promoting Hitchcock's TV persona 292
and queer theory 122
in South Korea 357, 363n2
Rope/Rope's End (Hamilton) 158–9

Rose, Jacqueline 131
Rosenbaum, Jonathan 212, 214
Rotha, Paul 17–18, 22, 95, 424, 426n6, 427n9
    The Film Till Now 17–18, 95, 426n6
Rothman, William 101–2, 107, 154, 206, 215–16, 319–20
    Hitchcock: The Murderous Gaze 18, 202
Roud, Richard 253
Royal Albert Hall 108, 110–11, 416
Royal Leamington Spa Courier 98–9
RTVE 386
Russo, Vito 116
Rutherford, Margaret 38–9
Ryall, Tom 18

SA/se (formerly Film Space 1895) 357–8
Sabotage (1936) 3, 260
    British critical reception 97–103
    and British critics 93–105
    and Graham Greene 97–8
    in Mexico 395, 398
    in South Korea 357
Saboteur (1942) 55, 80, 201
    in Argentina 408–9
    and *L'Écran français* 326
    in Mexico 396
    and Shamley Productions 282
    in Spain 388–9
Sabrina (1954) 356
sacred act of suicide 362–3
Sadoul, Georges 321
Said, Edward 109
Saint, Eva Marie 31, 78, 79, 385
San Diego State University 286
San Francisco 305–9
San Sebastián Festival 385, 391
Sanders-Brahms, Helma 331
Sans Soleil (1983) 357–8
sapphic modernism 49
Sarris, Andrew 3, 71, 80
    The American Cinema 256–7
    "Notes on the Auteur Theory" 63, 95
    Sabotage 104
    The Trouble with Harry 184, 188–9
Sarris, Andrew *The Man Who Knew Too Much* 264–6
satire 68, 73–5, 201, 411–12
Saturday Review 140, 142–3, 156n2, 212, 256, 262
Scarlett's Women (Taylor) 50
Schatz, Thomas 2, 44–5, 54–67
Schickel, Richard 149, 214, 284–5
Schober, Adrian 194–5

Scorsese, Martin 4, 285
    and Hitchcock's TV persona 293
    Vertigo and *Marnie* 143, 149–50, 419
    The Wrong Man 214–15
The Scotsman 97, 234
Scott, A. O. 360
Screen journal 63–4, 122, 145, 332, 372n1, 372n2
The Sea Inside (2004) 391
Secret Agent (1936) 39, 84, 93, 252–3, 260
    in Argentina 408
    British critical reception 98–9
    in Japan 364–7
    in Mexico 395
    music in Hitchcock's films 415
The Secret Agent (Conrad) 93, 94, 96–100
The Secret of the Fake Bride 334
Secret in Their Eyes (2015) 410
Seligmann, Nadine 276
Selznick, David O. 2–3, 32, 54–8, 62, 64–5, 303
    Mr. & Mrs. Smith 201, 204
    music in Hitchcock's films 417
    Rear Window 73
    Rebecca 43–52, 417
    reception in Communist China 376
    reception in Japan 364–5
    reception in Mexico 398
    reception in South Korea 355–6
    Rope 158
    Strangers on a Train 234
    and wartime Britain 421, 422
Selznick International Pictures 2–3, 43–4, 47, 52, 58, 83
sensational exploitation 59
sensational melodramas 84
sensationalism 345, 368–9
Seoul School of Culture 357
Sequence magazine/journal 17–18, 61–2, 200, 421, 425
sexual taxonomy 124, 126n5
sexual violence 243–7, 250n7
    see also abuse allegations
sexuality 195, 248–9, 332–3
    failed sexuality 191
    fetishism 124, 126n5, 358–9
    food and sexuality 248–9
    Marnie 154
    see also homosexuality; Oedipus/Oedipal complex; psychoanalysis; queer theory; voyeurism; women
Sgammato, Joseph 245
shadow, aesthetics of 366–7

Shadow of a Doubt (1943) 2, 4, 8, 54–67, 195–6, 201, 203, 229, 233
    in Argentina 411
    and auteurism 63–5
    and British austerity 233
    critical reception 54–8
    and *L'Écran français* 321–2
    Hitchcock's public image in Italy 347
    in Japan 367
    in Mexico 396, 398
    music in Hitchcock's films 415
    in South Korea 358
    USSR and post-Soviet Russia 351
Shadows of Glory (1930) 395
shadows in Japanese art and architecture 366
Shakespeare, William 36–7, 85, 87, 190
Shamley Productions 116, 272, 275–88, 303–4, 308, 311, 313, 315
Shanghai Philately 381
Shao Mujun 375–7
Shell Magazine 186
Shigehiko, Hasumi 371–2
Shijie dianying Dongtai (World Cinema News) 382n1
A Shilling for Candles (1936) 39
Shimizu Yasuo 372n2
"shock cut" 24
The Short Night (1976–1979) 290, 293
"showrunners" 282, 283, 286, 304
Siegfried (1924) 330
Sight and Sound magazine
    and *The Lodger* 17–18
    and *Blackmail* 22
    culture of film criticism, new cinephilia 151
    and *Downhill* 173–4
    and *Frenzy* 245
    Hwangsang ("Fantasy", or *Vertigo*) 357–8
    and *The Lady Vanishes* 40
    leading directors and their top ten films of all time 152
    and *The Man Who Knew Too Much* 263–4, 267
    and *North by Northwest* 80
    and Park Chan-wook 357–8
    and *Rear Window* 69
    Richard Winnington, summer 1951 229
    and *Strangers on a Train* 229, 233–4, 237
    and *The Wrong Man* 212
    and *Topaz* 254
    and *Vertigo* and *Marnie* 149, 151–2
Sikov, Ed 191, 196n1
Silence of the Lambs (1991) 122
"silent talkie" films 2, 415
The Simpsons (1994) 74–5
Sinyard, Neil 103, 258

La Sirène du Mississippi (1969) 334
Sisters (1972) 75
Sixty Glorious Years (1938) 33–4
The Sketch 233
Sketches of Foreign Cinema 376–7
The Skin I Live In (2014) 388
slasher-horror films 115–16, 119–20
    see also *Frenzy*; *Psycho*
slow art cinema 329
small-screen Hitchcock see television work
Smith-Cumming, Sir Mansfield 261n1
Smoke and Mirrors (2016) 391
Smoliński, Sebastian 118
Smyth, Jennifer 240
The Snake Puit (1948) ! 217
socialism 350, 367, 425
    see also Marxism, Karl Marx
Socrates 338–9
Somewhere in the Night (1946) 400
"Somewhere Over the Rainbow" 113
Song of Myself (Whitman) 195
"Sonnet 1" (Browning) 309–10
Sorogoyen, Rodrigo 391
The Sound of Music (1965) 356, 404n1
sound picture 2
South Korea 7–8, 354–63
    and Park Chan-wook 357–63
    Yeonggam ("Old Man") 354–7
Spain 8, 384–93
    Alejandro Amenábar 389–91
    Alex de la Iglesia, monumental location sequences 388–9
    Hitchcock as auteur 384–6
    Pedro Almodóvar and the new aesthetic movement 386–8
    preserving/promoting Hitchcock's TV persona 271
Spanish Civil War 386–7, 391, 400–2
The Spanish Jade (1922) 384
The Spectator 80, 97–8, 186, 263–4, 426n5
Spellbound (1945) 8, 31, 51, 58–9, 230
    in Argentina 409–10
    and auteurism 62, 65
    and Communist China 375
    in Communist China 376–7
    and *L'Écran français* 323, 326–7n3
    in Mexico 396, 398–9
    music in Hitchcock's films 415
    and Shamley Productions 282
    in South Korea 355
    in Spain 384–5
    USSR and post-Soviet Russia 351
Spellbound by Beauty (Spoto) 129

Spoto, Donald 94, 129–31, 154
    The Art of Alfred Hitchcock 149–50, 189–90, 200–1
    Frenzy 243–4
    Mr. & Mrs. Smith 200–1, 203, 208n1
    music in Hitchcock's films 419
    Topaz 259
    and wartime Britain 423
    The Wrong Man 215
spy films 84, 254–60, 350–1, 400
    James Bond films 83–4, 88, 252–3, 261n1
Staffordshire Evening Herald 234
Stage Door (1937) 35
Stage Fright (1950) 229–30, 237, 240n2
    and auteurism 62
    and British austerity 233
    in Mexico 396
Staiger, Janet 2, 68–77
Stalinism 350–3
Stam, Robert 73
La Stampa 345–8
Star magazine 347
Steimatsky, Noa 214
stereotypes 48, 87, 98, 112–13, 124
    see also idealism
Sterritt, David 83, 214, 418
Stevens, Brad 280–1
Stevenson, Robert Louis 121, 175, 355
Stoker (2013) 359
Storm Clouds Cantata 110, 416
The Strange Case of Alfred Hitchcock (Durgnat) 121, 173–4, 189–90, 201
Strange Case of Dr. Jekyll and Mr. Hyde (Stevenson) 121, 175, 355
Strangers on a Train (1951) 4, 188, 203, 229–41, 240n3, 264
    in Argentina 408
    and auteurism 62–3
    British austerity following the war 230, 233–4
    expatriate/ex-patriot 230–3
    initial reception in the USA 235–6
    in Mexico 396, 400, 403
    music in Hitchcock's films 415
    post-1951 reassessment in Britain/USA 236–8
    in Spain 387, 388
    summary/closing methodological note 238–40
    USSR and post-Soviet Russia 351
Straw Dogs (1971) 246–7
streaming services 271–3, 286, 386, 389, 394
Street, Sarah 70
Strick, Philip 71, 254
Strong Man's Love 350
The Struggle (1931) 257

subjectivity (*shutaisei*) 369
Sudetenland crisis (September 1938) 35
Suffragettes 33–7
    see also feminism
Sugiyama Heiichi 365–7
Sullivan, Jack 8, 29, 50, 70
    The Man Who Knew Too Much 111
    music in Hitchcock's films 414–20
    The Trouble with Harry 192–3
    Vertigo and *Marnie* 155
    The Wrong Man 220
Sullivan, Victoria 246
Sun Yi 7–8, 374–83
Sunday Express 14–15, 170–3, 185, 231–2
Sunday Post 39–40
Sunday Telegraph 210, 264
Sunday Times
    Hitchcock and wartime Britain 424, 427n7
    and *The Lady Vanishes* 32, 38–9
    and *The Lodger* 15, 18
    and *Rear Window* 69
    and *Sabotage* 95–7
    and *Shadow of a Doubt* 56
    and *Strangers on a Train* 229–30, 237, 240n5
    and *The Trouble with Harry* 185
    and *The Wrong Man* 212
Sur journal 409
surface criticism (*hyosho hihyo*) 371–2
surrealism 70
surveillance 335
Suspicion (1941) 8, 48, 51, 55
    in Argentina 408
    and *L'Écran français* 322
    in Japan 367
    in Mexico 396
    and Shamley Productions 282
    travels in Hitchcock's multiverse 314
Suspicion (1957–1958) 272, 274, 279, 282, 287n1, 287n3
The Swamp (2001) 411–12
"Sybilla" (1960) 284, 307, 314–15
symbolism 191, 204, 248–9, 306, 334, 387–9
    Blackmail 22–4
    food and sexuality 248–9
    inter- and /or ex-change of women in Farocki's *Vertigo* 333–4
    North by Northwest 81, 83, 88
    Pedro Almodóvar and Spain's new aesthetic movement 386–7
    Rear Window 70–2
    Rope 164
    see also idealism; psychoanalysis; religion

"Sympathetic Guidance: Hitchcock and C. A. Lejeune" (Miller) 20n4
Sympathy for Mr. Vengeance (*Boksuneun naui geot*, 2002) 358–9

Tacchella, Jean-Charles 321, 322–5
Tadashi, Iijima 365, 367–8
"A Talk on Film Directing" 375
The Tatler 100
Taxi Driver (1976) 149–50
taxidermy 410–13
Taylor, John Russell 108, 201, 244, 253, 380–1, 416
technicalism 376
"technicist bias" 161–4
Technicolor 107, 140, 159, 211, 322, 323, 399, 416
"The Television Films of Alfred Hitchcock" (*Cinema* magazine) 279–80
Television Limited (MCA) 281
television work 5–6, 113, 271–316
    Hitchcock's public image in Italy 347
    in Mexico 394–413
    preserving/promoting Hitchcock's TV persona 289–302
    Shamley Productions 279–88
    travels in Hitchcock's multiverse 303–16
    see also The Paradine Case
Temple of Doom (1984) 264
The Ten Commandments (1956) 211
Testament of Dr. Mabuse (1933) 330
Tewksbury, Joan 285–6
Tey, Josephine 39
That Hamilton Woman (1941) 232
The Woman in the House across the Street from the Girl in the Window (2022) 73, 75
Their Own Best Creations: Women Writers in Postwar Television (Berke) 283
Theodora Goes Wild (1936) 35
Thérond, Roger-Marie 321, 322–6
Thesis (1996) 389–90
Things to Come (1936) 101
Thirst (*Bakjwi*, 2009) 358–9
Thomson, David 115–16
The Thousand Eyes of Dr Mabuse (1960) 267
Three Days of the Condor (1975) 260
Three Guineas (Woolf) 35
Tiempo de cine 401
Time magazine 58, 68, 121, 142, 188, 212, 235, 242, 256, 283, 364–5
The Times 100–1
    and *Blackmail* 415
    and *Frenzy* 244
    and *The Lady Vanishes* 40n3

    and *The Man Who Knew Too Much* 262
    and *Sabotage* 100–1
    and *Strangers on a Train* 237
    and *Topaz* 253
    and *Vertigo* and *Marnie* 149
To Catch a Thief (1955) 62, 140, 144, 396, 401, 408
    in Mexico 396, 399, 401
To the Pantheon of Cinema: Textbook for the Film Analysis Course at Beijing Film Academy (Beijing Film Academy) 382n6
Toho Labor Dispute 369
Tokyo Olympics of 1964 370
Tokyo Story (1953) 152
"Tonal Design and Narrative in Film Music" (Neumeyer) 192–3
Topaz (1969) 5, 7, 88, 242, 252–61
    in Mexico 395, 397
    in South Korea 355
    in Spain 389
    USSR and post-Soviet Russia 352–3
Topper (1937) 35
Torn Curtain (1966) 7, 242, 246–7, 254, 256–8
    in Argentina 408
    and auteurism 63
    in Mexico 395, 397
    in South Korea 355, 363n2
    USSR and post-Soviet Russia 352–3
Total National Spiritual Mobilization Movement 365
Toter Mann (2001) 340
tourism 35, 334
Tourneur, Maurice 325
trade critics & trade shows 13–17, 40n3, 45–6, 56–9, 63–4, 94
    and *Downhill* 169–71
    Shamley Productions 283
    and *Strangers on a Train* 230, 233, 235
    and *Topaz* 254–5
    and *The Trouble with Harry* 184
    and *Vertigo* and *Marnie* 143
trade unions 217, 323, 355, 403, 404
"Trans Video Store" (Vargas) 122, 123
Transatlantic Pictures 158, 164, 176–7
"transfer of guilt" 179–80
transnational genre 329–41
transphobia 122–5
trauma and concepts of justice/injustice 216–24
travels in Hitchcock's multiverse 303–16
Trotter, David 18
The Trouble with Harry (1955) 3–4, 182–97, 266, 372n1
    in Argentina 408
    at the end of Hitchcock's career 195–6
    British reception 184–6

and *L'Écran français* 319
following Hitchcock's death, 1980 148–51
in Mexico 396, 403
"missing" or "lost" Hitchcocks 188, 292
preserving/promoting Hitchcock's TV persona 292
reception in France 187–8
reviews and critical studies 188–95
USA reception, early promotion and reviews 182–4
Truffaut, François 1–2, 6, 13
and auteurism 61–6, 107–8, 279
and character-based exploration 107
craftsmanship and character-based exploration 107–8
early queer theory 121
filming of literary novels 93–4
French reception 187–8, 319
killing of children in film 99–100
The Lodger 13
The Man Who Knew Too Much 107, 265–6, 416
#MeToo and angry nature 129–31
Mr. & Mrs. Smith 200
narrative and narrational tactics 69
North by Northwest 80, 88
Rebecca 44–5, 417
reception in Communist China 377
reception in France 187–8, 319, 323
reception in Italy 343–4
reception in Japan 367
reception in Mexico 401–2
reception in South Korea 356
reception in Soviet and post-Soviet Russia 353
Vertigo and *Marnie* 149–50
The Wrong Man 211–15
Turner Classic Movies 216
Turrent, Tomás Pérez 402–4
TV Chronicle 186
TV Guide 271, 274, 283, 285
TV Land 286
Twin Peaks (1990) 282

UCP *see* Universal Cable Productions
ultranationalism 368
  see also Nazism
Uncle Tom's Cabin (1852) 176
Under Capricorn (1949) 3–4, 175–81, 188, 229–30, 237, 240n2
in Argentina 408
and auteurism 62
and *L'Écran français* 326
in Mexico 396, 403
Under the Greenwood Tree (1929) 30
Under Western Eyes (Conrad) 94
unheimlich aspects 156n3

United Artists 43, 51, 58
United Nations 78, 81, 85
Universal Cable Productions (UCP) 293, 301n5
El Universal Gráfico newspaper 395–7, 399
El Universal newspaper 398–9, 402, 405n5
"Universal Pictures: Golden Collection" (2012) 353
Universal Studios 3, 55–7, 83, 141, 152
  and *Frenzy* 243
  Hitchcock's television work 273
  Italian film criticism 343
  Mexican celebrity culture 398
  preserving/promoting Hitchcock's TV persona 292–4
  and *Topaz* 252–3, 255
Universal-International 281
Universidad de Guadalajara Centro de Investigaciones y Enseñanza Cinematográfica 401
Universidad Nacional Autónoma de México (UNAM) 401, 403
University of Chicago 158
urban topography 336–7
USSR and post-Soviet Russia 7, 350–3
utopianism 202, 203

Vanilla Sky (2001) 391
Varda, Agnès 334
Varga, Chris 122–4, 126n4
Variety magazine
  and *Blackmail* 27
  and Hitchcock's TV persona 294–5
  and *Mr. & Mrs. Smith* 199–200
  and *North by Northwest* 78–9
  preserving/promoting Hitchcock's TV persona 294–5
  and *Rear Window* 68
  and *Shadow of a Doubt* 56–7
  and Shamley Productions 283, 285
  and *Strangers on a Train* 230, 235, 240n4
  and *Topaz* 252, 254, 258
  and *The Trouble with Harry* 183
  and *The Wrong Man* 210, 211
Vena, Dan 122, 124
"Venetian" women 49
"Vengeance Trilogy" 358
Vermillion Entertainment 301n5
Vermorel, André 321, 324–5
Vermorel, Claude 324–5
"Vertauschte Frauen" ("Mistakenly Interchanged Women") by Farocki 333–5
Vertigo (1958) 3, 7–8, 31, 80, 83, 140–57, 188, 192–6, 264–7
  academic film criticism 201
  and academic film criticism, 1970s and 80s 144–8
  additional artwork for 142
  in Argentina 408

and auteurism 62, 63
British critical reception 103
following Hitchcock's death, 1980 148–55
in Germany 330–1, 340
Hitchcock and Italian film criticism 344–7
and John Belton 257
and the male spectator 71–2
in Mexico 395, 397
"missing" or "lost" Hitchcocks 188, 292
music in Hitchcock's films 414, 418–20
and New German Cinema 329–41
and Park Chan-wook 357–63
preserving/promoting Hitchcock's TV persona 292, 293, 301n7
reactions during its initial run, 1958 140–3
and Samuel Taylor 252
Saul Bass's poster 141
in South Korea 357–63, 363n2
in Spain 385, 388, 390–1
television work 272–3
travels in Hitchcock's multiverse 305–12, 315
USSR and post-Soviet Russia 351
Vest, James 173, 187–8, 320
Victoria & Albert Museum 129
Victoria the Great (1937) 33–4
Victorianism 35–8, 113
Videla, Jorge Rafael 412
videotheque movement *see* cinematheque/videotheque movement
Vietnamese Heritage Museum 138n3
View and Plan of Toledo (El Greco) 305–6
Village Voice 63, 189, 264–6
Villaurrutia, Xavier 398
Violet, Roland 325–6
The Viper (1938) 323
VistaVision 107, 140, 399, 408
"Visual Pleasure and Narrative Cinema" (Mulvey) 51, 63–4, 71–2, 122, 137–8, 145
voyeurism 70–2
"Vengeance Trilogy" 358–9
see also Pyscho; *Rear Window*
VUFKU (All-Ukrainian Photo Cinema Administration) 350

Wages of Fear (1952) 141–3, 156n2
Walker, Alexander 237–8, 240n5, 249n1
Walker, Robert 63, 234, 237–8, 239
"walk-ons" at the start of films 5–6, 292, 301n2
Wang, J. 362–3
Wang Xinyu 380
Warner Bros 3, 159, 213, 232, 234, 240n2, 240n4, 398
wartime Britain 61, 217, 421–6
see also Nazism; World War II
Warwickshire Standard 98–9
Washington Post 235–6
Wasserman, Lew 271, 281–2
Watchtower over Tomorrow (1945) 271–2
Waterloo Bridge (1940) 356
Waterman, John 80
Waxman, Franz 50, 414, 416–17
Weimar era 37–8, 330–1
Weis, Elizabeth 30, 111, 415
"Welcome, Hitchcock!" exhibition (2016) 385
Welcome to Hitchcock (UCP) 293, 301n5
The Well of Loneliness (1928) 49
Welles, Orson 50, 56–7, 95–6, 321, 323, 356
see also Citizen Kane
Wen Hui Monthly 376
West Films: Monthly Magazine of Film Literature 377–8
West London Star 233
West Side Story 419–20
Westminster colonialism 33
see also colonialism
"Wet Saturday" (1956) 273, 274–5
Wexman, Virginia Wright 362
What Have I Done to Deserve This? (1984) 387
The Wheel Spins (1936) 34
When a Dead Woman Loves Two Men 334
While at War (2019) 391
White, Armond 71, 75
White, Edward 71, 215–16
White, Ethel Lina 34, 39
white femininity 362
White, Patricia 2, 43–53, 122
white privilege 109
see also patriarchy
Whitman, Walt 195
Whitty, May 2, 35–40
Wilde, Oscar 175
Wilder, Billy 195
Wilder, Thornton 55–6, 63, 66, 66n1
Williams, John 415, 417
Williams, Michael 18
Winnington, Richard 18, 61, 96, 229–30, 234, 424–6
Wirtschaftswunder (economic-miracle) 336–8
The Wizard of Oz (1942) 113
Wollen, Peter 86
women 31–42, 70, 362
abuse allegations against Hitchcock 39, 128–33, 136–8, 149, 154–5
adapting to 32–8
"fallen women" melodrama 175–81
female gaze 64–5
femmes fatales 131
lesbianism 49–50
male gaze 31, 40, 64–5, 107, 122, 137–8

#MeToo movement 128–39
misogyny 31–42, 72, 118, 133, 242, 245–7, 314
   in New German Cinema 329–41
   off-screen allies 38–40
   Original Six and lawsuit against DGA 288n9
   phallic feminine 117–18, 125–6n1
   Psycho and queer theory 115–27
   Rebecca, from 1941–present 43–53
   sexual violence 243–7, 250n7
   and Shamley Productions 283–5
   "Vertauschte Frauen" ("Mistakenly Interchanged Women") by Farocki 334–5
   Victorian women 35–8
   Victorianism 35–8
   see also feminism; heroines; patriarchy
Women on the Verge of a Nervous Breakdown (1988) 387
The Women Who Knew Too Much: Hitchcock and Feminist Theory (Modleski) 45, 51, 64–5, 83, 119, 145–6
Women's Steering Committee 288n9
Wood, Ed 125
Wood, Leslie 185
Wood, Robin 126n2
   academia, *Mr. & Mrs. Smith* 201, 204
   and auteurism 63, 65–6
   Frenzy 245, 248
   Hitchcock's Films 63, 66, 201
      Frenzy 245
      The Man Who Knew Too Much 107, 112–13
      queer theory, *Psycho* 121
      Rebecca 45
      reception in Mexico 401
      Rope 160–1
      Topaz 252
      The Trouble with Harry 189
      Vertigo and *Marnie* 145
      The Wrong Man 213
      Yeonggam in South Korea 356
   ideological criticism, *Rear Window* 72
   The Man Who Knew Too Much 107–8, 112–13
   narrative and narrational tactics 69
   North by Northwest 80, 83–4, 88
   queer theory, *Psycho* 116, 121, 124
   Rebecca 45
   reception in France 319–20
   reception in Mexico 401
   Rope 160–2
   television work 273
   Topaz 252, 258–9
   The Trouble with Harry 185, 189
   Under Capricorn 175–6
   Vertigo and *Marnie* 145, 150
   The Wrong Man 213
   Yeonggam in South Korea 356
   see also Hitchcock's Films Revisited
Woolf, Virginia 35
World Cinema 375–6, 377, 379, 381, 382n1
World Film News (1936–1938) 29, 426n4
The World in a Frame: What We See in Films (Braudy) 121
"The World Gone Wiggy" (Felleman) 194
World Vision magazine 381
World War II (1939–1945) 43–4, 125, 217, 230
   Blitz of London 230–1
   and British austerity 230, 233–4
   "le cas Hitchcock", Japan, 1946–1950s 367–9
   and Japanese cinema 364–5, 367
   London Blitz 230–1, 232
   see also Nazism
The Worthing Gazette 98, 101
The Wreck of the Mary Deare (1959) 84–5
Wright, Basil 97–8, 423–4, 426n5
Wright, Teresa 55–8, 62, 66n2
Writing with Hitchcock (DeRosa) 184, 194
The Wrong Man (1956) 3–4, 188, 210–26
   in Argentina 410–11
   and concepts of justice/injustice 216–24
   and *L'Écran français* 319
   film and initial reception 211–12
   following Hitchcock's death 214–16
   in Germany 330–1
   Hitchcock's indifference/ambivalence 212–14
   in Mexico 397
   in Spain 384
Wyler, William 321, 323, 325–6, 425

XXY (2007) 410

Yacowar, Maurice 18, 71, 104, 208n3
Yeonggam ("Old Man") 354–7
Yo soy Alfred Hitchcock (2023) 386
Yorkshire Observer 233
Young and Innocent (1937) 32, 39, 93, 415
young Turks 322, 425
Young-jin, Kim 357–9
YouTube 286
Yu Hyun-mok 356
Yumihiko, Nakahara *see* Nobuhiko, Kobayashi

Z (1969) 258
Zama (2017) 410
Zimmerman, Paul 245, 256
Zinsser, William 183, 216
Žižek, Slavoj 71, 130–1, 134, 190, 204, 260